HISTORY OF THE BRITISH LEGION AND WAR IN SPAIN

Alexander Somerville

2004 N & M Press reprint (original 1839). SB. 720pp.

8058 €32 $33 **£22.00**

This substantial book is both an unusual military memoir and a fascination exploration of an almost forgotten episode in Anglo-Spanish military history. The 'British Legion' of the title has nothing to do with its 20th Century namesake, but was the name of an expeditionary force raised in 1837 to fight in the First Carlist War - a bitter dynastic dispute. Don Carlos, brother of the deceased Spanish King Ferdinand, refused to accept the succession of his infant neice Isabella, and raised the standard of revolt in the ultra-conservative Navarre and Basque provinces of northern Spain. Britain and France, fearing instability, sent forces to shore up the relatively Liberal Madrid regime against the Carlists. The campaign that followed was messy, inconclusive, and, according to Somerville's account, characterised by incompetence, cowardice and even mutiny - mainly on his own side. The narrative switches between accounts of bloody battles at Irun and St Sebastian, comparisons with the Peninsular War fought over the same terrain only a quarter of a century before, and near-farcical episodes when the author makes no attempt to disguise his disgust with his own side. An inglorious episode in British arms by any standrad, it is scarcely surprising that the Carlist Wars are today terra incognita, even to military buffs. This book should go a long way towards filling a gap in our knowledge. It is accompanied by appendices listing the Legion's Nominal Roll etc.

Lt. Gen. Sir G. De Lacy Evans
G.C. St F. and K.C.B.

HISTORY

OF THE

BRITISH LEGION,

AND

WAR IN SPAIN,

FROM PERSONAL OBSERVATIONS AND OTHER AUTHENTIC SOURCES,
CONTAINING A CORRECT DETAIL OF THE EVENTS OF THE EXPE-
DITION UNDER GENERAL EVANS,—ITS MORAL, POLITICAL,
AND MILITARY CHARACTER,—ITS SUCCESSES AND RE-
VERSES IN THE ENGAGEMENTS FOUGHT, AND
HARDSHIPS SUFFERED, WITH NUMEROUS
ANECDOTES OF INDIVIDUALS,
ETC., ETC., ETC.

WITH AN APPENDIX, CONTAINING EVERY OFFICER'S NAME,
RANK, AND SERVICE, THAT WAS IN THE EXPEDITION,

And a Portrait of Lt. Gen. Sir George De Lacy Evans,
M. P. G. C. St. F. and K. C. B.

BY ALEXANDER SOMERVILLE.

LONDON:

PUBLISHED BY JAMES PATTIE, BRYDGES STREET,
CATHERINE STREET, STRAND.

1839.

This facsimile follows the inconsistent page
numbering of the original 1839 edition.

Printed and bound by Antony Rowe Ltd, Eastbourne

DEDICATION.

To the Officers and Soldiers of the late British Auxiliary Legion of Spain,

GENTLEMEN AND COMRADES,

However imperfectly I may have executed the self-imposed task of writing an account of our much misrepresented services, I am confident that from all of you I shall receive a larger measure of approbation than of blame. The faults and the merits of the work I leave to yourselves and the public to judge of; but allow me with every sentiment of respect to offer it for your perusal and correction, and subscribe myself, as I esteem it a honour to be,

Your obedient Servant,

THE AUTHOR.

PREFACE.

THE readers of this work will perhaps observe, but if
not they must be informed, that it was written and published
at intervals extending over ten months, and that consequently
the matter is in some respects, incorrectly arranged. The
Author commenced with the intention of confining himself to
the engagements fought by the Legion in order to prove that
these were equal to the battles of other armies in proportion to
the numbers engaged; but as he proceeded, he was led to take
notice of individuals and circumstances, other than those which
he intended writing of at first. The rule of narrative being
therefore broken through, he has gone on to sketch those occurrences which appeared most worthy of notice, without confining himself to narrative. To the fastidious, it is necessary
to apologize for such irregularities; but to those who read
for information, instead of criticism, he makes no apology: the
fidelity with which he has filled his sketches, he presumes to
think, will be more acceptable than mere correctness of form
without fidelity; and he has only again to observe, that situated
as he was, in the manner of publishing, accepting often, and
substituting communicated matter, for that which he would
have published from his own personal knowledge, it became
impossible to observe order in its arrangement.

Some notices of individuals have appeared, which, had the
work to be written again, the author has no hesitation in saying he would omit. His object was not to give offence to individuals either by unjustly depreciating one, or unduly elevating another; his object was not, even to offend by telling the
truth, where that related to personal character, and did not
affect the reputation of the general body; but as the highest

military authority of the day—the Duke of Wellington—has said (see his letters recently published,) that "every man is not a hero that wears a uniform," as the Duke declared this of his famous army, only two or three days after Waterloo, the author was the more willing to do justice to those officers in the Legion, who were heroes by exposing the misconduct of those who were not. He is aware, and regrets that public feeling has such a tendency, that to mention an act of dishonour relative to the Legion, is to make his reader or listener believe, that the whole were dishonourable, but having such a great authority for saying, that all are not heroes that wear uniforms, he has ventured to speak freely of the Legion's officers, trusting that allowance will be made for the many good ones, as was done in former armies, even in spite of the great exceptions made by the Duke of Wellington.

In a few instances, the reader will find the subject interfered with, by wood engravings, of which the author has only to say, that he is greviously ashamed. The Artists employed, were supposed competent to the work, and being treated with, in the usual way, the author is at a loss to account for the appearance of such abortions; he has only to assure his subscribers, and those into whose hands, the work may afterwards come that the greater portion of the profits of the work has been swallowed up by those attempts at illustrations; and if the *reader* is offended with their appearance, the *author* is not less so.

It has been frequently suggested that the work should either not have been called a "History" or if so, it should have accorded more than it does, with the common style and design of bistories. To this the author can only answer, that though the faults may be numerous, he cannot come to the conclusion that it is improper to call the details, even the most trifling, a part of history. Let it be understood, that he makes no pretence of his having conceived and executed his views perfectly; circumstances that controlled his materials, and perhaps his want of ability, added to his want of experience, would not permit him to do so; but he is still of opinion, that a " History" would be imperfect, however correct in style—philosophic in reflection, or eloquent in language, were it to neglect the *persons* of whom it treated. In this case, it has been the object of the Author to bring the details before the reader, which most other writers have overlooked when writing on similar subjects. How much he may improve when the honour of submitting a second edition to the public, has given him further experience in authorship, he cannot at present pretend to say, but he hopes to have an early opportunity of allowing the public to judge.

On another subject he has a few observations to make, and these he trusts will be of sufficient interest to warrant their being made here.

The personal character of an author who comes forward in his own person to publish his opinions of others, is at all times worth being enquired into; more especially is it necessary for an author to set himself right with his readers when he knows that his personal character has been made the rule of leading people to read, or keeping them from reading his work, much more than the merits of the work itself have been. It has for instance, been supposed that because the author had at one time been proved, or was supposed to have been proved to be a disobedient soldier,—that he must therefore be unfit to write fairly and freely on those duties which it appears he was himself incapable of performing. Now it so happens that he possesses the highest testimonials from officers of various ranks as to his exact performance of duty and unvarying soldierlike conduct in the Spanish service. He has it also in his power to prove that while serving in the 2nd Dragoons (Scots Greys) where it was supposed he so much misconducted himself that he was altogether unfit to be a soldier afterwards —that there he did *not* commit a breach of discipline, as that has generally been represented in the newspaper particularly in a paper called the *Weekly Dispatch*. From the period when that paper succeeded in dragging him into notoriety for its own peculiar purposes up to the present, he has looked with regret and shame on the position in which they placed him. Having *secured* him, according to their own words, to themselves, they proceeded to make a monopoly of their agitation, notwithstanding the frequent remonstrances from him, praying them to abide by moderation, or at most by truth. They did not do so; and when the supposed disobedient soldier would have proved beyond question that he had honourably performed his duty, he was prevented from doing so by two drunken lawyers who conducted his case; who having fought, torn each others clothes—broken the furniture of their hotel (for which, by the by, part of the " subscription for *Somerville*" had to pay) one of them proceeded to the Court of Inquiry, bullied the Judge Advocate, and sunk into drunken stupidity, during which some of the principal evidences in behalf of *Somervilie* were examined; and seeing which, *Somerville* declined calling the most important of all his witnesses. He might here add much more of the causes that led to his being maligned by the *Weekly Dispatch*; he might tell of how he was asked to give his name to a series of articles " cutting up the gentlemen of the army " (their own words) which articles they were to find a person to write; but how he indignantly declined to be made such a hack of; he might tell of the *Weekly Dispatch Public House* which was to be taken and *managed* for him, but which he declined; he might tell of twenty other causes of their mis-representations which shall shortly be told, but which do not properly belong to this work. At present however, it is necessary to say, that as a man and a soldier, he has been vilely misrepresented by that newspaper for its own purposes; and he considers a passing notice at least, to be necessary, he having the strongest confidence notwithstanding, to earn and retain the good opinions of the public, when he shall have shewn the source and the quantity of the misrepresentations issued by the *Weekly Dispatch*.

CONTENTS.

CHAPTER I.

CHAPTER II.

CHAPTER III.

CHAPTER IV.

CHAPTER V.

CHAPTER VI.

CHAPTER VII.

CHAPTER VIII.   •

CHAPTER XIII.

CHAPTER XIV.

CHAPTER XV.

CHAPTER XVI.

HISTORY OF

THE BRITISH LEGION.

CHAPTER I.

Introductory Remarks on the Object of this Work—The moral character of
the Legion—Origin of the War—Laws of the Northern Provinces—Remarks on
the recent Debate in the House of Commons.

AFTER returning from Spain to Glasgow in August 1837, I wrote
and published a work entitled " *A Narrative of the British Legion,
and the War in Spain,* " which being in many particulars so different
from any accounts that had hitherto appeared, drew the attention of
the public to it in a degree, that the first impression of between three
and four thousand were sold off in less than a month in the neighbourhood of Glasgow alone. It would be an unpardonable presumption to say its literary merit led to that extensive sale, but being
the first work that had appeared giving an unbiassed account of the
expedition, and that in a familiar way, wherein the soldier was brought
forward in his individual character, and the warfare seen not by Official Returns and Dispatches alone, but by those minute incidents
which are omitted in mere dry history—being therefore so written,
it became popular ; and for the benefit of other parties than the author
sold extensively. None of that edition having gone beyond Scotland,
and having been concluded much sooner than it would have, had its
publication been conducted to my satisfaction. I now offer my history of the Legion, to the people of England. It is not prejudiced
by any political bias, and as I served throughout the Campaign with
a character unimpeached with any fault moral or military, (which
some who have written about the Legion, and who were above me
in rank did not sustain,) I can venture to write about individuals

A 2

without the fear of being charged with flattery on the one side, or revenge on the other. As a careful observer of what passed around me, sharing in the varied fortunes of the service, I noted all that is worth knowing. There will be recitals of misery that may sicken the hearts of some, and there will be those details of horror, that will fill the minds of those who love the marvellous : but generally the events recorded, will be those that will set the conduct of General Evans — his troops — and the war in Spain in an unprejudiced light before the British public. This work will not attempt to prove whether the political interference of England with Spain is right or wrong, and consequently in giving the character of the Chief of the Legion, will say nothing of his side in the British Senate, for political prejudices are commonly so obstinate on all sides, that it would be vain to attempt to break them down. But there is something partly political that cannot be avoided, that is, the reports that have appeared in the newspapers, giving accounts of the different parties in the war, which from their conflicting nature, prove that they are either all untrue, or that if any are true, the others must be grossly false. One side represents the Carlist Army, as a band of mountain robbers supported by plunder, and fighting only for the worst of purposes— the perpetration of savage cruelties, and if a tale of horror can be got hold of, it is told to suit a political purpose, by those who are sent out to Spain to cater news for party newspapers. On the other side, the same partiality of reporting prevails, the Post contradicts the Chronicle, and the Chronicle the Post, and yet, as we found while serving in Spain, no newspaper ever gives facts as they are. It is true, that some of the correspondents to the London Papers were officers in the respective armies, and must have known many facts, but these naturally wrote to suit their own side, and not a few, as was the case in the Legion, were persons who had misconducted themselves—had private animosity towards the General, and some even were cashiered from the service; and immediately set up as "Foreign Correspondents " to the newspapers; that many of the reports that came home, were written by such persons is undeniable. Even while serving with a good character, in the full confidence of, and in daily communication with General Evans, an officer who held the rank of brigadier general, betrayed the Chief, and corresponded in a dishonourable way with one of the leading London journals. It is true this officer had to leave the Service with rather an indifferent reputation ; but he only came home to write openly what he had done disguisedly, and that from the most disreputable motives ; yet the public have believed him.

Again correspondents who are sent expressly out, are seldom where they can get correct information. The most of the Spanish news are written from Bayonne in France, and the sources of information are always uncertain. Even those who go near the scenes of operation, seldom go near enough. During our two years service, only one civilian as a correspondent of a Newspaper, was known to approach as near as he could witness how the troops were fighting ; and he unluckily got knocked down, and nearly buried by the earth thrown up by a common ball, so that he had the prudence afterwards, like all others, to keep farther back. But what was the consequence of that accident, a London daily paper, which, from its politics was considered favourable to the military character of the Legion, and for which this correspondent furnished news, contained an account of that single cannon shot, told in such a way as to appear the most if not the only remarkable thing that happened during the engagement ; and yet when I come to the details of that engagement, and give the literal facts without any colouring, and facts which will be verified by all who could possibly know their occurrence ; it will be seen how very different some of the conduct of the Legion was to what it has been reported in this country previously.

But why try to prove that newspaper reports of the war have been partial, when party politics were mixed up with the military interference ? No party will deny it. If the opposition journals, and such members of parliament as Earl Grey and Mr. Whitbread, could stand up in 1809 and denounce the Duke of Wellington and the army that gained those victories that British pride now boasts of, as a commander unfit to command, and as an army sustaining only a series of defeats and disgraces ; if they from opposition could say so then, which they did, may not Sir Henry Hardinge and others repeat the calumny against a whigish expedition now? It may be supposed the comparison is not good ; but it is perfectly just : for political opposition coloured every incident of warfare then, by and for the same means that it does now. It would not only be ungenerous and unnational, but it would be highly dangerous for any man who does not wish his head broken, to stand up in an assembly of Englishmen and say, that the armies of Wellington were not the gallant and the brave that all history now admits them to have been ; and yet were they not hurriedly collected and marched to the field (the 79th for instance, with five hundred recruits, went to Holland, and had not been drilled two months) ; were they not all of the same moral materials as soldiers are made of now ? It has been charged against the British Legion that it was composed of the scum of society ; if so, the British army is the same. For if in any village in England there is a young man more enterprising and less steady in conduct, perhaps more immoral than others, some sober person will say, " that fellow will go to be a soldier ; " another will add, " it is the only place fitting for him ; " and if he does enlist, all will say, " better could not be expected of him." Let any one who saw the detachment of the Legion going to Spain, and who supposed from their bad appearance that they were the scum of society, go at any time to the Ship in Charles-street Westminster, and they will see batches of recruits for all regiments in the British and East India service, and very much like those that filled up the corps, and afterwards choked the hospitals and the graves in Spain. So much for that particular portion of society from which armies are generally made up.

Still it would be grossly unjust to assert, that all those who go into our army are loose characters. Many young men join the army from causes of a different kind. But it is equally unjust to assert, that the Legion were all immoral characters. How often are the sympathies of the public excited by the distress of the agricultural labourers — the denial of relief to them when they are idle — their miserable treatment in Workhouses, &c.; and yet it was from this class principally, that the English regiments of the Legion were formed. I have heard many a tale told from the mouths of these simple countrymen, that would soften the heart of harder breasts than those of Englishmen, and would not allow calumny to lie on the moral character of the ill-fated Legion as it now does. A great number of those composing the Scotch regiments were also of an unfortunate class ; that is, the handloom weavers of the west of Scotland ; so that it was the force of circumstances, other than their moral character, that led many of them to go to Spain. As for the

Irish regiments, it was so indisputably the case, that they did not deserve the common term of reproach, that I shall only say that these regiments were formed almost wholesale from the rural population ; which to libel, would be to libel all Ireland ; and I believe few will deny at this day, that the Irish regiments are as good soldiers as ever entered the field, or are now in the British army. But if it is still insisted that the moral characters of those composing the Legion were worse than the efficiency of the corps required, I can only say, that those persons whose mere moral and religious characters kept them from joining such a corps as the Legion, would have been of least use in it. It is the rough-and-ready stick-at-nothing fellow, that is the best fighting soldier in such a war as that in Spain, or in any war. Those who would disprove this assertion, must know much more of the real character of active warfare, than is to be known by seeing soldiers in their barracks, or going through the evolutions of a field-day ; and especially they must know much more of what the war in Spain is, than that information which newspaper reports have yet furnished.

These observations are only intended to convey my opinion, that the Legion were not worse men morally, than other soldiers are As to their military reputation, many of the great and overwhelming obstacles which thwarted their efficiency, have not been known in this country ; but it is the object of this work to make them known. Yet before entering on the History of the Legion in detail, I would crave the attention of any unbiassed mind to this proposition. What could there be different in the young men of England, Ireland, and Scotland in 1835, from those of twenty-five years ago? We were drilled the same as the British army ; and for a longer period before meeting the enemy than many of the regiments who were under the Duke of Wellington. We were armed and accoutred from the Tower of London — our clothing made by the regular army tailors of England — our pay never fell into as long arrears as it did with the British army in Spain ; though it must be admitted that the moral effect of the credit of British and Spanish governments is very different. Our clothing was never so sore worn as that of the British in the peninsular war, else the testimony of old soldiers who served there is worth nothing. Therefore it must be asked again what difference could there be between British subjects becoming soldiers in Spain in 1835, and those who went there in 1809? all from the same classes of society, all of the same constitution physically and morally, and all disciplined by the same system of military law. I know no one can say why the Legion should have been cowards, and why the men of the peninsular war should not. Still such assertions have been made; and there are no parties in England who are ungenerous enough to reiterate these charges against the Legion so commonly, as that great mass of the population to which most of us belong. Our brethren of England of the working class, and those newspapers which assist them in repelling the foul charges of "swinish multitude," "unwashed ruffians," &c. &c., have been our most zealous assailants; repeating those charges of "cowards," "disgrace," and so on, which party hate only gendered against us. Refrain therefore, from branding a body of men with terms of reproach that are applied to yourselves by the same parties, from the same causes, and for the same purposes. There are charges against us that we will plead guilty to, and all the causes of our hardships and non-success will be laid before you; but "cowards" has no application to the Legion as a body of men. No one, however fastidious about military honor, has ever dared to call in question the personal courage of General Evans: still, though it will be proved that in fight he was brave even to a fault, and that with many of the obstacles that withstood him, he could have taken no other course than that which he took; it will be my duty to say some severe things of his character as a general out of the field, especially with regard to the hardships suffered by the troops, during the first winter of our service.

It will be necessary before beginning with the Legion, to give a sketch of what the war was, and in what situation the Christino and Carlist parties were when the foreign enlistment act was suspended, to allow British subjects to enter the service of Spain.

It is generally known, that Don Carlos claims the throne of Spain by right, and not from any factious motive, as some parties assert he does. By the laws of Spain, no female could reign until Ferdinand, father of the young Queen Isabella and brother of Don Carlos set that law aside, by making a decree in favour of his infant daughter. Had this abrogation of the Salicque law (as it is called) been agreed to by the Cortes and general voice of the nation, it would have been

more defensible ; but when it was known that King Ferdinand was
a man of weak mind, whose almost constant and dearest employment
was working with a needle—sewing and embroidering petticoats for
the Virgin Mary; and that his consort, the present Queen Regent,
was, and is still a woman of artful manners, loving and being loved
by hosts of lovers and political intriguers—and that she is believed
in conjunction with some of her Court favourites to have induced
her half idiotic husband to abrogate the law in favour of her daughter
and her own regency. When all these circumstances are considered,
it is almost natural to suppose that Carlos, the rightful heir would
claim the throne. But there is much more than the claim of Carlos
to the throne sought for by those who fight for him. The northern
provinces of Spain have always had laws peculiar to themselves
different from those of the south, and differing in many respects in
one part of a province from another part. These laws are called
fueros, which word in one sense signifies *laws*, but which in the
northern provinces always means " the rights of the people," or the
right of inheritance to property, coupled with the right of making
laws for themselves—being exempted from National taxes, and from
the general laws of Spain. On the kings of Spain ascending the
throne, an engagement was required of them by which they were
bound to continue all the privileges of the *fueros*, and then in addition to King of Spain, the title of Lord of Biscay was given to
royalty, and continued always in use in public documents as well as
common conversation throughout the Basque provinces where these
fueros existed.

There are no extensive landed proprietors in the north. Every
family have their cottage, orchard, garden, vineyard, and small corn
fields. The country is mountainous, and these cottages are to be
seen scattered on the sloping hill-sides peeping through their trees, or
basking in the sun, with their rivulets of water running down the
hill-side, which in Spain are always abundant, forming the Ebro, the
Nervion, the Urimea, or such rivers that wind through the valleys
below. The cultivation of these small farms is not severe labour, so
much of the produce being cider and wine. Hence the people live
at any time half idle; and as there is an abundance of the necessaries of life, there is no necessity for them doing more. They are
a different race altogether from the southern Spaniards, who are

little more than the serfs of grandees and are famed for indolence. The men of the north, are, as all mountaineers are—healthy, strong, sinewy, and brave. They are religious to an extreme, and no doubt, they in their local courts of self-government were a good deal under priestly influence. But if they were, it was an influence which they believed to be sacred as their salvation, and binding on them as the law of Heaven itself, and so long as they maintained their clergy and ecclesiastical institutions by a tax, which including all expences to which their land was liable, did not amount for an English acre to ten shillings sterling; and that land all of it equal, and much of it superior to the very best parts of England. It must be admitted that the inhabitants of the North of Spain had privileges not known in many other parts of the world.

Now, these are the people of which the Carlist army are composed. The government of the Queen sought to take away their *fueros*, and impose on them, laws and government burdens, the same as ruled the other provinces of Spain. Carlos, on the other hand, proclaimed himself Lord of Biscay, engaged to maintain the *fueros*, and let the people govern themselves as they had always done. Hence it is they fight for him. Hence it is the war is not ended, nor can it possibly be ended, until an army ten times the number of any that the Christinos have had, be marched against them! and who for such a cause would like to see it? The army of Carlos are the inhabitants of the land they are fighting on. They are defending their homes from the aggression of an enemy, when the southern Spaniard comes on them, and they have this advantage, they are hardy and swift of foot, their mountainous country protects them against cavalry or artillery, and they are so superior to any other infantry that they can go up one glen or mountain side, while an enemy is coming down the other, and there they can always choose whether to fight or not. Their policy is procrastination; for they know that they will tire out a government that must not only attack them but keep up a large army scattered in all parts of Spain, to watch them and keep down another body equally dangerous to that government, that is, the republicans. The Carlists know that, and their general tactics are, to hold those positions defended by rocks and rivers where five thousand assailants are no stronger, than five hundred who defend.

It is thus, that in a military point of view, the wisdom of General Evans having gone to Spain with such a small force may be doubted. As to the political merits of the interference, there may be conflicting opinions also, but it is only just to say, that the professions of the Queen's Ministers had much merit so far as they did not contemplate an interference with the *fueros* of the Biscayans, only these Ministers have been supplanted by other parties, and these in their turn too, have found successors : so that now it would be difficult to know on what principle the internal government of Spain would be carried on.

Thus far was this introductory Chapter written, when the debate in the House of Commons on the 13th March, occurred. Though by that debate the public have not gained much more information, the defunct Legion have gained something in character, at least, the calumnies false as they were ungenerous, were not uttered on that occasion.

The *special pleading* of some of the speakers to make out a case suitable to party opinions, caused quotations to be made in the most partial manner. The three months that we lay in, and around Vittoria, during which we suffered the most dreadful hardships, are always brought forward, and argued on as if the Legion had so suffered for the whole two years, And with these, assertions are made that have no foundation in fact whatever. It is said 250 officers quitted the service in disgust! Perhaps some of them might say they were disgusted, but I am bound to say they were disgraced first. 50 of that number were dismissed at various periods, for misconduct, and it is undeniable, that some of these have acted very prominent parts, as "correspondents "—authors, and wholesale calumniators of the Legion and its commander. Again a considerable proportion of the 250, were officers who had only one year's leave from the British and the East India Company's service, and who were obliged some of them (the gallant Colonel Apthorpe for instance,) much against their wish, to leave the Legion. As a proof what kind of disgust 250 were said to have left in ; I will mention one whom I knew, a Lieutenant, whose outfit had cost his friends a good few hundred pounds, it being more suitable for the showy parades in Hyde Park, than a campaign among the Basque mountains. One day as he smoked a Havannah, that perfumed the Biscayan air, and imprinted in the mud on the banks of the Nervion, the fashionable boots that had

been made to crush his toes in Bond Street, a concealed party of Carlists fired on us from a wood, as we marched past, we being then out
on a reconnoitring excursion. The dandy started, and it was said he
had no business whatever among the bushes that skirted the mountain pathway, but certain it is that by hurrying amongst them in
greater haste than honour warranted, the twigs drew off his mustachios and whiskers, leaving him with his former bearded face, naked
as it naturally was. Perhaps he might have overcome this disaster,
but unfortunately a little terrier dog that followed the regiment
snapped up the scented ornaments in his mouth, and ran playfully
along the whole line of the brigade with them ! Laughter was irresistible and the dandy's military heart was broken, so he resigned
and of course makes one of the number who are said to have quitted
in disgust.

A few more of these 250 were officers, who, by the accident of property being left to them while there, came home to take possession of it. One of these, a lieutenant, of the 8th Scotch Regiment
resigned to take the title and estates of a British Earldom; another, I
recollect, the heir apparent to the most ancient of the Scottish
Peerage resigned from being required to do so by family matters.
Yet these are all a part of those who are said to have quitted in
disgust, and if they are the publishers of their own story, they cannot
be much depended on.

It would be an easy, though unnecessary task to prove that almost
every statement made against General Evans in the House of Commons, was made and coloured for a purpose not the most honourable,
generally intended to lead civilians, who are unacquainted with the
details of warfare—astray. Yet General Evans attempted a line of
defence which must make all who served under him, and who have
held him hitherto in high respect, grieve ; for from political expedien-
cy, he defends the indefensible Cordova and Espartera, and we who
have a regard for the military character of the Legion, and who never
looked at him in any light but as a military Commander, must now
suffer the attacks of his political opponents, merely because he chooses still to be a partizan, and defend himself in a political capacity.

CHAPTER II.

Reasons for postponing the first nine months' History of the Legion to a future part of the Work—Action of the 5th of May at San Sebastian—Its commencement—the first Line of Fortifications taken—the different Brigades described—Charges repulsed by the Carlists from behind their Fortifications—The second Line of Defences taken—Arrival of the Phœnix and Salamander War Steamers with two fresh Regiments from Santander—the Phœnix opens a Fire on the Carlist Fort of Lugariz—the 4th and 8th land and are marched into the Fight at its greatest heat—a Breach made in the Redoubt of Lugariz—the 4th and 8th enter—Dreadful slaughter on both sides—Gallant behaviour of Captain Allez of the 4th—He falls—Reckless conduct of Corporal Oakley of the 8th, Private Smith, and others—the Westminster Grenadiers—their Charge—Adjutant M—— of the 8th a Coward—Gallantry of Smith, he is mortally wounded—Captain Shields wounded—Oakley shoots a Carlist Officer—Charging on the enemy—Running over wounded Carlists—the White House taken—Plundering in it—the Chapelgorris kill the Carlist Prisoners and the English try to save them—Numerous personal Anecdotes collected after the Engagement—Killed, wounded, and missing—Remarks on the Engagement—The General's Despatches, &c. &c.

In beginning the history of the Legion with the action of the 5th of May, 1836, I am beginning where all who have hitherto written accounts of the Legion, have left off. The share we bore in the war, actively, only commenced at that time, and continued for thirteen months; which, strange to say, has never yet been made known in detail to English readers. But the reason is obvious. Those officers who became authors, were nearly all of that class who left the service in *disgust*, as they are pleased to say; and the disgusted gentlemen were either all dismissed before the engagement of the 5th of May, or they had the natural propensity, common to gentlemen of delicate sensibility, to get disgusted as quickly after the first engagement as posssible; to avoid the danger of the second, third, fourth, fifth, sixth, and seventh, which soon followed, and in sanguinary succession, proved that those gentlemen who resigned early, were persons of prudent forethought.

It may be said, that the character of these persons make a part of the character of the Legion; but it is not so. These were the refuse of the Legion, from whom political partizans at home have taken their prejudiced information; and I never saw an officer quit

the service by his voluntary resignation, but the sneers of the soldiers followed him, even though he might not deserve to be sneered
at; so tenacious even were the men serving in the ranks, of the
honour of their officers. Had not the Legion's history been so
grossly misrepresented, we might in this have taken a view of them
from their landing in the country up to the fifth of May. But as
this work will go over the war, guided more by the nature of the
events than their date of occurrence, I have thought it best to begin
where our active services began, which was at San Sebastian, in
May, 1836; not but that the fatigues of the previous months ought
to be recorded, but because these are in every one's mouth, in and
out of parliament, without the other parts of our history being
known; but which I shall allude to hereafter.

After marching from Vittoria to Santander, at which place we
arrived on the 19th, 20th, and 21st of April, 1836, we had to wait
for some time; for before vessels could be got to convey all the
regiments, Spanish and English, that were proceeding to San Sebastian, it was the 4th of May. On that day the 4th, and two-thirds
of the 8th regiments, being the last of the Legion, embarked on
board the Phœnix and Salamander, British war steamers, and were
conveyed to San Sebastian. It was next day, early in the forenoon,
when they came within the reach of sound from the battle, which
was then going on. But we shall only let them hear the cannonade, and guess among themselves what it is. They are beginning
to see the clouds of smoke, and hear the distant roll of musketry,
and there we shall leave them for a time. Some, under the dark
presentiment of the fate they are about to fall under — others, in
their folly, making boast; and many, and perhaps the most wise,
making up their resolution to do their duty with honour, now that
they are in such a situation, but searchingly thinking on themselves.
We shall leave them there, till we go forward to the Legion, and
begin where the engagement began.

For some days previous to the 5th, plans had been forming for
the attack on the enemy's lines. The Carlists had a double line of
fortifications, extending from the river Urimea on the east to a deep
glen, which opens to the sea two miles westward. In that space
there were some villages on the heights, and a great number of
scattered houses, with stone walls enclosing small fields. Half a

mile from San Sebastian the first of their fortifications was formed, and then on heights above that were numerous others, some of them the natural defences of the ground, such as ditch banks, deep cut lanes, and so on, with breastworks, barricades of barrels filled with earth, and all the houses loopholed, so as they could fire under cover. Behind these, and separated in some parts by deep hollows, were other heights similarly fortified for musketry, but more strongly erected and intrenched for cannon. The main road from San Sebastian to Harnani went through that ground, and was at various places barricaded. The whole, as seen from the citadel, and as known to those who had been over the ground before the Carlists came there, was a series of fortifications, rising one behind another, and against which it would be no easy matter to direct a force with an energy sufficient to drive the enemy back.

Some counselled the General to pause a few days longer, as all the 4th, and six companies of the 8th, were not yet come forward, and as more Spanish troops from Santander were expected. The General, however, had seen the trifling way in which Cordova managed matters; and not deeming it proper to depend on his sending more troops, resolved to attack the Carlists with the force he had. It consisted of about five thousand British, and fifteen hundred Spaniards.

On the 4th, orders were promptly issued to the field officers, and by them given to the troops, that an attack would be led on next morning. What injunctions General Evans gave to his principal officers, or whether he gave any, was not known; but the different brigadiers thought fit to make observations on what was necessary for commanding officers to do; and these, in their return harangued their men. Some of them urged the propriety of being merciful to any prisoners who might fall into their hands; and one, Colonel Fortescue, of the Rifles, enjoined his men to conduct the reverse "Neither take nor give quarter," he said, "you will be fighting with savages, who will kill you if you are prisoners. Stand, to the last man, against them." This injunction was never believed by his men as wishing them to kill their prisoners, they rather thought that it was spoken at the time to deter them from trusting themselves prisoners, and that rather than fall into the hands of the enemy, to die in the fight. That is what the report of his speech was supposed to mean; and I only mention it because it has been made a subject of much warm dispute in parliament and elsewhere. Captains had their directions to give, and the interior of San Sebastian was that night all bustle. At one o'clock the regiments began to muster. It was a dark morning, and the showers of rain tended to keep the roads and fields in a disadvantageous state for the attack; and the men have since told me, that the dreariness looked so like the Vittoria mornings, when we marched out through the gloomy gates, so often expecting to fight, that they, from the similarity of the scene, could not fancy it more than a Vittoria excursion. " Close up, cover your files, and be perfectly silent," were orders given by officers of companies. At three o'clock the whole were moving out of the gates. The Light brigade, under General Reid, consisting of the Rifles, 3d, 6th, and Chapelgorris took the right of the enemy's lines, towards the river Urimea. The Irish brigade, consisting of the 7th, 9th, and 10th, under General Shaw, took the centre; and General Chichester's Brigade, consisting that morning of the 1st regiment of the Legion, two companies of the 8th, and about eight hundred Spaniards, (the 4th and remainder of the 8th, belonging to this Brigade, not being yet landed), took the left of the enemy's line. The convent St Bartolome was the point to which the different brigades marched, by the main road, previous to taking each their right, left, and forward directions. Some houses, two hundred yards in front of that, were the outposts of the Carlists, and the space between was neutral ground. Arrived at this point, all yet quiet, the enemy having no suspicion that they were so close upon them, it was deemed prudent to halt till the right and left brigades moved off, so as to make the attack as simultaneous as possible; and while that was being done, the 7th regiment on the road, stood ready to give and receive the first shots. The red glare of the enemy's picquets' fire, at a distance—the dark gloom of the wet morning, with the perfect stillness of everything around—not a cough, a whisper, nor a footstep heard, those who were moving forward treading with cautious lightness to get as near as possible, to be ready when the signal of attack would be given— and, as every man held his breath to listen for that order, all at once the sounds, " Qui vive ?" " Chapelgorri carajo," and a musket shot, were heard. This was the challenge from the Carlist sentry : " who comes there ?" and the answer of "Chapelgorri," accompanied with the common Spanish oath, and a well-aimed shot, which laid the luckless Carlist dead, and broke the silence of the morning. Forward! was the order of every commanding-officer to his regiment. A whole volley from the nearest Carlist piquet, and repeated by the different piquets all round the lines, kept up the noise, and the whiz of the balls was immediately heard — commanding officers called, "come on!" — aides-du-camp were galloping about with orders -- General Evans, in person, was in front of those farthest advanced — some were dropping down, giving a groan, and others fell silently dead.

The orders of the General had been not to fire, but to advance as close as possible, and charge with the bayonet; and this succeeded for a short time, till the first houses were cleared, out-piquets driven in, and so on; but as daylight began to show each party their opponents, and as the fortifications of the enemy seemed impregnable to such a small force, it was necessary, in some parts, to halt and fire.

The Chapelgorris are brave, and determined in fight; but that becomes a fault with them, when they forget that they are commanded by a General who acts on a studied plan. In this engagement they were absolutely wild to get at the Carlists, and where they could not run in with their bayonets, they fired, if there was only the slightest chance of killing, even though they were ordered not to fire. But it was different with the 7th Irish. Almost without firing a shot, that regiment advanced forward in the face of vollies; every minute some of their column dropping down dead and wounded, but going steadily forward, with the indomitable Swan at their head. He had been called a tyrant in his discipline, but he shewed himself now worthy of his command. He and his regiment proceeded forward, and actually took possession of the wind-mill battery, though five hundred loop-holes in the building had each a Carlist at it. It being still the grey of the morning when the 7th made their way over the stone walls into this place, the enemy might suppose, from the resolute way in which they had come up through their heavy fire, that there were many more than there really was. A great number of the enemy fell in and about these houses, but it was because they would not surrender themselves prisoners, but fought with the 7th, bayonet to bayonet. The conflict and the slaughter for a short while was mu-

No. 2.   B

tual, but the Carlists gave way. This was the first position of any
importance taken. General Shaw led them on with great ardour.
In this respect, every one who knows Shaw must allow that he has
all those attributes that are called bravery and courage. Onwards
he and his Brigade pushed. " You are doing nobly, Irishmen," said
General Evans to them about this time ; and the General himself
had only paused in his forward career for a few minutes, to send
orders to the other Generals, for the first line of fortification had now
given way, and a desperate effort required to be made to carry the
second. At these, however, there was something more destructive
to be done. Five pieces of artillery, from different posts of the line,
including the strongly-built and intrenched redoubt of Lugariz, were
now opened on the assailants. Musketry from every point — from
houses, through loopholes, in stone walls—from ditches, and from
all the numerous places that afforded cover, were now opposed to
them, and several attempts to carry the positions at the charge were
made, but repulsed with great determination by the enemy.

The Rifles, and the 3d and 6th, were getting their complete share
at the same time. When the 7th had carried the wind-mill houses
in the centre, the Light Brigade succeeded in establishing themselves,
and driving the enemy from other posts of a similar description.
About this time, Colonel Tupper, gallantly charging with his regiment, was shot through the arm ; but lest his officers and men might
be discouraged, he drew his cloak round about him, to hide it, and
led on his regiment for two hours longer, when, almost exhausted by
the loss of blood, and as he was again fronting a heavy fire, was shot
in the head. He lived a short while, and could say little more than,
" tell the regiment that I can no longer command them, but that they
are fit to be commanded by any one that will fight with them, and
that they will receive their reward in the well-deserved approbation
of their country." Tupper died shortly after, and was buried where
he fell.

Sharing the danger, and acting with equal vigour, the 1st and the
two companies of the 8th, under General Chichester, (but not very
well supported by the Spanish regiments,) assisted in the assault.

Colonel Fortescue, of the Rifles, was particularly conspicuous. At
different times engaged hand to hand with the Carlists, he continued
to fight, though he was wounded early in the engagement; his clothe

were literally torn off him. He had been going with his sleeves turned up, making his way sometimes through bushes—then over a wall—up to the knees in a gutter at one time, dragging his men through when they were sinking in the ditches and mud. "Mad Fortescue," he was often called after that time. He was a reckless fellow; and the very one to cut a figure in such warfare as he was now engaged in.

In attempting to charge, the 7th and 9th were repulsed three different times; each time being forced to retreat leaving numbers lying. A part of the 10th at last came to join them. Old Colonel (afterwards General) Fitzgerald headed the whole. A stone wall secured them for a time, from the enemy's shot; and over the wall the old fellow sprung, with a riding whip in his hand. The men attempted to follow; but as they got over the wall, volley on volley poured out on them, and battered them down as fast as they got over. The first of them thus falling so thickly, the remainder hung back. All the officers of the three regiments who were over the wall, fell, excepting Fitzgerald: he stood still, called them to come on—"Irishmen! tenth, ninth, seventh; Munster boys, bog-trotters, ragamuffins, come on with ould Charlie—I'll stand here by myself till I'm shot, if ye don't come." All this time the balls aimed at Fitzgerald were battering on the wall; and some of those who had fallen only wounded at first, were, now while they lay on the ground beside him, shot dead. When his last words of determination were heard, one Irishman sprung over the wall, saying, "soul, an' ye'll not die by yourself, ould Charlie." This was a familiar way in which his men (who were devoted to him) always addressed him; and following that one, all who were there charged. Several officers and a number of the men fell; amongst the former, Captain Thomson, of the 9th, a gallant thorough-going fellow, was severely wounded.

Through the united efforts of all who were in the field (for there were no reserve, every one being engaged), the second line of defences gave way; and the only obstacle of importance now remaining was the fort of Lugariz. To defend this, the principal strength of the enemy was now directed. The wet clayey soil—the continual charging and retreating—ascending and descending the steep hill sides, which the men had been exposed to up to this time, nine o'clock, rendered the attempt on Lugariz a mere killing of men, without the possibility of taking it. However, attempts were made: in one of

these, Captain Knight, aide-de-camp to General Chichester, fell, and
when the ground where he lay was again taken, his body was found
to have been bayoneted in four different places. Colonel Ellis, Major
Freestun, Captain Scarman, and other officers, distinguished themselves at this place; and the Rifles, 6th and 3d regiments, with the
Chapelgorris, were hotly engaged.

At this moment the Phœnix and Salamander, with the 4th and 8th,
entered the bay. Boats immediately crowded out, and brought them
ashore. Their knapsacks were thrown off on the sands—a guard
left on them—and, by the order of General Evans, delivered by his
aide-de-camp, the 8th first, and the 4th following them, were marched up; but along the sea-side, to miss, if possible, the sight of the
dead and wounded. But though that was the intent of the General, they met the wounded in vast numbers as they were carried into the town. Old Godfrey went on whistling, with his hands behind his back.—" Come on, you d——d grenadiers," he said, "and
you little beggars in the other companies there, come on; we'll let
them see, by and by, they hav'n't got it all to themselves. The General came forward, shook hands with the old fellow, and said—
" well Godfrey, I'm glad to see you're just in time : Chichester will
give you the necessary orders." " Scotchmen," he continued, " you
will not have much to do; but I know you will be proud to share
the glory with the 6th regiment. Your countrymen are carrying
everything before them," or words to that effect. He then met the
4th, and, no doubt, paid them similar compliments. The different
English vessels, under the command of Commodore Lord John Hay,
but especially the Phœnix, under the immediate command of the able
and gallant Captain Henderson, anchored close to the shore, and
opened a tremendous fire of ball and shell, on the fort of Lugariz.
At a distance of sixteen hundred yards, the shells were thrown with
the greatest precision. Cannon were fired in return at the Phœnix,
by the Carlists, but without effect. From the ships, bomb after bomb
made its loud hissing noise through the air, close over the heads of
our men; and exploding, as it reached the exact point, caused awful
devastation amongst the enemy.

" Now is the time, Godfrey," said General Chichester go up there
with your regiment, don't let a single shot be fired, march close up, and
pull the bayonets off the enemy's muskets through the loop-holes."

The 8th and 4th were then standing under cover : a few yards forward, by getting round the corner, would bring them under the fire. " Come, then, Captain Sheilds," said Godfrey, " mind what you have to do with your grenadiers. Follow me, men ; let nothing stop you. Serjeants Hamilton and Grey ; and you, Dingwall, Smith, and Oakley, on the right of the company, push on, and never mind who falls. The whole—attention ! with cartridge prime and load. See now you make no mistakes—not one of you fire a shot till ordered. Close well up. Pay attention to the command of your officers ; and let the officers pay attention to me. Silence ! you little beggars in the centre there, silence, Fix bayonets—carry your arms at the short trail—companies will follow in succession from the right. Grenadiers, right face—march—right wheel—double,' Round the corner the whole made their way—whiz, whiz went the bullets through amongst them—crash, crack went the cannon balls through trees, tearing up the ground on each side. Musketry rattled in all directions. Rockets made their way over head with a long train of blue smoke, and bursted in the redoubt, or slaughtered for themselves a way through a column or a line. The artillery of the Legion, the Salamander, and the Phœnix, with whole vollies of their heaviest cannon, battered at one angle of the redoubt. A part of it fell ; and a thirteen inch shell coming close over the heads of our men, knocking some of them down, though it did not touch them, bursted about fifteen yards before them, close in the inside of the breach ; and some others falling in the redoubt, and exploding at the same moment, turned all for a few minutes into destruction and disorder among the enemy ; and in these few minutes Lugariz was taken. Colonel Godfrey, Captain Shields, serjeants and privates, Dingwall, Smith, and others of the grenadiers, were at once in, followed by the regiment. At the same moment Adjutant Allez, of the 4th, and a party of non-commissioned officers and men, leapt over another part of the wall. The Carlists from the other side shot them as they got up ; and while the dead and wounded tumbled back from the top of the wall among the living ones outside, the 4th hesitated. Allez, left by himself, stood calling for the men to join him. A few more mounted the wall, and by the Carlists, who still stood taking sure aim, were shot. He was then, as some said, heard to utter an exclamation of determined defiance, and made a desperate rush at those of the enemy nearest him; but a ball through his heart laid him dead! It was a pistol shot from an officer; and it being just at the moment that the first of our regiment got footing inside, corporal Oakley of the company I belonged to rushed forward on the Carlist who was snatching up a loaded musket from the hands of a dead soldier, and stabbing the officer—Oakley made death doubly sure by shooting him also! Oakley was one of the most surprising young men that ever the British or any service possessed; but enough will be known of him hereafter so we shall leave him at present.

It is only just to the 4th regiment to say, that their hesitation was but momentary; and when it is considered that they had to climb over embankments so difficult of ascent that a few could only mount at a time, and these being shot dead as their heads rose among the shower of bullets from the interior, it will scarcely be said that they were *cowards.*—No; that epithet *can not*, and will not be used against them. Instead thereof, every one who had the common feelings of our common nature, must sink prejudices and be astonished, that such being their reception, they hesitated only for a few moments; and then in the face of death and over the accumulated dead and dying, they fought their way, bayonet to bayonet, man to man, with smoke, fire, and balls mingling and mixing up a terrific scene of grand disaster. The two regiments had gained their footing; and oh! the soul that loves the awful how it could have feasted there to madness!—The horrid grin of death that follows the mortal gunshot—the dead man trampled by the living one—the wild sound of the huzza and the oath—the guerilla's last revenge tearing with his teeth a wounded man, a musket or a stone, blood mixing with blood, and men yet unscathed dashing forward to meet their death;—such was the scene at this particular period of the fight, at this particular position.

But though this is a part, it is merely a part of such scenes. The seeming impossibilities that had over and over presented themselves had all been overcome; and that by a daring determination which makes men question when it is over how they could possibly dare to do what they did. At one period during the heat of the action, and when the second line had been partly carried, General Shaw was seen close to a fortified house, about to attack it with the 7th regi-

ment. This house being deeply entrenched around and loop-holed
so that the enemy could fire on the assailants, completely protected
in its interior, was one of the most formidable on that line of defences. The 7th had by this time done some desperate work, and
were just being re-formed by their commanding officer, Lieutenant
Colonel Swan, from the disorder consequent on having immediately
before carried a position in which many of them fell. Without
having had a pause for some hours, Colonel Swan received the following order from General Shaw,—" You will advance and at all
hazards take possession of that fortified house in front ;" and General Chichester having observed that position, ordered two companies of the 8th from his brigade to support the 7th. These
coming up under command of Majors Mitchell and Hogg, the order
was given to the 7th to advance. That regiment emerged from the
temporary cover of a house behind which they were formed: but a
shower of bullets from the fortification against which they marched
battered them down in front ; and they hesitated. General Shaw
became excited, and with that warmth of manner, yet stern resolution for which he is remarkable when in a fight, called out in a
voice of thundering loudness—" halt, the 7th shall not have the
honour of going, they hesitate," Then turning to the detachment
of the other regiment he said—" Mitchell and Hogg move up with
these companies of the 8th, and take that house from the enemy,—
let nothing prevent you ! " This was spoken in the hearing of the
men ; and no doubt the 7th were well enough satisfied to allow
their neighbours of the 8th to go first ; indeed the 7th previous
to this had been nearly shattered to pieces by their repeated charges
on places where it was impossible to gain a footing.

Majors Mitchell and Hogg, Captain Larkham and Lieutenant
Fiske, the only officers with that detachment of the 8th, led their
men on. The whole house was a blaze from its hundreds of loop-
holes ; fire, smoke, and showers of bullets fronted them. The gallant Mitchell, one of the bravest young fellows that ever unsheathed
a sword, and in whom the men put unlimited confidence fell mortally wounded. Hogg, his junior in rank, but not a whit inferior in
those qualities that make a gallant soldier, also fell severely wounded,
but both, lying amid the numerous wounded and dead who fell
around them, waved their swords and cheered the men to go on.

The cheer was gallantly responded to, when Captain Larkham and
Lieutenant Fiske also fell; and at the most moderate calculation as
appeared from the regimental returns, one half of the non-commissioned officers and privates mixed their blood with that of their
officers. By the assistance of some other companies from the Irish
brigade this fortification was soon afterwards taken, though with
great loss to the assailants.

By this time the reader will be aware, that the nature of the
ground on which this engagement was fought prevented anything
like that regularity of movement which is seen when regiments manœuvre on a field day. The innumerable walls and ditches rendered our cavalry entirely ineffective ; and the frequent unsuccessful assaults that were made on positions ere these could be carried
left many of our wounded men lying within reach of the Carlist
musketry. At one time the 6th regiment had retreated from an
assault on a fortified position, and two of their men were observed
lying on a dicth bank severely wounded; one of them had crawled
a considerable distance dragging his limbs, both legs having balls
through them ; and probably had the intention of rolling himself
into the ditch for shelter, as the enemy from their entrenchments
were popping away at all those whom they observed lying and not
yet dead. This poor fellow as he gained .the ditch bank, and
seemed about to seek shelter for himself in it, got a shot that
tumbled him in, and he never came out of it. The shot was through
his head, and he lies there still.

The other was a sergeant, and on some of the men observing the
fate of the one just detailed, they proposed to go out from where they
were in temporary cover, and bring in the wounded sergeant. " I'll
give any man a dollar that goes out and pulls him into the ditch,"
said one of the officers of the regiment. " I'll bring him here on my
back," replied one of the men; " it's what any of us ought to do
without payment; for I'm thinking some more of us 'll be lying the
same way by and by — hold my firelock some of ye, and I'll let ye
see me go for him." This fellow got the poor sergeant in his arms,
but he fell dead, and the sergeant was again left lying. Presently,
two more ventured, one after the other, and both in their turn were
shot dead also. These shots were observed to come from a quarter
where none of the enemy were suspected to be. An immediate

attack was made on that point, which was carried, the poor Carlists paying fearfully for what they had just done. That sergeant afterwards recovered, and the three men who were killed in trying to save him, were part of those who gorged that ditch ; many others having been tumbled into it, and the bank dug down above them.

About this time, the 3d regiment, commanded by Colonel Churchill, made a determined charge on a place that had been a long while resolutely defended by the enemy. The Carlist chief Segastibelza and his staff, were at this point. The red flag, indicating " no quarter," was hoisted above him, and all reports award to him the character of a brave chief. But here he fell ; and the flag that was meant to proclaim the bloody decree of Durango, was taken by Colonel Churchill and his regiment.

Perhaps the individuality of the Lieutenant General himself, should have been mentioned before this. For besides his orders as General, which he gave from the most correct judgment of the positions and the nature of the attack required to carry them, he was frequently seen in situations which he might have avoided as commander. When the attack was commenced in the morning, he was the first to mount the enemy's barricades, and sword in hand, cheer on the Irish brigade. At different times afterwards, he was seen in the very hottest of the fight, accompanied by his staff. Colonel Woolridge, and Lord William Paget, besides some others of his staff were wounded, while he was leading on these assaults in person.

By the time that the second line of fortifications were taken, many of our best officers had fallen. Some of those not so amiable, had also met with what had been promised them. At least I must say, that opinions prevailed that some of them fell neither by the enemy, nor by their *friends* ; yet my own opinion is, that if there were any such cases there could be very few. However, there were now fourteen field-officers, upwards of twenty captains, double that number of subalterns, with a proportionate number of men, amongst the killed and wounded. Colonel Tupper's regiment was now commanded by Colonel Ross, a brave and gallant officer; who was there, and in different engagements afterwards, distinguished in a most eminent manner. Still it was not easy to fill the place of such an officer as Tupper, who was one of the noblest veterans that had survived the peninsular war; but he fell there near to a monument that had been erected over the graves of some of the heroes that Wellington commanded; and he and others who saturated the ground that day with their blood, did no dishonor to the dust of those graves.

The brave Colonel Fortescue was also now amongst the wounded; and Swan, who was one of the severest disciplinarians in the service, and who had while drilling often got the silent curses of his men on his head in liberal measure, he too fell severely wounded, but not until every man who had the spirit of a soldier, had forgiven him for former severities. His incessant daring conduct that day — in front of every danger himself that he took his men to — melted the animosities of those whom he commanded, into admiration. General Reid was also wounded, and his brigade was now commanded by Don Belloso, a brave Spaniard, Colonel of the Oveida regiment.

There was one fellow not wounded, and I believe nothing gave more general grief than this person's escape. He was an officer of the 8th regiment, and though much of him could be said, we may at present pass him over by saying, that he was a most peculiarly ill-looking, ill-disposed man — cruelly tyrannical — drunk large quantities of brandy — flogged the men by the provost system without measure or regard to crime — went by the name of M——— — shewed himself a coward, and soon after for shame left the Legion; and is one of those who "quitted in *disgust*," as the gallant Sir Henry Hardinge has been imposed upon by false informants to say.

When the fort of Lugariz was taken, a great part of the Carlist army retired upon a point to which that part of the action with which I am more particularly acquainted, was now carried. The two regiments that had shortly before been landed, were fresh compared with the others, and were ordered to this point. It is unfair to particularise the incidents of one regiment more than those of another; but at the same time, as all details cannot be given, those occurring nearest the narrator will perhaps not be objected to.

Godfrey on getting an order to advance from where he then was, and seeing some other regiments likely to get before him, called out " come on my brave fellows! dont let them get all the praise to themselves--down this hill--over to yon houses--double, grenadiers, (the word " double " means to increase the pace from the quick step to a quick short trot). " Hurrah —hurrah—rah—ah—ah " the whole regiment yelled out, running off with their pieces at the charge. Hurrah one had again begun but was stopped by a ball going through his head. He fell close beside Oakley.—" What a fool you are," said Oakley, stepping over his body! " what a consolation to die with a hurrah in your throat! Do as I do, walk up to them quietly, and bid them take your compliments to the devil at once, making sure you send them on the right road—tal—al—al " he was beginning to sing, when he was stopped. " Who was that fell there," enquired the Captain of the company (Shields), " Oakley, sir " some one answered,—" poor fellow," said the Captain,—He's dead." " No, I ain't," answered Oakley ; and he resumed his tal—al—al, though a ball had struck the brass plate of his side belt, and by its force had knocked him down, and though others were dropping around him every minute.

The Carlists on a piece in front had rallied, and a heavy rattling fire was now meeting our regiments. Shields was cheering on his company,—" come on, my good fellows, come on," he exclaimed ; and had again called to them " come on," when down he tumbled. " Oh! the Captain's shot—the Captain's wounded," said some of those who were close to him. " No, I am not killed," said he, raising himself up, " but there is something wrong with me, for I can't hold my sword.—Oh! it's only through my arm—go on Robert with the company, and I will follow as soon as I get my handkerchief bound round it." This was his brother he spoke to ; he was ensign in the company.—There was always great love mani- fested between these two for each other ; but the younger Sheilds dashed on calling for the men to follow him and let his brother lie. The latter replied, " go on, go on," and starting up, took his sword in his left hand, gave a hurra and added " d——n the arm, let it go to mischief—my company must be the first to take your position, and I must be with them ;" and away he followed, cheer- ing with his arm shattered and hanging down ; but faintness soon stopped him, and he was carried out of the field. The men with young Shields were obliged to take shelter under a ditch bank until some others came up to their assistance, for the Carlists were stand- ing firm ; and a tremendous fire was now meeting them. To keep up a fire was all that could be done for a few minutes.—" Keep under cover men," said Mr. Shields, " but fire on, fire on."—" No," answered the dauntless Bob Smith, " I'll do anything you bid me as a soldier ought to do, but may I be shot this minute if I lie behind a hedge ; stand up like men and let them see us."

Smith was in every sense a soldier of those qualifications which are the distinguishing marks if an English veteran are to be supposed as constituting a soldier. He knew all parts of the artillery exercise—could elevate a mortar to throw a shell to a given distance —was a horseman—could perform the cavalry and infantry exercise in all its varieties, old and new—could fight with any one on any occasion—swore—got drunk, and had been punished by the provost for several acts of misbehaviour. Such was Smith, a native of Dundee, and one who had been fourteen years on foreign service in the British army. From the time he had been in this engagement his daring conduct had been in a peculiar manner conspicuous ; and now that the Captain was wounded and left behind, I believe that the men generally placed more dependence on Smith, although a private, than they did on any officer.

That company being in front had got near to a formidable barrier, which it was not easy to pass, and the Carlists, seeing the advantage, were mustering strong to oppose them. A few of the enemy had re-crossed a ditch, which on Mr. Shields observing he called out in his anxiety to maintain the position he had gained,—" down with these fellows men, down with them— mark that officer leading them on. Oh ! if I had only orders to charge on them ! what should I do Smith ? " Smith on being thus applied to for advice answered, " let us run on them, Mr. Shields ; let us run in on them ; don't let them come on us ; let us meet them on their own ground."

The Carlist leader was still persevering when Oakley, who had just at this moment come up, being much distressed by the stroke of the ball which had cut his accoutrements across the breast, but still wearing his usual appearance of gaiety, the Carlist officer continued to lead on his men, when the words " so much for Buckingham" were heard from Oakley, while he cocked, presented, took aim, fired, killed the Carlist leader, and spoke all in the same moment ! and still betraying no emotion.

Orders were then received by that party, to go forward and take the house before them at any hazard. It was one of those farm houses so common in the north. Standing slightly elevated on the hill-side and containing dwelling-house, stable, cowshed, pig-stye, dung-hill, cider, wine and grain-stores all under the same roof. A part of the 4th regiment were now sent here also.——The bugles sounded the well known field-calls for the onset. The officers waved their swords, and the men following them leaped over the walls and ditches, braving in front the battering balls that showered down from the orchards, and the farm house.

Among the first who led on, making their way over the opposing defences, was the brave Smith, and a serjeant and private of the 4th. Smith fell back mortally wounded in the breast, and the other two fell at the same moment, both wounded mortally in the head.

Amid fire, smoke and disaster, a mixed cry was then got up of, "to the white house,—to the white house—in on them—in on them, over the ditch—there's two, three, four of the Carlists lying wounded, oh! dont kill them—Ah! see the Chapelgorris killing them.—Oh! Lord I'm—I'm—shot—help me—the man's dead, never mind him—up to the house—take them prisoners.—Sut, sut, ut, ut, whiz, whiz, buz, buz,—oh! my leg, —there's Tam killed dead—hurrah—hurrah hur—oh! my—see how they, lie down there—what are we to do now? Stand a few minutes here behind the house, until some more come up---did ye see how Miller fell yonder?---and little Thomson how he was *winged* leaping over the ditch---now not a moment left men---into the house---over that garden wall---shoot---fire---down with these fellows---Oh! God my---my---take him prisoner---here now men follow me---dont let them escape."

Such were a string of running exclamations which were then made up to the time of gaining the entrance to this house. At the time that was gained; fire and smoke issued from every corner and crevice inside and outside the house. The assailants firing up stairs, and the defendants down; and the cry was—"up the stair—upon them—take them prisoners—fire—stab—fell—break his head—shoot that one that's got out of the window— see how they're carrying their wounded away.—Oh! God, who shot that woman—here's wine—here's pang (bread)—here's a priest's cloak—what's this?—d——n ye its silver, half and share—I share that with you, Drummond; I'll see you d——d first—give us a drink of that wine—I'll break

your head if you offer to take it out of my hand—open that box—
break it—there it goes—silver!—out with it—into my haversack
with it—what should I put it into your haversack for ? I'll put it
into my own haversack!—What's that Tom Wilson has ? a hen—
shoot that pig—Ben M'Neil's killed a cow with his bayonet—quick
quick, out with the sheets—smash the drawers to pieces—break the
lock—there's a Carlist beneath the bed—Oh! don't kill him—
there's another in a barrel—Oh! Jamie Gibson that's a shame to
kill him in the barrel, I'm not killing him but want that sash with
the dollars in it from his waist—Oh! don't kill that one, it's a
shame—it's no shame, did ye not see how our men were stabbed
yonder—turn down out of this house men—take your prisoners
to the General, but don't disgrace yourselves—I'll put my sword
through the first of you that I see touching another article in the
house."

These last exclamations came from officers, who, anxious to save
the character of their men from anything disgraceful, were now
urging those in the house to desist from plundering.

It being deemed unnecessary to take possession of more ground,
the troops that were farthest in advance on the retreating Carlists
were called back; and all the regiments were re-formed, and a
muster made to find out the killed, wounded, or missing.

General Evans on coming along the regiments was loudly cheered.
He seemed rather excited, but it was that excitement that no one
could mistake, pleasurable emotions. His clothes were dirty and
torn, as were those of every officer; for the mud being often knee
deep, and the rain continuing to come on, the whole engagement
had been fought under the most disadvantageous circumstances.
He took off his hat as he passed along, and continued remarking,
" you have done well all of you; you have made a noble beginning."

Some straggling shots were yet for a short while heard; but
these also died away, and melancholy silence succeeded. Parties
were seen here and there covering up the dead bodies; and at different places some of the wounded were found lying in ditches into
which they had crawled to save themselves from the shot of the
enemy. One man was found with *twenty-nine* bayonet wounds in
him, he having been taken prisoner and subjected to the amusement
of some of the Carlists, who were putting him leisurely to death

when they were suddenly surprised, and forced from their position.

The females of St. Sebastian, from the highest to the lowest rank, vied with each other in rendering assistance to the wounded men but their generous treatment of us in that respect and on all occasions will be more fully detailed hereafter.

The following is the " General Order " of the day relative to this engagement, and though rather lengthened it will, I trust, be found interesting.

Head-Quarters,
San Sebastian, May, 1836.

GENERAL ORDER.

The time requisite for obtaining Reports from the Commanders of Brigades and Regiments, enumerating the Officers, Non-Commissioned Officers, and men, who more particularly distinguished themselves in the glorious action of the 5th instant, and the necessity of classifying the names of those reported, has obliged the Lieut. General to postpone till the present moment, the duty so grateful to his feelings of expressing to the troops his deep sense of obligation for their noble and admirable conduct on that day.

The enemy's defences, after five months of preparation, had become a species of fortress, secured on either flank by a river and morass, and defended by what may be termed a garrison of three thousand men.

Before day-light our three columns of Spanish and British troops, under Brigadier-Generals Chichester, Reid, and Shaw, ascended, attacked, and carried in the most prompt and excellent manner, the enemy's first line of entrenchments.—A series of barricades, some deep ravines, and for the moment unsurmountable obstacles presented themselves to oppose any farther immediate progress against the enemy's centre and right.---What we gained however in that quarter was firmly maintained till the proper moment arrived for a farther advance.

In the meantime the 1st and 2nd Brigades and the Spanish Corps attached to them, still pressing forward, carried in a brilliant style that part of the 2nd line in their front where the 7th, 9th, and 10th

regiments established themselves although continually exposed to a
very heavy cross fire.

The whole of the 1st regiment with some detachments from the
7th, 8th, 10th, and Segovia regiments continuing in the same direction their triumphant career, soon lodged themselves notwithstanding
all the difficulties of the ground, close under the enemy's third and
last line of defence, the redoubt or battery of Lugariz. From this
point some heroic attempts were made to climb over the enemy's
parapets on the summit, led by Col. Ellis, accompanied by Majors
Freestun, Hicks, Thomson, Capt. Scarman, and other officers. These
efforts which were for a time ineffectual owing to the steepness of
the ascent, but still more to the extreme fatigue and exhaustion of
the troops from previous exertion, redounded in the highest degree
to the honour of those engaged in them. One of the chivalrous onsets referred to was headed by Capt. Knight, Aide-de-Camp to General Chichester, a gallant officer, who never went into action without achieving distinction, and whose loss is a source of the utmost
regret to the Lt.-General and his companions in arms.

At length the admirably directed fire of H. B. M. Ships under
Commodore Lord John Hay, and especially the Phœnix, Capt. Henderson, destroyed a part of the enemy's defences. The 4th and 8th
Regiments of the Legion, under Lt.-Colonels Harley and Godfrey
just disembarked from H. M. Ships, now mounted to the assault
through the breach thus made, and with the most cool and splendid
intrepidity, without firing a shot, rendered themselves masters of this
long contested point.

At the same moment the Saragossa and Oviedo Regiments, the
distinguished Volunteers of Guipuzcoa, the mobilized company of
National Guards, the 3d, 6th, and Rifles of the Legion, penetrated
the centre, carrying in rapid succession, several fortified houses, and
capturing the enemy's cannon in that part of the line. At this
point the Rebel Standard, erected in the centre of their works, indicating their intention of giving no quarter, became the prize of the
Westminster Grenadiers, under Lt.-Colonel Churchill. Here also
fell mortally wounded the Rebel Chief Segastibelza.—On the other
hand, it was in this last charge that Colonel Tupper received his
wounds. He was leading on his men with that daring ardour, which
those who knew him can conceive. He met the fate of a brave soldier,

—and his honoured remains now rest beneath the spot ennobled by his fall.

The victory was gained---the enemy fled utterly routed in all directions. The first proper fruit of this memorable action was the destruction of the enemy's works erected against this interesting city, and of placing it and its important bay in a state of permanent security. This preliminary is now nearly accomplished, and shortly the Lt.-General has no doubt but that farther successes await the troops.

The Lt.-General has now but to endeavour to express his sense, though inadequately, of the merits of those whose conduct shone most conspicuously on the occasion. For himself he claims nothing but that of having had the honour of being the senior officer present. It was an affair of straightforward fighting, and the end was distinctly gained by the intrinsic valour of all ranks, officers and men, Spaniards as well as British.

The extensive experience, superior ability, and unbounded zeal of Br.-Generals M'Dougall and Reid, are so fully known and appreciated not only in this corps, but in the British army, that the Lt.-General need only say, that to their advice and assistance on every occasion, and to their indefatigable exertions in forwarding the executive parts of the service, he is more indebted than it is possible for him to describe.

To Brigadier-Generals Chichester and Shaw for their constancy, decided practical skill, courage, and rare example, in directing throughl out the day the 1st and 2nd Brigades under their command, the Lt.-General will ever feel the deepest sense of gratitude. The prominent and conspicuous claims of those four officers in particular to a high and honourable consideration for their great share in the issue of this hard fought contest, are submitted to the Government, and will not be unattended to.

In the brief and hurried dispatch which the Lieut-General transmitted to Government at the close of the action, pressed for time, and nearly overwhelmed with fatigue, he felt unable to enumerate at the moment more than a very few indeed of the names of those who had distinguished themselves, and he therefore thought it more just not to do this partially, but to embody the whole as he now does in

No. 3.   c

one record which will be transmitted to the General-in-Chief and the Minister at War. [For the names see Appendix.]

The following letters are also of much importance. The first is that of Lord John Hay, one who would express no opinion that he did not feel strongly impressed on his mind as just. The second letter is from a French nobleman, General Count Harispe, who commands on the French frontier, a disinterested party, and one who possesses that knowledge of warfare which serving under Napoleon gave him ; and the third is the answer of General Evans to the French General.

Copy of a letter from Commodore Lord JOHN HAY, of His Majesty's Ship Castor, to CHARLES WOOD, ESQ., dated San Sebastian, May 5, 1836.

His Majesty's Steam Ship, Phœnix,
San Sebastian, May 5, 1836.
Sir,

I have the honour to acquaint you, for the information of the Lords Commissioners of the Admiralty, that at day-light this morning Her Catholic Majesty's Forces, consisting of the British Legion and about fifteen hundred Spanish troops, in all six thousand, under the command of Lieutenant-General D. L. Evans, moved out of this garrison for the purpose of attacking the insurgents in their intrenched positions.

I conceive their Lordships will not expect from me a detailed account of the various movements of Her Catholic Majesty's troops during these operations, the particulars of which are at this moment but imperfectly known to me.

I cannot resist, however, stating the proud gratification I experienced in witnessing the gallantry displayed by the British Legion on this occasion ; the intrenched position of the insurgents appeared impregnable, but one after the other were stormed by these brave men, in a manner that created one universal feeling of admiration.

It is impossible to report, with any accuracy, the amount of killed and wounded ; but from the most accurate accounts I can obtain at present, it is from five to six hundred, and a very large proportion of the superior and other officers wounded.

The insurgents' loss must have been considerable ; four pieces of artillery, and a stand of colours were taken from the insurgents.

His Majesty's steam vessels, Phœnix and Salamander, were enabled to render Her Catholic Majesty's forces most essential service. The precision with which the Phœnix directed her fire on the insurgents' lines destroyed one angle of their principal redoubt, which enabled two regiments of the British Legion to enter.

I have the honor, &c.

[Signed,]   JOHN HAY.
Commodore.

Charles Wood, Esq.
Secretary, Admiralty.

Count HARISPE's Letter to General EVANS.

Head Quarters, Bayonne, 7th May.

M. LE GENERAL,—I have the honor to transmit to you the annexed despatch, which his Excellency, the Spanish Ambassador, has sent under cover to me.

I hasten to avail myself of this opportunity of congratulating you on the action which you have just conducted under the walls of San Sebastian. I have known for a long time the position which you have carried. I was also made acquainted almost day by day with the preparations for the defence; I have been, therefore, enabled to appreciate all the difficulties which your brave troops have had to surmount. Whatever losses you may have experienced, the results of this combat do the highest honour to the British soldiers, and above all to their officers, who have given such brilliant proofs of devotedness and intrepidity.

It is my duty to tell you, M. le General, that in every quarter the news of this affair has excited the most lively sentiments of sympathy. For my own part I associate myself with all my heart to these testimonials of interest; and I can assure you that no person will be more delighted than myself—an old General of the empire—at the triumphs gained by the arms of his Britannic Majesty.

Receive, General, the assurance of my highest consideration.

[Signed],   COUNT DE HARISPE,
Lieutenant-General and Peer of France.

P. S. If I can be of any use to you, do me the favour to command me.

To General Evans. San Sebastian.

General Evans to Count Harispe.

M. le Comte.---I never received a letter more grateful or more flattering to my feelings than the one which you had the kindness to do me the honour of writing. I have taken the liberty of showing it to some of my superior officers, who are equally delighted with myself to find that we are deemed to have merited such obliging expressions from so high a professional authority, and one so fully acquainted with the facts.

With the momentary interruption of a sortie some months since, the insurgents had been diligently and energetically engaged from the beginning of December to the 5th instant in fortifying these lines. Till my arrival here, I was totally unaware of the strength to which they had brought them. In fact, considering them in conjunction with their adaptation to the very peculiar features of the position, and added to the nearly impracticable ascents, from the steep and swampy nature of the soil, they were the most awkward field defences to attack that it has fallen to my lot to observe. But they were not sufficient to resist the undaunted constancy and determination of the troops, Spanish and English, by whom they were carried.

You mention the satisfaction the successful efforts of the forces of his Britannic Majesty afford you, and the lively sensibility with which that feeling has been participated on the recent occasion in your part of the country. In return, it will not be displeasing to you to know of the total disappearance in England of those foolish and mischievous prejudices which were wont in ancient times to divide the two most enlightened and powerful nations; and that the firm alliance now so happily subsisting between our respective sovereigns, is universally popular among us. For myself I venture to consider this alliance as one of the most propitious events of modern times, the undoubted proof of advancing civilization, the best guarantee of the well-being of other states---and it is pleasing to think that even in her personal attributes, Her Majesty the Queen Governess of this country, is in all respects completely worthy of her illustrious and powerful allies.

Again, my Lord, I am desirous of offering my thanks for the generous and spontaneous favourable opinion you have passed upon the officers and soldiers engaged on the late occasion; assuring you, also, that there is no approval whatever, my comrades or myself, as soldiers, can set a higher value on than that of a veteran general so distinguished among the heroic chiefs of the French Empire.

I am aware that you have probably only intended your letter as an expression of your individual sentiments on a military action calculated to promote the cause in which you feel a sympathy, and I have perhaps to ask your pardon if I have endeavoured to convert this politeness into a means of additionally promoting, as far as in my humble power, the continued identity in policy and cordiality of reciprocal regard of our countries.

I have the honour to be, &c. &c.

(Signed)   DE LACY EVANS.

To General Count de Harispe, Peer of France.

One shirt, and a pair of boots, were served out to each non-commissioned officer and private, immediately after the action. The men were charged eight shillings in their accounts for the boots, and credited with a gratuity of eight shillings. The matter was simple enough, and there was a reason for entering them into the accounts, but it was impossible to make the men, excepting a few, understand that they had got the boots in a present, and they continue telling the story yet, that they paid for the present of the inhabitants of San Sebastian. They were satisfied they got the shirts, for these were not entered in their accounts. As some of those, whom the men blame in this affair, have enough of guilt on their heads without this, and not to let them bear it unnecessarily, I shall explain why their accounts were so debited and credited. The boots came out of the Quarter-master General's store, purchased by the inhabitants of San Sebastian, but not paid, and were presented to the Legion. Lest they might not be paid, it was necessary to charge the men with them; shortly after the money was got in payment, and the men were credited with it. Two months afterwards, I had a troublesome work to make this satisfactory, and all the others who kept companies' accounts, were no doubt situated in the same way. The men could not see how any thing could be a present, for which they were charged, and they could not believe that the money promised, could exist in figures. Those who did know, had full belief that the debit side was correct, but promises had been so often broken, that they gave no credit to the credit side of their accounts. They saw that these boots were in the store, to be served out to the Legion whenever required, to pay for which, there was a long arrear due to them already; therefore, it will be seen, that there was some reason to be displeased, at not getting the eight shillings in cash, although, at the same time, it was not an act of fraud, as many of them perversely contended it was, and by putting it into their catalogue of grievances, caused more discontent than there was a real cause for.

An order of the Spanish Government was also issued, awarding a medal to all who had been in the engagement. As these had to be cast, they were not got till the month of November following, until which time we shall leave them, as they created a good deal of stir at that time in the Legion.

The three classes of the cross of Fernando were conferred on Officers; the third class being conferred on Generals; the second class on Colonels, with whom, it appeared, a Captain of the Royal Navy was ranked; and the first class was conferred on Lieut. Colonels, downwards to Ensigns. Some of the non-commissioned officers and men, who had done any thing more than others, or as they happened to be in the favour of an officer, got the ribbon and cross of Isabella II. conferred on them. And nothing that General Evans did, or permitted to be done, did more mischief in the Legion, than these ribbons and crosses.

The following is the official return. Killed,—five captains, five lieutenants, five sergeants, one hundred and sixteen rank and file. Wounded,—two brigadier-generals, three colonels, two lieutenant-colonels, nine majors, twenty captains, twenty-two lieutenants, seven ensigns, thirty-three sergeants, five hundred and ninety-four rank and file. Total,---eight hundred and twenty three; seventy-five of these officers.

Four pieces of artillery were taken, and the red flag of "no quarter."

But, though this was correct at the close of the engagement, the fate of many of the wounded in hospitals rendered it incorrect; every day there being some of the wounded for the space of a few weeks, who found relief from their sufferings in death.

There is no scene perhaps can more effectually excite the soul than the pomp of military funerals, especially those following an engagement. The leaves newly green, on a lovely day of May, overhanging the slumbering waters of the deep, clear, Urimea—the sun shining in the cloudless blue heaven—the swell of the wave rolling from the Bay of Biscay, lazily dying away unbroken on the shore—the fields where the battle was last week, variegated by the millions of mountain daisies that seemed as if they had only hidden them-selves from the strife, and now put up their little heads to warm themselves in the sun, cheered on by myriads of merry singing birds, who assured them not to be afraid for the battle was over. Such was the calm lovely scene one day, when a mustering of officers of all ranks and regiments, Spanish and English, mixed with the principal inhabitants, were seen gathered in the streets and square of San Sebastian. The Lieutenant-General, not the most gaudy in his uniform, but calmly dignified, stood amid a host who surrounded him, ornamented in all the profusion of gold lace according to their rank, wearing their waving plumes : still, though the assemblage was gay in the extreme to look upon, a stranger could have perceived an unusual melancholy hanging over those who composed it. The lovely black-eyed Senoras filled all the windows and balconies. The mantilla floating gracefully over the bare head, neck and shoulders—the neat small foot peeping through the railings of the balcony—but no ogling—no killing with coquettish eyes were at-tempted by them—and no lovely deaths were made or thought of, so common at other times, by those of the gold lace and the scarlet uniform. There was to be a funeral. They were assembled to perform all the military honours, and the last melancholy duties, over the body of Major Mitchell. A regiment with the solid tread of five hundred, stepping in one, marched into the square from an adjoining street. The splendid military band of the National Guard and another gave intimation to those who did not see, that the dead body was now a part of the procession, for the high swelled soul-subduing notes of the Dead March in Saul, broke mournfully loud through the hitherto silent streets. The officers according to their rank, and according as they belonged, or did not belong, to the regiment of the deceased moved slowly away ;—but there were some who had been his dearest friends could not follow his body. One of these, Major Hogg, had fevered from the effects of his wound, and others, both men and officers, who knew and loved Major Mitchell well, lay now on the sick bed, and some on the bed of death, listening to the deep-toned sorrows of the slow march as the long procession winded round and round the high hill on which stands the citadel or castle of San Sebastian. Never was a better man, or an officer more lamented, borne to the grave; and though the people of San Sebastian knew nothing more of Major Mitchell than from seeing him a few days before the engagement, a gay, active looking officer, it must have reconciled many to the fate which awaited them—of being carried in the same manner to the same spot—to see the sorrowing tears fall from the on-lookers at every window in the town as the procession moved slowly past.

In a narrow nook of earth, high among the craggy rocks, on the north side overlooking the sea, was laid the body of Mitchell. It was the first deposited in that spot; but there are others now, who sorrowed at that time, mingling their dust there with his. The three rollies, which made the rocks ring above, and scared the sea gulls below—the prayer-book shut and the earth filled in—the word of command given, and the counter-march made; the soldiers, who had inly cursed a hundred times the "reversed arms" which pleased the eyes of the on-lookers, but cramped their joints during the weary ascent, now marched lightly back to some quick, gaily played march, which I never could help being ill-natured with, as it seemed to say, that the deep sorrow which they had played before was not real; and that funerals, like the most of other military shows, were a mere farce. But these things over, the sorrows of soldiers for an officer are ended. The letter to the grieving friends at home is, perhaps, only then written, and when they get it their sorrow takes firmer root; but we, who had to go home and bury some comrade of the ranks, less pompously, mount the guards and picquets in front of the enemy's line—or take the locks to pieces and sponge the muskets that had fired the funeral vollies—get all clean for an early, full dress parade on the morning—fight with the enemy again in a few days, either be killed or see others killed--- with again a procession of military funerals;---we, who were the actors in performances of such variety, soon became in feeling and disposition pliable to changes. We buried poor Smith in a garden, near the convent of San Bartholome, which was obtained for the use of the Legion; and many others soon gorged the place till no grave room in it was left.

I cannot pass from the funeral of Major Mitchell without correcting an error which has prevailed relative to his affairs, and which had a tendency to injure the reputation, or at least wound the feelings of those who acted as his executors. He was not a man of fortune, as was stated, nor did he leave money; his horses, &c. were sold off, and accounted for to the full satisfaction of his friends.

CHAPTER III.

Remarks on the honours conferred on the officers and men—Adjutant M——
Anecdotes of his flogging—The morning of the 28th of May—Grand Cannonade
The town of Passages described—taken by Lord John Hay—Artillery taken from
the Carlists—A bridge made by the British sailors over the Urimea—Remarks on
Cordova—The 2nd Lancers in a critical situation—gallantly rescued by Major
Martin—Extracts from the private journals of three different soldiers relative to
the foregoing engagements—their treatment in the hospital, &c., &c.

The general order, part of which appears in the last chapter, contained long lists of officers and men on whom honours had been conferred. Nothing was so productive of ill-feeling in individuals and general discontent as the manner in which these honours were bestowed ;—the most of those who got them had done nothing more than others ; and some of them not so much. The general orders required the names of men who had distinguished themselves to be sent to the Adjutant General's office; the colonels of regiments issued in regimental orders for captains of companies to give in a list of distinguished men,—this was complied with. A few were selected, for it was known that the honours would only be given to a limited number, and these few were generally those most in favour with the captain : others who were missed, but who did just as much as these, grumbled ; and, instead of the cross and ribbon being an incentive to good behaviour or bravery they were the cause of endless disputes, and envious hatred of one another. This I too frequently witnessed among the men ; and the officers were not better satisfied. The younger Shields, as brave and active an officer of his rank as was in the action of the 5th of May, was passed over unnoticed ; while the Adjutant, a Captain M——, before alluded to, got the cross and ribbon of Fernando, and was not within the whiz of a ball the whole day. On our retiring from the field he came and joined the regiment, nobody could tell from where, and immediately commenced bullying in his usual style for the men to "cover,"---"close up,"---"keep step,"---"slope their arms properly,"---to pay attention to what he was saying and so on. The Colonel on seeing him enquired where he had been. "Oh! Sir, I've been flogging up the rear all day" was the answer. To any one who knows what military service is, nothing may be said,---to those who do not know I will mention, that an Adjutant's place was a hotter one than this worthy put himself in.

The following will illustrate his character: — When the Legion occupied the villages in the neighbourhood of Vittoria, and when even sergeants were permitted to march a man to the provost, and give him two dozen, if he thought proper, this M—— was in the daily habit of punishing wholesale. It was common with him to march out twenty at a time, to be provosted—some of these for not being up out of their berths in the morning when he came round the quarters,— some of them for looking sulky, (and keep in mind this was in the hungry times, when it was not difficult to look sulky on a cold morning. Some of them laughed at him, for he had a long nose; his forehead lay sloping from his red brandy-tinged neb; and his chin, or the place where it should have been, seemed hiding itself from an upper lip that hung frowning over it; his voice, like a cracked trumpet, made the nerves shiver whenever he began his morning yell. One day he was ordered by the Colonel to take Smith to the provost; it was for refusing to pay a Spanish barber after he had shaved him, and for being noisy. For this M—— was ordered to give him two dozen. A file of the guard had come for Smith, and they were marching off. M——'s nose was redder and longer than usual, at least Smith thought so as they marched onwards, now and then giving a severe threatening look. He was tied up, and without saying anything, took his two dozen. "Weel, are ye pleased noo?" said Smith. "Give him other two dozen," replied M——. That was done, and nothing said by Smith. "Now, take him down," said the Adjutant, "and put up the drummer. By G—, I'll make you flog each other, time about till you do it properly; I've just a fine subject to practise on.--Go on, go on." "Will I?"

said Smith, " I'll not flog the laddie ; I'm a sodger, and if ye've an order to punish me, do it at once like a sodger." The drummer got two dozen for not flogging hard enough, and Smith was again put up. " I've given you two dozen," said M———, " as the Colonel ordered me to do, and I've given you two for your insolence." "Weel, gie me ither twa," said Smith, "its doost as weel to gie me't when ye're at it." "Go on," ordered M———, "give him other two, for this insolence." That was done. "Now," said M——— again, "as you have got the last two dozen for your own *pleasure*, I'll give you other two for *my pleasure.*— Go on, there,— go on quick,— go on with it." "Come, then---come on," said Smith, "come on, come on." This, which made the eight dozen, was also inflicted, and Smith, taking a look at the long-nosed Adjutant, that spoke something like future retribution if ever they "met by moonlight alone," said, after scanning him for a few minutes, "man, ye're an ugly beast." It must be understood that Smith was half intoxicated, which will account for his taking a severe punishment so willingly. At the same time, though drunkenness is an aggravation to a fault in a soldier, it will be kept in mind that he was punished against order and military law. It was an understood custom, though one not regulated by any standing order, that two dozen was as much as could be given for any single crime, without being tried by a court-martial ; hence the pretence of making each two dozen the punishment of a separate offence.

One day, M——— marched Oakley to the provost for some fault ; very probably it was for being in drink, for Oakley had few military crimes excepting that. " Adjutant M———," said he, "please speak aside a moment. I don't want you to stop the punishment, by any means — give me the punishment, but just do me the favour of a private whisper for a moment, before you begin." The Adjutant consented ; and his reason probably for doing so was, that a rumour was beginning to go about at the time, that Oakley was a scion of a family of high rank in England — that although only a young man, he had been an officer in a British cavalry regiment in the East Indies. These rumours were going about, and are a small, a very small part of his extraordinary history. Oakley whispered, "now, I never was flogged ; but as I am voluntarily in the ranks, and content with sharing the fate of other soldiers, I am quite willing to bear a punishment, but mark me, and mind no one hears us, by G—, you're a dead man by my hand. Duelling is out of the question. I've fought duels, and could hit a sixpence at a hundred yards, but that's folly.— Mark me, touch me with a lash — I'll say nothing — but you're dead, and there's the hand that'll do it, by G—." Oakley had an eye that could impart any meaning to his physiognomy at his will. "At this time," he told me, (for I got an account of the affair from his own lips,)—"at this time, I gave a look half wolfish, and the spiritless coward *begged my pardon*, and got on about General ——— being my uncle, and Colonel ——— of the, Royal Artillery, being my uncle, and that he would not punish me for their sakes. 'You low-spirited rascal,' 'I'll choke you — say a word — silence; d—— you, stir, and you're dead.'" From that time a truce was made with M—— and Oakley.

Early on the morning of the 28th, all was in readiness to make another attack on the Carlists. The Urimea, which falls into the sea close to the walls on the east side of San Sebastian, was, for a considerable distance, the boundary between the two parties. A bridge that crossed it had been destroyed. It has a strong current caused by the tide, and is only fordable at low water, and that at places where the sands are often shifting. This morning it was arranged that General Chichester's brigade, consisting of the Rifles, 1st, 4th, and 8th regiments, a part of General Jaureguy's division, consisting of the Chapelgorris, and two battalions of Spaniards, it was arranged that these should cross the river at day-light, covered by no less than thirty pices of cannon. On that part of the lines where the action of the 5th had terminated, General Shaw with his brigade was posted to prevent an incursion from the enemy. The remainder of the Legion, and the Royal British Marines, lay in reserve. Lord John Hay, with the Phœnix, Salamander, Gun-boats, and Marine Artillery, proceeded by sea from San Sebastian to the shipping port of Passages, four miles eastward.

What a scene it must have been, either for a poet or a moralist. The dull dark walls and gloomy castle of St. Sebastian receiving the first red tinge from the east; bushes newly leafed; flowers, dew, larks, and all the sweetness of a lovely summer morning on a lovely land. The Carlist columns dimly seen drawn up on the heights on the other side. The sea calm; the Phœnix and Salamander like two dusky

spots seen moving through the red of the horizon, almost indistinct
by the glitter of the water, stealing away by themselves. The cannon
drawn down to the water edge, but still hidden by walls or embankments from the enemy. Balls, shells, rockets, mules loaded with
barrels of ammunition, others with stretchers to carry the wounded,
regiments standing in close column behind walls and houses where
they could not be seen, all waiting for the word. General Evans
surrounded by the officers, white and red plumes waving, and the
horses prancing—

"Colonel Colquhoun, are you ready?" he was heard to ask, "let
your discharge of artillery be as simultaneous as possible."

"All ready," was the answer.

"Go then, General Chichester, and march down your brigade.
General Jaureguy will ford the river at the same time, and, if possible, march through the water in close column, and don't let the
men fire."

At this time artillery-men could be seen stepping forward and
stepping back, handing something from one to another, ramming a
pole into a cannon, and drawing it out again. Colonel Colquhoun
looking for a moment at the enemy through a glass, then looking
along a gun, doing something—starting off to another one—performing the same pantomime—a man at each of them with his
thumb on the touch-hole. This was seen at the time of such orders
being given to the infantry, as the following ;—" 'tention—shoulder
arms—by the left—steady there, steady—what are you about?—
carry your arms till you hear the word march, then stop together—
by the left—quick march." Such were the motions that could be
seen in Colonel Colquhoun and his artillery,—such were the orders
given to, and promptly obeyed by the infantry ; and in a few minutes
all emerged from the cover which had hitherto kept them from the
view of the enemy, and marched over the glacis (a green park)
towards the river side. At this time a considerable stir could be
seen on the other bank. The Carlists were immediately in motion
downwards to oppose the fording of the river. The English and
Spanish columns marched, when they came on to the glacis, in nearly
a parallel direction with the water, but at the sight of the Carlists
coming down, the following orders were given and obeyed—"Brigade,
right wheel," then "4th, left shoulders forward"—(a pause)—"for-

ward—8th, left shoulders forward—mark time the right there—eyes left—forward—move up these columns—wheel on the same ground, Rifles, 1st." At this moment a discharge of musketry and two pieces of artillery from the Carlists sent over balls whizzing and whirling, ripping the water and scoring the sands. That much was seen, but the report of their discharge was never heard. A signal by Colquhoun was given; the thumbs were lifted from the touch-holes; to each of these another man stood forward, pointed a burning match, and smoke, gun carriages reeling backwards, ears ringing, thirty pieces of cannon all off at once, mingled in their thundering sound with yelling cheers. The whole firmament was for a few moments in a quivering motion, then smoke, crack, one, two, three, the whole thirty shells bursting, some on a picquet, some in front, some in rear, and a good many in the centre of the enemy's columns. Slaughter, disaster, confusion, in a moment followed. Sponges in and out of the guns, charged again, elevated, fired. Every cannon now going off as fast as it could be loaded, fired, and sponged. In the water, horses snorting, officers calling "close up there," at the same time up to the middle in water themselves, holding on one by another; the little men in danger of being carried away by the stream, but by splashing, dashing, and swearing, they all got over, hurried to take advantage of the disorder the Carlists were thrown into by the tremendous cannonade, and, almost without firing a shot, cleared and took the positions before them at the point of the bayonet.

The Carlists, and, indeed, all the Spaniards, are very expert in carrying off the dead and wounded. They are careful not to leave one if they can possibly get him away; therefore, it could never be known how many of them were killed and wounded. At this time they were seen hurrying away the dead and wounded on their backs. They had to cross the Urimea, which doubled round behind them, and an impetuous onset was made by the Chapelgorris and our men to capture their artillery, and take some of them prisoners before they could get over the river. The Chapelgorris went on, but General Chichester stopped his men, "for," said he, "we do not wish to have any position beyond this where we now are at present; here we can defend ourselves against double our number, but if we go farther our lines will be too far extended for our strength." He saw also that they had succeeded in securing their artillery, and unless it had been to take it there was no use in pursuing, for the Carlists could bound up and down hills like goats, and leave the Legion, or any other soldiers excepting the Chapelgorris, far behind.

But there was some mystery about the two pieces of cannon, for it did not seem possible that they could have got them so hastily off. No more was known of them, however, till the following year, ten months after that time, when they were discovered buried in the earth. One was a twelve, the other an eighteen pounder, both of them brass, and very handsome dismounted field-pieces; where their carriages were, or whether there ever were any, we did not know.

As soon as Chichester's brigade had succeeded in dislodging the Carlists from these positions, the remainder of the Legion, and the Marines, crossed the river at the same time. Captain Maitland, of the Tweed sloop of war, and his sailors, set to work, and in a very short time had a bridge made across the river, at a place where it was one hundred and fifty yards wide, deep, and a strong stream running. This was expedition, perhaps, unequalled in the history of war in any part of the world; for let the reader picture to himself a bridge (as it really was) over which artillery, waggons, carts, horses, and six men at breast could go at ease on, and did go on for the next six months. The pontons, or long wooden boxes, sixteen feet long by four wide, and two feet deep, were all ready-made, but it would have taken the Spanish sailors, who made an attempt to do it, a whole day to lay them. Our gallant dashing tars, working like clock-work to each other, were into a small boat, had cables across the river, and made fast, before a few minutes were over, at the same time the pontons were launched into the water, hauled to their proper places, made fast to the main cables, at a distance of three feet from each other, long beams were laid across them, and then boards laid across these, close to each other, and the bridge was made. The Spaniards stood confounded to see it rise, apparently with as little effort as if it had been done by magic. Where, half an hour before, a deep and a broad rolling tide lay open, there was now a thoroughfare across, and it was immediately taken advantage of, in getting over artillery and ammunition. The Rifles, and some of the 1st regiment, were the only infantry of the Legion that now shared the engagement, but the English Lancers were hot at it. They charged the enemy on the Ametza hill, assisted by the Royal Marines; clearing the way there, they galloped forward, came up on some of the Carlists who were retreating on Passages, and drove them helter-skelter into the water, stabbing, cutting, shooting, and drowning them in mingled slaughter. However, though this was a gallant and furiously valiant charge, I believe Colonel Rait, who led it on, was found fault with, for had it not been for a circumstance which he knew nothing about, and could not possibly know, he would have been literally cut to pieces : what saved him and his Lancers, was Lord John Hay having entered the harbour, and effected a landing, and had actually possession of the place, that not being known even to some of the Carlists, who, it appeared, relied on that place being safe to retreat to.

On the heights above it, the Sarogossa regiment and a company of the 1st English were engaged ; the Chapelgorris also ; and, for a short while, the Royal Marines. Lord John had dashed in gallant style up the narrow inlet to the town of Passages, thundering his artillery about them, and with very little difficulty took possession of the town. The whole affair was one so comparatively easy, that it will scarcely admit of being detailed at greater length. I am very anxious to say something in favour of our gallant countrymen, the marines, and marine artillery ; but as this running fight of the 28th gave little opportunity for a display, and as there are other engagements to detail, in which they figured, I shall leave them at present.

An armed schooner, and five pieces of artillery, fell into Lord John Hay's hands, and some other military stores of no great value ; but the principal object gained was the getting possession of Passages. It was expected that great resistance would have been made, as it was a place of very much importance : hence the formidable prepa. ration of artillery, and the expedition with which the bridge was made ; but the panic caused by the overwhelming commencement, appeared to have spread to the remainder of the Carlist force.

Passages is a town of a very peculiar construction. It has as many houses as might have contained four or five thousand people, when they were inhabited. These houses are built against two im. mense mountains, the rocks often forming the back walls. A narrow street, at places *two* feet, and never more than six feet wide, runs up the centre, sometimes being arched over by the buildings, and sometimes by the rocks. A salt water lake, four miles long, and two broad, is spread out towards the south, and every house has a stair

a stair descending to it, the mountains being on the north side, rising between it and the sea. The place altogether is, in shape like the letter L, with a narrow outlet at the angle; this is a mile long, between rocks five hundred feet high; it averages about thirty yards broad, and is deep enough at low water for vessels of any burden to float, only there is such an impetuous stream, caused by the filling and emptying of the lake through this narrow gut at each tide, that vessels can only go with the stream. It being only a few miles from France, and communicating so directly with the open sea, this place was of considerable importance. It has been famed for smugglers and pirates, and so well is it hidden and protected, that no enemy could approach it from any side but by water, and then, if well defended, it could defy them.

Lord John Hay deeming it best to get possession of the port altogether, and not to be under the necessity of cruising continually on the open sea to watch it, as he had been for some time, made the attempt, and, as has been stated, easily succeeded in taking it. The connexion of the Carlists with the sea was now cut off in this quarter, and perhaps they would have found this a serious loss, had not the very pliant authorities on the French frontier permitted supplies of military stores and ammunition to reach them by that course.

From a height above Passages on the east, to San Sebastian, four miles westward, a line varying in its course as the rising grounds answered, was temporarily fortified, picquets placed, and so on: Lord John Hay, on the eastern part of it, with the marines; Jaureguy, with his Spaniards, in the centre; and Evans to the westward.

It is a question always asked, with a tone of impatient dissatisfaction, why General Evans did not, when the Carlists were on the run, follow them up; and the newspapers, at the time, appear to have considered it altogether unaccountable that he should have hesitated in pursuing the Carlists. A writer, in a number of a celebrated periodical, for the month of August, 1837, still complains of that, and in the same article condemns General Evans, because he allowed the enemy to turn his flank. Military men, especially those who have been, at any time, in the north of Spain, would not condemn General Evans for not running into the country. His

No. 4.   F

reason for fortifying himself before San Sebastian was to prevent the certainty of the Carlists flanking him. He had six thousand men, and, no doubt, could have pursued the Carlists farther than he did; but to have extended these six thousand as wide as would have scoured the country, there would not have been above *ten men* for each mountain pass, and the innumerable cross glens by which the enemy could turn round, and play at *bogly*, or bo-peep with them. Had General Evans gone on to Hernani, or Tolosa, which perhaps he could have done, the Carlists would have just come in behind him: if they did that, then his supplies of ammunition and provisions were cut off.

There is something so extravagantly ridiculous in the articles which have been written against the Legion, that, with rational readers, they must defeat their own purpose, for in going to an extent so far beyond truth, for the mere sake of mortifying an opposite party, can serve no useful purpose. The question of principle I shall leave General Evans to defend himself on. But I still maintain, that those who condemn General Evans' character as an officer and his mere military operations, do it in an entire ignorance of what a campaign is, either in its plans or details, or if they know that, they condemn him in their ignorance of the peculiar circumstances with which he was surrounded—and if these are also known by those who write the military character of the Legion and its General to condemnation, then they must write for a purpose which it may be as well not to notice. I shall give an account of our share of the war. as it really was acted, without regard to any party. A few scenes of the first act are now before the public; but that part of the drama of barbarous civil war, to which I was a witness, is not yet entered on. No civilian, nor even soldier, who has not been in active warfare, has any idea of what we did in Spain. Playing at soldiers with reviews and field days at home is a very different matter from being day and night before an enemy; and I am sure that those who would tear away every shred of reputation from us, of whatever quality, if they knew even a tithe of what we did with such a small force against every disadvantage, they would be generous enough to say that the Legion did *not* tarnish the military reputation of England, on the land of her greatest victories. No they would not. The graves of English soldiers who fell before San Sebastian, when the illustrious

Chief of the Peninsular war raised the military reputation of his
country—these graves were saturated with the blood of the Legion.
Give the cause what name is deemed deserving, but if glory is worth
anything, let those who fought have it, for they deserve it.

While General Evans had fought and beat the Carlists, even
without the co-operation of Cordova, although that had been promised, the latter *gentleman* lay basking himself in the summer sun on
the same mountains where General Evans had lain with his troops
in the dead of winter. In winter Cordova had kept himself in
quarters, with the exception of going once or twice out and precipitately returning again ; not being forced by the enemy, nor having
any dread of the enemy, but simply *because it was cold* to be out in
the country. At the same time the Legion lay night after night in
the open air in December and January, co-operating (as the phrase
is) with Cordova. Though he and his army were in good quarters,
we were starving with hunger and cold, which brought on the diseases, and gave rise to the horrid sufferings, which will be hereafter
sketched in the narrative of events at Vittoria. Now, when it
was summer, when operations were to go actively on,—when Evans
had hastened to San Sebastian, commenced hostilities and had so
far succeeded, Cordova still lay inactive, but, to make some shew,
went out to the hills in the warm weather that we had lain out in
the frost and snow. An action took place about that time, which
he got gazetted as one of importance, though, at the same time,
he intended it to be a disastrous slaughter of the second regiment of
English Lancers. In the month of January, General Evans evaded,
by a masterly movement, a trap laid by the traitor for the destruction of the Legion ; and now that the 2nd Lancers had been left
with him, while the remainder of the Legion was at San Sebastian,
they, one day found themselves completely surrounded by the Carlist
cavalry, artillery, and infantry. To have been in such a situation
without his designing it was impossible ; and so overwhelming did
the foe seem to be, that the commanding officer, finding his men
for a moment horror-struck, and being so himself, stood as if willing to surrender. Martin, formerly in the 8th Infantry, but at this
time Major in the 2nd Lancers, saw their situation and the hesitation of the Colonel, and it must be known that Major Martin is not
only *not* a common man, but a very extraordinary one. It is needless

to specify any particular department of military science or discipline, for he excelled in everything. He saw the dilemma the
regiment was in; in fact they were almost prisoners. " Charge,
Colonel————." he said, when he saw the Carlist battalions closing
around them. " How ? Where ? What, Martin, what's this ?
in confusion enquired his superior. " There's not a moment to
hesitate," replied Martin ; " Colonel—— will you give the regiment
orders ? Colonel————, I say, d——n you, will you let me take
the command then ? " " Oh yes, yes, but my dear fellow, there's
ten thousand men." " I don't care if there's a hundred thousand,
we must cut our way through them." This was the excited
dialogue that passed for a few seconds between the two. The
Colonel was a man that could drill well; was a good soldier when
every thing was going on easy, and had seen a good deal of service
in the British army, but placed implicit confidence in Cordova ; and
could not believe it possible at first that it was the enemy that surrounded them. Martin was an officer of decision. No sooner did
the other say, "yes, take the command," then he charged at the gallop, riding right up on a column of infantry, slashing and hewing
them down ; but it was supported by other columns in rear: and here
they found it impossible to cut through. " Squadrons, threes about,
gallop, charge, down with them," was immediately said, as he
wheeled his troops from that point, and charged furiously at a point
in an opposite direction.

Here also they were repulsed, but resolutely pressed on, slaughtering with pistol, sword, and lance. An opening for a moment was
made at another place. A squadron of Carlist cavalry entered ; they
were at the charge, and were galloping up in the rear of the English.
Some of the latter were unhorsed, but the greater part were still in
order. About they wheeled, and, again at the gallop, met the Carlists.
Such a collision would have been an awful one : it would have been
utterly disastrous to both parties had they met in an unchecked impetuosity ; but the Spanish horses reared, sprung to the side in
confusion, and the English cut down and rode over the first troop.
The remainder, so unexpectedly checked, had wheeled, and the infantry were opened to let them out. Martin, at the gallop, followed
them, his men throwing their lances into the rear of the cavalry,
riding over the astonished and partly disordered infantry, or cutting

them down with their swords. This was all the work of a very short
time; and the rapidity and fury with which they wheeled and made
the different charges appeared to paralyze the Carlists with astonishment. These had calculated on closing in on them, and taking
them prisoners; but this was not the end of the affray. After
getting clear, pulling up, and, being re-formed, they charged back,
exposed to a heavy fire. One of the Carlist field pieces, loaded with
canister shot, was just about getting the match to its touch-hole as
one of the lancers shot the gunner dead. Taking this from the enemy, they hurled their lances again on the infantry, and, at this time
some of the Christinos came in view, at sight of whom the Carlists
retreated. The work of the lancers had been short but very severe,
and they required to fall back; for, without any one to assist them,
it may well be supposed they required breathing time, exposed as
they now were to a galling fire. Some of the Christino battalions
took advantage of what the English had done, advanced, took some
of the artillery, killed a few more men, and took some prisoners.

And this affair, an advantage forced on Cordova by the bravery of
a handful of Lancers, he proclaimed in the Madrid Gazette, as one
of his battles; and the newspapers of the day in England gave currency to his dispatches. The whole was the work of Major Martin,
whose name he little more than mentioned: but though it was hidden
from the world by the traitor chief—no English correspondent being
at the place—the fame of his gallant conduct soon spread itself; and
I remember well the pride and boasting of the men with us in the
Legion, who had been of his company when he was Captain. Major
Martin was highly esteemed and respected by the men. There were
some eccentric traits in his character which made him very popular;
at the same time he was a very strict disciplinarian; but, unless a man
committed a crime of a very bad quality, he would rather give him
a box on the ear than let the provost give him two dozen. I know
he was a decided enemy to provo'ing, though he sometimes considered himself obliged to put in execution corporal punishments
decreed by a court-martial. He got the command of the Lancers,
and the rank of Lieutenant-Colonel, after this affair; the other one
having resigned, as the reader may suppose he was bound to do.
Colonel Martin performed some very efficient services with his regiment; but as it was in another part of the country, and none of the

English near them, I am unable to detail them farther at present; but shall, with great pleasure, take up his history when we come to the operations of the month of May, 1837, at which time he was again with the Scotch brigade; and I had the honour of being an eye-witness to his honourable and distinguished conduct---distinguished by bravery and humanity in very critical situations---and these qualities, combined with his varied qualifications, will I trust prove to the reader that my humble eulogium is not undeserved Cordova, continued such conduct as he now stands accused of. He had promised to act with Evans, but how he acted will be immediately seen. On hearing of the engagement of the 5th May, he, as I mentioned before, wrote a congratulary letter. When that of the 28th was heard of, Eguia, one of the Carlist chiefs, immediately marched on General Evans, drawing all the troops from before Cordova; the traitor allowing him to do so without taking any advantage of it. He lay basking in the mountains of Alava, while the Carlists concentrated their forces, and attacked General Evans, on the 6th of June.

Before proceeding to describe the attack made on us by the Carlists, and the severe conflict that ensued on the 6th of June, the following extracts from some papers written in the form of a journal, by a soldier while in San Elmo Hospital, and who was severely wounded on the 5th of May, may be given, and will, I trust, be found interesting — at least to those who study the theory of the brain.

San Elmo Hospital, May 24, 1836.

" Being wearied very much by having to sit continually in bed, Dr. Alcock has to-day permitted me to get writing materials, but says he is afraid I will relapse into fever.

There is a Chapelgorri just dying in the bed opposite; two Spanish ladies are watching him; he is said to be their brother; he is grinding his teeth, and calling for "*mas cortouches*," that is " more cartridges," and adding, " *Inglises, feugo, feugo*,"—(English, fire, fire.)

The Orderly tells me that I have been delirious ten or twelve days, and that I called for bayonets and fire the same way. It is strange, I now recollect that I had a long dream, and fancied myself a prisoner, which fancy must have arisen from the great dread I had of being taken a prisoner by the Carlists. My last sensation of consciousness previous to my awaking about eight days ago from stupor, was about eleven o'clock on the 5th of May. I had seen Captain Knight and some of our men, before that time, taken prisoners by the Carlists. I believe now when reflecting coolly on what my feelings were then, that the assurance we had of being killed, if taken prisoners, made us fight the more desperately.

I have just been told that Edward Rodger, whom I recollect falling by my side when we were going up the green field below Lugariz, is dead.—He was telling me at that time not to be afraid, for the bullet was not in Spain, that was to kill us.

I had some of the most strange dreams, I wish my dear sister C——— were beside me, as I dreamed she was. . I am writing a lot of nonsense, but shall write down what I thought, when I was what people call mad, and perhaps this will fall into her hands if I should die here."

May 27th.—" I had written the foregoing when General Evans came into the hospital to see us, and I laid away my paper, as the doctor said I was disturbing my brain, and I think it was true, for I have had some strange imaginations, the doctor said I was feverish. The General spoke very kindly. We are well provided with every thing. I never saw an Infirmary or Hospital in Britain better furnished or attended to than this is, only it is so dreadful, so many in torture, and so many dying every day. The General has sent in newspapers for any of us to read, who are able. He took off his cocked hat at the upper end of the ward, and said, " my dear fellows, keep your minds easy, all of you who are getting your limbs taken off, you will be well provided for when you go home to England." I hope it will be so. I have no fear for my part that we will not, because our fighting was so different to what all people expected, that their opinions of us must now be altered.

I had more doubts about our fighting than any of the Tories at home had. I never could have believed it. I always thought I was a coward ; and if any one knew what I thought when we marched out of San Sebastian that morning, I should be called a coward ; and yet I joked with some of the men as we whispered to each other coming out of the town, and have since got the cross of Isabella for bravery ; and I know my conduct did appear brave.

B——— F———, the corporal, whispered to me, "what do you think?"

and though I was actually arguing with myself whether I would pray or not, I answered, " Oh d---n it, if we die we must just die, let's keep up our spirits." This was dreadful; for I was calling to mind how perhaps my dear sister was lying in bed at home thinking on me, and I knew poor thing, she would be praying for me ; and yet when I had half begun to say " Our Father which art, &c." my thoughts rebelled, being ashamed to confess what I really felt myself to be, a coward. Immediately after I felt my heart beating tremendously, and I fancied that a ball was going through my head. Then it felt as if going through my leg ; whatever part of my body an idea fixed on, then I thought the pain was real in that part.

" Halt," was said in a low voice by the Colonel, when we had got along the sands near to where the first Carlist sentry was supposed to be. The word " halt" was spoken by captains of companies in the same low whisper, and then we were passing the word along in another whisper, to " secure arms," we having loaded previously, and it being now a rather heavy rain.

There was nothing but the still, deep darkness, save at a distance before us, about a mile, where the Carlists' red picquet fires were burning. One of our men had just whispered in my ear, " that it was all nonsense !" accompanying the observation with an oath ; " that we were only brought out as usual to be wet to the skin and starved." I did not answer, but inwardly wished that what he appeared to be dissatisfied with might be true ; when, as I thought, a flash of lightning came across our eyes. Some whispers of jokes and oaths half formed, were choked in the respective throats that essayed to bring them forth--- a shot at some distance from us rebounded, and then other flashes and shots, and a cry of " vivas" which we could hear proceeded from the Chapelgorris near the main road.

" Forward---forward---follow me men," was in a loud voice ordered by our commanding officer. " Oh God" I said to myself " support me now in body and mind" and again I said " no I will not pray." The balls whizzed past us and the whole sky was illumed by the flashes of musketry.

I felt the balls going into me, and I fancied eternity opened ; Heaven, and Hell alternately seemed spread before me, and I said " Oh had I never departed from the religious instruction of my dear father, with what confidence could I now turn my thoughts to Heaven," but I could not, even with the prospect of death, submit to my own conscience, I said " Oh God if thou exist convince me of it," and immediately I thought the conviction would be performed, by a ball striking me dead, and hurrying me before the Almighty. And again I thought no, my Reason has fully proved the impossibility of a spiritual existence in another life. A man fell down by my side, with a ball that appeared to choke his utterance, for he only said, " Oh God have mercy I'm dy---dy---ing---God---Oh my side." Some more were being knocked down, and it was therefore evident we were now open to the shot of the enemy, we were ordered to fire, which was done, then there was a bustle in loading ; my comrade R--- M --- sat down on his knees when charging his piece ; I thought it looked cowardly of him, but was nevertheless bowing myself down also, when a ball struck him on the shoulder knocking him over on his back, " Now," said G--- L--- who was next him, "had you been standing up like a man in your place you would'nt have got that." I stood, and though sinking almost in dread, said to Sergeant C--- who had lain down in a ditch to hide himself " Oh you coward."

At this a wretchedly ill-fired cannon shot, from the Castle of San Sebastian, intended for the enemy, struck amongst us and nearly covered us with earth, and immediately another from the Carlists struck almost at the same spot. Our buglers sounded the " advance" one of them had part of his mouth shot away, while he was sounding' " On men---come on," was the cry of our Colonel, and we followed him---the Carlist picquet retreating before us back to their intrenchments."

Here followed in this journal much of the matter which has been already given relative to the positions of the different regiments. But as even the private feelings, of a private soldier, must be interesting on such an occasion, we shall quote the following, which alludes to the period of the engagement when the second line of fortifications had given way.

" I do not know how it was, but my mind was now free ; I felt none of those dreadfully oppressive thoughts that had terrified me at first, and yet I thought I would be killed. I was all in a sweat. My arm was bleeding by the slight cut of a ball, and when General Chichester came forward to us at this time, and said, " Now my

young men forward again, I came out with "here we go." And immediately, I found we were led on to that seeming impossibility,
the taking of Lugariz. On going forward we lost a number of men,
and had to retreat. I looked about and I saw my dear comrade
M——in the hands of the Carlists, also the brave Captain Knight.
Some officers were calling out to the men to charge back again, for
the purpose of rescuing the wounded whom we had left, and who
were being put to death. I was one of those who charged; I remember of going forward about five yards, when I fell, a ball having
gone through my left leg below the knee. I immediately attempted
to get up, but I felt as if some person had struck me a violent blow
close above my right ear. It seemed as if done by an open wet hand,
I put up one of my hands to feel what it was, and felt it wet; but
though my .hand appeared bloody at first it assumed all kinds of
colours on looking at it, and the citadel of San Sebastian behind us
at a distance---and the sea---and the steam vessels which we had just
seen come to anchor a short while before, rose all up and swung
above me from the clouds.

"I made every effort to get from below them. At one time San
Sebastian came close down, and seemed about to smother me to
death. It did not appear larger than a person's hand, but on that
small compass I saw every street and house minutely. Sometimes
it spoke and lay close on my mouth and half choked me, then it
bounded into the air; and the hills, houses, ships, and trees danced
about up and down. Some tremendously huge giants, but that
changed their size now and then, until they were less than my little
finger, carried a house high among the clouds, and opening the
roof, emptied boiling water on my head! Then one of them making
himself very small, went over my throat, seeing which they all attempted to follow, and having striven for some time to decide
who should go first, they all bolted in at one house, ships, trees,
and mountains following them. I tried to call out, but could not:
for something black and heavy came over my face, and nearly suffocated me when I attempted to speak."

"How long I lay there I do not know; but though the whole is
like a dream, there was at times dreams within dreams, or a consciousness of having been dreaming. Frequently I fancied myself
as awaking from a long sleep and a confusion of visions. Once

when I awoke I lay by the side of a clear rivulet of water, near Lochleven, in Fifeshire. My sensations, at first, were, that I was still the boy that I once was, playing on the green grass and among the ferns, with my dear sister C——. My father's cottage and his cows, and the kail-yard, and the spring well, and the sunny stream were all there, but I could never enter the house. It receded from me as I went nigh the door; and, therefore, as I thought, my sister C—— made a bed for me by the side of the well, but always as she made a pillow of soft green grass for my head, there was an awful looking spectre came and removed me, and laid my head on a cold hard stone. My tongue and throat I felt gradually growing parched with fever, and my sister, who seemed more lovely than the form of any woman I had beheld, tried to lave the cold spring water on me, but was driven back by the spectre who said he was my ghost, and was very angry for my having left him, as he said, wandering amongst the graves and the hospitals of Spain in search of me.

"My visions then assumed another character; and oh—for my country, may dreamy visions only represent what I saw; may the brain which gives them birth, lie as low and as helpless as my disordered head then lay. The torch of war was lighted in my native land. As it is in Spain, province rose against province---town against town---son against father---and brothers slew their brothers. My father's house was in flames; I was a prisoner and in the hands of a victorious party, many of whom I recollect had been my schoolfellows. I saw my sister in their hands; they were murdering her: she called to me to save her; and bursting from the hands of those who held me, I uttered a cry of "fire, bayonets, blood, &c." and immediately the battle spread over city, village, and country, throughout Great Britain. I found myself rise into a mighty commander, and was standing on the highest of the Grampian hills, giving orders to the combatants. I ordered the dead to rise and fight; on which a skeleton came scrambling up the hill side, and taking one of his ribs in his hand, struck me on the head, and rolled me over the mountain. I then fancied that I fell from one end of Great Britain to the other, and saw nothing but warfare and blood. I felt myself die, but found that I could still speak, for I was loud in my demands to know what world I was to be taken to. My face

was wet, and I felt something like a sponge passing over my temples.
I looked up, and two men with red jackets were holding my arms
down by my side, and another person who wore a blue military surtout, was dressing my head, and telling me to lie still or my
wound would never get well. "Now my dear fellow," he went on,
"be quiet now; I think you are much better to-day; but if you
keep rolling yourself out on the floor that way, I'll be forced to strap
you down to the bed again. You see you have torn off all these
bandages from your head, and your wound is now worse than it was
twelve days ago — are you thirsty? — poor fellow — give him one of
these powders, Orderly — gently now — poor fellow! I think you're
much better to-day, are you? Do you know I extracted the ball
from your leg yesterday? no, my dear young man, you didn't know
but you will soon, if you lie down quietly and sleep; your fever is
not so bad now, is it?" I enquired where I was, and received some
answer about my being in San Elmo Hospital. I farther asked how
long I had been dead : and was answered that I was not dead, that
I had only been dreaming. I then began to be convinced that I
was really still alive, for I felt ravenously hungry. The surgeon
told me to lie still and sleep and that he would order something nice
and nourishing for me when I awoke; and charged the orderlies not
to talk to me, else I would relapse again into a fit. He and they
then left me.

Though I could not speak but with a severe effort, I still persisted
in being better informed of how I came there, and kept moaning
"oh will nobody speak to me,"—when I heard a voice close to me
saying "Ah old feller you're ungry now are you? I s'pose you thought
as you were in t'other wuld!" I turned myself towards him, and
saw a head peeping from amongst the bed-clothes of another bed
two yards from me. There was a red night-cap on the head, I looked at it for some time scarcely being able to speak, and not being
sure if it was safe to speak to a mere head with a red night-cap on
it—but he went on.

"What was you a calling fire,—bayonets and blood," that time as
you rolled on the floor for? You wont sleep, and you wont let any
one as is near you sleep—strike me blind but I wished t'other night
as you would croak and be done with it, you got up sitch a gallows
noise, you brought all the Ho-de-lies in the 'ospital into this here

ward, and that b——y chapelgorri in the bed at the window carajos (swears) night and day since he was brought up from the operation ward."

" How long have we been here ?" I enquired.

" How long !" replied he " let me see—why, a faughtnight to-morrow. I thought as how you were not knowing yourself, wot you was a saying all the time, you talked so much b——y scotch gammon. Don't you know as how 'Oskins, and Williams, and Bill, and Jerry, brought you to Sin Sebestian on the 5th of May, and laid you on the street, and wouldn't fetch you in, 'cause they thought you had croaked. S'help me G— you would have been put in the dead-house, had not that Spanish young 'ooman as comes and 'quires for you every day since that, brought you 'live again."

I lay and said nothing, but began to question myself if it was possible that I could have been twelve days in the Hospital. The last thing I recollected of the battle, was the charge on the fort of Lugariz, but I believe I soon fell asleep, and allowed my loquaciously ill-natured companion to talk to some one else.

Half awake and half asleep the next night passed over, and in the morning I was lifted out of bed, when I saw for the first time, all the ward as it now is. 'Twas visited by the surgeons, and soon after by some Spanish ladies, who come here almost every day. One of them, I am told, has been very kind to me. Many of the beds, sheets, and blankets, were furnished to the hospital, by the families of San Sebastian.

There are eighteen legs, and ten arms awanting in this ward. We have between eighty and a hundred beds in it, rather too close, but still it is airy and comfortable.

May, 28th. This is a dreadful morning, the most awful thunder that ever I heard, was nothing compared with the cannonade that shook the walls, and windows, this morning at five o'clock.

One of the Lancers took two Carlist prisoners, but was shot in the thigh, the ball lodging in the hip joint, yet he held them both, until assistance came. He has just been brought into the hospital, and is in dreadful pain. One of his comrades has come up to see him, and has a letter for him, which has just come from England. The sufferer is not able to read it, and the other cannot, and as it is not possible that he can live long, I opened it and read a part of it to him.

but he begged me not to read any more, but to keep it, and if he died, to write to his father.

Poor fellow, it says that his friends did not know until lately, that he was in Spain, and that his father had hoped that after paying thirty pounds last year for his discharge, from the Enniskillan dragoons, he would not have enlisted again. But as such dreadful accounts are in the newspapers at home about the Legion, and as his mother and sisters are like to break their hearts about him, he (his father) will do all to get him off, if he is willing to come home. The letter says " even your poor brother's orphans cry for you, though they never saw you when they see us in such grief, and your poor mother wondering at night if you have a bed to lie on." It was at this passage that the poor wounded Lancer desired me to stop, for he could hear no more.

June, 1st. M—the Lancer died yesterday, and was buried to-day, with the full military honours. All military funerals are imposing spectacles, but that of a dragoon is particularly so. The horse on which he was wounded, bore to the grave his empty boots stuck in the stirrups, (with the spurs in front) and his helmet—sword and accoutrements. The deep melancholy notes of the regimental musicians, told us what streets they went along, and the three volleys have just been heard below San Bartholomew Convent where they have buried him. How I am to write the letter to his friends I do not know.

CHAPTER IV.

The scenery and localities around San Sebastian—The duty of the Legion at this time—The morning of the sixth of June—Objects of the attack—Its commencement—The 1st regiment's sentries shot, and piquet driven in—The 1st retreat—General Chichester taken by Carlists—cuts down those who take him—The Chapelgorris and Chapelhurris—Dreadful fighting between them, and awful atrocities—Alza retaken—General and severe fighting—Two priests leading on the Carlists in their canonical robes—One of them shot—Remarkable bravery of Oakley—Cowards hiding in a ditch—The 4th English regiment fires by accident on the 8th Scotch—Charges led on—General retreat of the Carlists—Great slaughter—Houses taken—Plundering—The inhabitants flying—Remarkable anecdotes of individuals—The dead—The wounded—Mounting piquet in a wood among the dead bodies—Retrospective view of the whole.

From the 28th, of May, until the morning of the 6th of June, there had been no remarkable occurrences on the lines before San Sebastian. The Legion, with the Chapelgorris, and some other Spanish regiments belonging to the division of Jaurreguy (El Pastor or the shepherd as he is called) were extended from the convent of Antigua on the right (north-west) to the village and heights of Alza on the left (south-east) over a distance of four or five miles. Farther to the 'eastward and considerably to the rear of Alza, was the position of Lord John Hay—the town and port of Passages. In the diversity of hill and valley—river, and green woody mountain—villages—cottages— vines—orchards—fields of maize—luxuriant wheat, and beans odoriferous in leaf and bloom, there was a beauty of rural richness, mixed with the grandeur . of romance, in this part of the country, that no tongue can tell, or pen adequately describe. Ere the soul can be softened to mingle its sympathies with, or feel, the fullness of enjoyment, sensual, and intellectual, arising from the Spanish summer, it must be seen—for then only can its power be felt. We have our mountains, but there are no vines, and corn-fields, on their summits, We have our cottages—our green woods, and our rivulets but they do not unite the wild romance and the luxuriant softness of the north of Spain, The white walled cottage, lies in its orchard, winking from a more dazzling sun than ours—the mountain, and the valley, wear one greenness, and the river and rivulet have the maidens of the country at all times washing in the clear running water, This last peculiarity makes a part, and that not the least interesting of every Spanish landscape, The river in the valley below, and the streamlet that gathers from the innumerable springs along the mountain side lovely as they naturally are, would fall short of their beauty and interest were the clean linen not on their bushes, and the young black eyed beauties of the villages not bathing their uniformly handsome limbs in their waters,

The Urimea which comes winding through the mountainous country, and falls into the sea on the east side of the walls of San Sebastian, was for a considerable distance our boundary with the Carlists at this time. We were quartered on its eastern bank, in the houses, and villages at some distance from it, and mounted our piquets on an irregular line of heights, immediately in front, overlooking the river. Each morning as the day dawned, the regiments turned out of quarters armed, and accoutred, and having " fallen in," as the phrase is, lay under arms lest an attack might be made by the enemy until about seven o'clock, when if all seemed quiet they returned to quarters, had the day's rations of bread and beef served out, cleaned muskets and accoutrements, washed shirts and white trousers, relieved the guards, and picquets, paraded and drilled, went on fatigue duty, to cut wood, built fortifications, and so on (but this last species of military labour will be found more fully detailed hereafter.) Such were the positions held, and such the duties performed in May and beginning of June, 1836, by the British Legion. To be what is called inactive while lying before an enemy is unaccountable to those who read of a campaigning at a distance. It is ever an unpardonable neglect of duty in a commander if he sees the enemy and does not attack. The relative strength, and situation of positions are never thought of; the parties are only estimated by the numbers on each side, mountain, glen, river or fortress is nothing--- never thought of---the questions at the fireside, and in the reading room is---" Why dont they fight? they are doing nothing." Well let such questions be asked again as they were asked then about Evans and the Legion and the same answers will be returned even though the best army of the same number that was ever armed, or the best commander that ever commanded were there , that answer was, that an impossibility stood between us and a successful attack on the Carlists on the heights they then occupied, yet that did not preclude an engagement. We lay advantageously open to their attack. They had lost some of their most important positions, the town and heights of Passages, and having lost these, their communication with the sea in that quarter was cut off with the apparent possibility that Lord John Hay and General Evans would make an attempt from that place to extend to the frontier of France, only a few miles distant which attempt if successful would cut off all supplies for the Carlists in the province of Guipuzcoa. To prevent this, and smarting under the recent losses of the two former engagements the Carlist Chief Casa Eguia resolved to attack General Evans, which he did with great energy evidently intending to re-capture Passages.

It was on the morning of the 6th of June, 1836. The regiments of the Legion, and the Spaniards with them, had as usual turned out at day-break, and were under arms at various places along the lines fronting the enemy. Before sunrise a slight attack was made on our picquets, which were placed on and near a hill called the Ametzagana. This was a position a little to the left of our centre, but the attack was only a feint; their object being to draw our forces to that point, while their real intent was to attack and take by storm the height on which stood the village and newly erected fort of Alza. This if successful, would have been to the Carlists most important as from it Passages could have been attacked, and if not taken at least battered to pieces by their cannon.

When the false attack on the Ametza had ceased, the volleys died away : and their smoke had mingled with the dewy morning mist ; when the sun had risen in full radiance, the larks had mounted to their song, the music of millions of birds had succeeded the martial reveille of drums and bugles that daily ushered in the dawn, when these peaceful signs were seen, the fair Spaniards who come out early to wash in the rivulets and carry water to the town, began gaily to their pleasant toil, and the regiments of the Legion piled arms. Some lay down to sleep wrapped up in their great coats— some lighted their pipes and smoked—twos and threes who had known each other at home, lay down together, and talked about what was in the last letter they had got from their friends. A sigh came from one as he thought on a mother, or a sister—an oath polluted the lips of another, as he in bravado swore that if the Carlists would only fight he would not give a d—.Some hungry ones enquired if the Muleteers had come with the rations, and to the great satisfaction of these, and to the neglect of all other thoughts and employment with the whole—thebread was served out. The keen mountain air and early rising made it always acceptable, and though there was the beef and the allowance of wine to get, with many, the bread disappeared at once accompanied only with a draught of clear spring water which was always to be had in abundance. When the first three hours after sunrise had thus passed and we had returned to quarters leaving the piquets on the lines only, a cry was heard of " turn out"—" turn out." The drums rattled, and the bugles in all directions sounded the respective regimental calls—the " dressing call"—the " turn out the whole"—the " fall in" and the " advance" all at once to which they added the well known " double quick" which told that there was something of pressing haste required.

Hurrying down the old stairs of the houses—and crowding in mo. mentary confusion to get on our accoutrements, and hold of our muskets—there was a mixture of voices from the officers calling—" my

No. 5.   E

sword—my boots—my horse—saddle my horse—Serjeant A — Corporal B — down with that company—fall in men—fall in—number from the right—tell off right and left," amongst which, men were swearing " that's my musket you have"—" no I'm d—d if it is"— " that's my great coat" " let your great coat go to mischief—you'll not need a great coat long"—" aye there'll be pills for some of us in a little" and some whispers of " I hope that——that gave me two dozen yesterday, will get payment for his trouble."

On coming out we saw the volumes of smoke rising in the direction of Alza, and immediately in front of us in the direction of our piquets. There was a continued rattle of musketry that extended itself like a long thunder clap without intermission, and every few moments a loud rebound rose above the rattle, which told of the shot and the direction of the great guns.

At Alza, the 1st regiment, formed what might be termed the garrison, for the church and other houses were all loopholed (that is perforated with holes for muskets to fire through) but it was not sufficiently fortified at that time, to justify troops to remain within as it could be easily surrounded. It was on this village the attack commenced. The piquet of the 1st regiment lay about 400 yards outwards, and a little beyond that were the farthest advanced posts. Two of the sentries on these posts were shot by the Carlists who had crept up under the cover of an orchard—the other sentries fired, and ran into their piquet. Immediately that, amounting to about fifty men turned out and met the Carlists, and for a short while made a stout resistance, but had fourteen men killed. The remainder, as was their duty, retreated to their regiment, leaving some of their number by the way wounded, who, when the Carlists advanced, soon met their deaths—being, bayoneted without ceremony. Two pieces of cannon, an eighteen, and a thirty two pounder, opened on Alza, under cover of which the Carlists came boldly up. A sentry that stood at the back of the church was struck by the first cannon shot, having both feet taken off by it. The same ball coming in contact with the corner of the church, bounded off again, cutting one man in two pieces, and taking off the arm of another, General Chichester one of the bravest and most skilful officers that the British service is possessed of, commanded the 1st brigade of the Legion, and he fortunately was at Alza when the attack began. He lined the wall of the churchyard with the 1st regiment and despatched his aids-du-camp for other assistance. But the Carlists consisting of the Navarrese regiments the bravest, and by far the best soldiers in Spain advanced against the dreadful fire which the English met them with, and before more of the Legion could come up had forced their way through some fields, and with the greatest resolution and bravery, amidst a severe loss of killed and wounded on both sides—took the positions of the 1st regiment. It was said the Navarrese had volunteered to lead the attack, and they did it nobly, one of their officers daringly came forward followed by others and seeing General Chichester within reach, seized him on his horse, disdaining for the moment to take meaner prisoners in preference to a General, but which they could at that time have done easily. Chichester's pistol was ready and laid one dead! his sword first on one side and then the other, cut down those who had seized his horse, and springing from amongst them came out—rallied the 1st regiment and with the others who had reinforced him retaliated fearfully on the Carlists. Slaughter was mutual. The Carlist General afterwards stated in his dispatches that his loss at this point " was unusually severe."

The regiment first ordered to march to Alza, to strengthen General Chichester was the 8th, that which I alluded to as being suddenly turned out and seeing the attack on Alza at a distance. Godfrey, our Colonel, led on the instant he received orders, but the Carlists were not so easily dislodged from the ground they had taken. Emboldened by the success of the regiments that had taken Alza, they made a resolute attack on other points ; one of them was at the western extremity of our lines, but perhaps deeming it unimportant to carry that point and believing that all their forces would be required in the direction of Alza they withdrew from the west; on observing which, General Evans ordered his disposable troops in that quarter to come round to defend the Ametza and assist in retaking the village and heights.

In this the Chapelgorris more especially rendered themselves conspicuous, whether for daring resolution in going forward on an enemy—deadly hatred to their Carlist countrymen—relentless cruelty to all prisoners who fall into their hands—savage rage even vented on the dead bodies—or any other quality of either bravery or barbarity they are alike conspicuous—unmatched and unmatchable by any military band save one, and against that they were now opposed. The Chapelchurris or " white caps" of the Carlists, and the Chapelgorris or " red caps" of the Christinos had met. The most of them though on adverse sides were known personally to each other. Many of them were relations of the same families, and some now opposed in the deadly strife were even brothers. They were nearly all natives of the province of Guipuscoa, which is on the frontier, and this being the guerilla land, to which the most noted robber-bands of the Pyrenees belonged, the two armies had respectively their share of these mountaineers the most active and brave—lawless and savage, that ever slew, or were slain in warfare.

They met on the hill side beneath Alza. We at some distance but on rather higher ground had met the Navarrese, and were for a time kept back while they also stood, checked by our fire. The ground was rough, woody, and intersected by numerous hedges, so that it was difficult to advance, but this enabled us to keep our ground the better against the numbers opposing us. The green sunny fields, and the orchards of yesterday were now a blaze of fire and smoke. We saw the Chapelgorris driven back and those in front of us emboldened by that, made a strong onset to force us, but a heavy and steady fire scattered them on the earth as they came forward. The Chapelgorris rallied and their opponents in turn retreated, the wounded being left lying. As the victors came up to them the bayonets were dashed into dead bodies by those foremost, while others more leisurely put cartridges into the mouths of the wounded and blew them up—pinned the bodies of two dying ones together by a bayonet—cut off heads holding them up in the air to the enemy—and perpetrated other atrocities too horrible to be told.

The retreat of the Carlists was but short. They retaliated the full measure of slaughter and barbarity that they had suffered, for the Chapelgorris were again compelled to give way. A few of these being cut off in the corner of a field, could not by any possibility escape; and they were seen to close with their assaillants. Shortly afterwards on the ground being retaken their bodies were found, but mixed with almost an equal number of Carlist dead, the two parties having slain each other mutually. A Carlist officer was lying gasping while an antagonist had seized him by the cheek with his teeth, the latter was dead having been stabbed by the officer, but still held fast and thus was the cause of the Carlist's death, who, but for this would have made his escape not being otherwise wounded This officer was immediately recognised by some of the Chapelgorris as the once powerful chief of a guerilla band in which some of them had been subordinates. He had split the band at one time for a bribe, which caused them now to be on adverse sides, and the one who had seized him in the manner described had been second in command under him—had met him that day—was disarmed, but had wrestled with him and thus played his part of the mutual revenge.

There was an " *advance*" sounding by our bugles. Two companies of the 6th regiment with great bravery joined the Chapelgorris and driving the enemy back with considerable loss on both sides took possession of part of the disputed ground.

Our own and the other regiments of General Chichester's brigade advanced also, and after having gone forward for some distance against a heavy fire there was a general charge made : and the Carlists tremendously peppered by shot, and bayoneted in their retreat, abandoned their ground and fell back on Alza. Perseverance on our side soon drove them from that position in like manner.

As they retreated they set fire to the houses, so as these might afford us no shelter; and with the smoke arising therefrom, and that from the now general engagement, which was shared in by all the Carlist army and all the regiments under General Evans except two, we had got so completely enveloped in the thickness that it became difficult to know our own troops. The sound of the bugles in some degree served to direct us, but the thundering noise nearly drowned these. The 4th regiment had been ordered to support the 8th when that went forward on Alza; but being unexpectedly repulsed for a short while, and the 4th not knowing our exact position, they mistook us for the enemy, and fired on us. It was fortunate that they were soon apprised of the mistake, for some of our bravest fellows fell by their bullets ; and we not knowing but they were the enemy, that had got round our flank, were about to fire in that direction, or, perhaps, retreat from our position. This did not arise from any want of caution on the part of those commanding. It is extremely difficult in such a fight as that, for any one in command, to know distinctly where the different regiments are detached to, when performing light infantry movements, and especially as we had ad-

vanced in the smoke considerably farther than we should have done.
The Carlists stood firm at this place, and were soon observed re-
advancing on us again; and not only headed by their brave officers
but by priests in their canonicals, holding aloft the symbol of the
holy cross to lead them on to slaughter. They advanced, though
rather cautiously; for we observed the priests did not take the very
front, but by their gestures seemed encouraging the troops to go on
before them. A part of the brigade in which I was, lay in a place
where the Carlists certainly had not expected us to be, for they
came close up, while we were strictly ordered to keep down out of
sight, and not to fire until ordered. The priests were mounted
on horses; and it was with much impatience that some of our men
were restrained from levelling a rifle at the cross. But the order
was given at last, and vollies poured in on the hapless Carlists who
fell in all directions; some scrambling into the ditches; some retreating through gaps and over walls. The priests fell also; but
were seen in the disaster to get to their feet again, and as swiftly as
the lightest footed Guerilla betake themselves to a hasty flight.
"Forward—forward, men—fix bayonets—charge." were ordered
by our officers, sounded by the bugles, and instantly responded to
by the men, Spanish and English;—the first with their *vivas*, and
the last with their *hurrahs*; sending up a wild shout of triumph as
the whole dashed forward on the disordered Carlists. One of the
two priestly leaders rid himself of his holy robe and shovel hat, to
make himself either lighter for the flight, or less conspicuous for
those who fired in his rear. The other priest, on hands and knees,
was making his way through a gap, in the bottom of a bramble
hedge, but stuck and could neither get back or forward. The poor
old man kicked and sprawled, but to no purpose; and then he
prayed for mercy as Jock Watt, a huge grenadier, pricked him behind with his bayonet! but that likewise availed him nothing.
Jock was not very murderously disposed in ordinary times, but he
had little respect for a priest; and seeing silver buckles on his shoes,
a silver cross, and an ivory crucifix, with strong suspicions or hopes
that there was something else, he had thus pursued the priest, and
was standing swearing in half Scotch and half Spanish oaths for him
to "deliver up," giving him at the same time some very ungentle
touches with his bayonet. Others were approaching, and Watt

thought, that as he was not beyond the need of a pair of shoes, he would be surest of the silver buckles by putting on the priest's shoes, and he immediately made the action follow the thought. Another denuded the reverend gentleman of his cross and silver spectacles. One or two had rifled his sash, and had taken his money; and others, as they came up and halted for a minute, sought for something else; but none had yet offered any farther violence. The Carlists, at some distance, rallied, and perhaps supposing him slain or a prisoner, and having the dread of perdition for themselves if they allowed the body of a priest to become the prey of the heretic English, they came back on us with great resolution, but unsuccessfully; for we firmly withstood them, and a straggling chapelgorri happening to come near, his eye caught the priest. The "red cap" gave a wild *carago* (the common Spanish oath)—fired a shot—followed the bullet wound with a bayonet stab—smashed the skull of his victim to pieces---leaped on the body, grinding his teeth, and continued to pound down the head and breast bone of the priest with the butt end of his musket! Thus perished the poor priest; and thus is a correct specimen of the English and Spanish soldier given. The English soldier fights well at any time when he is ordered. The Spaniard fights bravely only by the impulse of revenge or rage. The Englishman will take either a silver buckle or a cross from those within his power, but rarely does he carry passion to the destruction of his victim; at least I have seen many honourable exceptions.

About this time, Colonel Godfrey of the 8th, had dismounted from his horse, in order to lead his men through an orchard where the branches of the fruit trees were too low to admit of his riding. The animal was left by itself, and the regiment having moved some distance from it, and then fallen back by another part of the orchard, the horse stood about half way between us and the Carlists.—Two or three of the latter were advancing to make a prize of it; but by some of our men, one of them was shot dead—or apparently so, and another wounded. Then a party of six belonging to our light company volunteered to go for it, expecting no doubt to be rewarded, but principally to shew their daring before the regiment, for we were then standing looking on, waiting for orders. As these six emerged from under cover, into the view of the Carlists—the latter fired, and four out of the six fell. "Let the brute alone," said Godfrey, "if he will stand there like a fool, let him,—I'm not to have my brave young boys shot for nothing." At this a Chapelgorri offered to go for the animal, and was bargaining for the number of dollars he was to have as a reward, on which Oakley who had previously distinguished himself, said with an oath, "no Chapelgorri shall go, and leave me behind him, afraid! if he can venture that length for payment, I know who will do it for honour.

"A dollar with you Oakley, you dont go half way," said one.

"What a fool you are to bet with me," replied Oakley, "if I be stopped before I go half way who will pay you?" and saying this he started off.

"My allowance of wine to yours," said one "he does not get up," "Done," was the reply.

"A dollar to a pisetta, (that was 4s and 4d to 10½d) he does not come back," said another—but no one would take that, for the dust knocked up by the Carlist's bullets, was at this moment seen rising around Oakley's feet.

He got hold of the horse—but the animal was fractious and began rearing! Bets then went on rapidly—wine—bread—beef—tobacco —and tobacco-pipes being hurriedly hazarded on the chances of his getting back to the regiment, with or without his prize.—He fell : but only for a moment, for the reins by which he led the horse were literally cut through by a number of Carlist shots having been fired on him at that moment. The regiment cheered—the Carlists in sight of him fired, and the balls flew thick, when one of them striking the horse, caused it to scamper inwards to us, and Oakley having been out about seven minutes, and exposed to a continued fire of about fifty of the enemy, who were at the head of the orchard—returned in safety, having only fallen when pulling the animal onwards by the reins, at the time these were cut away.

A pause had been made for a short while, to allow some regiments time to mount the steep ascent which we had now left partly behind us.—A universal cheer rose wildly through the woods, as the bugles sounded the "advance," but for a moment only was it heard.

A deafening thunder of musketry, and the rushing roar of rockets blazing over our heads, drowned the hurrahs of the English and the vivas of the Spaniards. Some who hurrahed, suddenly stopped and fell down without uttering a word. Some exclaimed "my leg," "my head," "my," "my," and were left to groan behind. The hedge-rows, and the fields, and the houses, that had hitherto been lying clear from smoke in the sun and the south wind, beyond where the battle had been, now emitted smoke and fire,—while in our rear the strife was dying. There only being the burning ruins of the cottages —the groans of the wounded—the surgeons cutting and dressing— the skulkers—and the plunderers. Around us were the ill-fated dead and dying of the enemy, and the cheers and vivas of our own troops as we pushed on and drove back the retreating foe, beyond the positions held by them previous to the attack on us in the morning. At a distance in front were the inhabitants hurrying off their cows, and pigs—the elder children leading the younger—the mother with the babies—her sheets and shirts hastening after them. The dusty coloured bakers who had been busily preparing the Carlist rations in some of the houses, were seen making their escape with each a bag of flour or bread, assisted by the retreating soldiers. Ours in turn shared the bread and the wine, and whatever could be had, as they came up to these houses. Some dared to advance farther in front than others for the mere purpose of being first at the plunder, and some were behind where they should have been at the hedge sides, and among the ditches, into which they had tumbled professing to be wounded.

One of these, an officer, was observed by some of his own men. Two or three of them immediately turned on him, and threatened to shoot him, if he did not come out of his hiding place.

"You Coward!" exclaimed a young man named M'Intyre—a clever soldier, who was taken prisoner in a subsequent engagement and shot by the Carlists"—"you coward come out or I'll shoot you." Come here an' see him now, some o' you. I'd kill him sooner than a Carlist." A number more collected round him, and he would perhaps have come out of the ditch had he dared, but every one as he came forward cocked his piece, with the bayonet fixed on it, and swore he would shoot him.

"Oh, no, men, spare me, spare me!" was the prayer of the fugitive.

"You rascal, what did ye flog me for?" said one.

"Aye, d—— ye, What did ye flog us for?" said another.

"Spare me, men, spare me!"

"And my bounty," said M'Intyre, " ye borrowed it, and never would gi'e me't again ; and got me provosted in Vittoria for askin't frae ye, because ye said I was insolent.   In-so-lent ! d—n ye, I'll put a ball through ye ; ye're a disgrace to the regiment."

"Oh no, Colly, Colly M'Intyre, spare me, and I'll do any thing for you.   I'll give ye an order on the paymaster to draw my pay— only spare my life."

"Shoot him : put a ball through him," said one.   "No, wait, let him write Colly's order first," said another.   "Oh yes, the order, gaur him write it, an' then we'll dispatch him."   "Oh you vaga-bond,—dinna let him out o' the ditch," called out two or three more who came forward.   "D' ye mind when ye sold the pang, old lad ? we're upsides wi' ye noo."   "As sure's my name's Wylie, I'll shoot 'im."

A resolute young man, well known as a clever forward soldier, named Wylie, in the light company, uttered the last threat, and cocking his musket, with the muzzle close to the poor lieutenant's breast, gave him a most determined look as the lock sounded click. "Oh men, make me swear to anything and I'll do it, but spare me."

"Well then, swear you'll pay Colly."   "Yes."—"And that ye'll never get another man flogged."   "Yes."—"And that ye'll never speak o' this."   "Yes."

This rough and unceremonious form of taking an oath to these engagements was going on, when some other men started another officer hiding.

"Come out o' the ditch," they were continuing to call to him, and some of them, seeing a trick going on, kept attracting his attention to themselves by threatening to shoot him.   A considerable quantity of powder, in broken cartridges, had been left by the Carlists in the place where he was standing.   A rascal behind him was making a train to it, and when he got it long enough to be out of danger, fired his musket into it.   The report of a shot close behind him made the frightened man start round to see what it was.   At the same mo-ment the loose powder. and the cartridges, exploded.   Head, feet, beard, and altogether singed, and partly in a flame, he gave one ter-rific roar, and jumped out of the ditch.   Happily for him there was not time to carry the persecution farther at that period, for the bugles were sounding the "advance," and Godfrey coming in sight ordered his men to fall in, marched them forward again into the fight.

Half an hour's sharp firing succeeded, during which a few of the men fell who had been most conspicuous all the day in being foremost on the enemy. They had at this time gone up to a house at the edge of the wood, and received a heavy volley through a hedge. This house was taken, and was in that part of the lines made the out-post, and continued to be some months afterwards,

The scene of plunder that now ensued far exceeded that of the 5th of May. One cause of its excess was that they had got possession of a wider space of fields, orchards, and houses, and all fell to be pillaged by the hands of those who had taken them. In some, both men and women were found. The latter vociferously called out " Viva Inglises,—viva Isabel segunda." That was a cheer for the English and the Queen : but their new cry, poor things, was too plainly a forced one, and it purchased for them very little favour.

The enemy in this engagement, lost above one thousand men, and Evans nearly half that number. The difference arising from the Carlists being the attacking party, which is extremely disadvantageous on such ground.

The Carlists, thus defeated, after a very determined attack with their best troops, the Navarrese, must certainly have found the war for the time look hopeless ; for the reader will not fail to keep in mind that this attack was a concerted one, all the strength that could be brought to that quarter having been done by the passive permission of the Queen's Commander-in-chief. Thus repulsed, they must, of course, have looked to the prospect of regaining these positions with dismay, or rather I should say they might have been supposed to be dismayed ; but they made another attempt, not such a resolute one certainly, but though more cautious, not less daring.

This was on the morning of the 9th, before daylight. The Royal Marines and Marine Artillery occupied a height to the eastward of Passages ; a temporary fortification had been erected, for here Lord John Hay had taken up a position as soon as he took the town on the 28th of May. To take this the Carlists ventured to attempt, not by cannonade and storm, for they were directed by better judgment than to attempt that. All the forces in Spain put together, would not have taken it by fighting, so inaccessible was the height, but they resolved on trying it by stratagem.

The Carlists brought up some columns of their best forces during the night, and after getting them up the steep hill-side, and partly under cover of some of the rocks, they were re-forming into columns, from having scrambled the best way they were able, and, no doubt, were about to put their plans into execution, though it never became known what theoe plans were.

It happened that the officer of the Marines' guard was visiting his sentries just at the moment that the first glimpse was got of the enemy, as they gathered under their partial cover. He did not allow the sentry to fire, which, no doubt, the latter would have done ; but ordered him to remain perfectly quiet until they were more distinctly seen. This officer communicated immediately with the commanding officer. The latter directed the sentries to remain without challenging, and the whole force to get under arms. This was silently done, and the guns drawn from the embrazures of the mud fortification, and each loaded with canister shot, then quickly and quietly pointed to the doomed foe. Every marine, loaded, stood at the 'ready' with his musket through the loop-holes of the fortification, and waited for the order which was to be given. In a short while the Carlists began to move from where they had formed, and by their movement, seemed as if intending to surround the place, and devour the sleeping garrison before their sentries could give the alarm; but, alas! for them, their daring had led them to destruction. The order was given within — " Fire! " one whole volley of artillery and musketry was discharged at once, and over the rocks, dead, wounded, and living, tumbled mingling in confusion. There was not even time to follow them with a second discharge, for they so suddenly disappeared that there was not a living one stood to receive a second shot. Descending down to the lower ground, the marines followed them, and for a short while kept up a slight engagement as the last of them retired. It could not be ascertained how many were killed, for they carried some of the dead and most of the wounded away ; but the marines got some of them to bury, and some dead bodies lay unburied for six weeks after that time between the lines, no party venturing to put them under the earth. At the same time that the marines fired, another division of Carlists made an attack on Alza, where they fought on the 6th, thinking, no doubt, that if the height on which the marines were, was taken, they would soon regain Passages; for it was reported that the Carlist chief, Eguia, who was now making these attacks, was exasperated almost to desperation at those who had so easily given way on the 28th of May, when Passages was taken from them. Alza was now defended by some artillery and two or three regiments — one of them, the 4th, was engaged with the enemy for a short while, and no doubt would have received it hot enough, had not the disaster of the division that had made the attempt on the marines, become apparent to those who attacked Alza. The latter, therefore, fell back, and Eguia bethought himself of employing his brave Navarrese in another quarter to more advantage. They were brave troops, and it is a pity that such bravery as they displayed in battle, should have been clouded by the crimes of the unnatural war. About the same time an attack was made on the western part of the lines where General Shaw commanded, which was repulsed principally by Colonel Colquhoun, and canister shot. The 10th regiment was engaged for a short while, but the whole affair was of little consequence, save to shew, that frequent attempts were made to regain what they had lost. But the necessary precautions that had to be taken with such a small force, on lines extending over so much space, (though amounting to nothing with the readers of foreign news,) were very hard work for the troops.

About this time, considerable numbers of our men deserted across the lines to the Carlists. A great number of placards, containing the following, were at different times found about the lines, in such places as our men got hold of them. Whether any actually relied on them or not I cannot say, but it is certain, more men deserted about this time than at any former period, and had less reason to do so for ill usage.

"TO THE SOLDIERS OF THE BRITISH LEGION!!!

"From the General in Chief, in the name of the King, his Royal Majesty Charles V.

"SOLDIERS!

"For the sake of yourselves keep silence!

"I have made you no offers until now that I find myself enabled to perform whatever I promise. If you join our army, who, fighting for the right and legitimate claim, which I have on the crown of Spain, you shall have everything that a soldier requires, receiving the reward which I now promise you. Many of your comrades have joined our ranks; they can tell you how they have been received by us, and what kind of treatment they have. Follow their brave, their bold example; we will receive you with love and affection ; you will then join our brave soldiers, who fight for our God, our religion, and our King.

" You will be rewarded as follows :—

" To every sergeant, corporal, or soldier that presents himself to me, and joins our army with his horse and arms, fifty dollars ; and he will be enrolled in our British Legion, where he will receive the best treatment.

" He that joins with his horse alone, thirty-five dollars.

" If he joins with his arms alone, ten dollars.

" And he that comes to us without arms, five dollars.

" Every sergeant, corporal, or private that joins us, bringing with him from thirty to forty men, shall be made an officer.

" If he joins from with forty to sixty men, he will receive a lieutenant's commission.

" If he brings over from sixty to eighty men, he will be made Captain, and the officers, sergeants, and corporals that are required to fill up the troop in his company, shall be made from the men who join with him.

" Any man who is the means of bringing over 300 men shall receive a commission as Lieutenant-Colonel in the British Legion.

" Soldiers ! By your joining us quickly you will be the means of putting an end to this horrible warfare. You have before you a noble career. Come, then, and enrol yourselves in the ranks of the legitimate Sovereign, and I pledge my royal word that all I have promised shall be performed.

" EL CONDE DE CASA-EGUIA,

"The General in Chief of his Majesty's Army.

" *From Head-quarters, 10th June, 1836.*

" Comrades ! You are now serving in an unlawful cause ; you are commanded by a set of officers, who are neither soldiers nor men, and who disgrace the name of Britons, by their cowardly conduct in the field, and their brutal treatment of their men in the camp. Here! if any man distinguishes himself as a brave and respectable soldier, he will have a fair and equal promotion from the ranks.

"From the British Legion in the service of his Majesty Don Carlos."

One of the most annoying deserters was a piper that had gone from the 6th regiment, near Vittoria, and now came frequently to the front of the Carlist lines, and played on the bagpipes.

As soon as we had taken up these new positions after the engagement of the 6th, the well stored gardens soon became a prey to the rapacity of the Legion. I was one day, while writing up the company's accounts in the captain's ledger, witness to an incident of rather an amusing character which took place outside the window. Three of our men who did not possess the most delicate appetites had got, as they thought, some fine young cabbages, and cooked a large quantity of them, which having salted, peppered, and buttered well, they began to eat.

"Eh man, they're capital," said Jock.

" Famous," replied Geordie.

" We manna let ony body ken where we got them," rejoined the third.

As they had sat down close below the window where I was writing, their observations and the smell of their mess, mixed together, caused me to look out above them.

"Na," said Tam Wilson, "we manna let Warsaw's Last Champion, and Sandy M'Gregor, and Ben, ken, for they'll tak' them a' at yince." (these were three noted gourmands.)

"An' that Simervel, for gudesake dinna let him ken, for he'll no' only eat the half o' them himsel, but he'll tell the hale regiment after he's saired," said Geordie.

"Wha d'ye mean,?" asked Tam.

"Whisht! him up there that's makin' up the books," replied Geordie. D——me, I had the finest bed o' ingyans the other day, that I wasna gaun to speak about, an' I doost let him see them, an' yesterday he had them twice, an' the day a' the company has them."

" He's a gutsy sow," said Jock Watt.

"An he canna haud his tongue," rejoined Geordie; "w en he gets onything he maun aye tell a' body where he got it.'

They had, at this last remark, eaten about the half of their quantity.

"What ails ye, Tam?" asked Jock, "ye 're no done already, are ye?"

"I dinna think they 're gude," replied Tam.

"I 'm turning staw'd tae," said Geordie.

"Faith there's naething wrang wi' me," said Jock, and continued a few minutes longer, but then laid down his spoon, and rose and commenced to vomit, which was carried on by the three in concert.

"Somebody's puttin' something in amang them," said Jock.

"Naebody could d' that," replied Tam.

"We're push'nt," said Geordie.

All three retched violently, and were soon surrounded by a number of the company, among whom I mixed myself, inquiring what was wrong with them. They would not tell at first where they got the cabbages but on getting worse, and likely not to need any more messes, they told where they were growing.

"Cabbage! did ye tak' yon for cabbage? yon 's tobacco," said two at once, who had been beguiled before with it. This solved the cause of the sudden sickness. They did not begin to another mess for a few days.

The next engagement of the Legion was in the vicinity of the town of Fenntarabia which lies near the mouth of the Badossa on the border of France. This took place on the 11th of July; but as preparations were making for some days previous and as I find some entries in my journal relative to events which occurred at this time, which entries were written in our quarters on the heights of Alza while lying before the enemy. They contain some particulars which will be interesting, therefore I shall quote them in the next chapter, previous to leading the reader over the lofty mountains which we ascended on the 10th and 11th of July 1836 to make an attack on the Carlists at Fenntarabia.

CHAPTER V.

Notes from a Journal—Piquets before the enemy and desertions—Court Martials and punishments—Narrow escape of one falsely accused—Anecdote—Fleas—Tailors in trouble—General Evans and the Royal Marine Officers—Evening of the 10th of July—Getting under arms—Morning of the 11th—March to Fontarabia—Attack on the Carlists—The engagement described—Retreat from Fontarabia and Return to Passages—Desecration of the Church—Author meets a Carlist spy—&c.—&c.

June 18th, 1836.—This is a glorious day among the old ones. All the Waterloo men are getting an entertainment at the expense of the old officers in honour of the anniversary of the great battle. There are altogether three or four hundred of them in the Legion, who wear the honours and can tell the tales of the Peninsular battle fields. I respect, nay almost reverence, an old soldier; and yet there are not three hundred fools in the Legion more contemptible—borish—and of greater hindrance to the efficient services of the younger men than these are, who pretend to know every thing; still there are a few of them noble old veterans. I am at present non-com of the piquet while scribbling this, and am sitting on the very spot where old Serjeant Deans fell on the 6th, and within twenty yards of the grave where he and others are now buried. The recollection of this arrests me while about to libel the old fools with their true characters. Deans was a remnant of the 42nd, a survivor of Egypt and Waterloo—wore four different honours of the English service, had a pension, came out here, fought gloriously on the 5th of May, was foremost all day on the 6th of June at the head of the *light bobs,* and fell dead with two musket balls in his temples at once, almost when the last shots of the engagement were fired. What a career! Egypt and Waterloo had spared him; and he fell here, as they will say in England, without glory!

There are an abundance of song makers in the Legion; almost every company of every regiment have their songs, celebrating their own share of the engagements. One of them which I have just heard recited is very good poetry, only it unluckily happens to be measured by the same versification as the beautiful, inimitable lines on the *Burial of Sir John Moore.* Yet, though it might, perhaps, be unreadable at home, it is extremely effective here. Here, where

No. 6   *7

we 'see the enemy's bayonets glancing in the sun in the opposite
wood—where we are surrounded by the graves gorged with their
dead, and here where we see every tree and orchard-bush scorched
by the fire, and shattered by the bullets of the late fight. The
author of this piece, though I do not know at present who he
is, must be, to a certain degree, a poet,—he says, after some spirit
stirring verses descriptive of the battle.

"They sleep on the mountain—the warrior host,
  Where the warrior's fate consigned them ;
They lie in the place where the grave and the ghost
  Are all that you now will find them.

They came from the mountain with valiant hand,
  For a valiant spirit swayed them ;
But they dared to brave a British band,
  And they lie where the Britons laid them."

I am afraid there is something more of them left than the "grave
and the ghost." We were fired on this morning when planting our
out-posts at day light, and I see something like two battalions drawn
up at a distance, near a house in a wood, just now ; I wish they
were ghosts. I would rather be in a church-yard by myself at midnight than here as I am, with a corporal and nineteen men, if yon
battalions should think fit to pay us a mid-day visit in this wood,
    June 19th.—I had been thus writing when a shot went off yes-
terday, and a cry from the sentries of "fall in the piquet"—then
another shot, and one of the sentries coming in calling "Sergeant
—men—men—for God's sake be quick—there they are—Andy's
shot dead on his post—and they're up—coming on us in thousands—
thousands—oh, men, we'll be killed!" The piquet was alarmed,
and to tell the truth, my heart would have leapt out of me had it
been able to find its way, it bounded up and down so with such un-
controulable thumps! and yet, I do not know how, I was able to
d———n the fellow to be silent, and order him back to his post, and
the other men to stand steady. It was all very alarming, for we
are on the extreme left piquet—the outpost, and the captain, and
the sub. of the main piquet are half a mile from us. The captain is
a clever fellow ; the sub. is a fool and a coward; so I am glad now
it is all over—that the latter, as he should have been, was not here.

I have not been able to find out yet the cause of the alarm, nor how the sentry was shot; and Captain E———of the piquet, has orderd me to make the one who came in a prisoner.

June 20th.---I am now in a dreadful dilemma. Two days and nights on piquet at once, from the scarcity of men and overwhelming amount of duty. Mounted with about two hundred---was told off with one corporal and nineteen to this post, and now I have only eleven ;—three are prisoners---one is dead, and the others have not been seen since last night. Deserted, they must be, no doubt of it. Goodness! what am I to do. I expect nothing short of a court-martial for having lost so many men off my piquet ; or if not I must appear as the convicting witness, which is nearly as bad, against one who was asleep on his post, and two for being drunk on duty. The others are either absent drinking, or have deserted.

To explain the foregoing notes I have now to add, that one of those men who did desert, has since our return to England, met me, and enjoying a laugh at the adventure, which I care nothing for now, but which was extremely grievous to me at the time, says, that the firing, the day previous to his desertion, was occasioned by four of them having stolen down the wood from the piquet, intending to go over to the enemy, but, that the sentry on the out-post challenged them, and threatened to fire if they proceeded further. At the same moment, a small party of Carlists who had remained in the bushes, much nearer than was suspected, after day-light, fired on them, and shot the sentry. This he explains by saying, that he and others had made full arrangements with a Spaniard, at Passages, a Carlist spy, and that had the piquet been all of the right sort they intended to have told the whole of us of the bargain they had made with the traitorous agent; but suspecting that to be dangerous, four of them ventured by themselves, creeping among the bushes until observed by the sentry who threatened to fire on them if they went any further. The sentry was shot by the Carlists, because they, expecting the piquet or a part of it to desert, had hid themselves before day-light, within gun-shot of that post for the purpose of protecting the deserters from being retaken or shot while attempting to come over. Not knowing that then, and not being certain if the Carlists fired at them, the four came running in through the wood to us as if they had only been strolling in the shade of the trees as they were at liberty to do, and joining in the cry of alarm that was given, took their muskets from the pile, and assumed a share in the consternation of the piquet.

Next evening as he reminded me, two of them got leave to go for water and beans, (beans at this time being every day pulled from the fields in immense quantities by the Legion,) the sentry on the out-post, in the direction of the water spring, being one of the four conspirators of the day before, went off his post along with them taking his musket and accoutrements. They approached the Carlists ; he who was armed was about to *reverse* his musket previous to their appearing in full view of the opposite sentry, but the latter seeing a head and a musket amongst the bushes fired, and the man who received the bullet was so severely wounded as to die soon after. The other two knowing the danger of returning, and expecting to be shot also the moment they presented themselves, were now dreadfully alarmed, but they had no time to hesitate. The next two minutes had not passed until the Carlists' picquet surrounded them ; they performing the sign of the cross upon their knees, and surrendering themselves in the earnest tones—bad Spanish—and profound terror that their perilous adventure inspired. They found as they deserved to do, that the exchange of service was not to their advantage. The poor fellow who was wounded received no medical attention whatever, and after being stripped by the Carlist soldiers of his accoutrements—clothing—even his shirt, he was left among some straw where he died, as the other two believed, on the third day after their desertion.

And this was the very day too that I, subjected to the most painful apprehension on their account, was to attend a court-martial as evidence against some other offenders, not very sure but the military crime of being sergeant of a piquet, and losing nearly one half of the men, might be charged against me as a punishable offence : this occurrence arose from a sum of money, an unusual thing, having been then issued to the Legion, on the receipt of which a good many put it to an imprudent use. Court-martials and flogging, was the consequence, and the most unpleasant duty that can devolve on a soldier is that of being a convicting witness in a case where he is fully assured from the nature of the crime, that the lash will follow. At this time I was in that painful situation

The most of soldiers, however ill behaved they may be, have like other people, some sympathising comrades or friends ; and even these, though the Articles of War are beyond all moral justice imperative and summary, can often serve the unfortunate criminal in a very important manner. The sympathising comrades, whether from friendship or an expectation that it may be their own case next day—will hunt about for exculpatory evidence—will go and beg of the witnesses against the prisoner to be merciful—will apply to a non-commissioned or a commissioned officer to give the accused a good character, or if none of these applications are successful, they will at least sympathise and have pity for the sufferer in his agony.

But as in most other departments of life, there were men with us who had no friends, who had entirely worn themselves out of comradeship from some cause or other. To be a soldier in Spain—to be in danger of not only a flogging, but the sentence of death, and not to have even one pitying friend was indeed dismal. Yet there was such a person. He had been once convicted and punished for thieving by a court-martial : and often suspected of and punished for the same crime by his comrades, and there is nothing be it known in a soldier's life, that is of a more damning quality in the eyes of his fellow soldiers, than stealing from a comrade. This man was of a morose forbidding disposition, cared for no one, and no one, man or officer, cared for him more, than to compel him, to do his share of regular duty. At midnight on the 18th, I had gone round the sentries, as was my duty, to see if they were all alert. This man was asleep ; on which he was relieved by another—stripped of his accoutrements—marched over to the main guard and there confined a prisoner. A good many of the men expressed their satisfaction at seeing him "in for it" as the term was ; one or two I heard admitting that "poor devil he'll be able to feel pain on his back as well as any of us," still they added "he's a disagreeable, ill natured, thieving wretch, let him take all he gets." Now I was aware that some of the more expert thieves had turned the blame of thieving on him many a time, when he was innocent : indeed, I believed then that there was not a more honest, or sober man in the regiment. Sometimes they stole things and put them into his knapsack for sport, and the frequency of these accusations, and his general sulky manner, had made the captain of his company promise that the first fault he was in would be specially reported to the colonel; and the colonel himself had heard of the ill-fame of this despised man, so that now there could be no hope for him but the utmost severity.

The Colonel and Adjutant inspected the prisoners, as these were paraded before them on the morning of (I think) the 20th. The greater part of them were confined for having been drunk; which drunkenness had followed the issue of money after a considerable period of no-pay. Two or three of them got two dozen lashes each, and the remainder who had not been on duty, were, after a severe reprimand, set at liberty. Those who had left the piquet and had been found drinking, were all ordered for trial before a court-martial, which was then assembling. The Colonel, on seeing the man who had slept on his post, among the prisoners, exclaimed, "You d—d rascal! *you* are there, are you?" The Adjutant responded, "Yes, the sulky vagabond, he should have been here long ago." The Captain of the company to which the men belonged was passing at that moment, on his way to the court-martial, of which he was president. On seeing this unfortunate prisoner, he turned round and said, "You brute, are you there too?" The Serjeant-major was ordered to turn in the prisoners again into the place of confinement. He stood at the door, and as they passed him, took this one by the shoulders, giving him an ill-natured push, saying, "go in, d—n you." The provost serjeant was also there; and he likewise uttered an oath and a contemptuous epithet, in ordering this prisoner to go in. The other prisoners said, "You sulky, ugly beast; had you not been among us, we would have been, perhaps, let off with the rest."

I had been sent for, and got a violent storm of oaths from the Colonel for my unhappy piquet, and was ordered in a peremptory tone to go and give evidence against them to the court-martial. At the same time I saw the Adjutant and Serjeant-major looking out for a suitable place for the afternoon's parade. They were in a small green field, where there was a lovely cherry tree with its ripe fruit. They examined it; and immediately after, a regimental order was issued that the regiment would parade at five that evening; each captain to march his company from the different quarters, and form in this field. The object of this was at once obvious. We would be formed in hollow square round the cherry tree; the men to be punished would be tied with their feet to its root, and their arms extended to its spreading branches, and there the punishment would be inflicted.

Many were the applicants of that morning; all beseeching me, as I was principal evidence, to say something in favour of their comrades who were to be tried. Alternate prayers, bribes, and threats, were offered in behalf of every one, save the man who had no friend. Had it been otherwise — had any sympathy been excited in his behalf, it is probable that I should have treated his case the same as the others; but he seemed to stand so dismally alone, amid the unpitying, universal sneers of the regiment, that I felt painfully sorry that I had confined him at all; and yet I had no alternative, for there were others had seen him asleep besides myself.

I consulted with the Corporal, who was the other witness, about what could possibly be done; but the answer was, instantly, "done! what would you do? Is not there some of the best chaps of the regiment to be tried for only getting drunk, and that sly rascal, a thief, that took my white trowsers off the hedge and hid them in his knapsack, and stole my shirts — him! the vagabond — there's not a man in the regiment likes him, and I'm d—d if I try to save him; let him have his whack."

"The man that stole your shirts, and put your trowsers in that poor fellow's knapsack," I replied, "is one of those that you call the best fellows of the regiment—one of your own dearest comrades. I knew that long ago; and but for the aversion I have to be a prosecuting witness, I would have had him punished for it."

As I went towards the house where the court was assembled, I passed the prisoners going in charge of the provost, and two or three file of the guard. The court had not been constituted, and we had to wait for about half an hour; during which, some serjeants of other companies, who were attending to give their men good characters, kept pressing me to give my evidence as favourably as possible for them. I took this opportunity to whisper to the friendless man, that I would try to save him if I could. That moment, the sour face, that had forbidden by its aspect every friendly feeling in others, brightened up; but as I passed away saying nothing more, it fell into its natural cloud of ill-humour, probably from his supposing that I had only mocked him.

The trials went on. They were short; as the charges against

the most of them for absenting themselves without leave, from the piquets, and neglect of duty, were easily proved, the punishment for which could not have been obviated by any favourable evidence. The Colonel was in a foaming rage—swearing—filling his nose with snuff— blowing it out, and refilling without intermission—stamping up and down, and finding fault with every thing, and every person, which ill humour had been occasioned by so many men misbehaving themselves.

While the court was consulting on what punishment should be awarded to the first five, who had been tried in a batch ; I was outside and accidentally met the raging Colonel. As I was generally in very good favour with him, and had never incurred his displeasure up to this time, I thought of venturing to speak for a mitigation of punishment for the soldier who was to be tried next, which punishment could not be inflicted—be it known—without the Colonel's approval.

" You d—d scoundrel how dare you speak to me," was his answer to my salute, as I approached him, but had not yet opened my lips— " Provost-Serjeant" he continued, " cut off this fellow's stripes— let him be reduced to the ranks--I'll try him by a court martial ; the scoundrel—to mount piquet with twenty men—get one shot—let one fall asleep on the very outpost—three desert to the enemy—and five get drunk—d—n you, rascal, are you not afraid of me." Had he been less furious I might have been inclined to have shrunk a little. As it was, although not very prudently I confess—I answered " No Sir—I'm not afraid of you." His grey glaring eyes flashed with rage—his very mustachios had terror in them. I stood at the position called in military phrase 'tention, while he eyed me from head to feet, and from feet to head, and then fixing his eyes upon mine, stared at me fast without speaking. The provost-serjeant, who was an obsequious slave, or rather knave, that delighted in being the instrument of any man's punishment or humility, came to perform the operation of reducing me to the rank and pay of a private, by denuding my arm of a certain badge. But the Colonel said " No, I'll not reduce you, but by G— I'll flog you." I was not much afraid of this last threat, for I knew there was no real crime on my part, only he might have reduced me—as he could any one that he chose to be offended with.

I turned and went away, and he probably relenting a little, called me back, and enquired what I had wanted to say to him. I answered that there was a man now to be tried, for sleeping on sentry—that I believed the corporal was at that moment proving him guilty—and that I had wished to remove from the colonel's mind, the common impression—but unjust one—that the man was a bad character.

"Say nothing about him," was the reply. "I have ordered him to be handed over to a brigade court-martial, from which he will receive three times the punishment which I could give him by a regimental one, why! he has the worst character in the regiment—and you will have the assurance to come and speak in his behalf."

I then explained what I believed to be the real character of the man and told the Colonel what he did not know before, that the poor fellow was the object of every one's mischief, and that I could now prove that the flogging which he had formerly received, was undeserved, as I had heard some of the young mischievous ones boasting of the way in which they had got old Buffer, as they called him, to catch it, and how one of these had frequently threatened to *snitch*— or tell who stole the bridle which Buffer was flogged for.

"Now go away and do not annoy me—I'll not punish *you* but by —by my—must I swear?—I've a good mind to do it," was his reply.

But whether he had a good mind to punish me, or a good mind to swear, I did not wait to hear, for his head was shaking ominously.

Five o'clock came.—The regiment was paraded. A hollow square formed round the cherry tree. The minutes of the court-martial read, the sentence—one hundred and fifty lashes to each of the prisoners, to be inflicted at what time and place the commanding officer thought fit—was by that supreme ruler of a regiment fully approved of, and he following his approval, gave the order to the first one— "strip sir."

There were one hundred and fifty lashes administered to each of the five prisoners, beneath the cherry tree, and five patients were sent to the hospital.

On that being over, the Colonel ordered the other prisoner to be brought out, and on his appearance addressed him thus. "So you thought fit to lie down and sleep in front of the enemy's sentries did you?"

"It was my third night out of bed," was the reply.

"Your third night! how?" enquired the commanding officer.

"Because Sir, I am oftener on duty than any other man—they all cheat me of my turn. I was on the Casa guard on monday night —the regimental guard on tuesday night, and was sent out of my turn to the piquet on wednesday."

"Why did you not report that?"

"Because you would have flogged me."

"What makes you fear that?"

"You flogged me once before Sir—when I came to tell you of my shoes being stolen—and the captain another time got me tried by a court-martial for stealing his horse's bridle—when I had only come to his quarters to tell him that there was a plan laid to rob him."

"And do you know who robbed the Captain?"

"Yes I do Sir."

"And why did you never tell?"

"Because the Captain flogged me for coming to tell him."

"Why did you not tell that to the court that tried you?"

"They ordered me to be silent and would not let me speak."

"Why then did you not tell me when I inflicted the punishment?"

"You would'nt allow me to speak."

"Now do you deny the common character which every one gives you of being a thief?"

"I am not a thief sir."

"You are sure?"

"I am sure—but you may find it out sir by enquiring whether ever I was proved guilty or not?"

"Why your comrades tried you and found you guilty—by a company court-martial—did they not?"

"The court was not fair Sir?"

"Why not?"

"Because there are only six thieves in the company, and they were the six members of the court that tried me."

"How do you know that the six were thieves?"

"Because they stole the things themselves, that they tried and punished me for."

A number of other interrogatories and answers brought out some interesting facts, that so completely satisfied the colonel that there was a conspiracy of ill feeling towards this man, and taking into consideration that he had been on duty out of turn, he set him at liberty adding " you may thank the serjeant of the piquet for that." The poor fellow, I believe, continued to have a feeling of deep regard for me ever after—though I had done nothing but a very bare duty in saving him from a brigade court-martial.

Ten months afterwards when the fort and town of Irun were stormed and taken—when amid the wild ravage of the plundering riot which succeeded the stormy assault, and valiant defence,—the unhappy women fell a prey to the overwhelming flood of srime ; I saw this man with a baby in his arms nursing and endeavouring to soothe it, while the mother had become the helpless victim of men more brutish than he was. Such is, sometimes, the falsehood of physiognomy ; for I remember having seen at that moment one of the best looking men—clever—and bearing a good character, in the commission of the basest of crimes, while the man of forbidding countenance seemed actuated only by the softest affection, and most honourable humanity.

During the month of June, and early part of July, the duty of the Legion consisted in mounting the piquets before the enemy — guards on the regimental quarters—turning out before day-break to be ready for prompt defence—drilling once or twice a day—washing shirts and white trowsers at the rivulets, and in boiling beans ! As the houses were so completely overstocked with certain insects called fleas, so much so, that we went out to the sun-shine, where they became powerless, and brushed them off our clothes with a handful of grass—many, the greater part of us, chose to lie outside during the night in the orchards to escape persecution. Each regiment had a number of tailors and shoemakers always at work. The tailors particularly, had been extremely annoyed by the small gentry, who claimed a right of habitation with them ; as their berths had become —from the nature of their repairing trade---a kind of head-quarters for each company's fleas. For a while, two or three tailors together shifted their places each day in order to cheat the fleas of yesterday, then they separated and wrought singly to prevent au undue accumulation ; but all these tactics of manœuvre availed them nothing, each unhappy tailor had still more than sufficient to torment him.

The inventive talents of a Scotch and an Irishman, who wrought together, were one day combined to out-wit the fleas. They ascended

an apple tree that spread out its wide boughs on each side, and
which extended the clustering fruit to the dew and the sun---while its
canopy of leaves shut out the scorching heat.   The now luckless
fleas---if they made a leap at all, had many chances to miss their
footing and fall to the bottom.   This succeeded admirably.   Where-
ever there was a thick wide spreading tree in the orchard you would
be sure to find a tailor or a shoemaker perched in it, the latter with
their whole kit of implements.   On descending, the tailors to avoid
the hosts that inhabited the grass at the root, made a hasty escape
to a distance,   Some of them who had a good tree with flatly grown
branches, roosted in it all night.   Of this sort was that of the two
whose genius first made the discovery of this escape from persecution,
the hot sun of the day-time, and the damp ground, and green grass
of the night.   A third one, who was always their comrade---but for
some days had been employed elsewhere, came and as usual with
him, sat down at its root, which had been their old shop, knowing
nothing of the new.   The two who sat aloft soon discovered their
friend and enjoying their joke as they thought, allowed him to remain a prey to the hungry myriads that had been for three days starving among the grass,   He endured for a while, but at last, taking
flight to find a new place of peaceful business he was informed of the
new system, and laughed at by those who had been watching his
persecution.   He was an old soldier, a remnant of Badajoz, and had
seen too much mischief, for others to laugh at him with impunity.
Night came on.   The two, on a bed of grass and leaves which they
had gathered and spread on the branches of the tree, wrapt themselves in their great coats and fell asleep.   Old Joe, to enjoy his
turn of sport, collected a quantity of straw at the root of it, threw on
leaves, hemlocks, and other combustibles that would make smoke,
and then set them on fire.   There was first a coughing heard, then
an exclamation of " Och, Holy Jasus, the house is on fire."   The
other, being still covered over head, and less of the smoke having
reached him, grumbled in his Aberdonian dialect, " fat are ye gaen
on at that wy? fa eer heard o e tree in e open field gaen a fire?"
But the Irishman, with an expression of half-prayer and half-oath,
bounded from the branches to the ground, ran to some distance,
where a whole company were collected to see the sport of *smeekin
the tailors,* as they called it, and turning round to look at the de-

struction of the nest, stood repeating the names of the saints until seeing the plight of his unhappy comrade, he left off the calender, and shared in the unpitying mirth. Poor Sandy was not so clever in descending, being an older man, and being completely enveloped in flame and smoke he rolled down in the midst of it, and was dragged out beardless, hairless, and half-choked: exclaiming, "fat's this o't? fat 'ill I dee? dinna kill me, geed Carlists—dinna kill me;" supposing, no doubt, that he was in the hands of the enemy. He was vindictive, as he had some cause to be; and old Joe did not venture to come in contact with him for some days.

About this time, General Evans issued an order to the effect that officers of the Royal Marines would always be considered superior in rank to the officers of the Legion, and take precedence of them in the following ratio. The officers above the rank of Colonel in the Marines were to rank with the Generals of the Legion. The captains with the colonels, and the subalterns with our captains. It was a foolishly weak and unmanly prostration of dignity in General Evans thus to succumb to the prejudice of a few persons who snarled at him. One of the officers of the Marines wrote frequently to a London newspaper, complaining of the shocking indignity of their being associated with the Legion. But what to him must have been the indignity, as he was a young, fashionable aristocrat, was the obligation he found himself under to wrap himself in his cloak and soil his polished boots by mounting the piquets of the Ametza hill. His letters are only worth referring to, because in England, people have been misled by them. The genuine English officers that had seen service in the Marines were never ashamed of being along side the Legion. It is true that some unpleasantness might arise to them if they happened to be on duty where an officer of the Legion, who had once been in the ranks, could now command them. But such cases were very few, or, perhaps, never occurred at all. And had such unpleasant associations of aristocratical pride on the one hand and veteran merit on the other occurred, nothing but the unmanly conceit of the gentleman of Marines could have been injured by it. As a fair example, we may consider the case of Mr. Sked. He had been twenty-eight years in the Royal British Artillery, was known to be one of the best practical and most scientific gunners of the service, yet had never risen higher than a sergeant, and never would have risen higher had he continued twenty-eight years more in the British service. He went to Spain, was for some time a serjeant-major of infantry, and then got promoted to a commission in the Legion Artillery. His services in that corps were most efficient. It might have been unpleasant to a gentleman, born with a silver spoon, to have been in the same quarters or at the same mess with him; but in the battle-field, where every shell thrown by Sked, told on the enemy's lines and fortifications with the most precise effect—where practical science and undaunted courage were united in conflict with the enemy—even the gentleman—and he sooner than any one else would shrink beside the superior skill and experience of the veteran old soldier.

Yet, allowance must be made for these prejudices of British officers to a certain extent. It is not themselves as men, but their education, and the usages of society that inspires them with their ungenerous estimate of rank. Though I believe there was no vulgar associations in Spain that made them so uneasy as the vulgar Carlist bullets with which they sometimes came in contact :—it must be admitted that they had a right to consider themselves superior in dignity to the officers of the Legion. I never met an officer of the Marines, or one of the Royal Navy, while in Spain, without saluting him with the most profound respect, taking it for granted, while I knew nothing to the contrary, that they were full of that honour which we are accustomed to believe them to possess. But General Evans to have depreciated the dignity of the officers of the Legion, to flatter them, was mean ; unjust, so far as men who had any regard for the honour of the service was depreciated, and altogether mischievous in its effects. It caused ill-feeling and light esteem for the General's own character to spring up among his officers, while those whom he intended to propitiate only laughed at his good nature.

The 10th of July, 1836, was a lovely summer day. Wheat was ripe. Apples hung on the bending boughs of the orchards in their countless millions. Beans had been rich and plentiful, but they were now thinned, and the fields presented only the prematurely leafed stalks. The thousands of men who had by these increased their otherwise scanty rations, were all now in the full enjoyment of renovated health. No army in active service could appear better than the

Legion did at this time. The discipline was strict, but it only tended
to improve that military appearance on parade which has never been
exceeded by any regiment, and which the Legion then exhibited to
great advantage. There was a roughness in our style of living,
cooking, and eating, that some at home might have laughed at,
but we drank our daily wine to our dinners which they would have
been fond to partake of; and we wore white trowsers, clean belts,
carried polished muskets, and performed the evolutions of the field,
with a correctness that would have excited the respect and admiration of all who know what soldiering is, in this country, had they
seen us; yet we lived a rough and uncertain life.

The evening of the 10th was calm and beautiful. The river, woods,
fields, and mountains, seemed sinking asleep in a lovely melancholy,
as the sun drowned himself in the great Atlantic. The ships of
foreign trade were losing their time, and lay lagging on the Bay of
Biscay. Some of us, as we looked at them, sent a sigh home to
England; knowing that there were at least some who responded to
it. I was sitting among some green bushes, watching the dying
glory of the sun, a blackbird that caroled close behind me, and some
young Spaniards that gamboled by the side of the rivulet, while their
dark eyed eldest sister was wading barefooted through the dew, calling them to come home to bed. There was a holy vision of my own,
our happy home before my mind's eye, and I was luxuriating in
dreamy recollections, when the startling bugle sounded for orders.
In a minute it was followed by officers calling for their serjeants, and
servants; amongst others I heard my name, and starting up, saw the
rocket brigade — mules loaded with ammunitions — stretchers to
carry the wounded — and the quarter-master's mules of different
regiments, with three days rations of salt beef and biscuit. The
bugle which had sounded was now silent, but there was a running
about, and a multiplicity of orders giving, taking and retaking, that
plainly shewed there was something in progress; especially as the
buglers had been ordered not to sound, lest an alarm might be taken
by the enemy. This was suspicious; and the most of us had some
apprehensive forebodings.

The mules in hundreds carrying mountain guns, and all kinds of
munitions marched past us, kicking and crushing, while the muleteers in smothered oaths endeavoured to keep the movement noise-

less. Canteens, which we did not always carry with us were hurriedly served out, and every man told to take care he had it with him, as the march we were to have would require us to carry water. This seemed mysterious, the sea was on one side of us, and the enemy on all the others.

It became dusk, and we turned out; all smoking of pipes, and lights of any kind were forbidden.   The salt beef and biscuit were divided, and some put them to a masticating process before their time, probably being in doubt if they would eat them at all if they did not eat them then.

For nearly two hours we stood under arms, wondering where we were to go.   Companies were told off in subdivisions, in sections, in threes, and in right and left files, all in whispers.   We saw aides-du-camp galloping back and galloping forward, as if giving orders.   At last the order to shoulder arms, and march away was given, and we moved off after the rocket brigade and mountain guns, towards the town of Passages lying two miles eastward.

The road to that place from where we were, was extremely bad, and it being a dark night, the march was very tiresome : going along the sides of deep declivities, ascending at one place, and descending at another, halting till some mounted officer passed us on the narrow pathway, and crushing our way past mules loaded with ammunition at another place. In the narrow streets of Passages we stood waiting till regiments in front of us got across the water, which was about one hundred yards wide, but in which there is always a strong tide running.   This is the inlet from the sea that runs between the high mountains mentioned before.   All the boats that could be manned by sailors from the different vessels under Lord John Hay, were ply-ing between the two shores, getting us over, and they were not long about it. I heard questions asked at them about where we were going but they of course knew as little in that respect as we did ; only that the steamers to which they belonged, with a number of gun-boats, were to sail for the coast of France, as soon as we were all over to the other side.   With great difficulty we made our way up the steep hills that rise to an immense height above Passages.   The road was so bad that those officers who were mounted had to dismount and lead their horses, and even then they could scarcely make their way up the steep ascent.

A little before daybreak we got up to one part of the height where there was a level, and halted; there were other hills to ascend before us, but we did not know that we had farther to go. On this first height which we ascended, we piled arms and lay down; I fell fast asleep, as did many others, and had a sound slumber till the bugles sounding the regimental calls of the different battalions roused us up. The sun was just peeping his red edge above the horizon, shewing us a beautiful morning, the 11th of July. The Chapel-gorris went forward as a skirmishing party and then the 10th regiment moved off, their band playing the tune of *" take me while I'm in the humour."* The other regiments, British and Spanish, marched forward in succession, excepting the 7th Irish; and 1st English, which were left keeping the lines at San Sebastian. When we had proceeded a short distance the Carlist piquets fired on the Chapel-gorris, and we supposed that the engagement had begun; but the Carlists retired, and we did not see anything more of them for some time.

As we crossed this part of the lines, which was the ground within the range of the British Marine Artillery, we saw the remains of the havock which they had committed on the Carlists, when the attempt had been made, on the morning of the 9th of June, to surprise the marines. One of the bodies was lying on the narrow path, out of which we had not room to step to a side. It was a dreadfully loathsome sight. A piece of a shell had taken a part of the head off, and the whole body was exposed to the sun, and filled the air with a sickening effluvia; other bodies were lying near the same place, and it was astonishing how a love of the marvellous drew almost all those who could get away, to go and look at them, when we halted in the narrow road to let other regiments get forward.

Marching onwards, and when further along, to where there was a full view of the sea, we saw the Phœnix, Salamander, Gubernadora, and Isabella steamers, with about a dozen of gun-boats, making their way along the sea-coast. We were now on a very high ridge of mountains, the north side of which sloped down a distance of three miles to the sea, and rose almost perpendicularly on the southern side.

We marched along this height about six miles, and began to suffer thirst severely from the salt beef and biscuit. The canteens which

No. 7*   G

we had been served out with did not hold in the water, and now there was none to be had but far below us, where it was seen in streams issuing from the side of the mountain, and pouring over the rocks, Grass, and other green plants, covered the hills to their very summits; the flocks of sheep and goats had been browsing, but were driven away as we approached. It was perhaps as well for the owners, but we were not in a way to have molested them much, for we marched in close column, which caused us to be very tired, in the suffocating heat of the sun, but which gave each Colonel full command of his men on a small space of ground, in the event of any of them attempting to fall out without leave.

On the highest pinnacle of the ridge we halted for a short while, and breathed a fine fresh breeze that came over from the south. Here we had one of the most splendid views that the human eye perhaps, ever beheld. Stretched down below us were fields of wheat, yellow, and mixed with the green of orchards; and *beans* where no Legion had been. There were heights and hollows, we afterwards found; but at the distance we looked down, all seemed a beautifully spangled plain. Farther eastward was France, all as lovely, but not more so; and between the two countries the Badossa branching off on different sides, or rather gathering in its branches, lay intersecting the earth's carpet like silver cords. I do not know what others felt on beholding it, but I thought the sight an unfortunate one for the energy required for fighting. It made me thoughtful. Cottages lay peeping out of the vines, and other fruit-trees that shaded them from the sun; and between us and these we saw the people hurriedly taking in their cows and sheep. All at once, these lovely cottages emitted the smoke and fire of murderous musketry : the hedge rows had lines of smoke and fire blazing through them. A long roll of thunder began, and was kept up, and warned us, who were still spectators, that the mortal strife had begun,

Feuntarabia lay beneath us, near the mouth of the river, and at about a mile's distance the steamers commenced throwing shot and shells into the town. The gun-boats came up the river, where it was about a mile broad, and continued firing, sometimes on the town, and sometimes on the Carlists on shore.

What the real object of this was, would be difficult to state. The Carlists had been successful, farther south, against the Christinos, and a descent was threatened by them into the province of Santander; perhaps this was to attract them from these quarters to a point that they would be naturally anxious to defend. Other reports were, that Cordova had communicated with Evans, and desired him to make that movement, in order to assist him in some plan of operations. Whether these reports are correct or not, it must be quite evident that the object was not to take the town of Feuntarabia, for that could have easily been taken. If nothing else could, the steamers would have battered it down: but that was evidently not desired, for we observed that the most of the shots were sent in directions where they did much less destruction than they would have done by falling in any other place. These were, as we supposed, intended only to let the inhabitants know what the ships could do, if they thought fit to employ them.

General Evans was very unwell, and appeared, from his sickly look, to be unable to endure the fatigue of going into action with an enemy: he was even then and for a month afterwards, considered dangerously ill.

The 6th and 10th regiments of the Legion, the Chapelgorris and the Oveida regiments of the Spaniards, were the first who descended from the heights along which we had marched, and began the engagement. A bridge about a mile from the town, and about two miles from where we, the other regiments of the Legion, were halted, became the principal subject of dispute, and consequently the centre of the action. General Shaw, who led on the regiments just mentioned, had got between the bridge and the town, and thus opposed the Carlists as they hastened from the interior of the country to aid in the defence of Feuntarabia.

As we, who were outlookers from the summit of the lofty mountain, beheld the scene below us, it was truly magnificent. In the bay, at a mile's distance from the town, were the Phœnix, Salamander, and four other ships of war, with about sixteen gun-boats, emitting their volumes of smoke, throwing shells into the fortifications, and shaking the air with their loud thunder. On the opposite side were our regiments; and from that quarter a long unintermitting rattle of the lighter thunder ascended to our ears. From a wall skirting a road on the Carlist side of the bridge, a heavy fire of musketry scattered the 6th regiment as that advanced on the position; and the

10th, following to go down on the town, were similarly received as they approached this point. Colonel Ross of the 6th, a gallant soldier, who formerly served in the 23d of the British service, fell dangerously wounded, and with him several of his officers. One of these, Captain Calder, whom many men loved and all admired, got a musket-shot in the shoulder, and soon after fevered and died. Colonel Beatoon of the 10th was also wounded. But these are the names of those whose wounds got the pleasing salve of promotion, a place in the Gazette, and approbation in General orders, applied to their wounds. There were others of lesser name, but not less brave, fell unknown and unhonored.

"We cannot pass to the town until this position on the other side of the bridge is taken, for we shall get between two fires, and perhaps be cut off in our retreat should we not succeed in entering," was the observation of the general of the brigade ; "therefore we must cross and get possession of that side to secure our flank." The hurrahs then rose amid the other din—bayonets were fixed, and with men dropping dead and wounded on the bridge ; about three hundred of the 6th and Chapelgorris, got along the narrow pathway to the opposite side. This was a brave, and so far as could be ascertained before attempting it, a judicious design on the part of the assailants ; but they grievously mistook the situation and the numbers of those on the other bank of the river. Three battalions, of from six to eight hundred men each, rose from their concealed positions, and received the handful of Scotch and Chapelgorris. The cheers that had hurrahed them onwards—which they had first raised themselves,—which other regiments now on their way down to support them joined in, and which we sounded in loud hurrahs from the top of the mountain on beholding the venturous band—these cheers changed to the sudden outbursts with us of "Oh! see yon! Oh God! see how they're driven back—they're prisoners--surrounded —why don't the third charge ?—see the red-coats of the 6th among Carlists—hurrah for the lancers—see how they gallop down to the bridge—ah! the Carlists are on it—they're in the water—the 6th leaping in—drowning—Carlists, Chapelgorris, and 6th, all mixed together over head—drowned—the Carlists have got to this side— they're shooting the Chapelgorris in the river—hurrah for the marines—the marines are down, and the lancers—ah! glorious—over the bridge—see the Carlists now leaping into the water—shot and drowned."

Such were the outbursts of interjecting sympathies with us, as we stood spectators of this wild conflict; a conflict furiously maddened by the ferocity of the principal combatants on each side; that is, the guerilla "red caps" of the Christinos, and the guerilla "white caps" of the Carlists, having met; but unusually disastrous in slaughter; from the narrow ledgeless bridge and the bank of the deep river having been the stage of action. Rather than be prisoners, the brave 6th, who had led the van in crossing, leaped into the water, some being at once drowned, others being shot as they swam to the opposite side.

We could see, even at the distance we were from them, that some of the tartan scarfs worn by the 6th, had become the trophy of the enemy. These were triumphantly waved in the air, held up on the muzzles of the Carlist muskets, while at another part those who had the red-coated prisoners in their power, and were now assailed by our lancers, 3d and 10th regiments, were seen stabbing and shooting their victims; Spaniards as well as English. There was a universal burst of impatient demand broke out through our brigade, to be led to the assistance of those now engaged, meeting their own death in avenging the death of the others. I can bear testimony from personal feelings, though not the most courageous and always brave, a man will at such times lose the inferior feelings that make him a coward, and be filled only by the swelling passions that shew themselves to the world as daring courage. It is painful to be a soldier, a witness of a fight, ready at any moment to be marched forward on danger, which as a soldier of the ranks, you seldom know the real character of: but be a witness, as each of us were then of the conflicting parties, their respective positions and strength, the mutual slaughter, with misfortune on your own side and unfair treatment on the other, and then the feelings that burst into a voice through our regiment of reserve, can be appreciated.

I had no fondness for bullets, and when I have heard them whiz about my ears and seen blood issuing from the cut of these unseen emissaries of death, I have thought myself a fool in not having been more prudently economical of my adventure. But at that time with such a scene before us, witnessed as it was by the people of the French frontier, crowding on every tree and house-top, to be witnesses of the fight—by the French army, who, drawn up to prevent a breach of neutrality, stood spectators of the engagement; with such a conflict before us, pending before such witnesses, is there any one will question the reality of our desire to fight, when I say, that individually (with perhaps a few exceptions) we burned to join our comrades, and collectively as regiments, and a brigade, demanded, by our cheers, to be led on.

" Rifles, 4th and 8th, 'tention—with cartridge,—prime and load" was ordered by the respective commanding officers; and then the intermediate words of command having been given, " forward" was ordered. We could see that General Chichester was in an impatient and dissatisfied mood at having been kept so long on the heights doing nothing while the others fought. But his impatience subsided into an apparent heedlessness of what was going on, when he, as he was moving his brigade forward, received orders to remain where he was.

We were thus, by that order left on the heights, mere witnesses of the whole day's proceedings.

The Lancers made an effective charge on the Carlists who had passed to our side of the river, and the 3rd and 10th regiments took quick, and for some time, successful advantage of the cavalry's assistance.

Alternate success was on each side until after mid-day, when the tide ebbed, and afforded the Carlists a fordable passage across, which they took advantage of at some points where none of our troops were in a situation to repel them. By this they, in some measure, outwitted the 3rd regiment; and succeeded by firing on the flank to force its retreat.

This, though seemingly an advantage to them, reverted on themselves with disaster. Two companies of the Royal Marines were standing in a position where they were not seen, and being ordered not to fire, though the enemy was within reach, they stood until the Carlists had come within pistol-shot. A volley in front of the unsuspecting and boldly advancing enemy was given; and ere they could recover from the confusion, it was repeated, and they fell back to their own positions by the river.

Shortly before this, the bridge also became the possession of the

Carlists; thus leaving them a free access to the town. But they did not establish themselves on and around it but at an expense of life on both sides, that caused General Evans to decline carrying on the fight, as he by his dispatches at the time and Parliamentary speeches since explained,—that he had no object to gain farther than to attack the Carlists, and attract them to that point, to give Saarsfield and Espartero an opportunity of executing some operations in the south.

The noblest daring which the Carlists ever displayed before us was at the time they took this bridge. They had a harmless cannon of eighteen or twenty-four pounds, in the direction of Irun, about eight hundred yards southward, but, from the unskillfulness of the gunners, it wrought no farther mischief than to create some slight alarm as its balls plunged into the river, or took an idle flight into the air. This added some noise and smoke to the battle, and nothing more. But, what they wanted in skilful science, in the management of artillery, they, in an eminent degree, possessed in bravery, and their active abilities in the practice of guerilla bush-fighting.

We saw them approach the bridge three successive times and thrice retreat, leaving their officers, who led them, lying on the road, by the bullets of the 9th and 10th regiments. A fourth time they were seen to face the same heavy fire, led by an officer on horseback. He waved his sword, cheering them on, but he also fell when near the centre of the bridge, and they were again driven back. They only succeeded by some of their regiments fording the tide, at a place where they were not opposed, and coming down on the flank of the 3d.

Had the object been to force the town of Feuntarabia, that could have been done, for if nothing else would have succeeded the gun-boats in the river, and the ships from the bay, could have battered down its fortifications. They appeared to have only fired to shew what could be done, as most of their shots took effect on places where the least possible injury could follow.

The garrison thinking they could do something even against the British Navy, kept firing idly at the Salamander with a gun from a round tower. For some time this attracted our notice but seemingly no notice from the steamers for they continued firing on another place until in answer to one of the balls that went skimming the water astern of the Salamander, and another which went through her rigging she bounded off two or three of her heaviest guns with balls, accompanying them with one of her heavy shells.—We saw the latter burst —and a cloud of smoke and dust rise—but when these cleared away there was no tower— she had levelled it, and probably buried those who had been firing, in its ruins.

General Evans had been sick for some days previous to the 11th, and during this day he was unable to occupy himself otherwise than on his camp bed. In the evening he was conveyed to one of the steamers and went round by sea to San Sebastian.

About sun-set all had become quiet, and the dull air hung heavily over the place of strife, until the thickening twilight absorbed the smoke in the general darkness.

We mounted a range of piquets along the side of the mountain— the whole of the regiments lying among the rough furze until morning. A heavy fog by that time, had wet all the furze through which we waded, and large portions of that having been burned a few days before—we came through it on our march home, and had our white trowsers—to the great grief of the clean soldiers, and gratification of the dirty ones, blackened by its soot—the light, and grenadier companies of the 8th covering the whole as skirmishers on the rear.

This harassing excursion and valueless engagement lost to us, about two hundred men, with double that number to the Carlists; they having had more killed at the bridge skirmishes—by the lancers —and by the vollies of the marines---than they had been able to kill of ours.

On our march back, the houses which had been the piquets of the Carlists were burned---the dead bodies that had lain a month unburied, as mentioned before, on the neutral ground, were put into scanty graves and the whole descended the steep mountain side, and were quartered in, and around the town of Passages.

We found that during the previous day the Carlists had made a successful attack on the Ametza hill---one of our formidable line of positions — had taken it from the 1st regiment, and now had it in their possession, which it continued to be for some months after.

General Shaw who had been principal in active command the day previous, was now the cause of much annoyance both to General

Evans and to the Legion. A letter appeared in the London Courier the week following, giving an account of the engagement --- with particulars that could not have been by any possibility furnished by any one but himself. It contained hints disrespectful to General Evans, and a great deal of matter trumpeting forth the high services of General Shaw. An explanation was required --- a quarrel ensued, and after another disclosure of those peculiarities of character which will come within the province of my record in the next chapter---he resigned,---came home and published " memoirs of his life," and put forth statements relative to General Evans and the Legion, that will be found discussed in this work, towards its close.

When we came into the town of Passages on the 12th of July, there was an allowance of spirits due to some of the regiments. This being served out---and many of the inhabitants giving the men liquor in consideration of their having come off a tedious mountain excursion---a considerable proportion of the men got into a state slightly inclining to intoxication. *Buttons* were passed off in large quantities on the inhabitants! that species of imposture being up to this time unknown in Passages. These were easily managed, for there is no nation where money is known, that has a confusion of coins like Spain. They are so varied in shape and value---and having often no stamp on them whatever, our " smashers," when they went to a strange place had little difficulty in passing the buttons of their great-coats ---with the eyes cut off---for pisettas, and half pisettas. Some who were more expert, or perhaps had known a little of the art at home, made moulds, and stamps, and carried on a lucrative manufacture. It was by the assistance of these devices, that some of the brandy which had made the quarters of the regiment rather tumultuous had been procured during that afternoon and evening.

On coming into quarters, I mounted guard with four men, on a stable containing the colonel's and some staff horses. This was always the best guard, as there was not much trouble, and generally a non-commissioned officer was preferred to this in proportion to his favour with the sergeant-major---or adjutant. Yet though the duty of keeping guard on the horses was easy, the charge, and the trust was important, for it was no difficult matter to get a horse sold in Spain, and horses at this time were much in request among the secret agents who traded for Don Carlos in the service of the Queen. I

had overtures made to me to sell the whole, and go that evening to
Carlos; but before giving the particulars of these overtures, I must
digress from the running narrative of events, and give a scene from
the interior of the church of Passages.

The regiment to which I owned alliance was peculiarly happy that
night, and had got the church for quarters. As usual, those that
were enjoying themselves forgot those who had no enjoyment, these
were the guards, who being on duty dared not stir from their respective charges. We had waited long for our rations being sent to
us; but these not coming, I at the urgent request of my comrades,
and at the instigation of sundry hungry suggestions of my own, ventured to pay a visit to the regiment to forage for our necessities. On
entering I was saluted with cries of " knock him down," " keep him
out," and to the first expression the action was suited to the word,
ere I could tell them that I was on the harmless errand of looking
for my bread and beef. They had supposed from my accoutrements
being on that I was sent with some authority to quell the general
riot; so on getting to my feet, I found for the consolation of a broken head, that I was not to consider myself injured as an individual
but merely as serjeant of the guard. It was not easy for me to distinguish the pain of a broken head in my official, from my individual
capacity; but I saw it was wise to say nothing.

The church, like our English Cathedrals had a space of its interior
open, without any seat furniture, and covered with tomb-stones, laid
flatly over the graves of the thousands of monks who had been deposited there for the last five hundred years, On these, parties
were dancing Scotch reels to the music of the regimental musicians;
others were fighting. With some the battle had ended: their seconds and their seconds' seconds having fought, and they were now
having a glass in a *manly way!*, shaking hands; while with others,
who had been discussing the engagements of the 5th and 28th of
May, 6th of June, and the one of yesterday, the moral was giving
way to the physical argument, the unmistakeable sounds of " a
ring—a ring " were heard from a score of those who supposed the
best argument to be the best man. A dozen of " Highland Flings "
and " Flowers of Edinburghs " were going on at once. Reels followed reels—songs musical and sweet, mingled with those uproar-
ious and wild. On the altar, stood my friend H———, commonly

called the *Champion,* awfully tragic in gesture, giving *" A Cheftion to the Highland bound."* In the pulpit was one who sung the well known Scotch song—*" A maid gaed to the mill ae nicht,"* and imitated the clapper of the mill with his hands on the board before him. Beneath, was another singing the *French* and in presbyterian mode reading the line; while in another pulpit—an orator stood with a few special auditors giving — " Romans — Friends — Countrymen," &c.—In the confessors' vestries were social parties sitting on the floor, with a canteen—full—half empty—or altogether empty as the case might be—joining hands and singing *Auld lang syne.* Some of these were discussing how the wind was to be raised again to refill with brandy or aguardiente (pronounced akadent) the canteens. One would say " your pads Jock vendy them—you have two pair," " no," would be the reply, " I'll no vendy my sapattas, or pads, or whatever ye ca' them,---(these were shoes) but I'll vendy my chimese," (pulling out the breast of his shirt) " but its mucho porco I doubt it 'll no vend," (he thought it was too dirty to sell,) another proposed his *her,* and whispered where *she* would be disposed of adding that he would go and lift another one as soon as it was dark ; --- that was a musket for which, from one to ten dollars might be got according to circumstances and another to supply its place stolen from the quarters of another regiment. A few were standing in a knot, arguing whether something they had got was silver, I asked what it was, at one who had inspected it and was turning away with an air that seemed to depreciate its merits --- he answered " it's a little J——s they 've got but he's no worth a d——n he's only lead !" being disappointed at finding that some relics and images which they had taken from a place of sacred deposit, were not so valuable as report gave out all these things to be. In the marble basins among the holy water were messes of salt beef steeping, and men washing the salt off it. Outside were numbers employed in cooking. Fires were burning between two stones over which strode the kettles with the foot, or head of a wooden apostle, sticking out in front of the blaze. Add to all that unhallowed revelry that thus desecrated a temple of God the noise made by the organ. Its notes from the high gallery mingled mournfully loud with the bedlam below. As a number crowded round it, and contended for the priviledge of making noise, a listener would have expected on hearing a few notes, that there was to be something musical --- but suddenly it gave a discordant howl as if rebelling against the profane hands that touched it, and ultimately amid the riot, it was broken and became silent.

A fight gave way to a dance --- a dance to a fight. --- The *Champion* had given " Warsaw's last," from which he got his name, and was now giving Grecian Statues --- which with his finely formed Herculean figure and a classic taste, he could represent in a superior manner --- only his shirt which served his naked figure for drapery, was rather dirty, but in the dim distance it harmonised with the dingy saints who surrounded him above the altar-piece. Having scanned the whole --- laughed at some --- been disgusted with others --- and admired the Champion's performances, I could stay no longer, but was under the necesity while he yet stood in character, to go up to him and put the unclassical question of what he had done --- with my mess of beef. He was representing Hercules, and being suddenly transformed from the Greek to himself, he took the lid off a camp kettle which he held in his hand for a Mount Atlas, and taking therefrom my ration of salt junk. I received it, and departed to my guard musing thoughtfully on what I had seen.

On returning to the guard I met Colonel Godfrey, whose natural ill-humour was soured in a double degree by the fruitless expedition of the previous day, and the tumultuous mirth which now abounded among the men. He returned the common military salute which I gave him by halting me, and letting one of his stormy passions like a bomb-shell, burst, oath-full, in my face. Though his oaths were the most originally poetical, even sublime, with only a slight inclination to the ridiculous, and therefore of a quality that excited terror in the timid, and amusement in the confident, they cannot be recorded : but I must say that I scarcely ever heard Godfrey swear without my feeling some of those indefinable enjoyments of pleasing terror, floating in the region of imagination, which some minds will recognise by recollecting certain passages of Milton or Montgomery. Often on the dull parade, when the monotonous sound of every day drill had palled the mind into a lazy obedience, I have been re-stimulated to energy, when the battalion was repeating for the fiftieth time, the " deploy into line," or the " change front to the rear by the wheel and countermarch of subdivisions round the centre," by hearing Godfrey thunder out " halt,"—stopping the whole battalion until he poured ire on the head of some poor wight; who had, thinking he was hidden in the centre, tried to ease the left arm by the support of the right; or, as was not unfrequently the case, had taken that opportunity to shift a voracious flea that fed luxuriously while he marched at attention. Sometimes wearied by three hours unremitted drill, these interludes that startled and refreshed like a thunder blast on a lazy summer's day, made some of us enjoy the vigour of the next hour. Once, I remember, he stood at about a hundred yards distance in front of the regiment, giving his word of command with that powerful voice and melodious cadence that peculiarly distinguished him; when suddenly, as the battalion was performing an intricate evolution which we had re-performed over and over until perfect in it even to sickness, the word "halt," like an unexpected bomb bursting over head, brought every right foot even with the left, and all remained steady. There was half a minute's unbroken stillness, during which, every officer and man (for officers were not exempt from his public rebuke), inly questioned himself whether he was to be the object of the storm that was just mustering to the bursting point. At last a low growl, then a distinct *damn*, then three or four made into one, forming an adjective that ear had never heard nor tongue before pronounced, formed his preface. He went on; "you long white-headed grenadier, the left but one of the third section; and you little beggar in the centre of the rear rank of the 5th company, must I halt a whole battalion for two who will not pay attention to my orders? Put that *flea* off your nose, you white-headed scoundrel; and *you*, you little beggar, put the thumb of your right hand on the seam of your trowsers, and not in front of it! Now mind me—the whole—quick-march." This was literal; though it must be supposed he could scarcely distinguish the small insect on a grenadier's nose, at the distance of a hundred yards; but sundry twitchings of the head, and the frequent unsuccessful attempts of the unhappy man to smuggle his hand to his face, gave proof to Godfrey that the only cause of uneasiness must have been the tormentor already named; who, having confidence in the strictness of military law, was tickling and taking its dinner off Jock Watt's proboscis.

At the period I referred to before making this digression, I must confess I stood before Godfrey with some sensations of awe; for, from the state of dirt and confusion in which every man was, consequent on the excursion of the previous days, and the too liberal supply of spirits that day, he had good cause to be displeased. Besides I had been absent from my guard which was not allowed, and his stallion had been kicking with one of the staff horses, and had received the worst of the engagement, which last occurrence was most unlucky—for the only *friendly* companion of our commanding officer was his grey horse; that he would see get his *rights*, while, as he has been heard to say—and uniformly shewed, he did not value generals—colonels— officers or men—Spanish or English, but with one equality of estimate. As occasions required, he damned them all, but he loved his horse, and as some of the staff were forced into the same stable with it, he would not have expressed any sorrow had *his* broken their legs. But the grey had got the worst of the kicking riot; the sentry was giving the victor a slight touch with his bayonet to urge a renewal of the conflict, two of the guard were looking on and laughing, the other was insinuating himself into the favours of a Spanish girl, who chattered from an upper window on the opposite side of the street, when the colonel came on them, and I had been against orders, absent. I was an unhappy man; only there was so much misbehaviour to punish that night, that he did not know well where to begin. Had he ordered our confinement, there were none to relieve us on duty, so he only swore and threatened; but little did he suspect how near he was putting me in a mood that made me listen more favourably than I would have done to certain proposals which were shortly after made to me.

For nearly two hours after he had gone away I kept walking to and fro on the street in front of the house on which we kept guard, partly from a curiosity to observe a Spaniard who appeared to be observing me,—partly to watch if Godfrey was coming back—to prevent the men stealing away—and partly to study and muse on all these things, and the busy incidents of that and the last two days. The Spanish officer, in a large military cloak muffled round his head, passed and repassed me frequently; part of the walk that I had been making, was below an archway and where the overhanging rocks made it then darker than it would have been at twelve o'clock, for it was not a very dark night. He contrived to pass me always near this archway, and sometimes I involuntarily made my elbow touch

the hilt of my bayonet, just by way of making myself doubly sure
that I had it. At last, thinking I might as well be within, I went
to the door of the house where the guard was and tried to open it,
but found a difficulty by the muskets being set against it inside.
For two or three minutes I kept fruitlessly poking my bayonet
through the open seams to push them away. I then turned round
to see if the mysterious Spaniard was still walking about, when, to
my horror, he stood so close to me that I almost touched him on
turning. The ideas of a knife running into me, and of running my
bayonet into him; and again, that he was perhaps a ghost scared
from a visit to his skull and marrow-bones in the church, ran all
through my brain in a second. "What do you want?" I inquired
in the best Spanish and the bravest tone I was master of, at the
same time taking a side step, and pointing my bayonet a little in his
direction. He took hold of my right arm, and I gave a sudden step
farther to my left. A more courageous hero would have perhaps put
the bayonet into him, but I preferred stepping back and again asking him what he wanted. Without speaking, he stretched out his
left arm, and, as I thought, held out a pocket pistol and was about
to fire at me. One will summon a great deal of energy to postpone
his last moments, and I seized hold of his hand to avert the ball that
I thought was about to go through me, but it did not hold a pistol.
It was a hand wanting three of the fingers, and the remaining one
was pointed out. On hearing him speak, I immediately recognised
a monk of the convent of Castri, a town distant sixty miles from
where we then were, and where we had once been quartered for a
night—when I made myself acquainted with this monk, who, as he
told me, had been a soldier in the time of the French invasions, and
had lost three of his fingers by a brother guerilla; in fact, he was soldier, guerilla, monk, or what ever suited him, as it afterwards proved,
though he appeared to me at that time to be a holy man. He asked
me to go and have some wine with him as we had been formerly acquainted. I hesitated before complying, but ultimately went with
him round the corner of one house, and up the back outside stair
of another.

It was then past midnight, and, though all Spaniards go to bed
early, the inhabitants of this house were moving about, and appeared
to be making ready a supper on what was an extensive scale compa-

red with the common Spanish frugality, and the number of persons
who were there to eat it. I saw the whole company ; there appeared
to be four military gentlemen, including the monk, and three ladies,
two of them young and one old. They were above the common rank,
and had something to do by sitting up so late, for they were well
dressed, and enjoying themselves doing nothing, while servants were
at work in the kitchen, which I saw as I passed — a thing not common with the Spanish ladies ; besides, the house had the appearance
of being of the genteel sort. Why I was introduced to the guests,
and why they paid me kind compliments, I could not conceive. The
monk had said that he only wished me to go up and have " un poco
vino," (a little wine,) but they insisted on my partaking of supper
with them. A thought crossed my mind, and no sooner did it enter,
than I got up and would not stay a moment longer. I suspected they
wanted to detain me till the horses were stolen, and I knew that the
other men, being in the stable, were not to be trusted, for they had
lain down nearly half intoxicated, and none of them, I knew, would
be ill to advise to leave the stable for the sake of getting more brandy.

Promising to return, I went down, and found every thing safe ; but
I roused some of the men up, and whispering to one whom I could
confide in, told him there was something to be done, and he promised
to watch until I would return to him. In going up again to the
house, I was taken into another apartment, and the monk accompanied me, while a jug of wine, bread, and a good proportion of a fine
smelling stew, were set before me. The monk tasted it, perhaps to
shew me there was no danger of being poisoned, gave his lips a
smack, said " bueno" (good), and beckoned to me to go on. I did
not require much pressing, for " Warsaw's Last Champion" had given me a very small mess of beef. I was anxious to know what the
monk was engaged in now with the army, but he did not give me
any direct answers, more than that he was an officer, which he said
he was obliged to become again from the necessities of the times.
He told me he had been at Bayonne, in France, since we had been
in Castri, and was expecting to go to Madrid on important business of a private nature as soon as he could get leave, and asked me
how it was that I was still only a non-commissioned officer, for I had
told him before that I expected to get some promotion above that.

On saying something about it, he pointed to the stripes on my arm, and said " *estos ne valer nada,*" (these are not worth anything), and then he held his tongue, looked stedfastly at me, shrugged up his shoulders, and said in a low interrogative tone, " Do you like to be a soldier—no more than common soldier in British Legion?" He paused for an answer, and as soon as I got my mouth emptied, I said, " No," and recommenced eating. He looked again at me, and asked if the other men on guard would like to have their supper. I told him that I was sure they would. He then said, " go for them," and again looked for a minute, and said he wished to say something to me, but still hesitated to begin. After a few minutes of silence, he asked how many horses were in the stable. I told him, three. Then he asked how many men were on guard. I told him, four besides myself. " Bueno" (good), he replied, and was again silent. After a pause, he asked if I had any particular comrades in the regiment. I answered, not any that were very particular.

I was then leaving him to go for one or two of the other men, and he called his servant by the name of Juan, who accompanied me, as if to prevent my falling down the stairs in the dark. I observed, however, that a few whispers had passed between them ; and Juan, when we came near the stable-door, asked me how many horses there were, and how many men on guard. I told him, quite unreservedly, although I was conceiving to myself what they would like us to do. Juan was a little dexterous fellow, about five feet and had a great deal to say on different matters. He pointed through an opening in the houses, to where the Carlist picquets were, and kept " carago" ing (swearing) at the Carlists, and at the end of every observation, he gave me a squeeze on the arm, and added, " me un diablo, tu no sabe?" that is, " I'm a devil, do you not know?" the last word was drawn into a long tone, during which he pinched my arm very hard I answered that I knew, on which he clapt his hand on my mouth, uttering in an under tone, "silencio." "Yes, I'll be silent," I replied; "but how could the horses be got across the water?" (it was two miles broad in the direction of the Carlists.) He put his hand again on my mouth, and said " silencio," and went on telling me what could be done. I found that I had taken up the hints of the monk in their right meaning, and that an opportunity now offered, if I chose, of getting a conveyance to Carlos ; but how far that was

No. 8.   H safe I did not know : besides, a thought of deserting had never before entered my mind. The other young man that was on sentry, and who was keeping himself awake till I returned, was one that I knew could form an opinion on the merits of the proposed adventure as well as any one could, so I whispered all my proceedings to him, and he at once said, like a sensible man, as he was, " waken up the chaps, and let us go and get some o' the stew." I reminded him there were two of them which we could not, by any possibility, trust with such a secret, for they would begin to speak of it to every one the next day. He had the same opinion of them, so he and another followed Juan by my desire, and I wakened the other two, charged them not to sleep, for I expected the Colonel, and that I had been called away with a " file of the guard," to do something.

When I got to the house, the two had a jugful of wine before them, a tumbler of brandy, and were driving away with little ceremony at the stew. The monk then called me aside, and asked where the others were ; I told him that I had left them below, that I did not want them to know what was going on, for I could not trust them. He stared, and asked what I could not trust them about. I told him there were a dozen that I could get in the course of a day or two, that would suit better than these down below. He said nothing ; I then went on, and said, that I did not think it possible to get out of town that night. He was silent for a few minutes longer walked twice round the room, and then took hold of my arm, gave me a look, and began thus, " diablo (devil) you think me want you desert for Carlistas—senor (sir), me an officer of our Queen, senor— me no Carlista," and he clapt his hand on his breast, then crossed himself before a crucifix which was hanging in the room, as I supposed, for the purpose of atoning for the sin of telling a lie, as quickly as possible. Then he called for Juan, whispered a while with him, inquiring, and being told, no doubt, what passed between us when we were out. At the conclusion, he said audibly, " bueno." Juan departed, giving me a significant smile as he passed. The monk then said, that we could be kept out of sight for some days, if we chose ; that the horses could be conveyed away that night ; but as they had to be taken across the water, it would be safer for us to remain concealed till a more fitting opportunity, as there was not a possibility of being discovered, there being a way of getting from the house to the lake that nobody knew of but those that the house belonged to, and that it had been used for far more dangerous purposes at other times, and never was found out. Curiosity had led me to know this much from him, and now that I had become fully possessed of his confidence, I did not know how with safety to myself to get out of it. Having once made the disclosure of his being a Carlist agent, he followed it up with very close and convincing arguments. To these I seemed to pay the greatest attention, but I was at the same time busied in contriving how I was to manage to get myself and comrades out of the dilemma we were in. My difficulty was heightened a good deal, by hearing one of them bawl out, " where's Somerville ? d——n me, I'll gang to Carlos as fast's he likes ; if I dinna, d——n my soul; what d'ye say, Ned ? Ned was the sagacious one, and though I did not hear him speak, he had interfered to keep the other quiet. I requested of the monk to be allowed to confer with them, which he assented to, and after making them acquainted with what had passed, I asked what we were to do to get out of the scrape. " Sell *auld daddy's* (Godfrey's) horse," said the noisy one, " and let us go ; there's no pay here, and as for the sides, we may as well be wi' Carlos as the Queen : I wou'dna gie't twa thochts." Ned considered that it was very dangerous ; that if he was going to desert, he would rather go across the lines sometime when he was on sentry, and I concluded, that it was best to think on the safest plan and act upon it. I suggested to the monk what could be done if an extensive plan was put in operation for coming over with a large number at once, and especially if the Carlists would promise to send the men home to England. I said, that I believed the greater part would desert, in fact, almost march over in a body. He was pleased with the idea, but the chance of getting the horses was what made him anxious, and especially as he was to leave Passages immedidiately. I was under the necessity of promising to do all that I could towards getting a band to accompany me across at another time, and by this means we got away from them. I suspected the monk was ready for the march, as we heard a few days after that a number of Spanish soldiers had deserted that night, and had taken arms, ammunition, and other things with them. I ventured to call at the house about two months after that, but I saw no one of the party save the old lady, and she either did not or would not know me. I pressed on her to recollect the time, and described the persons of the monk and Juan : she still said she never had seen me before. She thought it proper to conceal her knowledge of that night, as well as I and the other two men did, for it was not for a long while after that period that we ventured to speak about it in the regiment.

On the morning of the 13th, there was what is vulgarly called " *the devil to pay,*" and a good many devils got paid for their last night's riot in the church and about the town. We got all ferried across the narrow inlet, and proceeded towards San Sebastian.

The 6th regiment went and took up quarters on the western extremity of the lines, at the convent Antigua, and kept the same place during the summer and ensuing winter. Of that convent, the regiment, and individuals in it, I will require to allude to frequently, as the 6th acted a prominent part there during the winter. The 7th regiment were quartered next them, in a city of small huts, which they built for themselves, on the ground near the wind-mill, which place they took so gallantly on the 5th of May. Their town was called " *wee Ireland,*" and many a scene of a stirring description took place there. Excepting the 6th and 7th, the other regiments changed quarters frequently.

At the period of our returning from Feuntarabia, there was nearly seven months' pay due. I should rather say we had been seven months without a settlement, for many of the men, instead of having any pay due, were in debt ; to such an amount had they been served with clothing and necessaries, For three months in Vittoria, and (except when I was left in Santander sick), up to this time I am writing of, I had kept the company's accounts, and had therefore the means of knowing some of the secrets of the ledger. The accounts were balanced every month, and the debt or credit of each man carried forward. Not having seen their accounts for six months, it was a difficult matter to give them a satisfactory explanation. All the companies of the 8th regiment were the same as the one I had to do with, and all the regiments of the Legion were the same as the 8th. A dollar (four shillings and fourpence), had been put to each man's account as a gratuity for the action of the 6th of June ; and this, especially to those who were in debt, caused a great deal of discontent. It had been paid in cash to the paymasters of regiments, and was given to the men in figures on the credit side of their accounts, and was one of the causes of the mutinous rupture which took place in the Legion, which I am just coming to.

Another cause of discontent was the men seeing whole pag₅s filled with *dittos* in their accounts, articles having been given to them without restriction in Vittoria, which they sold as fast as they go*t*, and in consequence now found themselves in debt; but as these were few, compared with those who had considerable sums to draw, the main cause of the discontent was their getting no money at all, and that was the greater grievance, now that the *beans* were nearly all done. The orchards were all loaded with apples, and all the country was an orchard, mingled only with gardens and small fields. Indeed, the orchards and the corn-fields were the same, for the trees were planted in rows about sixty feet asunder, and the wheat or beans were growing all round them. There being therefore an abundance of apples, messes of them in all shapes were tried by those that hunger and ingenuity prompted to make experiments. They were roasted, boiled, stewed, salted, peppered, buttered, sugared, and tried without any thing at all, just as the whim or ability of the parties admitted; but none of these messes would do. The apples were green, and though they were a lovely sight hanging in thousands on a million of bending trees, yet they were not a substitute for the beans.

CHAPTER VI.

Mutiny in the 8th Scotch—Paraded before General Chichester—The result—General Shaw makes a speech to them—Mutiny in the Lancers—Sixty of them Prisoners, guarded by the 10th Irish—The 8th arm themselves, and rescue the Lancers—8th and 9th sent to Santander—Twenty-five of the Scotch sent prisoners on board the Castor Frigate—Mutiny still continues—Payment of the Arrears—Riot and Intoxication—Flogging—Half of the regiment lay down their arms, and refuse to serve at Santander—The 6th do the same at San Sebastian, and are imprisoned in the Castle, &c. &c.

Our duty about this time was as easy as ever we had it in the country; but as there was no money, and the promises of payment having been over and over again broken, it was the daily conversation among parties washing their trowsers at the rivulets, going away seeking *forage*, or lying down in the green shade of the trees to hide themselves from the sun.

On the morning of the 16th, the 8th were paraded, and had "fallen in" in line along the road leading from San Sebastian to Passages, a short distance from which were our quarters. It was reported that we were to march to the height of Alza, about two miles distant, to relieve the 1st regiment. We had been on parade about half an hour, waiting for the Colonel coming, and I observed a considerable buzz of whispering going on, notwithstanding the order of Captains of companies now and then to their men to be silent. A corporal Dingwall remarked to me, "this'll be a serious affair—the boys seem to be determined." I asked him what it was, for I had never to that moment heard of any thing that they were going to do. In fact, as I learnt afterwards, they studiously kept it a secret from me, and I believe for the following reasons. First, That I would, if I took any share in a mutiny, be marked as a ringleader. Secondly, That I had said over and over again, at former times, when *strikes* were spoken about, that I would do all I could to prevent them, rather than join in them. And, lastly, I was supposed to be in favour with the Colonel, and therefore not fit to be trusted with the plans that were laid. However, to do those justice who were the promoters of the strike that was about to take place, I must say, that so universal was the feeling of disaffection, and so little argument did it require, that at nine o'clock the night before, when the report came out that we were to march, the proposal had been only then first made, about refusing to obey orders.

At nine o'clock, the Colonel came riding up in front of the line. When near the centre he paused a minute, took a pinch of snuff (which was his custom), and, in his usual loud and commanding tone, gave the words, "Parade, 'tention." The whole line, as if one man, obeyed the order. "See that the line is properly dressed, Major Hogg," he said.

Hogg obeyed by calling, "Eyes right—dress up the centre of the 5th company—back the left of the grenadiers—No. 4 up a little— back the first three files on the right of the light company—steady." The Major had gone through these orders, or something similar, and Godfrey took another snuff, left the half of it lying on his mustachios, and gave "Shoulder arms." The right file of the grenadiers were the only two men who shouldered. Godfrey stared,

and stood about half a minute silent; then he said, " Is my word of
command not heard ? Lieut. Sheilds, did you hear my word of
command, on the right there ? " " Yes, Sir," Sheilds answered.
" Very well," said Godfrey. " Battalion, shoulder arms." All
remained the same as before. He called for the Majors, and asked,
" Do you, officers, know what this means ? " " No, Sir, I don't."
they both replied. " Very well—very-well : I'll see what it means
before I'm done with you : I dare say you think you'll have it
all your own way, do you ? We'll see. Battalion, shoulder arms."
Not a man moved. He rode up to the right of the regiment. " Mr
Sheilds," said he, "do you know why the grenadiers don't shoulder?"
"No Sir," was the reply. "Shew me your right section, Mr Sheilds."
That was done. Godfrey at this put on an awful look of sternness,
and gave the order, " Right section of the grenadiers by themselves
—the remainder of the company stand fast—right section, shoulder
arms." They obeyed. He went on.—" Second section, shoulder
arms; " they threw their muskets to " the shoulder ; " and the
third and fourth sections did the same on being ordered singly by
themselves. He then went to No. 1 company, and said, " Must I
begin with you little beggars in the same way ? The whole company
at once—now mind (he spoke in a hurried tone), I'll run my sword
through you if one of you hesitates a moment ! No. 1, shoulder
arms." They shouldered, and he spurred his horse to the front of
No. 2, and without any observation, in a towering passion, gave
" No. 2, shoulder arms ; " and then off to No. 3 the same way. At
this time the light company on the left, and the one next it, No. 6,
gave a cheer, and repeating the hurrah, the grenadiers caught it
also, and " ordered arms," that is, took the musket from their
shoulders, setting them by their side in the position they were before
shouldering. No. 1, and the other companies, in like manner, followed. Godfrey stood confounded—the first time ever I saw him
look at a loss to know what to do. He stood for a minute silent,
and then began thus, " I see there is something amongst you that I
know nothing about. This must have been going on to an extent
for some time. I suspect you officers have heard of it before, and,
if it is so, you have treated me ill in not mentioning it, for if you
had, this might have been prevented. Now, will any one just be
kind enough to tell me what your grievance is ? " As none were

willing to speak, from the fear they had of being considered ringleaders, all were silent.   He then said, " Will any of you non-commissioned officers tell me? " Some of them answered that it was the
want of pay.   Godfrey replied that he knew that to be a grievance,
but that he wanted his pay also, and that he had laid out three hundred pounds of his own money on the regiment, and went on at
length in arguing the absurdity of their behaviour in refusing to
obey his orders on parade.   He then inquired if there was any other
cause of discontent, because, if the pay was the only thing, he would
immediately go to General Evans, and represent the case, and see
what could be done.   John Brownlee, one of the grenadier company,
said that he could only speak for himself, but that he understood
there was an intention of making them serve for more than one year,
&c., and went on with that unfortunate question which afterwards
caused such disturbance.   The most of the men considered that the
time to speak of that was not yet come, which caused poor John to
stand all the brunt of it himself.   Godfrey said that Brownlee should
not only not serve more than one year, but that he would not be
allowed to serve one day longer; that he would be sent home as
soon as a vessel was going to England, and that he would go with a
bad character.   John replied, that when on his passage out to Spain
he threw a written character overboard, not supposing that a good
character would be of any use to him in the Legion, and that if he
went home with any character at all, it must be a bad one, for nobody would believe any thing else.   John was stripped of his accoutrements and his stripes taken off (he was a corporal), and sent into
San Sebastian a prisoner, where he remained for some time, but was
afterwards liberated.

Godfrey finding the regiment in such a state, went away and
ordered the Captain of companies to march home their men.   Immediately a regimental *union* was formed, and a regular system of
delegates from the different companies established.   They met, and
made arrangements for carrying out the *strike*.   At these confer-
ences many grievances were brought forward; but it was agreed to
waive all others and stick to that of obtaining their pay.   A depu-
tation to go to the 6th regiment at Antigua convent, and Lugariz
battery, was appointed, and request the co-operation of their brethren of the 6th.   Amongst other matters it was agreed to let non-

commissioned officers act as they chose, but all others were to be bound to act in *union*, that they would turn out in the mornings in the usual way, before day-light, as that was for their protection before an enemy, and that they would mount the " casa guard," that was a guard on the quarters of different companies, but that they would do no other duty. I may perhaps be allowed to mention, that on being requested to form one of a *committee*, I considered it not only necessary to decline, but to accompany my refusal with a *protest*, and " *reasons for protest*," which reasons were founded on the matters mentioned before at the beginning of the mutiny.

About three o'clock in the afternoon it was announced that General Chichester was on the sands, and wanted to see the regiment, but that they were not to be accoutred. They went, and the General began asking what was the reason of their disobedience. No one spoke. He then said, that he pledged his honour that those who did speak to him, would not suffer in consequence ; he only wanted to have an explanation from them. On his asking again what they wanted, a young man in the light company, named Conolly, an Irishman, stepped out and gave the General a salute, and began.

" General—no more I've no larnin', I'll tell ye's. We've been soldiers now about a year. You know all what we did in frost and snow—how we marched about with you, starving in hunger, General. Then you know how we fought on the 5th of May, and the 28th and 6th of June, and no more we did'nt fight at Feuntarabia, we were there to fight. You've praised us—General Evans has praised us—every one has praised us. Now, General, we are not able to live any longer on flattery—the *banes* are all done, General, and we must have something more in their place." Some others followed nearly in the same strain.

" Will you do your duty if you get your money ?" the General asked ; " yes," the whole called out. " Then it shall be got for you this night, I shall raise it in San Sebastian some way for you." A cheer followed this, and the whole broke off.

About six o'clock, a parade, in " heavy marching order," was ordered, and the regiment " fell in," where they were in the morning. Captain Kymer, the paymaster of the regiment, was on the right with a mule, and a heavy bag of dollars on it. The regiment

was called to "attention," "shoulder arms," and "right face,"
which they obeyed, but on getting quick march," all stood fast but
the drummers, sergeant-major, sergeant, and the first file. Godfrey came up and marched the grenadiers by themselves ; then the
first company and so on. Those in the rear gave a cheer, and the
front halted. Nothing could be done, so we were again dismissed.
The money was there, or at least a part of it, but the men were determined not to march in any direction without getting it all, except into San Sebastian ; so when we had any parades, Godfrey
was under the necessity of taking the regiment to the glacis (or
green) before the town. Chichester had called the 8th cowards,
when he found that they still stood out, and the men complained of
that to Godfrey. He, willing to do any thing for a propitiation,
quarrelled with the General about that, and we were then, to please
us, as they thought, put into General Shaw's brigade.

The first parade we had to meet that officer, was on the glacis.
He came, mounted in full uniform. The regiment formed square,
and he, in the centre of it, began thus : " Scotchmen," at this a
faint murmur of a cheer was heard among the non-commissioned in
the centre of the square, who had been instructed to get it up, but
it was put down by a hissing, "whisht," and Shaw proceeded. I
cannot pretend to give his exact words, but the purport was, first,
an address to those who had been in Portugal with him ; and that
day happening to be the anniversary of a skirmish, he went on describing this *glorious* anniversary, and appealed to them about what
he had done in Portugal!" One man called out, "what did you do
wi' the *funny box* ?"* " I pledge my honour, men," "Is it your
honour, you speak about ?" he was again interrupted by some fellows, who were called to silence by Godfrey. "There are good
men amongst you, but you have got too many tailors ; d——
my blood, I could give my honour on it, the half of you are tailors,
for tailors are all lawyers." At this a laugh burst out, in spite of

---

* This was a box which he caused to be made for depositing fines in which he
levied from the men while in Portugal. He was then Colonel of a regiment,
and kept a key—his Adjutant kept a second key, and his sergeant-major a third.
The soldiers named it the *funny box*, and well they might ; what became of its
contents was best known to the three key keepers !—the men pretend entire ignorance. On saluting him with a recollection of it at San Sebastian, he took no
notice of it but went on.

sundry scowls from Godfrey, and I did not hear a few of the sentences that followed, but he concluded with, " your lawyers! I'll hunt them to h——."

Godfrey, I observed, burned with an affronted face, for Shaw had given out, in San Sebastian, how he would manage the Scotch, and a number of the staff officers had come out to witness the result. The men hissed, and Godfrey, in the greatest hurry, gave the word of command, " re-form column at quarter distance,' then " open column from the front," and wheeling into line, formed four deep, and marched to the convent San Bartolome. We were quartered there for a short while, and one *real* a day (about twopence halfpenny) was paid each man. Some of the companies occupied a pile of buildings that formed three sides of a square, at a short distance from the convent. Here twenty-five of the lancers out of sixty, who were prisoners, were brought in to be tried by a court-martial, under the following circumstances :

The question of, whether we were engaged for one year or two, was beginning to be spoken about, and the lancers, whose period of one year was now expired, had been discussing the matter among themselves. Colonel Kinloch, their commanding officer, issued an order for all those who were not wishing to serve for more than one year, to give in their names. Sixty of them did so : their horses, arms, and accoutrements, were then taken from them; they were marched into San Sebastian, and quartered in the town, allowed to go about at liberty, until all at once four companies of the 10th regiment were brought in, and marched them out to our quarters, to be tried by a court-martial.

The reason why there were only sixty gave in their names was, that they were the only ones who had not been engaged specially for two years. They had been hurried in among the others on leaving England, and were in the same situation as the Scotch regiments were, as to the period of service.

The 10th brought them out of San Sebastian; twenty-five of them were charged with mutiny, and all the preliminaries of a court-martial had been gone over, and the first prisoner's trial was going on. Some of our men had been in the town, and were told that the lancers *depended on the 8th for getting justice,* especially as the 8th were known to be about to claim their discharge on the same grounds.

From our quarters we were looking down above them, and all at once
I heard the whisper go round, " on your accoutrements, men." It
was repeated from room to room, from company to company.
Some were lying asleep, and some were sitting at their dinners, and
some were cooking; but all in a few minutes were accoutred. At
the stair some one called out, " fix bayonets," and immediately
the clanging of bayonets was heard, and through the long passages
and lobbies where they were crowded, with the butt-end of their muskets on the ground, a forest of bayonets were seen sticking up among
the heads. Something more was seen, that spoke a direful purpose.
They were loosening the " ten round packages" of ammunition, and
here and there you could hear the ring of a ramrod give a stifled
sound, which told that a charge had been put into the musket. A
cry was heard of " the 10th are loaded!" and this was a signal for
every one to load. The alarm was taken by some of the officers ;
they rushed in at the door and stood at the foot of the stair, bran-
dishing their swords. " Villains — cowards — traitors — rascals —
Scotchmen — brave fellows — disgrace — shame," were uttered by
them, and mingled with the more loud and deafening hurrahs in the
stair. All round through the large building the cheers were re-echo-
ed by those behind, who did not see what was going on in front.
" Down on them — charge them out o' that — fire !" were heard, accompanied with all manner of menaces and imprecations ; but the
last word — fire !" was an awful one. Some of the officers below
drew out their pistols and presented them, and at the same moment,
those in front, making their way down the stair, step by step, as the
swordsmen retreated, cocked their firelocks. Twenty more had
pointed their muzzles over the balustrade of the stair, and had their
fingers at the triggers. It wanted only one more reckless than the
others to fire, and a shower of bullets would have poured down on
those who daringly withstood the infuriated numbers coming against
them. Piece by piece, those in front made their way down ; even
the cries of, " fire on those in front if they don't go on," were heard
from behind ; and at last, by the force of numbers, they cleared their
way, and rushed out into the yard, overset the tables where the court
was assembled, and mingling, one company with another, filled the
yard.

I had been in a corner at a turn of the stair, crushed against the wall as they passed me, and I now took my place at a small window that overlooked them. The most of the members of the court had disappeared; I only saw one, and he, when the mob rushed out and tumbled over the tables, chairs, and papers, stepped back a pace, pulled out his cigars, picked the best one — took a look of what was going on, lighted a lucifer, touched the cigar—folded his arms across his breast, and puffed out his smoke. Colonel Kinloch, demanded the officer in command of the 10th, who was outside the square, to march in his men on the 8th, and disarm them. The cry was raised that the 10th was coming round, and a rush was made to the place of entrance to meet them. That regiment, however, refused to interfere, the officer in command saying, that he must have higher orders before he could act; and the men, when they heard that the 8th had turned out, shook the priming out of their pans, and unfixed their bayonets.

Godfrey had been sent for, and, in the meantime Major Hogg, and some other officers of the 8th, had come and got the men to fall in by their companies, and marched them outside. On Godfrey arriving, he neither bullied nor flattered, nor entreated, but just said, " you've succeeded in affronting me at last: come away from this place, and let us go over the river out of sight," and some other remarks to the same effect. He promised forgiveness to the whole, if they would only now behave themselves, and each man was paid half a pisetta (or five pence farthing) a day, as long as we continued there, but that was not long, for we were sent to Santander to prevent farther mischief, and the lancers were kept prisoners, but not otherwise punished.

At this time every thing was going wrong with the Legion. The General was sick. The 1st of August was coming on, when the 6th were to lay down their arms, their year being out; and the 8th in addition to having been mutinous, were to be so again on the 19th of August, when a large proportion of them had their year made out, and had completed the term of service agreed on with General Shaw, and that officer was urging General Evans to use " harsh measures," as he expresses it in his letters, but Evans would not take his advice, and was throwing blame on Shaw for not having engaged the Scotch regiments in a way that would bring them under law.

When one of the Royal birth-days had been held, on which all

the troops got double rations, and on which a great deal of powder
was wasted by firing salutes from the battlements of San Sebastian,
we were suddenly counter-marched coming from parade, and an attempt was made to get the regiment on board a steamer.   We
went on well enough a short distance, till on going towards the
harbour, a cheer was got up, and all halted with the exception of
those who did not join in the mutiny before.   General Shaw came
with other officers, and began to flatter about " Scotchmen--brave
fellows," and so on.   " To h——— wi' Shaw ; ony body but Shaw :
where's our Portugal siller ? where's our land we were to get ?" was
heard assailing him from different quarters.   He went on swearing
by " my honour," and " d——— my blood," the common oaths
that were always in his mouth, and made the most reckless promises about what he would do for the Scotch : a volley of hisses
scouted him off ; and after Godfrey and the paymaster were seen
with a heavy chest going on board, the regiment went cheerfully.

We arrived at Santander the next day, and on preparing to dis-
embark, M'Knight went round the vessel getting five men from each
company for a guard which he was going to mount, as he said.
Some of the officers knew what he wanted, and picked out the sort
of men required, and others did not know, but just took those standing first on their rolls for duty.   These, amounting to twenty-five,
were kept on board, and were very proud to think they were getting some fine guard, as they were rowed away in a boat alongside
the Castor fiigate ; but to their astonishment, on going on board,
they found themselves prisoners, for having been ringleaders in the
mutiny.   To be a prisoner on board " a man-of war," has something
dreadful in it ; and, perhaps those who read this are pitying the poor
fellows who were imprisoned with a marine sentry over them on
board the Castor : and a very fine story of the cruelty appeared
shortly after in the English newspapers.   I shall let their sufferings
be known.   They got clean shirts, and soap to wash themselves,
in the first place—a regular ship allowance of biscuit, tea, beef, pud-
ding, and all the other things that the marines have ; besides the
sailors, pitying the *poor fellows*, gave them tobacco, and an extra
share of every thing.   They had hammocks and blankets, a luxury
that Bauldie Thom declared he had never had between that and the
time of leaving Paisley.   When they had been there about three

weeks, Godfrey went on board, and said he would pardon them, if they would promise good behaviour ; if they would not they were to be sent to a Spanish prison. This last threat induced them to promise good behaviour, else they would have been content to be prisoners long enough, for all the Legion would have liked a turn of the Castor.

Different far, was the regiment on shore during these three weeks. We had landed on a Sunday, and the gay holyday people of Santander flocked around us. Godfrey begged of the men, if they were going "to begin again with their ——— nonsense, to go out of the town first," and not to affront him there.

Santander has a row of fine houses fronting the bay, which is only connected with the sea by a narrow inlet. This street is half a mile long, and looks fully equal to the best streets of our new towns in Britain, only the buildings are something in the London style, being of brick, and deceiving the eye with imitations of stone, in plaster work. Santander is the only place I saw in Spain that has an old and a new town—that infallible proof of an increase of trade and population ; and notwithstanding all the disadvantages of war, it still maintains a good commerce. It has several churches and convents ; one of the former is very splendid, and in one of the latter the Court of Inquisition was held when that bore sway in Spain. For a number of years the practices of the Inquisition have been put down by the growing dislike of the public ; but it was only three years ago it was entirely destroyed, which was done by the people on some exciting occasion, bringing out all the ancient furniture of torture and execution, and burning it in the market-place.

Having got two leagues out of the town on the Vittoria road, and several attempts at a halt having been made, against the will of Major Hogg, he being in command while Godfrey remained in the town arranging matters with the paymaster—when several attempts to halt had been made, the whole at last made a stop in a wood, and refused to go a step farther without their pay. Hogg could not even persuade them to go half a mile farther to the intended quarters, until Godfrey and the paymaster would come up with the money ; when that arrived, they moved onwards to a straggling village, and were quartered in the different houses, about twenty men to a house. For a short while the people attempted to keep the men from pulling the apples and pears, which hung in great abundance; but presently, chuckling of hens and squeeling of pigs attracted their attention, and they let the apples go, to protect the pigs and poultry. Godfrey called a parade, and addressed the regiment thus : — "Men, I am suffering you to get your own way, because, all you want is your money, and that I have now ready for you; but I tell you, the money will not be paid if you destroy these people's property. Do you think I'm afraid of you, because you have got your own will for a short time?—No! you will find I am not—I swear by the (here followed two or three sentences made entirely of new oaths)——, every farthing due to you will be paid before this time to-morrow; but with the same oath I swear, that not a fraction will you get if I see another *single sign* of insubordination. You were called cowards by the Brigadier-General when you disobeyed my orders first—you complained to me, and I, knowing you were *not* cowards, demanded from the General why he dared to cast such reproach on the character of my regiment. He repeated it; I challenged him—dared him—and would not rest till he retracted the foul imputation; but now, hear me, you *shall* submit. I've wrested the money from those that intended it for other purposes, to pay you, you will have it; but remember—" A cheer was beginning to get up. Godfrey quickly raised his hand, checked it, and said, "Do not make these sounds, they are unmilitary—unmanly, and should never be heard on a parade; obedient silence is what I want. There is only one hurrah for a soldier, and that is when he charges the enemy with his bayonet. You have given that cheer—I joined in it; and I tell you, that twenty-five years ago, when I fought in these provinces with those whose fame is immortal, I never saw better determination to fight than I have seen in you; but you have disgraced it—yes, men, your conduct since is a disgrace; our enemies in England will turn it against us for disgrace—they will forget that we have fought well, and say, that the Legion are a mutinous rabble; let us prove them liars." He paused a few minutes, and then resumed, in a mild tone, "you non-commissioned officers and men, who have large balances due to you, three days after this when your money is all done—when you have been robbed and, are in the *horrors*, without any money, you will say, "I wish I had sent five pounds of it home to my mother or my sister." I know you will; I would rather send it to a sweetheart than spend it here. I'll undertake to remit the money to London, and get you drafts on your agents, payable there, which you can inclose in letters to your friends. Now be advised by me, men—but if you will drink, which I know some of you will, take wine, and eat well; be kind to the people, and pay them for every thing. You gentlemen, who command companies, will go immediately to Captain Kymer, take your accounts and your pay-sergeants with you, and get your money." After a good deal of trouble in making out lists of debts and credits of men present and men absent, and calculating English into Spanish money, Captain Shields and I, as his clerk, got the money (about one hundred pounds in all varieties of *Spanish coin) for our company, and others did the same. Early in the morning we began thus,—the Captain with the money before him, and the clerk telling him how many dollars, half dollars, quarter-dollars, pisettas, half-pisettas, reals, and other varieties of coin, the man had to get as he came in.

One would say, who had a good sum to receive, "never mind bein' particular, hand here the *dinero* (money); faith Saturday nicht's come at last!" "Aye, Bob," another would reply, "this is the *big pay*." Some of another sort would come in; Jock Watt was one of them, I remember. "You've *ninepence* to get, Jock," I informed him. He answered, "weel, I dinna ken hoo that is, there's some 'o them we 'rhee pound, an' me only ninepence." The reply was, "you have had seventeen pair of shoes, twenty shirts, four pairs of trowsers, besides many other things." "What did you do with all these?" the Captain enquired. Jock did not wish to be examined on that point, but lifted his ninepence, and said, "it's a' yin, there'll be plenty o' them drunk in a wee," thus insinuating where he would get money. Some were wise. "Warsaw's Champion" gave the Captain back two pounds, and many a time he and his friend Sandy could buy the produce of the dairy, when others looked hungry on. But to pass from particulars, the riot began; I got through with my task after mid-day. Those who had got pounds were lying drunk and pennyless. Some who had got none had fifty dollars. For three or four miles around, the roads to the wine shops were crowded. Through the fields and on the roads they were lying dead drunk. A party would be seen rifling

No. 9.   I

them : then another would come who had just awoke, and finding himself stripped naked, he took off their clothes, or as many of them as he wanted. Then one, two or three with money, would be met by a stronger band—they had immediately to "deliver up," and they in turn served others the same way.

At all the wine-houses, but especially at one on the road-side, three or four Spaniards filled the wine out in large jugs. It cost about fivepence a quart, and that quantity intoxicated any one. Some bought small barrels, filled them, and went out to a field and drank, and gave to any one who would, or could drink; others broke the jars and paid for them, and insisted on the owners taking more money than they asked. Hosts of beggars, young and old, male and female, came flocking from all quarters ; coppers were thrown about in profusion ; boys got half-dollars by diving over-head in tub-fulls of wine. Some of the men bought whole pigs, and roasted them in a piece on bonfires : and people with articles of sale gathered from all parts of the country. Godfrey rode about, pressing all the bullock cars into the service of carrying the drunk ones home to quarters. A dozen of these cars creaked away with their loads at once—naked and half naked, all one colour of mud, and dyed with red wine ; and as these went in, others awaking up in stupor, were wending their way back to the wine-house.

Such was the state of the regiment for six days. On the fourth from the commencement, Godfrey issued an order that his indulgence had ceased; that any one who was not on parade next day would be considered absent without leave, and would be punished accordingly. Many of those who had been strolling about all the time were afraid to come in, and it was not till the sixth day, that some of these made their appearance, and then they were brought under a guard of Spaniards. A court-martial assembled immediately, and tried them on the heinous charge of, "losing, or making away with their arms, accoutrements, and regimental clothing, and for being absent without leave." They were brought on parade, and the trial and sentence read to them. Two hundred lashes each was their doom. The one whose name was first, received it, and the others were pardoned ; and as there were still some absent, Godfrey sent orders about by non-commissioned officers, that if they would come back during that and the next day, he would pardon them.

They all took advantage of the amnesty, and returned. New white trousers, boots, caps, and other necessaries, were immediately brought from Santander, and they all got once more rigged out, and returned peaceably to regular duty. I heard but one opinion, and that was universally expressed, that they would rather serve without pay, than have another repetition of such riot.

From where we then were, we marched to the convent of Corban, and took up quarters for a few weeks. While quartered there, we marched into Santander one day, to be present at the proclamation of the Constitution. A grand display of processions, ringing of bells, mingled with the other demonstrations of rejoicing, common in our own country, followed; and we, after standing six hours under arms, and marching through the town, returned to the convent, and received each, one *real* (2½d.) as a present from the inhabitants of Santander.

While all this had been going on with us, those at San Sebastian were not very tranquil. The 10th regiment had a mutiny, and for nearly a whole week refused to do any duty; and the 6th having completed their one year's service, claimed to be discharged and sent home. General Shaw finding himself in an awkward position, by having brought the Scotch into the country without any form of enlistment, resigned, but not before he had done all he could to bolster himself up by advising General Evans to take " prompt and. hard measures" to compel them to serve. In one of his letters the following passage occurs, (it is dated July the 21st;)—"You will hear of a letter the General had from Madrid, saying the contract is for two years, and not for one. I have been advising prompt and hard measures : but although there is mercy in this, the General will not listen to it. I am made president of a court of inquiry, where I shall have a difficult part to act : but I do not care, I shall do my duty fearlessly." This court of inquiry was inquiring whether or not the men had been enlisted for one or two years. He was president, and, knowing that he had never specified any time, and every man telling him so, he admits that he advised prompt measures, which Evans would not listen to. I shall not make a single comment, part of the " prompt measures" was by bringing the other regiments of the Legion who were engaged for two years—who therefore never thought of refusing to serve—and ordering them to ;" prime and load" over the 6th, which they refused to do. He asked some of them if they would be satisfied to abide by the opinion of Lord John Hay, aud they agreeing that they would, an interview with his Lordship was had, when that distinguished and honourable man gave the following view of the case :—That they were not bound to serve for any particular period, and that he considered General Shaw was greatly in error in having acted so loosely with the con-tract ; but that he thought as the Spanish Government insisted on two years, they had better continue to serve rather than be in the country doing nothing, for they could not expect to be allowed to go about at liberty without law or restraint ; and it was quite evident they would not be sent home before the others.

Another letter from Shaw, (dated 11th August,) contains the fol-lowing :—" Upwards of 400 of the 6th regiment have laid down their arms. I think the remainder will do so on the 6th of September; and I believe the whole 8th on the 15th of August. Pray, be very prudent just now in expressng opinions, or you will floor me."

Well did he know that he was about to be floored :—but I shall say nothing more about him : he tendered his resignation under the plea of having been charged by General Evans for being the corres-pondent of the London Courier—so he would make it appear ; but the awkward facts that came out in the court of which he was pre-sident was the principal cause. However, I have done with him about that matter. I will only add, that he was a man apparently thirty-five years of age ; five feet seven—firmly and well formed ; his eye particularly indicated restlessness ; his whiskers, which ap-peared to cost him some trouble, were reddish yellow. Altogether he was what is sometimes called a smart, clever man. He was nervous, I mean, easily excited, and could not help showing this de-fect even on the most trivial occasions. He shewed forwardness; but it was always where he could be seen with effect. The wish to be thought a brave man was stronger than the qualities that are called bravery. To be a man of the world he lived temperately, but had a habit of swearing that was rather unmeaning and vul-gar ; " by my honour" and " d—— my blood" being his common oaths.

On the 1st of August, the 1st regiment, and a few companies of the other English, made an attempt to take possession of the Ametza hill, a strong and commanding position which had been taken on the 28th of May, and which the Carlists had retaken from the 1st regiment while the others were at Feuntarabia. At this attempt on the 1st of August they were met very unexpectedly by a strong column of Carlists, and, after finding the latter immovable, they had to retreat with considerable loss. It was said that this had been done without an order from General Evans, and that he had reprimanded those connected with it.

On the 19th of August, a number of the 8th gave up their arms, and were left behind us at Santander. They were joined by those of the 6th, but the most of them returned to their regiments within a few weeks after that time. Those who did not, continued there as prisoners during the winter, and suffered the greatest privations that it is possible for human beings to endure. Guarded by Spanish soldiers—fired on, and some of them wounded when they offered to rebel—restricted in food to twelve ounces of bad bread a-day, and water. Their great coats had been taken from them, and they lay there on the cold floors, without any thing to cover them. This is one side of the story. They enjoyed liberty, and got full rations until they got up a system of going out during the night, plundering houses, gardens, fields, and persons; in fact, any thing they could fall in with; also, they found their way into a cellar below the chapel of the convent, which had been unopened for many years, as the thick mould on the doors and wine pipes indicated. It was supposed that the wine was the remnant of the stock of the monks who precipitately left the convent of Corban when Napoleon took possession of it and its immense riches. To break into the cellar, find wine in it, broach the casks, drink and be intoxicated, was one short act; but it did not end there. While some were nearly drowned, the wine having at one time run till it was two feet deep in the cellar, and the drinkers, for want of vessels, lying down and drinking out of the pool, pushed into it overhead, and pulled out again by those behind them—while this was going on, a party attacked the interior of the church, tore and destroyed a splendid assortment of paintings and music, and were only arrested in their madness by being fired on. It is true, I believe, that the worst of these were not the men who suffered for it; but those who did suffer, suffered

in consequence of these things being done ; and, it is only just to
state, that the most of those complaining of imprisonment, were
persons connected with these outrages. But I must leave them at
present.

On leaving these we proceeded to a town called Santona, about
six leagues or eighteen miles from Santander, and lying in the direction between that and San Sebastian. At this place, and in its
neighbourhood, we had many interesting adventures, mixed with a
good deal of flogging. One day, no less than six men got a hundred lashes each for various misdemeanours. The vines here were
in an abundance, far surpassing any thing we had seen ; and, for the
first time, we saw groves of orange trees. Nothing is perhaps more
lovely than the orange groves. The trees are generally thirty inches
round the trunk, they are altogether about thirty feet high, the
branches beginning to spread at ten feet from the ground. They
are so thick and bushy that light is scarcely seen through them;
but the eye rests pleasantly on their yellow fruit which hangs in
rich variegation on the tops of the branches. However, there was
one great drawback—though they were ripe, they were so sour that
they could not be eaten. I saw some of our gourmands take a look
at them—pull a few—take a bite—wink—screw their mouths—
throw them down—look up at the trees again, and come away,
saying, "it's a pity they're sae soor."

We marched one day into the interior of the country in pursuit
it was said, of a Carlist band, but we did not fall in with it. A
General Gaurea, since killed, commanded the detachment, which
consisted of the Chapelgorris, other two Spanish regiments, and the
8th and 9th of the Legion, in all about three thousand men. We
ascended the most stupendous mountains which are to be seen in
any part of the north of Spain. The rich vallies that were covered
with the luxuriant Indian corn and vines we left below us, and made
our way from one high ridge to a higher, until [we literally looked
down on the clouds. To the very summits we found patches of cultivation. The streams of water that issued out of the rocks, and
foamed over the sides of the mountain, were delightful. In the
compass of about four miles I noticed nine of these springs, which,
had they been united, would have made a considerable river. Far
below us we could see the villages and church spires like motes, and

though the actual distance could not be more than about two miles,
we were told that the inhabitants of the region we were in, never
held correspondence with these places, the nearest practicable path
being above twenty miles. Besides the sloping sides of the mountain, there were perpendicular rocks, 1000 feet in height. From one
of these we had a view, partly real and partly illusive, which surpassed any thing that has perhaps ever been witnessed by any traveller. The grandeur of the illusion arose partly from the accident
of the morning mist lying down below us, and might be visited often
without being seen to such advantage. Through the cloud of mist
there was an opening which shewed us the valley below, all glittering in morning sunshine. A bold precipitate rock, a miniature of
the other mountains, with a flock of wild sheep picking the scanty
green that was here and there patched on it, was seen abruptly
raising its crest at the head of the valley. It stood at the mouth of
a great glen, and split the river that came rolling out. A little village at the bottom of its eastern edge seemed so like as if it had run
in there for shelter from the impetuous torrent, that I could not help
having a glow of affectionate love for it. That was as it appeared
on the first day of our march. But at this time, when we were on
their summit, early on the second morning, I, with a few more,
during the time of a halt for resting, walked towards the highest
precipice to have a look over. We went forward cautiously to the
edge, expecting a dizzy quivering of the brain when the vast vacancy of space would open to us, but we saw nothing at first save a
white floating cloud, about a hundred feet beneath us ; it could only
be known to be mist from its incomparable softness. A few expressed disappointment. "It's no height to look off here," one of
them said. "It's the mist the for," exclaimed a second, "we can
see nothing for the mist." A third, when he had looked a few
minutes, turned to me and said, "would ye no' like to jump in ? "
This feeling is a strange one. Byron says, in picturing some vortex
of wild floods from a height,—

> " You cannot gaze a minute,
> Without an awful wish to plunge within it."

My friend and I were filled at the same moment with the same wish ;
but it was not an "awful wish" in desiring to plunge into the soft
bed of mist. When he spoke to me I had the most luxuriant sen-

sations of delight in fancying myself falling in. But the grand
effect of the view was the accidental opening of the cloud, which
shewed the clear world below. At this I could have believed any
story of enchantment. The vision of Mirza was realised. All exclaimed, in admiration. My poetical friend said nothing for some
minutes, but stood wrapt in his own contemplations. I asked him
what he thought of it when it had gradually opened, and was slowly
shifting and revealing new objects. He answered, "If I was a fairy
to sit an' ride there, an' look down, or to swing on yon white
streak!" I felt the pleasurable idea, and was disposed to express
the poetry of my imagination, which I did by wishing that I was one
of the eagles which we saw at a distance, hovering on the wing,
wheeling their circuit, then " shaving the air," and hovering again,
(" staunin' on naething," as Jock Watt called it.") " How I should
like to be an eagle," I said, and was about to proceed, but Tam
Wilson stopped me by interposing, " aye, ye wad soon pounce down
on yon sheep, if ye was," and this produced a laugh at my expense.
The clouds gradually separated, and, mingled by turns, I could fancy
there was an uncertainty with them whether to hide or open the
lovely vale to the eyes that were strained to measure the spoil it contained. We saw to great advantage the protection that the country
affords in war to those who have possession of it, for from this
height we had a view of the mountains, passes, rivers, and all the innumerable intersections through which one party may go on to the
end of time, if they choose, decoying, eluding, and menacing another.
We halted at a village during the night, which the Carlists left on
our approach, and which they came back to when we came away,
and other places between that and Santona were deserted when we
passed and repassed, the bells of the churches and convents being
rung when we made our appearance at a distance, warning the people
of our coming. We were afterwards informed that at one of these
places both cavalry and infantry were within the church, at the time
of our marching through beneath the portico of the door. We also
heard that General Gaurea knew that, but did not wish to molest
them ; and it was also said that Godfrey, on hearing these reports,
raged and swore, and threatened Gaurea with a court-martial for
having harassed the troops two days for no purpose. This was
natural for Godfrey : it is also natural for Gaurea to be called a trai-

tor or a coward by those who love to read of battles, if the case was
as these reports had it. But I think there was something else that
was natural. Gaurea was among his native mountains — the play-
fellows of his childhood were the old people of the villages—he had
been long absent from them, an exile for many years in England,
where his own family had been born and educated; but he had
hunted and fished among the hills and streams of that district;
perhaps he had loved some one who might still live there. He had
worshipped God in the church where they were hiding, and to deluge
the altar with blood where he had knelt to pray, to burn the village,
and root up the remnants of his home! To have done that, he
must have been a monster, which would have been worse than any
imputation that was thrown on him.

At Santona, we left some more men, whose year's service was out
on the 5th of September, and who refused to re-engage for a second
year. They were treated in every way as prisoners as soon as we
left them, and that without any outrage having been committed by
them, as had been the case with those at Corban.

CHAPTER VII.

State of the Legion after the Mutiny — Commencement of the Attack on the
1st of October — Turning out — Hurried Preliminaries, &c — Marching within
shot of the Enemy — A Cannon Ball goes through the 8th in close column —
Coolness of Colonel Apthorpe, and others—Jokes on the occasion—Another 32
pounder from the Carlists does extraordinary execution — Colonel Colquhoun of
the Artillery — Tremendous disasters among the Carlists from his shot and shell
—The Carlist Cannon on the Ametza dismounted—Gallant charges of our Lancers—The 6th engaged—The 8th, &c.—Rifles, 9th, 10th, and the English Regiments — General Evans wounded — Rockets — Officers of our Rocket Brigade
killed — Proposal to take the Ametza Hill, and remarks thereon — The Carlists
fall back at night — Burying the Dead — Getting into Quarters — Anecdotes
&c. &c.

By the time we returned to San Sebastian, which was on the 10th
of September, perfect order had been restored to the different regiments. None of them had been so outrageous as the 8th, but all of
them had been, more or less, out of order, in getting their pay and
spending it. But all was now regular soldiering; drilling twice a
day on the sands, mounting guard and piquets at the different regimental quarters, and on the lines before the enemy. New jackets

and trowsers had renovated the appearance of every regiment, and so strictly military were all the details in every respect, that the most fastidious must have been satisfied with the Legion's military appearance.

The 8th was commanded by a Colonel Apthorpe, Godfrey being now Brigadier-General in the place of General Shaw, resigned. Colonel Apthorpe was an able officer of the East India Company's service—had obtained a year's leave, and was passing that time in the Legion. He was in every respect a gentleman, a good man, and a good officer, and under his command we were, and had been, for a short time, on the 30th of September.

I remember that was a beautiful evening, and about the time of piquet mounting, which was sunset, I and my friend the *Champion* had taken a walk along the lines—had been up to a house where the nearest piquet to the Ametza hill was mounted, and had passed some time in conversation with my cockney friend, Bill Oliver, had a quartilla (a pint) of akadent amongst us, and then returned home, pretending to be in admiration of the red west, and every thing that is to be seen on a fine evening of autumn. I lay down and slept soundly, and Bill Oliver had done the same thing, as he told me afterwards.

About three o'clock on the morning of the 1st October, Bill had been called two or three times to get up and go on sentry, still dreaming that it was not his turn, and the corporal was continuing to bawl out "Sentry go," that being the technical phrase for giving the alarm to those asleep on such occasions. "Sentry go" was repeated, and immediately Oliver found himself bruised, broken, and buried. A cannon ball had knocked in a part of the house where the piquet were lying, and had silenced the corporal with "sentry go" in his mouth by nearly knocking off his head. A scramble was instantly made to get up to their feet, when a second ball, a thirty-two pounder, played crack, and crash through the roof, hurling the tiles about them. All were getting hold of their muskets as quickly as they could, and hurrying down stairs. The whole could not get on the stair at once, but were crowding to the top of it. Another ball from the first cannon dashed through amongst them, killing and wounding, and while the panic increased by it caused the crowd at the top to hurry over each other, a second from the thirty-two carried away the stair, tumbling them down headlong. These were what, if fired from our side, would have been called four *beautiful* shots, and any of those who got time to think, wondered what Carlist gunner could have sent them. The rascal! he was a deserter from the Legion—had once been in the Royal Woolwich Artillery, and was now with the Carlists, directing their artillery from the Ametza hill. This was the beginning of that eventful day's work. Wilson (that was the gunner's name) will be heard of immediately, when I have described another part of the attack.

About the same moment the cannon from the Ametza opened, the sentry on a post farther down than the piquet-house was killed by a Carlist musket-shot, and following that, columns of Carlist infantry marched up, and drove back our different piquets with a murderous fire. The piquet of thirty men in the house where the cannon balls had come, and were still coming, maintained their post against the Carlists with great valour, in a kind of court-yard, in which the house, with some others, were situated; they rallied from their first panic, and fired through holes in the wall against a thousand of the enemy who surrounded them. Their regiment (the 3d or Westminster grenadiers) was quickly turned out, being quartered near by, and came up to their assistance. At the same time, the rifles hurriedly joined them, many of the men and officers not having time to button their clothes. Some of them who had been lying fast asleep, and had seized their rifles before their eyes were well opened, met their deaths as they came out; but they made a desperate resistance to the Carlists, and kept them in check till stronger reinforcements came forward.

The 6th and 7th were quartered to the westward about two miles, and the 8th were in some scattered houses, about half a mile from where the fight was begun.

I had at this time rather an onerous duty, that of colour-sergeant; of course it was my business not only to start myself, but to make others get up as quick as possible, our officers being at the time quartered in San Sebastian. " Sergeant S. turn out your company," I heard the Adjutant call as he ran through the houses, at the same time he was calling out " bugler, d——you, bugler, sound." The bugler was heard calling " where's my bugle?" and then getting hold of it, was seen running about naked, sounding that ominous call, which is termed " *turn out the whole,*" and which is never sounded but in cases of great emergency. Adjutant O'Driscoll, who had succeeded M'Knight, was the cleverest and best Adjutant we had in the service. He was chasing the poor bugler from house to house along the river side, where we lay, making him give the alarming *rouse* at every door. At the same time, there was no mistaking the cause of the early alarm; the cannon rebounding, and the rattling musketry at a distance, told too plainly what it was.

" Bang up—jump—rouse—on your accoutrements—turn down —there's the Carlists at the back o' the house—d——you, stir yourselves." " What 'll we get up the noo for?', was the drowsy reply of one. " What are ye pu'ing the big coats aff us for?" was the wakening question of two. The bugle was heard routing again at the bottom of the stair. Again the poor non-cons. such as myself, bawled out, while they accoutred themselves. The greater part were beginning to start up ; and when they listened a few moments, and had uttered, " what 's a'-do ? —mercy, hear to that—faith there's something gaun this mornin'," there was a general folding of greatcoats, forcing of feet into perverse shoes by turning up the heels and knocking the toes on the floor. A general mixture of voices saying, " that 's my coat ye're folding ;" thae's no' your coat-straps, " " they are my coat-straps ;" " oh, I've an awfu' sair head," " I canna get my coat on for the byle 'at's on my arm ; oh, Sergeant——, I wus ye wad send me to the hospital ;" and the thundering roar of, " silence, you men, every company's turned out but ours ; we're last, as usual," at the same time we were perhaps first. From the moment the first sound was heard, ten minutes had not elapsed till all the companies had fallen in outside. At a distance, on the road leading to San Sebastian, mounted officers were at the spurred gallop, riding out and riding in. General Evans, on a gallant grey charger, was seen darting along for an instant up through the fields, over hedge and ditch, followed by his staff, riding a furious steeple chase in the straightest direction for the point that was atacked. General Chichester followed by his aides-du-camp, took another direction. Our regimental officers came running and riding, according as they were field officers, captains or subalterns. The Colonel said, in a hurry, " fall in with your companies, gentlemen. Is that mbulance and ammunition getting out?" (this was the surgeons'

baggage, stretchers to carry the wounded on, and barrels of ammunition.) "Yes, sir, was the reply. One of Chichester's aides du-
camp came gallopping down a narrow lane at a break-neck pace, and
ordered, "Colonel Althorpe, march up the 8th—no time to lose."
The Colonel gave the order, "battalion, 'tention, with—cartridge,
prime and load;" that done, he went on, "right, form four deep—
close well up—quick march." Two dozen of fifers and drummers
whistled and rattled the tune of, "A' the blue bonnets," and in a few
minutes we found ourselves marching along the top of a rising
ground, where there was an earthen bank, about four feet high, on
our right hand, which sheltered us from the Carlist fire. The balls
were chipping off pieces of earth, cutting the twigs, and spinning
over our heads with a long singing noise, and consequently most of
us thought it was just as well to keep down our heads a little. In
the corner of a field, we got the following orders from the Colonel :
—"Close column," "order arms," and "stand at ease," which is
(as I may inform some readers) to take the musket from the shoulder,
set it down by the right side, clap the palm of the right hand on that
of the left, then shift the fingers till those of the right covered the left
with the thumbs inside, drawing back the right foot a little, and
keeping fast the left foot. This was to "stand at ease ;" but soldiers have to be particular not to ease themselves by moving, unless
the additional words, "stand easy," are given.

We had received this last indulgence, and were looking about,
past a corner to get a glimpse of what was going on. I saw Major
Hogg give his horse a sudden spur, at which it sprung to a side ; a
cry of "oh !" and a buzz was heard for a moment. The officers
had been standing in a group, and they were now lying scrambling
on the ground : the companies forming the left wing of the regiment were in disorder, and pieces of stone and earth were falling
down above us. A cannon-ball, from the Arretza hill, twelve hundred yards distant, had been sent down by the excellent marksman,
Wilson. Major Hogg saw it coming, and saved himself and horse,
by springing to a side. It took the ground just at the Colonel's
feet, ploughed, for a distance of five yards, a furrow, twelve inches
deep, in the grass field amongst the feet of the officers, threw the
stones and earth about, rose, and bounded through the column,
striking a man, named Duncan Campbell, on the hip, cutting him

in two pieces—breaking the arm of another—knocking the musket
out of the hand of one, which knocked down half a dozen men,
breaking a leg and some ribs. The ball having done that, bounded
off in the air, and fell, no one knew where. I saw the stones
coming down above us. " Oh, my head," one was saying. " Am I
much hurt ?"   Captain Robertson asked : a stone had cut him severely on the face.   There were a number of stone wounds ; and the
men were rather amazed ; at the same time, the officers not severely
injured, but only tumbled over, were scrambling to their feet. " Be
steady, gentlemen—be steady," Apthorpe said. Presently another
whistler from the Ametza struck a little to our right, throwing up
the earth to a height of sixty feet. " Be steady men—be steady,"
he continued, " they may fire long enough before they touch us
again."   At the same time he went a little to where he had a full
view of everything—where he was openly exposed, and pulling out
his pocket telescope, took a survey of all that was going on. " That's
a ration return," said one of the men.   " I wish they would send
another with the rations, then," was the reply.

At the moment of these observations, the following circumstance
occurred.   An officer on horseback—a Chapelgorri a few yards in
rear of him—another soldier a small distance from the Chapelgorri,
and an Englishwoman a few yards behind him, were in an open space
of ground between us and a house that was about forty yards distant.   The woman came there looking for her husband, who was in
the Lancers, and who, as she had been told, and as was the case,
had been killed in one of the gallant charges that were then making.
The others, officer and men, were passing that particular spot on
some duty, and were fully exposed to the view of the Carlists on the
Ametza hill.   We were out of sight, but saw the officer and the
others passing us, and having nothing else to do at the time, we
were passing remarks on them : a heavy ball whirled past them, and
after having cut up a piece of a hedge and shivering a tree, it
plunged itself into the earth.   One of our men remarked, " that
was near them;" and another added, "what a crash it made through
the hedge ! "   A number of voices from an opening, where a view
of the Ametza could be obtained, gave a sudden indication of having
seen something by the suppressed tone and hurried utterance of
" there's another, there's another—it's coming this way—clap low

down." We instinctively looked for it, and perhaps fancied our heads going off, when all at once, the horse and four individuals mentioned, fell down, and the ball bounded away, having lightly touched a hard road. " Did you ever see anything neater than that?" one observed ; "it minds me of the nine pins," said another. ' 'I would be proud of that fellow's personal acquaintance," was Oakley's observation, alluding to the gunner, whose excellent practice was making these first-rate shots. The nose of the horse was first carried away by the ball, then it entered the animal's breast, explored the regions of his inside, and made its exit behind, leaving the rider unhurt. It next took off one of the Chapelgorri's legs, he being on a piece of higher ground. Then the one behind him being on lower ground, was knocked dead at once, and the ball travelling a little farther, came in contact with the woman, committing an inexpressible injury. Her wound was not mortal, but it was extremely dangerous, and I believe, afforded the medical officers an experiment, perhaps without a parallel in the history of surgical operations. It s only due to Mr. Alcock, and other eminent gentlemen of the hospital, that they at all times exerted themselves humanely and skilfully to save the wounded, and that in this case they did so particularly, and were eminently successful.

While these cannon shots from the Carlists, directed by a skiiful hand, were doing execution in different parts, our artillery, principally under the direction of Colonels Colquhoun and Shaw, was playing its disastrous share of the day's strife. There were cannon planted at different points along the lines always ; but the fieldpieces were kept in the town, mounted, and ready to be taken to any point at any time. The work in getting these out, and up to a height over broken wet ground, was not easy ; eight, and sometimes twelve horses were dragging them—drivers spurring and whipping —sticking fast in a gutter—the different men belonging to the gun working with levers and their shoulders to give assistance.

"There, now, my good fellows," Colquhoun would say, (dismounting from his horse, and assisting with his own hands,) "that's the way to do it, never mind soiling your clothes, put your shoulders to the wheel—this way—here goes." In that style he would assist and encourage the men in an emergency, though I should mention, his common habit was to speak very little. Without any loss of time, the pieces were at work, and in full play, with shot knocking down houses, and shells killing those that were outside.

At a distance the Carlists were marching in close column from behind a house, and coming round it on their way to the line of engagement in such perfect order, and so openly exposed that they did not seem to be on the look out for anything in the shape of cannon shot. Colquhoun measured the fuse, saw the shell filled with its proper proportions of powder and so on, ordered the gun to be charged; elevated her to the range of his scientific calculations ; then turned, and called the attention of the gunner, to the house, at fully a mile's distance, and the battalion marching past in column. "You see yon house ?" " Yes, Sir,"—"Yon column ?" " I do Sir."—" That shell will take effect six yards from the north corner of the house, four feet from the ground in the centre of the column—fire !" The man at the breech lifted his thumb from the touch-hole—all shut their lips and pressed their teeth to save the deafening shock—the match was applied, and the volume of fire and smoke issued—the air trembled, and the shell, faithful to the science, and obedient to the wish of the infallible master of the art of bomb-shell practice, took its rainbow curve through the air, and exploded, as near as could be observed by all whose eyes and telescopes were directed to the point, at six yards from the north corner of the house, four feet from the ground, in the centre of the enemy's column. Colquhoun, when he saw the disaster and confusion it occasioned among the Carlists, turned round and said, "there's no difficulty in doing that, now go on." Taking observations for all the other guns, he gave the minute directions necessary, and left them thundering, and proceeded to another quarter.

Here he was standing on an elevated position taking observations, and it was now evident that he was doing great havoc among the enemy's infantry ; their artillery on the Ametza, which was all this while battering, first at one point, and then another, but always with precise effect—was now directed against our artillery. The Carlists' infantry were lower than Colquhoun's position : but the Ametza was considerably higher, and, therefore, they had the advantage of elevation. He stood viewing them with a telescope. One of their heaviest pieces emitted its volume of smoke in his direction, which, to a practised observer, tells at once where the ball is bound for. The well directed emissary of death passed with an awful concussion of air near his head, and struck the gun immediately behind him, killing one of the men, and wounding one or two more. He continued his observations till satisfied, by knowing what he wanted to know. Another ball had followed, and it was said General Evans came to him and asked his opinion of the Carlist gunner—whether he thought him an Englishman or not. Colquhoun replied, "there can be no doubt of who he is; I've been taking a close observation of him, and I am just about to let him know that I am acquainted with him." "Remove these wounded men," he continued, addressing some of the others, "but don't trouble yourselves with dead ones; come, my good fellows, we'll give them something for that." This last part of his sentence was spoken in reference to another crashing ball that thinned some trees, and wounded one of the horses of the General's staff. He elevated for the Ametza three pieces that went off at once, when the smoke of the shells, which two of them threw had cleared away, all appeared confusion and dismay for a while on the Ametza; and when their guns were again manned, they were seen to be directed by a Carlist officer of artillery; what his fate was remains uncertain; but his best piece of artillery got a blow from Colquhoun, the ball going into its muzzle and splitting it, as was afterwards learned, when some particulars about that day's engagement became known. Thus the enemy's artillery were comparatively quieted, and shortly afterwards were completely silenced.

This was part of the work up to about ten o'clock in the forenoon. During that time a determined conflict was going on with the infantry of both parties, but especially on the Carlist side, for on ours there seemed only a desire to defend, with the exception of what was done by the Lancers. The 8th not being particularly engaged during the morning, in doing anything but looking on, or lying in reserve, as it is called, we had an opportunity of seeing the charging of the Lancers to advantage. Their horses were at this time in fine condition, and when it is known that the regiment had been formed of men carefully selected—principally of those who had been in British cavalry regiments, or men likely to make good dragoons, and had been regularly and well drilled: also, that there were a number of names ending with " woiski," those names which

No. 10.　　　　　　　　K

at once tell of a nation whose warlike valour and experience would be a guarantee for their bravery before an enemy; also there was Antonio Fourori, and some others similar in character, though not so remarkable in personal history. He was a Venetian by birth, had fought in native revolutions, afterwards under Napoleon — again with General Mina, and others; then he became one of the Parisian heroes of 1830—got a pension—visited Bayonne and the frontier— fell into the hands of the Carlists in 1833—was jcompelled by Zumalacarregui to serve as a dragoon, which he and the others taken with him did. In 1834, he found his way into France, and was suspected of designing republicanism—fled to England—joined General Evans in 1835; and was, on the 1st of October, 1836, in the engagement which I am describing. A lance and a sword were playthings to him. He was a first-rate horseman, was six feet, with an eagle eye, looking over a forest of mustachios, and a beard that hung down on his broad chest, and had a brawny arm that could have done deeds of more than ordinary magnitude. Such was Antonio Fourori, and of such others as I have mentioned, were the Lancers composed. They were commanded by Colonel Wakefield, an officer who was strict in discipline, though not so tyrannical as Colonel Kinloch, their former commanding officer, but every whit as brave and efficient before an enemy. Kinloch was a tyrant, but at the same time a clever officer and a hero in courage. Wakefield on the other hand was as clever, less tyrannical, and distinguished, nay almost reckless in courage.

On the morning of the 1st of October, the Lancers had been, of course, early called out by the sounds of " *boot and saddle*," from their trumpets. We saw them charge in gallant style on the southeast side of the Ametza hill, we being to the northward. The Carlists gave way, until they came behind their breastworks, at which it was rendered impossible for the cavalry to follow farther, and necessary for them to retreat, being exposed to a heavy fire. The sight of horses going back without riders, and men without horses showed too plainly what they were exposed to. The Lancers went through their evolutions in beautiful style; some of their charges, wheeling and retreating, were as regularly performed as ever the same has been seen with any cavalry regiment on a field-day. It must be remarked, however, that there was only one point, on the line of attack, where the operation of cavalry was practicable, and that only partially so, else the Carlists might have suffered much more than they did,

The forming of the square, and preparing to receive cavalry, in the style of British field exercise, is not known with the Spaniards on either side, or if known it is seldom practised, for I do not remember to have seen a Spanish regiment go through that manœuvre. Their mode of warfare is regulated by the nature of the country in which they carry it on. The whole of their fighting is in the light infantry style, though not so regular as ours. Instead of retreating to, and forming square when attacked by cavalry, we never saw them yet engaged without having either a natural or artificial defence to fall back to for protection. They fire whenever there is the slightest chance of killing, and on either side, if a Spaniard sees his party getting the best of it, he will be very daring, and he is as cowardly when success is reversed. Whatever reports may have reached this country about the Legion's fighting, I claim the credit for it, that while the system of drill was strictly taught as it is in the British army, and the Legion drilled with great perseverance and success, to perform all the field manœuvres, there was a necessity, from the nature of the country, and the style of fighting, both of the Carlists and Christinos, for the Legion to adopt in an action a part of the Spanish system; but there was one part of it not adopted. The Legion was disciplined to follow the General's orders —to keep a post without flinching, if ordered to do so—not to fire, though some of the enemy could be killed, if ordered not to fire; and to advance, if ordered, against all seeming disadvantages. I claim credit to the Legion for having acted strictly under such a system of discipline.

The 6th regiment, about nine o'clock in the morning, was brought from the western extremity of the lines, leaving the 7th Irish to defend that part, after having warded off a feigned attack, made, no doubt, to distract the attention of General Evans, by making it appear that the attack was general along the lines.

The Carlist chief, however, required all his available force to concentrate on one point; the object of which was, as he afterwards explained himself, to carry by storm the village and fort of Alza. The Chapelgorris, 2nd Spanish light infantry, 1st regiment of the

Legion, and a battery of the Legion's artillery repelled the attack there, and rendered the attempt to storm that position hopeless. The Carlist General, Eguia, admitted, in his dispatches, that the repulse his division received there was "unusually severe;" and, that having his artillery on the Ametza (which is about 1200 yards to the north-west of the height of Alza), he deemed it proper to advance under cover of his cannon in that part—for what object it is not stated—but it was, no doubt, to cut off Alza and the regiments forming its garrison from the remainder of Evans's force, and thus perform a part of a plan of operations which the Carlist Generals, in conjunction with each other, were said to have contemplated at this time.

The 6th regiment having come from Antigua convent, on the extreme west, as mentioned, were marched into the fight near to where the Lancers were. Let any reader suppose, for a moment, what his own feelings would be, to come to a certain point, which they did—stand there awaiting orders for a short while, during which the cavalry were seen attempting to charge on ground where their attempt was ineffectual, and exposed to a dreadful fire of musketry—then to be ordered to go and face the same fire, only because it was deemed possible for men on foot to scramble over the obstacles while horses could not get over. To see a regiment of men march on to encounter such a reception which they saw before them, without a sign of hesitation, would for ever silence the calumnies of cowardice. That regiment got the word of command to go forward. They had to go a short distance under cover, and, all at once, by the turn of a lane, they were brought under the open fire of the Carlists.

Leaving the rifles, 3rd 9th and 10, which shall be particularised, I shall proceed with my personal observations. The 8th were ordered to move away through some orchards, for the purpose of coming into action near to where the 6th and lancers were. Our way just lay in a direction where it was possible to be shot, without that strange consolation which men feel on such occasions of being able to shoot others in return. I observed also, that, as it was along a wooded declivity that we passed, and that, as it was evident the higher up we were there were more balls flying about, and the lower we kept ourselves there were fewer.—I could see that a good many had the instinct to take the lower side of a tree when it stood in the

way, even though it took more time to go round it than the upper
side would have done. Our friend on the Ametza hill had got his
eye on us, (this being previous to the dismounting of his guns), and
an awful rush of a cannon ball, smashing trees, snapping the tops off
some, lopping the branches off others, hurled over our heads. Did
ye see that?" one said, "three balls into a tree at once?" "Oh,
help me up some o'ye, dinna gang an' leave me," were the beseeching words of an esteemed young friend of mine. He had fallen, and
was addressing that request to another comrade beside him. I turned
round to see what was wrong with him, for I knew his voice, and he
was a young man of such an amiable disposition, that I had conceived
almost a brotherly affection for him. "Puir Jamie Macdonald!" I
heard some of them say. "What's wrang wi' ye, Jamie, my man?"
I inquired. "Oh, it's through me, it's in my side," he answered.
I had to pass on, being under the necessity of not only keeping my
own place, but to endeavour to make others keep their places; and
he was carried to the surgeon. His clothes were carefully unbuttoned,
to get at the wound. The surgeon asked where it was, and the
young man groaned, scarcely able to speak, that it was in his side.
"I don't see it, my man," the surgeon replied. In fact, there was
none. Now, this was not a singular case, for such occured frequently
but it was a vexing one, for the young man no doubt felt the imaginary wound as acutely as if it had entered his body. Such wounds
are occasioned sometimes by spent balls, that being balls whose force
is so far spent that they produce a contusion only; and sometimes
these wounds are produced when a ball in full force strikes a man a
severe blow obliquely, and bounds off without entering. I mention
this case only as an illustration of a species of danger to be met with,
which many readers are perhaps not acquainted with. A ball entering the body, is not felt acutely painful for some time, unless, perhaps, in a vital part. These spent balls, on the other hand, produce
a more acute and immediate pain, while they are generally laughed
at. Indeed, I knew men sometimes suffering severely, and because
the ball had not cut the flesh, only bruised it, they would rather suffer in secret than be laughed at. I believe my young friend felt
himself affronted as long as he was in the regiment after that occurrence, though he did not need to feel so, for he was severely injured.

Passing for some distance in the direction we were going, we came up to the San Sebastian division of the national guard, standing in the wood. It consisted of about a thousand citizens. Numbers of the inhabitants belonged to other regiments, such as the Chapelgorris, and on ordinary occasions followed after their business, going only out to reviews on holidays. On this occasion, all these were with their respective corps to which they belonged. But the national guard was a regiment of itself. It was composed of all sorts, in dress, size, age, and profession : generally they wore the belt round their waist the same as the Chapelgorris, which contained two rows of holes, in which were carried their ammunition. The convenience of getting hold of the cartridges, when loading, and the ease with which a light infantry corps, especially rifles, when they are extending and running about, can carry their ammunition in front of them, is decidedly better than the heavy pouch which hangs on the hips of all British soldiers.

I felt particularly interested in seeing the citizens of San Sebastian in arms, not so much because there were many of them shopkeepers whom we were in the habit of seeing in their shops, nor was it from their variety of character; but there was a sweet assemblage of sisters and daughters about the woods. These were meeting the wounded as they were brought off the field, and performing all the kind offices to the dying men that the soft sympathy of woman is ever ready to perform. The beauties of San Sebastian are not without the common dangers to hearts that are vulnerable. On this occasion as we marched towards the fight cheered by their cries of " Viva l'Ingleses," I believe there were some of us forgot the coming danger for a short time, to revel in the luxury of imaginary love. They seemed so peculiarly lovely amid the surrounding circumstances, that an on-looker could have wished to go into the fight, or not go at all, just as he might have the affections that looked through the black eyes to win or had already won them. I observed one particularly. She was the younger of two daughters of a merchant of considerable note in San Sebastian. There was combined in her person, the whole of that beauty that poets have embodied in the words *fairy*, and *angel*, and she bent so tenderly over the body of a dying Englishman, as she prayed for his parting spirit (an office performed readily by all Spaniards)—washed the blood from his temples, and gave him a cordial to drink, that it seemed uncertain whether she whispered a prayer, or gave him a kiss! whichever it was, the one or the other, or both, there were some who saw her, who could have been content with a wound (not too deadly) for the sake of such tender consolation. But it was a passing scene. Some saw it for a moment, as if Heaven had permitted them a parting glance of earth's choicest pleasures 'ere the worldc losed on them for ever. A short counter march—a wheel to the right, and a run at double quick, brought us under the fire of the enemy, and death which had by this time thinned other regiments, commenced among us.

Shortly after this, some men of the Rocket brigade passed us on horse back as they were going forward with their rockets to another position; the Carlists being now rather inclining to retreat. One of them, whom I knew, and who recognised me as he rode along at a gallop, exclaimed, " halloa, old feller, any message as you vishes to send for t'other wuld ?" Whether he meant that he would send a message by his rockets, which, before this, had sent off a good many, I cannot say, but he had scarcely uttered the words when he was sent off himself by a Carlist musket-ball going to his heart.

Lieutenant Bakehouse, who directed the rocket-brigade, and who had up to this time performed most efficient service in the engagement, perceiving that he could do little more with his rockets— as General Evans would not allow the Legion to advance farther than the positions held before the attack—sat down, and with Col. Colquhoun was taking some refreshment. Both had been in the heat of the fight from its commencement, and now that they sought a few minutes repose, and had gone partially out of danger, a ball struck Bakehouse—he laid his head on Colquhoun's breast, and ere the question of "what is vrong with you ?" could be put, he was dead.

Lieutenant Bakehouse was a clever officer, much respected by officers and men. He was buried a few days after the action, on the rocky height, behind the Castle of San Sebastian, where Major Mitchell and others lie; and since, a neat marble tablet has been erected over his grave, by his brother officers of the artillery.

During the action, General Evans got a ball through one of his ears. He was continually exposed, riding about from one place to another with the greatest imaginable coolness. It would almost make one superstitious about fate to be an observer of the misses and the hits. It is no exaggeration to say, that a thousand balls must have passed within a few inches of Evans that day, from the continued exposure of himself before the fire of the Carlists; and this was the only one that touched him.

There was one peculiarity about this engagement: it had only been one of defence; no ground had been taken, and consequently no plunder. Some observed it was "no job" to let the Carlists attack us—that we must be at them, for then there would be something got. Oakley, and one or two others, were those only of the 8th who had got anything, and what they got was by going contrary to orders, and joining themselves to the other regiments that were engaged, and assisting to charge the Carlists from some houses where there was spoil, but to what extent I cannot say; only they were able for some days to perform that slang miracle of "raising the wind," which most people know the meaning of.

I cannot pass from this without giving another trait of Colquhoun's character. He is well known to the scientific world as the inventor of some important discoveries in the art of gunnery, and as a military engineer generally. About this I shall say nothing, because I am not sufficiently informed of particulars to explain it, and because his extraordinary merits have at length (after being long neglected) been noticed in a quarter where he will thrive, that is, under the influence of the Lords of the Admiralty, and the Master-General of the Ordnance. But the trait of his character, which I wish to record, is one of a class that is generally deemed too unimportant to mention in connexion with genius. It was this:—Colonel Shaw, from a refractory temper, that made him at all times unpopular, refused to let his men have their rations, although there had been several opportunities for them to take refreshment. At about four o'clock in the afternoon, Colquhoun was seen approaching Shaw's battery of artillery, and that gentleman was at a distance out of sight, refreshing himself with his dinner. One of the gunners proposed to the others,—" s'pose I speaks on it now to Cu'nel C'onn, what do you think he would say?" "Why," replied another, "I don't think as he wouuld tie you to the carriage wheel, and flog you for it." Colquhoun heard this, and inquired what they wanted to say to him. He was told, and immediately ordered "cease firing" to one of the guns, bidding the others to go on meantime, and adding, that those at his battery had not only got their regular rations, but the double allowance that General Evans had caused to be brought from the town for every corps, and that he had sent for a third allowance, at his own expense, for his men. This was one part of his character. Another was that he would never allow flogging among those under his command, while it was a practice with the other never to miss an opportunity to inflict that punishment from the time he went into the Legion till he left it. There was scarcely a crime among the men under Colquhoun, which, of course, arose partly from their different treatment, not perhaps altogether from the want of that punishment, as from the kindness that they were governed by in its stead.

Colquhoun at this time returned to England, and was sent for by his late Majesty, and had a lengthened private audience ; during which, it was said, the King enquired particularly about the French, their conduct with regard to smuggling stores, &c., across the frontier to the Carlists. He was only a Major in the British service, but he got the rank of Lieutenant-Colonel on this occasion, and was immediately sent out to Spain, with a battery of Royal British Artillery, which is rated on the books of the ship Castor as a part of her crew—England being bound, by the quadruple alliance, to assist the nations of alliance with a naval force only. Some of the correspondents of the London papers wrote home about the contrast in the behaviour of the Royal Artillery and that of the Legion, but the difference of conduct and character must have arisen principally from their commanding officers. Those of the Legion, when under Colquhoun, behaved as well as those from Woolwich, and when they fell into the hands of the other Colonel, they became similar in character to the others.

I shall conclude this Chapter with an extract from the General's dispatch to the commander-in-chief, Rodil. A great deal of it is missed, which refers principally to the commencement of the action ; and that part where he refers particularly to the Lancers, and Colonel Colquhoun's artillery also left out : what follows contains information which I have not previously given.

Extract from General Evans's Dispatch.

" The conflict continued about twelve hours : our troops were full of ardour and confidence, and we might probably have seized on the enemy's cannon, but having already gained a decided success, and inflicted a severe punishment on the rebels, I did not desire to throw away, for an inadequate result, four or five hundred additional men, in killed and wounded, which it might have cost to storm the steep and entrenched heights before us, particularly as it does not enter into my plan to retain possession of that position.

"The complete order and intrepidity evinced by the officers and men, Spanish and English, on this occasion, appeared to me worthy of far more veteran soldiers, and will, I hope, meet with her Majesty's approbation. It was one of the best contested actions fought by the troops of this corps since I have had the honour to command them.

"From a variety of sources, I am led to believe, the enemy's loss cannot have been less than 1000—reports from their partizans carry it much higher; but the truth upon this point cannot be ascertained. Ours in killed and wounded is rather under 400, including 37 officers. Some deserters have come over, who represent a consternation to exist among the factious, from the number of their killed and wounded.

"I have to express my best acknowledgements for their gallantry and conduct, and for advice and assistance they afforded me, to Major-General Jaureguy, Adjutant-General La Marchant, Brigadier-Generals Chichester, Van Hallen, Fitzgerald and Godfrey; to Colonels De Lancy, Jockmus, Quartermaster General Bellow, and to the officers of my personal staff; and I would be much wanting were I not to express my obligations to Colonel Wylde, his Britannic Majesty's Commissioner with the Spanish army; nor should I omit to include in this acknowledgment, Lieutenant Vicors, of the Royal British Engineers and the detachment of the Royal British Marine Artillery, under Lieutenants Pike and Savage, who rendered on this occasion distinguished service.

Note to the foregoing Chapter.

The Author begs the attention of subscribers particularly to this note, especially as some omissions in the account of the engagement of the 1st of October have been made, and as he has hitherto confined his description of the engagements merely to personal observations, he has now the satisfaction of stating that arrangements have been made to illustrate this work with cuts, and that these will immediately appear with the succeeding numbers. The cuts will not be an ornament to the first page of each number merely, but they will be correct views of the different places, and events spoken of in the text. As a view of the *Westminster Piquet-house,* in which the 3d regiment so gallantly defended themselves—and a view of the ground on which the Lancers Rifles 6th 9th and 10th regiments were engaged on the 1st of October will be given, the Author has omitted the share of these regiments in the action, until the views are prepared.

As many officers of the Legion, have honoured him with their correspondence to give additional value to this work, he is able to promise to the public much general information which he did not at first possess. He returns them thanks for that correspondence, and requests that any information relative to the Legion will be forwarded to him, at the publisher's as early as possible, as sketches of the lives of the officers and men who were in any way distinguished will be given, authenticated communications respecting them will be made use of.

CHAPTER VIII.

Introduction to a new Series of incidents—Captain H. of the Lancers and Corporal Tucker—Sergeant Deana—his punishment, &c. &c.

Having thus given a running sketch of the principal engagements in which the Legion fought during the year 1836; we shall now take a review of the personal history of the most noted Characters in the Service, and record their behaviour as it was manifested in their respective regiments, from the time of enlisting in 1835 until the various periods of their being killed,—their dying of disease, —their desertions or discharges.

In thus taking up the lives of individuals, many of whom will wince from the peculiarities of their characters in the Legion—I disclaim every imputation of animosity. I should in justice to many individuals have commenced my work with the sketches which are now beginning, and in not doing so, charges have been made that there was a wish to conceal some of the black facts that stained the service of the Legion, and which are engraven on the minds and on the backs of many of the poor wretches who now throng the miserable cellars of St. Giles's.—Who only bore up against the sufferings to which some of them were subjected, in the hope—aye even the poor soldiers of the Legion had hope,—that one day they would obtain justice in England, against those who not only trampled humanity, but overstepped the not very humane British Articles of War. We have officers now in London, and English society have admitted them in the shape of gentlemen, who not only punished men with undue severity, but literally committed murder. Startling as this charge may be, it is true. I, the author of this work, am, with other witnesses in a condition to prove this charge against two Officers now in London: one of them high in rank in a regiment of the British service. But let the reader bear in mind that I as zealously defend the general body of officers from the common imputations thrown against them, by the poisoned rumour that has spread in England, relative to the Legion. Because nothing had been spoken of at home but those matters that deteriorated from the military honour of the Legion—this work began at the period when the honour of the service began, and having given a faithful record of the events up to October, 1836; we shall now illustrate these events farther by writing the character of several officers and men who figured in the different regiments.

The first to be noticed is the 1st Lancers, commanded at one time by Colonel Kinloch; at another, by Colonel Rait; and lastly, by Colonel Wakefield. Colonel Kinloch was more severe in his punishments than almost any other Colonel in the Legion. Colonels Shaw, Kirby, Swan, Tupper and others carried the provosting system to an unwarrantable extent, and what made it worse than otherwise it would have been was, they deputed the power of punishing to inferior officers. Men were even sometimes punished by non-commissioned officers; sergeants, who, by the favour of officers, got promoted, ere they knew "right face" from "left about," but these will find the injuries which they wantonly inflicted: rise up against them in their turn.

It would be difficult to convince readers who know nothing of military life, of the necessity for severe restrictions on men, especially in active warfare, but if all civillians were convinced of that necessity it would still be difficult to convince them of the enormity of crime committed by individuals in petty command, in and about Vittoria during the winter of 1835-6 on the poor wretches emaciated with disease and suffering the starvation of cold and scarcity rations ; bad in quality and restricted in quantity. It may be supposed that when hardships were common to all that a fellow-feeling of kindness would have prevailed between officers and men : In many honourable instances it did : but amid the general suffering there were some who were able to live in comparative luxury, and who seemed to have minds seared against common thefeelings of our nature. Among these was Captain H—y, of the Lancers. Let us follow a narrative of his conduct, with the sufferings of some of his victims, for a few pages. H—y had been Riding-master at one time in the 7th Dragoon Guards, and is well remembered in that corps, still,—one of those who suffered by him in Spain, and who did not survive to see the author of his sufferings afterwards disgraced, was a corporal Tucker. He was the son of the landlady of a tavern :—somewhere about London, but which is unknown to me :—called the *Marlborough Head*. He was a young man well educated, and so far as I ever heard, well-behaved. Some whim led him to join the Spanish service, and for a time after going out, while the treatment was still as good as that of British soldiers, he, like others, did not feel much hardship. The march from Santander to Vittoria came, and following it the dreary and hungry winter. Tucker was reduced to a skeleton, and the common disease accompanied by the biting frost had seized his feet. He lay for some days on the bare floor of the nearly roofless,—doorless,—windowless,—and altogether fireless old convent, in which the Lancers were quartered :—unable to move, wrapt only in his cloak ; the sergeant major, a person named Casey, accused the poor fellow of skulking. Captain H——y reiterated the accusation and ordered Tucker to be forced to his duty. Unable to stir, he pleaded to be left alone to die there ; but they would not give him even that indulgence. He was dragged from his corner, and the most horrid scene presented itself. As a proof of his inability to rise, there was a mass of filth and vermin collected about him, he being wasting away in a flux which, at this time, by the poisonous ingredients mixed in the bread by the Spanish bakers, and other causes had affected nearly all the men in the Legion. Poor Tucker, in that hopeless dying state got *four dozen lashes* by order of the Captain, to force him to his duty ; the Captain swearing that there was nothing wrong with him. Let the reader of this suppose the possibility of a lively gay young man, used to the fastidious correctness of London manners, lying down in such a state; and persisting in it for mere laziness,—impossible ! yet he lay as did thousands of others ; many of whom were similarly punished, only he was more fortunate than some of them, for death relieved him from his misery. He was taken to the hospital,—if the bare walls of an unfurnished house can be called an hospital : and both his legs were cut off while the punishment he had received, was still smarting in his flesh. At this time a letter came from his mother, in answer to one he had sent home informing her where he was. The grieved parent did not know where her son had gone when he left home, and now that she did know, her grief was even heavier, for the reports of the horrors of Vittoria had, at that time, reached England. The letter contained mixed expressions of motherly love and bitter sorrow, which were read to the dying man. Two days after, his body was carried to the gorged holes where the dead were unceremoniously thrown in, and this was the end of a gay youth who had aspired to be a soldier. Alas ! the end of many others was similar.

If I have said aught that offends the relatives of the unfortunate man, I assure them it is with reluctance, and from no want of consideration for their wounded feelings: but the act—the act of duty—of holding up to scorn that person who moves in London society, now as a gentleman, and who thus accelerated poor Tucker's death, could not have been performed, I presume, by saying less than I have said. Let us proceed to another case.

In the peninsular war, there was an officer in the Commissary's department, named Deana. He had a son who enlisted into the ranks of the 15th Hussars, and served for some years in that corps with a blameless character : it is he of whom I am now to speak. Some of the officers who served in the same corps, have since borne testimony to the excellence of Deana's character. He, after leaving the 15th, went out to Spain ; and among the profusion of promises that were made in this country, without measure, he had been promised the rank of Sergeant Major. These promises were so profusely made to induce men to go out, that it became impossible to realise the hundredth part of them. Deana, for some time found himself only a private; but being decidedly a clever soldier, and a fine looking man, he soon got promoted. To those who know him, I need say nothing; to those who do not, I may mention, that he was the first dragoon of the Legion who turned out, full accoutred and mounted, to be inspected by the Spanish generals; to shew to them what appearance an English lancer had, in full uniform, previous to the regiment being drilled and equipped. Also, he drilled the regiment in the use of the Carbine; which, with all parts of cavalry exercise, he performed to perfection. It will therefore be seen, that he was a valuable man to a regiment in the infancy of formation. How was he treated afterwards? the following will show, though I must omit many particulars. The long and weary march of the Legion, from Santander and Bilbao to Vittoria, brought the worn-out regiments within the black gates of that last named city, late in the evening of the 5th of December, 1835; the supply of the rations having been irregular, and the march a circuitous route, keeping us more than a month among the mountains (though a widely circulated London newspaper, whose Editor sits writing his opinions in an easy chair, asserted lately, that the Legion never had a march that could even tire the men, while it was in Spain). Night clouding over the dull, dark Vittoria, hid the sad visages of the wearied soldiers, as they crippled along the streets. It is true, the inhabitants cheered the sunken spirits of the hungry Legion, as it entered the town; for a profusion of illuminated devices were erected over the Santa Clara gate; and bands of music playing the national hymns, with the *vivas* of the people at their windows, seemed to welcome the weary soldiers who had traversed the mountains for more than a month, to enter and share the friendship of Vittoria. Even the cheering inscription of, " To the generous English, who fight for the liberty of nations," was emblazoned; and certainly as the Legion passed beneath the gateway, it had the effect of exciting hope. But the ruined convents, of which there was an abundance about Vittoria, were allotted as quarters to the *generous English*. Without bedding of any description, the wearied soldiers lay down on the cold damp stones, being overcome with fatigue, and arose next day shivering in agues and dysentery. From this commmenced the direful plague that thinned the ranks, and spread despair over many a poor wretch, who had thoughtlessly left his friends and a comfortable home to be an adventurer, but who up to this time, had kept hope alive, thinking he would one day return. Now, there was nothing about the fireless damp convents, but white sleety snow outside, and black misery and dying men within.

Amongst the thousands who suffered severe sickness, was Sergeant Deana of the Lancers, whose narrative I am pursuing. He was, in the first place, reduced to the ranks, by Captain H——y, for having said he was unwell and not able to come to stable duty, the morning after their arrival in Vittoria. Deana shortly afterwards was in a skirmish, when a charge was made on a party of Carlists, in the direction of Salvatierra. His horse came down with him, and he being severely disabled by the fall, was for some time under medical treatment. He had a valuable watch, and being about to die, as was thought, the Captain and Sergeant Major, who in all things went hand in hand, embezzling stores and money, as well as plundering the men through their accounts, &c., made an attempt to get hold of this watch. Deana was married; and it should have been mentioned sooner, that his wife was one of the very few industrious, and well-behaved, among the many women who left England to share the Spanish campaign. She wrought hard, and by making a little money was enabled to keep her husband in a billet where there was a bed. A species of annoyance and ill treatment towards the poor woman was unremittingly kept up by the two heartless persecutors, insult followed insult during her husband's illness, until one day a demand was made peremptorily for the watch. She refused to part with it. A few hours afterwards, Captain H——y came to the billet, and said, "Deana you must go immediately to your duty, I will have no skulking like this."

"I am not able to walk through the room," he replied.

"Well, you must walk to duty or else to hospital, I shan't allow you to stay here," was the retort.

Let the reader keep in mind that there was at this time no hospital, save the old houses, in which thousands of dead and dying were crowded, without beds, lying on the bare floors—the dead ones

EXECUTION OF DON JOSE ELGOEZ,

For poisoning the Rations of the British Legion, with a View of Santa Clara, the principal Street in Vittoria. p. 186.

No 11.

eaten with rats, and the living with myriads of loathsome vermin—
medical officers themselves sick, or worn out with fatigue ; and
every day a host of helpless objects being admitted with frost-bitten
toes and other diseases, receiving no medical assistance whatever,
but who generally lived about a week and then died.

Deana replied to Captain H——y,—" Sir, you may do with me
what you think proper, but I cannot move."

The Captain went away, and in a few minutes the guard came
and he with it, and took Deana off to the guard house,—which guard
house was nothing more than an open lobby of the convent, through
which the snow drifted, and the wind blew without intermission.
Here the poor man lay three days, and was then taken before a
court martial. One of the members of this court, was Captain,
afterwards Major Baker, son of the coroner for Middlesex. This
officer's name is mentioned because he begged of Deana, *not* to mention his name, for he would be ashamed to meet his friends after
having been a party to such disgraceful proceedings.—He said this after
Deana had proved himself brave and well-behaved, beyond what most
soldiers are, and what some of these officers proved themselves to be.
But having been a member of a court martial, of which he himself
was ashamed, I think it is only just to mention him.

Deana was sentenced to receive two hundred lashes, and had not
Captain Hargrave, formerly in the 15th Hussars, who knew the
good character of the prisoner, interfered for him : he would have
received the two hundred. As it was, he was taken out and in his sickly
state, got one hundred lashes. He then fell into a fever, and became
insensible for twelve days.

The poor man when returning to consciousness, was asked by
the disconsolate woman, if he recollected his having been flogged ;
on which his horror at the punishment, knowing that he had done
no crime—was so dreadful that he declared that but for the interference of his wife, he would have destroyed himself.

About a month after this he had in some degree recovered, when
a guard of men was sent to bring him out of the town to the village
of Arangues, six miles from Vittoria, where the Lancers were
quartered. The poor persecuted object was a shadow of death.
He trembled on his emaciated limbs, and his back was still a
blister of raw wounds. His wife accompanied him, and was

assisting to lead him along, when Captain Cumberlege, a brave
and humane officer, met them, expressed surprise at seeing a man in
such a state come out of bed ; and gave him permission, by his order
to return to Vittoria. The sick man was not able to return, but sat
down among the sleety snow of January, on the road side, (the accompanying soldiers having been sent on to the regiment by Captain
Cumberlege.) Night was falling on the wife and her sick husband—
the dull dreary road was losing all its straggling passengers—and
the hours when wandering Carlist bands or guerilla peasants came
prowling about for plunder, had set in on them. At a distance, the
sound of horses' feet and voices were heard. These approached, and
proved to be Captain H——y and two or three other officers. Deana
was ordered to get up from where he lay and go on. He told the
officers the state he was in ; and his wife begged in tears to have
some assistance for her husband, and to be permitted to return with
him to Vittoria. H——y swore if she did not go back herself to
the town, and leave her husband to do his duty with the regiment,
he would cut her to pieces with his sword! at the same time dismounting and taking hold of Deana (who had risen to his feet as well
as he could to salute his brutal superior), shook him—pushing him
across the road, backwards and forwards, while the poor woman
kept the feeble man from falling, until the dressing that was on his
lacerated back was torn off, and the blood and matter, by the violence done to the wounds, were oozing through his shirt and jacket.
They were forced onwards, and coming at last to Arangues they
joined the regiment, and lay down in the damp, clay floors of the
dilapidated houses, for this being one of those places where the
Christinos are at one time, and the Carlists at another ; the wood
of the roofs and doors is burned to make fires for the present tenants,
and to afford as little shelter as possible to their successors of
the opposite party. Next morning Mrs. Deana was in a fever,
which led to delirium, and she did not recover for nearly two
months. Her husband was in the greatest agony, his shirt adher-
ing to his skinless back, not able to move himself : and no person
and no ointment to dress his wounds. They returned to Vittoria,
aud after many hardships, with which we might swell a volume,
both recovered—marched to San Sebastian—and he had an opportunity of nobly distinguishing himself in the various actions with
the enemy that followed.

It will be recollected, that in the chapter the trial of a number of the Lancers for mutiny was mentioned, when the 8th regiment armed themselves to rescue the prisoners.—Deana was one of the accused; and the circumstances were the following:—

The Lancers, like many others, had signified their determination not to serve for more than one year. A regimental order was issued by Colonel Wakefield for all those who wished to retire at the end of one year to give in their names. More than one half of the Lancers recorded their names as desired by their Colonel. They were taken into San Sebastian, and after a few days a general Court-Martial assembled in Misericordi hospital, the place where the 8th were quartered, outside the town, and was about to try the Lancers who had given in their names in compliance with the regimental order, for mutiny. An aggravation of the charge against them arose, however, from their refusing to march out of the town. Their year had expired: and they resolved among themselves not to go out of San Sebastian. They were marched to the gate, Captain H———y's troop being in front. They had formed four deep, and on coming to the gate, the four right hand men in front stood still. Any of the others would have done the same; but this accidentally, of course, caused these four to be marked as ringleaders. These were Corporal Montgomery (formerly a Scotch Grey), Deana, Daniel Tobin, and Alexander Pearson.

It was then ordered that a regiment of infantry should be brought in to march the men of the Lancers out as prisoners. The 7th and 9th were thought of, but these regiments knowing the nature of the business, and being resolved not to serve any longer themselves, absolutely refused to march one step towards San Sebastian. The 6th and 8th Scotch were in a state of mutiny at the time—they could not be depended on;—the other regiments were on duty, save the 10th Irish, and that corps having been at a distance, where nothing of the mutiny was known at the time, four companies came primed and loaded, and marched out the four prisoners to be tried. The members of the Court were Major Stevenson (President), Adjutant-General La Marchant, Major Baker, Captain Heley, Lieutenant Middleton, Lieutenant Francis, Cornet Ryan, Cornet Heley, attended by Colonel Wakefield. The men were sentenced to receive, Montgomery and Pearson, five hundred lashes each; Deana and Tobin three hundred lashes each. Though a form of a Court-mar-

tial had been gone through, yet the men had been, as is common
with most court-martials, condemned before they were tried, for all
the flogging apparatus was brought out, and put in readiness previous to the trial commencing. The result was what was stated,
when describing the mutiny in the 8th regiment. That corps (the
8th) turned lawlessly out, armed themselves, rushed into where the
Court was assembled, overset the tables, and put a stop to the
proceedings; and it was not deemed prudent to put the flogging into
operation.

These mutinies being at last quelled, and the men returning,
peaceably to their duty, the action on the 1st of October was fought.
Deana distinguished himself gallantly that day, was immediately promoted to Sergeant, and the first general order which it fell to his turn
to write in the order book of his troop was one stating that the services of Captain H——y, of the Lancers, were dispensed with, and
that he was therefore cashiered from the service! and for what?—
Cowardice!—absent from the engagement without leave. Fit termination to such services as his had been. Mrs. Deana, by frugality and great industry, saved a considerable sum of money in the
Legion, and with her husband is in a profitable business in East-
street, Walworth, London.

It would not be doing justice to the character of H——y nor to
the men who suffered by him were I not to mention some other circumstances attending his misconduct, not that I think it necessary
to write more in proof of what he was, but to shew what overbearing officers may do to injure a regiment—an army—even the whole
campaign, and the cause for which it is waged.

The men galled to desperation under him, deserted to the enemy.
One day a sergeant and six men were on piquet, and rode across
the lines to the Carlists. Their names were Sergeant Bailie, Privates
Brush—Barryman—Knowley—Davies—Hutchine, and another; one
of these had not mounted piquet in the usual way, but Bailie having
with the others determined to desert, came down to the quarters,
said that he required another man for piquet—got the one he wished
to have, and proceeded to disclose the secret to him. A Corporal
Cox was with them who would not desert on account of his wife who
was with the regiment. They did not insist on his going—but
loaded their pistols and carbines, and swore that if he moved until

they were across the lines, they would turn and fire on him. They got safely into the Carlist country, and received sixty dollars for their horses and arms, that is £13 sterling, a small sum certainly for a horse, saddle, bridle, iance, sword, carbine, pistol, belts and ammunition, but a good sum for men who had not handled money for more than six months, and which could be possessed by merely riding half a mile: with the chance al so of getting home to their own country. These men got safely home, as did most of those who deserted; the Carlists sending them into France, and the French sending them to England.

This desertion tollowing close on some others created much excitement among the officers in superior command. It was alleged that Captain H——y's ill-treatment of the men was the cause, A kind of Court of Inquiry, though not a regular one, was appointed to enquire into the truth of these allegations, at which the Captain himself was present. The enquiry proceeded by the men being severally asked in his presence if he ill-treated them. They all as might have been expected, declined making any charge, believing it to be better to bear old insults rather than provoke new punishments by telling the truth.

Another unfortunate man cf the lancers was a Sergeant Fletcher, This man's history was as extraordinary, as his end was melancholy. I shall relate a few passages of his biography.

A few years ago, a Captain Moss of sporting notoriety, was well known in the county of Nottingham. He had been an officer in the British army, had retired, — married a lady of fortune, and kept a splendid establishment of hunters, &c. Among other whimsical methods he took to spend money, was the driving of a stage coach, which he purchased and drove himself between Derby and Nottingham, carrying passengers free. He also distinguished himself by performing the character of Rob Roy in the Nottingham theatre, and some other places. When last about that part of the country, he was forty years of age, and will be remembered by many people particularly I believe by Mr. Hutcheson, Mr. Pearson, and Mr. Wilmot, of Nottingham, with whom he was intimately connected. He was a man though extremely eccentric, of quick sensibility, and when as a matter of course his fortune began to fail, he felt an unwillingness to seek support of those friends whose sober counsel he had probably laughed at when in the stream of his career. His wife had the prudence to retain her income for herself which enables her still

to live in independent affluence, in the town of Southampton.
What were the causes of difference between him and his lady, or
whether there were any substantial grievances existing between them
other than those that we may suppose would arise from his eccentric
habits, I am not sufficiently informed to say. But in the month of
July, or August, 1835, he joined the 1st Lancers of the Legion in
Spain, under the name of Fletcher, and was appointed sergeant. He
was a tall fine looking man, with large black whiskers, as I remember, and was highly respected by several gentlemen of rank, who
were in the service, and who had formerly known him. Through
some of these he was about to be promoted to a commission, which,
no doubt would have been speedily done, had not the indiscretion of
those who formed the different regiments choked themselves overfull
with officers, many of whom were worth nothing ; which for a time
rendered it impossible to take advantage of the services of those
useful men who were found serving in the ranks, Time, hardships,
and other adverse circumstances soon thinned their numbers, for
they came straggling home at various periods in *disgust* as they have
said, and thus openings were made for men of usefulness. That
Sergeant Fletcher would have had a commission, is certain had he
not during the winter which followed our formation, been taken ill
with the common diseases.

It it is painful to be a witness of human misery, of whatever kind
or whosoever suffered by, but in the case of persons whom you know
to have descended from the luxuries of life, to pine in want and woe,
I think few people will have as much revenge in them, as deny that
the degree of suffering is increased in such persons beyond what it is
in those when the distance between prosperity and adversity, has
been less.

Fletcher, in the month of February, was confined to his desolate
berth, unable to come out. He lay along side or near where Corporal Tucker was. Mr. C———, assistant surgeon in 1st Lancers
was sent to visit him and report if he was sick. It must be mentioned that Mr. C——— was one of those persons whose unaccountable conduct cannot, by any possibility, be explained, unless we, in
charity to his character as a man, suppose that some mistake was
made in taking him out to Spain as a surgeon; for certainly there
was no one in the Legion acted a more conspicuous part in degrading

the character of the service than this Mr. C———; but as there were so many honorable exceptions among the medical gentlemen there, we shall only give this youth a passing notice. He was ordered to visit Fletcher, which he did, and accused him of being drunk. The poor man could only groan a denial, when the charge of drunkenness was repeated, and a threat made that the provost and the cats would be sent up to him. It should have been stated previously, that this same assistant-surgeon made a similar report of poor Tucker's disease; when that man's legs were cut off two day's after.

Fletcher, however, was too ill for any one but C——— to have given such an opinion, and, therefore, he was not punished by the "cats," though in many cases, and in almost all the regiments, the "cats" were applied oftener to the sick, in their first stages of illness, than physic was; this is literally true. Let Colonels Shaw, Swan, Godfrey, Dixon, Kirby, Thomson, Boyd, Kinloch, or doctors Jenner, Coleman, Gannon, Taylor, Murphy, and a score of others deny it if they dare in the face of gentlemen who were officers in the same regiments with them, who maintained honourable characters, and are now suffering the shame that attaches to the officers of the Legion generally for a few having been so brutal in their behaviour.

Fletcher's case and surgeon C———'s opinion of it were reported to Dr. Lardener, the regimental medical officer of the Lancers; that gentleman immediately went to the sick man, and pronounced him to be in a high fever—ordered his removal to the hospital; and sharply reproved Mr. C——— for having so trifled with the dreadful sufferings which were then overwhelming the illfated Legion. Fletcher, when Dr. Lardner came to see him, was lying with an old dirty bed which some kind friend had procured for him, slit at the one end, into which he had crept for warmth. He wore his clothes and was altogether in a loathsome state of filth. He was taken to what was called the hospital, and died in two days from that time. There were no military funerals in Vittoria. It was not often that as many men could be had from the hard duty of piquets and guards as could bury the dead; for bodies accumulated in hospitals sometimes to a hundred at once. Some of the Lancers went for the body of Fletcher and laid it in one of the holes that were dug as general receptacles at the back of their quarters in San Francisca convent; but the feeble men were not able, as they have told me, to cover it with earth that same day. During the night a storm of snow came on, and by the time that had melted, there was not much of poor Captain Moss, alias Sergeant Fletcher, left to bury; the rats who fed on the Legion had, in less than a week, consumed the corpse, leaving only the meagre skeleton. Sergeant Major Tilbury, of the Southampton division of Yeomanry Cavalry, and many others, now in England, are persons who knew poor Fletcher well, and can give some more particulars relative to that dreadful period of the Legion's service should any reader of this wish to enquire.

CHAPTER IX.

Bread poisoned—Desertions and Spies discovered—Bakers convicted and executed—Anecdote of Colonel Kinloch—A party of infantry escorting rations taken prisoners by the Carlist Lancers, two of them and a woman make their escape, &c. &c.

WHILE the Legion lay in Vittoria during the first winter, there was nothing to vary the languid dullness save the excitement produced at times by deaths and desertions, when these happened as they sometimes were—to be attended with peculiar circumstances. We had been suffering extremities of human misery for nearly three months, when events occurred that caused great excitement amongst us. There had been at this time about fifteen hundred buried in Vittoria alone, besides what had died at other places. In the hospitals and other houses, there were nearly two thousand sick, while the most of the regiments were lying in that state which might be called convalescent, the greater portion of the men having had the fever. We lay shivering in the unfurnished houses, cold, dirty, and emaciated, gnawing the morsel of tough sapless beef, and devouring the black sour bread with a greediness that none but those who have suffered starvation can conceive. There was an allowance of spirits called aquardiente, (about one third of a pint) given to each man, and though this was unwholesome ill tasted stuff—having some resemblance to the very worst kinds of brandy and rum, when mixed together, yet the extreme cold caused men to drink it with a greedy gratification. To the horror of the dying victims, and consternation of all, it was discovered that this naturally unwholesome liquid, was mixed with poisonous ingredients, principally white lead. That the bread was poisoned with various deleterious drugs; besides straw—bones, (human and others), and chalk having been ground to powder and mixed with the flour of which the loaves were baked. The immense quantity of rations required, compared with the means of supplying them, about twenty thousand Spanish soldiers being in and about Vittoria at that time, prevented the bread from being baked properly; and often kept us a whole day without having any of it. Hence this raw stuff, which by being thrown against the wall, would stick to it like mortar, was voraciously consumed, and hence the universal disease, and great amount of mortality that destroyed so many of the Legion. The hungry jaws stood aghast! the stomach craving, and the lean visages looking at the black bread for a time with some refused it; but there was no alternative, bad as it was, there was no other, and it had to be eaten. This wholesale murder of the Legion by the Spanish bakers, was not discovered, however, until one of them had been arrested, and found guilty of another crime of treachery. This was Don Jose Elgoez, chief contractor for the Christino army. He was with his assistant in trade, accused, convicted and executed under the following circumstances.

Amongst some of those who deserted, was a man from the 7th regiment of the Legion, who, after having found himself safe and better treated as he alleged with the Carlists, wrote a letter to one of his late comrades in the 7th, persuading him to desert also. The letter contained instructions for getting safe out of the town to the Carlists, which could only be obtained by applying to Don Jose Elgoez the head baker. The man who received this letter, either unwilling to run the hazard of deserting—content to stay where he was, or expecting some reward shewed it to a Captain, who suggested the propriety of his going to the baker, and making a bargain. This the man did, and acting on the instructions of Captain Byrne agreed to bring a sergeant and a few more men whom he knew to be anxious, and only waiting an opportunity to desert; While Captain Byrne communicated his information and intentions to the colonel of his regiment and the brigadier-general. On the evening of the 24th of March, Captain Byrne having borrowed a sergeant's clothes, proceeded with seven privates of his regiment, of whom he that had the letter was one, to the house of Don Jose, and told in secret whispers that they were now ready. At the same time orders were sent round to the various guards on the gates to be on the alert as their assistance would be required during the night or early in the morning, by a party of peasants who would be going out at one of the gates as was expected.

The baker was very kind to them, and his assistant or foreman immediately began to get them covered with Spanish cloaks and other clothes so that they might have the appearance of Spanish peasants, who alone could get egress at the gates. The party, provided with the necessary mules and disguises, proceeded under the direction of the foreman to one of the gates as if going out for forage of some description. The gate was opened, and the luckless conductor had got his party outside the walls, thus making the act of treason complete,—when the concerted signal was given; the guard rushed out, took the party prisoners, and then without any loss of time proceeded to the house of Don Jose Elgoez, made him a prisoner, likewise seized all his stock in trade. In his possession were found the poisonous drugs, which had never been suspected before; but, which were now found on analization to be mixed in the bread.

This created great excitement in every quarter and among all classes of people. The criminals were both tried on the charge of treason, in being Carlist agents, and pronounced guilty. Great ransoms were offered for their lives. The principal of the two was very rich; he offered, it was said, to advance money to pay up the whole of the arrears of the Christino army if they would spare his life. Villa Real and other Carlist chiefs corresponded with Cordova, and begged his life, he having been a man of great importance in the province of Alva for a number of years. Cordova and the other authorities were inexorable, though it was said, that the large offers of money was beginning to stagger justice in them, but that General Evans interfered, and demanded that the criminals be given up to execution.

In accordance with a usual Spanish custom, the two prisoners were taken to the plaza, or principal market-place, and on two different days were stripped naked and beaten with rods. This is the manner in which all flogging is executed in Spain. The criminal, whether a soldier or a civilian, is laid with his breast on a drum, a piece of wood, a stone, or whatever is easiest got, with his back 'upwards, he lying nearly horizontally, only having a slight bend to tighten the skin. Two persons with long rods, one on each side come on alternately.

Don Jose and his accomplice in guilt received that punishment twice, previous to their being executed by the *garrot*. This instrument is peculiar 'to Spain ; and its operation is certainly the most expeditious and least unseemly way of putting criminals to death except shooting, that is now in use. The performance of choking by it is simple ; and if the French still insist that it is more vulgar than their method of cutting the head off, it is undoubtedly not so disgusting as the English mode of hanging.

A platform is erected some three feet in height, and a strong pole is driven through its centre—a seat is also added, and on this the criminal is placed with his hands tied, and resting on his knees. The *garrot* is then affixed to the pole at the proper height, and the circular iron, (attached at one extremity by a rivet, on which it moves), placed around the throat. A central piece of iron, with grooves, passes through the other—resembling in appearance a patent cork-screw. The handle is a transverse piece of iron, and when this is turned by the executioner, the screw advances closing the opposite extremity of the circular piece or neck band, in the same proportion. One half turn is sufficient to produce instant death—and the head inclines forward, over the chest, supported only by the iron which encircles the neck.

On the morning of the 28th of March, the two flank companies of each regiment and the 1st Lancers, marched into the town of Vittoria, to be present at the execution. After a delay of nearly five hours during which we were all tired by standing in the plaza or square ; we formed around the platform, fixed bayonets, and stood at attention. The muffled drums beating a dead march were heard, and the two criminals attended by about twenty priests, were seen moving slowly down an opening made purposely in the ranks of the military. The baker it was said paid largely for his salvation, for in many of the churches the service for the dead was performed all the day, while around the scaffold the attending clergy prayed with great perseverance and apparent earnestness for him. The Chapel-gorris on the other hand crowded the balconies of the houses, and cheered with derisive shouts the appearance of the prisoners on the platform. Don Jose ascended first, and after speaking for about two minutes with his confessor, and taking the sacrament, his hands were bound down—the collar was put around his neck—the execu-'tioner gave the handle of the screw a turn, and the ill-fated baker was dead. Immediately after, the other was brought up, and the same operation was as speedily performed with him; the Spanish soldiers shouting loudly as the screw got the extinguishing turn. A cloth had been thrown over the faces previous to the execution : it was now removed, and the faces were seen bare without any distor-tion of the features or even discolour of skin, which proved that the death must have been instantaneous. The bodies were left on the scaffold for three hours, to be gazed at by the mob that gathered around, and a spectator who did not know the nature of the death, would have supposed them to have been two men sitting comfortably down to be shaved.

About this time an incident in the life of Colonel Kinloch occurred which deserves to be recorded. The Colonel was a man whose taste for a military life consisted mostly in his love of gaudy display. There was no horse pranced more proudly beneath a gallant rider than did the steed that bore Colonel Kinloch. No romantic warrior—not even King Murat—displayed more splendour in plumage and trap-pings than the gallant Colonel K. did. One morning as he headed his lancers through the streets of Vittoria, and led them outwards to Salvateira, the fair Spaniards beheld him in admiration,—they crowded the balconies as he rode along—and the dark eyes and soft hearts recorded the impression of his matchless figure. The soldiers saw his plumes wave and his horse prance, and enquired or told each other who he was. English officers envied ; and Spanish offi-cers accorded their admiring respect for the honour done to their cause by the service of such a noble and gallant looking Englishman. The balls began to whiz ; and what was at first a mere skirmish was growing into a sharp engagement. The Lancers were ordered for-ward. The Colonel began to think himself rather too conspicuous ; for the distinguishing ornaments of himself and horse, which had attracted the Christino eyes to admire, now drew the sharp-shooting eyes of the Carlist fusileers to pay him dangerous compliments. He dismounted, and ordering his servant, who was in the rear with another horse, to dismount also, he exchanged, denuding himself at the same time of his feathers, and putting on a sober unostentatious forage cap! Murat fought in the battle-field with a dress and manner as theatrical as if he had been on a stage—and he became a king. Poor Colonel K., who aspired to be that immortal hero's parallel, put on his forage cap,—gave the command to Major Rait, —did not fight at all, and thus became nobody. Such is sometimes the different fate of aspiring men.

The following Extract is from the Journal of an Officer of the Staff relative to this engagement, and some other events.

January, 16th.—Yesterday there was a grand movement of the troops; the English marching forward from the villages they occupied, in the direction of Salvatierra;—the French Legion and Cordova, on the road to France:—and the division of Espartero, on that of Bilboa. At an early hour, Cordova found himself engaged, and the action lasted until midnight, It terminated, however, without any decided advantage to either party, each occupying its own ground the close. To-day, a good number of wounded have come in, (about 150), and a few of the French Legion. The English, on the right, had but little work, the principal force of the Carlists having been collected in the centre of those three roads already named. One or two only were killed, and two officers, and three privates, wounded. A gallant charge was made on this occasion by the Grenadier company of the 3rd, who drove half a battalion of Carlists, at the point of the bayonet, from a wood of which they had taken possession, at which they at first showed symptoms of determination to hold. At the close of this charge, the officer commanding it, Captain Fitzgerald, was wounded in the leg, and borne off the field. Of nine officers of the Queen's army wounded, there were two of Cordova's personal staff,—one a Captain Santrago Y'Hoppe.

January 19th.—This day the Spanish and English head-quarters returned to Vittoria, the several divisions of the combined army having fallen back upon the villages they had previously occupied. An attempt at an advance was indeed impracticable, by reason of

'the dense frost and fog, that has continued to prevail for several
·days. The only casualties that have occurred since the 10th, have
been the deaths of a Sergeant of the 2nd regiment, and a young
man of the Commissiare, (a Mr. Street), both of whom were shot
in advance of the troops, while entering a village they supposed to
be perfectly safe. The bodies are said to have been immediately
stripped, and shockingly mangled. The servant of Mr. Street, a
man of the 7th, who was with his master at the time, had a most
narrow escape, having received at least a dozen lance wounds in
various parts of his body. So closely was his contest with the man
who attacked him carried on, that he repeatedly grappled with the
lance, in a vain endeavor to wrest it from his enemy, whose horse
he twice threw down by passing under him. He is now in the hospital for the wounded here, and with every fair chance of recovering.

January 22nd.—Vittoria may, in truth, be said at this moment
to be the city of death. Day after day, the poor fellows of our
Legion are carried in bullock carts, to their graves, and all they have
to cover them is a sheet;—the officers, long unpaid by the Spanish
Government, being utterly unable to afford their men the customary
means of interment. The prevailing fever has at length been pronounced by the faculty, to be typhus of the worst kind. Whatever
it be, it is making fearful ravages in the Legion.

Captain Santrago Y'Hoppe, Cordova's Aid-de-camp, who had
died of his wounds, received on the 16th, was buried yesterday, and
the manner of interment pleased me much. Instead of the lid of the
coffin being screwed down, as with us, it was carried separately by
four bearers. The body itself, partly visible above the edge of its
last tenement, was habited in full uniform,—the arms were folded
across the chest, and the features, placid to a degree, seemed
rather to wear the repose of slumber than of death. The cocked hat
placed on the top of the head, moreover, lent to the whole an en-
semble as touching as it was military in effect, and, as a soldier, I
felt that thus I should wish to be borne to my grave, after falling in
the field of glory.

January 24th.—To day I rode out with Colonel Wylde, (who has
been almost constantly with the Legion, and who, by his sound advice, based on his intimate and accurate knowledge of the country,
and of the contending parties, has, on more occasions than one

considerably advantaged our cause,) to see the conbined force of
Spaniards, French, and English, who were making a demonstration
in front of the castle of Guabara; but all their efforts to draw the
enemy out proved ineffectual. With the black flag flying at the
top of the building, they prudently kept themselves under cover of
its walls, content, as usual, with exchanging a few shots. Two parties of cavalry, however, met, and in a successful charge by that of
the Queen, a Carlist Lieutenant-Colonel was made prisoner. He
was immediately run through the body by a dozen lances, in revenge,
as the Spaniards said, for the brutal murder of Mr. Street. The
movement towards Guabara was intended, principally, to cover an
advance of Espartero. The day was exceedingly fine, and the *coup
d'œil* offered by the various divisions and brigades in position, highly
picturesque : nor was the effect less striking, as they moved off, in
succession, to occupy the various bivouacks of the morning.

January 26th,—The true position of the Legion, which I have
cursorily touched upon, some few days since, on the 16th, 17th,
and 18th, was as follows :—On the 15th, Evans received Cordova's
order to march to the Salvatierra road, and engage the attention of
the enemy at a small village then occupied by them, called Mandigar,
while he moved by the centre. Four Carlist battalions made their
appearance, one of which only had possession of the village, from
which they were driven several times in the course of the day. True
to his instructions, which were to act chiefly on the defensive, the
Lieutenant-General caused the regiment then engaged, to retire upon
the main body. This emboldened the enemy, who threw half a
battalion in advance, into a wood at the foot of the village, from
whence they kept up a smart fire. It was at this crisis that a company of the 3rd were thrown forward, who, with the usual war cry,
dashed into the wood at the point of the bayonet, and cleare d it,
although opposed by double their number. *Par parenthese*, we may
as well remark, that the 3rd, or Westminster Grenadiers, are part
of the "Isle of Dogians," whose original appearance excited so much
mirth among the Tories, and whom I had the *honor* to command at
their first formation. Night put an end to the partial contest, and
the General retired, as commanded, into cantonments.

On the following day, having heard a continual firing on the left,
in the direction Cordova had taken, he moved the Legion to the

THE ESCAPE OF MRS. MILLAR FROM THE CARLISTS.

Page 196.

No 12.

heights of Zoazo and Marietta, about a league and a half from Cordova's position, there to await any order that might arrive from the General. But, although there was an incessant fire kept up throughout the day, no directions were sent to General Evans, as to what course he was to pursue ; here, therefore, they bivouacked. On the close of the 18th the Lieutenant-General, still uncertain of the actual position of Cordova, determined on taking a party of Dragoons, and, with his staff, repair across the enemy's country to ascertain the true state of affairs."

The village of El Burgo was for a few days the quarters of the brigade to which I belonged, and in that place we suffered all the privations that human beings can be supposed to endure. It was the middle of January. Snow, frost, hunger, and filthy vermin were literally destroying us, and on getting within the walls of the ruined houses as we entered El Burgo, we considered ourselves fortunate in getting such good quarters. This was occasioned by the three previous days which had froze and snowed incessantly while we lay all the time on the heights of Arlaban awaiting the movements of Cordova the commander-in-chief. During these three days we had got nothing but a lean bullock which our pioneers of the 8th met with by accident, and which, divided as it was among five hundred men and officers, offered but a meagre meal. There was no bread to be had and the lean tasteless beef was eaten by some, myself, among others, without any cooking whatever. General Evans and the Legion being betrayed by Cordova, left to perish if they chose among the snow,—which numbers of men did lose their lives by,—we conceived, even the ruined huts of El Burgo to be palaces as we entered them. It was one day while we were in this place, that an event occured which I must relate.

The morning parade, and two hours drill, had just been dismissed, and the unremitting universal regimental question of, " do you see the muleteers coming yet," was being asked by every one, and of every one that was met in the village. The muleteers and pioneers of the regiment had gone to Vittoria a few miles off, for two days, bread and beef which was due to us, and griping hunger caused every one to be on the outlook for their return. Mid-day came, and afternoon came—but not the *pang* and the *carne*, as it was called in spanish. Officers and men all enquired what could be keeping the muleteers.

At last an alarm was raised that cavalry, at a gallop, were seen coming into the village ; the alarm spread, and men running to see swore at the cavalry and asked, why were the mules not coming with the rations. What had appeared to be cavalry at a distance, resolved itself into one solitary rider, who came flying at full speed calling, " Oh Bob Millar ! Bob Millar ! did you ever think to see your wife in this guise?—Oh Bob take me off the horse," This was uttered in a hasty exclamation, as a horse foaming in sweat and splashed with blood gallopped past the guard house, where a sergeant Millar was on guard, —carrying on its back, as he had just time to observe, his dear wife Nancy. Her long black hair hung wildly around her, and the cap that held on by one string streamed behind.—" Bob, oh Bob stop the horse," was heard indistinctly again as she glided away, and poor Bob standing astonished,—but she was gone. She sat in regular masculine style astride the saddle, and all eyes were strained after her. Rations, and hunger were forgotten for the moment, for every man was confounded at what he had seen. The horse at last writhing in agony and having nearly bled to exhaustion was intercepted in ¦his flight by some soldiers, and Mrs. Millar dismounted. At first there was mirth as her husband and others came running around on seeing her in such a plight ; but the extraordinary pace at which she had rode, and the wounded horse caused suspicion to arise that something serious had happened. Her first explanations confirmed the suspicions. Mirth, at her unfeminine ride suddenly subsided into grief, for the causes of that grief were twofold. The mules,—rations, —pioneers, quarter-master-sergeant, and muleteers had been taken by a detachment of the Carlists cavalry, and she had seen most of the men slaughtered, and the mules and rations marching off to the hungry Carlists, previous to her escaping.

At this intelligence, the whole regiment sorrowed for their poor comrades, but no doubt those who were most hungry, had the severer grief. One of the party, sergeant Bayne, on seeing the Carlists spring from their ambush, drew his sword, and ordered his own men to stand fast. They could not by any possibility have withstood the Carlists, these being about fifty mounted horsemen, while the party attacked consisted only of thirteen armed men on foot, and about a half dozen muleteers who were not armed. Yet though some of them might have escaped, none who were there attempted to run.

The quartermaster was with them, who on being ordered, gave up his sword without offering to defend himself. Bayne, the sergeant of the party, was ordered to submit by a Carlist officer, but instead of giving up his sword he ran the officer to the heart with it, and called loudly to the other men to fight to the last. There were five or six of the Carlists brought to the ground by our men, when one prisoner (the quartermaster), had only been taken and only three killed. The Carlists seeing such determined resistance, closed on the handful of men, and soon slaughtered them; but not until, as they themselves admitted, Bayne had killed three of his assailants with his single sword. This gallant fellow received a lance in his left arm at the beginning of the affray, and he now fell overpowered, and was literally cut to pieces, his body being found afterwards dreadfully mutilated. Three or four. of the others were taken prisoners alive, and with the quartermaster, were put to death in the most brutal and torturing manner in the Carlist's quarters, in presence of several Englishmen, who were at the time in the camp of Don Carlos.

While the party were securing the prisoners, after having killed Bayne, and were also gathering the mules with their loads together, they gave Mrs. Millar, who was one of the party, the quarter-master's horse to hold. While they were engaged in collecting their spoil, and in pursuing two pioneers, who, being mounted on mules and not having been up with the party, had escaped, she mounted into the saddle, and starting at a gallop, made off. One of them sprung a lance into her horse, and some others fired, which, having wounded, made the animal gallop the more furiously; until, as was before mentioned, she reached the regiment at El Burgo with the dismal tidings.

The two who were making their escape by not having been with the party, were now in an alarm doubly frightful, as they did not know, on a division of cross roads, which to take. They knew that one led to the Carlist lines, and the other to El Burgo; but not having been that way previously, they could not determine which to take. Venturing some distance on one of the branches, they met a peasant of whom they enquired: he told them to go direct forward. From the situation of some hills at a distance, they supposed that they were wrong, when they met with two other peasants (or paysàns, as the word is pronounced in Spain); one of these immediately in-

formed them that they were wrong, while the other insisted they
were right, and urged them to go forward.   At this moment, some
of the cavalry were seen coming at a distance behind.   One of them,
named Thomson, said he would go straight on at all hazards; the
other, named Dennis, dashed off the road into the field, in the direction of the other road; seeing which, the peasants tried to stop him,
and kept up a pursuit, as there were some hedges in front which
they probably thought would enable them to come up with the prey;
for it is likely, that seeing the two separate, they thought of taking
one a prisoner, and sharing the booty of wine which the mules carried, between themselves, or of carrying it with the prisoner to the
Carlist army.   Dennis saw them pursue, and heard them call to him
to halt; he saw the cavalry making in his direction; he saw the
hedges before him, and again on looking behind, he saw Thomson
on his mule, leaving the road which he probably discovered to be
the wrong one.   Dennis whipped his mule to a gallop.   The distant
sounds of shots, and the long whizzing of two or three balls passing,
proved to him the necessity of speed, as the pursuing party were now
within shot of him and were firing.   He observed a gap in a hedge,
at some distance to the right of the direction he was taking.   Towards
this he turned the mule, and waved to Thomson to make for it also,
by a direct course from where he then was through another field.
Thomson either did not observe the signal, or could not get the mule
across the ditch which skirted the road; for Dennis, on making the
gap which he had turned aside for, and which let him out of his
pursuers' sight, turned round and saw Thomson entering the field
through which he himself had come, and three Carlist lancers had
just entered at the same time, and were crossing to intercept him.
As nothing more was seen or heard of Thomson, his fate can scarcely
be doubted; especially, as a woman belonging to El Burgo told us
that one of the *Ingleses* was lying dead in a field—which field, on
inquiry, we found to be the one spoken of by Dennis.   He corroborated Mrs. Millar's account of Serjeant Bayne and his party, so far
as he had been able to judge from the distance of two hundred yards,
from which he had witnessed their conflict.   Dennis, shortly after
this, went into the hospital, and died of the common destroying malady of the time.

From sheer necessity, we had to go a plundering that night to get something to satisfy torturing appetites, as we had by this means lost our rations. The 4th regiment had their supply and very much to their dissatisfaction, the General of the Brigade ordered them to share the half to us. That, for men who had nothing for two days amounted to about eight ounces of bread, and four or five ounces of lean beef to each,—this was soon swallowed, and then we set out to look for more. My company and another fell in with a calf, which within twenty minutes of being discovered was divided into above two hundred stomachs. Some knowing ones suggested, that where there was a calf, there was probably a cow also. This hint was acted on. The cow was discovered, and ere the place of her late residence was known to one half of the brigade, she was no more— save the horns and skin. Then flour was discovered, and again another cow, which with two or three pigs, made altogether one of the most luxurious nights of feasting that we up to this period had enjoyed in the campaign.

CHAPTER X.

Extract from an Officer's Journal — Awful execution of the Chapelgorris — Melancholy end of Sergeant Rielly—Dreadful atrocities under the Durango Decree —Lancers taken prisoner and burned to death—Miseries in Vittoria farther described.

The following is from the journal of an officer, which has been forwarded to me.

"Vittoria, December 12th.— This day (Sunday), has been re_markable for a cruel tragedy — one which will long live in the memory of the brave, although it must be admitted, lawless Chapelgorris. The facts connected with it are as follow : —

Some time ago a party of these latter attacked a Carlist village called La Bastide, in Alava, and succeeded in driving the enemy out. A priest, who was among the number of fugitives, was shot in the act of flying with the Carlists; and the Chapelgorris, on their return to the village, plundered the church, and drank wine out of the chalice. A representation of this fact was made known to the Government of Madrid, with this important alteration in the true version of the story,— that the priest had been murdered in the church,— and simply with a view to subsequent spoliation. Espartero, the commander of the division here, was accordingly written to, and strongly censured for having suffered the commission of such an outrage. The measure he immediately took to justify himself, and punish the offenders, was fearfully summary. The whole of the Chapelgorris were this morning marched a few miles on the Miranda road, and, without being in the slightest degree aware of what was in preparation, were ordered to ascend a rising ground,— the same where the French batteries were planted which did so much execution during the advance upon Vittoria by Lord Wellington's army. Here they found a body of 6,000 infantry, the horse artillery which had preceded them from Vittoria, and a considerable number of cavalry, already drawn up. Having completed the ascent, they were halted, and ordered to pile their arms, from which they were commanded to move some distance. The cavalry now rode up between the Chapelgorris and their muskets, forming a guard to these latter. Then, for the first time, the poor fellows began to form a suspicion of what was intended against them, and several moved as if to repossess themselves of their arms; but the cavalry drove them back, and they were left helpless. Espartero, who commanded in person at this scene, now ordered that lots should be cast for decimation. The command was obeyed, and the unfortunates stood apart from their astonished and indignant comrades. The first ten of this devoted number were again selected, and these were inevitably to die. Among them was a fine young man, a Frenchman, and, as his comrades assert, a nephew of Lafitte. This youth, scarcely nineteen, was an object of general interest, both from his appearance, and the earnest manner in which he avowed his innocence of all crime that could possibly lead to such an end. But his judge was inexorable, and he was compelled to share the lot of his companions. His fate once decided, he thought only of dying as best became a brave soldier; and when told to turn his back to the firing party, he refused, saying that he was no traitor, and that he had too often faced the bullets of his enemies, to fear those of his comrades now. Then, waving his cap, he tossed it in the air, and told them he was ready to die like a Frenchman.

Thus have perished ten of our old San Sebastian friends. It happens, unfortunately for them, that General Evans is absent, or his intercession with Espartero might have obtained them their lives,

December 16th.—The affair of the poor Chapelgorris has been the subject of general conversation in the Legion, for the last few days. and the conduct of Espartero disignated as any thing but merciful. Even Jauregui himself is deeply chagrined and pained, it is said, so much so, as to be obliged to keep his bed. It is a singular circumstance that a nephew of his own, in the ranks of the Chapelgorris, stood eleventh, originally for the list for decimation; but a yet more remarkable fact may be recorded. Among the ten who received the fatal fire, was a young man to whom Jauregui was particularly partial; —the only ball by which he was hit slightly grazed his ear or neck, sufficiently to draw blood, and he had the presence of mind to throw himself down, and continue perfectly still, as if struck by a mortal wound. Here he remained until the troops had withdrawn, when he was removed to the quarters of Jauregui, where he is at this moment; and where the gallant El Pastor declares he shall continue unharmed and untouched.

A visible change has been effected in the manner of the Chapelgorris generally. To the sprightliness and enjouement of character, which distinguished these men from all other spanish soldiers, has succeeded a reserve and dispiritedness, that proclaim how much, and how deeply, they have felt the tragic occurrence of Sunday last, This force has hitherto been composed of a mixture of Spaniards and foreigners; but, within the last two days, the whole of the latter, chiefly French and Italian, have been taken from the corps, and moved off, with the intention of being sent to their respective countries. This may be politic, but it will sadly lessen the efficiency of the corps, on whom great reliance has hitherto been placed :—not the less, for having these same Frenchmen and Italians of their number. Many of the Spaniards are dissatisfied with the arrangement, and, as all are volunteers who may quit the service at their pleasure, it is supposed not a few will disband themselves, and return to San Sebastian, at the first favorable opportunity. To day I conversed with one of them, and he declared, with tears in his eyes, he would no longer remain after what had occured. He was at the affair of La Bastide himself, and although he admits that he and his companions plundered the church, and drank wine out of the chalice, he swears positively that the priest was killed in fair fight, and while fleeing with the Carlists, —both parties having sustained some loss in killed. He moreover asserted, and repeated his assertion, that so far from Espartero being dissatisfied with their conduct on that day, he was the first to encourage them, by exclaiming, " Good, Chapelgorris, good ; you have behaved well." But, he added, with strong emotion, produced by the recollection of the recent fate of his comrades,—" it is only to shield himself, and court favour with the government, that he has done this deed."

Among the many misfortunes that befel the Legion at this time, and particularly individual soldiers, perhaps the most distressing was the fate of a lancer named Rielly. This man, before going to Spain, had been a bricklayer, and lived in Chelsea, where I believe he was well known among his fellow-workmen. The lancers were one day exercising their horses outside Vittoria, when that of Rielly became restive, and though he was a good rider, almost unmanageable. Being only in "watering order," his bit was not sufficiently powerful for a fractious-tempered and hard-mouthed horse, which, on the animal breaking off with him, rendered restraint impossible. From a cross canter the speed increased to a gallop, and that in a direction outwards from Vittoria. The men at first thought that Rielly had given his horse head, purposely to tire him ; but they soon observed that the rider was making every effort to pull up and could not. Suspense became painful. Onwards the mad animal bore, direct into the Carlist lines. Some suspected that he had intended to desert ; but others who knew him better would not believe that ; especially as his wife and children, of whom he was extremely fond, were with the regiment in Vittoria. Suspicions of his design to join the Carlists were at last completely allayed, and unmingled pity for him filled every one who heard his fate. It was ascertained that the horse having gained a height where there was a descent in the direction that his unchecked career tended, and Rielly finding it impossible to pull up, as he was now descending into the Carlist camp, threw himself off, and was making the best of his speed on foot to regain his comrades, when a party of Carlists pursued, overtook, and carried him into their quarters. Here his fate was soon decided. The bloody decree of Durango did not spare even this hapless man. Death, cruel, abominably cruel in its execution, was instantly inflicted, or at least commenced, and in presence of English officers who were in the service of Don Carlos.

I disclaim any political partiality in making the remarks which I am here forced to make. Even I have elsewhere stated my opinion to be, that many of those who make up the ranks of Don Carlos, had a cause for which they were, and are still fighting, that was as sacred as the religion, rights, and privileges of the Basquese could make it. But let holy justice keep us from mingling our sympathies for these brave, deluded, and ill-fated people, with the cause of Don Carlos, and the object of many of the chiefs who fight in his name. Legally, I believe he has a right to the crown of Spain; religiously and morally, he has none; nor had he before the present struggle commenced. His whole life had disqualified him. Now his deeds, more black in infamy than any recorded among the iniquities of ancient tyrants, have to an inexpressible degree heightened the disqualification. We might there let him wither in the hatred of mankind, after we had warned readers to beware of valuing the Carlist cause by the claims of the Basque peasants, were there not other parties with whom we are closely allied, that it becomes imperatively a duty to allude to in this record.

Michael Burke Honan who wrote a book called the " Court and Camp of Don Carlos," and who has been for some years reporter of Spanish news to the *Morning Herald*, with Lord Raneleigh and other Englishmen witnessed many of the executions under the Durango decree. Lord Raneleigh, Captains Dixon, Henningson and many other officers, whose enthusiasm of opposition to the government led them to join the Don, have long since returned to England, tired of the wasting, fruitless, and interminable war. In justice to these officers we may charitably suppose, that the horrid atrocities committed in the Court and Camp, in which they were adventurers, prematurely disgusted them. But there is not one case of an English prisoner having been saved by their interposition, though they were witnesses to the murder of many. Mr. Honan and the correspondent of the *Post* may have interposed, I believe in one or two cases they did; and though unsuccessfully, still they are entitled to the credit of intended humanity or momentary sympathy for a victimised fellow-countryman. But what value are we to put on their humanity when we consider, that the two last, for a small sum of money, scarcely an income that would rank them with a respectable English tradesman, have witnessed the barbarous executions under the Decree, and have not only withheld the truth, but have misled their employers and that portion of the English public, which read their correspondence, by giving reports utterly false. They saw Reilly brought in a prisoner ; they had seen the cause of his being in the hands of his enemies and their friends. He implored mercy ! the Spaniards, who knew not the English tongue, might suppose that the incessant prayer of their victim was for the mildness of mercy, but they did not know that he prayed for his wife and children ;—they did not know that he appealed to the Englishmen, who stood by, to interpose for him. But these Englishmen knew, and though they might not have been able to save him, which I believe they were not, for the decree was irrevocable, still they saw the manner of his death, and never made it known to England. He died under the Durango decree as did many others. This was known in England ; and the knowledge filled our country with humane disgust. But the history of New Zealand, or Algiers, or even the Spanish Inquisition itself, of which Don Carlos is the worthy champion, have not afforded cases of barbarous atrocity greater, if even parallels, than those executions under the Durango Decree. In some cases the victims were shot when there was no time to get up a spectacle of public amusement. The execution was sometimes hastened to a merciful conclusion by a prisoner being accidentally killed when the first operations began ; or at other times designedly slain, by the chances existing of a rescue from the Christino enemy.

The prisoners when taken were commonly conveyed some distance into the interior, or at least as far inside the Carlist lines as the public exhibition could go on without danger of interruption. The modes of putting the victims to death were various, according to the ingenuity of the priests, who were mostly charged with its infliction, or the diabolical whims of those who were appointed to inflict the torture. In the case of Cunningham, Donaldson, M'Gregor and M'Leod who were taken when unarmed from the 6th regiment, the execution was inflicted by two demoniacal priests, and other people brought from a distance for the special purpose; merely because they were considered as adepts in the art of torture, or were devotees of religion, Cunningham, on proving himself to be a true Catholic, was favored by instant death ; which Mr. Honan of the Herald says he was a witness of. He mentions that the first one, which must have been Cunningham, faltered a little, and seemed about to sink from nervelessness, when it was speedily over with him ; but that he did not see the death of the others, having retired from the awful scene.

It is undeniably true—and many officers and men now in England will recollect that the deserters who came into San Sebastian told the circumstance—besides some of the people of Astigarraga when we afterwards took these places, that *three* of the four men were not shot as the first one was, but were kept two days for public amusement and to prove the faith of devotees. Also there are men now in England who were at that time with the Carlists and can prove, that, when the first one (Cunningham) was shot, there was a cry of disapprobation from a crowd of people, who had collected from distant parts to do themselves *an holy office* by having a hand in the death of the heretical prisoners.

God forbid ! that I should be suspected of giving offence to the professors of the catholic religion in this country by refering to these atrocities which I am about to describe, and which were mixed up with religious ceremony. But such outrages on all laws divine and human having been committed in Spain, in the camp of Don Carlos, in the name of the catholic religion, and politically supported, as his cause is, by those parties who are on the opposite extremity in this country—I fear not the hostility of catholic, or protestant—the religion of the one, or the politics of the other, or the prejudices of both ; for humanity and reason will rise superior to cruelty and superstition equally in the catholic as in the protestant. The Spanish catholic priesthood were perpetrators of the most abhorrent crimes, because a party demanded their superstitious support for political purposes. The organs, or instructors of English protestants, were daily witnesses of these abhorrent crimes and kept them hidden in hypocritical obscurity because to do so was suitable for *their* political purposes. The political knave of England, and the religious murderer of Spain have one cause. If the crime of the Spanish perpetrator was blacker than that of his English spectator the other sunk into, comparatively deeper crime when he stood by to see the immolation of his own countrymen on the altar of religious and political fanaticism, merely because they were protestants or at least not catholics.

They were all put to death because they were prisoners taken from an enemy which was barbarous enough, and is the sole and only cause of any disgust that exists in this country against Don Carlos among his political partizans, —— But that does not include the crimes of Carlos — Neil Cunningham was a prisoner, but being a catholic he obtained the mercy of instant death. The others were not catholics, therefore, a share in their death was a virtue. Public notice was given of the intended immolation that the priests had got a sacrifice, and devotees crowded from the surrounding country. The three men, Robert Donaldson, Walter M'Gregor and Donald M'Leod — the two first from Glasgow, the latter a native of Inverness—were tied up each to a pole and were stripped naked. A priest approached, made the sign of the cross and cut off the right ear of one. This was a signal for others to follow, so as a wound was inflicted there was no particular rule to observe; but it is a disgusting fact provable by witnesses who saw it and incontradictable by Mr. Honan, of the protestant Morning Herald, or any other correspondent ot English Carlist newspapers, that the religious virtue of the devotee was in proportion to the nature of the wound inflicted. The greater pain, or even indecency—but indecency was covered by heavier shame—or the greatest ingenuity, shewn in maiming the victim, was the greatest virtue.

How can it be told, but told it must be, that even females were known to purchase great reputation for devotion, by cutting the bodies with scissors—the naked bodies of these three men, in a manner that brings crime to a climax, and excites disgust to the extremity of abhorrence. One of them died in about an hour, having bled to death. Another prayed to be out of pain, six hours after his fingers and toes had been cut off: and the third, (supposed to be M'Gregor from the description of his person,) was still lingering the second day, having been upwards of forty hours tied to the post in the public green, outside of Hernani gate. To prevent his being killed too soon, a priest stood by him, not allowing any more wounds, after the first day, to be inflicted; but pronouncing a blessing on all those who came forward to spit on the victim, or offer some other insult.

Such was the execution of these men, taken on the 4th of March, 1837, when having left their picquet to get wood at some old houses to make a fire for themselves and comrades, they were unexpectedly seized by a party of armed Carlists. These had frequently observed the English piquet send down men to the old houses for wood, and had at this time secreted themselves during the night, when seven unsuspecting men went down as usual to provide fuel. Two of the seven were not in the house, and theretore escaped. Another was taken, but was recognised by a Carlist soldier, who had formerly made acquaintance with him, when both happened to be on the extreme out-piquets. The man belonging to the Legion had given the Carlist tobacco, and received favours in return, in a very dangerous way certainly, but still by a friendship, that by the accounts of old soldiers has been often made up between the piquets of opposing armies. In this case, the Carlist soldier recognised an acquaintance; and as he and others said afterwards, they would have let the whole escape, had it not been for the officer who commanded their party: but on hurriedly rounding the houses to make off with their prisoners, the Carlist gave the other a push behind him, and told him to *vamos* (to be off). The officer in a minute after, observed him running, and ordered this same man who let him off, to fire. The Carlist fired, but missed intentionally, and the officer not deeming it prudent to discharge any more muskets, as they had four prisoners, these three got leave to escape. Captain Wood, who saw them at a distance, could have destroyed the whole by the discharge of a shell from Lugariz battery; but deeming the death of his own men no retaliation, he suffered them to go, and they were speedily out of sight; he hoping, that his forbearance in not firing might obtain mercy for the men. How he was deceived has been already detailed.

I have particularised the execution of these men : instead of saying anything more about Rielly, as the manner of his death was uncertain; but deserters from the Carlists agreed, and men who deserted to the Carlists and have now come home, agree in saying, that such a man taken prisoner under such circumstances, was put to death by the Decree.

Shortly after him *eleven* lancers fell into the Carlists' hands, when outside of the gates of Vittoria, looking for forage. I am unable to give the names of these poor fellows; only one of the party of twelve —named Montgomery, who has been alluded to elsewhere, on coming to the gate, refused to go out, as the appearance of the country,—

they being on foot and unarmed—was dangerous. Montgomery returned to the regiment, but the other eleven never ; their deaths were even more horrible, if horror could be increased, than those that have been mentioned before. They were tied to trees, and fires of green wood kindled that would not burn too soon nor extinguish life speedily :— the Carlist soldiers amusing themselves by throwing in cartridges into the fire, exploding them about the tortured wretches. And while such inhuman barbarity was the almost daily exercise of the Carlist executioners:—the correspondents of newspapers on that side withheld information of such monstrous cruelty· I believe they did not see these things done,—that they did, does not agree with any reports they have given, or whch I have ever heard. But they knew of such executions, and at the very time they were making and spreading infamous reports about the Legion killing prisoners.

At this very time some English newspapers contained accounts of 130 Carlists having been put to death in cold blood, by the Legion.

Even this came before parliament for discussion, and was gravely asserted on the authority of these correspondents, by Lord Londonderry. So far from that being true, the Legion at this time, had never taken a prisoner ;—nor up to the time of being disbanded and returning to this country, was it ever known that a spaniard had been slain by one of the Legion, excepting in the open field of fight.

A dispatch of the commander-in-chief, of Don Carlos's army, dated Februray 3rd, refers to another batch of prisoners being taken. They were also lancers which may be accounted for by this :—that none of our infantry were allowed to go out of Vittoria, unless marching under command and armed, while the lancers having their horses and almost no means of getting forage for them, were not only allowed to go out, but were under the neccessity of going.—The Dispatch is as follows :—

" Excellent Sir,

"I have received the following dispatch from General Don Bruno Villa Real, dated yesterday :—"This morning I sent out a detachment of cavalry on a reconnoitring party, in the direction of the fields of Salvatierra, and the environs of Vittoria. Two soldiers, belonging to the lancers of Biscay, whose names are Juan Bautista Arostoguira, and de Moya, actually advanced to the gates of Vittoria, *and although*

only armed with their swords, made four English lancers prisoners,
who will *this day be shot.* You will be pleased to make the extraordinary brave conduct known to his Majesty, and entreat that the
two soldiers may receive the bounty of one real pay day, for the rest
of their lives.

(Signed)   Count de Casa Eguia."

Now, here are four men taken unarmed, but the Carlist General
omits that circumstance, or else it is omitted by the English correspondents, for this is their version of the dispatch, and they are to be
shot,—so says the General. To have said any thing else in a dispatch
would have been a hazard, for the Carlist Generals could distinguish,
between shooting a prisoner and giving him up to the religious murder of the priest, that is, they could see the effect that religious
sacrifices would have on the public mind, in the other nations of
Europe, and, therefore, he would say they were to be shot, whether
he intended shooting them or not, because shooting was a matter of
course. There are causes, however, to make it be suspected that
they were not shot ; for whenever the priests demanded prisoners for
immolation, these prisoners if not Catholics were with few exceptions given up to torture and a lingering death to excite the fanaticism
of the brutalized mob of devotees.

The Catholic religion is in itself as blameless of these infernal atrocities, committed by some of the priests, as the English Conservatives
Herald and Post are blameless of the mercenary acquiescence of
Honan and others, who are in their pay, and bearing the name of
English Protestant Conservatives, have connived at the disgusting
barbarity of priestly murders.   Let the distinction be clearly understood.   The political allies of Carlos in England, will shudder at
the bare supposition of being partizans in such a cause, bloated as it
is by such abominations.   They are incapable, as a body, of sympathising with such a bloody faction.   But absolving the body of Conservative politicians from a guilty knowledge of such crimes, I must
also declare that the numerous professors of the Catholic religion in
this country, are as blameless of an adherence to such enormities. To
be Conservators of English institutions, and Conservators of the Inquisitorial institutions of priest-ridden Spain, are very different,

THE STABLE HOUR OF THE 1ST LANCERS, — THE COLONEL'S DAILY AMUSEMENT.

No. 13.

though such a paradox exist among our politicians. And to be professors and followers of the Catholic religion here, and followers of it as practised politically in Spain, is no less a paradox, and will be charged, though wrongfully, against all Catholics. It is such men as those who have been sent out to correspond with the Conservative press, that are criminal. They may not have seen these savage executions, but they knew well of their frequent perpetrations and hire—base mercenary hire, caused them guiltily to keep England in ignorance.

I publish truth ; let it be denied or disproved, or let Englishmen not only withdraw their sympathies from such a cause as that of Don Carlos, but denounce it. The last course only is the alternative, to wipe from the protestant conservatives of England the damning blot of having been acquiescing parties, through their agents, to the priestly butcheries of a religion they pretend to abhor. Let not a hypocritical morality or a sense of military honor, lament that Carlos should have put prisoners of war to death, that was comparatively no crime ; but let England's protestants absolve themselves from their alliance with the inquisitorial deaths, and diabolical tortures of the Catholic priests, perpetrated in the name of religion, on English prisoners.

I am at present referring to a period of the Legion's service when severe charges must be made against General Evans, and were it not that he afterwards, as commander, redeemed his character with the Legion it would be impossible to ward off in any way the abuse which has been so liberally hurled against him. At this time he was culpable in a high degree, and his misfortune of having been often blamed unjustly relative to other periods of the service does not seem a sufficient reason why we should, in a false mercy, hide those faults of which he ought to be accused.

I would ask him if ever he saw the interior of San Domingo or San Francisca convents ? or did he ever personally inspect the quarters of the troops in Vittoria ? was he ever in the convalescent hospital, at the back of Santa Clara, or was he ever in any of the hospitals ? If he had any dread of infection in going into the hospitals he ought not to have had such fear ; for he who could expose himself so coolly, often unnecessarily, to the enemy's balls should have exposed himself to the dangers of disease among his men. But it was not the dread of the mortal diseases;—it was a dread to see men so overwhelmed with wretchedness that kept him from inspecting the quarters; and, therefore, I conclude he never knew our real state of suffering which he ought to have known. As I have a black picture to draw, in which he is not the only one blameable although the chief, I shall quote from a journal to which I have already referred as an authority, because the writer of it was an officer of high rank. My account of Vittoria miseries, with the names of some officers who not only aggravated, but, to a great extent, created them will come with greater force, when this officer's passing remarks on the *facts* of the sickness and death have been read. I shall give the *causes* of that sickness and death; so let those officers who have accusing consciences prepare to wince. This officer says

" February 30th. — A long hiatus in my journal: thank God, it is not an eternal one. I am just recovering from typhus fever, which has continued to rage through Vittoria with increased violence. We have lost upwards of 700 men and 40 officers, exclusive of those who have died elsewhere, *since Christmas.*

Death has ceased to be looked upon as an extraordinary visitor, and the common question among officers, is,—" Who is dead to day?" alluding to themselves. Among those attacked is Colonel Kinloch, of the Lancers, on whom the command of the brigade of cavalry has recently devolved : — An officer of some standing in the British service, and a great favourite here. I attribute my attack to mixing much with the convalescents, in my unenviable capacity or Commandant of Vittoria, assigned me prior to my illness. The officer who succeeded me, died a few days afterwards, although I had left him in perfect health. Two other captains, who, like myself had been much with the the convalescents, died also. As for the men, the mortality amongst them is truly awful. Nearly half of my company of the 2nd are dead; and officers and men are, by general order, buried without military honours of any kind, For nine days I was totally insensible, and attribute my eventual recovery to the unremitting care and attention of Mr. Duplex, surgeon of the Rifles, whose assiduity to me while his patient, I feel great pleasure in acknowledging. He, poor fellow, had scarcely pronounced me out of danger, when he was attacked most seriously by the same malady himself, and is, at this moment confined to his bed, although recovering. It is remarkable that twelve medical officers have fallen victims to this cruel disease.

The natives of Vittoria, long exempt, have caught the epidemic at last ; and, it must be confessed, few of us have the humanity to grieve at it, for they have been uniformly disobliging. When Mr. Duplex was first attacked, he was with his regiment, some miles out of town ; and when brought in, in a litter, suffering much, he was kept for four hours in the streets, opposite the entrance of the *casa,* on which a billet had already been obtained, before he could gain admission and even *then* a party of Spanish soldiers were compelled to force the door.

But this is no solitary instance. Before I was taken ill, a servant came to me one evening, stating that his master, an assistant surgeon of cavalry, on outpost duty, was dying in the street, the people of his former billet refusing to take him in. I hastened to the spot, and found the officer insensible, as represented ; but vain were my attempts to gain an entrance. The woman of the *casa,* who was even a greater vociferator than her husband, said he had no right to come back to them, having once left his billet. To cut the matter short, and fully resolved not to concede my point, I went to the alcalde's, at no great distance, and procured a billet on the same house. Even with this I could not suceeed in getting the poor officer in, without exposing him to great inconvenience, from the incivility of the inmates ; and I was obliged to exchange his billet to another quarter of the town. But repeated instances have occurred of the sort, all showing the disinclination of the inhabitants to accommodate us in the slightest degree.

But God knows, the people of Vittoria have not so much reason to complain. Billeting is confined solely to the officers of the Legion. Unlike the Spanish troops, who are completely housed, the men, while here, were put into convents, damp, impure, and unhealthy ; and two regiments (the 2nd and 5th, since broken up for their weakness,) had no other place whereon to lay their wearied bones, than the damp cold stones of a church, which has literally destroyed them. The effects were not immediately felt, but they failed not to develope themselves at the proper season. The hospitals were filled with these unfortunate fellows, and the other day, the 2nd regiment, admittedly the finest in the service while at Bilbao, could not muster 150 men on parade. The Spanish authorities, moreover, instead of seeking to ameliorate the condition of these men, by furnishing beds and blankets, threw every obstacle in the way ;—and through them principally, I have no hesitation in stating, the Legion is not what it might have been expected. To crown all, there has been no pay for months, and even the rations have been very irregularly issued.

March 5th.—Sad changes in the Legion during my illness ; the 2nd and 5th regiments have been broken up, and the officers and men transferred to other corps ,—all in consequence of their having been infamously billeted in a cold church, in the midst of winter."

That is a statement of facts by an officer; but only a part, and a small part of the facts with few or none of the causes. He states, that his fever arose from his frequent visits to the convalescent hospital, and his intercourse with the sick; this I believe, but whence arose the sickness ? when the malady had once begun, many men not predisposed to disease were seized as is the case with healthy people in all epidemics, and suddenly cut off—and no measures were taken to keep the healthy from coming in contact with the sick; but not only was there a want of care—there was an unrestrained prodigality of corporal punishments, that by inflicting wounds on able-bodied men caused them to go into the hospital to have their backs dressed, from whence many of them never returned. As an instance Colonel Kirby of the 1st regiment had twenty-one men tried by court-martial and flogged on the march between Bilboa and Vittoria. Eleven of these were flogged at Brevaisca for having sold some of their regimental necessaries, which is undoubtedly criminal in a soldier even though he may have purchased these nescessaries out of his pay. But there was this in extenuation of *their* making away with their kit or parts of it. They had been on a long weary march, daily ascending and descending untracked mountains, and they were starving from the scantiness of rations; therefore, hunger, which could be appeased by the disposal of some of the extra necessaries that had worn them out on the march, and that hunger craving sharply in men who had hitherto lived in comparative luxury—such hunger among such men may be supposed to have soon decided them to sell their oppressive loads that they had carried on their march. For this, eleven were stripped naked among the frozen snow outside of that wretched town, Brevaisca, and got punishments varying from one hundred to three hundred lashes each. I (the author of this work,) happened to come to that place about a month after these men were flogged, three of them were dead—three or four had a fever, and I having caught their fever also, remained there for another month, when only *two* out of the eleven were alive. I found nearly four hundred men at that place all left behind the main body by disability of some kind, but two thirds at least—and I state this after consulting a proper authority, were left unable to march and carry their accoutrements, from having been flogged. And what became of them.? between *eighty* and a *hundred* only left the place alive, and many of these were maimed by frost-bitten feet, and other diseases. This was a fearful result of corporal punishments, and to prevent the men's backs being wounded so as they could not carry their knapsacks, the lash was applied often after that time, to another part of the body— more painful to the sufferer, and more disgusting to the spectator; but less detrimental to the numerical strength of a regiment. This is one instance of how the malady that raged in the Legion, was fed ; but not how it originated. The officer whose journal has been quoted, states that the 2nd and 5th regiments were broken up from having been reduced by excessive sickness. I know that was true, and it was also true, that they lay as he says, on the bare floors of the cold damp convents in the middle of winter. But why does he not draw a picture of Colonel Swan of the 5th, drilling his regiment in the middle of winter.

Colonel Swan formed—drilled, and commanded the 5th from its formation in September 1835, until its dissolution in February 1836. It was scarcely in existence five months. He began to drill in September with upwards of seven hundred men. He could not muster, not even number the half of them in February. To *inure the men to hardship* he created sufferings in addition to those which all other regiments were exposed to from unavoidable circumstances. In the frosty or rainy weather, among the wet slush or the drifting snow, he took his regiment out to drill, and if there was water or marshy ground to be found, that was taken in preference to any other. His regiment was light infantry,—hence to drill properly he required a wide space of ground. It was common for him to march to the outside of Vittoria two or three miles and have his men extended over fields to the distance of a mile from the one flank to the other. If he saw a sheet of water, he made them go through it,—if a ditch swollen full with the soft snow which men could not get over was nigh, he would extend, and manœuvre around, purposely causing them to wade it. If he saw men trying to avoid a pool of water, he would halt his battalion, and make these men go through the water by themselves. Sometimes he would " form close column," and " wheel a quarter circle," or " change front by the wheel and counter-march of sub-divisions round the centre," in a pond, merely to make the men wet themselves ; and one day particularly, which all those of his regiment who survive remember well,—he saw some of them picking their steps in going across a running brook, and to punish them he deployed into line in the centre of the rivulet, and put the regiment through the manual, and platoon exercise, and then marched them home to occupy the " *bare floors of the cold damp convent !* " not only the *bare* floors ; but the bare stone floors, in which by a general order, no fires were allowed to be burned lest the men should pull down the wood-work for fuel, and thereby give offence to the inhabitants of the town.

In battle, a braver soldier than Colonel Swan, never unsheathed a sword to lead on a regiment, and I have elsewhere recorded his bravery shewn in the action of the 5th of May, when he commanded the 7th regiment. This merit I shall cheerfully record to every officer who deserved it. In some preceding sketches we have been noticing the conduct of officers who were tyrants, and cowards—the most despicable of all military martinets. In the case of Colonel Swan, we see an officer who was a tyrant the most severe and uncompromising—who set at defiance every feeling of justice and humanity and who for his own amusement seemed to make havoc of the health, life, and very existence of his soldiers while in the conflict of bullets and bayonets he did not seem merely, but actually made death a plaything.

Many a man died of a broken spirit. The want of bedding—the damp and cold, and the bad rations did much to wreck the physical system, but there was such a thing also as a man being broken hearted, and dying in despondency.

I remember well a young man named Alexander Halliday. A

more sprightly and pleasant looking youth, standing six feet two inches in height, never graced his birth place, the city of Edinburgh. He was, I believe, a carpenter by trade, and with no intention of going to Spain, accompanied some acquaintances to Glasgow to see them go on board. As the assurances of Colonel Shaw and others who recruited there, were often repeated, that the campaign would not last three or four months, or *six* at the very utmost. Many young men joined to go over to Spain for a three month's *spree*, or as an Englishman calls it a *lark*; consoling themselves that they would *aye get their meat and claes*, and six months pay to come home with if nothing else, and " as for fighting" they would say " we'll neer see a shot fired the *Carlists* 'ill gie up wheneer they see Evans land." Among such as these were some of Halliday's young friends. They pleaded hard that he should go with them, *that they would all come back together*, and that it would be fine sport. Halliday, I am told, stood on the shore of the Clyde for a few minutes, thinking if he would leap into the boat that a'ready contained his companions, and at last resolving, made a spring and stood with his tall manly figure among the crowd going to Spain.

I saw him when he wore the uniform of the regiment, and with the blue Scotch bonnet and tartan plaid; (for Swan's regiment the 5th was called Highland light Infantry,) he looked so well as a soldier that I do not recollect to have seen one in any corps ever look better.

I saw him on the march to Vittoria, and when others were tired climbing the pathless mountains, and were desponding— he, on the right of the regiment, and by that means in front, went cheerfully on, his gaiety cheering those who marched before them. "Never mind lads," he would say, "we'll be climbing Arthur's seat some May morning, with our lasses in our arms to gather dew" (alluding to a custom that is observed annually by the young people of Edinburgh, in going to the top of the hill called Arthur's seat,) "never mind being dry," when some one would complain of thirst, he continued, "we'll get a drink when we go to Habbie's Howe," such were the cheering observations of Halliday to his comrades, which told that though encouraging others, *his* heart and affections were behind him.

I saw him gay and lively in Vittoria, his whiskers were trimmed with care, and his mustachios, jetty in colour, and luxurious in growth might have made a French exquisite envious.

I saw him a month afterwards in what was called the hospital. His features were languid, thin, and ghostly. He lay with his great coat over him, and in a hollow low voice, was moaning, " oh my feet they're nipping off me with the cold, oh spread something on me some of ye," and surrounded by a number of others who were crawling close to each other for warmth. He was unable to rise, and had never had his clothes off him from the time he went in, which was then a fortnight. The hair that had curled, and been shaded over his finely formed brow, and the whiskers and the mustachios were now clotted with vermin that literally hovered over him, and others, among the mass of filth in which they lay. His glazed eyes and wan skin shone through the matted hair, and he kept groaning, " oh my feet ! oh my head's ill !

I saw him a week afterwards when I, as Corporal of a party went to bury the accumulated dead bodies, when among *thirty-five* which we found in the dead house, I was looking for that of Robert Williamson an intimate friend of my own, and found it, the head eaten away with rats, laying beside that of poor Halliday whom I could not have recognized but by his clothes, and a letter in one of his pockets which came from his relations in Scotland.

There was the end of the gay and manly looking Halliday. A dysentry and frost-bitten feet, caused by wading among water and lying down in the cold convent, without any change of clothing, had rendered him unfit for duty, He was taken to the pestilent fever-house, where the floors of every room were crowded ; and like other's with a flux wasting him away was left there to perish.

There is enough in this single case to condemn Colonel Swan's overdrilling. But this is *one* only. The provost system of flogging bad as it was in all the regiments, was carried to an extremity in his. Men and non-commissioned officers who were in the 5th, assert, that they do not remember one day passing at Vittoria, without some of the men being flogged.

He heard no plea for mercy from, or excuse for an offender. Even the captain of a company dared not if a man was taken out of the ranks to be flogged, urge anything in defence. " Take that man, give him two dozen—three dozen---or four dozen," as the case might be was ordered, and the provost sergeant and drummers with the cats, were always ready.

The manner of inflicting the punishment was, to order three men to fall out of the ranks, besides the one to be provosted, No. *one* of these three stood upright, the offender's *trowsers* were loosened down, his arms were put over the shoulders of No. *one*, No. *two* took hold of his right arm, and No. *three* his left, and drew his body close to the back of No. *one*; sometimes if the victim was refractory, and did not take the punishment quietly, an additional man or two would be brought out to hold his feet.

This mode was resorted to if no trees were at hand : but commonly if there was a tree, the man to be punished was tied there.   The *lower parts* of the body were also flogged, rather than the back, because the back, when cut, rendered them unable to carry their knapsacks or accoutrements.

But it was not with him alone, that all the ill-treatment of the men of his regiment originated.   He had some officers who appeared striving to outdo him.   One of these named Landers, formerly a Linen Draper's shopman in Dublin, as I have been told, was probably the worst, the very worst of any that disgraced the Legion, and helped to destroy the 5th regiment.   I could write much about this person.   He was at that time a Lieutenant, and got command of a company when his captain was sick, which he literally got flogged from *right* to *left* save *nine* men, that is the whole company of about seventy was punished by the lash during the weeks that he commanded it, except *nine* men.   He was afterwards shot in another regiment, by the men of his own company, so much for Landers.

Such then, was a course of creating disease and deaths, and though chargeable on Colonel Swan, I cannot see how General Evans can escape censure.   But the General pleads guiltless, because he did not order, or superintend in person these punishments, and that he softened down some and altogether remitted many of the sentences of court-martials that were submitted to his approval.   My opinion is, that he did an injury to the efficiency of the Legion's discipline, by *not* putting in force some sentences of general court-martials; for, let it be understood, that it was only general court-martials that came before him for approval, all other sentences were carried into effect, previous to their being reported to him.   It was in the provosting system, by which any officer or non commissioned officer, the latter by reporting a man, even to a subaltern, could have him flogged, and in the minor court-martials that the abuse of punishing existed.

There were commanding officers who sought then, and seek yet to obtain credit for humanity, by having remitted the sentences passed by court-martials. One of these was Brigadier General Shaw, and though there were several others, a few remarks on his conduct may suffice to illustrate the evils produced in military discipline, by a profession of unreal humanity.

The members of a court-martial have no alternative, but to pass a sentence in accordance with the Articles of War. General Shaw frequently ordered a court to sit for the trial of cases, that some officers would not have thought of bringing to trial, merely that he might have the pompous show of reading the proceedings of the court to a parade, and declare that the sentence was too severe, or, that the man was of good character, and therefore would be pardoned. This at first view might seem harmless amusement if it was not real humanity; but instead of being either, it produced fearful effects on the general discipline of a regiment. Often, also, men who were sentenced to three hundred lashes, got one hundred and fifty; or if sentenced to two hundred got one hundred and so in proportion, General Shaw or the Colonels who followed this practice, saying, that he or they, considered the offenders had got enough. Now the feeling in the man who was thus saved half the torture, and the feeling of the whole regiment or brigade, as it might be, that looked on was naturally, that the commanding officer was a merciful man, and that the members of the court-martial were most unmerciful. The effect this feeling produced was abhorrence in the mind of that man who was tried and *partly* punished against the officers who sat on his court martial, which in not a few cases in the Legion, rancled in the victim's mind, until he avenged himself by becoming the assassin, of these officers on the battlefield, where honor should have prompted to other deeds. At the same time that a commanding officer thus got credit for a spurious humanity, he was the actual and direct cause of punishment; for as all military readers know well, the criminal that is referred to a regimental court-martial has been, or at least his crime has been examined by the Colonel in the orderly room previous to the trial being ordered, and when ordered to be tried by a brigade court-martial the General of the brigade has likewise been acquainted with all the facts of the case *or ought have been*, and either might have ordered the accused to be tried or not as he thought fitting. The only thing to be ascertained by the trial is, whether the man is guilty of the crime charged against him. The magnitude of that crime has already been weighed, for it was according to its weight that he was sent to a regimental-brigade, or a general court-martial. General Chichester, who in many cases appeared to me to be too severely ready with summary punishments, and was the strictest disciplinarian, but at the same time the most efficient of any of our brigadiers ; never tampered with men's hopes and fears in punishing them. If a man committed a crime under Chichester, he knew that nothing could save him from punishment, but then he was not tried by a brigade, if a regimental court-martial could take cognizance of the crime. The consequence of this was that no man calculated on punishment as a chance, but expected it as a certainty, if his trial had been ordered by Chichester, for that officer would not send a man to trial, until he had first investigated the case himself, and then if guilty, not a lash was spared.

Many will think he was severe. I often thought so ; but I must state the effects of his system :—The men under him consoled themselves by saying, " well, if he is hard on us he does not make fish of one and flesh of another, we always know what we've to get from him." Under some of the others the greatest speculations of betting &c. went on among the men when one was tried whether he would be punished or not. I have known some of the gamblers leave off card playing or refuse to play at night, " because" said they, " there's to be a court-martial to-morrow, and we must keep the *coppers* we've won for it !" If the case or cases to be tried were well known, bets of a " guilty" or " not guilty" sentence went on freely, when the officers, who were to be on the Court as members, but especially the witnesses, had been all carefully weighed according to character in the minds of those disposed to speculate. The amount of the sentence was not so much betted on, for most men in each regiment knew what the sentence was for different crimes, there being scarcely an alternative left in the power of the Court. But the grand betting took place on the question of how much of the punishment would be inflicted. Some knowing ones could tell by the very manner of a colonel's riding when he came on parade, or by the sound of his voice when he called the regiment to attention, formed square, fixed bayonets, shouldered arms, and said " pay attention to the proceedings of a court-martial." In different officers the tone was different; but many speculated in their minds, and endeavoured to anticipate their success by guessing whether the Colonel was in a mood to inflict, to bid the drummers come on heavily; or the reverse—to punish in whole, to remit in part, or grant a pardon. So uncertain were the chances of punishment, that men who could thus bet their daily allowance of wine—their trifle of daily pay, and after that their tobacco and their pipes, which in Spain were valuable, on a comrade being punished, might also, if disposed, commit crimes on speculation themselves. That such was the case, I in the situation I held, which was between the officers and the men, between crime and punishment, between the authority of superiors and the ill or góod feeling existing in the ranks, between the devil and the deep sea; I, in that situation, had better means of knowing the amount of crime reported and not reported to superiors, and the effects of punishment than any other individual in a company had; and I may presume to say, that, having taken much care to study these matters, I knew better than any one, from the Colonel downwards, what the effect of different modes of punishment had been. I have heard much said of the uncertainty of civil law, and the consequent evils,—let these be discussed by those who are competent, I shall only state, that no soldier should ever have it left to him to calculate on punishment as a chance. Let punishments be modified so as to meet the measure of the crime as near as possible—to restrain the criminal, and at the same time not overstep humanity; but let these punishments be sure to follow or else never bring the criminal to trial; for one escape of a guilty man has an effect incalculably more injurious on the general body of a regiment than if the criminal had not been accused of his crime.

CHAPTER XI.

The drumming of Casey, a private of the 7th out of the Legion—His subsequent fate—Flogging of a Lancer, named Nash; his death in consequence—An officer's description of Brevaisca—The Author's description of the same place—Affecting narrative of the death of James Ritchie—his disinterment by the Spaniards, &c.—Notices of Dr. Jenner and others at Brevaisca.

HAVING referred to General Shaw's uncertainty in punishing in the last chapter, and mock humanity, by which the recoil of the severity of the law came on the members of the court-martial, I shall relate a circumstance of which he boasts in his published letters, but which he is not likely to know the subsequent result of. It is a case wherein he dictated to a court-martial what sentence they were to pronounce on a man who was guilty of thieving, and was altogether one of the most disgusting punishments ever executed.

This man's name was Casey, he belonged to the 7th regiment, and had stolen some articles off the staff baggage : after being tried by a brigade court-martial, General Shaw, who commanded that brigade, had a full parade one day at the extremity of our own positions, and as nearly in front of the Carlists as he dared to advance, Casey's trial and sentence were read. He was taken out to the front, so that the Carlists might see if they were disposed to look ; but they had not seen it as it afterwards appeared ; and there, being put on the back of a man, his hands and feet being held fast by the others, the drummers gave him one hundred and fifty lashes, cutting his back dreadfully. " For," said General Shaw, " let them see where he is going, that we have been flogging him ;—do it well— that's what I do it for." After being flogged, a rope was put round his neck, a loaf was given to him and an old great coat. A drummer leading him outwards for about fifty yards, with others behind beating the *Rogue's March* made the finish so far as the ceremony went. The brigade marched off ; the sentries on the out-posts having orders to shoot him, and he being assured, that if he returned he would be shot, was left to his fate. Shaw, who has a great propensity, with a miserable ability, to speechify, delivered an address, directed to the man, but loud enough, and in a position where he could be heard by the brigade, of which the following is a literal copy.

" Now your friends are waiting on you yonder. I have brought you up here to flog you, that they might see how we punish thieves. Tell them we shall soon be with them, but not on such a friendly visit as yours is. We shall have the pleasure of seeing you there, but *remember it will be as an enemy*," &c. &c.

I have only made this quotation because of its stupidity. A General of the brigade attended by Aid-de-camps, and surrounded by Field officers—plumes waving in his cocked hat and his sword drawn, making a speech to a man who had been, and was about to be treated with a punishment to which *death* would have been mercy—to mock

that man with sarcasm pointless though it was, was cruel, and to conclude with an idealess nothing which was gravely uttered so that the
wondering soldiers might hear that he actually contemplated a fight,
and was sending over a message to the enemy, was worthy only of
his common foolery. To drum a man out of the regiment at home
is always considered a disgrace. But if a soldier has no sense of honor, or would suffer any degradation to get rid of a military life, which
many would who are in the army, the disgrace of drumming out and
the present of a shilling, which is given, becomes to the happy criminal,
not a punishment but a boon ;—the man may have friends to go to, he
may work, he may beg, or at the most, he will not be murdered by
the first one he meets, if drummed out of a barrack gate in England.
But how monstrously cruel was it to have induced men to go to a
foreign country, and though this man did commit a crime—which
crime at that time had many extenuating circumstances,—fatigue,
hunger, &c. how cruel was it after torturing with the lash, to force
a man away on the pain of death to where, his persecutors knew not
whither. To have abandoned him in an Indian desert among tigers,
or to have left him in the tide among the crocodiles of the Nile, where
it was possible he *might* have escaped, would not have been so very
inhuman ! but to leave him to the certainty of meeting *men* more
cruel than either the beasts of the desert, or the monsters of the Nile ;
with no possibility of escape, as they thought, was the perpetration of
the ingeniously *humane* General Shaw.

The brigade marched away, and Casey thinking he might follow
the Chesterfield maxim—that of making the best personal appearance,
the best recommendation to strangers —took the rope from about his
neck ! and anxiously anticipating the future, moved slowly towards
the Carlists. He sat down in a hollow and rested a while, washed
the blood from his back—put on his jacket, and wistfully debated
with himself what he should do. Peeping about on one side and
then on the other among the bushes, to see if any one approached :
it occurred to him that he was more likely to be shot by that stealthy
way of letting himself be seen, than if he went speedily forward and
therefore in a terror of dread and uncertainty he moved onwards. A
house at some distance was before him, nearly hidden among the
trees and expecting it contained the Carlist picquet he made for it, intending to profess himself a deserter, and thereby, if possible, purchase
favor. On entering this house, however, he only found an old wo-

man who was busy with some household affairs. The moment she saw
him she said he would be murdered if he stopped a minute in her house,
as she expected the soldiers in immediately, whom she knew to be
looking out for stragglers, that were invariably put to death. Casey
told her that he was a deserter, that he had come over to join the
Carlists, that he was a christian, &c. still the old woman implored
him to be off—to go back to his comrades as he would assuredly be
slain, the moment the Carlists saw him if he remained there. He
had not long been in argument with her and himself, about what he
should do when the soldiers whom she expected made their appearance, one of them entered, to whom the old woman told that, this
was a deserter, pointing to Casey, and that she was the more sure of
it, as he had had time to return but would not go. The Carlists then
questioned him, and being satisfied that he had come designedly to
them ; they gave him share of their *pochera*, a mess of stewed beans,
oil, and garlic, which all classes eat in Spain, and which the old woman of the house had been preparing for them.

He was then taken into the interior, joined the other English who
were there—got a musket and accoutrements, and fought in three
successive engagements against the Legion. He had endeavoured
to get passed into France with other English deserters who were
sent there, but having made himself a useful soldier at first to gain
favor, they would not permit him to leave their service ; but as a
reward they promoted him. He undertook, sometime in the month
of July, 1836, to pass himself into the quarters of the British Legion, near San Sebastian, and to take a correct view of all the defences, gather information, &c., and return to the Carlists ; which
he succeeded in doing so far, and probably would have altogether
accomplished, had not he, to satisfy his curiosity, paid one indiscreet visit to the 7th regiment, his old comrades. He had learnt to
speak good Spanish,—good enough to deceive any Englishman, and
wearing the dress of a Spanish peasant no one had, for some days,
taken any notice of him. On going to the 7th he had the intention
of making arrangements for an extensive desertion, but some of those
who had supposed him dead long before, made so much friendly
mirth at his return that he was discovered, arrested, and immured in
the castle of San Sebastian. Here he continued for some months,
but, continuing to profess that he had deserted from the Carlists,

VIEW OF THE CITADEL AND WALLS OF SAN SEBASTIAN.
The River Urimea and the Pontoon Bridge thrown across by the English Sailors during the Action, 28th May, 1836.

No 14.

intending to rejoin the Legion, he was at last liberated, put on board a ship, and landed in England.

I have also the painful duty of recording the dreadful punishment of a young man named Nash, which punishment was inflicted at the instance of Colonel ——— of the Lancers. But, before proceeding to detail it, I must, in addition to all that has been said of this nameless torturer of soldiers, state, that the limits of this work would not admit of a tenth part of his heartless tyranny; therefore a stable sketch has been engraved which is given on page 209. It represents, what was, with very few exceptions, the daily scene in the stables of the first Lancers, while that corps had the misfortune of his command. To some readers an apology may be necessary for having introduced anything that has a tendency to disgust the sensitive; but to represent what the Legion was in Vittoria is to disgust every reader, military or civil; although, to tell the truth, if then the sketch of the stable scene be repulsive, it is at least painfully true.—The men are represented brushing down their horses; one is tied to the post of the stall, is stripped, with the shirt hanging over his head, and is receiving a four dozen punishment very probably for no crime that moral justice would take any cognizance of. Colonel ——— is superintending its infliction; and Captain —— is bullying over another man, and pointing to the punishment with a savage threat as was usual with him. Should any officer think himself offended by that illustration, he may console himself, if his conscience is at peace, that he will not be unjustly accused; but, on the other hand he will, if deserving, be contradistinguished by a record of his good behaviour. I am undertaking a painful task, but it must be performed. The unmanly propensity to punish men for the simplest faults in some of those who commanded must be exposed, however much the subjects of exposition may wince. I, at the same time, invite the youthful aspirant to a military life to look at that engraving. I, the writer of this painful explanation, have often felt a burning enthusiasm when reading about battles. I have, with a warm imagination, followed to the fight, and when in mere childhood I have longed to be a soldier. But it is a truth in the moral and military history of soldiering, that those young men who are of the quickest temperament, readiest to admire the evolutions of the grand parade, and be fired with rapture in contemplating the battle field, have ever been the worst every day soldiers. Such minds are impatient of controul—that strict and severe subjugation, that, from the nature of military obedience, is necessary to preserve it. I, therefore, present these sketches to my young readers. I could tell of the wheeling squadron and the charging line, and these will be spoken of in their turn; for, never was a regiment of dragoons more efficient in fight than these lancers were at a subsequent period; but to intoxicate the youthful mind with the romance of war is to commit a moral fraud, which almost all descriptions of a campaign have hitherto been. For one hour of the day when the gay parade is seen, how many dull toilsome hours of unvarying polishing and cleaning has the soldier to endure under the insults of superiors—to whom if he looks *even only sulky* he is guilty of a punishable crime. Though there is no such flogging in the British army, at present, as that which was inflicted on the Legion daily, at the time I am writing, yet it was as bad in the Peninsula war, and it would be now were the army in active warfare. Therefore, again, for one glorious day of battle, which the enthusiastic youth may long for, how many dull every day parades and marches has he to endure— how much sickness and toil to undergo, without the soothing voice of a mother or sister—how many comrades who burned with military ardour like himself, has he to see flogged for crimes which were but harmless sport in civil life! I am now about to tell a tale of a young man, a native of London, who, from his childhood, longed to be a soldier. Let all young men read it; it is short.

The name of this man was Nash. He joined one of the early detachments of the Legion, and full of health and spirits he landed in Spain. There was not one more gay, nor more full of hope than he was. In uniform he was smart, and soldier-like beyond fault. He had succeeded in being what he had always wished to be, a soldier; yet his feelings were warm, and a lively recollection of those soft affections that grieved for him at home, caused him, as he said to be often dull and thoughtful. The winter of 1835 came on, and he, like all others, felt its severity. The regiment was on the march to Burgos from Santander, and on halting one night at a village not far from the town of Brivieska, he and another man having a little money, and nothing being sold in the village where they were quartered, resolved on venturing to the neighbouring town to purchase something for themselves and comrades. They went, and while there, were taken up as prisoners by a provost guard, for being out of quarters after tattoo. In vain they represented that they had come from a distance, and were about to return. They were confined until morning, and sent to their regiment under an escort, as prisoners—were immediately tried by a drumhead court-martial, as the regiment was about to march, and sentenced to receive two hundred lashes each, on suspicion of having intended to desert. They represented that it was to buy bread, chocolate, and some of these necessaries, that they had gone ; and as it then appeared that Nash only had been possessed of money, he was held as the most guilty of the two. He who, as the men all asserted to me, risked himself to go and spend his money to purchase chocolate to give away among his comrades, to make at least one warm breakfast on the snowy march, (for they had nothing but biscuit and salt beef,) he was now tied up to a tree on the road side, to be flogged in front of the regiment; the other being pardoned. Nash stripped, and tied fast by hands and feet, received one hundred and fifty lashes. He had been tied up against a tree where there a was a joint of a broken branch protruding, and which joint was between his breast and the tree. During the infliction of the punishment, his writhing and twisting, caused by the excruciating pain, made this part of the tree rub into his breast, which wounded him so severely, that when taken down, they, mercifully as they thought, having forgiven him fifty of the lashes, he was found to be dangerously ill. He was carried to Brivieska, and thus parted from the only friends that he had, his comrades, he was put into the Spanish hospital. For some days he lingered there, but his raw wounds both on his back and breast, which had been inflicted among freezing snow, and were thereby frost-bitten, began to mortify ; and among strangers, unknown, unsoothed. and unmourned, he died. I believe, hitherto, his relations did not know what became of him ; but though a painful assurance to give, I must tell them, that this was his end, and these the circumstances of his death.

This town, Brivieska, where Nash and about two hundred more died, is a miserable place. I shall quote the notes of an officer, giving his opinion of it, and then write my own experience ; for if he felt the wretchedness of the place so dreadful, with a *braziero* to warm himself at, and with a horse cloth, as he says, below his heels, and

that in a house ; what must we, the soldiers, have been, in an open
dilapidated convent, without any fire, any covering, any bed, and no
dinner. He, the officer, had, what he calls a poor apology for a dinner ; we had none ; for our meat, trifling as its quantity was, was
eaten raw. But more of that after the officer has given his sufferings in this place, and they were certainly bad enough. Oh ! how
it made the *dandies* shrivel their noses at a military life ; he says :—

" November 12th.—Brivieska is one of the most wretched places
under the sun—the houses are miserable—the people are miserable
—all they possess seems to be of the most miserable description. Of
the comforts of life they have no more idea than a Hottentot, and
there is an apathy of manner about them, in the midst of all their
filth and meanness, which provokes and vexes even more than their
poverty. The fact is, however, that a strange anomaly presents its
self in all of Spain we have yet traversed. Amid the rude mountain-
of Biscay, where the cultivation of the soil is limited to the occasional
patches of valley that spread themselves, at intervals, few and far between, at their base, the peasantry are of sturdy, cleanly, and healthy,
even characteristic, appearance ; while on the other hand, in proportion as our advance has been extended into districts teeming with
every evidence of fertility and richness, not only the peasantry, but
the inhabitants of the towns, have universally presented the most
pitiable pictures of squalid misery :—and this the more despicable,
inasmuch as it springs less from want of means to remedy the evil,
than from a natural indolence and inaptitude for all improvement.

November 13th.—This morning I arose benumbed with cold, which
had kept me awake the greater part of the night ; and on looking
out of my window upon the Plaza, was for some time at a loss to
conceive to what quarter of the globe I had been, as if by enchantment, conveyed during the last twelve hours. First Russia, and next
Switzerland, suggested themselves to my imagination ; and finally,
the snows of America, amid which I had passed a couple of campaigns in my early youth. But there was wanting the inspiriting air
of liveliness, and vigorous action peculiar to the inhabitants of these
climes, as well as the internal comfort to be met with in their homes.
The Plaza was covered with a deep snow—the mountains in the far
distance, and the tops of the houses were clothed in the same cheerless garb ; and when I looked around my wretched room, and beheld

nothing but a brick floor, without carpet of any description—the naked square of its walls unbroken by a fire—I confess I shuddered
at the prospect that awaited me.

Had it been the close of December, one would not have cared so
much, as each succeeding day would have brought with it the certainty of a proximate and enlivening spring. But the 13th of November only, and in Spain, to find one's self regularly imbedded in
snow, and half congealed with cold, with the probability of something
worse, was more than the anticipation had been prepared for. From
the melancholy contemplation of my apartment, I turned my gaze
again upon the Plaza, and had already begun to derive some shadow
of comfort and hope from the snug appearance of our soldiers, as they
issued forth to parade in their warm great coats, apparently regardless
of the weather, when that trifling consolation was taken from me, by
the picture presented by the natives themselves.

Shrinking, trembling, with chattering teeth, and in a half torpid
state, these latter moved through the Plaza, to their several avoca-
tions, either in their shops or in the market place, with an air of in-
ertness that gave to the scene around an aspect even more dreary
than it was. Nay, what heightened the misery still more, were the
very cloaks in which all—inhabitants and peasants without exception
—were inducted, to preserve them from the effects of that cold, old,
tattered, threadbare—and mostly resembling in color, the "sere and
yellow leaf," which tells, in language not to be misunderstood, of the
unpromising advent of blear-eyed winter; these were drawn around
the faces of the drooping crowd, in a manner to conceal every thing
but the eyes; while, as an additional protection, across their mouths
and noses were tied handkerchiefs, remarkable for any thing but their
purity of color :—the very sight of these was sufficient to petrify
one.

With such a prospect before me, it is not likely that I should fail
to look with some degree of despair upon my return to my miserable
billet at night, after performing the duties required of me during the
day. Nor was that apprehension ill-founded. After finishing a sad
apology for a dinner, I am now warming both my toes and my nose
over a *braziero*, which I have managed to procure, yet in which
there is infinitely more ashes than coals. The window of my room is
hermetically closed, to keep out as much of the cold air as possible

and a horse-cloth is placed under my chair to receive my heels—the toes resting upon the *braziero* ; my servant's regimental great coat is on my back, and yet despite all this luxury, all this comfort, I can scarcely hold the pencil that traces my note. We are allowed wood, it is true ; but, alas ! where are the chimnies in which to consume it ? And yet these Spaniards talk of liberty. Ye Gods ! who would accord liberty to men so far besotted—so far behind all the rest of mankind, as not to know the comfort of a cheerful fire ?

November 16th.—The weather still continues fearfully cold, and its effects are the more sensibly felt, inasmuch as there are no means of escaping from it. Yesterday I rode out to the villages of Cumino and Quintinillia Bon, occupied by the 2nd brigade. Nothing could exceed the wretchedness of these hamlets ; even the billets of the officers were of a description not to be surpassed in misery by the worst hovels in Ireland. On entering that of General Chichester, at Camino, I found him just returned from a visit to the regiment of his brigade at Quintinillia Bon, and bent nearly double over a *braziero*, shivering with the cold air that rushed in from a window which had never known the luxury of glass, yet which when closed, left the room in utter darkness. As I brought with me the change of route to San Domingo, a large town situate about seven leagues to the south-east of Brivieska, it may be presumed I was a welcome visitor. This morning that change was effected, leaving the distribution of the Legion as follows :—1st and Light Brigades (Evans' and Reid's) Brivieska ; 2nd and 4th (Chichester's and Mac Dougall's) San Domingo ; 3rd (Shaw's) Villania ; Cavalry—Pradanos, one league from Brivieska, with orders to move in a day or two to Burgos."

Such then, is this officer's account of that dispiriting visit to Brivieska. But unpleasant as it was to officers, and I readily admit they had severe hardships as gentlemen, still their sufferings as human beings, were easy compared with the misery of the soldiers. He speaks of the "miserable apology for a dinner;" but any dinner was a luxury compared to absolute starvation, which I insist many men at this time were suffering. And though the *braziero* was a cheerless fire, still it was a fire, and he had the privilege of "bending two-fold over it," while the soldiers had no fire whatever, but lay on the bare brick-floors of an immense untenanted and unfurnished convent, or stood shivering on picquets and sentries among the snow. No officer

was absolutely without resources of some kind, therefore a little
tobacco, even though it might not be the real Havannah, was sweetly
pleasant in such circumstances compared with want.   When a person used to a luxurious living, descends from it to the mere necessaries of life, he suffers a hardship that the person living on frugal fare
cannot sympathise in, and if both descend in company to a coarser
food than the common necessaries, the former still suffers most; but
if both are left without food of any sort, or so little of it that excessive hunger rages in them, I conceive they will suffer alike.   Also if
the gentleman who has been used to warm himself in a carpeted par-
lour, and the ploughman who has enjoyed a bare hearthstone, are
both perishing among snow, their suffering must be equal according
to their physical constitution, but if, as was the case with our officers
that the gentleman can get something to eat, and have a fire and a
horse-rug beneath his feet, he is immeasurably more comfortable than
those who died from starvation and neglect.   I cannot better prove
the horrors suffered by the soldiers, than relate a few facts that came
under my own observation, and which related partly to myself.

By order of the Colonel of my regiment, I had been some weeks in
rear of the main body in charge of the regimental baggage, and had
at last after much weary anxiety reached Brivieska, with other bag-
gage-guards and detachments on our way to re-join our respective
corps. A battery of artillery was also on the line of march to Vittoria,
and the whole baggage and detachments, were under the command
of Colonel Shaw of the artillery.   Many of the men had been left
sick behind their respective regiments, and were now in a weakly
state, forced to march onwards to Vittoria.   I know that most of
them were anxious to go forward, for we had all suffered so severely
by cold, sickness, and the want of regular rations, and supposing the
main body to be faring well in front of us, no one that could go on
thought of staying longer behind.   I was myself, in a slow fever, and
could not have by any possibility kept up, had I not been in charge
of a baggage waggon, on which I laid my musket and accoutrements.
There were only two days out of eleven, which it took us including
stoppages, to go from Santander to Brivieska, on which there was
no flogging.   I saw men throw themselves down on the road-side
declaring they could not come on, but the lash was indiscriminately
applied, and probably Colonel Shaw *did* feel a reluctance to flog these

men, those who are able may form what opinion they choose, and can place these punishments to the account of Colonel Shaw, or to the account of the unavoidable consequences of war. If the latter, it behoves every father to teach his child what the horrors of warfare are.

I cannot pass without remarking, that in England those publications which most loudly denounce corporal punishments, feed themselves and intoxicate the minds of youthful readers with selections from writers on battles, and other exciting scenes of war. Often does the same paper contain denunciations of military cruelty on one page, which justly excites the sympathy of an extensive class of readers, while on the other side, there are those soul stirring incidents of the campaign, that more than anything tends to upset the steadiness of youthful minds. In war, *glory* and *cruelty* are inseparable, not the cruelty of the lash to the backs of worn-out soldiers, that *is* separable from glory, but numberless indefinable encroachments on humanity, that none but the soldier can feel: and he does feel them more terrible than even the lash itself sometimes. I contend therefore, that every poet or historian, or newspaper writer that represents war, as virtuous or honourable, or excites the passions by partial visions of its glory, are guilty of a crime committed on the whole human race.

I saw men sick and when they lay down the provost guard that brought up the rear applied the nine tailed cats, to every one they came to. A poor fellow, I remember, named Stenhouse, belonging to the town of Dalkeith in Scotland, told me one night that he did not think he would live long, for, said he, "I *am not* able to go on unless I get a ride on the baggage waggons,—I fell down on the road thi' day, and man, I got two dozen, and though I fell ahint again they had my *breeks* loosed down a second time, when Mr. Brown your officer stopped them, and said he could see by my face that I had a *fiver*; Oh man! what will I do? I canna' leeve this awfu' life,—I think it would be far better to die at once;" some other observations passed, and I being feverish myself his dispondency fell heavily on me also. Next day I was with the waggons considerably in front of the detachment, when having halted for some time, two men who had been flogged that morning for declaring that they were not able to march, were brought up to be put on the waggons, as the surgeon pronounced them to be in a fever. I called to mind the sickly state of

Stenhouse, and wished him to be put on also ; but the sergeant in charge of them said " did you not hear what has happened" and before I could enquire, he told me that Stenhouse had shot himself ! I went back a short distance and saw his body. It was alleged that he was contumacious and sat down, declaring that he would not move on, and that they might do with him what they chose. For this he was again flogged, and pushed onwards, but watching an opportunity he went off the road, loaded his musket, put his chin on the muzzle—pushed off the trigger with his bayonet, and blowing his head to pieces ended his earthly misery. About a ton weight of small stones were gathered and laid above the body, as we had nothing to make a grave. Five months afterwards we repassed the same road, I with some others, during a halt went to look at the spot where the body lay, bones were scattered about bleaching on the bare black mountain. A river that rises close by dashed its way over precipitous rocks, and on its banks two ravens sat on an old stump croaking in company. He had wandered often on the banks of his native Esk, and was, as I have been told, a poet possessing fine sensibility, and a passionate lover of one of the fairest young maidens that are to be seen in the neighbourhood of Rosslyn castle. A real, or a supposed slight made him in self banishment flee from the wildly romantic, but peaceful scenery of Rosslyn swayed by an ardent immagination to forget love, in the danger of the battle field !—but he lies ingloriously on one of the highest, blackest, and most desolate mountains of the Asturias, a few leagues from the solitary little town of Aceita.

Within a few days of this man's melancholy death we, got into Brivieska, many more being sick and sinking into despondency were laid down never to rise out of the old convent, which the troops had occupied some weeks previous to our arriving. I had during the eleven days slept mostly at night in one of the waggons, not daring to trust some articles of which I had special charge, to any one on the baggage ground, the necessities being too urgent and the facilities so easy to steal and sell to the Spaniards. I was now, however, obliged to abandon my charge to the chances of any accidents, or design, and betake myself to the convent, where I lay down on a small portion of straw that a comrade named James Jack procured for me. The frost—wind was piercingly cold ; it howled through the broken roof and doorless apartments with a dismal fierceness, while we lay shivering in our clothes. The first night and the day, and the second night passed over without any one, so far as I know, coming near us, or any rations being had. The second day it was announced that bread and beef had been got, but that none would receive their allowance unless they attended personally, at a certain part of the convent, it being considered that many of the men were shamming sickness, in order to be left behind. I had only eaten some small morsels of biscuit, not amounting altogether to a pound weight during eleven days, but had drunk water immoderately until a dysentery had rendered me so weak as to be incapable of going up or down the convent stairs.

I can remember that my only desire was for water; and as that could not be got but from outside the convent, and a guard being placed to let no one get out during the night, on any pretence, I suffered a most dreadful night of fevering thirst. Dreams of delirium sometimes carried me to the home and friends that seemed anxious to soothe and administer relief; but at short periods I again awoke with a burning brain, and feet that were literally frozen. James Jack made an attempt in the morning to procure something for me, but could not succeed; as a person named Ramage, who acted as Serjeant-major, would not deviate in the smallest degree from the order which he said he had got, not to allow any man his rations who did not attend personally to draw them. My comrade Jack got his own, and after striving fruitlessly to boil his morsel of beef in a small mess tin, by gathering particles of straw and blowing them into a blaze beneath it, there being no wood or other fuel; he brought it to me willing to share what he had got. It was scarcely warmed, and there not being any such a thing as salt, it may be supposed it was nauseous enough; but I burned with thirst, and that rendered even the unseasoned foul water delicious. That day passed heavily on, and the next night came with a delirium of ghostly visions. On both sides men lay as ill as I was, and all lay huddled together, to generate and retain warmth. Morning came, and for the first time a medical officer. This was Dr. Jenner, a relative, I was told, of the celebrated physician of that name; but it matters little whose relation he was. He ordered all the sick to be paraded in one of the galleries for his inspection; but some of these, among whom I was one, were unable to move from where they lay. In another apartment where there were sick men, I heard some of them groaning and calling " Oh Doctor Oh ! do not flog me, I cannot get up ; " and some, who were well, came in urging us to go out before the provost came, for Doctor Jenner was flogging all who did not get up. Presently he made his appearance, and ordered us to turn out, saying, " do you think I shall go into your filthy pigsties ? Here, some of you men," addressing himself to those who were moving about " tumble that fellow off that straw, and put it outside ; if they will lie there, let them have the bricks for a bed." We were then taken outside, to the corridor or gallery by assistance ; and I having stood until my limbs shook from weakness, waiting in my turn to be examined, sat down. He accosted me with " Now I know what sort of medicine will cure you; I have it here : (pointing to the cats,) so just come and let me see what is wrong with you ; come away now, come away; I dare say you are very ill." He spoke this in a tone of mock pity ; then bursting into a passion, as I endeavoured to crawl towards him, he said, " take off that night-cap ! throw it away, away with it—now, don't look so d—d dying like—I shall have none of this." And after examining my tongue and pulse, he ordered me to get four dozen lashes, adding, you're a d—d skulking vagabond ; there's nothing wrong with you. See you lay it well into that fellow, provost ! "

I certainly did not believe that this man could seriously intend to punish me, being sure that as a medical officer, he must have known that I was in a high fever ; nor did I think that Colonel Shaw and other officers who were present, would allow any sick man to be punished : for though they had applied the lash freely on the march, they had always the excuse of flogging the men up, to prevent their falling into the hands of the wandering guerillas, that infested the mountains over which we came. Now we were at a town, where, if not able to march, we could be left behind under medical treatment. But there were some of these men punished, and I believe that I should have shared it also, had not a young officer, ensign Brown, interfered in my behalf, by stating that I had been sick all the march, and, that though wearing a private's coat, I was a non-commissioned officer by my Colonel's order, and that they therefore could not inflict a punishment on me in that manner. I could have told them that, but being indignant at the infamous insult of Dr. Jenner, I had resolved to say nothing. I am sorry to state, that I never had an opportunity to thank Mr. Brown for his humanity; for I was then taken away to a kind of hospital, and before I joined my regiment, he had fallen a victim to the deadly malady. Also another friend that treated me kindly during the march, to the utmost of his power, was Sergeant Bayne; whose heroic death was mentioned in a previous chapter, when he and a party with rations were surrounded by the Carlists.

Colonel Shaw, his artillery and the detachment, then moved onwards to Vittoria, and I, with only two acquaintances, James Ritchie and Robert Smith, was left behind among a crowd of nearly two hundred in an old unfurnished house in Brivieska. This Smith was the same who had been flogged by Adjutant Macknight so severely, as mentioned in page 42, and who fell mortally wounded foremost in the fight on the 5th of May.

I must here note, that there was a Mr. Greenwood, a surgeon belonging to the Rifle corps, who laboured zealously for the recovery of the men, but having no medicine save a trifling quantity of inefficient powders he could not effect much good, only it was a consolation to a sick man to know that he was pitied if nothing else. And I must admit that some consolation arose to us from seeing Dr. Jenner carried away in a delirious fever to the Spanish hospital, assailed by the questions of " who is skulking now ?" Not so much that any man really rejoiced at his being taken ill: but that we were pleased to be relieved from his unmanly maltreatment.

For about two weeks I lay in a dark corner, with no covering but my great coat. There were three poor wretches along with me, whom I never saw, but with whom I afterwards got acquainted by hearing them speak in the dark; for it was a recess in a room to which we had crept to be out of the drifting snow and wind that whistled unrestrained through the house. One of these men was named Rolles, as he told me, and had once kept a tavern in Gravesend, and afterwards an hotel in Scarborough. He kept himself alive for a long time by talking about his famous dinners, and enumerating all the " hot joints, shoulders, &c." that he had cut in his time. The other two, who were both from Devonshire, responded by soliloquies on their former good fare also; and I beginning to feel my-

self less feverish, though so weak that I could not rise to walk, felt
a pleasure in listening to them that I could not now easily account
for. The two Devonshire men had been left behind their regiment,
(the 2nd) from having frost-bitten feet; and they now lay night
and day in that corner, never making their appearance in day-light.
About ten days after I had gone there, one of them fevered, and the
other fell into a raving delirium without, as I believe, any particular
disease. My proximity to them made me very uneasy; so creeping
from my corner, I found my way to another part of the house, and
lay there five days. At this time, I began to force myself to move
about, for I observed, that all those who lay huddled in corners invariably died; while, in moving from place to place, wretchedly
cheerless as the house was, others saved themselves, I made a visit
to the three whom I had left in the dark recess, to hear if they were
still living, when I met the man Rolles creeping on his hands and
knees, covered in the most loathsome state with filth and vermin
that I had seen any one in there; and, certainly, beyond a degree dreadful beyond what can be conceived or believed in this
country. In that state he had laid talking night and day about his
chaise and pair that he once kept; about his visits to France; his
great Christmas dinners and holiday fetes! Now his glaring eyes
and ghastly face presented themselves to me as he came creeping
out of the den of filth! He was leaving it, he said, because the
other two had died, and the rats were eating them beside him.

I had by this time made the acquaintance and friendship of Mr.
Greenwood, the surgeon spoken of, and I went and brought him
from an apartment where he was, shivering over a charcoal *braziero*.
He took a light, and on entering the dark corner, the two Devonshire
men were lying in such a position that left no doubt that the delirious one had strangled the other in the fever. They were thrown out
into a garden at the back of the house, the snow being so deep that
they could not be buried; and they lay there a fortnight. Having
gotten a better berth for myself, I procured one for Rolles; and many
a weary hour he whiled away for myself and others, by juicy descriptions of, how to carve turkies—make French stews, &c. But,
poor fellow, the ghosts of turkies and legs of mutton only haunted
him with a kind of platonic torment out of the world. He died soon
after the period I at present refer to.

When I went first into that house, I was attended now and then by my comrade, James Ritchie, who, though sick, was not quite so ill as I then was. I had now missed his visits to me for more than a week, and did not know where he was; but searching about, I found him wrapt in his great coat, and as he told me, very ill. There was a strong healthy man named Larry, a native of Shetland, who had been left behind his regiment, (the 6th,) for being what was called "daft," perfectly intractable, to be made a soldier of. This man was a melancholy instance of the evil effects of martial law being applied without variation to all varieties of men. He had no idea of cleanliness making a good soldier, nor had he heard that order, and neatness, and implicit obedience, were far higher qualities in soldiering, than the fearless dash-away, careless-of-every-thing, fighting qualities. Colonel Tupper had flogged him over and over for being disorderly in his dress, and not sufficiently polished and clean on parade. These punishments only made Larry worse, and he was ultimately left behind as being useless to the regiment.

I had now an opportunity of observing his qualities of mind, and I must say that a more kind hearted being I never knew. Nothing was too much for him to do if it was to serve another. He lifted and cleaned the sick men—carried out the dead ones on his back, and night or day went cheerfully to the assistance of any one who desired him. My friend Ritchie was wasted away to the last quiver of life when I discovered him, and my first object was to secure the services of Larry, by offering him my small allowance of wine daily to attend Ritchie. But he would not sell his services; he looked at me earnestly for a few seconds and answered " do you think *I* would take your wine? na, na lad; I'm a queer chap, but I am no greedy." It was only next day that I found Ritchie cold and stiffened; Larry having had so many to attend to during the night, had forgotten him, not hearing him make any noise for assistance.

I had a great respect for Ritchie, and there was only one duty now that he was dead, which I could perform, that was to get him buried, and not left to be destroyed by the rats and other vermin, as some bodies were then lying. I proposed to Larry that we should descend into the garden by a rope from a window, there being no other entrance allowable to us, and dig a hole among the bushes, and deposit the body. Larry answered that he thought of a better plan,

which was, to take the corpse during the night to the Spanish cemetery, and lay it in one of the open graves that were always ready
made.   I acquiesced, and getting the assistance of Smith, we carried
the body---or rather they carried it, for I was scarcely able to walk,
and got it over the wall about eight feet high, and put it in a grave,
where there was the dead body of a Spaniard.   It is a custom with
the people in Spain, to bury more than one body in the same grave,
and they frequently put a small quantity of earth on the first one until another is ready.   It was a grave of this sort in which Larry and
Smith laid my poor friend Ritchie, while I kept watch outside to
see that no visitors to the church-yard made their appearance
to stop them.   Smith told me that they hesitated a little whether
they would leave the clothes in which Ritchie died, on him; but
Larry considered that it being so very cold, and havning nothig to put
earth into the grave with, that it would be a shame to take off his
great coat; so laying him quietly down above that of the Spaniard,
he was left and we returned home through the dreary streets, we
having chosen a late hour at night purposely to avoid interruption.
Indeed we knew too well that none of our dead men were allowed
to be buried in consecrated ground and to get Ritchie buried in that
way, it was absolutely requisite for us to do it in the way we did.

Next day I was descending the dark stairs of the house which we
inhabited, when hearing some person coming up the stairs as if carrying a heavy burden :—I enquired who it was.—

" It's me.—is that you?" was the answer, and responding enquiry
of Larry.

I answered that it was me, and getting to the same part of the stairs
where he was, I enquired what he was carrying.

" It's Ritchie," he replied, " he'll no stay yonder ! for I had got him
lyin' outside the Kirk-yard the now; an' he was laying on his face
as if he had fa'n comin oer the dyke."

I was astonished, and began to believe that Larry was, as his comrades asserted *daft*.   But the body being positively there, and Larry
re-asserting that he found it laying outside the cemetery. I concluded
that the friends of the deceased Spaniard, must have been attracted to
the grave by our feet marks among the snow; and that on discovering the body of an Englishman which they would readily distinguish
by the clothes being on; they, for the eternal peace of the Spaniard

who lay beneath him, took his body out of the grave. I asked Larry what was to be done, (after giving my opinion of how he had been thrown out), adding that there was no use in taking it up stairs again. He seemed for some minutes to be estranged in thoughtfulness, and then asking me if I would get Smith to help him, said, " I'll let you see me cheat them this time." As the Spaniards have no dread of resurrectionists, and never stir out of doors after sun-set, especially in a cold night, we had only to make a slight reconnoissance, when seeing everything quiet, Smith and Larry again got the corpse into the grave-yard, I occupying the post I had the night before. In about quarter of an hour, they returned to me, and I was then informed that according as Larry had planned, they had taken up the Spaniard, put Ritchie's great coat on him and reversed their situations, the latter undermost, and the former above.

The day following that there was a complaint made to the Alcalde, that an English soldier had been laid in a Spaniard's grave. This led to the Magistrate giving an order that persons should be appointed to make graves in a field outside the town, and also an order for the removal of the heretical body that had been unlawfully and sacrilegiously laid *above* the Spaniard in the consecrated cemetery. This order was obeyed, and a service for the dead performed to redeem the body that remained in the grave from the contamination it had been exposed to. It will be scarcely necessary to add, that the body of Ritchie kept possession, and that the Spaniard travelled. In the other place allotted to us, for the next three or four weeks I assisted in the interment of some every day ; and my readers will probably regret with me that one of the number was poor Larry.

This young man had travelled from the Shetland Islands in the summer of 1835, to work at the southern harvest-work, and as he told me it was a mere money speculation, his changing his route and going to Spain. He said, that he had never been farther from home before than Lerwick, which is on one of his native islands : but on coming so far south as Edinburgh, which he considered nearly the utmost limits of the world, he was induced to enlist for Spain, being told that he would be back in *three* months, and that besides saving his pay, he would get about ten pounds then to come home with. This he said was far more than he expected to make at the harvest, and besides, as they told him it was in a ship that he would go to
No 15.

Spain, he thought of necessity that Spain must be nearer Lerwick
than where he was, for he found himself very near the end of the sea
at Edinburgh.   Some of those who were recruiting, seeing his simplicity, played on it, and he was by that means kept in humour until
fairly in Spain.   The foolish and mischievous, then made sport of his
simple ignorance of mankind.   The officers demanded his attention
to soldiering—the Colonel flogged him, and as was a common case
in all regiments, many of the accomplished rascals wrought mischief
and swore it on him, and by that means had him punished.   He told
me, and some of the men who knew him, corroborated what he said
that in four months he had been eleven times provosted, and once
flogged by sentence of a court-martial for having lost his musket,
which some thieves had no doubt stolen and sold to the Spaniards.
The court-martial awarded him one hundred and fifty lashes, all of
which he got, and the eleven provostings amounted altogether to
upwards of three hundred more.

He was the most warm hearted and affectionate being towards any
one who befriended him, or rather did not work mischief on him that
I ever knew.   When he has been working amongst all sorts of sludge
work, and some one who did not need his assistance playing a trick
on him, or calling him a " brute," which they did, I have immediately
entered into conversation with him, when he talked of his friends and
put the never ceasing questions of when I thought we would get
home—how far it was from that to Lerwick, &c.   To have told him
that he must go to London, or Edinburgh, before getting home made
him stare.   I have seen him stand still after I had mentioned these
places, and think for a few minutes, and in a very earnest tone say,
" but where are we ?" and then add, " if my Mother had seen me
come away, I would'na mind stayin a while."   Yet with all his very
innocent knowledge of the world, he possessed a great deal of
natural vivacity, shrewdness, and even wit ; only he was so thoroughly
out of his own moral latitude, and had been so stupified by the severity
of martial law, that he was to a common observer, a fool.   Kindness
might have made such a man a good soldier, though I believe it
would have been thrown away if extended to some of his more ingenious comrades.   The first information I had of his death, was from
Mr. Greenwood, the Surgeon, who had seen him die, and shed tears
when he told me.   Larry had supposed himself at home in his deli-

rium of fever, and in a kind of broken language which he spoke in —but which I am not able to translate, was telling all what had been done to him "at the far away places," associating the name of every place he mentioned with Edinburgh, believing that, and the other towns he had seen in the west of Scotland to be at the outside of the world.

Peace to the grave of Larry! I carved his name, and that of his native place on a flat stone, which I put beside his grave, but it is probably not there now, as all the feelings of the people manifested towards us at Brivieska, were the reverse of kindness and respect.

While referring to my unhappy stay at Brivieska, I may mention that a Major Edwards, a kind hearted old soldier, was in the town commanding the depot. Ultimately those of us who recovered were not so badly off, as he succeeded in getting some money from head quarters which was laid out in purchasing coffee, and ingredients to make soup for us. I had a hand in the drawing of the rations from the commissary, and as we did not often know the exact number of living men we had to eat them, and the commissary had a more imperfect knowledge, it may be supposed, we commonl erred on the side of the extras. Major Edwards soon after went to take command of the depot at Santander, where he died.

CHAPTER XII.

Extract from an officer's Journal relating to Mr. Wilkinson.—Extract from Wilkinson's letter in the Morning Herald of 11th March, 1836.—Quotation from his pamphlet exposing the real state of parties in Spain.—Career of Zumalacarregui—his death.—Intrigues among the priests.—Don Carlos and the character of writers, &c. &c. &c.

THERE were some other officers at Brivieska, and their conduct at that time and subsequently, having made them conspicuous ; I shall give a sketch of one, a Mr. Wilkinson. In the first place I may quote a note respecting him, which appears in an officer's journal which I have before me. "March 30th, 1836. At Ona I chanced to see the *Morning Herald*, of the 11th, containing a letter from Mr. Wilkinson, alluded to in a former note, as having gone over to the enemy. Of this long tissue of farrago I shall briefly notice one passage, which is that wherein he says, "I had left all my kit behind me, and only brought my baggage." Now, as it appears from his letter, that he only took Mrs. Wilkinson with him, we may fairly presume that she is the "baggage" alluded to. How far she deserves that character, may be learnt from the following short history of the lady, about whose honor so much fuss is made. The *now* Mrs. Wilkinson came from Scotland, the mistress of an assistant-surgeon of one of the Scotch regiments, who, when we marched from Bilbao, supplied her liberally with money, to take her back to Scotland. Instead of going to Scotland, however, she went round to Santander, in the Mazeppa steamer, where, between her present husband, (or somebody else, for I am not quite sure,) and another officer, who had been dismissed the service, a regular battle took place, as to who should claim priority in the lady's favor. Ex-lance corporal of the Portuguese service Wilkinson, however, bore the palm from his adversary, and married his prize, who tramped it with soldiers, and soldiers' wives, (occasionally dressed in the habit of a man,) as far as Brivieska where Mr. Wilkinson was left in depot, and where, it appears, he was dismissed the service,—not for "building churches !" It would hardly be fair, under any other circumstances, to enter upon the *vie privée* of the lady, but when her husband states that he was dismissed for upholding the *honor* of his wife, and attacks, in such bitter terms, both the Legion and its chief, it cannot be too distinctly known how nice must have been his sense of that honor ! His wife, by this time, we are assured forms one of the brightest ornaments of Don Carlos's *choice* little court at Onate. I heartily wish the *soi-disant* king joy of such an acquisition."

The foregoing is quoted not to expose Mrs. Wilkinson's alleged infirmities, but as these remarks have already gained publicity, I quote them here in order to do justice to Mr. Wilkinson. I am not acquainted with him personally nor have I had any correspondence with him ; but I remember his being at Brivieska, and my opinion of him, was then, that he was as gentlemanly and as honorable, in his moral and military character, though he *had* once been *lance corporal* as most of those who had been born gentlemen, and were his contemporaries in the British Legion. Mr. Wilkinson possesses very superior talents, and the fact of his having taken a young female who was basely and cruelly deserted, not liberally provided with money to go home as is asserted—but cruelly deserted in a foreign country, after liberally spending her own money on a false seducer—to protect this young woman by making her his wife, and upholding her character as his wife, and his own as husband, was, if not prudent as an officer, at least honorable as a man. Mr. Wilkinson challenged to mortal combat, some of those who insulted him for his alliance with this woman ; they refused to fight because he had once been a soldier in the ranks, and as I have been informed he very properly gave them a hearty castigation, first for their insult, and then for their cowardly excuse, and thus got his own dismissal from the Legion.

But it would be an injustice to Mrs. Wilkinson having once alluded to her, were I not to state farther that setting aside her first folly and embarkation in the Legion which was an enterprise too romantic for a female, she had many amiable qualities. At the time that men were starving with cold and hunger, and dying as has been sketched in the preceding chapter, she voluntarily, zealously and efficiently assisted them, and in different cases prevented men from being heartlessly flogged, by her entreaties in their behalf. It is improper I admit that a *woman* should make any officer swerve from the performance of duties devolving on him : but when those duties are the execution of orders disgraceful to humanity, and derogatory to the honor of commander, executioner, and victim ; the interfering sympathy of a woman, is no disgrace to the pliant husband that gave way to her.

Mr. Wilkinson having been dismissed from the Legion, went over to the Carlists, and after getting there, was solicited to write a favorable account of what he saw to the English newspapers. It will be readily believed that if he wrote anything, it must have been laudatory of his new friends the Carlists, and abusive of the Christinos ; for he would not dare to write anything else. In his letter published March 11th, 1835, he gives the following account of how he got to the enemy's camp :—" I walked out of Trevino in the middle of the day, in company with my wife and a late brother-officer a particular friend ; my intention, (unknown to him) being at the time only to reconnoitre the road, but not immediately to go on. Having, however, proceeded a good way from the town, I thought it was better to go on, and being sure no pursuit would be made while my friend was with us, we requested him as he complained of being fatigued, to remain at the top of the hill, till our return from the valley, which my

worthy friend most unsuspiciously did. Pray Sir, send him one of
your papers if you accept this communication, that he may know his
guard is relieved. We gained the mountains, and began to scramble
over them, a patrol of Christino Lancers passing on our right. We
soon found some peasants working, at one of whom I presented a
pistol offering him four dollars to take me to the Carlists, and declaring I would shoot him in case of treachery. He led us through
the mountains about five miles, when suddenly several soldiers resembling the Chapelgorris ran out of a copse towards us. Uncertain
what they were, I held my pistol to our guide, and drawing my To-
ledo, placed my forage cap on its point crying, *Viva Carlos V !* *Viva Carlos V !* was the answer. We blessed God for our deliverance
and exchanged congratulations with our new friends, who conducted
us to the picquet which turned out to me. I refrain from mentioning names and places in the immediate vicinity, suffice to say, we
proceeded into Alava, passing near Vittoria, and laughing at the
Christinos."

Mr. Wilkinson was presented in due form to Don Carlos, and was
directed not so much by request, as by order or special command, to
write to England exalting the Carlist cause, and decrying that of the
Christinos. That appears from a pamphlet which he has since published, to make a quotation from which, and thereby do justice to
his character, I have introduced his name into this work.

He takes the most correct view of all parties in the war which has
yet been published, and having been on both sides, not as a traitor,
but by ill-treatment forced to exchange, it is likely his information
was superior to most others. Besides, at the commencement of this
work I laid down the same line of argument as to the merits of the
Spanish quarrel, and thereby, I am aware, alienated the friendship
of many who adhere more firmly as partizans to certain sides, than I
do ; so that now to that man I gladly avail myself of the lucid, and correct historical remarks of Mr. Wilkinson, in support of my view, and as
explanatory to those who may not yet be aware of the position in which
parties stand in Spain. He says :—

" The war commenced by the attempt of the Spanish government
to deprive the Basquese of their immunities, and was then the struggle of a free people for independence ; whereas now the principles of
the people are changed, and the war is the effort of a faction to force

upon the Spanish nation the odious tyranny of an usurper. It was also no less preposterous for the Spanish government during its infancy, and while its very existence might be deemed precarious to attempt a conquest in which very powerful sovereigns have failed, than it is presumptuous for the Basques to support the Spanish Pretender against the liberal governments of Europe. Whosoever therefore now supports the cause of the Queen Regent, as being that of the liberties of Spain, must upon the same principle, commend the Basques for having resisted her encroachments upon their liberties; and whosoever supported the Basquese in the beginning of the war, must now condemn them, and advocate the cause of the Queen Regent, if reason be his criterion. But what have political partizans to do with reason? I am so far from admitting it to be a proof of a man's constancy to a political creed, that he has uniformly adhered to the same party, as to consider it impossible for such an individual not to have betrayed his principles, if ever he had any.

The Basques did well to defend their liberties, but their policy in attempting to force Don Carlos upon the Spaniards was erroneous: they fight for freedom at home, and absolutism abroad.

The provinces of Biscay, Alava, Guipuzcoa, and Navarre have, as is well known, enjoyed during immemorial ages, peculiar immunities, varying in the several provinces, but being generally, that they tax themselves, and are governed by their own laws, administered by the Alcaldies of different districts, who are freely elected by the people. The affairs of the province are settled by a junta, or meeting of all its Alcaldies, which is the government mentioned by several ancient writers who also quote from the language, that with some slight inversion of phraseology, is the same to this day. We trace the language, government, and customs, antecedent to the Roman conquest, through the Gothic monarchy, the Mahometan era, and thence through all the vicissitudes that have distracted Spain.

This freedom has rendered the Basques far superior to the Spaniards, though less favored by climate; yet man, the noblest work of nature, seems to flourish best under an inclement sky, the mind strengthening with the body; and liberty, with which only true greatness can be achieved, finding her securest home in uncertain climates and in mountainous districts.

The towns of the Basque are generally superior to those in other parts of the North of Spain ; the agricultural resources far exceed the consumption, and commerce being free, the affluence and comfort of the people were extraordinary: so false is the assertion that ignorance led them into the field ; knowledge led them, a just appreciation of the blessings Providence has bestowed upon them, liberty and mountains.

This superiority of the Basques stirred the black bile of the Spaniards, and what they lacked virtue to imitate, their characteristic envy rendered them desirous to destroy. The regenerators of the age also cast their eyes upon the Basques, and beheld a people happy and independent, under a government immemorial as their mountains. The idea had something heathenish and antediluvian about it, shocking to every modern theory. The inhabitants of the provinces lived, each free peasant, under the shade of his vine and fig-tree ; for *they* had never heard the names of Malthus and Martineau.

To gain popularity therefore, by gratifying the envy of the Spaniards, and indulging the meddling propensities of the regenerators of the age, the Queen Regent deprived the Basques of their liberties ; so that one of the first acts of a government professing liberal principles, was to subvert all that could be found of true freedom in the Peninsula. The compensation forced upon the Basques was, that they should participate with the Spaniards in an experimental lately defunct Constitution : considerations of justice and experience were as cobwebs before the new broom, and liberty was the war cry with which the Christino army entered the provinces, to burn, to massacre, and enslave. Every town was occupied, every pass secured ; the people groaned beneath the pressure, but their fetters were so extended and so weighty, that it seemed desperate to attempt to break them ; yet their minds revolted, though their bodies were restrained ; nor was a champion lacking to his country in her hour of persecution and abasement.

The renowned general Zumalacarregui, then colonel in the Spanish army, being exasperated at some ill usage of the government, suddenly left the Christinos to head a few hundred peasants in the mountains, with whom he defeated the detachments sent against him, and entered several villages ; the country people flocked to his standard, being mostly armed with sticks ; yet he continued conquering, till from the wrecks and with the spoils of Spanish regiments, he had armed his soldiers. He now defeated the Christinos wherever he found them, put to flight whole divisions of their best troops, headed by their most experienced generals, who have three times successively taken the field against him ; stormed strong garrisoned towns, and drove their scattered army hither and thither as he pleased. As he marched he conquered, as he conquered he re-established the ancient free government ; the juntas of the several provinces raised monthly supplies accòrding to the army estimates, the troops were regularly paid, and the army provided with artillery and all necessary equipage, from the defeated Christinos.

Zumalacarregui at this time nearly determined to accept the crown of Navarre, which the people were ready to confer on him, and altogether separating the four provinces from Spain, to govern them as Don Thomas I., King of Navarre, and Senhor of Biscay. How unfortunate for his country, that a mistaken principle of allegiance and a devotion to legitimacy, excusable in a Spaniard, induced him rather to invite over Don Carlos, who was thus received by the Basques on condition of upholding their privileges! They conducted him to the tree of liberty at Guernica, and seated him beneath the canopy of its branches; the national cap of the provinces, now uniform in the army, was then placed upon his head, amid the acclamations of an assembled people; whose immunities he swore to maintain, and in whose hearts observance of this oath would have for ever rendered him freely, greatly despotic.

The firmness of the Queen's goverment was admirable, as its error in provoking the war must be condemned. Its energies increased with the imminence of the danger; new armies were levied and other generals tried. Undismayed by reiterated reverses, it continued to pour troops upon troops into the provinces; and as they were destroyed, others started up, like hydra-heads, to replace them. But the spirit of the soldiers no longer corresponded with the determined policy of the government; they were now so accustomed to defeat, as to consider success impossible, and the very name of Zumalacarregui palsied their resolution.

Thus far we have seen the Basques, fighting in the cause of liberty headed by the greatest general Spain has ever produced, unanimous among themselves, and triumphant over all their enemies; we must now note the Carlists, contending as a faction, and observe with what saintly guile absolutism is substituted for liberty as the principle of the war, how, to the interests of individuals composing a paltry court, the sacred cause of the public is sacrificed, trace the infant steps of the inquisition and remark how the priestly foot was first placed in the stirrup of state affairs.

The first thing done by the sycophants of the faction, was to set up a mock court, appointing a ministry, with secretaries, clerks, &c. The priests began also to be busy, having a firm hold on the weak mind of the Pretender, a great many pounds of candles were burnt, and pious evolutions innumerable, exhibited. The contributions raised by the juntas were of course transmitted to the court, and the troops began to grumble at not receiving pay. This roused Zumalacarregui, who appeared at court to the consternation of the clerical, and official cabal, and threatened to shoot them all, confessors, ministers, secretaries, and clerks, unless the pay of the army were immediately forthcoming. The confessors, ministers, secretaries, and clerks disgorged their plunder, and Zumalacarregui, having proved the crime against them, only spared their lives at the prayer of Don Carlos, neither during the life of the general did they venture upon a repetition of similar embezzlement.

The design of Zumalacarregui was to take Vittoria, and march immediately upon Madrid, but Don Carlos desired that he would first take Bilbao (some negotiations depending upon the capture of that city) which accordingly Zumalacarregui invested, and must have taken, but for the wound he received. He enquired of Dr. Burgess, an English surgeon, who had gained his confidence by performing successfully many operations which the Spanish surgeons declared impossible, if the wound were dangerous. Dr. Burgess answered it was a trifle and that he ought in a few days to be on horseback, but if he permitted two Spanish surgeons, sent by the king, to attend him, their treatment might kill him, though the wound would not. Zumalacarregui would not dismiss these men, because they had a royal order to attend him, and Dr. Burgess took leave, being aware the Spaniards, would, if he staid, make him answerable for the life of the general. I cannot exactly describe their treatment, but, although the bone had not been shattered, they put splints upon the leg, did not extract the ball, and poured into the wound some liquid, which gave great pain and caused much inflammation. Dr. Burgess,

notwithstanding the danger which he shared with the patient, would
have generously remained, but that he conceived, to be present during their proceedings would be to connive at murder, neither could
he bear to witness Zumalacarregui's agonies under their treatment.

The event justified his suspicions : Zumalacarregui died immediately after drinking a cup of coffee, and was hastily buried without
being opened, Dr. Burgess being refused permission to examine the
body. The grief of Don Carlos and of the army was sincere, and
fear compelled the court party to dissemble their satisfaction, which
however they afterwards discovered, affirming that Zumalacarregui
had been too independent, and more regarded the cause of the provinces than legitimacy, in fact, that it was well he died as he did,
being no longer wanted, for the king had an army of thirty thousand
men, all the rough work of the war had been done, and general
Moreno could finish it. I have only further to observe, that one of
the surgeons who attended Zumalacarregui had deserted from the
Christinos, that immediately after his death peculation recommenced
and has continued to this day, the troops scarce receiving any pay,
although the juntas raise monthly contributions for the purpose,
which money, besides what the English Tories and the Northern
Powers may have sent, the confessors, ministers, secretaries, and
clerks are so loath to part with, that it would break their hearts to
oblige them to disburse it.

Confident in their expectations of an approaching triumph, all
the offices of Spain were disposed of in advance, and the distribution of nearly every individual place settled among the courtiers of
the Pretender; the old officers of Zumalacarregui were displaced and
superseded by Castilians and Andalusians, the immunities of the
Basques became a very uncourtly theme, and the inalienable prerog-
atives of legitimacy a favourite topic : indeed, the people of the
court seemed to regard the Basques as encroachers and liberals,
miserable hinds, too much honoured by permission to toil in the vineyard, of which their betters were to enjoy the fruit. Absolutism was
the order of the day.

The liberal governments of Europe, which must have sympathised
with the Basques, had they contented themselves with maintaining
their liberties, were thus necessitated to oppose their attempt to re-
establish absolutism on the Spanish throne, in the person of Don

Carlos and aided the Queen Regent accordingly. Thus was the
war re-commenced upon a new principle, for, at the time of the formation of the British Legion, the provinces were nearly cleared of
Christinos, neither, had the Basques rested there, could any intervention have been justifiable; but they resolved, after having vindicated
their own liberties, to enslave all Spain, which the quadruple alliance,
with great reason, would not permit.

The arrival of the Legion struck terror throughout the faction,
with the single exception of the Pretender, whose confidence in the
generalship of the Virgin Mary is unbounded; but the ridiculous
exaggerations in the Carlist bulletins, concerning the reconnoissance
of the 30th of August, 1835, had their intended effect of diminish-
ing this panic.   Contrary to their expectations, they retained Hernani, only because it could not have been the Spanish general's
object to take it, and the British lost two men, who were multiplied
to eight hundred in the Carlist account.   A number of scarlet coats
were also made and distributed, that it might be believed they were
taken from the slain English, and I saw an officer's commission, in
which it was stated, that he received his promotion for his gallantry
in the battle fought on the glorious day of the 30th of August, when
His Majesty's arms were blessed with a decisive victory.

I am the more particular on these details, knowing the extreme
apprehension felt by the government of the faction; lest the true
state of things should appear before the public, which induces them
to take every precaution to prevent unfavorable reports from leaving
their territory; they are especially anxious also concerning the British press, and seize every opportunity of persuading any stray Englishman who may chance to enter the provinces, to write something
for the cause; of which solicitude it is a singular instance, that the
very prime minister of the Pretender condescended to express a particular desire, that I would write to the *Morning Herald* when I first
entered their country, and Don Carlos himself requested a sergeant,
who deserted from the Legion and whom he made an officer, to write
to his friends in favour of the cause.   They will escort any person
connected with the Tory Press throughout the country, and if the
season be spring or summer, will bid him observe how green the fields
and trees are, how the peasants are busied in their occupations, and
appeal to every cow and pig on the road as a proof of abundance.

All this while, the individual has no opportunity of ascertaining, by general inquiries, the real state of things ; he is feasted and wheedled by the people of the court, writes as they wish, and leaves the country with the idea that he is competent to pass a judgment upon it. At the same time, their severity towards any whom they suspect may write against them, is altogether as great : all letters must be read before they quit the country, or are delivered to parties resident in it ; nor dare any person question the accuracy of the *Gazette of Onate*, when it so grossly exaggerates the loss of the Christinos, as on the 30th of August, 1835, on pain of being imprisoned as a well wisher to the Christinos.

Since the death of Zumalacarregui, their troops have scarce received any pay, though the estimates went monthly to the juntas, and the necessary supplies have been raised ; the displacing so many good officers and substituting others, strangers to the language of the troops, had also a very bad effect in the army; its discipline daily declined and its efficacy deteriorated ;—plunder, which Zumalacarregui had completely put a stop to, recommenced, and in a few months the soldiers became banditti ;—priests also, whom he would never permit to meddle with affairs in a clerical capacity, many of them held commissions, being consulted on all occasions, began to exchange their humility of demeanor for extreme haughtiness, till things came to that pass, that every officer was expected to salute a priest whether he knew him or not; they interfered with military, civil, and private affairs. Such a man must be promoted for his piety, and such an one cashiered or reprimanded by his military superior for not confessing. The time of Don Carlos was much occupied with complaints about unmarried girls being with child, and officers intriguing in their billets ; and more than one delinquent was convicted of having corrupted chastity with a franc, and has received a royal order to make atonement by marriage : but what I admire is the address of the priests in keeping clear of the noose with which they are throttling the laity. The priests have mistresses, with whom they live as man and wife, and are often surrounded with a number of interesting little shavelings, styled nephews and neices, yet no one is scandalized ; the holy man can give absolution to his beloved, and I remember an instance of two sisters doing duty with a priest, she who was very near her confinement being relieved by her sister.

The name of a consitution is odious to the faction, and Don Carlos is too honest a man to hold out any promises of this kind, his
avowed determination being to conquer the Spanish crown, and
reign more absolutely than his ancestors, in conjunction with the
inquisition. Now the king of Spain was never king of the Basques,
but only their Senhor, and it was against the sovereignty of the
Spanish crown, which the Queen Regent endeavoured to enforce,
that they took up arms; yet we see they would impose upon the Spaniards a yoke much heavier than they themselves rejected, and as
this attempt has prevented their now enjoying their liberties, by
forcing the Spaniards, who commenced the war as aggressors, to
continue it upon a defensive principle, also by disgusting the French
and English governments; it must be admitted, " that the Basques •
did well to defend their liberties, but their policy was erroneous in
attempting to force Don Carlos upon the Spaniards; they fight for
freedom at home and absolutism abroad."

The Spaniards fight upon similar principles, for their own freedom
and the subjugation of the Basques.

This may be considered a corollary to our first proposition, yet
the subject being one that requires ample discussion, a few additional
facts may be useful.

The attempted usurpation of the Queen Regent's government, towards a brave and free people, was no less atrocious than impolitic,
and is rendered utterly detestable by the savage cruelty with which
it was partially effected. The proclamations of Mina and Valdez
roused that spirit they were designed to overawe. *Death to any
surgeon who relieves a wounded rebel,* (this is the only humane part of
the proclamation,) *root up every vineyard, burn every cornfield, cut
down every tree, level every house ! Let neither age, sex or condition
be sacred in your sight, for our gracious Queen devotes the rebellious
provinces to rapine, to slaughter, to fire !* Is it wonderful that the
Basques hate the Spaniards, and will endure every privation for independence, any tyranny but their's ? How could poor villagers refuse
rations to armed Carlists ? If they refused they would be destroyed
by the mountaineers, and the rations taken also ; if they yielded
they were to be butchered by Mina's blood hounds. Thus were the
Queen Regent's adherents alienated, and the entire provincial population rendered hostile to her government : so that, had not the

Basques encumbered their cause with the Pretender, that just cause must have long since triumphed, and in its triumph all who profess liberal principles must have participated.

That the Spaniards are right, in supporting the Queen's government against the faction, is no less obvious, than that they erred greatly when in an evil hour they meddled with the immunities of the Basques ; for, not only would the success of the Pretender extirpate every germ of liberty in their institutions, but the flaming zeal of inquisitors, fanned by revenge, political inveteracy, and the exultation of recent conquest, would out-herod any hitherto recorded atrocities of their diabolical tribunal : not a corner of the kingdom would be free from its researches, nor any individual too exalted or too mean for its observation ; neither do I speak hypothetically, as of what might be expected, but positively, as of what would certainly be, for, when I was at Segura, Colonel Ceballas the commandant, gave warning to all officers to be circumspect since he had spies in every billet, and upon the report of one of these spies, doctor Burgess was imprisoned with me six months, most of the time in a filthy lousy jail; the accusation of the spy being, that he had jocosely said, children were baptized in England with bacon and brandy, and offered to receive the sacrament without confessing. We were detained after our innocence, in other respects, had been established, according to the Spanish law, which lays the *onus probandi* upon the defendant, who must prove his innocence, not even the commander-in-chief daring to speak in our behalf; although I heard he expressed much sympathy for us. Don Carlos declared, that for a murder he would have forgiven us ; but concerning such horrid impiety the law must take its course. Well nigh reduced to skeletons from starvation, we afforded subsistence to vermin that fattened upon our blood, like the priests upon the exhausted country, in this condition, treated with great brutality, we were marched barefooted over the mountains, to be examined about paltry matters, till badgered well nigh to desperation we showed front to our persecutors. I was desired to sign a declaration, that I did not know the difference between right and wrong like the Spaniards, never having been instructed in the doctrines of the apostolical, evangelical Church of Rome. My reply was, that according to a text in scripture, *if the blind lead the blind both must fall into a ditch.* That the Spaniards were too ignorant to instruct even the ignorant, and that I was an unworthy member of the apostolical, evangelical, protestant catholic Church of England. The next question was, how could I call myself a christian and be a rebel to the church of Rome; and my answer was, that I could not be a rebel to that church never having been its subject. We were marched back to jail. Afterwards at Tolosa, the Doctor's examination was renewed, a list of questions being sent by the Pretender's confessor to be categorically answered; some of these questions were ridiculous, others casuistical, but the Doctor quoting Scripture repeatedly disconcerted his interrogators, and floored them at every reply, like a jack in a box, till they came to the question—What is the protestant religion? The religion of Jesus Christ was the reply, and it acted like a *vade retro Sathanas* upon them; the interpreter ran out of the room as if he had been exorcised; and a courier was dispatched to Don Carlos with the protestant's confession of his faith.

The priests are foremost in the war: they not only pray but even fight for Don Carlos, and would they do this but for a conviction that his cause is their cause, and that the re-establishment of absolutism would be accompanied by that of the ecclesiastical power with increased wealth and even exaggerated abuses? All former church revenues the clergy would, of course, resume as a right, then seize upon what remained as a prize of the war, and after avarice should be glutted, revenge would require to be satiated: yet this would be but one consequence of Don Carlos's success—his rapacious adherents must be rewarded—his brigand army satisfied. What private resentments might not be gratified under political pretences? what treachery! what confiscation! what massacre! The tyrant, the priest, and the bandit all tearing the bleeding vitals of their country! Yet, when all should be slaves, despotism could encroach no further; there is blood and wealth in Spain to glut even her clergy and her brigands;—thus could the faction completely crush every other party, the tranquillity of desolation might reign, and the vulture when gorged might slumber;—but this the faction cannot do even if successful,—therefore its triumph would commence an era of civil wars the most dreadful Spain has witnessed.

However unjustifiable, then, may have been the attempt of the Queen Regent to deprive the Basques of their liberties, as most un-

MAGNIFICENT PASS OF PAN CORBO,

The Boy Maxwell shooting a Guerilla who has rode off with a Musket.

P. 266.

No. 16.

justifiable it was; the Spaniards have a far more dangerous usurpation to apprehend from them, and fight upon similar principles with them; viz, their own freedom and the subjugation of others.

The Basques are losing their liberties by espousing the cause of Don Carlos.

It is scarce possible for a people to fight the battles of absolutism and retain its freedom, as the Basques are now discovering. Two governments exist in each province, the Pretender's and the junta's, neither for some time did the court party venture to interfere with the native power; but when, after the death of Zumalacarregui, Castilians and Andalusians were placed in command, when some Basque chiefs had been conciliated and others overawed, when the clergy had taken up their position, encroachments commenced by Don Carlos sending two priests as members to the junta which immediately expelled them and sent a strong remonstrance. Don Carlos apologised, but made it his request that, during the war, the priests might be members, and the junta yielded the point. The arbitrary imposition of fines now used by every commandant followed; these fines at first were to be transmitted to the Junta, but soon became a court perquisite; the power of imprisoning civilians was the next usurpation, and the jails are now filled with persons obnoxious to the court; yet according to the immunities of the Basques, which the Pretender had sworn to uphold, the king of Spain could neither interfere with the junta, impose fines or imprison any denizen. It may appear surprizing that the army endured this, but be it remembered the army is not what it was in the days of Zumalacarregui; it *then fought* for independance, *it now fights* for plunder, superstition, and subsistence. As Louis the XIV. said *the men most follow the rations* The soldiers of Navarre act in Guipuzcoa as in a hostile country those of Guipuzcoa would do the same in Navarre; the soldiers are in fact banditti. The resources of the provinces are also fast failing, and those enormous contributions, to raise which the wretched peasant toils and starves, are embezzled by individuals of the court faction.

The consideration of the long arrears due to them may also induce the troops to fight for Don Carlos, since, that they will be paid, when he gets to Madrid, they have been assured, and, too stupid to understand the fallacy, they believe the fable. To consummate the misfortunes of the Basques, to give the death blow to their liberties, the execrable inquisition is now established in their country.

Imagine Don Carlos absolute king of Spain, acting with the inquisition, possessed of power to attempt what his faction can at present but contemplate; would not the court of Madrid be the rendezvous of French Carlists and jesuits, the very focus of diplomatic mischief, a perfect workshop for foreign conspirations? Imagine the Spanish army reorganized and disciplined by German officers, and consider how much easier, in case of a general war, for the Spaniards to invade France, then for the French to invade Spain, owing to the frontier ground. The idea of the Spaniards invading France seems ridiculous, but, be it remembered, that the Spaniards, although now the most miserable, inefficient troops, in Europe, were once the best disciplined. Their material is the same, why should not their discipline be recovered? Absolute governments are often favorable to military progress, and it was under an absolute government that the Spanish army achieved its high reputation formerly. Indeed, no doubt can exist, but, that were Don Carlos to conquer the Spanish crown, the object of his policy would be to get on foot a numerous, well disciplined army; and this he would easily do with assistance of the Great Northern military governments. If France have therefore, any reason to fear the Northern Powers in the existing state of things how would she be situated, were their apprehended invasion supported by a Spanish crusade?"

CHAPTER XIII.

The miseries of the women following the Legion.—Death of an Irishwoman and her child.—Anecdote of Zumalacarregui.—Description of the pass of Pan Corbo.—A guerilla shot by a boy named Maxwell near the pass.—An extraordinary meal round the picquet fire.—Descriptive narrative of some of the officers of the 10th regiment, Lieutenant H——ington, Ensign Q——ll, Lieutenant Jo——-ce, Colonel Ebsworth, Major Shaw, Count Kalling, with King Bernadotte of Sweden's treatment to him, Captain De B——ce, Colonel O'Connell's behaviour, the British Commissioners engagement with him and address to the Legion.—Denial of that engagement by Lord Melbourne.—proof of it by a letter from Colonel Hogg.—Personal sketch of General Evans.

THE quotations in the previous chapter from Mr. Wilkinson's pamphlet are so truly correct, as regards the *principles of* the Spanish quarrel, that I considered it best to quote his own words, lest in-giving my own, coincidence of opinion and the fact of his having had precedence of me in publishing, might have seemed an illegal appropriation on my part.   I therefore take leave of him, having as I wished, done what I could for his character, hitherto unjustly maligned.

To pursue a narrative of the horrors of warfare, I shall relate a circumstance illustratrive of the awful hardships suffered by the weak and sickly men ; more especially the women, and their children who bring up the rear of a march.

The fewer women there are following soldiers on active service the better, and though in the British army it might seem severely inhuman to part soldiers and their wives as was often the case in the late war, yet it was an act preventing much of the awful heart-rending misery that attends female life in a campaign.   Who can read Sir John Moore's retreat but with a soul-sickening shudder at the horrors attending it ? and yet we in the Legion had some cases of wretchedness, not less horrible, without the same unavoidable causes.   But before any of these can be rightly understood I must explain the circumstances in which the women, more especially those of the Irish regiments, were placed.

A most reprehensible laxity had prevailed in raising the Irish regiments, by permitting vast numbers of women to follow their husbands ;—indeed to get men to fill up the regiments, whole families were taken over to Spain, and when the great march took place which was that from Bilbao to Vittoria over the trackless mountains, these women were commanded to stay behind.   Some insisted on following the main body of the Legion, and did follow ; but a number amounting altogether to between four and five hundred, with about two hundred and fifty children, of all regiments, nearly three hundred of them belonging to the Irish brigade were sent by sea to Santander, to come up by the main road with the baggage to Vittoria.

It would have been impossible to have separated these women from their husbands but by means of a subterfuge ; for they were sent to that place not to rejoin the Legion by an easier road but to be sent home to Britain.   Some will exclaim this was charity, and perhaps it was ; but though these people have been called the outcasts of society, there were strong feelings of family affection existing in them, which lost none of their strength when they discovered that they were by a cheat separated from their husbands. Some consented to go home, some were forced on board of vessels, others would not consent, and would not be forced ; they had followed their husbands they said by permission of those in command—they had sold off every remnant of a home previous to coming away — the husbands being promised, especially if an old soldier, advancement in Spain if he would only join the expedition, and the wife, the special patronage of those who were to be officers — therefore they insisted on rejoining their husbands. There were to be washing, dressing, and *cooking for the mess* — all manner of money-making means ! Alas ! vain vision of wealth ! Home the women must now go, or starve — perhaps be subjected to the most brutal indignities by those at whose mercy they were treated.

At the Convent Corban, where they were congregated there was a dreadful scene. At times the eye might see a well-dressed English woman wearing her yet undecayed silk dresses, she being under the special protection of some of the numerous officers or their assistants, who were conducting the staff and regimental stores, and thereby living by means of their plunder, not unfrequently being the agent who transacted sales tor stolen stores between them and the Spaniards. Again some might be seen, who had disposed of their better clothes, to get food for themselves and children — they having no protectors' or not accepting of that service. Then there were those who had been ill-clad from the beginning, some of them sick, lying in loathsome neglect of cleanliness with children squalling around, all of them left more to chance than to any regular allowance of rations Whenever a detachment of men marched from this depot to join the Legion, a few of those women in favour of persons who had authority got leave to go on to their husbands, while a large number of others fruitlessly strove to follow but were not allowed.

On the 5th of December, 1835 I proceeded from Corban with a detachment, having some baggage specially in charge, consisting of the Colonel's of my regiment, and a box of General Evans's. Numerous were the applications, and overwhelming the entreaties made to me by women who had trudged along the road with their little all on their backs to help them onwards, as at a certain part of the road there was to be a stop to their progress, made by not allowing them to cross a river where barges were employed to take the detachment and the baggage across.

We came up to the place on the evening of the first day's march, and were quartered on the banks of the river. Next morning we were early astir getting ferried over ; sentinels being placed to prevent all women save a favoured few from getting into the barges. One poor woman with an infant was loud in her prayer to be taken across, "Och ! Colonel dear," she exclaimed, " dthe blessing of your own childer on your head ; take me over dthe water — Och, Holy Mother Mary, it was yourself and little Jasus knew the hard hearts o'dthe world — Och ! Micky dear, why but you took me wid ye ? " and so on was her prayer. She was forced out of the barge, but continued to keep hold of it with one hand while it was pushed off dragging her into the water. After being wet overhead, she was taken out, and with nearly fifty others was left there, to find her way back to Corban, or remain and die where she was.

This woman however, had got over by some means, and travelling all that day and night, (the 6th of December) came up on the 7th with the straggling sick and worn-out men who formed the rear of the detachment. She was in a fever, and had not some of the muleteers contrary to orders put her on a waggon, she must have then perished on the road-side; as it was, she did not survive much longer. The 7th of December poured in rain, and she being sick, having received no sustenance, and having been in the wet and cold, and suckled her infant which was also dying—fell into delirium, and in that state lay on the jolting waggon steeped in wet.   It was ten o'clock that night before we got into quarters ; the artillery, to save themselves from the rain having taken up the quarters intended for the infantry, and the latter, having had to go ten miles farther than their intended destination for the day.   The early part of the night was an united hurricane and deluge. We occupied an old house in which the water ran knee-deep, which had been the summer habitation of bullocks, not being even a shelter for them in winter. Some of us gathered stones together and sat on them all night, others scrambled to the joists and cross beams and perched themselves there, all of us drenched with rain and afterwards freezing with cold.   The night howled dismally on, and united with it the cries of delirious fever from the dying woman, as she lay in the bullock's stall to which we had lifted her, made the night-tempest peculiarly wild and awful. Some of us endeavoured to soothe and nurse the infant, but it was past that strength of life, when any thing which could be administered to it was serviceable. It died in the arms of one of my comrades, and at about six o'clock in the morning she was discovered to be dead also.

There remained only one duty for us to perform, and as we were to march at daylight, we hastened to fulfil the office. The hurricane had subsided, and the thick clouds were now breaking up, and showing the feeble light of a wintry morning's moon exhausted to her last quarter.

The new made cataracts dashed over the craggy mountains, and swelled the foaming stream that rolled past. By the light of the wane moon, we laid the babe on its mother's breast, one of our comrades said a short prayer, and two others dug down the bank of a ditch above them. In two hours afterwards we with our knapsacks on our backs, were winding our way up the mountain road that overlooks the valley of their solitary grave. The husband of this woman I afterwards heard died in Vittoria.

As the name of the brave Carlist general Zumalacarregui was introduced in the previous chapter, and as the reader whatever his partialities may be, cannot have other feelings than respect for the character of that great man, and sorrow for his death, I shall introduce the following anecdote as given by an officer of the Legion, it refers to the bombardment of Bilbao, where Zumalacarregui received his fatal wound.

"The day previous to his attack on Bilbao, he sent into the town, intimating that if there were any English ladies who wished to quit it, he would allow them until eight o'clock on the following morning ; but that after that hour, no one would be allowed to leave, under any pretence whatever. Emboldened by this act of courtesy on the part of the Carlist chief, one or two of the residents inquired if similar permission would be accorded to a certain number of Spanish ladies as well, Zumalacarregui demanded to know how many, and on being told twenty, gave his consent, stipulating only that these ladies should place themselves under the protection of the British flag. The terms were complied with, and the parties quitted the town, thus escaping all the inconveniences of the siege. It must not be forgotten, that Zumalacarregui added, on giving his assent, that, in the event of his being fired upon by the Queen's troops from the town, he would not return that fire, until the ladies were embarked, and out of danger."

There is also another anecdote respecting him, which will illustrate the character of the warfare that is desolating the Basque provinces ; and will shew that while the Carlist chief forced by necessity resorted to the guerilla laws of raising money, that is by plunder—he was able to turn various accidents into a supply for his Exchequer. The following, if it does not make him quite so amiable as might be wished by his admirers, will bear rehearsal from the sympathy that all must feel for the love of an uxorious husband towards a pretty wife. It was told by Captain Clarke an officer of the staff, who had been on a tour of examination along the Lagrono lines, and is thus related in an officer's journal :—

" On Captain Clarke's return from Pampeluna, he stopped at a small village, the principal posada (or inn), of which was remarkable for the beauty of its hostess. Nor was the style of that beauty Spanish, (Spanish beauty few of us have had the bad taste to admire, however our romantic cockney tourists may descant on it,) but essentially and touchingly English. The husband was exceedingly fond of her, and indeed testified so much attachment, as to render it a matter of remark to his guest, who, in the course of subsequent conservation, elicited the following fact :—

" While Zumalacarregui was traversing this part of the province, struck by the beauty of the woman, he carried her off to the mountains, where she remained for some time. Filled with grief and despair, the unfortunate husband sent to the General, entreating the restoration of his wife. Moved by the appeal, Zumalacarregui at length consented to do so, provided within a certain time, 1200 sheep and 700 dollars were sent to him as the price of ransom. The poor fellow had great difficulty in raising the amount ; which, indeed, was more than he was worth. But affection will conquer much in favor of its object ! The money was obtained—paid into the hand of Zumalacarregui, and the delighted Spaniard once more strained his beautiful wife to his heart. " Ah," said he, with a look full of love, as, on concluding his little history to Captain Clarke, he patted her cheek, "you know you were not worth half the money I paid for your restoration." But her expressive eye and malicious smile, directed to her guest, at once said,—" Don't you believe him."

On page 257 is represented a view of the magnificent pass of Pan

Corbo. The road leading from Burgos to Vittoria goes through this
singularly wild chasm dividing the narrow space with a struggling
stream, the waters of which chafe with surly froth the sides of its
confined channel, as if irreconcileable to the companionship of a road-
way. The rocks are of a height that fills the imagination with sublimity, more especially as from the turns of the approach their grandeur opens unexpectedly to the eye. The road wends through this
pass for nearly a mile, the chasm varying from 50 feet to 100 yards
in width, and the rocks rising to a towering height so gigantic in
majesty that the hovering hawks—though of the largest kind, seemed
only as floating motes in the air at midway distance to the top. In
some parts of the rocks, there were openings, as if caves had been
chiseled out, on the face of an unbroken perpendicular of 500 feet,
which no human hand could have touched; but which were no doubt
formed at the great convulsion that cracked this immense mountain
in twain; although in conformity to common superstitions, these
caves were believed by the people to be the work of supernatural art.
We heard more than one account of their formation, and of the sanctified nature of those who had in former times inhabited them; but
as there were even then a race of beings who had a hidden home in
the rocks, not often visible to travellers, save at unwelcome seasons,
I suspect that they are only the present generation of the same sort
of inhabitants that have always been there from the antiquity of time
to the present day—that is, a race of guerillas, or robbers.

It was, I think on the 15th of April, 1836, that, on the Legion
marching through this pass, and as usual some of the men being sick,
or tired, and thereby unable to keep on with their regiments, two
young men, one of them a mere boy, were left behind. As the quarters for the night were not at a great distance in front, and as the
rear-guard was bringing up all stragglers, those who did lay down
on the road-side, were not thought to be in any danger, especially as
the inhabitants of the surrounding district were supposed to be on
our side. The two youths alluded to, were both in a fever, and had
been told to rest by the road-side until the baggage would come up,
with which they were to be conveyed onwards to the first hospital.
Being overcome with fatigue, they fell asleep, and while in that condition, were espied by a guerilla from some part of the mountain,
who, mounted on horseback, came and awoke one of them, This

was the youngest of the two. named Maxwell. The guerilla at first offered to buy their ammunition, muskets, and accoutrements; but Maxwell refused to sell them, and on being urged to do so, replied that he dared not, even though he were willing, as the want of a single round of ammunition, alone, would cause him to be flogged. The guerilla then seized hold of Maxwell and wresting the musket from him, remounted his horse and galloped off; but the boy, (for he was only about fifteen years of age,) caught hold of his companion's musket, loosened his ammunition pouch, bit a cartridge—primed, loaded, took aim, and fired. The guerilla had got to the distance of two hundred yards, when Maxwell's well directed bullet overtook him, which lodging in his hip joint, brought him to the ground. The one who was asleep, being startled by the shot, got to his feet, and, with Maxwell went forward to the wounded Spaniard and retook the musket, the guerilla praying earnestly and loud for them not to kill him. Some Spaniards from a distance witnessed this incident, and were hastening to the spot, but Maxwell, and the other prepared by reloading their muskets and betaking themselves off towards Pan Corbo. What might have farther ensued with them and the Spaniards is uncertain, as at that very moment a troop of lancers came to their protection.

It was on the same line of march and near the same place alluded to in the foregoing paragraph, that a rather ludicrous incident befel some men of various regiments, who, being quartered in the same village were mounted on their respective regimental guards near each other. As usual, the small ration allowance of biscuit, which was allotted on the march, had long before night been consigned to the actions of unsparing teeth, and the stomachs were now in an uneasy state of emptiness, which of all things to men enduring the langour of a midnight guard is the most painfully wearisome :—As the counterpart of that, nothing was so agreeable as broiling a piece of a pig or a calf when these could be obtained, and whiling off the cold nights by burning our fingers with the picquet fire in laying on —turning—taking off, and tearing with our teeth a piece of the illegally slaughtered and rudely cooked carcase. A small drop of *arquadiente* would sometimes be laid hold of, and would stimulate the story tellers, to enliven the whole by recitals of all manner of tales.

When no *arquadiente* could be had, a pipe of tobacco would be subscribed round the the picquet as an inducement for some one to begin and tell stories. But if in addition to a good story there was roasting, and broiling, and frying, round the blazing picquet's fire, the night went off in such a way that no one regretted it being his turn to be on picquet.

The relief had gone round, and some of those who had come off sentry were, when warming themselves, telling about something that had kept moving about near their post all the time they had been out, and though they pretended to make light of it, they had, as could be seen, laboured under a heavy load of fear; some one suggested that we had better go out and see what it was, no one saying what his thoughts were, but every one thinking secretly that perhaps it was something that *might* be eatable. I was one who went out on the expedition of discovery, having the privilege of making a pretence of visiting the sentries to see if they were alert. At the place spoken of, we listened, and after some minutes heard a sound, which came from a small enclosure, round which, there was a wall six feet high. From the top of this, by the weak glimmer of the moon, we perceived a calf and at some distance from it a cow, which, as we concluded were there, from their portion of the peasant's house of which they were at other times inmates—being that night filled with our men, baggage, and other stores. There was a general order which decreed a court martial and punishment to all who stole from, or molested the inhabitants; but though this order was often put in force to the utmost of its severity the chances of detection were so few, when all were combined,—that we, sharpened in enterprise as we were, by hunger—never hesitated a second in passing a silent decree of death on the calf. I call it a silent decree, for no words were spoken; four of us who had ascended the wall saw the prize at the same moment, and we understood the customary rules so well, that we went simultaneously over, laid hold of what might have been the young hope of some poor family, and holding his, her, or its mouth to prevent noise; three bayonets grazed each other's point in its heart at the same instant. In a few minutes we had the carcase to the other side of the wall, and before ten minutes at the most, nearly every man of the picquet had a piece broiling on the fire, the incense of which ascended actively to the nostrils.

The mastication began, and went on pleasantly, one or two remarking it was very tough, and the whole shewing that it was, by the sundry twistings of their head and energetic tugs which they took at it; yet the eating of it was agreeable, for each had cut a piece from the carcase—had skinned it for himself—broiled it a little, eaten a little, put it again on the fire, and again taken it off, burning his fingers and mouth with such delicious juice that he did not know whether it was tough or not, though an onlooker might have seen it was. There were, however, two or three laying asleep, who, having had no special friend to wake them, had been all the time in vacant unconsciousness of the midnight feast, and only awoke at last by their olfactory nerves being impregnated by the odour of the burning bones which were now laid on the fire to be consumed, so that no remnant might exist in the vicinity of the picquet house for evidence to a court-martial.

One of these who were too late was a Scotchman, and another was a cockney of the purest breed, who, had many a time turned up his nose with delicate dislike at more delicious flavours than he now felt saluting him. But circumstances and habits arising therefrom, rule tastes more than nature does, this man, as he told me, had been a nobleman's valet once, and when in Spain he many a time called to mind the substantialities which he had despised at a hall table, because of some seeming error in carving or cooking.

He woke from his sleep, and surveying the heap of burning bones for a few minutes, snuffed up the smell which he pronounced to be precious fine, and then asked "What has all on you been up to?"

"Nothink as I knows on," replied one, who having gorged himself thought he could indulge in a persecuting joke at his less fortunate comrade.—"What's them 'ere as you're a burnin of"? was the farther enquiry of the hungry man, who, turning over the bones with a piece of wood, continued, "strike me blind! but you've been a doin it slap."

"Vy, only roasting and eating a jackass," said the other,— "that ain't much:" (thus making a farther joke as he thought.)

"I knows better," returned the hungry one, who, getting to his feet, started off after two Scotchmen, one of whom had only uttered "what a deevil of a fine stink!" and who were both without more ado, following the direction which they got to the carcase, or rather the place where it had been.

"Eh! aye! mun," said one of them, in his native Kirkaldyisms

" here its haid—fa'th we'll have potted haid made the nicht ;" " or,"
said the other, " what wad ye say to tripe ?—we'll gie down e brae
to e burn an clain e tripe, I've a bit o' braid i my haversack, we
can pit it in e bree and mak e kail o't an let him tak e haid an e
feet to himsel."

This last part about letting him take the head and feet to himself was alluding to the Englishman, who, groping about in the
dark for a piece of the remnants, demanded if they would not leave
him " none on it."

To work they went to cook up the last atoms of the calf, for
neither they nor any of the others knew that there was a cow in the
neighbourhood, else she would have been soon victimized, and the
poor peasants relentlessly robbed. The two Scotchmen had their
tripe dressed and boiling in a camp kettle ; the Englishman had got
a cut off the neck, had eaten it, and was preparing another. To
enable him to select the best of what little remained, he brought the
head close to the fire to see what could be done with it.

All eyes were fixed on him for about half a minute ; and some who
had been speaking held their tongues. Gradually he relaxed his
strength from a cut which he was making with a knife, and turning
the head over once or twice, looked round on the faces about the
fire, which were all directed to him and the calf's head.

" What lang lugs that calf has had !" said one of those who were
boiling the tripe.

" Dong it !" said a north of England man.

" Dogzond !" said a south of Scotland man.

" Let me see that foot laying behind you," said I, and the foot
was handed round to the no small horror of those who had eaten
their fill, and disappointment of those who had only expected to eat.
The grey face, long ears, and uncloven hoofs demonstrated beyond
doubt that we had eaten a donkey. One or two made an attempt
to discharge the unclean supper from their stomachs ; but the most
of us thought it as well to let it remain now that it was eaten.

In some future chapters, I purpose giving personal sketches of the
officers of different regiments. The following sketch of some of the
10th Irish is from a gentleman who served in that corps with honor
to himself and the regiment. He says :—

The 10th, or *Munster Light Infantry*, was raised chiefly in Cork.

General Evans took the first Colonelcy of this regiment to himself ; and on more than one occasion shewed undue partiality to it. The Lieutenant-Colonel was O'Connell, formerly a lieutenant and adjutant in the 73rd, when commanded by his father, Major-General Sir Maurice O'Connell. He was a good drill, but was too fond of favoritism among his officers ; his favourites, too, were contemptible, —not that the writer of this sketch has any personal feelings of dislike in the matter, for he had reason to feel otherwise, but some of these favourites of O'Connell having notoriously exhibited the *white feather*, it becomes a duty on all who write on military affairs to expose the evils of favouritism.

In the action of the 5th of May, Colonel O'Connell being posted by order under cover of a wall, to direct the storming parties which went forward at various times, and in various directions, on the fortifications, retained his favourite officers with him in rear of that wall, although their respective companies were engaged in the front fight, and were conducted by other officers. One of the *worthies*, who lay beneath the shelter of the wall, was a Lieutenant H——ton, and another was Ensign Q——ll ; the former having been acting captain, in charge of a company, which was now commanded and led on in the action by his junior. How these officers, under the nose of their colonel, escaped being tried by a court-martial for cowardice I cannot say ; but their conduct became a matter of common conversation among the officers, more especially that of H——ton. This gentleman was openly called a coward by a spirited young fellow, Lieutenant M——k——r ; and H——ton, as a matter of course was obliged to send a message to him, but after, as it was said, his second refusing to negotiate with the second of M—— to fire with horse dung or some such harmless substance, and hearing of the determination of M—— to have a shot, he by some means withdrew his challenge, and got out of the affair, H——ton, whose sole recommendation with the Colonel had been his profusion of flattery and ability in singing a good song, now found these qualities avail him little when his notorious cowardice became known amongst his brother officers. He soon after found a ship going to England, and slipt away quietly by permission of Colonel O'Connell.

Colonel Ebsworth, who was shot in a mutiny at San Sebastian, while on the Spanish staff, was one of the most gallant and intrepid officers in the 10th regiment. He was, when in that corps, senior Major, and had his breast decorated with orders of merit acquired by his gallantry in Spain and Portugal. He was a strict soldier, but most honourable and just.

Colonel Shaw (not the officer of that name who was in Portugal nor he who commanded the artillery,) but one who was a Major in the 10th, was a brave old fellow, and had served for a long time as Lieutenant in the British Service. He mas enormously fat, and by his weight very nearly became a prey to the Carlists one day. This was on the 16th of January, when the heights of Arlaban were abandoned by Evans after Cordova had so disgracefully left the Legion and its commander to perish, among the snow, or by the overwhelming numbers of the enemy, Major Shaw and the wing of the regiment to which he was attached, were closely pressed by the Carlists. The poor old fellow became breathless on ascending a hill, and having for some time struggled, at last gave himself up saying they must just have me I can go no farther, some of the men thought of carrying him, but on attempting it was found impossible, and he was left to his fate; but the Adjutant seeing him lent his horse, Major Shaw was thereby saved to drill well and fight well after that time.

A comical individual in the 10th was a little fellow—a Lieutenant J—ce, who was always skulking from duty on pretence of being ill. This personage will account too for strange reports that appeared in the newspapers at home, about the gallantry of certain officers, while it was notorious in Spain that these same officers had either not been in the fight at all, or if they had, their behaviour had been notoriously unofficer-like. But a relation at home connected with the press could do much (as witness General Shaw's bravery trumpeted to the world by the *Courier*, the first news of his daring deeds being known in regiments which he commanded, by news from London!!)—Lieutenant J—ce was a hero according to the newspapers. In the accounts of the various actions, his brother officers read such intermingling sentences as "Lieutenant J—ce greatly distinguished himself in this gallant charge;" "Lieutenant J—ce led on his company to the attack;" "Lieutenant J—ce was one of the officers who bravely led the assault, and whose bravery obtained much praise." In fact Lieutenant J—ce was distinguished for every thing, but being able to do his *duty*. He ultimately got promoted to the command of a company through interest at home ; which interest obtained for him also the cross and ribbon of Fernando. This was bestowed on him five months after the 5th of May, for gallantry in action with the enemy on that day, at the solicitation of an Irish peer. Indeed many of these *orders* were bestowed through favoritism, and thus exhibited some of the weakest points in General Evans' character. But this being obtained by the brave J—ce was all ; for Colonel O'Connell was indignant at the order being bestowed on him, while other officers, who had been recommended, were passed over ; and those who had received the order refusing to wear it because of the degradation they felt at Lieutenant J— ce, caused a deal of unnecessary, though common, discontent, and rendered it impossible for him to shew it off in Spain whatever he may do in England.

Count Kalling, of the Royal Swedish Guards, was a captain in Colonel O'Connell's regiment (the 10th) and was twice severely wounded, having distinguished himself gallantly in several engagements. Unlike our British officers, on coming home, though they had been in Spain by special permission, some of them at the special request of the English government, Count Kalling was summoned before King Bernadotte, and besides receiving Swedish decorations for his bravery in Spain, was rewarded in a more substantial way. But Bernadotte was bred a soldier, and knows what *merit is.*

Another Swede in the 10th regiment was just the counterpart of Kalling—a notorious coward and bully. This was Captain De B——ce, who went out to Spain in gold lace, and talked like a hero, a man whose prowess alone was a regiment to the service, but who ended, like most talkers, in being nobody at all. He had the presumption also to call himself the *Honourable* Captain De B——ce, though his highest post in Sweden had been a riding master. He was brevet captain in the Rifles when he first came out, and afterwards got full captain in the 10th ; he is now what time and circumstances have made him---an adventurer, living where he can ; but, setting aside his swelling *brag,* he was otherwise not amiss as a comrade in the camp.

In addition to the foregoing, which is inserted here as written by an officer in the 10th, I must state, that my opinion of Colonel O'Connell is such, as to raise him very high in my respect. He was unquestionably a brave officer; and his conduct, as commonly known, rendered him very popular with his regiment. Afterwards, as Adjutant-General, and charged with the formation of the new Legion, he became more conspicuous; and I am persuaded, had he been supported by the Spanish authorities, he would have proved himself an efficient commander.

These remarks on Colonel O'Connell enable me to introduce a subject which, from its date of occurrence, would have filled a place in the latter pages of this work, but which requires publicity at this moment, from its relation to circumstances now engrossing the attention of those who take an interest in the affairs of the Legion, more especially in the settlement of its claims. Colonel O'Connell undertook the formation of a new Legion, and to induce the men of the old to enlist with him; he promised that should their pay fall into arrears for any time more than three months, he would embark his men for England. The British Commissioner Colonel Wylde, who, be it understood is not acting as a military officer in the war, but simply the agent and commissioner of England watching the progress of affairs; he on the 7th of June, 1837, delivered an address to the regiment in which I served, in presence of Colonel Hogg our commanding officer, and Colonel (by that time General) O'Connell, the chief in command of the new Legion then forming. It was the assurances contained in this address formerly made by Colonel Wylde and now repeated, that caused O'Connell to take the new Legion under command, which caused Hogg and others to act under him as officers, and which caused many of the men to re-enter the ranks after the first period of service had expired. It will be seen then, that this address has an intimate relation to the character of General O'Connell. It was as follows—

"Men, your time of service is now about to expire, and I have to inform you that the British Government has suspended the foreign enlistment act for one year more, to allow such of you as may choose to remain in the service to do so.

"Men, I know you have suffered great hardships—very severe hardships, indeed; but you have also gained for yourselves great honour. I can assure you, in England your efficient military discipline is justly appreciated. Now, although you have had great hardships during part of the first year of your service, the Spanish govern-

No. 17.

ment have at last settled all your claims ; or, if you have not been paid, you will be to-morrow. *All other engagements, I am authorised to say, will be fulfilled—I can assure you, the British Government will not suffer your claims to be neglected. I am fully authorised to say so.* Therefore, men, I think you are in no danger—none whatever, in engaging to serve for one year more. Your pay will be paid regularly to you ; and you know the character of Colonel O'Connell, who is to have the chief command—you could not serve under a better officer, that I know you will all admit. Well, Colonel O'Connell is to command you, and he will withdraw you from the service if ever your arrears of pay is allowed to extend over three months. Also Colonel Hogg is very anxious that a large number of you should stay, and I really think men, you could not do better. I have seen you in arduous situations, and I can tell you—and I am not telling you so to flatter you—on the honour of a British officer, I tell you, that no soldiers could have done better than you have done. I am proud of you, your country is proud of you, and it would be a blind mistake of you, men, to go home just now. Nearly one-half of the working population are out of employment, and cannot obtain it in England. Now, I do think, men, you could not, under these circumstances, do better than stay. Besides, I may mention too, that General Evans being now at home, and in parliament, will be of great service to you. All the representations from me in your behalf, I know will be favourably attended to. Now, just make up your minds, and go to your Colonel, or to any other Colonel ; you can choose what regiment you like best—but just go and agree to stay another year, and I have no doubt we shall see matters in a more prosperous condition than they have been."

The lines in Italics convey certainly a distinct pledge, that the government of Great Britain was security for the Legion being fairly dealt with, at least we were made to believe so in Spain. And let it be borne in mind, that Colonel Wylde is an officer of undoubted honour and probity. We were aware that the foregoing speech was intended to flatter us, Still the military, as well as moral character of Colonel Wylde, was considered such a certain guarantee, that a doubt never existed in the mind of any one, but we would be honorably dealt with if we renewed our services.

In answer to a question from the Duke of Wellington, it was stated by Lord Melbourne, that Colonel Wylde was the accredited agent of the British Government. Latterly his Lordship has denied that Colonel Wylde ever made such a speech as that referred to, and the Morning Chronicle of June 20th 1838, asserts in a leading article, that the fabricated address of Colonel Wylde had been satisfactorily contradicted &c. Now as I was the person who committed that address to writing as soon as we came off parade at Astigarraga where it was delivered, having been assured of its correctness—and having been the first to publish it in this country, though with a very different view from that entertained by some of those who have republished it; for nothing has occurred which I regret more than the factious use made of the grievances of the Legion, by the opponents of Government; but being the reporter of that speech in my sketch of the war called "A Narrative of the British Legion and War in Spain," and being confident of its accuracy—I was astonished to find an unqualified contradiction given to it, first by the Prime Minister, and then by the Prime Ministerial organ.

Application was made to the Colonel of the Regiment to which it was addressed, and he being an officer above all suspicion, honorable and independent, and not one of those who are denominated (though with much injustice) by the Morning Chronicle as factiously discontented, but an officer living unconcernedly in the privacy of his family, not meddling with any of the Legion's affairs, but having served honorably throughout; he corroborates that report in the following terms:

Gilestown House,

Strokestown,

County Roscommon,

June 20th, 1838.

Having been called upon to state if the address of Colonel Wylde on the 7th June 1837 to the 8th regiment B. A. L. under my command was correctly reported, in the "Narrative of the War in Spain" by Sergeant A. Somerville; I can have no hesitation in saying, as far as my recollection serves me, it was so. The words made use of by that distinguished officer may not have been exactly those asserted in the report alluded to, but the substance was the same.

GILBERT HOGG,

Colonel, late commanding 8th Highlanders, B. A. Legion.

Though this letter is rather out of place in this part of the work, it is still, of that immediate importance, that those who may read these sketches in a volume will perceive that, as this work was published at intervals, to have waited to the conclusion, would have been a delay, which, to the numerous officers and men who are starving in London now, would have been unserviceable, while its being published at this time may lead to an interference 'in their behalf, which it is clear the government is bound to undertake. Besides as it was on the strength of this pledge of the British Commissioner, that Colonel O'Connell assumed the command of the new Legion, and as I was exemplifying his character as an officer, it is not improper to step forward twelve months to get hold of those circumstances that illustrate a character imperfectly appreciated in an earlier part of the service.

He acted to the very letter of his agreement, and while he taught his soldiers that he was a strict disciplinarian, and would not be trifled with by them, he also proved that he would not submit to the trifling of his Spanish superiors. O'Connell was an officer who loved to cut a dashing figure. He is a tall soldier looking, black mustachioed –duel fighting—steeple chasing—horse racing—love intriguing—and point of honor quarrelling soldier—who at any time might be an honorable acquaintance, but a very dangerous one to those who do not like to make as free with pistol shots at twelve yards distance as himself.

It may seem to some an unpardonable omission to have neglected a sketch of the personal appearance of the Lieutenant General, up to this. Many people know him in London as a member of parliament; and may deem a descriptive sketch superfluous, but I may state that his hesitating and rather awkward manner of an irregular mode of oratory deteriorates greatly from his appearance at a public meeting, or in a debate in parliament, while as a soldier every characteristic served to make him popularly admired, so far as a commander can be admired by those beneath him. He is a native of the west of Ireland, and, was before going to Spain, notwithstanding all that has been written to the contrary a soldier of experience, having served on the Quarter Master General's Staff in the Peninsular war. He is dark complexioned, and when his black mustachios grew he was more like a Spaniard than an Englishman. General Espartero is so like him, that both Spanish and English soldiers mistook the one

for the other; only there is more soft complaisance in General Evans'
face. Espartero punished mutiny by shooting every tenth man—and
this is all the apparent difference between the two, General Evans
does not look like the man that could do that. There is a thoughtfulness in his face, that often seems like melancholy; but when he spoke
to an officer, it had a smile, though I have sometimes thought the
smile more assumed than natural. I have seen soldiers put themselves
in his way—I have done it myself, to have an opportunity of saluting
him, for there was not an officer in the Legion returned it so kindly,
and so directly to each individual, as he did. He is five feet ten
inches in height, well formed, and apparently forty-five years of age,
but has altered five years nearer old age while in Spain, though now
he looks much more cheerful. In riding, he did not study fine effect;
he had the finest looking English horses, but all of them appeared to
know that their rider did not care for capering or prancing. His
horse walked steadily, or started off at a full gallop, leaving his staff
to canter after him. When he had a horse shot (which happened
several times in the engagement), he immediately mounted another
which the orderly would hand to him, and stand in the same place,
or move to a situation more dangerous, as circumstances required,
giving out orders to his aides-du-camp as he dismounted the dead,
and got on the living one. He permitted commanding officers of
regiments to punish as severely as they chose by regimental courts-
martial, and mitigated the sentences of general courts-martial,
as these came under his own immediate sanction. He had too
much kindness in his manners, and tried to please every body. The
electors of Westminster, the Spanish Government, and his own soldiers, had all different and diametrically opposite interests in him.
He did not wish to have criminals shot, as that would have been unpopular in Westminster, but he suffered his soldiers to die in thousands, with hunger and cold, rather than be too importunate with the
Spanish Government. He aspired to be a champion of the freedom
of nations, and he found that it was not possible to organise an army
without being a tyrant.

I have paused to reflect on the last sentence; it comprehends all
that General Evans was or would have been, even though completely successful in the objects of his expedition;—Yes even though he
had been the peer of WELLINGTON or SOULT and had become the
idol of fame—he would have been, for he could be nothing else—

a tyrant. With every wish to soften the aspersions cast upon him, where justice admits defence I will defend him. As a brave soldier, zealous though thwarted, skilful though betrayed, contending in a severe toil of physical and intellectual energies, against opposing difficulties, he did as much for the cause in which he was engaged as any other man could have done in the same circumstances. But —there comes a *but*—he was a tyrant by profession, by voluntary choice, and I am sorry to add, that all his patriotism, and liberality professed in England, seemed to be forgotten and lost in his military character in Spain.

In page 153 of this work, mention is made of a number of men being prisoners in the fortress of Santona for refusing to serve more than one year. The following details of their imprisonment is given, first, in justice to the men; second, in contradiction to a series of letters widely circulated through the newspapers by Deputy Commissary General Black; and third and more particularly as shewing what difference can exist, and has existed between real and professed liberality, between a man advocating an extension of humanity in the laws of England, and practising beyond the inhumanity of the laws of Spain,—between a political creed on the hustings and the Articles of War in the camp—between General Evans as a man and General Evans as a soldier;—but as the man and the soldier are allied in this case, we cannot allow the last distinction. General Evans must shrink under the exposure of the following Chapter, Deputy Commissary General Black has taken unworthy means as will appear to whitewash Evans, therefore the General must thank the Deputy for drawing out all the particulars of this disagreeable subject from me.

CHAPTER XIV.

The imprisonment of eighty soldiers at Santona—Letter to the Courier Newspaper, in answer to Deputy Commissary General Black—Remarks on other documents published by Mr. Black—Statement of Major Stewart sent to General Evans—Reply to that Statement—Remarks on Major Stewart's character as impugned by General Evans.

THE following letter written by me at the special request of some of those men who were imprisoned in Santona to the *Courier* in answer to statements, some of them grossly incorrect, made by Deputy Commissary General Black, will explain so far, how these men were treated, and in what measure they deserved their treatment.

London, 4, Brydges Street, Strand,
June 12, 1838.

To the Editor of The Courier.

Sir,

On a subject to which you have devoted space in the *Courier*, for a series of letters from Mr. Black; I trust in fairness, you will insert this *one* in reply. In his letter marked No 4, he makes a grievously severe charge on the characters of the men of the Legion —either all the men, or that portion of them who were imprisoned at Santona (he does not state the limits of his accusation,) but, I, knowing the circumstances attending the imprisonment of the eighty men, at Santona, much better than Mr. Black knows or could possibly know,—beg to correct him, and I do it the more earnestly, because he has partly hidden, and partly distorted the truth of those circumstances which he *did* know. He says. "A few stern admirers of military law, may be of opinion that many of these men should have been "shot dead," according to the sentence of the court-martial, and this perhaps would have been their fate in the British army, but most of you will allow that it was both humane and proper to spare their lives, even though they may have been obliged to carry coals on board a steamer, and carry wood to cook their rations. Yet these incorrigible culprits are paraded before the Lord Mayor as a spectacle to excite public commiseration, and sympathy, and provoke indignation against those who had treated them with such lenity."

Mr. Editor,—These men were never tried by a court-martial, nor did they receive any sentence as stated here, nor was there any crime whatever charged against them. I shall tell you how they were imprisoned, and as all of them at Santona belonged to the regiment which I served in, and a number of them to the same company of which I was at the time pay-sergeant, I presume that my knowledge of their case deserves credit.

These men were a part of five hundred who sailed in the Killarney steamer from Glasgow on the 5th of September 1835, on which day their service began. I went out in that vessel, and I solemnly declare, that none of the men on board were enlisted for any specified time, *so far as I knew,* and the conditions of service stated that the period of service might be for one or two years, as the person engaging chose. By no agreement having been made, both parties in the contract were at fault,—both the men and the officers engaging them. But I for one, resolved on the expiration of the first year, to serve to the end of the campaign, and besides as the officers of my regiment know well, I laboured for some weeks among the men, persuading them to re-enrol themselves for the service. Money was supplied to me to expend in recruiting these men, and as there was not one who claimed to be discharged, that I did not try to have enrolled whether successfully or not, it may be believed that I knew the individual characters of them all. This recruiting had taken place previous to their one year being up, so when that expired, which was on the 5th of September 1836, the regiment was paraded, and all the men who claimed to be discharged, and had not re-enlisted, were ordered to "fall out," and form up at the right of the regiment. As some of those officers who had enlisted the men in Scotland, alleged that an agreement for two years had been entered on, and the men denying it, each man was brought separately to the orderly room, and was there sworn on the Bible, whether he had engaged to serve for one or two years; most of them swore they had not been engaged for any specified time—some that they had engaged specially for *one*—none of them admitted having been engaged for two years. Their accoutrements, ammunition and muskets, were then taken from them, and afterwards their great coats. Now mark this,—Mr. Black says,—

"That they should have been in want of clothing, cannot be to you cause of surprise, knowing as you do that soldiers removed from the superintendance and controul of their officers, will sell the shirts off their back, and the shoes off their feet, *even when not of the superlatively dissolute habits of these men.*"

The *italics* are Mr. Black's. I am sorry, truly sorry, that a person who had the good fortune to rise from a very subordinate situation, to be Deputy Commissary General, and thereby became entitled to

the respect commonly paid to gentlemen, should have written anything so much at variance with truth as this paragraph.   In the first
place, the men's great coats were taken from them although these
were their own, and they were left imprisoned in the fortress of Santona.   I know the apartment in which they were kept, well, my
company having been quartered in it for two weeks.   It was dark---
with a damp clay floor, in which these men never had a fire; and had
no beds save boards.   They were not permitted to get out, excepting when going to work with Spanish sentries primed and loaded
over them.   They at the time of being imprisoned, were entitled to
their second year's clothing, which the other men got, and which they
(the prisoners) were much in want of even then, and became more so
when, never having any change, they were overwhelmed with vermin.
So dreadfully filthy were they, that some of them took stones to chop
their shirts merely to kill the vermin, others took off these rags, and
threw them away, trowsers and jackets were in the same state, and
these being nearly worn out at the time they were imprisoned, it may
be supposed that men lying night and day in their clothes, would
soon wear them to rags.   Mr. Black insinuates by a sarcasm, that
all they were required to do, was to carry coals to a steamer, and go
for wood to cook their rations.   Had he said *the steamers* and that
without much intermission, he would have been correct in that part.
And as to carrying wood, they went climbing a mountain some
miles distant for wood to supply the whole garrison and state prison
department.   They did not carry it to cook their rations, because
bread and water did not need any cooking, and they had no other allowance for some months.   He quotes a document which at the end
of six months, states, that they had got six ounces of meat *alternated*
with pork, with rice, and three quarters of a pound of biscuit daily,
for the previous five or six weeks, that is, they got three quarters of
a pound of biscuit or bread, with six ounces of rice one day, fish
another, and meat of the same weight, another.   What prison fare
in England is reduced to that scale? but they aid not get even this,
for a period of four months ! they got three quarters of a pound of
bread without anything else save water, and as I recollect well, the
water is nearly salt, Santona being surrounded by salt water, and the
wells being lower than the tide.   Farther, the men were not of
" *superlatively dissolute habits.*"   My attention was called to Mr.

Black's letters by a man who was imprisoned there, and who is in a situation in London at this moment that none but a man of superior education and character could fill. Besides, as the regimental books of our regiment will shew, some of which are in my possession now, only thirteen men out of these prisoners had ever been charged with a fault of any description at any time in the service. Eleven of these men belonged to my company, only one of whom had, previous to that time received a punishment; and only two more of the eleven had been at any time in a guard house during their year's service. Why, then does Mr. Black speak of their liability to have been "shot dead " by sentence of the general court-martial? I solemnly declare, these men were never accused of any crime whatever when imprisoned there, other than I have stated; and they were only kept there to be forced to return to their regiments. Frequent offers were made to them, viz. that they would get up all their arrears of pay, if they would enlist for another year,

I must, however, make another remark, and that is, that I did not enter into the feeling expressed at the Crown and Anchor meeting, so far as it was made a subject of political discussion; far less did I join in the groaning towards General Evans.—I have as high a respect for the General as Mr. Black can possibly have, and I presume I have lately been rendering him as much service by writing a good deal of truth. Also I have served through the campaigns in all the varieties of hardship and danger not only without blame, but receiving from my officers the meed of an unstained military and moral reputation, therefore I feel the sweeping charge of Mr. Black who was until latterly a very humble person in the Legion—come with painful impropriety either against the whole of the men, or against those, some of them my dearest friends, who were imprisoned in Santona.

To a newspaper I have probably written too much; but in one which has found room for five letters from Mr. Black and the threat of a sixth, I trust this, the only one which I shall trouble you with, will find a place.

ALEXANDER SOMERVILLE.

But, besides these men at Santona, there were a great number more at Santander; at first about four hundred, subsequently reduced in number to about one hundred; the other three parts having rejoined their regiments.

The following letter is quoted by the Deputy Commissary General, and is introduced by a statement, that he obtained a copy of it from General Evans ; and that it " is the best exposition of the ground_ lessness of these imputations," referring to the treatment of the prisoners. How unfortunate for the General's character that this letter should have come before the public !

Santona, Nov. 9th, 1836.

Sir,—I have the honour to inform your Excellency, in reply to a letter addressed to me by Colonel Arbuthnott, referring to one he had received from your Excellency—

1st. That the original cause of the detention at Santander of certain men of the 6th and 8th regiments of the Auxiliary Legion, commenced in their laying down their arms, and absolutely refusing to march with their corps.

2ndly. That the reason of their close confinement, at the convent of Corban, was rendered imperatively necessary by their gross outrages and depredations on the persons and property of the inhabitants in the neighbourhood, when suffered to go at large ; and—

3rdly. That the cause of their being fired at and wounded by the Spanish guard placed over them, was produced by their frequent attempts to escape, which, had they effected, would have led to the perpetration of fresh outrages.

I have the honour to be, Sir,

Your Excellency's most obedient humble Servant,

CÆSAR TOURNELLE,

Commandant-General of the Province of Santander.

I, the British Vice-Consul at this port, do hereby certify to all whom it may concern, that the signature set at the foot of this letter is of the true hand-writing of Cæsar Tournelle, Colonel of Artillery, and Chief Commanding Officer of her Catholic Majesty's Forces at this city.

Given at her Brittannic Majesty's Vice Consular Office in Santander, under my hand and seal, this 9th day of November, in the year 1836.

JOSEPH M MONTALVAN, Vice-Consul

To his excellency Lieutenant-General De Lacy Evans, Commanding in Chief the British Auxiliary Legion, &c., &c., &c.

That letter is either a fabrication, or too stupid to have been published. We who were in Spain know very well that General Evans did not require to send to Santander for information. The General was at San Sebastian, and the 6th regiment was at San Sebastian; the men of that regiment who refused to serve two years were disarmed on the 1st of August, (they did not lay down their arms, their arms were taken from them.) A Court of Enquiry sat to examine their right to be discharged;— they were sent to the Castle and confined there by the General's order ;—then they were embarked on board a steamer, and sent to Santander, a distance of one hundred miles or so from San Sebastian, and there imprisoned.—Could all this be done, and General Evans have to write to Santander, to be informed *why* these men were detained there? Certainly not. These men did not refuse to march with their regiment; their regiment was at San Sebastian with the General, and did not march at all, nor was it under orders to march; therefore the Commandant of the province of Santander could not write such a letter to San Sebastian without getting his information from San Sebastian, from which he got his prisoners. Those of the 8th regiment were disarmed at Santander when we had no orders to march, and were sworn on the Bible that they had only enlisted for one year. This was on the 19th of August—the others were disarmed at Santona in like manner on the 5th of September, *their* year being up that day; and the regiment returned to San Sebastian, the head quarters of the General, on the 10th of September ;—could General Evans be in ignorance of these men being left at these places until the month of November? He could not. There were parades, field-days, and reviews; regimental and brigade " states " sent in daily, weekly, and monthly; so that he could not be in ignorance *one day* of the diminished strength of a regiment. But, suppose that he had not known why the men were left behind,—suppose he had not sent the 8th regiment away from San Sebastian purposely because too many men getting their discharge from the service should not be at one place ; —suppose that he had not sent the Spanish regiments, that accompanied the 8th, with orders to fire on the latter if necessary ;—suppose that if he had not known any of these things,—what are we to think of him if he did not know the causes of the men's imprisonment, until the Commandant's letter of the 9th of November reached him ? But he knew well. I will give him credit for being a better commander than not to know : besides, the Adjutant-General was too strict in his duty, to let the chief remain in ignorance one day.

And, what does this all amount to ? Why, that letters were either made in Spain, or have been manufactured in England to obscure circumstances, that must have disgraced the General's character as a man and an Englishman, though his fame, as a soldier, had been the idolatry of his country. But we must be fair with him ;—he did what other commanders would have done. He does now what other commanders have done—he hires subterfuges for defence. And be they who they may, that have become famous in war, they rose by setting at defiance every tie and right, and every affection and law of humanity.

Humanity is a sweet word, but it is a concentration of feeble impulses when struggling in opposition to the romance and glories of warfare. It is dazzled into obscurity in the heroes of the wars of France and England, and it is heard in condemnation of Evans only, because his battles and carnage were too small for the marvellous.

But having made this digressive observation to shew that in his severity—unjust and tyrannical as it was, he did as other officers would have done, or at most as they commonly have done in such a situation as his ; I must proceed with *his* special condemnation on other grounds than military usages. Here is a medical certificate of the health of these prisoners, forwarded after, as will appear, the surgeons signing it had been specially instructed what to say.

Santona, Jan. 17, 1837.

" We, the undersigned, do hereby certify to have examined the (80) eighty disarmed English soldiers at Santona, and do pronounce them in good health, with the exception of nine men in hospital labouring under itch. And we learn that during the six months the above prisoners have been in confinement at Santona only (1) one has died.

" We also beg to add, that we have been informed that the food allowed has been for some weeks past (6) six ounces of meat or bacalao (salt fish), alternated with pork, with rice, and from three-quarters of a pound of bread or biscuit daily : and from their diet or confinement do not appear to have materially suffered."

HENRY BOWERS BUNNETT, Hospital Assistant.

CAYETANO DE VILLAR, Military Surgeon of Santona.

The tone of this certificate shews that it is not the unbiassed result of a medical investigation, but an attempted proof that certain circumstances have not taken place; proving that they (the surgeons) had not been appointed to report on the health of the prisoners without knowing what kind of report was required. But here is the statement of Major Stewart relative to this medical examination, a gentleman of strict honor and integrity. He says, after giving an account of why, and how he interfered in their behalf—

" Three days after this representation had been made by me, *private* and *secret* steps were immediately taken to have the miserable wretches at once embarked for England ; but first undergoing a medical examination with rigid instructions to the medical officer to make a special report of their robust health, and a similar report to be made by the embarking officer. Five of these *robust fellows* died at the depot immediately after their release."

The medical certificate says only *one* had died, and Mr. Black dwells with triumph on " only *one* " in the *Courier* newspaper; but Major Stewart's statement is, that so emaciated were they by their prison treatment that, on going to the depot at Santander five of them died; which I know to be true.

But if medical officers could be found, who accused a man of being drunk, when he was in an epidemic fever, and within a day of his death—when medical officers could be found who would mock a man writhing in agony with the toothache, by strapping a piece of simple dressing plaister on his belly, telling him that soldiers had nothing to do with toothache, and when the man thus insulted tore off the plaister and threw it away, the surgeon got him punished by four dozen lashes for his insolence ! when a surgeon who could do that and similar disgraceful acts, which some did, but which for the honour of the profession the greater part of those in Spain were not capable of doing ; it is not impossible that a certificate should have been drawn up pronouncing men who had lain all the winter filthy and naked, starved with cold and hunger, over run with itch and vermin, beaten with rods by the Spanish overseers, forced to go in their naked state through snow—ice—water, and over the mountains to carry wood, when medical officers could be found to perpetrate such other indignities, it is not very surprising that two should have been found to pronounce these brutally treated prisoners in good health.

But Major Stewart's statement as laid before General Evans, and the answers returned him, will speak for themselves, only I must explain that besides these men confined there for no crime, there were five or six under sentence of a court-martial, and what we now complain of is, that the men accused of no crime suffered the same as the criminals, and that all of them were treated in a way unbefitting human beings to suffer.

Statement of Major Stewart.

On the 14th of January 1837, in company with Captain Jamieson, Commander of the " James Watt" steamer, I went ashore at Santona and visited the prison, where the different men of the regiments of the Legion were confined.* They were locked up in a room of about 35 feet by 20 to the number of 84 or 85 persons, on entering which, a sight, such as I never before witnessed, presented itself to my view. —It was perfectly dark, the window shutters being fastened to exclude as much as possible the piercing cold, the snow being still on the ground, which when opened I saw those wretched men huddled together on guard beds, as close as they could pack themselves with the only covering of *one* rag between every two men.— Many of them knowing me immediately started on their legs perfectly naked and implored me for assistance.† I thought it a good opportunity of advising them to return to their duty and harangued them at some length, I, at the same time told those under sentence of court-martial that I could hold out no hopes to them of release as I was then out of the service, but that I would endeavour to get them clothed. They, then, to a man declared they would return to their duty provided they got a suit of clothes to appear like *men* instead of *beasts*. Captain Jamieson and myself subscribed some money to purchase them some tobacco, an article they cried out for more than food.—My particular motive for visiting the prison arose, in consequence of the melancholy picture which the Governor of Santona drew of those unfortunate misguided individuals.—" That

---

* Many of these men made affidavits that they only entered the service for one year.

† One young man in particular who was Col. Arbuthnott's orderly sergeant, whilst I was Assistant Commandant at the Depot, came to me and declared he distinctly enlisted *but* for one year, agreeable to the first article of the conditions of service : this poor lad is of good family—Frazer is his name.

they had been living on half rations of a bad quality for some time, but latterly they would have been totally destitute was it not that he advanced money out of his private purse to purchase provisions for them, which, as he could no longer do, not having been reimbursed that which he had already given, they must in a few days be without food."—

These poor wretches (as I have before said without clothes,) have been compelled to work at the vilest labor, such as carrying coals for the supply of steamers, cleaning the streets—carrying water, &c. with Spanish drivers over them, who unmercifully beat them with sticks and they would be obliged to eat their food raw did they not cross a rocky mountain, *barefoot and naked* in the depth of winter, to cut firewood, a distance of a league or a league and a half.—

I then left them, promising as a fellow man and a British subject, I would bring their situation to the knowledge of the Commandant of Santander, to which place I was going.—

On my seeing Colonel Arbuthnot walking with Commodore Henry, I immediately communicated to him the melancholy situation of the prisoners at Santona particularizing their *nudity* and their being eaten up with *itch and vermin*.*

I had the pleasure in consequence of hearing an order given to a medical man (Mr. Bunnett Junr.), to proceed by the "James Watt" to Santona to inspect and afford medical aid, and also that clothes for each man should be put on board for the use of the prisoners.

On my return to Santano on the 17th Jan., 1837 I again visited the prisoners and found the men clothed, with a few exceptions, I again asked them if they were still willing to return to their duty, and they declared they had already subscribed their names to a paper to that effect, which they told me they gave the doctor to submit to the Commandant of Santander.

On this last visit to the prison I was also accompanied by a friend, Mr. Renwick, of the Commissariat department.

A true copy of the statements sent in by me to Lieut. General Evans

CHARLES STEWART,

late Major 1st Regt. British Legion.

---

* "Commodore Henry of the British R. N. on hearing me describe the state of these men, said very emphatically to Col. A. by G—d you and Evans will get yourselves into a nice mess about these men, Col. Arbuthnott very coolly said, there are none of mine there."

THE PRISONERS AT SANTONA CARRYING COALS TO A STEAMER.

Copy of a letter accompanying the statement.

San Sebastian, 23rd, January, 1837.

Sir,

With reference to the enclosed statement, which I do myself the honor of laying before your Excellency, I respectfully request you will be pleased to take into consideration the deplorable situation of the persons in question, which, as an officer once in the same service with them as a British subject and a fellow man, I beg leave to bring to your notice, in the hope, that, as they are willing to return to their duty, you will in humanity release them from their present confinement and debased situation.

I have the honor to be &c.,

CHARLES STEWART.

Late Major 1st Regt. British Aux. Legion.

Lieut. General Evans.

Reply of the Military Secretary.

Head Quarters, San Sebastian, 24th June, 1837.

Sir,

Your communication of yesterday's date to the Lieut. General has been referred to the Adjutant General.

I have the honor to be &c.,

(Signed)   G. F. HARMAN.

Lieut. Col. Mil. Sec.

To Major Stewart.

Copy of the Adjutant General's Letter.

San Sebastian, 24th Jan. 1837.

Sir,

Your communication of yesterday's date to the Lieut. General relative to the prisoners of Santona, has been referred to me. I therefore have it in command to request you will inform me, by whom you were authorised to draw up such a statement since you are no longer in the service of Her Catholic Majesty, and consequently can have no title to address the Lieut. General upon subjects connected with duty, and much less of a nature to imply censure upon the public authorities; moreover having given a promise that upon your being recommended for the advantages of the 4th and 8th articles of the conditions of service, you would proceed to England in the " General Evans Cutter," and as orders have been issued to all retired officers to quit this garrison, you will be pleased to consider yourself under orders to proceed this evening by the " James Watt Steamer" to Santander.

You will have the goodness to acknowledge this communication.

I have the honor to be &c.,

(Signed) J. G. LA MARCHANT.

Adjt. General.

Major Stewart.

San Sebastian, 24th Jan. 1837.

Sir,

I have to acknowledge the receipt of your letter this moment received, and beg leave to reply to that part of it which refers to my pledge of proceeding to England in the " General Evans Cutter," that as the Deputy Commissary General brought a debit against me relative to my accounts of the depot at Santander, I was compelled by the decision of the Board of Claims to proceed to Santander to procure Vouchers in support of Disbursements made by me whilst Assistant Commandant and acting paymaster of that depot; and that on my return by the only conveyance practicable, the Cutter had sailed for England, otherwise, provided my claims had been settled, I should have been more than happy to have left this country.

I have &c.,

CHARLES STEWART.

It will be a difficult task—though a task imposed by the laws of justice and honour, for General Evans to explain why he thus treated with indignity such an officer as Major Stewart, more especially when that indignity was undisguisedly intended to smother complaining humanity. The Adjutant-General says " *I have it in command* (from the General of course,) *to request you will inform me by whom you were authorised to draw up such a statement, since you are no longer in the service of her Catholic Majesty, and consequently can have no title to address the Lieut. General upon subjects connected with duty, and much less of a nature to imply censure on the public authorities.*" What could there be more dictatorial in *Russia* than this? What more absolutely illiberal in the *Inquisition*? yet this proceeded from General Evans!—eight men were suffering the vilest degradation *without trial*, in a secluded fortress, unseen by any one who could

speak their language, until Captain Jamieson the commander of a
British Steamer, and Major Stewart, formerly an officer of the British army, having put in at that port, went ashore from motives of
curiosity to see the town and fortress,—not until the authority of
common humanity, prompted these gentlemen to represent the dreadful sufferings of the prisoners, did their misery find a voice of sympathy! and then to prevent farther interference, Major Stewart was
peremptorily ordered to leave Spain.

To give this circumstance due weight, the character of Major
Stewart as an officer, is of importance.

He entered the British service when a mere youth, in 1816, and
became Adjutant of the 69th regiment in India soon after.   Military
readers know well, and I may inform civilians, that, though many
British officers get posts and promotion for which they are not qualified, none of them are *adjutants* unless fully competent to the arduous
duty ; — it is no favour to obtain the adjutancy of a regiment
farther than that holding the situation, is a proof invariably correct,
that the officer doing that duty is a clever soldier, especially on active service.   Major Stewart was in his early career appointed also
to be Staff Adjutant, and served throughout the most of the campaign in the Deccan, under Generals Sir Thomas Munroe, and Sir
Theophilus Pritzler.   He was wounded at the storming of Sholapore ;
and having had nearly eleven years active employment in India, it will
be seen that his experience as a soldier, must be considerable.   He
was applied to, as one likely to be practically useful to go out to
Spain, and he consented to leave a settled situation in London by
the promises, and with the hope of speedy promotion.   This he soon
obtained ; for there was scarcely an officer or man in the Legion,
who did not perceive the efficient services of Major Stewart particularly in the 1st regiment, in which he was for some time Captain and
adjutant.   The complete state of discipline to which that corps was
brought in a very short time, chiefly by the drilling of this officer,
justly entitled him to promotion, and he received a reward so far by
being appointed Brigade-Major under Brigadier Evans, an elder brother of the Lieut. General.   In the month of March, 1836, Major
Stewart was sent from Vittoria, to organize and command the depot
at Corban Convent, Santander, which, from two Assistant Commandants, Colonel Renwick and Major Edwards, having previously died

there, had fallen into a state of chaos, from which it could only be
redeemed by an officer of energy and experience, such as Major
Stewart.   Great quantities of baggage and stores of all descriptions,
with batches of recruits coming out, and invalids going home, were
collected at this place, and the embezzlement of the stores, had
arrived at that state of prodigality, that would have baffled any common man to have arrested.   The following incident is a small part
of what was going on.

A person named Hughes, who was quarter-master, and another
named Jupp who acted as his assistant, had the charge of these stores,
which consisted, in the first place of all, or nearly all, the gaudy uniform—necessaries, and super-necessaries of officers, who had been
obliged to leave their luggage behind them, in the month of October
1835, when they marched from the sea coast across the mountains
to Vittoria.   These were the splendid outfits from Jermyn Street,
Bond street, and other places that had been furnished so profusely to
the officers ; in some cases by their relations, and in others by the
military tailors,(not yet paid) on the strength of the bills of Spanish
agents.   These, and vast quantities of soldier's clothing, consisting
of boots, shirts, flannels, and all kinds of regimental necessaries,
with muskets and ammunition, were at Corban, and were under
process of plunder, and spoiliation by Hughes, Jupp, and their
associates, when Major Stewart came to take command.   His first
enquiry at Hughes, was to have the books and accounts delivered
over, but that gentleman answered there were no books! (Major
Stewart did not know then, nor does he know yet, as I believe, that there
was a fire made one night in one of the cells of the convent, in which
these unresisting but dangerous witnesses, the books—were put out
of existence).   The Major next demanded to know what stores were at
the depot, and was told that there were only some trifling *odds and
ends*.   He had his suspicions, from seeing numbers of Spaniards,
men and women, crowding near the convent every day under pretence
of vending small wares, when, as he knew, nobody had any money
to purchase from them.   In fact these people had been supplied
daily with the plunder of the stores which women belonging to the
depot, and in the employment of Hughes and Co, carried out to them.
This plundering had been rendered more disgraceful too, by the most
heartless treatment of the poor wretches of invalids. who were collected

about the convent. The persons who were the real plunderers—who sold even the bread and wine at times which was allowed to the invalids—got up court martials, and a provost system of their own, and flogged the poor wretches—whom they were starving—under pretence of plundering the stores; so that their own misdeeds might be less likely to be detected.

Major Stewart with an acute perception, fixed his suspicions on another quarter than those who were blamed and frequently flogged at the instance of Hughes, Jupp, and that gang; he fastened his suspicions on these persons themselves, though for a few days he said nothing to indicate what he thought

He had no one to apply to for information, therefore he made himself his own spy. A large apartment that had once been the refectory of the convent, was immediately beneath his own room, and in this apartment, all that remained of the Legion's miscellaneous baggage was deposited. The Major made a small opening so that he could at any time have a bird's eye view through the floor of what took place beneath. The same day that the hole was made, he was having a peep, when Messrs Hughes, Jupp, and their clerk entered, and began to undo the fastenings of some portmanteaus. The articles were tossed out, and various shirts, stockings, boots, and things more or less valuable were inspected. Jupp seeing nothing that took his fancy, contemptuously turned the contents of his trunk in again, and proceeded to another in search of golden epaulettes, or something that would take the market readily; the others were going on in the same way, and Major Stewart to make his discovery effectual, went and got the Adjutant of the depot, to come and have a peep also, so that the latter might be a corroborating evidence. This done, the Major descended the stairs, and going to the door of the store-house found it bolted. As usual the sentry was walking with his musket and fixed bayonet outside keeping out all but those who had the privelege of entrance, and who were those that were then within. The Major demanded admittance, but no answer was made from the interior, nor was the door opened, though he repeated his demands, until the guard which he had sent for came, and received from him in a loud voice, that echoed through the convent the order "*prime and load.*" As there could be no mistaking his intention of discharging a volley of bullets through the door to burst it open, the delinquents within, thought it was then as safe to come out, which they did by opening the door and presenting themselves in conscious guilt before Major Stewart and the guard of soldiers, some of whom had been flogged at the instance of these same Messrs. Hughes, Jupp, and Co., on suspicion of robbing the stores when on sentry. Major Stewart immediately ordered them to lead the way to their quarters where with the assistance of the guard he found bales of linen shirts, barrels of boots, bales of great-coats, and an immense number of valuable personal effects belonging to staff and regimental officers, all hidden and deposited in secret places, some shuffling excuses were at first urged, but the manner of Major Stewart held out little hope of favor. Sentries were placed over them, and as there were some batteries of artillery at Santander, the requisite number of English officers were found, and a District Court-martial was constituted, which awarded to each of them three hundred lashes.

This punishment which in all cases is a degrading and brutal mode of taking vengeance on criminals, was inflicted on these persons with as little of accompanying pity from the spectators, as any criminals were ever doomed to suffer under. This might savor of vengeance on the part of the witnessing soldiers; but it is questionable if there is not less justice than vengeance in all punishments within the bounds of English law, either civil or military, and less pity than gratification in all who are spectators of punishment.

Be that as it may, there were a considerable number of those who saw Hughes and Jupp flogged, saw them with that spirit of satisfaction which developes the moral ingredients from which it springs in certain people, when we hear wishes expressed that any one inflicting injury on another, should get the same thing in return; such as a flogging officer should be flogged himself, and so on. This quality common in a certain kind of men, and prevalent in almost all women, though not a benevolent ingredient in the moral constitution of either, was fully alive to gratification when these *gentlemen* were flogged; for at their instance, men had been punished for having even insinuated that dishonesty kept from them the due allowance of rations; and men were flogged by them also for robbing, or at least for being suspected. The criminals themselves prayed for mercy, but Major Stewart was inexorable, and if he had inclined to leniency, he could not, for Colonel Arbuthnott the Commandant of Santander, and the superior of Major Stewart, had ordered that not a lash was to be spared.

It is necessary here to make a digressive remark on Colonel Arbuthnott's severity in flogging, as Major Stewart has been blamed for inflicting punishments which were ordered by the superior officer ; one of these was on the clerk of the depot who was among the plunderers of the stores. The instrument with which this man was punished was the man-of-war cats, which are commonly used in the infliction of two, three, or four dozen lashes in the navy but not more. I am not aware which of the English ships of war the cats were procured from, whether from the Castor, Royalist, Salamander, Phœnix, or Tweed, though I have heard that they came from the Castor : but there can be no doubt that the officer lending that instrument out of an English ship of war, was committing a breach of duty, which is punishable if any one in authority were to look on it as a crime, which however, is not likely. Major Stewart has been accused of procuring this instrument ; but it was Colonel Arbuthnott the brother-in-law of General Evans, who borrowed it from the man-of-war and forgot to return it until by frequent use it was worn so as to be good for nothing. The clerk, who was first flogged with this instrument, was sentenced to receive three hundred stripes and got nearly one hundred when being dreadfully lacerated, he was taken down from the triangles by Major Stewart and sent to hospital ; after recovering he was brought back by order of Colonel Arbuthnott to receive the remainder of the three hundred, but Major Stewart told him, secretly, to faint when the punishment began, which he did, and the surgeon in attendance having had Major Stewart's secret instructions also, pronounced the man to be unfit to receive any more punishment. This man who had for some months been almost a king in Corban by virtue of his office, was then dismissed the service.

Two months after this I saw these cats in daily use at Corban convent, under the direction of a Major Fitch, who succeeded Major Stewart as Assistant Commandant of that depot. One morning there were seventeen men flogged by this fearful instrument : their crimes were mostly connected with the following circumstance.

Colonel Arbuthnott, who had a house and military establishment as Commandant at Santander, rode out one day as he occasionally did, with his lady and some other attendants to Corban convent, a

distance of nearly four miles across a heathy common. On returning
the lady dropped one of her diamond earrings, but having been galloping on the heath out of the usual track she could give no opinion
of the place where the article fell. Early next morning all the inmates of the convent, sick, lame, and lazy were turned out on the
heath to look among the grass over a space of four miles for the earring, a reward of five dollars being promised to those who found it.
The search had scarcely commenced when some lynx-eyed Legionary
caught sight of the glittering diamond among the furze, but he probably debating with himself whether he would conceal the treasure
or give it up, allowed the general search to go on for a considerable
time. Honesty at last overcame him, and he and some others proceeded towards Santander to return it and receive the reward, telling
the others that they need not look any longer as the earring was
found. It was given up, and the reward was promised to be paid
soon after, as from unexplained circumstances it could not be paid at
the time : Major Fitch who formed the vision of himself bowing to the
lady and presenting her with the trinket if it could be found, was
outrageous when he knew that some of the men had gone to Santander with it themselves. The holiday which all the invalids and soldiers were enjoying on the common, which was indeed a holiday, as
at other times they were closely kept within the walls of the convent,
among an overwhelming swarm of fleas :—Major Fitch who had once
been a lieutenant of Marines, having converted Corban convent into
a man-of-war with all the rules, usages, and strict discipline of a hulk
—this holiday was suddenly interrupted by the offended Fitch ordering all the men to be brought back to quarters immediately. Some
of them ventured to enjoy the sun, fresh air, and relaxation from flea
torture a little longer, not dreaming that the Major had any cause of
displeasure ; they therefore lay among the furze until they were
brought in as prisoners along with those who had gone to Mrs.
Arbuthnott's with the diamond earring. These last had supposed
that they could draw on the forbearance of military severity for
a few hours, more especially as they considered the Commandant in
their debt, the promised reward not being paid; Major Fitch thought
otherwise ; he being incensed at not having an opportunity of visiting
his proud superior on business that would have less formality than
usual, took vengeance on all those who did not obey his first order to

come in, by shutting them up in the guard house during the night, and bringing them out next morning to the number of seventeen, and giving them punishments varying from two to four dozen lashes with the naval cat. Among these unfortunates were those who found and delivered the lady's earring; the Major not recognising, as has been observed, any alliance between the debt of the Commandant to them, and their debt to the Commandant's military law. The Commandant, however, took a different view of the case; he considered that there was a close connexion between his debt to them, and their obedience to strict law; for on the plea of their having misconducted themselves, he decided that they had forfeited their claim to the reward, for finding his lady's diamond, and accordingly did not pay them. Thus these fellows were regularly'done for, the Major flogged them because they gave up the diamond to its owner, and Colonel Arbuthnott did not pay the reward because they had been flogged.

To return to Major Stewart. That officer had wrought a complete reformation in organising the depot at Corban; though Colonel Arbuthnott took, and got credit for the reformation that was effected. It was notorious that during the whole of the preceding winter, the men lay in the open corridors and galleries, windowless and doorless, with the snow drifting on them, and nothing was done to save them from the inclemency of the season until Major Stewart came, and ordering all carpenters, bricklayers, glaziers, &c. to be set to work—put the convent in a very short time into a habitable state of repair. He also set gardeners and others to work, and cultivated the gardens that were laying waste around the convent, so that two important purposes were served; first, the quarters were made comfortable, and an abundance of vegetables were produced for the use of the depot, and second, and more particularly the men who were pining and every day dying in filth, starvation, disease, and despondency, were renovated in health, for let it be kept in mind this depot consisted mostly of invalids and sick men; Major Stewart also drilled them twice a day, which drilling they were enabled to endure better in connexion with their work, than they could when confined to quarters and doing nothing.

Thus far the efficiency of Major Stewart as an officer was manifested. He has been blamed for severity in punishing, and General Evans has been known to complain of his severity; but the punish-

ment in many cases were not Major Stewart's they were Colonel
Arbuthnott's, the relative of the Lieutenant General and the dictator
of what punishment should be inflicted. It is known that Major
Stewart refused to inflict the punishment as ordered by Colonel
Arbuthnott, and this in fact was as much a cause of his being removed from Corban as any other, though the Lieutenant General in
an order for Major Stewart's removal states, that " as he cannot allow
an officer so useful to the service, and one of such extensive practical
experience as Major Stewart to remain in the depot; the Lieutenant
General is therefore pleased to command that Major Stewart shall
proceed to join his regiment at San Sebastian immediately," &c. &c.
This commendation was only just, and afterwards when Major Stewart
was treated with indignity, and demanded to know if he had given
any cause of offence; the Military Secretary, Colonel Harman, returned
for answer, that he had it in command from the Lieutenant General
to say that nothing impugning the character of Major Stewart had
come to his knowledge.

As to the value of this officer's services, and the way in which he
conducted himself, together with the estimation he was held in by
the men, it may not be improper here to state that, as he brought
the depot from a chaos of the most disorderly materials, to a state of
complete order and discipline, so that depot fell into its original element of confusion under his successor, although the lash was used without an exception every day of Major Fitch's command. Here was a
proof that it was not the severity of Major Stewart's discipline, that
had made him successful, while there is also a proof that he was beloved by the men, from the manner that all those who knew him
talked of him ; and a remaining, and strong proof, that, had he been
very severe without any qualification, he would not have been favoured with the good will of the soldiers unless he deserved it, was,—
that the second Assistant Commandant in succession from him, that
is, the one that succeeded Major Fitch—whose name for the sake of
his relations, I shall not mention, though I may state he was the son
of a church dignitary now deceased—was the brother of the High
Sheriff of a midland county in England, and had been an officer in a
British regiment of dragoons ; — this gentleman who was deemed
worthy to be Assistant-Commandant of the depot, so conducted himself, that on his passage to England in charge of a batch of invalids,

he was thrown overboard in the Bay of Biscay, and there left to shift with " the blue above, and the blue below," as he best could.

Major Stewart had sent to England for his wife while he was at Corban, supposing himself likely to remain there ; but the truth is, that he was looked on with envy, and General Evans knows who represented the necessity of his being removed from the depot. Mrs. Stewart was seized with typhus fever almost as soon as she landed, and had only been able to rise for the first time from bed, when her husband received the order to proceed immediately to San Sebastian. Any one who knew Major Stewart will allow at once that he was not the officer to hesitate a moment on receiving an order, yet as it is known that he tenderly loved his wife, and she having infant children with her, it may be supposed that he was grieved to leave her, an entire stranger, behind him. Scarcely had she recovered sufficiently to follow him to San Sebastian, when he was engaged in the sanguinary action of the 1st of October, 1836, and received a musket shot in his breast, which for the time put him in the greatest danger.

His efficient services were now rewarded by eight junior officers being promoted over his head, on which he immediately tendered his resignation, which was accepted ; but with the assurance "that nothing whatever impugning his character had reached the ears of the Lieutenant General."

It was then that Major Stewart having to go to Santander, went to Santona in company with Captain Jamieson of the James Watt steamer, and saw the prisoners in their wretched state of filth, nakedness, and disease, and prompted by humanity he laid the statement of their condition before General Evans, to which he received the answer demanding to know " by whose authority he had presumed to send a statement about the prisoners, &c."

Now the truth may as well be told in full. Colonel Arbuthnott was the brother-in-law of General Evans. He could not endure the evidence of Major Stewart's good government which went to condemn his own former negligence, and Colonel Harman was Military Secretary to the General at this time and is a person who rendered himself so obnoxious to all the officers, save a few favorites that even now he dare not let himself be seen in England as there are nearly a dozen of unanswered challenges from officers demanding satisfaction for in-

solence which he used towards them with impunity in his office under the General.   And lastly, General Evans though not naturally
a harsh tempered, or tyrannically disposed man, was so much defici-
ent in some qualities as a Commander, that those who had his ear
for the passing time, could sway him to any side and overturn any
former favorite.

Thus was the Legion for a time deprived of the experienced services of Major Stewart, and thus was it that a person who had been
originally a clerk in a merchant's office, afterwards an agent in the
West Indies where he was reduced to extremities from conduct, that
the law of libel forbids me to write—who came and offered his services as a clerk in the commissary department going to Spain, and
who subsequently became Deputy Commissary General Black ;—
thus was that Mr. Black who, ignorant even of the mere rudiments of military duty, highly promoted, and enabled now to write
with all the pomp, and assurance of a military authority impugning
the character and conduct of officers, many of whom served in the
Peninsular war, and some of whom, like Major Stewart, more lately
in the East Indies; all of them superior in military experience to
himself.

In the foregoing narrative of circumstances relating to the Santona
prisoners, we have some of the weakest points of the character of
General Evans unfolded to us, and I should be willing to proceed to
those scenes of bustle and bloodshed which occurred subsequent to
any period which I have yet alluded to, and which admit of narrations
more interesting to general readers, as well as more honorable to
General Evans as a soldier; but there are some other matters that
must be noted as we pass.

CHAPTER XV.

Remarks on General Evans and Sir Hussey Vivian's memoranda—Dr. Guthrie's regulations, remarks thereon—General inspections in Vittoria—Disgusting
spectacle in the streets—A funeral—Description of the common appearance of
the convalescents—Anecdotes of several individuals, of various kinds—Pedro
Hamilton's duel, and Pedro Hamilton cudgeled, &c. &c. &c.

PREVIOUS to going out to Spain General Evans was favoured by
Sir Hussey Vivian with a memoranda, suggesting regulations to be
observed in the formation of the different regiments, all of them of

great importance, but the greater part of which were not attended to. Sir Hussey, suggested that there should be no flank companies distinguished from the others, such as *light* companies and *grenadier* companies, as the existence of these excited jealousy and other ill feelings in the remaining companies of the battalion. General Evans, however, instead of observing this rule, had not only flank companies, distinguished by peculiar favors from their commanding officers, but he had all kinds of distinctive appellations to the different regiments; that,—though many of them were only harmlessly ridiculous shewed a weakness of mind, and ignorance of, or inattention to the prejudices of mankind. He had the 3rd Westminster Grenadiers—many of them as good soldiers as ever carried muskets, but not a few of them at the same time any thing but *grenadiers*. He had the 4th " Queen's Own." He had the 5th or " Highland Light Infantry," few of whom ever saw the Highlands until at a distance when sailing out of the Clyde for Spain. He had the 6th, " Scotch Grenadiers," who were as much misnamed, and as often laughed at as their Liliputian brethren in arms from Westminster. The 7th "Royal" Irish, and the 9th Irish, and the 10th " Munster Light Infantry" were named rather more appropriately, because they were in reality Irishmen ; but to have followed Sir Hussey Vivian's suggestions would have been much better, that was to have no distinction of countrymen, for as the departure from that suggestion proved, — discontent and continual disagreement, fights, brawls, broken heads, and inefficiency in discipline were, to a great extent, the result. The 8th were also called "Highlanders," though one third or more were recruited in the north of Ireland, and a considerable proportion of the others thought it no compliment to be styled by that name, which did not belong to them, and for which they had no regard more than for other names. The 1st, was a good fighting corps without any particular distinction. The 2nd was not long in existence. But the *Rifles* of every corps in the Legion were most exposed to danger—fought best—had most men killed—and from their common good conduct excited more emulation without any peculiar name, than any of the others.

But had the departure from Sir Hussey Vivian's memoranda ended there, General Evans might have been pardoned. He departed from absolute rules of conduct, which could not have been dispensed with without subjecting him to a criminal charge of neglect. This was in proceeding to Vittoria from Bilbao, without any arrangements for the treatment of the sick.   He did not obtain a regular supply of rations, nor proper quarters for young troops on the march ; yet on that point, as it was a bold enterprise to lead a young army through a circuitous route among the mountains, to form a junction with another army, by eluding the powerful foe that commanded the main road—we may forgive him ; he depended on the Spaniards for faithful service in getting rations, and the fault of not providing them properly, was theirs.   But he calculated on the good health of his troops, and even with the good health had no sufficient hospital arrangements ; for it was not until the month of March, (he having left Bilbao on the 30th of the preceding October,) that a medicine chest was forwarded to Vittoria, and even then there were no proper hospitals, or stores to form one ; although two thousand men were sick at once, and the whole of the troops were in a deplorable state approaching to disease from the neglect of cleanliness—want of bedding—bad rations, and continued exposure to the freezing cold.

About the beginning of March, he issued a general order, and had it printed and distributed among the troops, which contained extracts from regulations drawn up by a Dr. Guthrie, to be observed by colonels of regiments, captains of companies, and regimental medical officers, in promoting the comforts of the men.   There was perhaps, never a greater mockery of misery than these regulations, as published in this order, though the fault was not Dr. Guthrie's.   That gentleman understood the diseases likely to arise from the neglect of certain rules, and had provided for the undue occurrence of disease by pointing out what rules were necessary to be observed,   The spirit of these ran thus : —

"That a warm breakfast should be provided in every case, even where the cooking of dinners might not be easily performed !—That the men should never lay within eighteen inches of the ground, and at all times should be provided with clean straw," and several other similarly sensible suggestions.

But what was the case at the time this order was issued ?   There were no warm breakfasts, nor breakfasts of any kind ! the morning's duty began by the regiments marching out among the snow to drill, or to what was called a Carlist hunt among the mountains, sometimes with their twelve ounces of raw poisonous bread in their haversacks, to be eaten on the march, and sometimes with nothing, the rations not being had from the commissariat till the evening, when wearied or worn out the men devoured the sour bread and morsel of tasteless beef, and lay down without either straw or beds on the floors—crawling to each other for heat; enjoying existence only when kind darkness hid the surrounding wretchedness, or kindlier sleep rendered them unconscious of hunger, and cold, and gave them in some homely dream a review of their formerly inappreciated happiness.

At the time of these regulations of Dr. Guthrie's being issued in general orders, accompanied as they were, with strict injunctions to medical officers of regiments to see that they were carefully enforced, we expected some alteration from the state of wretchedness in which we then were, to take place, and for a few days hopes were excited; but these died away; for no improvement whatever, in our quarters or rations took place. The months that we had passed in, and around Vittoria, had been unceasing and unvaried starvation, and they continued so until we left that (to us) unhappy place.

If General Evans intended that order to be followed up with a substantial alteration of treatment, he must have been deceived in some quarter; but the opinion among the troops was, that he was not sincere, and that feeling was strengthened more by one single peculiarity in his behaviour than any other circumstance,— that was his never visiting or inspecting the state of the regimental quarters, or the hospitals himself. He had two or three times an inspection of the different regiments in the Plaza, or square of the town, when great pains had been taken to have these all paraded clean, and in full regimentals. There, with his gaudy staff-officers attending him, the waving plumes, the fresh scarlet, and the glittering gold, all unsoiled as they were when first fitted on in Bond Street, he walked round the ranks, while the band played the " *General*," or the " *British Grenadiers*," or " *Hurrah for the bonnets o' blue*," as the case might be,—the balconies graced with Spanish ladies—and the scene all lively and gay — and then rode home to the next street to dine with his own, and the Spanish generals — while we returned to our old convents to enquire if the bread was not got yet — carry sick men into the hospital, and dead ones out — or kill, each man, a few hundreds of the lice that had been feeding undisturbed during the parade as we dared not scratch ourselves before the General.

Another mockery of humanity at this time were Sunday parades to hear prayers! to hear prayers read on the same parade where were heard groans accompanying the provost's lash. It is true the officers who thus blasphemously mocked Heaven, and outraged their fellow men, were few; but one of them resorted to this form of sanctity so frequently while he otherwise violated every impulse of moral honour or honesty, that it would be an injustice not to name him, that was Brigadier General Shaw. The poor fellows who were in Portugal a few years ago, have a lively recollection of this person's assumed sanctity, with which he prayed for the *Mercies of God* on the same ground, with the same square formed around by his men, where the triangles had stood a few minutes before, or were again to stand, with a victim praying for mercy from *him* whose ear heard no appeal,—whose grey twinkling eye, looking small and cunning, fastened its unkind glance, with unnatural satisfaction on a suffering criminal.

Another who dared once, and only once, to lift his unholy voice was Colonel, afterwards General, Godfrey. This was at the village of Aranguez, in which his regiment among a few miserable huts were quartered. One Sunday morning while scudding showers drove along the black sky—when the knee-deep gutters surrounded the ruinous village, the unbreakfasted soldiers were paraded for inspection, and to their astonishment Godfrey appeared with a prayer-book. He, a man who never uttered the simplest sentence—who never gave the word of command and never had, previous to that, appeared on a parade, but accompanied with the most fearful oaths,—now formed the battalion into a hollow square, and giving the common words of command without any oath for once, began to read prayers. He proceeded for some time, when a few of those in one of the rear ranks began to twitter. His keen eye detecting their confused features, he said "so you think fit to laugh, do you? you think to make me swear! stand steady, there." He resumed the prayer. Twittering continued, until stopping again he said—"Sergeant Major, take these fellows off and give them two hours drill, drill them well now—I'll not flog them, but I'll drill the life out of them, the scoundrels—be steady, and silent there, or by the living G—." This was enough. He found praying on parade and swearing would not do :—the adjutant took the prayer-book home.

No. 19.

It was the same day, on which was one of these reviews that the following incident took place. The incident was no unusual one, nor do I need to quote any officer's notes for it from the scarcity of such occurrences, for I saw many similar ones almost every day myself, but as I find this recorded by a Mr. Aynge, I give it in his own words.

"I was standing at the window of my billet with Lieut. Payne, when a cart drawn by bullocks passed along the street; it was loaded with dead bodies from the hospital to be deposited in the field for the dead, behind San Domingo Convent. There had been a sheet covering them, but it was turned off by the wind, and the arm of one hung over on one side; while the leg of another hung to the other side, and was grazing on the wheel. It had continued to hang on the wheel all the way down the street, and it was now rubbed till the bone was protruding. We called to the Spaniard who drove the cart to halt and put it in, but he only looked behind—he being as usual in front of his bullocks, shrugged his shoulders, and then went on. Disgusted at the sight, and indignant at the Spaniard we went down to the street, and forced him to halt until we put the limbs of the dead men into the cart, and the sheet decently over them. This occurred in the main street of Vittoria at mid-day."

The foregoing was quite common; and I may here quote from some notes which I took myself about that time, of occurrences, but which notes were stolen from me in the town of San Sebastian; but which, as a proof perhaps that they were not much worth, have been returned to me since I came to London. Had I been in possession of these notes sooner, I would have quoted more frequently from them. The following is a funeral:—

"I have just seen the funeral of a Spanish officer of high rank: the corpse was borne along with two full military bands playing, one in front, and the other in rear of the attending procession. A train of priests with lighted candles three feet long, and from two to three inches thick followed by a vast number of Spanish and English field officers, among whom, were General Evans and his staff—formed the mourners. There is a pure melancholy comes over the mind as the slow step and martial music winds onwards to the grave. I had such sensations of the unreal as the rich uniforms and gaudy plumes passed before me, and the subduing music more softly mournful than I ever

before heard, melted through my imagination—that I was for some
time unconscious of what I was listening to, until the last of the
scarlet uniforms had passed, and close behind them was a cart be-
smeared with filthy soil with the driver holding back the mule which
drew it, so as not to force its way among the officers of the procession,
which it seemed striving to do. In this cart were the bodies of four
English soldiers naked and coffinless. They were being carried to
the grave, but they formed no part of the grand funeral.

Such was the state of the enfeebled victims of this dreadful epidemic, produced by the want of the commonest comforts of life, that
in what was called the convalescent hospitals where the remnants of
those who had survived the first attack of fever were congregated,
they lay crowded together with wan and ghostly visages doing nothing but killing lice! The vermin were clotted in their hair, and a
stranger to the place on entering, saw them lying or sitting with a
rug about them, and a part of their clothes off at the usual employment. By the time the jacket had been thinned a little, it was time
to begin on the trowsers, and when these had been the field of half an
hour's slaughter, the tormented *convalescent* Legionary began again
on his jacket! he seldom had a shirt to trouble him. Some of these
had a relapse of fever, and under that second attack they commonly
died, indeed almost without an exception.

I remember to have seen a young man named——no, I must not tell
his name, who had been one of the smartest dandies that ever cut a
swell out of London, or perhaps in the metropolis itself, strange turns
of fortune took him to Spain, and at this time he was one of the convalescents. I saw him in a corner by himself killing his overplus.
He struck me as being peculiarly philosophical in his manner of putting them to death. Being refined beyond other men in all things,
he was refined even in this. The most of the others crushed the
little animals to death the moment they got hold of them with their
fingers : but the broken down *exquisite* did not touch them with his
fingers. He had two needles which he used similar to a fork and
knife, in lifting the bodies and laying them down on a flat stone,
within a circle made by gunpowder. When the amount to be immolated for the day had been gathered, he made a general destruction
by blowing them up in a gun powder plot, and throwing the piece of
stone with the ashes, outside the house. This, I should have scarcely

mentioned, had he not lived to re-appear as the peacock of his tribe, which he is at the moment of this being written. He did not afford any matter for comment on his character as a soldier, for he came home soon after this period ; but he will have the comfort of seeing that I have not altogether forgotten him.

I saw a man named William Douglass among them ; he was not convalescent, but assuming the first symptoms of fever, having been sent to this place when the regiment to which he belonged was going out on a day's march to see what they could find among the mountains; he not being deemed sick enough to be sent to hospital. Douglass had been only twelve months before this time, owner of, as he expressed himself to me, " twa o'e bonniest shuppys (ships) that e'er carried e king's flag in e Pentland Firth, an' as bonny a wifie as might be seen on e water side." In fact he had been a man of considerable property, and as I have been informed since, *was* the owner of a schooner and a brig, but lost them by the failure of some speculation. His wife was the daughter either of a late, or the present Consul of Demerara. He told me that the sudden failure of his speculations caused her to return for a time to her friends, and shame and beggary caused him to go to Spain, he not being friendly with her relations as they were in a superior rank of society. We called him the black Douglass, from his peculiarly dark eye, and the raven forest that covered his face. He was a steady and seemingly very sober man. I saw him two days after he went into the convalescent hospital, and he was then beginning to have active symptoms of fever. I was one of a fatigue party that were burying dead bodies about a fortnight after, and I found his among them.

There were at times a painful performance of duty fell to the share of those who were well. To give some idea of it, I may sketch a part of one day's work, premising, that though this is written in the first person, and descriptive of what I, and my party did, it is applicable to all the regimental fatigue parties from different corps that were employed in Vittoria :— I find my *notes* written shortly after this time, commencing with the following remarks.

To each company there had at first been a few beds, though there were always a vast number of men lying without them, but at this time these had been taken away to the hospitals, and there were no beds or blankets in our quarters. General Shaw takes much credit to himself for having furnished the hospital with six hundred beds and blankets, which he says by great exertions he managed to obtain for the use of the dying. He did right in giving the beds to the hospitals; but he neglects to state, that the great exertions he made was only to send fatigue parties of convalescents to collect all the beds in the different quarters of the regiments one day when the whole Legion had a march to the country; and it was ascertained that above two hundred of the blankets had been sold to the Spaniards, by those who had been charged with conveying them to the hospital. * *

In the morning, parties were at work clearing the passages and corridors of the snow that drifted in at open windows, and the rubbish that accumulated by the shaking of the old convent in the gusts of wind. There was no drill that day, and there had been none for two weeks previous, for the snow covered every part. In the long galleries of the convent, single companies might have been drilled, but winter seemed so inveterately withering and cheerless, that no officer thought of troubling his men, for if he did, he must needs bestir himself. All was dull weary idleness. The pioneers went out in search of rations early in the morning, waited three or four hours, on the turn of the regiment to be served, and were perhaps not served for ten hours. Quarter-masters of English and Spanish regiments, drawing rations for upwards of twenty thousand men, crowded about the different public stores and bakers' shops, in competition. Some of them would purchase the turn of being served from another one, and the knave selling it went either last, or caused his regiment to want rations for that day. While the Quarter-masters were, with the pioneers of the different regiments, thus employed, the men in quarters had a hungry idle time, waiting on them coming. "Are the pioneers away for the *pang?*" was the first question with every one in the morning. "Is the *pang* come yet?" was the question kept in continual repetition during the forenoon. "Is the *carne?*" "Yes," the answer would be, "the cooks are cooking it." The Spanish name for bread is *pan*, and sometimes pronounced *pang*, hence the familiarity of that name amongst us.

To see the cooks at work outside, a few would go to the open windows of the rooms, which on one side of the convent were so cold that no one could inhabit them. To get a glance of the kettles boiling was purchased by standing for a few minutes in the frost wind, or in the sleet that was battering in.   Shaking, and trembling, these spies would return and report progress, to a crowd who lay huddled together to keep themselves warm.   If there was not a good fire, or if the kettle of No. such a mess was running over, or if the cook had been seen tasting the beef, or if he had some suspicious ones about him warming their toes, all, or any of these matters, were reported to the main body inside, who listened with the greatest anxiety to any report.   What increased the anxiety was, that there was a guard on the outer door, to keep all in but non-commissioned officers or men, going out on duty, and as the honesty of the cooks was not to be trusted, and hungry fellows going about the fires warming themselves, suspicion caused them to be narrowly watched.   It was a melancholy picture, but it was mixed so often with the ludicrous, that one could not help laughing at it.

If you ventured to look out from the open gap, where a window should have been, you would see in a temporary shade, with half a roof, the cooking going on.   There was one cook of a company could not get his fire to burn, for the want of dry wood, another had drowned out his fire by accident : he had lifted the half door off its hinges, from some Spaniard's house, or brought away his bullock car, and was now breaking them up.   The Spaniard would come in search of them, take out his knife, grind his teeth, and utter with vehemence the common Spanish oaths, then half a dozen of our men with pieces of wood in their hands, would chase him away.   It was at the entrance to a field where the dead were buried.   Four men carrying a dead body, or sometimes a long train of ten times as many men and dead bodies, came straggling past from the hospitals.   Very few could withstand the temptation of warming themselves at the fires, and taking a look at the kettles boiling ; the bodies, in the meantime, were laid down, and some of them got leave to lie there, the party making off without them.   Between that gate and where the graves were, you would at any time see bodies lying unburied, left there sometimes from the hole being full, having twenty or more tumbled at random into it ; and sometimes left there by those who, having an opportunity to " skirt," as they called it, threw down their load and went away : but not to their quarters, rather, perhaps, to sell the " stretcher," or bier, on which they had carried the dead body.   Our cooks just being in the way, were often supplied with fire wood by that means, giving a piece of beef out of the kettles, to the hungry fellows who, with themselves, ran the risk of being flogged. Perhaps before they got back to the hospital, the sheet which had covered the body would be sold also.

Looking out from the convent, we would see these things going on, and that day which I am particularizing, I had been attracted to the cold side, where the open windows of the second story overlooked the cooks and the burying ground. Some of the men had come in saying, that there was a *vendy* going on, that being a cant term they had made from the verb " to vend," which in English and Spanish is similar in pronunciation and meaning. It was extremely cold, and a shower of fierce hail was giving them an excuse for taking shelter. They had the body of an officer in a wooden box. It had perhaps been intended to give him the ceremony of an English funeral; but neither priest nor layman had ventured to wade through the snow to officiate, and, therefore, six men were carrying the box by themselves. The wet slush was knee-deep, and no grave had been made : four other bodies were lying farther down in the field unburied. The pioneers had not come in with the bread, and as it was eleven o'clock, and every one hungry, pressing orders had been sent out to the cooks to be quick. Their fires were nearly put out by the sleety rain that poured on them, and there was no wood. " Seize that coffin," said some of them, and it was immediately done, the body tumbled out, and in a few minutes the wood blazed below the kettles. " It's of no use to let him lie in the gutter with linen sheets about him," one of them suggested, for he'll be no worse than others, though we take them off. This was also agreed to, and a Spaniard that lived near by, was, at the time we looked out, making the purchase. Some of them took up the corpse to carry it down to be in company with the other naked ones; but as they were passing us, the heavy shower of hail came on, and one of them said, " I'll go no farther." " Nor I," replied another, " he was a bad one at any rate, let him lie there." Our cooks and they divided the unhallowed spoil; and I remember one of them treated us to a little salt that day, which he purchased, none having been got for some days before.

When the foregoing had just finished, the bugle was heard sounding, what every one thought at first was the ration call, and that therefore the pioneers must have come with the *"pang."* The call for fatigue duty was similar ; and this was for a fatigue party of two non-commissioned officers, and twenty men of each company, and I heard myself ordered for one. I repaired immediately to my berth, to secure my knapsack, and other articles, and to give directions for the safe keeping of the half loaf when it would come, for it now ran a precarious chance, if the bread was served out in our absence. The adjutant, Macknight, with a face that had mixed in it the blue of a cold day, and the red of aguardiente and brandy, hurried the orderly sergeants to fall in their men, and get them marched away ; to where, we did not know, but none were willing to go till the beef was brought up; and ready or not ready, it had now to be devoured.

Double price paid to a menagerie to see the wild beasts feeding, procures a sorry sight compared to our exhibitions on such occasions. The beef had been probably that of a lean cow, or if not, it had been a wrought bullock. It should have been twelve ounces, but it included the bones of the lean animal, which generally weighed more than all the meat that was on them. Besides, officers had got the best and by a great deal the largest messes cut off in the stores; store-keepers and pioneers had got their choice of quantity and quality, so far as it would afford; cooks had been tasting, and doing some other things with it, as before mentioned, and its quality and all these matters taken into account, diminished it considerably in bulk. From twelve ounces, it was now barely six eatable ones. There was the water it had been boiled in ; but it was not soup, for there was very seldom salt in it, and never anything else, save at times about an ounce of bread to each pint, and of that there was a pint to each man, for the kettles allotted to each mess would not allow of more being made, suppose the quality of the beef had allowed it. With such a dinner, and no breakfast before it, the ravenous appetites were sharpened, but not satisfied. Each mess, as it was divided and subdivided into single allowances, was scanned by eyes that could have detected one fibre too much. To the nicety of a grain was it divided, and for a few minutes all was noise and bustle, as the pieces were laid out, and every one getting his share by lot. One turned his back, another pointed, and called, " who shall have this ?" " Yourself," would be the answer ; and if these two fellows were not well watched, they sometimes tried for a big one to themselves. If there were any better than others, these were touched the first and second times; therefore, the second question of, " Who shall have this ?" was generally answered by " *myself* ;" but there was a law made amongst us, that whenever " yourself," and " myself," appeared to be in concert, they were to be called over again by another person.

This Legion dinner of ours occupied, as may be supposed, a very short space of time, and the Adjutant, aware of that, had waited till it was over. To get a party turned out for duty of any sort, was a very difficult matter at a time like that, when there were so many sick, for though I have been describing the hungry and the healthy ones, there were, every day, some who required to be carried to the hospital, and the dreadful suffering from frost-bitten feet made many of those who could eat well enough unable to walk. In such a case it was extremely difficult to know how to act with them. There were some who lay huddled together in corners, and were a moving mass of vermin and filth, who would never stir but at ration time. Although they had no particular disease, some of these lay there in that state till they died. Macknight was one whom it was difficult to escape ; he used his authority with very little regard to who deserved or did not deserve punishment ; and I never saw a more shameless application of the provost than he used that day on all the luckless wights, who either would not or could not get up.

After getting the required number paraded, and all told off into squads, we marched away to the general hospitals, for the purpose of carrying the sick to other houses, and for the purpose of getting some of the dead put out of the way, for they had accumulated to an awful extent during the snow storm, from their not having been regularly buried.

An intimate friend of mine, (Williamson,) had gone into the hospital about two weeks before ; I had been twice to inquire how he was, but could not find him. This day my first object was to look for him amongst the living, but not seeing him, I, with a few others, who were removing the bodies in the dead-house, turned over a number of them to look for his corpse. There was not one body that was not mutilated more or less by the rats, vast numbers of which infested the place. About the last body we lifted was that of Williamson, who we supposed must have been dead a long while, as he was very much destroyed. I would not have known him but for his clothes, the face being literally eaten away. As we proceeded to remove some of the sick, a horrible scene presented itself; dead and dying were mixed together. In one apartment, eighteen lay together on the floor, six of whom were dead, and the rats, not scared by those who still groaned in life, had began their part of destruction. Only one man was sensible, and he said that he would have come out of the place but for his feet, these being blue and mortifying at the time we saw him. He said the orderly who put him into that room, and who had given a little assistance at first, came in, and lay down himself one day, and soon after died, and no other person had visited them till we came. The feet were what death generally finished with. Agues, dysentery, and fever, were the first diseases that brought the victims to the hospital, but as soon as they were there, the feet immediately became diseased, a pain that is indescribable seized the toes and soles. If any thing touched them, the patient would roar out in agony. Some of them got their feet amputated, and survived; but the greater part of those who were thus diseased, died as soon as the blue began to make its appearance, which was generally when the fever began to abate.

A surgeon who was there pointed out to us those who were to be removed. Any who were dying, or likely to die soon, were left, but they were too far gone to be sensible of the hopelessness of their situation. As they lay close to each other, for the sake of drawing heat, the first one that stirred himself would touch another one's feet, and he, starting with the pain, would communicate it to the next, and so on, and thus a continual cry and moaning was kept up. It was varied sometimes by a few minutes of stillness succeeding to some raving wretch, who had just found relief in death, but others succeeded in turn to make their last struggles, and the noise was again renewed. It was mingled sometimes with calls for a mother or sister to come, and give them water, or, as I heard one say, "mother, make the pillow soft." Poor fellow, he had got his knapsack below his head, but the edge of its boards were cutting him. We made it easier, which caused him to lie quiet. I saw him die soon after; his mind seemed to have wandered in delirium where it had fondly loved to be when he was well. Another one wrought himself up to a sitting posture, and appeared in a violent passion; after speaking angrily for a few minutes, he paused, then burst out a-crying, and said, " will ye keep me waiting a' day on ye; will ye no come and die at once. This strange language caused me to look a while at the emaciated face of the dying man; he appeared to fall asleep, having wasted himself away. Others were making their last struggles, and I could not help philosophising as an involuntary witness to such a scene, but some circumstance in the street recalled me to recollection, and I left that horrid place. I got my day of fatigue duty over, and though our regiment was employed at that work for a week, burying the dead, and carrying the sick to another hospital, I got some other duty to do, and did not see the continuation of that horrible wretchedness.

The disease destroyed more English than Scotch, and more of the Scotch than the Irish. Most of the opinions that I have heard given, account for the difference in the mortality, to have arisen from the former habits of life, which differ in the English, Scotch, and Irish, and I believe these are partly correct, but not wholly so. The 5th was composed of the same sort of persons as the 6th and 8th, and yet the deaths were three times more in the 5th than the 8th, and double in amount to those of the 6th. But there was a cause. The 5th had been put into quarters, where they lay on damp stone floors, with the roof so much broken, that they were never dry, in the time of either snow or rain. Besides, Colonel Swan, though he was a very clever officer, carried his drilling too far; as was stated in an account of his conduct at page 214.

During these months of mortal malady, the officers suffered equally with the men, and some of them old veterans of the Peninsular war, who had outlived the dangers and fatigues they encountered when contending with the formidable hosts of Soult;—now fell an inglorious prey to an epidemic, engendered by neglect and starvation. One of these, a Captain Havelock, formerly of the 43rd, (British Service,) died of fever. He had fought at the celebrated battle of Vittoria, when Joseph Bounaparte was defeated, and is remembered by some old soldiers to have distinguished himself on that sanguinary occasion. Now, within a short distance of the ground where he had spilt his blood twenty-five years before, and to which the martial souled pilgrim turns with excited veneration,—he lies among a heap of dead, to whom circumstances not deserved, have forbidden the accordance of glory. Captain Havelock was to have been buried with martial honors, and the party commanded by a captain, conveyed the corpse with the due formalities to the grave yard ; but on arriving there among snow wreaths and ice, it was discovered that no grave had been made. The body was laid for the night in an adjoining house, and next day put beneath the earth by some shivering convalescents, without ceremony.

At this time the officers would have had some of their arrears of pay, but General Evans, at the desire of Senor Mendazabal, as was said, consented on the part of his officers, to forego for a time, the first quarter's pay of 1836, to allow the distressed minister to make a new evy of troops as decreed by the Cortes. This was afterwards paid by bills on England in the latter end of May, and was the only money received by regimental officers, during the year 1836; and it is questionable if that would have been paid then, had not the successful engagement, in which the Legion fought on the 5th of May, filled the Spanish executive with a temporary enthusiasm. The Staff officers, however, including the medical department, were allowed four month's pay after that, which caused, and very justly, much discontent among the regimental officers, who were always at hard duty ; some times not under the shelter of a roof at night—seldom in a bed, and never in comfortable quarters ; while the Staff occupied the best houses and bed-rooms in San Sebastian, at all times, and had many opportunities of obtaining the supplies of life through their intimate acquaintance with the inhabitants, by making love to wives and daughters, &c. &c.

But we may now turn from the gloomy details of the misfortunes of the Legion, to some of the less painful incidents that varied the scenes of the campaign. In the 4th or Queen's Own Fusileers, there was an officer named Pedro Hamilton, whose parentage, rumour, and his own love of title and notoriety have blamed on the Duke of Leinster. If blamed deservingly the Duke has no great credit in his hopeful offspring. Pedro was in some respects a genuine Irishman, he could not live without a fight, but he unfortunately mixed more of ill nature than of what is called Irish *humour* in his frolics ; in fact, Pedro had the character of being a dead shot in a duel, (though that became rather questionable,) and he was beyond doubt, a regular knockdown at the cudgel ; but at that he met his match, for as he was never one entire day or night without a quarrel with some one, so was he often the victim of his own mischief.

One of his duels was with Lieutenant Fanning, of the 4th. The cause of quarrel had originated like all Pedro's brawls in one of the *café's* (taverns). He, however, had the advantage of all his opponents, for he invariably inflicted a summary thrashing on them at the first stage of the quarrel, making sure that whatever the chances of the duel that was sure to follow, might be, he had gained a part of the thing called satisfaction. He had done so in this instance, with Lieutenant Fanning, by giving him some unhandsome blows by way of enforcing his side of the argument, and next morning, Mr. Fanning called him out to decide the quarrel with pistols.

They were attended each in due order by a second, Pedro, by Mr. R———, an officer of the commissariat, and Fanning, by Captain St. L———. The usual preliminaries having been gone through and the gentlemen placed, Pedro looking very unconcernedly, took from one pocket a cigar, from the other, a flint, steel, and tinder, and producing a light, commenced smoking with as much composure as if he had been in the café. This assumption of coolness by such a person as Pedro, who had acquired a fame for fighting duels, must have been anything but pleasing to Mr. Fanning and the gentleman who was his second. The signal was given, and both fired, but neither bullet taking effect, Pedro, who had made sure of his man, seemed rather surprised. A second brace of pistols were resorted to, and he taking his cigar in one hand, and gently trimming the ashes from it with the other, continued smoking; and taking their positions, both got the order and again fired. This discharge was as harmless as the first, and the second of Lieutenant Fanning, walked that gentleman off the ground, while Pedro raved and swore at the pistols, not attaching any blame to himself. This duel got Pedro some fame for coolness, but that was soon dispelled by another event in which poor Pedro got the worst of it by a great deal.

A party of officers belonging to the 4th regiment, were invited on board one of the British ships of war, then lying at Passages, in the month of September, 1836. The 4th was quartered at the time at the village of San Pedro, or Spanish Passages. This party was very pleasantly entertained, through the hospitality and liberal frolic of the mess of the cock-pit, where, generally speaking, the most mirth is going on in a man-of-war. Pedro had a glorious opportunity to indulge a common propensity, and as usual, when drinking, his

bullying qualities got vent. He fastened on an old officer, the adjutant of the 4th, who, having been wounded in action some months
before, was carrying his arm in a sling. This officer's name was
Firman. He had served long in the British service, and bore an
excellent character, particularly that of being an inoffensive man,
and one not disposed to quarrel. Pedro and he disputed, the former
refering to his dignity as being the son of the Duke of Leinster,
and the latter reminding him that a gentleman proud of his parentage, ought to respect the fame of his mother as well as the rank of
his father; and that if, as he said, the Duke was his father, decency
ought to prevent him from boasting, and thereby implying the dishonour of his mother, &c. On their way to the shore in the boats,
Adjutant Firman holding a cane over Pedro's head, told him in
usual duelling phrase, to consider himself horse-whipped, and that
though he had never before quarrelled with any person for nearly
thirty years which he had been in the British service, still he was
determined to punish Pedro's insolence, and that he referred him to
his friend Captain Pearce for farther communications. The moment
they stepped ashore, Pedro knocked the Adjutant down, and as usual
was drawing in advance for *satisfaction*, by giving him a repetition
of blows. Mr. Firman being wounded, could make little resistance,
but luckily for him, and most unluckily for Pedro, a Captain Thomson
was there, who, ringing a good cudgel about the assailant's ears,
knocked him to the earth, and with strong and willing arm, inflicted
such a punishment on the Scion of Leinster, as that worthy had
never before received, but had sometimes given.

Pedro finding himself completely mastered bawled murder, and
prayed for mercy, but no mercy hung on the blackthorn stick of Captain Thomson; nor would there have been, as the case seemed, had
not Captain Pearce laid hold of Thomson, and allowed Pedro to get
up and run. The latter still bawling murder, ran to the quarters of
the colonel, but that gentleman had heard too much of the complain-
ant to pay any attention to him, Pedro then ran into a house, and
tumbled himself on the first bed he saw making a pityful noise, as
his wounds saturated the bed with blood. Unfortunately for him it
was Captain Pearce's bed that he had gone into, and that officer
making his appearance, poor Pedro had to get out and make off to
save himself from another drubbing.

Next morning Captain Pearce received a hostile message as the friend of Firman, from Pedro demanding a meeting, and Captain Thomson had also a challenge demanding satisfaction for various injuries inflicted by his cudgel. Both declined to meet Mr. Pedro, and a general meeting of the officers of the fourth regiment having decided that Pedro was no *gentleman*, he was turned to the right-about from that regiment, having been compelled to send in his resignation. For some months after, he frequented the road leading to San Sebastian, from the quarters of the 4th; and unaffronted, made his way into company, always taking share in a quarrel when he could get any one inflammatory enough to fight with him. Like one of his countrymen who is said to have exclaimed on leaving home from a fair " Blur an agers ; isn't it a shame that a poor fellow cannot have a bit of a fight,—I'm disgracing my family, I'm blue moulded for want of a bating ; is there neither frind nor inimy to stand again me, I don't care if it's frind or inimy if I get a fight.'

But it is a warrantable supposition to say, that perhaps the officers of the 4th were willing to get rid of Pedro on other grounds than that of being *no gentleman*. He was known to be a *dangerous shot* in duel practice.

CHAPTER XVI.

' Duelling anecdotes continued—Major Macduff and Captain Maturin, with original remarks—Major Garmon and Captain Chadwick—Surgeon Barret and Assistant-Surgeon Mackay—Two Sergeants of the Lancers, &c.—Defence of the conduct of General Evans in a matter where he has been falsely accused of the misappropriation of money—The building of batteries—Occurrences on the outposts—Burning picquet houses and destruction of a family, &c. &c.

THOUGH the coolness of Pedro Hamilton was remarkable when duelling, and when, for anything he knew, he might have got a bullet in his head, that coolness was more than matched by Major Macduff of the staff, in a duel with Captain Maturin of the 1st Lancers.

Macduff, having in company made an observation reflecting some discredit on an officer whom he did not name, was called on by Maturin to explain if the observation applied to him. The explanation being demanded in rather a pompous way, Macduff did not choose to explain, and the usual hostile meeting was the consequence. Maturin came on the ground smoking a cigar, and wearing that coolness which, to a timid opponent, must have been productive of uneasiness. Macduff on seeing him, pulled out a cigar also, and walking up to him—asked in a polite manner to be obliged with a light! which request was complied with, the antagonists returning to their respective grounds, each puffing his smoke. The signal being given, Maturin fired directly at Macduff, but did not touch him, and the latter fired in the air, and then walked up to the other and said. "My observation *did not* apply to you." Both then left the ground good friends!

I am here inclined to quote a remark of Dr. Paley's, relative to duelling, although I am well aware it is of little use, save to shew what that divine's opinion in his moral philosophy relative to this code of folly was. He says :—

"Duelling, as a punishment, is absurd ; because it is an equal chance whether the punishment fall on the offenders or the offended. Nor is it much better as a reparation, it being difficult to explain in what the *satisfaction* consists, or how it tends to undo the injury, or to afford a compensation for the damage already sustained."

This philosophy I repeat, is of little utility ; for all people have made up their opinions on the folly of duelling, save one class, and so long as that exists as a class, it is a task of utter hopelessness to attempt to redeem it from its present moral nothingness. Men whose brains are deadened by tobacco smoke, and whose blood is inflamed by other intemperate indulgences—whose midnight is gay, and whose morning is gloomy horror—who live in an alternate round of mirth and misery from which they cannot escape, but by offending the society of their profession; who wound the honor of others, and have their own wounded studiously, and merely to maintain an *honor*, which is a violation of the laws of nature. Such persons, are as hopelessly beyond the control of the higher influences of the mind as the Indians, who are said by phrenologists to be incapable of feeling, or believing in Christianity. But there is this difference, the Indians according to the organic laws of nature, will advance in the scale of rational beings in the course of future generations if they are educated, just as the originally insignificant Dhalia is rendered by cultivation, the richest of the florist's collection ; while the enfeebled class

PEDRO HAMILTON'S DUEL,
AND HIS SUBSEQUENT CUDGELING BY CAPTAIN THOMSON.

No. 20.

of beings who are insensible to every impulse, save the lower propensities of human nature will decay into idiotcy.   That is, were
their offspring to follow the same degenerating habits as themselves,
or were they only to intermarry with beings of their own moral order.
It is now an established truth, that mankind will degenerate from,
or progress to a given standard of morality, as the animal or moral
faculties are allowed to lead the way.   With that portion of men
who cultivate the art of quarrelling as a science, among whom duellists are commonly found, the lower propensities reign supreme ;—for
it is the gambler—the seducer—the swindler—or their hired bully,
should they be cowards themselves, and their *victims*, that fight duels.
It is true there have been some exceptions, men of high intellect,
standing well with the world in moral reputation, have fought duels.
Mr. Canning, and more recently the Duke of Wellington, may be
instanced; but they may be fairly presumed to have been involuntary duellists, constrained to conform with fashionable usages, merely
from their station in fashionable life ; though it must be admitted
their example had a fearful effect in producing a succession of pig-
my imitators.   The persons who are dangerous to society, from the
exercise of the duel-code of honour, are those who nightly do nothing
but dress, smoke, swear, drink, talk, and dream of animal gratification.   They do not fight duels every time they quarrel, but they
quarrel often, and *talk* of fighting always; hence *Combativeness—
Destructiveness—Love of Approbation—Self Esteem—*and other low
propensities are always excited, while higher qualities of the mind
lie dormant, and would in time become extinct, only the world is
saved from a race of feeble minded sensualists dwindling into a barbarous degeneracy, by those who would be the forefathers of such a
race, marrying into purer blooded streams of the human family.   To
despise and hold in contempt, therefore, as many do, this class of
persons, whose names make up two-thirds of the Army List, and a
majority of whom fill the clubs, divans, and saloons of London;
who, in fact, have their imitators, though inferiors in rank, scattered
among the companies of the parlours and tap-rooms of the public
houses—to despise them, is not enough, for they become fathers
of an enfeebled offspring, whose want of intellectual capacity and
predominance of animal propensity will tend to the certain degeneracy
of the race.

These observations may be objected to, as not lying altogether in the narrative of Spanish affairs; if so, it must be called to mind, that before digressing, I was recounting some of our duels, and though there could be nothing more calculated to excite an admiration of bravery then the whole history of Major Macduff's life, still his coolness in the duel was folly. He said something which was either disrespectful or not, of Captain Maturin or somebody else, and before he would say if he intended to criminate the Captain, he would have a shot. Knowing there was no cause of enmity, he went up to his antagonist and asked to be obliged with a light to his cigar. The captain *obliged* him with the favour, and next minute fired a bullet at him. The major performed that act of generosity that is so much lauded as honourable in duelling, by firing in the air, and then they renewed, and continued their good friendship. Major Macduff was a very kindly feeling man, and had no necessity to stand a shot to let people know that he had courage, for his life as a soldier had proved that. The following are some of the incidents of his military career. I knew his private character well enough to regret that such a man should have been a soldier.

He fell severely wounded on the field of Waterloo, and had been tumbled into one of the pits dug for the dead, when a party who knew him, took him out to bury him more honourably and consistent with the bravery he had displayed. He was then discovered not to be dead, and with careful treatment, he recovered. What he was between that and entering the Legion, I am not informed. It was generally believed that he was the officer who gave the gallant Carlist General, Zumalacarregui, his death wound, the wound that was said to have been afterwards poisoned by the priests. If Major Macduff had the misfortune to hit this brave man, I am sorry for his good aim. It was said to have been done while the General of the Basque people was reconnoitering near Bilboa. It appears Major Macduff having had *interest* at home, left the Legion and returned to England, and was appointed to an office on the military staff in Scotland, but not being able to enter on its duties for some months after the appointment, he took a passage out to Spain, in one of the steamers, just to see how his friends were getting on, by way of passing the time. While there, on this excursion, the attack on the town and battery of Irun, which will be hereafter detailed, took place

and he appeared with General Evans, as a volunteer. When, after
two severe days fighting, the defences were carried, and the bloody
conflict was, street against street, and house against house, in the
town, a number of Carlists retreated into a large building, where,
after defending themselves for a time, they exhibited a white flag,
as if wishing to surrender. An officer who was an eye-witness, says
in a sketch of the parts of this attack which he has favoured me with,
and which I did not see myself;—

"When the flag appeared Major Macduff and several of the Sappers
went forward to speak to the Carlists; that moment they presented
themselves in front of the house a volley was fired at them and the
brave Macduff fell never to rise more!"*

Duelling in the Legion had become so common that the first
question on officers meeting in the square or placa of San Sebastian
in the morning, was " well who've been out this morning ?" some of
the quarrels were serious, others arose out of a contemptible wrangling about precedency of rank, and some arose from more contemptible sources still.

Mr. Gannon, one of the Staff Surgeons, was what the world
would call a gentleman, and he was so far as I know, justly entitled
to the appellation. A Captain Chadwick, was his dear and bosom
friend, and as the phrase goes, was also an officer and a gentleman
of honor. The Captain called at Mr. Gannon's quarters one evening,
and not finding his friend at home, he to leave an evidence of his
having called, put a certain indelicate article into the bed, which he
found standing beneath it. The doctor on coming home and finding
it, demanded from his servant to know who had been there, and being
informed, a *friend* was dispatched immediately, demanding a pistol
meeting. They met on the sand hills, which was the usual ground for
satisfaction—which was the ground too, where the batteries had been
erected by Sir Thomas Graham that effected the breach in the memorable storming of San Sebastian, and where fragments of shells, skulls

---

*Those officers and men who fought in the actions of the 10th, 12th, 14th, 15th
and 16th of March, and in those of the following May, would oblige the Author
by sending any particulars in their possession to him, addressed to Mr. Pattie, 4,
Brydges-street, London ; as his own personal observations in these engagements
were confined to what passed near himself, and he is anxious to do justice to all
regiments. To those who have already transmitted documents to him, he returns
thanks, and will make them available.

rockets, and cannon, still lay strewed about, contrasting strangely with the puny conflicts that daily occured with us on the same ground ;n the shape of duels. Mr. Gannon and Captain Chadwick fired at each other seven times but did no harm.

The next pair of combatants that are worth mentioning, were Surgeon Barret of the 9th, and assistant Surgeon Mackay of the 1st Lancers. Mackay had been assistant to Barret in the 9th, and at that time they had frequent bickerings, but could not fight very well from their professional and regimental connection. After being separated, they met again by accident in a Café, had as usual a quarrel, and next morning met to decide the out-cast by bullets. Mr. Barret declared before going to the ground, that he would break Mackay's leg, " Now I shall let you see me leg him" he said, " I'll just put a ball in his leg for his impudence." Mr. Mackay assured *his friends* that he would shoot Barret in the head. They took their ground— got the signal—fired, and to the astonishment of the attendants Mackay's leg had a ball in it, and the peak of Barret's cap was shot off. This was rather close, some of the braggadocios thought, so there was more prudence manifested in the challenges for some time afterwards, especially among the medical officers ; for it was among the *faculty* that the most of the duels occurred.

Previous to this, an officer of the name of Murphy, shot a brother officer in a duel, and on the effects of the deceased being put up for public sale among the officers, as was always the case with the effects of officers who had died, Mr. Murphy appeared at the sale, and competed with the others in purchasing the clothes of his dead opponent. The forage cap among other things was knocked down to Murphy, and he wore it on duty and off, for the next six months ; there is no accounting for taste in some persons.

In page 300 it is stated, that Colonel Harman, the Lieut. General's Military Secretary, had the challenges of nearly a dozen officers, for his haughty and overbearing behaviour, and that these were still unanswered ; but I find that the gallant Colonel did answer one of them, and at the first shot from Colonel M'Cabe, who was his antagonist, got a ball through his mouth, which carried away both rows of his front teeth. This was certainly a good cause for not responding to any more of the dozen challenges.

Duelling in fact, became so fashionable that, as is always the case

in prevailing fashions, the inferiors imitated their superiors. Two
sergeants of the Lancers went out to fight one morning with their
holster pistols, each attended by a second, and according to usual
formality, with a medical attendant, who, in this case, was their fellow
equal in rank, the regimental *hospital sergeant*. They exchanged
shots—missed—shook hands—came home, drank a few glasses of
aguardiente, and were good friends.

Whatever faults may be attachable justly to General Evans as a
Commander, there are some with which he is unjustly blamed. Towards the autumn of 1836, a sum of money was put in his hands
for the settlement of the arrears due to the officers. He was at this
time in a peculiar situation. The troops had mutinied in consequence
of non payment, and after overcoming many disheartening obstacles
he had got them reduced to order and obedience ; and what was important, had the second yearly regimental clothing, and many other
necessaries served to them. Active discipline, not often unnecessarily
severe—cleanliness, good health, and most correct soldier like duty
were now the characteristics of every regiment.—But there was a
great want in having suitable positions, whereon the limited number of
his forces could maintain themselves against a superior force, should
that come against him. He set working parties to erect defences
and as these could not labor without some other support than the
very meagre meal which the ration allowance made, he issued to
them a small sum of daily pay. This was the money that at the
time was destined for the officers ; but the General put it to this use,
believing that the Spanish Government would give him credit for it.
This turned out to be the contrary of what he expected, and he was
accused of the misappropriation of money. The following is the
balanced merits of the case :—

The officers were entitled to their pay, and it was at first an injustice to them not to receive it ; but the positions which he held
were widely extended, he had relieved San Sebastian from the siege
of the Carlists, the place which above all they were anxious to get
possession of, and which had they got, the unstable footing of the
Queen's forces in the north would have been altogether untenable.
In relieving San Sebastian, and in maintaining his acquired positions
he had lost a greater proportion of his men in open fight than fell in
any single engagement during the celebrated Peninsular war ; there

had been no want of fighting, and no want of the abilities in fight that Englishmen are ever ready to claim as peculiarly their own. The General then, to prevent all that he had done from being undone by the accidents of a heavy opposing force—a sickness such as that of the year before among his men—a mutiny if they should not be paid—any, or all of which occurrences might have caused him to lose the positions he held, and thereby have laid him open to blame, began to build defences on a line of heights extending irregularly about eight miles. Great quantities of tools for fortifying uses, had been sent from England, and he was only fulfilling the original design of the Spanish Government—the design that they must have had when these were ordered from England—in putting them to a useful purpose. As already stated, he could not make men work serviceably, but by giving them some additional allowance above that of the starvation point at which they had been previously living—always except when they ate up the gardens and the bean-fields.) The working parties consisted of a fourth part of the men, each day, and were allowed a sum rather less than 3d. and about threefourths of a pint of wine (extra), which might amount in value to about twopence more. This, trifling as it may seem, produced a wonderful effect on the health and condition of the men. Though they had got all their pay formerly, it was paid in such a way that more harm than good resulted from it, being issued at lengthened periods in a sum, many of them had not prudence to preserve it one day, and some could not, had they been willing, as the most powerful and most numerous party who had spent their own, would have taken it from them. Then, when they had nothing, some ventured on selling their extra shoes, trowsers, or shirts, for which they frequently got flogged, but by which they managed to have a temporary supply of food. This caused them to be immediately served out with new articles to replace those sold, which articles were placed to their accounts, and with many of them amounted to more than their regimental pay. It was thus then, that the issue of the small sum in payment of work, produced such beneficial effects; for it being paid every night when the parties left off work, they were always too hungry to put it to any other use than that of purchasing something to help their allowance of rations. Batteries were built—breastworks thrown up, and the whole line of defences completed in a manner that rendered it

impossible for the Carlists to retake these positions; and General
Evans was only waiting for the movements of the other Queenite
Generals and weather that would permit his advancing on the
enemy, to break up the temporary cessation of hostilities—yet,
the Spanish government say, that he misapplied the money given to
pay the arrears of his officers, though even now a comparatively
small force is able to keep the Carlists from approaching San Sebastian merely by the strength, and judicious arrangement of the defences thrown up by General Evans. It will scarcely be credited that
the amount of labour performed by the Legionaries, was so great as
it really was; for be it understood the money expended on it bore
but a fractional proportion to the amount of labour. Many of these
men, from previous necessities, wrought with an anxiety, that they
would have been unwilling to shew at home, especially as an extra
allowance of wine was at times given to those who were most industrious, and not a few of them, who from their hatred of soldiering,
volunteered to labour, wrought hard for the mere privelege. All of
them were more healthy, more steady in habits, more cheerful and
obedient, and seldomer committing punishable crimes, when at work,
every second or third day, and getting a more proportionate quantity
of food, than they were at any former time.

The food they were then enabled to procure, was commonly used
in this way. At six o'clock the bugles would sound for rations, and
about the same time for fatigue parties to parade. The companies
of a regiment, would be dispersed among houses, over a space of
half a mile or more. The orderly sergeant of each company, having
warned all the men by name the evening before, who were for fatigue
next morning; (working parties not regular artificers or sappers or
miners, being always styled fatigue men in military phrase); these
being warned by name, turned out immediately on hearing the bugle.
Others had been warned to be ready to go for the bread, which was
had thus soon to enable the men to get it with them to their work.
Some would eat it all dry as it was, and moisten it by the spring-
water that always runs plentifully in northern Spain. At a later
hour of the day the beef was served out to companies, and then
divided into individual portions. This last, however, was only done
in some regiments, but from my experience in controuling these
troublesome affairs in a company of men, I found it was much better

to allow each man his rations uncooked. The men then associated together in messes of three, five, six, or ten, as they chose, making choice of their own associates; this answered better than by telling them off in messes of eight or ten by the alphabetical roll. Those messing together by choice took care to have their mess made up of names scattered through the alphabet, so that when the A's, B's, and C's were on fatigue, and the K's, L's, and M's on guard or picquet, and the N's, P's, R's, and S's preparing to go to relieve the picquet, there would be the D's, E's, and those at the end of the alphabetical roll at home to look after the interests of the mess; to see that the allowance was fair—to keep it from being stolen—to cook it—to draw the ration of wine, and keep it for the absentees, &c. When, on the other hand, where the messes consisted of men taken off by tens from the alphabetical roll, which is the regular military practice, it was rare to get as much unanimity created among them as to admit of practical sociality.

All the men at this time, not above a certain sum in debt, received daily one Spanish *real* or 2½*d.*, and this in most regiments was laid out in the same kind of messing as just detailed. Some commanding officers caused chocolate, vegetables, salt, &c. for the mess, and pipe-clay, blacking, and soap for cleaning, to be bought by pay-sergeants of companies, and dealt out; but we found the money was more economically expended by the men themselves, who made chocolate or coffee, or took cold water to breakfast, as they thought fit; who made their own choice of vegetables, and used rice as they chose—made puddings according to ability and taste—in fact, did as choice led them, so far as military discipline would permit a relaxation of standing orders. The consequence was, less quarrelling among the men, easier duty for corporals and orderly sergeants, who were liable for all mistakes in the serving out of rations, and less suspicion on the part of the men towards pay-sergeants, and indeed all superiors who were often suspected, and sometimes justly, of cheating them in all things which are served out and charged for in their monthly accounts.

The mode of cooking was very rough, but the daily drill, when not at the batteries, the unceasing work of cleaning and brightening for parades, after coming off day guards, and night picquets, and the sharply wholesome breezes from the Bay of Biscay skirting us

on the north, or from the rocky mountains rising above the vallies
on the south, all tended to make the frugal meal agreeable. Agreeable, even though the coffee was drunk out of the kettle lid, the
meat eaten off a slate or tile taken from the roof of the house, or
what was as common torn wolfishly with the teeth. It was agreeable,
because there was no more than a necessary supply, leaving always a
little craving for more, which more excited hope by our looking forward to a loaf " *the first thing*" in the morning. It was wholesome
to be in Spain then; we had been starved the previous winter, and
thousands were sacrificed from neglect; now we were as a body
of men, in better health than could have been enjoyed by any other
system of living, especially when we got the luxury of blankets,
a luxury for which we very gratefully thanked Lord Palmerston, and
for which we had reason to be thankful. So good was the general
health in the latter months of 1836, and up to the disbandment of
the Legion in June, 1837, that the *doctors*, as has been shewn a few
pages back, had little to do, and did little but offend each other,
give, and receive *satisfaction*. That applys more particularly to
regimental surgeons. The hospital staff had always their hands full,
from the numbers who had at various times been, and were afterwards wounded.

The fatigue parties at the batteries were under the superintendance
of a subaltern from each regiment, whose duty it was to march his
men regularly to work and home again, and be answerable for the
performance of a certain quantity of labour. Above these, were
officers of engineering skill, all of them clever and scientific; indeed,
two or three of them were considered gentlemen of very superior
abilities, and yet I have seen them make themselves ridiculous,
through their want of a knowledge of the first and simplest practice
of manual labour. One of these, a Major Macintosh, who could no
doubt do every thing on the most correct mathematical principles,
who could apply the scale and the compasses to measure the minutest
fractions in the depth of ditches, and the slope of embankments;
ascertain the fractions of the square or the cube, tell the difference
of a ball's velocity between a hundred and a thousand yards from the
cannon's mouth—measure the rocket's flight to any given distance—
in fact, do anything that was scholastically scientific; but he could
not understand why one Irishman should be able, only to work with

his face to the west, and another only with his face to the east, when both were alike employed throwing earth to the north side of the ditch they were working in. He could not see why one man felling a tree should be able to cut it only on the lower side, if it stood on a slope, and another who was used to handling a hatchet, could cut it off either the higher or lower side. He made a man be punished for disobedience of orders, whom he told to begin at a certain corner of a breastwork, and pare the turf smooth with his spade ; the man having begun at the opposite corner, choosing, as he urged in his defence, to work with *his face foremost.* He could not work with a pickaxe or shovel himself, which few can who are taught to take *command* of workmen, and yet none, to direct work efficiently, should be so ready at handling pick, spade, saw, or hatchet, as an officer of engineers. A blunder creates distrust in his other abilities, and the men under his command, laugh at him in his absence, and if forced, by military law to obey him, their obedience has the sour mixture of contempt for his science, and hatred for his authority.

" What are you about you men with your faces this way, and that way, some turned in one direction, and some another in that manner, can you not begin at equal distances, and stand all one way, throwing the turf as I told you ;" were his questions addressed angrily one morning to some sons of the Green Isle, who, beyond all Her Majesty's loving subjects eating the sweaty bread earned by working with picks and shovels, are the most dexterous at using these instruments gracefully.

" Och sure, its not soldiers we are now yer honor—its diggin wid dthe shovels we are, sure nare a one knows better nor meself how to dig dthe turf," was the response of an offended member of the *Munster Light Infantry*, who had that morning gaily thrown off military restraint—stripped his jacket—loosened his stock—turned up his trowsers, and begun with national pride to shew his superiority in handling a shovel. The Major could hear no answer, he knew only that they were soldiers, that he commanded and they were bound to obey ; but he learned afterwards, that some men from habit, and some in obedience to a natural law which no habit could overcome, wrought with their left hands foremost in lifting earth with a shovel, and that some from the same law of causes, wrought with their right hands foremost, which led them to turn in particular directions.

The Carlists opposite to us erected works on their heights and hollows also, but in doing so they had several disadvantages to contend with, which we had not.   Our artillery kept firing on them, throwing shells whenever a working party made their appearance, which, exploding among them, wrought frequent and severe disasters.   It was astonishing nevertheless to see how coolly they treated these dreadful visitors.   They kept men on the look-out, who, on the moment of the flash of our cannon, gave the alarm and the whole working party dropt to the ground ; the shell then had some chances of going past them before it exploded, and many chances of not doing much injury to them if it did explode, as all shells are calculated to take effect before falling to the ground, and when they do fall unexploded, they can be lifted and thrown into a hole or ditch if the person making the daring adventure is not blown to pieces too soon.   The moment one of these passed over them, the party started to their feet, waved their caps, and cheered.   They bore the annoyances in the same cheerful way for nearly six months, and during that time there were weeks when a continued firing of cannon was kept up along our lines·

To those who may enquire the utility of this waste of gunpowder and bombshells, it may be explained that the nature of the ground was such on both sides, that to fortify it, was to make each hill like a castle, and these hills commanding the valleys and ravines beneath, to fortify them was to oppose completely any progress into the interior on the Carlists' side.   With these in front and the sea in the rear, General Evans might have been effectually shut out had he suffered these fortifications to proceed quietly ; he did not do so, and this, with the expectation of being requried to advance immediately,—an expectation lasting for a period of two or three months, to form a junction with Espartero the Commander-in-Chief, were the causes why he so zealously opposed the erection of the enemy's works in his front.

The Carlists, on the other hand, opposed him similarly, and whenever an opportunity occurred of firing on our workmen with musketry, they, to a certainty availed themselves of it.   Latterly, they had cannon which played on our working parties also ; but having only round shot they did less harm to our men than ours did to them by the shells.   The balls were almost sure to pass over-head if a sharp look-out was kept for them, and the men warned to clap down ; this precaution was closely observed, and though some men were at times injured, the greater part of the Carlist cannon shots, at the erection of these works, did little more than cover a few with earth, who might be lying beneath the bank of the ditch on which it struck.

There were many interesting incidents occurred on the out-posts during the progress of these erections ; the following is from an eye-witness. General Chichester who was always on the move, the first to detect anything going on wrong, and the first to make wrong things right, came up one day to the Queen's battery, (this was one of the forts erected by Evans all of them being named after some Christino place or person, who happened for the time to be popular.) Lieut. Skedd an old soldier, who had seen twenty-eight years service in the Royal British Artillery, who had gone out to Spain as Sergeant Major of Infantry ; but who had by this time got the tardy justice of a commission for his very efficient zeal in the service, was in command of the guns and small garrison, at this fort. General Chichester, on applying his glass to a point on the Carlist lines, and looking intently for a few minutes, in an enquiring tone, said, " Skedd, what are these people about over there ? you must not allow them to throw up works so near us as that, just send over a—let me see—a shell among them, and if that won't do, give them one or two more." There were a number of our own men working in and around the Queen's battery, and these being withdrawn from danger, a twenty-four pounder was quickly charged with a shell, elevated, and fired. The missile took fearful effect, for it was evident the enemy had not expected one, they being at a distance of sixteen hundred yards, and on the opposite banks of a deep hollow and winding river. That was immediately followed by an eighteen, which obedient to the unfailing practice of an expert gunner, plunged into the hapless party of Carlists with an explosion that strictly fulfilled its mischievous mission. In a few minutes we could see them by the naked eye, hurrying down a green slope by the edge of a wood carrying off the wounded men. At seeing these, Lieut. Skedd prepared another shell, but Chichester said no ; don't by any means fire among their wounded, only fire when they're working, for we must prevent them from doing anything so near as that."

Shortly after, another shot was prepared to send over, as the luckless party had recommenced their labour. Some men of the 4th regiment who were at work completing our own defences, were talk-

ing to each other about the fine shots,—" Skates a gellas old feller !
what a higher he has in his ead to hit 'em such a precious way off,"
said one—" how they make me start, them big uns, when they goes
off," said another—" Start," interjected a third, "you starts hat
hanythink—you be 'fraid on 'em !—I, be'nt 'fraid! I lies as nice here
as can be, and lets 'em go over me,"—and so on he was going, when
the order " stand clear there! out of the way you men in front !"
was given; which was the prelude to another shell from Skedd to
the unfortunate Carlists. Obedient to the order, and their own organs of cautiousness, the men who were at work in front of the guns
retired, all, save the one who as he said had lain down where he was
when the previous shots had gone off. There was a minute of hesitation after the gun was elevated, and the match ready, owing perhaps,
to something that was seen among the party to be fired at. The man
who had lain down, and who was not afraid, probably thinking that
the cannon was not to go off, raised his head to see; but the same
moment the match was at the touch-hole—the smoky cloud rolled from
the muzzle—the rebound shook the air—the shell was on its demon
course, and his body lay lifeless; his head was—no one knew where.

General Chichester said, " never mind now, it cannot be helped;
but I shall put an extra non-commissioned officer on duty here, who
shall be answerable for all heads, or he shall lose his own." When
this order and rather uncomfortable assurance had been given to
a sergeant who was ordered to perform the responsible duty of
being answerable for all accidents of this kind, the officer in charge
of the working party was heard exclaiming, " there now be done with
that grave you men, how long will you be about it; get that body
buried at once, and go on with your work, or by G——I'll stop your
wine."

This was one passing scene of the great melo-drama of war! let
us shew another more deeply tragical.

On a sloping hill side, variegated with orchards, whitewashed
cottages, trailing vines, streaming rivulets, and smooth patches of
green fields, the Carlists were daily seen passing from their quarters,
on a more southern ridge, to a line of picquets, which they had
established at the summit of the mountain, skirting the sea coast.
This mountain had its rounded north-eastern base planted in the
Bay of San Sebastian ; had an extended line of rocks stretching to
the north-west to a head-land that stood out, bidding bold defiance

to the surges of the Bay of Biscay, and a more gentle southern slope, softened its inland aspect, by dipping itself into a morass, at the mouth of which in rough weather, the furious tide lashed up the froth, and in fine weather, the feeble waves died away on the sand hills. On one side of this morass, were the western extremity of the Legion's outlying picquets, and on the other side were some houses roofless, and shattered by cannon shot. Behind these and beyond the cannon's range were the cottages, vines, and orchards, on the sloping hill; and above on the very summit were the Carlist picquets, the principle of which was formed at a tall column, that had once been a light-house; but which now served them for a tower of observation, and a shelter from the storms that were daily scudding along the coast. The convent Antigua, was the nearest building on our side to the morass, and was tenanted by the 6th regiment. Sentries had been nightly placed on the sands beneath it, to observe the enemy, lest they might secretly pass during the night and surprise our men in quarters; but these sentries were sometimes found dead on their posts, having been shot from the opposite side, where the Carlists were enabled to conceal themselves among furze and bramble bushes.

On the 17th of November, 1836, an order was given to a party of the 6th regiment to cross the morass, at a place where the tide ran into it, as there might be least opposition there, proceed to destroy the houses that had sheltered the Carlists, and burn the furze in which they had often hid themselves. It was a mild breathless day on which, after parades and drill were over, the mind could fall into melancholy and think of home, more especially could the feelings soften on such a day, when the desolated villages on our side were contrasted with the peaceful repose of cottages on the opposite sloping hill. I was passing into San Sebastian about noon on that day, and I remember to have marked to myself the peaceful scene that lay beyond our cannon range, where the cows and the calves grazed, the children played, the white walls sparkled through the green trees, and the busy Spanish females were washing their white linen at the spring wells; these were seen by the eye as we passed along, and the mind, at least mine, could not resist an ideal ramble among my own Lammermoor hills.

I came out of San Sebastian towards evening; the citizens were crowding to the walls, and soldiers of all regiments, Spanish and

English thronged to see the sight. A rattle of musketry like low
rumbling thunder was heard, with at intervals, a heavy cannon rebound, and all the western sky was obscured in dark smoke. The
cottages that smiled peacefully at mid-day, were now smouldering in
their black ruins. An old woman, the grandmother of a family, was
brought along as a *captive* to be deposited in San Sebastian. The
soldiers of the 6th were returning with their booty of pigs, calves,
flour, linen, and various articles of household furniture. Men of
other regiments had gone voluntarily over, even unarmed, and having
been exposed to the Carlist shot, some of them being wounded—
were now seen returning loaded with spoil. Cheers from the
Spanish soldiers—congratulations from many of the Spanish
civilians—thanks from their own officers for the boldness and success
of the excursion, were plentifully showered on the plunder-laden soldiers of the 6th regiment as they came home to quarters. But
though the Spanish people loved to see such sacrifices made of their
neighbour's property on the Carlist side ; though the necessity of our
party, according to the usages of war, demanded the destruction of
the *enemy's* shelter ; there was a deep crime of tragic dye committed
that day, which no warlike usage can palliate, and for which there
can be no refuge for the accusing consciences of the suspected perpetrators, but in the self-assurance of innocence. Mankind, and
God will record judgment against them, for a mother and her infant
family were burned to death in the flames that consumed their own
house. It was the old grandmother of the same family that was
dragged a captive into San Sebastian; and it was her cow, and
calf, and pigs that were carried off and butchered to feed the riotous
spoilers in Antigua Convent. The following are the particulars.

At three o'clock in the afternoon, a party consisting of about two
hundred of the 6th regiment, forded the branch of the tide beneath
the convent, and made their way up the opposite hill side. The
Carlist sentries fired on them, and they in return, shot two of the
Carlist sentries. On these shots being heard, the picquets descended
from the light-house and other stations, to meet and repel the aggressors, and a sharp skirmish ensued ; the cannon sending over
some shells from our side, but which were not effective, and were
therefore discontinued, owing to the bushes covering the parties and
causing an uncertainty of who were Carlists and who English. The

poor people who inhabited the cottages shut the doors on themselves when they saw the skirmish begin, and trusting to the defence of the Carlist soldiers, they remained to look apprehensively on. For some time they might have entertained considerable confidence, as the defending soldiers withstood the assailants : but at last the former gave way—retreated to the heights—left the houses unprotected, and the triumphant spoliators began to plunder. All the domestic animals were quickly seized on ; the cows and the calves—the little calves destined to be the future family cows, and which, up to this dreadful day had been the favourites of the little children, were dragged out. The fowls flew to their common roosting place to escape being caught ; but musket shots filling the house with smoke, and smashing the tiled roof, brought down the feathery flutterers, and they were quickly appropriated to the capacious haversacks. The cat scampered from one corner to another, to escape persecution, and at last turned her face to the spoilers, with her yellow eyes glancing mixed fear and defiance, but even the cat fell a sacrifice to destructiveness. The chests containing linen were forced by the butt ends of muskets and bayonets—the locks broken, and the old well hoarded store of contents tumbled out. One portion of destroyers ransacked the upper floors and found flour, bread, bacon, and beans—the family food. Others stripped the bed of blankets and sheets, and carried away kettles, frying pans, pitchers, jugs, and plates, while another portion had hold of an old woman, who alternately crossed herself—clasped her hands—prayed and assured them that there was no money—they all the time surrounding her with bayonets pointed to her body, and swearing in oaths of mixed Spanish and English, that they would kill her if she did not give them the dinero (money.) In hearing of her cries, were her daughter, and daughter's three children hiding themselves in an upper part of the house—where they had not been discovered. The husband of this wife, and father of these three innocent young victims of war, was far away in some other province fighting for his KING, or perchance he was already slain. No brother remained :—they only had been left clinging to the family sanctuary of home.

She, the mother, dreaded a crime, and she dreaded too truly—that wild passions subject unprotected females to, and this with the infants clinging to her in fright, caused her to remain hidden ; while the old

No. 21.

grandmother, either too feeble to escape to a hiding place, or thinking
herself safe from violence, trusted to the forbearance of the plunderers.
But, not even grey old age saved her from being made the victim of
crimes—black, deep, and nameless. She was dragged to the door,
and taken away from her house down the little foot-path that led to
the spring well, and carried off a prisoner to San Sebastian.

When the house had been spoiled, and the old woman was pulled
out at the door, the soldiers fulfilled their orders by setting it on fire.
Two of them discharged their muskets into the straw that lay in the
bottom of the bed, but these not having the desired effect, another
soldier took a shovel, and lifting the fire that had all the time been
burning peacefully on the hearth, put it into the bed, and in a few
seconds the lower part of the house was in flames. To make destruction sure, the straw and bundles of fire-wood that lay scattered about,
were lighted in other corners of the house, and these also blazing
furiously, the once lovely cottage overspread with its vines, and surrounded by its shrubs, now crackled, and blackened the sky. And
the woman with her children, afraid of, and expecting every violence
but death, lay unknown to the destroyers in an upper part of the
house. As the fire and smoke approached her, she was, with her
infants, heard screaming, and with all on fire below, was the next
minute seen forcing herself through the tiles of the roof. Some men
now risked their lives to save her from that destruction which they
themselves had kindled, but too late. Her hold of the tiles was frail,
for being stifled by smoke, she could not hold—she fell into the
burning mass, and with her infants, was never more seen. While
that house was burning, another was ransacked, and set on fire, but
so far as was known, no person was in it. This dreadful outrage
has been softened a little by General Evans having reprimanded the
officers who commanded at it, —urging that they overstepped their
orders, and by some portion of the facts having been denied ; but
the whole case was as here related. The old woman was re-con-
ducted across the lines next day, to the side from which she had been
taken, and it was said she was frequently seen hovering about the
ruins of her house. General Jaurragui, surnamed El Pastor or The
Shepherd, who is a Christino General, sprung from the people, though
nominally for the Queen, felt grievously offended with General Evans
for having ordered, or permitted, or at least not punished the com-

mission of this outrage ; which, more than anything, had a tendency, and that justly, to alienate the support of the Basque peasants from the Queen's cause :—

> " Ah ! monarchs if ye knew the mirth ye mar,
> Not in the toils of glory would you fret ;
> The hoarse, dull drum would sleep and man be happy yet."

CHAPTER XVII.

The 9th regiment—Captain Mackay's wound, and its treatment by Surgeon Mahoney alias Dirty Jack—Officers leave the hospital in consequence of Captain Mackay's death, and thereby affront Dr. Gannon—Lieut. O'Connor of the 9th, his mysterious disappearance on the 5th of May, his sword, cloak and cap lost, his cowardice discovered, the order of San Fernando bestowed on him, &c—Lieut. Keogh's cowardice, he runs away from the fight, escapes censure through the friendship of General Fitzgerald—Remarks on Fitzgerald's conduct—Ensign Bezant, his ill treatment, his general good conduct, bravery, and death—Captains Cotter, Thompson, Allez, Lieut's. Thornton and Stack, on the 5th of May, and conduct of the light company of the 9th—Mr. Street, of the same regiment—History and character of General Fitzgerald—Other extraordinary characters, Owen Kelly and a Carlist officer, Kelly's quarrel with Major Lister—Kelly's conflict with the Spanish guard, in the streets of San Sebastian, &c. &c.

At page 16 is an account of the beginning of the battle of Ayetta, fought near San Sebastian, on the 5th of May, 1836, and in the pages following, a general sketch of the engagement throughout, is given. To give all the circumstances that break off and mingle with other matters, in sketching an action with the enemy, would be to travel from the action itself into other affairs, I have therefore given the early engagements in which the Legion fought, a merely general sketch, reserving the greater part of the particular details to be gathered up in the present history of different officers. On the 5th of May, the 9th Irish were perhaps the most severe sufferers in the fight, and if no other estimate could be formed of the bravery displayed by that regiment, the numbers of killed and wounded might, as usual in all battles, suffice to found an encomium. The number of killed and wounded, however, is not a just criterion ; for equal valour may be displayed, without equal disaster ; but in the case of the 9th regiment of the Legion on the 5th of May, this criterion of estimating valour was just, for bravery and loss, were parallels.

The first officer who may be mentioned, was Captain Mackay, who, at the head of the Grenadier Company, led gallantly on, to the first assault, and was wounded early in the action by a musket ball striking obliquely on the back-bone. Being examined by the surgeon on the field, the wound was pronounced severe, but not dangerous, as the ball had not entered further than cutting the thin fleshy substance that covers the spine, and he was carried into the hospital of San Sebastian, to have the wound dressed. The crowded state of the hospital kept the surgeons more than busy for some days, and it was not until the painful period of a day and night had elapsed, that Captain Mackay's wound was seriously examined. Unfortunately for him this examination was the work of a person assuming the name of *doctor* and Assistant Surgeon Mahony, but better known in the society of Saffron Hill, as *Dirty Jack !* How he came to be a sur-geon in the hospitals where there were many really clever professional men I cannot say; but he was there. On seeing Captain Mackay's wound, he immediately pronounced it dangerous, though it was really not more than a scratch and slight contusion ; and discovering the lodgment of the ball, as he said, he commenced the work of extraction. Poor Mackay lay groaning beneath the operation, and that grew more and more painful, as Mr. Mahoney cut in with his knife—took a tug and a pull with his nipping instruments—cut deeper—took another pull—cut again, and pulled, and tugged again ; under this poor Mackay lay groaning, and the operator continued digging deeper and deeper, until Dr. Barret, who came accidentally in, knocked the knife out of his hand and told him that he was ex-tracting one of the joints of the back-bone ! What had been nothing more than a slight wound, was now mortal ; Captain Mackay died next day.

Here was the end of an officer as brave and as good as ever held a commission in any service. In his manners and common behaviour, he was a gentleman, as well as by birth and education ; and what was rare with an officer strict in discipline, he was beloved and grievously regretted by his men.

This occurrence may excite curiosity in some people, by their wishing to know what became of Mr. Mahoney, but all that happened him was his being removed to one of the *wards* in which the wounded *non-commissioned* officers and *men* lay ; and there left to operate to the full extent of his curiosity and ingenuity—studying anatomy and dissection gratis. Some of the superior officers demanded that a Court of Inquiry should examine into the causes of Captain Mackay's death, with a view to Mr. Mahoney's dismissal from the service, but against any enquiry the following objections prevailed. *First*, Mahoney was a favourite. *Second*, to convict a medical officer of such a blunder, would be to lay the whole medical establishment open to animadversion. *Third*, Mahoney if dismissed, might become dangerous as a newspaper correspondent, as he had a tendency to tell stories, and *fourth*, he was prevented from killing any more officers, by being transferred to practise on lives of inferior value. The only uneasiness excited by his manslaughter of Captain Mackay was in the minds of about a dozen other wounded officers, all belonging to the same regiment (the 9th), and in the mind of Dr. Gannon, the chief medical officer of that hospital; and that uneasiness was manifested in this way. Dr. Barret, the regimental surgeon of the 9th, went into the apartments occupied by the other officers, as soon as he had arrested the knife of Mahoney, and said, " Gentlemen if you stay here, you'll be all murdered;" and the officers who had been cut and maimed by Carlist bullets without shewing any fear as we are bound to believe, quailed, and that naturally at the prospect of being butchered by surgical knives. Accordingly those who were able to walk out, went; and those who could not go, sent for men from their regiment, and were carried out, to be attended by their regimental surgeons. These had all left, and their beds were standing empty, when Dr. Gannon came round in the morning to visit them. His usual even, and gentlemanly manners were ruffled into a tempest of passion, when he was informed of the affront offered to the hospital department by officers preferring their regimental surgeons to the hospital staff, and he demanded that they should be compelled to return; but General Evans taking Captain Mackay's death into consideration, did not give any orders in the matter, and Dr. Gannon after swearing that he would challenge them to give *satisfaction* as soon as they recovered, ultimately pocketed the affront, and did nothing in the affair.

Another officer who was singularly treated on the 5th of May, who got the Cross and order of San Fernando, and who has been recorded as one of the bravest of the brave in Captain Thompson's book, (" Twelve months in the British Legion,") was a Lieut. O'Connor.

of the 9th.   There was a Captain O'Connor in the 10th regiment. and a Lieut. O'Connor in the 4th, but those persons must not be confounded by their names ; for the two latter were in character different from the first.   The O'Connor that I at present refer to, is Lieut. Dan O'Connor of the 9th, who fell behind his regiment just at the time of the word "*forward*," being given at the commence· ment of the attack, and mysteriously disappeared until General Shaw discovered him running at full speed without his sword, cloak, and cap, leaping the ditches calling "where's my men ?—och General dear, I've been a prisoner, and I've bate six of the Carlists meself, with me fists—och General give me a sword till I fight !"   He had not been seen for nearly five hours until making this dashing appearance ; and as a reward for this bravery General Shaw recommended him for, and procured for him the order of San Fernando.   In *Shaw's Memoirs*—(an extremely amusing work to those who know the au- thor,) this Lieut. O'Connor is mentioned, and is spoken of as being a clever young man, one of the best leapers and swiftest runners in the Legion, and that he—General Shaw, author of *Shaw's Memoirs* gave him—the order of San Fernando.

What room does this give the detractors of the Legion, to found their common calumnies ?—to be writing of an engagement and the bravery of the officers, and to state in conjunction with these, that an officer rewarded with the highest mark of merit bestowable in the Legion, was the swiftest runner, &c.,—is to strengthen the belief that none of the officers were distinguished for bravery,—which be- lief is not just; or that Mr. O'Connor had something else to recom- mend him, than that mentioned which is not true,—that, orders were not fairly distributed, which is partly true—and that General Shaw was himself a weak man to be gulled by Lieut. O'Connor— which is wholly true.   To put such a thing as an officer getting a military honour for being a good leaper and runner, into a book in which people were to seek for information about the war, is ridiculing the whole of the officers,—but more especially is it derogatory to General Shaw's own character, when it is known that this same Lieut. Dan O'Connor was an arrant coward—deserted his regiment—hid himself in the ditches during the fight, and was never within whiz of a bullet during the day.

Dan, was a darling for fun and frolic, when he had it all his own

way, and had thus made himself a favourite, particularly with old
Charley Fitzgerald, at that time the Colonel commanding the 9th, and
afterwards General of the Irish brigade ; but Dan did not like bullets·
He gave out that he lost his company and regiment, in the darkness
of the morning, and that he had frequently after that encountered
the Carlists hand to hand—that they took him prisoner ; but that
after keeping him for some time he made his escape from them,
leaving his sword, cloak, and cap in their possession.   This was
an unusual way for *Carlists* to deal with *prisoners*, and certainly
seemed problematical so far as Mr. O'Connor was concerned ; for
his regiment had been in front nearly all the morning, and he had
not been able to find it, and join in the regimental fight. His absence
had been particularly remarked in the regiment too, as he was one of
the subalterns of the grenadier company—that, to which the ill-fated
Captain Mackay belonged, and as the other subaltern fell in the fight·
the company had to be mingled with others for the want of an officer to command it.   The problem of Mr. O'Connor's single handed
battle with the Carlists might have remained doubtful to some people
—though not to his brother officers who knew his braggadocio manners—had not some inquisitive persons gone into his billet, and
found stowed away in a corner—the cloak—sword— and cap, which
he asserted the Carlists had taken from him.   Captain Thompson of
the same regiment—a brave little fellow—(the son of the political
Colonel Thomson,) was severely wounded in that sanguinary engagement, and he has subsequently published a work entitled "Twelve
months in the British Legion," wherein he gives credit, and currency
to the story of Lieut. O'Connor having engaged the Carlists with his
fists, and what was more,—overpowered them ! and more still came
off un-shot, and un-bayoneted by those looking on ! I would not
have said so much of this boy Dan and his exploits, had he not been
honoured with the Fernando ribbon, which, other officers fighting
bravely to the last shot, and then falling wounded, did not
receive.

Then there was Lieut. Keogh of the same regiment. This young
gentleman was a great favourite with Colonel Fitzgerald, and got
into, and out of disgrace in the following manner.

When the battle began, he became so alarmed, that he ran off the
field, and made his way into San Sebastian, as if suddenly overcome

with madness. In fact, no one who saw him, thought any thing else
of him than that he was mad. But the bustle and crash of the
battle, and the thoroughfares in the town becoming crowded with
wounded men dying, and raving as they died, gave people enough
to look at, without their taking much notice of the cunning youth
Keogh, who feigned sudden insanity. Captain Middleton whose
bravery was rather doubtful also, and a cleverly gallant young man,
Ensign Bezant, belonged to and continued with the company from
which the runaway Keogh absconded; Bezant when fighting with
bravery, fell severely wounded ; but I shall have something to say of
him that will excite a lively interest in the next paragraph. Let us
follow Keogh. This gentleman was, as already stated, a favourite
with Colonel Fitzgerald, who more than any other officer dealt in
favouritism. He could do or undo anything for any officer, according as that officer was in his favour or not. Keogh was charged by
Captain Middleton, with having deserted his company, and was also
threatened with a court-martial. The latter threat would have
beyond remedy condemned him, had it taken place ; but Colonel Fitzgerald stopped it, by urging Keogh to *challenge* Middleton, for having called him a coward. This was done, and as understood, no
injury to the pair resulted from it, for it was said they fought,—no,
not *fought*, but fired with leadless pistols ! adding shame to disgrace,
so far as Keogh was concerned ; but affording a pretext for staying the
proceedings of the court martial, as Mr. Keogh was now alleged to
have proved himself, not a coward.

There is in this transaction a concatenation of the disgraces connected with the code of honour. Keogh, has run away from his
regiment, but he is one of the Colonel's *fancy men*, and, the Colonel,
to save him from being dismissed, exhibits the want of honesty and
honor, in the following manner : *First*, in shewing that he deals in
favouritism, and is therefore not honest. *Second*, that his favourites
are not honorable men—but in this case, one is a most degraded
coward. *Third*, that he thwarts justice by interposing to prevent a
court martial. *Fourth*, that he does not appreciate the worth of a
man who has done his duty honorably and then added to that honor
by exposing a coward. *Fifth*, that he takes up the coward's defence,
excusing himself, that the coward is a *man of good family*. *Sixth*,
that he resorts to a course that places an honorable man's life in

jeopardy; only, that *Seventh*, he makes himself dishonest, by conniving at farther cowardice, that of cheating even the laws of duelling, by letting the pistols be charged with blank cartridge. Then, *Eighth*, and most particularly, he sets an example to younger officers, by shewing that all this duplicity can be covered by a duel; they knowing well that if any one called the Colonel's honor in question that person would have to respond to his challenge, which, as a matter of course would result from an accusation.

General Evans, saw that Fitzgerald did not behave honorably to the officers beneath him, but then, Fitzgerald had always this reply ready if Evans said anything. " Either I or he must leave the regiment; if you prefer Mr. Such-a-one, to me, you may do so; but I cannot serve with him," then the good-natured Lieut. General Evans gave way, and by this means the unfriended young officers were borne down—some of them brave spirited young men; while such as O'Connor got the ribbon and cross—and Keogh was taken under special protection. There were also two young Fitzgeralds, sons of the Colonel, and these were able to turn their father into any mood; at least, one of them could, and he was mostly engaged in a quarrel with some one or other of the officers. He was the main cause of the ill treatment of the youthful and brave Ensign Bezant of the 9th regiment.

This young man was the son of a Major Bezant, of the British Service, and went to Spain, full of that enthusiasm that made other young men, like himself, prefer an active military profession abroad to a nominal one at home. In every department of duty this youth displayed superior energies, and acquitted himself in fight and out of it, in a manner that would have brought applause and preferment to any other person, and to himself, had he been free of the influence of an ungenerous superior. He was wounded on the 5th of May; he fought bravely, and was all the day in the same company that Keogh ran away from; but he got no recommendation for a reward of merit. Previous to that, he had quarrelled with one of the young Fitzgerald, and ever after the old one subjected him to those small, but irritating persecutions that a Colonel has so much command of; but against which, a sufferer cannot found a substantial complaint. He was harassed with undue picquets and guards, getting always that picquet that might be in any degree more inconvenient to an officer,

than another.   He was more than once or twice placed, not intentionally as a favour, in situations where the fight was the hottest;
but on the discovery being made that this pleased the young man
best, that nothing more agreeable to him as a soldier, whatever he
might feel as a man, could be done, the case was altered ! once he
was placed under arrest on a groundless charge the night previous to
a general engagement, merely to prevent him from gratifying his
propensity of shewing more bravery than most other officers.   This
was not the direct work of General Fitzgerald, for he was by that
time a brigadier, but it was by the order of Colonel Cannon the officer who succeeded in the command of the 9th, the protegé of Fitzgerald and in every thing so far as regarded favouritism his exact
pattern.   Cannon even took up the favourites that his predecessor
had cherished, and continued the persecution of those that had been
formerly proscribed.   Bezant had seen almost every officer, of whatever description of character who commenced on the same scale with
himself, promoted to be Captains : some had been promoted to companies during the first year, who had like him, began as Ensigns, and
yet at the storming of Irun, the last fight under General Evans, he
was only a Subaltern,

It was the evening previous to this engagement, the evening of the
15th May, 1837, that Colonel Cannon placed Mr. Bezant under
arrest without giving any reason whatever for having done so.   Almost every other officer of his regiment had received the order of
Fernando but himself.   At each succeeding engagement he had
risked his life, more and more recklessly, to obtain this reward.   He
seemed to have but one ambition, that was to have the cross of
Fernando to shew his friends on coming home.   Vain as the ambition
may have been, still it must not be altogether sneered at by the more
soberly philosophical.   He had been *taught* to look on military
honour as the highest premium of superior enterprises, and he went,
I believe, against the wishes of a fond mother to Spain.   Perhaps
being conscious of superior abilities, he, to fellow officers, such as the
young Fitzgeralds, made himself obnoxious; but be that as it may
he found ungenerous enemies, for he was not promoted.   At the approach of the last engagement, he found himself also disappointed,
where, as he had expressed himself, he was determined to have the
order of Fernando, if nothing else, the secret ambition being to shew

at home, that though not promoted, he had won something by the
inheritance of those qualities that had honoured his father, and of
which his mother had been justly proud to see in her young boy. All
mothers are fond of their froward boys—the very fears engendered
by the untamed spirit of the reckless youth, makes the maternal
breast more fond. It would have been a pleasing return for the
mother's anxieties, had her son only come home with the Spanish
cross, simple as that was; and he, in his own mind, felt so. Determined that he would not have the imputation of being behind his
regiment, he disobeyed orders, and joined his company on the 16th,
when the attack on Irun commenced. He was for some hours in the
heat of the engagement, and displaying his usual courage and intrepidity in the storming of some fortified houses, when a cannon shot
carried off both his feet, leaving only the shattered bones hanging by
fragments of sinew and skin. According to general orders, the
wounded were carried to France, this engagement being little more
than half a mile from the French frontier, and we being critically
situated should a retreat across the country become necessary. Four
men of the hospital transport corps had got poor Bezant on a stretcher
or bier, and were carrying him away, with a blanket and his cloak
wrapped round him, when General Fitzgerald came alongside of
them, and enquired who they had got. The blanket and cloak,
saturated with blood, shewed that it was some poor fellow with a
dreadful wound, and the general on being told it was Mr. Bezant,
enquired farther what was the nature of his wound. The men told
him that his feet were knocked off by a cannon ball, and that he was
fainting from loss of blood: "*The devil mend him!*" was the reply
of General Fitzgerald, who rode away after giving this last testimony
of a heartless want of the commonest feelings of mankind.

He was carried across the river Badossa, to the French side, and
besides being attended to by some of our own Medical Staff, was assisted by the skill and humanity of the French surgeons, who exerted themselves in behalf of all our wounded officers and men, from
their own spontaneous kindness, as well as in compliance with the
orders of General Count Harispe, commander of the French Army
on the frontiers. Next day death closed the career of the young
man! and the 57th regiment of the French line, buried him with
military honours. There is something in this last act, that soothes

the feelings; though ill-treatment haunted him even to death, yet he escaped the last malignity which he would have too probably met from his brutal superior of the brigade—he would not have felt it, but it was well he escaped it—for others did not escape indignities offered to them even when dead! He had fallen into the hands of the French, who did not know that he was not a favourite, but who too honorable to have abated their generosity had they known—buried him with honors which were deemed due to an officer wearing English uniform, and to one who had fought with that bravery which at a mile's distance they had been spectators of the previous day. No officer, in the Legion, had been so ungenerously treated as Mr. Bezant, while living, and none were so highly honored when dead. This may, perhaps, prove that the friendly feelings now existing between France and England, are not exclusively the offspring of *English* good sense and generosity, some of them are *French*.

As a contrast to the officers who proved themselves cowards in the 9th, may be mentioned Captain Cotter, afterwards Lieut. Colonel in the same regiment, and Captain Allez, brother to the brave Adjutant, of the 4th regiment, whose death is noted at page 21; also Captain Thomson, Lieut. Thornton, and Lieut Stack, these last four were all wounded at one time, when attempting to charge with a party of their regiment on the Carlist breast-works. Captain Cotter commanded the light company of the 9th then, and gave the first practical display of that bravery that so peculiarly distinguished him in subsequent engagements, particularly in that where he lost his life, which will be detailed hereafter. On the 5th of May, he was at the head of his gallant company and made his way over the enemy's breast-works and into fortified houses, which never could have been carried but by him or his equal in wild daring courage The opposing force, many times the number of those who followed him, were confounded; and probably, thinking that the assailants were much more numerous than they were, gave way the more readily. But, brave as Captain Cotter was, and resolute as was his chosen company of men, it is only just in a narration of warlike events in which they were distinguished to tell all the truth. On entering these fortified houses they spared none who fell into their hands;—beneath beds—in the inside of barrels--on the rafters of the roof--up chimnies, or in any other hiding place, the ill-fated Carlists, who, supposing themselves overpowered sought safety in concealment, were all sacrificed. The light company of the 9th had the distinction of having taken a position, held by troops five times their number, having fulfilled the order to go forward and stand at nothing; but they also had the distinction of having literally fulfilled the other part of the order, which was not to *mind taking prisoners.* This order, however, be it known, was not a general one ; it came from some of those beneath General Evans, and, it is but just to state, that he took precautionary measures to prevent such a slaughter of prisoners afterwards. Yet, on that morning there was sad havoc in these houses, and the glory gallantly won by Captain Cotter and his company, was tarnished by the unnecessary slaughter of the enemy.

Another gentleman who held a commission in the 9th, and was distinguished for singular conduct, was a Mr. Street. This officer was bred to the medical profession, and practised as a surgeon in Don Pedro's service in Portugal, in which service was also a patron, Colonel Shaw. A very efficient cure performed on Fitzgerald, was the cause it was said of Mr. Street being taken into favour, and after going to Spain,—of his getting a commission in the Legion.— Colonel Fitzgerald soon got him [promoted to a company, of which he was captain for a considerable time, and was distinguished by his wonderful sagacity of discovering when an engagement with the enemy was likely to occur, as it happened with a rare exception that he was always taken suddenly ill about that time, and that he recovered as soon as it was over. We had one or two in every regiment of this sort ; one I recollect was in the 8th, and fell sick like Mr. Street of the 9th, when " coming events cast their shadows before," but Mr. Street's sickness on the 9th of March, 1837, and his recovery on the 17th of the same month, was the most remarkable case of sagacity ; I am sure most people will think it remarkable when it is known that the Legion had a general fight on the 10th, advanced and fought partially on the 12th, 13th, and 14th, fought a general action severely and successfully on the 15th, were hand to hand with the Carlists, and defeated on the 16th! Mr. Street being convalescent, and able to join the shattered regiment on the 17th. That regiment too, that had sacrificed its brave Cotter and others on the battle-field of the previous day.   Ah, Mr. Street ! it was convenient, but not honorable.

But having run over a few of the most notable officers of the 9th regiment, it will be proper to give a sketch of the most notable of all, the head of the corps, namely, Colonel, afterwards Brigadier-General Charles Lionel Fitzgerald.   This gentleman was a Major in the British service at one time, though long ago, and has been celebrated since, in one of the most extraordinary crim. con. cases that ever occurred within the limits of British law. • He is Major Fitzgerald who figured about twenty years ago at Castlebar and Dublin, in a case that was at the time pronounced as the most extraordinary that had been in an Irish court, and which up to this time remains unmatched in, or out of this country.   It is not my province, however, to give a history of that affair.   The judge who presided at one of the trials where Major Fitzgerald was plaintiff, recommended the newspapers of the time not to publish it, as it would not only offend the public decency, but that from its unmatchable ingenuity, as a means of persecuting innocence for a price, it might excite others void of moral feeling to imitation ; it is therefore not in my way to give further explanations of that case.   Some years before that, there was also a famed character in Ireland, named George Thomas Fitzgerald, who was the greatest dueller of his day ; who in almost every duel wounded, or killed his man ! in a number of instances the latter result followed his deadly arm.   He was sometimes wounded, or supposed to be, in vital parts of the body himself ; and some of the more dexterous duellers took him up designedly to inflict retribution, but they failed ; he was discovered to wear, which he had always worn, a case of chain armour next his skin.   This gentleman encased in his steel armour, was hanged at Dublin for a robbery.   It would certainly be unjust to throw any blame on his nephew Charles Lionel Fitzgerald, late Colonel of the 9th regiment of the Auxiliary Legion ; for a nephew could in no way be answerable for the faults of his uncle. But the family likeness having descended so exactly, in person and manners makes the family history worth alluding to.   That Colonel Fitzgerald was not blameable with such offences, as those committed by his relative is true ; but the difference was to be ascribed more to the altered state of society, and the laws rather than to any other circumstance of character.   In Spain where any restrictive law for such as himself was almost nominal, he had sternly absolute laws at his command, with which he could punish or persecute those beneath him.   But after what has been said of his way of treating gentlemen who held commissions with him, it will be unnecessary to add much more.   The men suffered in the same manner, and yet many of them were devoted to him, for he made such havoc of officers, and sometimes rewarded the most unworthy criminals so manifestly to the injury of better behaved men, that he became popular from the very causes that should have made him obnoxious.

Allusion has been made to his sons, and it may not be improper to state that they are " chips of the old block."   The youngest, by his father's interest of course, returned to England three different times during the campaign, once on leave of absence, another time on recruiting service, the third time for some unknown purpose, but what was most remarkable, during these periods of absence, three different battles were fought.   It was not an unamiable trait in a father's character to save a son if he could ; but it was brutal to treat the sons of other fathers who were not there to defend them, as he did.*

The 7th regiment of the Legion was also Irish, and like all other regiments, whether Irish, English, or Scotch, it had its share of uncommon characters ; the most noted of any in the 7th or perhaps in the whole Legion was Owen Kelly, one who never feared the face of man, and as he was not much disposed to Godliness it may be said " he feared neither God nor man.

Kelly had been a smuggler on the coast of Ireland, and had been inured to danger and fatigue from his boyhood ; in those desperate enterprises which have framed characters peculiar from all other classes of mankind.   Those who have seen Owen Kelly, have seen

---

* It is perhaps not generally known that Sir George De Lacy Evans has along with that title to himself, managed to procure appointments under the government for the most of his superior officers.   As many of these as could be thrust on Lord Hill were sent out to Canada, some of them zealous and efficient officers, whose drilling will be no joke for the Canadian militia, at least if they drill as they did in Spain—Colonel Swan, for instance ; see page 214 of this work.

It is said that Lord Palmerston strove hard for an appointment for General Fitzgerald, but Lord Hill was immoveable in his resolution, not to re-admit that gentleman into the British army, and that in consequence, the Foreign Minister got him appointed, a short time since, to a consulship in the Mauritius.   The mouths of the higher ranks of officers are therefore all, or nearly all closed, and the complaints of the inferior ranks are disposed of, by their being comprised in the general denunciation of " *discontented individuals.*"

the last remnant of the Captain Grant's, the O'Ncil's, O'Brien's, and others of chieftain fame, and those who have read of these famous robber chiefs, and have formed pictures of their stern features—the sinewy limb—the athletic form—the impervious nerve—the sable beard, and the eye like dark night reflecting its own lightning— have seen Owen Kelly. I shall at present confine my sketch of Owen's Legionary exploits, to a few instances by no means his masterpieces, but still, of a character interesting enough to be read. The first, however, causes a digression to be made, and another person of extraordinary bravery to be introduced ;—that is a Carlist chief, or if not altogether a chief, an officer of high rank. His name was said to be Don Junot Bassilla—something—the surname being almost unwriteable to a pen that follows recollection, and altogether unpronounceable to an English tongue, from its being a composition of nearly half the consonants of the alphabet with a vowel to each three or four ; which consonants, like the rocky mountains in the North of Spain, at places piled on each other without intervening vallies—present themselves as insurmountable obstacles to those not acquainted with them.

On the 6th of June, 1836, the severe attack by General Casa Eguia, was made on the troops of General Evans, as described at 81 and the following pages. In this engagement, a brave Carlist officer, • the one referred to, was conspicuously exposed in the early part of the day leading on his men. He was repeatedly in front of them, and between the two fires, where he waved his sword, first flourishing it in defiance of our side, then turning towards his own followers, taking off his cap, and with that and the sword seemingly cheering them to the attack. As the fight went on he came nearer us, and certainly, had the soldiers followed as resolutely as he wished to lead them, they would have had the ground in their possession, which, as it was, we kept. Though thick showers of bullets flew about him he continued for a considerable time in that exposed situation, making his approach nearer and nearer, until *Owen Kelly* presenting himself in front of *his* regiment went forward and met the brave Carlist. The parley was not long ; the Carlist brandished his sword and gave a furious defiance to his antagonist ; but Kelly levelled him with his first stroke and left him dead. This was the first act of the deed, and in military phrase, it was honorable ; but the

No. 22.

THE PLUNDERING AND DESTRUCTION OF THE PEASANTS' HOUSES ON THE 17TH OF NOVEMBER, 1836, BY
THE 6TH REGIMENT OF THE LEGION.

See Page 336.

second act, which in an equal, if not in a greater degree, was as brave, was not, in military language, equally honourable. Kelly, turning again, towards the enemy, after leaving his dead opponent, observed his uniform to look useful, and making action follow thought, he returned and commenced stripping the Carlist; and though bullets from the brave Don's followers battered round Kelly, he did not desist, until he had made himself proprietor of the *trousers* as well as the several other articles of clothing and accoutrements; which trousers, Owen Kelly, it is said, wears at home now.

Owen had a countryman in the Legion, a Major Lister who is also a military man; but one of a different class from himself. Kelly, was the stern soldier who made deadly strife a profession; Lister, was the martinet, smart, handsome, clever and conceited. Kelly, the bull-dog! Lister, the ladies puppy! They came into wrathful contact in the public square of San Sebastian.

Kelly had given some offence at a public meeting of the officers, which was held relative to the pay question, by animadverting rather freely on the character of General Fitzgerald, who undertook the onerous duty from General Evans of keeping the Legion quiet until the chief got away ; or of keeping them full of promises for some weeks, until a number of them had been induced to re-inlist in a new Legion. This work of smothering discontent by deception, was the main department of Fitzgerald towards the close of General Evan's command; it was far from being satisfactory to either officers or men, as there was so much of a daily shifting duplicity, necessary to hide realities, and Owen Kelly was one who gave imprudent vent to his suspicions of foul-play. The *reporter* of what he said at a meeting of officers, was Major Lister, and the Major also had the temerity to order Mr. Kelly to consider himself under arrest. Kelly having no assurance of this arrestment being legal, and not caring much if it was, went about as usual until a Spanish armed guard was set on him, to take him on board a steam-boat to be conveyed away a prisoner. The Spaniards supposing that he was some unhappy being that would quail before them, marched down the street clearing away the mob of people who had collected as spectators; and seeing these make way, and among them a number of English officers, they became bold, and with fixed bayonets drove the mob into the doorways of other streets.

They had not yet seen Owen Kelly ; but at a corner as they passed along, he presented himself, and drawing his sword, stepped to the middle of the street, and opposed their farther progress. With bayonets on their muskets pointed to him, they attempted to pass for the purpose of surrounding him ; but he struck consternation into them, by parrying the bayonets off with such force that on the muskets being knocked from some of them by his blows, they fell back a little. Having once made them give way, he followed his advantage, and ultimately charged the whole party, consisting of from fifteen to twenty men, through the streets ; they running and he pursuing amid the cheers of the onlookers. As the Spanish soldiers were likely to turn out in greater force and with firmer resolution to make Kelly prisoner, some of his friends persuaded him to surrender peacefully, and go aboard the steamer in the harbour, until the disturbance had settled down a little. He did so ; but came ashore next day, when meeting Major Lister in the market-place, he went forward to him, and asked if he was the officer who went for the Spanish guard. Lister was not sure how to answer, and declined saying anything. Kelly flourished a cane in his hand, as if not unwilling to give Major Lister the weight of it ; but went away without touching him. The moment he was gone out of the square, the Major flew into a violent rage as other officers gathered round him, and swore that he would go for his sword, and that he would run Kelly through the body if he came back to bully him in that manner. And saying so, he set off to his billet, buckled on his sword and reappeared in the square. Some one told Kelly, and *he* immediately set off to the house where he was quartered, and in which there was at the time a number of officers. On entering, he walked to where his sword was hanging, and taking it down girded it on, without saying a word to those about him. Some of them dreading the consequences, laid hold of him exclaiming, " pray Mr. Kelly consider what you're about ! do not Mr. Kelly ! pray do not take your sword &c." But Kelly throwing the tiny hands that feebly held him, from him like straws, uttered not a word, but descended the stairs—walked along the street—entered the market place, went up to Major Lister, and said, " so you went for your sword did you Major !—Draw !" In every window, on every balcony, as well as in the crowded colonnades of the square, an immense number of breathless expectant observers strained their eyes. Kelly had drawn his weapon ; but the Major stood motionless and mute. Eyeing him intently for about a minute, and seeing he was not inclined to risk the combat; Kelly returned his sword, uttered contemptuously the expression " *oh you Coward*," and wheeling about, strode majestically away.

When he had quitted the square, the Major relapsed into his former rage, and swore that he would not degrade his sword by running it into the body of such a fellow ; but, said he, " by G— I'll shoot him." So hastening up to his billet, he provided himself with a pair of pistols primed and loaded, with which he returned to the congregated officers, who by this time were beginning to see some amusement in the matter, and demanding to know where the scoundrel had gone to, he assured those about him, that he would blow Kelly's brains out by G— he would. A messenger conveyed intelligence of this to Kelly, who, also got a pair of pistols, and reappeared in front of Major Lister; but the latter was not disposed to fight, and the former again walked away.

CHAPTER XVIII.

The 3rd regiment—Colonel Churchill, his general character—The 3rd engaged at Arlaban, and incidents relating thereto—Major K—— of the 3rd, alias, the Hero of Rathcormac, his conduct at Arlaban, and death in Vittoria—The deserters Richardson, Johnson, Mahoney, and Salmon—Ensign Chadwicke, his bravery, and death—Captain Jackson, and his son Lieut. Jackson—Adjutant Keevil disgraced on the 6th of June—Major Maclaine—Colonel Churchill making Corporal Brown an officer—Lieut. M'Intosh—General Shaw and Mr. Wilkinson.

THE 3rd regiment, or Westminster Grenadiers, was commanded by Colonel Churchill, an officer of whom nothing important claims a record, save that he was a gentleman, in the most strictly respectable sense of that ambiguous term. He was also a brave soldier when occasion required his bravery ; but he frequently, rather too frequently assumed the character of the merely gentleman-officer, deputing to others those duties of detail which should have been performed by himself ; which more particularly should have been performed by himself, as the faults of these inferior officers have caused his character to suffer. I allude principally to the faults of Adjutant Keevil, who was a clever and excellently qualified officer in regimental and company drill, but who did much mischief in other respects to the corps, as he harassed the men most vexatiously beyond what was requisite for discipline. Colonel Churchill is also a political partizan holding liberal opinions, and expressing them oftener than some of his friends have thought necessary. At one time in San Sebastian, where General Evans gave a public entertainment, some of the officers (from military enthusiasm I believe), proposed the health of the Duke of Wellington, on which, when the cheering that always follows that toast had subsided, and the glasses had been refilled, Colonel Churchill rose and gave the health of *Daniel O'Connell, a greater man than the Duke of Wellington.*

As this was a controversial subject, according to the opinions of different men, it may be supposed that Colonel Churchill had not all the table on his side ; a rather noisy debate ensued, which was only put down by General Evans interposing his opinion, that as soldiers they could only drink His Grace's health as a soldier, and that as such he stood above all other men. Colonel Churchill got rather the worst of his own dispute by this expression of the General; but he is a man not ready to give in to any opposition, and he continued to recur frequently to political affairs, when in company with those who professed to be his opponents in opinion. He is likely to be known in the political world soon, as his property—liberal opinions—and active talents seem to make him ambitious of public life, and an expected opening has attracted his attention, and the attention of his political friends to get him into parliament. But let us have a passing inspection of his regiment, and its services in Spain ; for it is only his military character that my sketch comprehends.

Very few officers of the Legion have been so highly eulogised as Colonel Churchill, and though he eminently deserved high respect, yet it would be unjust to the character of his rgeiment to take no exceptions. In the 3rd more men died than in most of the other regiments, and fully as many deserted from him as deserted from other corps. Sir Henry Hardinge has said in parliament, that Colonel Churchill was a gentleman of education, and that he therefore did not punish men by the provost system of flogging, that is by ordering or permitting his officers to order three or four dozen lashes to an offender without trial. But the mode of punishment that Adjutant Keevil used, was most dreadfully severe so much so, that men were

heard to declare that they would suffer any other punishment in preference to being harassed and drilled to death.   Keevil as has been
said was clever, but he treated men most unjustly ; he did not forgive
an offence when it had been atoned for, but continued to impose
extra duty and withhold common indulgences from men, until their
spirits sunk and carried them into the diseased hospital, or irritated
them so much, that they sought refuge in deserting to the enemy.
When any money was got for the partial payment of the troops,
Colonel Churchill was always more anxious to lay it out on the or-
namental equipments of his regiment, than in procuring any additional
supply of food ; he got woollen paddings for the breasts of the regimental dress-coats, to make the chests of his grenadiers look full ;
but left their bellies to shrink with a meagre allowance and uncertain
supply of bad food.   Yet in many other respects Churchill was an
excellent Colonel, he discovered when too late, that he had entrusted
too much to an officer who abused his confidence.

On the 16th of January, 1836 the 3rd regiment had a sharp fight
with the Carlists, and acquitted itself very creditably.   Being the first
fight at which all the Legion were present, though not all engaged,
the officers and men of the 3rd looked back on that day with considerable pride, as their regiment had had the honor of shewing the
others what a real encounter with mortal foes was.   On that occasion
the Colonel was not engaged, Major Campbell having command of
the party ; but though whisperings, injurious to the Colonel's reputation, were at that time on the lips of those disposed to slander; he
has been so eminently gallant in fight since, that his not having been
with the fighting party of the 3rd, on the 16th of January, can only
be mentioned to give me the power of explaining that he remained
with some companies of his regiment, which were destined for a
bolder enterprise, than were those who did fight ; but that the General
recalled these, not deeming a waste of life justifiable until he knew
what Cordova, the General-in-Chief, was intending.

This is the engagement that has been frequently referred to, as
that fought on the heights of Arlaban, when General Cordova retreated and left Evans by himself on the snowy mountains, exposed
to all the rigours of winter, and the want of rations and what might
have been more dreadful still, with the enemy surrounding him
without his being informed of their positions, and Cordova's retreat.

Evans was manœuvering until he received instructions from Cordova, and it was then that he got engaged with a battalion of Carlists. A few hours of sharp firing and two or three resolute charges from the 3d regiment was the amount of it; for Evans very magnanimously refused to send more men, though these were at his disposal, than would cope in number with the enemy in front of them. The Companies of the 3rd went briskly in, on the Carlists, and the latter retreating, a running guerilla fight was kept up for some hours. At midnight the party were withdrawn, and General Reid to whose brigade they belonged, took up his quarters in an old dilapidated house on the skirts of his position. Having invited a few officers to share a basket of provisions and a few bottles of wine with him, which his servant had brought from Vittoria, and one of these officers having survived subsequent disasters, I am enabled to give a short description of the General's supper party, as this officer has furnished me with the following notes.

"My company being engaged during the afternoon, and the captain being severely wounded, I, as subaltern, was ordered to take command in his place. Perhaps as we had been rather hotly engaged, General Reid wished to give us some mark of favour, as on coming off the field, I was ordered to mount guard on the General's quarters with my whole company. This was indeed a favour; the men got into a hayloft, and though there was no hay in it, they lying only on the bare floor in their clothes and accoutrements, they were so comfortable, compared with the other companies, that both they and I were envied, at being ordered for duty. A heavy hoar-frost fell, the air was thick and dark, and the hungry worn-out men of the companies, officers as well, lay outside on the snow, the icicles hanging from their hair and the frost when any of them sat down holding their greatcoats to the ground. *"

This was literally true. The colonel of the regiment. I was in (Godfrey), had lain for some time, and attempted to sleep; but when waking in a shivering fit, he found his hair frozen to the earth, and so strongly, that he could not turn himself to either side, until some of the men extricated him. We were all similarly frozen, and believing that we could have got quarters in a neighbouring village, much grumbling prevailed; but the next day shewed the wisdom of General Evans in not taking up quarters in the village. The Carlists had nearly surrounded it, and as Cordova had retreated, would most assuredly have cut off our retreat. Therefore bad as the snowy mountains were, they were the safest quarters that we could procure.

Being on guard, I was invited to partake of the General's supper along with a few other officers. The only part of the house where we could make anything like an approach to a table, was where there was a dunghill, over which some cloak or great-coat was spread, and around which we sat and ate our cheerful repast. We gathered a few stones to sit on, and got a scanty fire, which was certainly all miserable enough, but which was peculiarly pleasant to us, contrasted with the state in which so many thousands were lying almost frozen to death outside."

This, is from the officer who was one of the supper party. Then here is what one who was otherwise employed says—one who was trying to save the wounded men from the dreadful effects of the weather. He remarks.

"The night of the 16th of January set in, and when the soldiers of the 3rd had been brought from the field, elated as they were by having so successfully routed that portion of the enemy that had attacked them—when exhilirated by their success they had talked away a good part of the night in mutual congratulations, some of them at last made the accidental enquiry of "where are the doctors and the wounded men ?" The question was repeated, from the men to non-commissioned-officers, and from these to their superiors, when to their utter dismay, nobody could tell where the wounded were, the doctors being also missing. Major Campbell, and a troop of lancers, immediately set out in search of them, and after a considerable search, found the regimental surgeon, his horse and a wounded man lying in a ditch. The surgeon (Mr. Kearns,) on finding the regiment had been with-drawn by some other road, attempted to go for assistance, and to save one man at least, should the others fall into the Carlist's hands which seemed to him likely, he took one on his horse, but had not got many yards when in the darkness the animal tumbled into a ditch with them, where all three lay unable to extricate themselves. The Carlists were close at hand, and no doubt would have soon despatched the whole, had they known of such a feeble party being lying so near them. On Major Campbell, and the lancers finding them, they were assisted to the regiment, and Colonel Churchill with his usual humanity immediately gave up his quarters for their accommodation. A consultation had then to be held to decide what was necessary to be done with certain patients whose wounds were severe. One of

them was a lad with a severe compound fracture in the leg, who by
one surgeon was pronounced beyond the hope of surviving the night
in any case, by another, certain to sink, if immediate amputation was
not performed.   It appears, however, that Mr Kearns must have had
another opinion as he, being regimental surgeon decided on the
case, and the young man is now using his limbs at home nearly as
well as ever he did."

In the 3d regiment, was a Major K——, who on ordinary occasions talked well of himself, and indeed, was commonly supposed to
be a man of considerable energy.   On the day that the regiment was
engaged at Arlaban, as just detailed, when General Evans seeing
that they had gone far enough from his own positions—when in fact,
night coming on, rendered it necessary that they should be re-called
—but, when the Carlist's bullets were still flying thick, and cutting
up the earth in an adjacent field, Major K—— was ordered to gallop across that field, and order the wing of the regiment that was
fighting under Major Campbell to retire.   For a few minutes Major
K——'s horse reared and pranced with him, while he whipped and
spurred, and not being, as he said, able to make it go, he turned and
told General Evans that perhaps some other officer would go as his
horse was so violent and unmanageable.   The General rather surprised
to hear an officer presume to excuse himself from any order, told him
again to go; but the Major's horse began again to kick, and bore its
rider backwards,—not one step would it move to the front.   " Oh,
I see how it is," said the General, " *if you wont allow your horse to
go forward*, I must send another officer."   The Pay-master, Captain Edwards, of the 3d, being at hand, offered to ride across the
fields, though it was of course no part of his duty to do so; but the
General's aides-du-camp being at that moment dispatched in other
directions, or in some other manner employed, Captain Edwards was
sent to order Major Campbell to retire. The Major enquired if he was
to march at once to the rear, or if he was to fire and retire by degrees
Captain Edwards told him he had no commands on that point, but
that he would go back for orders.   Having got the required order,
he rode again to Major Campbell, and thus by having to return
again, caused him to cross the same field four times, that Major
K——'s *horse* would not set a foot on once.

Believing that Major K——had not been willing to go where he

was ordered, General Reid, to whose supper party before mentioned, he had been invited, sent to him, to intimate that his presence at supper would not be desirable. It is common in all ranks and professions of life, for imitation to take its law from superior rank, indeed, few tendencies of society are more uniformly correct, not even is the needle's point to the north more certain than this : and we in the Legion, were no exceptions. When the Brigadier General declined the honour of the Major's company, all the inferior grades of officers soon did the same, and the poor Major was shaken off, even by the Subs. He had not been the most amiable of men, nor the most agreeable ; for, having been in the British service, he often boasted of his superior knowledge and experience. The first, no one would deny to an officer, who, like him had been an Adjutant in a British regiment; but he, being too young to have been a hero of Wellington, his brother officers naturally doubted his experience. It was however, known to some of his friends, and from them, the knowledge spread to almost every person in the Legion, that he had been in the wars previous to his joining the Spanish service,—that he was in fact nothing less than one of the officers who was in the celebrated tithe fight of Rathcormac. Having boasted too often of his warlike experience, the most of which had been the storming of widow Ryan's house, andthe capture of tithe-pigs, his brother officers made a joke of him, and for some time previous to his entire failure, which caused his exclusion from General Reid's supper party, he was styled the *Hero of Rathcormac.*

The remainder of his history is melancholy. Soon after the 16th of January, he caught the fever that was then thinning the ranks, and went into the town of Vittoria. There the horror of being slain by the Carlists haunted him, and he called incessantly for some one to keep them off. At one time he sprung out of bed, seized his sword that hung by the wall, and, but for the swiftness of his servant, would have killed him, believing in his delirium, that the servant was a Carlist. A few minutes after, he was dead ; having sprung from a third floor window to the street.

When the Legion was occupying some villages outside of Vittoria, six men deserted from the 3d regiment to the Carlists. The leader of these named Johnson, was a man who un-surpassed in activity, and a thorough knowledge of drill, was yet so unsettled in his behaviour as to cause more trouble to the officers than a dozen of other men. Of the six, two were rather indifferent characters like himself, and the others were very well behaved, only goaded to seek a chance of escaping from the Legion, by the severe treatment of Adjutant Keevil. One of them was named Salmon, and had been a soldier in the Royal British Artillery before going to Spain; but more of him hereafter.

It will be recollected that in the Ninth Chapter, an account is given of the bread being poisoned, and of the apprehension and execution of the bakers. The person who is there alluded to, as having written a letter from the Carlist camp to a friend in the 7th regiment inducing the friend to desert, was a man named Richardson. He had been Quartermaster-Sergeant in the 7th, and had deserted from the Legion when in the neighbourhood of Bilbao. His letter to his nephew, who was at the time in hospital, caused the traitor Don Jose Elgoez to be apprehended, and excited some suspicions against himself in the Carlist camp. On Johnson and his companions going over, they found nearly two hundred English with the enemy, mostly deserters from the Legion, among these was Richardson. Johnson being a clever drill, got the party put under his superintendance, and soon gave such satisfaction to the Carlists in drilling well, that he was made Adjutant. In the course of three or four months, his party by frequent additions of deserters from General Evans, amounted to nearly four hundred. The treatment of the Carlists however, was no improvement on that of their own regimental officers; they were not paid, not well clothed, often knocked about and beat by Carlist soldiers without daring to complain, in some cases were put in prison, and some others were taken and shot without even the form of a trial. This made them resolve to escape if possible from the Carlists; even if they could not manage to get into France, and so leave all parties; some of them had proposed going over again to the Legion; among these was Richardson. This intention was secretly whispered about in order to get them all prepared; but Johnson acted traitor, and on his evidence, Richardson and some others were arrested, condemned and shot. Soon after that, Johnson from some misbehaviour broke down in his new power also, and being discovered robbing a house, was shot through the thigh by the inmates. He recovered, and has subsequently returned to England.

Another of his party was named Mahoney; he was the servant of Lieut. Stack at that time in the 3rd, afterwards in the 9th regiment. Mahoney robbed his master of a doubloon £3 12s. when he deserted, which being a part of the company's money, and that being scarce at the time, was a loss not very convenient to Mr. Stack. After many vicissitudes in the Carlist service, and in making his way through France, Mahoney found himself in London; and is now employed in the neighbourhood of Tooley Street.

Salmon, another of the party was altogether a different character from the others. By the information gathered from men who have been in the Carlist camp, I find that it was him, and not Wilson, as mentioned in the Seventh Chapter that directed the Carlist Artillery, from the Ametzagana on the 1st of October. He is there mentioned as being supposed killed by shells thrown by Colonel Colquhoun. The more correct statement of the facts is this :—

Salmon being an excellent gunner, as his practice on us that morning fearfully proved, was working the Carlist cannon as chief gunner, and had up till about ten o'clock in the morning, kept a heavy fire on the Legion. It was about that time an explosion was heard among the Carlists, as mentioned in the dispatch of General Evans, but which explosion remained unintelligible to us; it was, however, a dreadful event in the life of poor Salmon, as is now ascertained. By the negligence of his assistants, a large quantity of ammunition was lying open, and as is supposed, one of Colonel Colquhoun's shells coming unexpectedly near it, it exploded; or if not ignited by the shell, some carelessness among themselves had allowed fire to communicate with it. On observing this, a Carlist general came galloping up, attended by a priest, a number of whom were always in attendance as spiritual aides-du-camp to the chiefs. The trembling culprits by whose negligence the explosion had been occasioned, when fiercely interrogated how it happened, answered by pointing to Salmon, and pronouncing *L'Ingles*. The general turned to the priest, as if willing to take his opinion on the matter, namely, if it had been done by accident or design, and whichever way, by whose fault. The priest pronounced the Englishman a traitor, and the same instant four Carlist Cacadores got the order, prime and load, and in a few moments more, they were levelling their pieces at Salmon, and the sanguinary command was almost fulfilled, when, a heavy shell from the Legion Artillery fell into the battery, and arrested their purpose by blowing about a dozen of them to pieces, among whom was the priest! There was a minute of confusion, but there had been too many similar visitations during the morning, for this to be heeded much.

The enraged General stung with the prospect of defeat—galled by these successive disasters from our Artillery, and seeing an immense quantity of his own ammunition blown up, was more furious in his command that Salmon should suffer instant death. The soldiers also, to whom he gave his commands, had all the fury of excited passion, caused by the disaster of the former minute to impel them to take revenge on Salmon; and even among the smoke and confusion they rushed on him with their bayonets. But where was he? The moment the, disaster was caused by the shell, he had sprung from the platform on which were the guns—scrambled to his feet beneath the embankment, and was now bounding down the hill-side towards the lines of the Legion. He had cleared above a hundred yards ere he was observed, and had thrice as far to run until he gained the English; but when discovered, a number of Carlists fired after him, and the balls flew thick in his rear, yet he did not fall; on he went and again they fired, and yet they missed him. Among those who fired, was an Englishman, and the next moment a Carlist sergeant plunged a bayonet into him, as he had seen his musket to be levelled higher than the heights, that would have struck the fugitive. The same sergeant instantly seized a musket, fired—and Salmon staggering a few yards farther, rolled on the ground. He was dead at once; for it was discovered after, that the mortal bullet had gone through his brain. There were two or three more gunshot wounds in his body, but these were either received after he fell, or had not been destructive of his ability to run. He had got within one hundred yards of the English Rifle regiment when the mortal ball overtook him.

In the sanguinary conflict of the 5th of May, that which tried the military virtue of all the Legion, the Westminster Grenadiers were severely engaged. Colonel Churchill shone out in eminent bravery on that occasion, and the most of his officers nobly supported him. He was three different times compelled to retreat by the opposing foe; but as many times did he rally his regiment, and was at last completely successful. Captain Glazier was perhaps the most distinguished, and at each of the repeated onsets was seen with Churchill, heading the men in a gallant style. Among the most distinguished of the other Officers were Major Campbell, always brave; Lieuts. Jackson, and Chadwicke, and an Ensign, the younger brother of Lieut. Chadwicke. There is something in the history of the youthful Ensign, that specially claims notice.

He had been for a time in the Navy as a Midshipman; but for how long I am not enabled to say: he was only about eighteen years of age on going to Spain, and therefore could not have been long at sea. But whatever time he was there, he had been nursing a darling ambition, which not finding scope enough in the now peaceful Navy, led him to join the Spanish expedition, in which was his elder brother.

Those who knew the two Chadwickes, remember their youthful appearance, as they were seen on the 4th of May, the day previous to the engagement. The elder had been with his regiment from its formation, and was at this time a Lieutenant; the younger had only arrived from England, having quitted the British Navy, merely that he might be in more active service, which an enthusiastic devotion to a military life prompted him to seek.

On the 4th of May a mother in the county of Cornwall, having parted first with one son and then another, sat fondly conjecturing where they would be, and what they would be doing,

On the same day, they walked in the Plaza of San Sebastian among a host of gaily accoutred officers all full of life, and animated by a coming event! The youngest, handsome in figure, smart in uniform, and more boyishly youthful than any other officer on the parade, attracted more than ordinary attention. "That's young Ensign Chadwicke of the 3rd," said some one who answered an enquiry.

Next day the mother's thoughts were still on her youthful sons. But where were they? The following note gives a melancholy answer.

According to military usage, which gives the junior Ensign the regimental colours, the younger Mr. Chadwicke carried those of the 3rd regiment on the 5th of May. He was soon observed by those about him to have a valiant spirit. In the different assaults on fortified houses which were carried by the 3rd, the colours were always in the heat of the fight, and often nearer the front than moderate prudence would have warranted. As the conflict was not uniformly successful on the side of the assailants,—although they became ultimately victorious—it was found necessary to retreat some distance to a partial shelter from the heavy fire in front. On this occasion when the regiment had fallen back in disorder, the colours were seen waving, as if fastened to a particular spot. Balls flew thick around them, and were perforating the waving silk; but still they kept the same place. " Save the colours," some of those exclaimed who were falling to the rear, and saw the flag still waving where it had been planted ; and exposed to the thick flying musketry of the enemy, some men attempted to get hold of them, and there discovered young Chadwicke lying bleeding from a musket shot in his loin ; but still holding the flag above his head. He was solicited to quit the colours, by one who caught hold of them to carry them back ; but he would not.—He was ordered to quit them ; but still would not; and as the whole party with himself were nearly prisoners, the Carlists being almost laying hold of them, he was lifted and carried to the rear still holding fast by the standard, and waving it over his head. On the regiment again rallying he attempted, but was not able to move forward, and some other Officer then took his place, and performed his duty. Poor Chadwicke had performed nobly his first act and his last; he was carried into the town, and was there discovered to be mortally wounded. His brother had been also severely wounded, and was lying suffering great agony, when the dying youth was taken into hospital, and laid by accident along side of him. The wound of the younger hastened his life fast to a close, and that of the elder, only left him strong enough to observe the youthful brother dying.

He died, and of any martial scene which we witnessed, his funeral was perhaps the most soul-exciting. The colours which he had so bravely carried, and retained even after his death-wound, were laid on his coffin. The regimental band, and the muffled drums led the mournful procession, while a long array of mourners followed, mixing the rare accompaniments of gaudy display and real grief. The procession wended along the circuitous path, that leads round the rocky hill on which stands the citadel of San Sebastian. The very sea seemed listening, and when "earth to earth, dust to dust," had been

solemnly uttered, and the vollies which paid the last honor to the
dead, and startled the lonely seagull, had been fired ; the remains of
this hero of tender years, were left to rest in the narrow nook of
earth behind the castle.

His brother recovered, and some of those who then mourned for
the illfated youth, have been laid in the same place.

One of the subalterns of the 3rd regiment wounded on the 5th of
May, was a Lieutenant Jackson. This young man was also an enthu-
siast in the profession of arms. His father had been an officer in the
Royal Marines, and on the youth going out to Spain, the father
followed and got a captaincy in the 6th (Scotch) regiment. The
wife of the latter, thus having her husband and son in Spain, had her
hopes all away, and she was destined to suffer severely. The elder
Mr. Jackson got appointed to command what was termed for a time
the invalid battalion, but he shortly after died, and though his son
applied frequently to the pay-master of the 6th regiment for his
father's accounts, there was some unaccountable objection made to
their being given up. A settlement was put off from time to time,
and had not been effected when the young man fell mortally wounded
on the 1st of October. He died, and was buried at the same time
and place with Lieut. Bakehouse, of the Artillery, formerly mentioned. Their graves were beside those of Chadwicke and the brave
Major Mitchell who fell on the 5th of May, and who I believe was
the first interred there. The deaths of a husband and son were, to
the wife and mother, a severe affliction, and it is said that she has not
been able yet to get any satisfactory information of their accounts, a
matter which has many parallels in the Legion's history, but which
would have been otherwise had pay-masters and commanding officers
kept their accounts in a more honest shape than they generally did.

When the attack by the Carlists on the 6th of June following that
of the 5th of May occurred, Adjutant Keevil, who had too often and
too long made himself obnoxious to his regiment, wrought his own
disgrace. He was in San Sebastian when the action began, and
continued there on some pretence of business, though more than one
order had been sent to him by Colonel Churchill requiring his immediate attendance. When the fight was over, he made his appearance
and was then ordered back to his quarters as a prisoner under arrest.
The option of resigning or standing a court-martial was given

him, and he choosing the former, came home to England. His history since is short and mournful. He died in a low lodging house literally of starvation.

Many severe remarks have been made by persons unfriendly to the Legion, on the promotions of officers from the ranks. With a very few exceptions, these remarks have been equally ungenerous and unjust, for the officers who were elevated from the ranks in the Legion, proved themselves an unanswerable argument in favour of merit being the standard of promotion. Take Major Maclaine in the first place. This officer had been at one time a private in the Royal British Artillery. He obtained a commission in the Legion, and became one of its best officers; indeed, an officer that would have been an honor to the military profession in any service. He had some portion of conceit about him, which probably in a person of haughtier birth, would have been called high breeding, and it only wanted that appellation in him, because he had not been high bred. One of the principal incidents that befel him in the Legion, was his being in the Westminster picquet house, as the picquet was called which the enemy attacked, and which the 3rd regiment so gallantly defended on the morning of the 1st of October, and having had his brave and effectual conduct on that occasion disputed by Major Lister. Both these officers were at that point of attack, and it was generally allowed that even the officer doing least had won credit for gallantry that morning, but these two disputed the merit of having defended the position, until reinforcements came. To settle this, a court of enquiry was ordered to take evidence and decide; and that being done, the decision was in favour of Major Maclaine, even so much in his favour, that it left Major Lister with a less share of the merit of having defended the position than he would have had allotted to him, and would have retained, had no dispute existed. Major Maclaine enjoyed the confidence and high respect of all the officers.

Another officer of good reputation raised from the ranks was a Mr. Brown. The tale of his promotion is told among the other officers with some humour, at least by those who had no good will to such promotions. He was raised through the interest of Colonel Churchill, who as has been said, was a liberal in politics, and who in accordance with his professions practised liberal actions. He had seen Brown as a corporal to be a clever soldier and worthy of promotion, and had
No. 23.

therefore recommended and procured for him a commission. As will be readily supposed, a man serving in the ranks of the Legion could not be transformed all at once into a gentleman with a superfine surtout and epaulettes, gold lace, &c., and that therefore the first stages of the transformation must have been rather ludicrous. Lieut. Colonel Wakefield of the 1st Lancers having been in company with Colonel Churchill when the corporal was made an officer, described the ceremony afterwards to have been in this way.

Colonel Churchill called his orderly, and that official making his appearance in due time and with due respect, the colonel said, " orderly, send Corporal Brown to me immediately." The orderly disappearing to fulfil his mission, Churchill turned to Wakefield and said, " this Corporal Brown that you will see just now, is one of my best men. I have got a commission for him."

Corporal Brown came in, and with a long lean body and thin visage, thin either by nature or hunger, or perhaps both, stood at attention before his colonel, expecting with wonder what was to be done with him. The latter, full of that manner and tone, which as a commanding officer and a gentleman he never forgot, because nature fitted him to wear them ; and with that liberal condescension which accorded with his political professions, though rather inharmonious with surrounding circumstances—said " Corporal Brown, I have ordered you to attend here, to inform you that you were recommended to his Excellency the Lieutenant General, as a fit person to hold a commission in Her Catholic Majesty's service, and I have farther the pleasure to inform you that his Excellency has been pleased to appoint you a Second Lieutenant of my regiment. Lieutenant Brown, will you do me the favor to dine with me this evening ?" The astonished corporal stood for a moment and eyeing the brown sapattas on his feet, his red jacket which had been worn day and night for the preceding six months, with a piece of calico peeping from the elbows, which, though rather impure was still his best shirt.—The astonished corporal taking himself into consideration, pondered on the reality or delusion of his being *Lieutenant* Brown. But the condescension of Colonel Churchill eased the momentary perplexity ; for the Colonel having done the official part of the interview broke into a more familiar colloquy. Mr. Brown proved himself a good officer, and is at the time of this being written (August 1838) Adjutant to the company of English Artillery, which still remains in Spain, and which is, and has been the most effective in good services to the Queen, of any corps sent out of this country.

When General Evans issued a general order to the effect that all meritorious men would find a ready recompense for good conduct; he promoted a man named M'Intosh as an instance. This officer proved himself rather an exception, and is one of those referred to as a dishonor to the commission he held. He was, however, a clever officer, and also a brave one, his error of conduct was therefore not without the accompaniment of some merit, though at the same time it must be pronounced disgraceful. Being on picquet one night he, with the men under his command, went across the lines, and attacking some peasants' houses, plundered the inhabitants and on these making some resistance—murdered an old man the father or grandfather of one of the families. They brought off their booty and having fired a few rounds of ball cartridge to let it be heard that they had done something, told next day their story of having been attacked by a Carlist picquet—their having driven it back, &c. Mr. M'Intosh among other things, had obtained possession of a silver cup, which, with a quantity of linen, he sent into his quarters in San Sebastian. After going off picquet and getting home, having received thanks for his ready efficiency the night before in repelling the attack of the *midnight marauders*, he was displaying his booty to the people on whom he was billeted. To their horror they saw the silver cup of their own family, the long cherished treasure of their father, and the linen marked with their family name. The same day information was conveyed to them that their father's house had been robbed—that he was murdered—that their sisters had been polluted, and that the family home was in ruins. An investigation was immediately demanded by the authorities of San Sebastian, and which being made traced the guilt of the robbery, and the entire blame of the incursion to the picquet of the 3rd regiment, and of course to Mr. M'Intosh who commanded it. He was dismissed; but afterwards permitted to re-enter the service as a volunteer, and again got a commission He is now a pauper and an inmate of one of the metropolitan workhouses.

Another officer whose conduct is said to have proved that persons without high connections or high pretensions, are unfit to hold com—

missions, was Mr. Wilkinson, the officer who went to the Carlist camp with his wife, and whose pamphlet I have quoted in a preceding chapter. He resigned his commission in the Legion, through the ungenerous treatment of Brigadier General Shaw, or rather he was dismissed through the misrepresentations of that officer. His case, though not lying wholly within the range of my present sketches, is yet so full of interest and involves the character of the Generals of the Legion so peculiarly, that something farther must be explained, so that shame may rest with the General to whom it belongs.

It appears his treatment in the Carlist camp was good, until a circumstance, diabolically ingenious, caused the Carlists to arrest and imprison him, and thrice make preparations for putting him to death. General Shaw, who, not satisfied with having deprived Wilkinson of his commission, and from mere caprice, expelled him from the service, blasting whatever hopes he had founded on it—pursued him with his hatred even beyond that, and for no better reason, according to the General himself than that Wilkinson had been only a corporal in the Portuguese service, and had now the audacity to be an officer. Having his head always full of some project, continually doing, or talking of doing something that no officer but himself would have thought of, Shaw wrote a letter one day, and had it conveyed to near the Carlist positions, and there dropped, in such a place as they were likely to find it. It was addressed to Mr. Wilkinson, and was as nearly in the following words, as can be recollected—an exact copy not being to be had.

"My dear Wilkinson.——How is it we have not heard from you lately? We got the deserters sent over by you; but were disappointed at not finding more, in consideration of the money furnished. We have still confidence and believe you to be doing the best for us you can. But that Plan of the Carlist defences, and the State of their strength have some important omissions. I hope you will remedy these by making such amendments as may be necessary from subsequent alterations in the affairs around you. We are rather impatient at your inactivity; for we certainly expected more success to follow your eminent abilities when we sent you over. Be so good as attend to this. You will receive your money in the usual way—

        Yours my dear Sir——"

This letter being found, and opened by the Carlist officers, caused

Wilkinson to be immediately arrested and thrown into confinement. He lay in that state for a considerable time, and was twice ordered to prepare himself for immediate death! but something was deemed necessary to be done in the way of finding out his accomplices before shooting him. He was at last taken out for execution, when fortunately for him, a superior officer of the Carlist army, who knew more of English letter writing than to believe that the style of that was genuine, suggested, that it was most probably intended for the destruction of Mr. Wilkinson, and that if so, nothing would please General Evans better than its being deemed genuine. Thus, General Evans lost character even with the Carlists by a diabolical scheme of General Shaw; for such things would naturally be credited to the account of the Chief of the Legion by those who did not know the genius of some of his officers. In the Spanish war, prisoners have been put to death on both sides—confidence has been betrayed on both sides, and men of all parties have become the victims of treachery—but a more infamous scheme to destroy an enemy, even deserving death, was never devised by any Carlist or Christino partizan than this.

The friends of Lieutenant Keogh are informed that the author is engaged in getting correct information on the subject of cowardice charged against that officer. The whole proceedings on which Captain St. Leger and others founded their opinion were irregular, and in the author's view, seem to aggravate the case of Lieutenant Keogh, yet he willingly gives that officer the benefit of the denial that has been made on his behalf; namely, that the act of cowardice as related in chapter 17th is "false and scandalous." The affair will be found fully balanced with the evidence for, and against Mr. Keogh in the appendix to this work, and in the meantime, the author is willing to let the public believe that he has published a "a false and scandalous" charge, rather than that Mr. Keogh should suffer in character until his guilt is established, and that cannot be farther entered on in the body of the work, as the document from which information was taken will be found appended among others at the end. The author, however, assures these, and others who complain, that it arises from no love of persecuting defenceless individuals as has been insinuated that he has thus exposed the names of certain officers. In the case of Lieutenant Keogh, the notice arose from the notoriously unjust conduct of General Fitzgerald towards other officers who did their duty well, while it was alleged that Lieutenant Keogh was favourably treated although he neglected his duty. It seems certain, that Mr. K. was absent from the engagement, but whether *with*, or *without* leave, whether *on duty*, or *not on duty* in Sebastian where he was seen, shall be hereafter determined. General Fitzgerald asserted that Lieutenant Keogh had an order to go into the town ; if so, General F. is more awkwardly situated than he was supposed to be, and the Adjutant-General, as well as General Evans himself, were all guilty of irregularities which they will not like to see exposed in the history of their courts-of-enquiry and courts-martial.

The Pedro Hamilton, who figures on page 321 and whose duelling propensities are detailed in this work, is not the gentleman of that name, at present in London —nor is he a Scotchman—he is, as he loved to say himself, a natural son of the Duke of Leinster, and is at present, (August, 1838,) in Ireland.

The reflection on the character of the officers of the 4th regiment, namely, " that they were willing to get rid of Pedro, on other grounds than that of his being no gentleman—that he was known to be a good shot, &c."—was not written by Major Stewart. That officer has no alliance with the author, whatever ; every line of this work, humble though they may be, are written by the person whose name is on the title page, excepting those marked as extracts. The encomium on Major Stewart's character, though offensive to some parties, the author still deems just ; it was called forth, not from his having any connexion with Major S., as is alleged by some correspondants ; but from the illiberal treatment of Major S. by General Evans, when the former interfered in behalf of the Santona prisoners, an interference more deserving the encomiums of any lover of humanity, than all, even all the actions of any single individual in the Legion. He was a severe and a strict disciplinarian, it is admitted ; but some of the officers of the 1st regiment will perhaps recollect, that in the excursion to the Ametzagana and its picquet houses, as mentioned in the following chapter—that when other companies plundered, and spoiled the people's furniture and committed crimes brutally infamous, which it would be a pollution to write—when one officer could only take back with him *three* men, the whole of his company being beyond his controul among plunder—Major Stewart marched back his company entire, not a man having been permitted to touch an article. Now this is the *men's* own report. They did not like Major S., certainly, and this was one of the causes, but it was not the terror of the lash that wrought that ascendancy ; others flogged as much as he did, but had no controul over their men in such cases as that just alluded to. It was his unrelaxing attention to duty leading as well as forcing, that made Major S. so successful in his discipline, I am sorry that any act of undue severity ever tarnished his otherwise honourable reputation ; but, it is because one party denounces him for severity, and another made him suffer for his interference in behalf of the ill-treated prisoners of Santona, that his name is introduced, and his reputation defended in this work, other, than in these relations, he *is* entirely unknown to the author, and the insinuations of certain parties are therefore groundless.

CHAPTER XIX.

The Rifles—Lieut. Colonel Fortescue, and Captains Atkyns, O'Rielly, Jeffrey, and other Officers of the regiment on the 5th of May, Corporal Withers, &c.—The 1st of August, the Ametzagana taken and lost, conduct of the Officers on that occasion, Colonel Apthorpe, Major Stewart, Captains Stapleton, Rigg, Harris, and others of the 1st regiment, Captains Atkyns and Brown of the Rifles, their adventures—Anecdote of a Rifle Officer on the 1st of October—The siege of Bilbao by the Carlists, taken by the English Seamen, and British Marine Artillery—Christmas—Preparations for the general engagement in March, &c. &c.

THE Rifle corps of the Legion have yet to be noticed, and if my humble sketches are in any measure a compliment to them ; that compliment is paid with sincere assurances of high respect for their military reputation. If degrees of merit belonged to the regiments of the Legion, the Rifles possessed the highest. Many convincing proofs were given by themselves, and many might now be recorded ; but I shall at the present time notice only a few.

On the 5th of May, Lieut.-Colonel Fortescue having taken the command, which the Baron de Rottenberg resigned two days before —which he resigned, as some said, not very honorably, an action with the enemy being expected ; but which I believe he resigned from his suffering a painful disorder, which at that time, was daily growing worse, and which had he continued longer on duty, and such duty as was expected, would have cost him his life :—Colonel Fortescue having succeeded him in command of his regiment, had a glorious opportunity to display that reckless gallantry, which philosophers may call folly; but which the lovers of perilous bravery must admire. At a time, when the contest had lasted about three hours, and the success of the combatants had been doubtful ; the enemy repulsing with fearful effect, the gallant attacks of different regiments of the Legion on some houses in which they were entrenched, the Rifles came up to a point at which a stand was made by the assailants. The 6th regiment under Colonel Tupper, had twice made an attempt on these houses, and finding them surrounded by ditches, and the ditches fortified by musketry ; besides two pieces of cannon being at a short distance, so ranged that grape and cannister shot could meet the assailants, they had been forced to fall

back, each time leaving a large number of their men behind them ;
General Evans had come from some other point of the attack, and
exposing himself to the enemy's fire, stood up on a wall and waved
his sword to cheer the men onwards.　His example had no effect,
the 6th were shattered to pieces, and Colonel Tupper who never
shrunk from anything within possibility, however dangerous, told the
General the position was impregnable, unless there was cannon to
batter a breach.　Colonel Fortescue coming up with about two
hundred of his regiment, the remainder being killed, wounded, or
holding positions which he had already taken ; offered to go forward
and take the place that the 6th had twice attempted unsuccessfully.
He had no sooner made the proposition, than Captains Atkyns,
O'Reilly, Lieut. Jeffrey, and others, volunteered to lead the attempt.
The men also volunteered to go forward, and being led out of the
partial shelter where they stood, they were at once under the fire of
the enemy.　Colonel Cottoner of the Chapelgorris cheered on his
brave troops, and pointing to the Rifles, told his men to follow the
English ; but the Chapelgorris who rarely halt when it is possible
to go forward, hesitated there, having previously made the attempt
and found it impossible.　Colonel Cottener, however, followed the
Rifles, and when some of the most resolute of the Chapelgorris,
were rushing forward, against their consciousness of the impossibilities before them, he fell severely wounded, and they retired.
The Rifles went on, and as they went, they strode over the dead of
the 6th regiment, who had previously charged on the same ground.
Most of the latter had a number of balls in them, the Carlists from
behind the walls, having marked them as they lay wounded and
unable to get into cover.　The tartan plaids which they wore, were
now strewed about among blood, and some of these were waved
from the walls behind which the enemy were entrenched ; they
having come out and stripped the dead within their reach.　The
naked body of Lieut. Balfour of the 6th was seen dreadfully mangled,
he having been at first wounded, and then slain by the party that
stripped him.

　　The Officers of the Rifles say, that on looking back they saw their
own men mingled among the dead of the 6th, and between what
were killed, and wounded, or had rolled into the ditches to save themselves from the dreadful shower of bullets that scattered among

them, they had lost about two thirds of those that had formed the party five minutes before. About fifty were up to the position; but to their horror and consternation, no possibility of entrance presented itself. A ditch surrounded the houses, and behind it was a wall perforated with loop-holes, through which hundreds of muskets vomited fire and smoke. Similar discharges came from the windows above, and the gallant but ill-fated party looked at each other, as their number was every moment lessening. The Colonel had not got forward, having received a severe wound by the way. Captain Atkyns was also wounded, and some of the men faithful to him, as he well deserved, were carrying him to shelter. A gallant young man, Corporal Withers a native of London, had among the many brave ones there, shown himself particularly forward; he cheered on the others, and amid that deadly fire and strife, as he had frequently done during the morning, he took aim with his rifle, and struck a Carlist Officer who was at a window cheering his men to repel the assailants. Undaunted by the numbers falling around him, Withers reloaded, and fired at the very muzzles of the enemy's muskets, and sent his bullets through their own loop-holes. When retreat became the only alternative, and the most of the surviving party were retreating, Withers fell dead at the side of his Officer, Lieut. Jeffrey. And this young Officer himself, (at that time not quite eighteen years of age,) had gone to the very walls of the fortification, though he got a musket shot in his belly on coming first under the fire. He had gone on with his hand on the wound, and now was nearly the last person retreating. Along side of him was Captain O'Reilly, who, when they had gained their retreat about half way, started with a wild leap from the ground, and fell backwards. Jeffrey looked behind him, and poor O'Reilly lay with his head split in two pieces. The next moment, a bullet struck Lieut. Jeffrey beneath the shoulder joint, cutting open the arm-pit. He had but a few yards farther to go until he would reach a partial shelter; but before he gained that, a third bullet made its way through the calf of one of his legs. Exhausted by fatigue, and the loss of blood, he sunk down, after telling what the position of the enemy was, and that the attempt to storm it was impracticable; and his wounds being examined, it was found that the first bullet had entered near the ribs on the left side, and had barely missed the intestines in its progress to the back; that it had there made its exit, carrying with it a part of the buckle of his sword belt. This was a singular wound; Lieut. Jeffrey having received no injury to any part of his intestines, though the bullet had made its rough ingress and egress at the two extremities of the ribs on the left side.

On the disastrous proof that the position was beyond the power of infantry, the General dispatched Lord William Paget to order up the Artillery to that point, and the moment his Lordship rounded a corner to gain the road by which he was ordered to go, his horse was shot beneath him. The Carlists at that place continued for a while unmolested, taking aim at any one who casually came within their reach, and popping bullets from behind their walls into the remnants of the rifles who shewed any signs of life as they lay scattered among the dead of the 6th. This position was afterwards taken and fearfully did the poor Carlists pay for those they had killed of the English. Captain Newcombe, a brave officer, the only one of the Rifles who had returned from that disastrous attempt unhurt, succeeded Colonel Fortescue in command of his corps for the day. The other officers wounded in the Rifles that day were Captains Costello, (an old soldier of the peninsular war,) and Durie, Lieut. Durie, second Lieuts. Barker and Hanbury.

An occasion on which the Rifles were smartly engaged, was the 1st of August following the other engagements spoken of. The Ametzagana, a hill which has been frequently referred to, had been taken by the Legion on the 28th of May. The Carlists re-took it on the 11th of July, when a small force was left protecting the lines in the absence of the main body which was on that day fighting and preparing to retreat from Feuntarabia. General Jaurregui—(*the shepherd*)—gave an order that the Ametzagana should be re-captured from the Carlists, and for that purpose, about three companies of the Rifles and as many of the 1st regiment were picked out and ordered to the assault. Nothing had been done in a superior style to this by either of the regiments; but it wanted much of that credit which it would have obtained had not General Evans dissented from the propriety of taking the Ametzagana at that time. Captain Rigg of the 1st, led the front, and being closely followed by Lieut. Colonel Apthorpe, Major Stewart, Captains Harris and Stapleton of the same corps, and Captains Atkyns, Brown, and others of the Rifles, the hill was speedily in possession of the Legion. It was deemed necessary however, to go farther than merely getting possession of the hill ; the picquet houses ranging in its vicinity, were also attacked, and it was at these where the smartest contest took place. Colonel Apthorpe pushed on with a company and took possession of one, while Major Stewart as anxious to signalize himself, went farther, and scattering the enemy took possession of two houses which he supposed would be then required for the out-picquets of our lines.' To his surprise, however, he heard a *retreat,* and he withdrew his men.

On the *retreat* being sounded, the Carlists, more swift of foot than any that contended with them, were soon on the rear of the English. Indeed it seemed on such occasions that they sprung up in the ditches and hedges around their retreating foes as beings not natural, so difficult was it to account for their sudden appearance on the heels of those who had a few minutes before been pursuing them at half a mile's distance. Captain Atkyns of the Rifles, the same who was distinguished, and severely wounded on the 5th of May, had been endeavouring to collect his scattered company. He had left the most of it at some point under charge of his subaltern, and was proceeding forward to recall some of his men who he supposed had not heard the *retreat.* Seeing a number of Spaniards a short distance to his left, he walked up to them, and he having a dark regimental uniform, thought that they might mistake him for some lingering Carlist stealing away to meet his party, and lest they might by that mistake, give him the compliment of a bullet, he uttered as he approached them, the common test word " *Viva Isabel segunda,*" to his horror and dismay, " *Viva Carlos Quinto*" was the reply, and ere he could form a thought, of what he might say, he was seized by two stout fellows of the party, and his sword stripped off. Astounded at finding himself thus unexpectedly among about a hundred of the enemy, and that, an enemy that spared no lives, he was beginning to reflect what would become of him, when he saw Captain Brown coming walking up also ; Brown happening to throw a glance before him, observed the unhappy Atkyns in the grasp of his foes, and wheeling about, as well became him, he took flight while the whole party discharged a volley of balls after him. He still ran on, and the officer of the party being engaged in trying on his new prize —Captain Atkyns' sword—the latter perceived the men to be attracted to the hasty flight of Captain Brown, while at the same moment they were all seizing hold of cartridges to re-load for another volley, and ere they were aware, he sprung from their grasp, and dashing through the group like a fox from his cover he was bounding onwards over hedge, ditch, bank, and scaur, when the rattling volley rose loud behind him, and the bullets scattered over head, and around his feet ; yet he was untouched. Other bullets came hissing past, but they went idly in the air, and he got back unharmed, only being stripped of his sword. Not so Captain Brown; one ball grazed his thigh, and another shattered his hand, yet even with these he was fortunate. Two or three of the men were missing, who were never more heard of; they were probably not so lucky, and therefore got what the two officers narrowly escaped from. Three wounded Carlists had been taken prisoners, and were sent into San Sebastian to the hospital, when the English got first to the top of the hill, and their treatment may be contrasted with that received by our men in their hands.

It was said, that General Chichester ordered the Ametzagana to be evacuated, and other reports say, that the Carlists chased the English from it by the suddenness of the retreat, and the disorder, consequent on the men having gone too far in search of plunder ; whichever report is true, it is certain that the Carlists re-occupied the hill within four hours of their losing it ; and though nothing was more bravely done or could well be, than the taking of it, in the same proportion—there was nothing more dishonorably lost. The companies of the 1st regiment, had fourteen men wounded on the excursion, and the Rifles, about as many; among whom, was a Sergeant Major killed, who was shot from the top of the hill, when making his descent after the Carlists had regained it. This hill was in their possession until the 10th of March the following spring.

On part of the ground of this fruitless excursion, the general action of the 1st of October was fought. We may here remark, that the Rifles were again severely engaged. Captain Jeffrey, who was Lieut. on the 5th of May, and who was so severely wounded, had recovered during the summer and was again wounded on the 1st of October. He is a handsome young officer, and, as was the case with many, who did not possess his peculiar gracefulness of person, he had won the affections, or at least, agreeable attentions of a young lady of San Sebastian. Nothing could be more kind than the attention of all the females of that place to the wounded; and Captain Jeffrey, will perhaps, admit, should this ever reach his eye, that he was not sorry on the 1st of October at getting a *nice* wound, that sent him a few months into his billet, on the sick list—nor, will any one doubt his satisfaction, when it is known that he was billetted on a lady whose lovely daughter was the fair minister of cordials, and the many little tender attentions that made a wound endurable. Some of the men who were witnesses of Captain Jeffrey's wound, on the 1st of October, tell an anecdote of it, which is worth noticing.

A musket ball struck him on the cheek, a little above the edge of the mouth and lodged by his ear. Mr. Duplex, the skilful and attentive surgeon of the Rifles, with his assistant, was engaged, taking out the bullet by the way at which it entered; Captain Jeffrey, suffering that, rather than he would allow a slight cut to be made to let it out. The surgeon said, it must be cut; "No," replied the youth, "I'm ugly enough, as it is, with one hole in my face;" and the surgeon again tried to make the ball return by its own entrance. But, when so engaged a heavy cannon ball came in among them, throwing up the earth with such violence and causing such a concussion in the air that they were all knocked to the ground, and the young officer, who was so anxious to preserve his beauty, was obliged afterwards to submit to having the ball cut from his cheek as there was not time to parley longer with it. It was said, the young lady fainted, or nearly so, when she saw her lover brought in wounded; but, whether from the distress of grief for the pain he suffered, or joy, that she was to have the dear occupation of nursing him, as Haidee did Juan, I am not informed, but she performed the sweet task :—

> " And every day, by day-break—rather early
>   For *Jeffrey*, who was somewhat fond of rest;
> She came into the *room*, but it was merely
>   To see her bird reposing in his nest;
> And she would softly stir his locks so curly,
>   Without disturbing her yet slumbering guest;
> Breathing all gently o'er his cheek and mouth,
>   As o'er a bed of roses, the sweet south."

On the 16th of December, 1836, orders were issued to the 6th, 7th, and 8th regiments of the Legion, and to some regiments of Spaniards to be in readiness to march next day. The sea was behind us, the enemy in front and on our flanks, therefore we could have little doubt of the direction in which we were to march, particularly as these regiments did not know but the whole forces on the lines were ordered to move. During the night preparations were made, and the turnout anxiously expected, as whispers said that we were to move forward on the left positions of the enemy before daybreak. Towards midnight, when ammunition and mules were being got ready, a light was seen to ascend into the air from some house in San Sebastian, but from what particular house no one had been able to mark. On this appearing, lights of the rocket kind blazed at intervals from one extremity of the Carlist lines to the other, and by that means spread the alarm, that they were about to be attacked. That they had agents in the Christino garrison had been always suspected, and was now proved beyond doubt; but the most vigilant of the authorities in San Sebastian were either unable or unwilling to detect them, for they were not discovered; indeed the belief prevailed that the traitor was the Alcalde, or chief magistrate himself. The intended attack was put off to another day, and as it was only to take possession of the hill on which stands the Light-house, a position not deemed important, General Evans, at the suggestion of Lord John Hay and General Jaurragui, left it unmolested, to the satisfaction of those who would have had the most work and the least glory, amongst whom, I was one.

For nearly two months previous to this, the Carlists had drawn a great part of their forces from the different provinces towards Durango, which is a village easily defended, about six miles from Bilbao, and which Don Carlos has made his chief residence while in the north of Spain. Bilbao is well known as the commercial town of greatest importance on the north coast, and was, of course, important to the rival parties to contend about. Carlos had been first proclaimed King of Spain, and Lord of Biscay, in Bilbao ; but before he had an army, the Queen's party took possession of it ; and as there are a number of English merchants and French about it, and these having much influence with the other inhabitants, and choosing rather to court the protection of their native countries through the ships of

war that lay there for the protection of English merchant men,
Bilbao, by these means, became a Christino town.

The Carlists had, in November, got the command of the river
Nervion, and from the sea up to the gates of Bilbao, which is perhaps six or eight miles following the river, they held the town of
Portugalette, and all positions on both sides. They surrounded
Bilbao also on the other side, and commerce was thus completely
stopped. The inhabitants were reduced to distress for the want of
provisons; and Espartero fruitlessly contending with the Carlists on
one side, to drive them back and give relief. General Evans was
applied to, but refused to send any of his troops, because he had a
stronger force before him, and had defended himself against a
stronger force than that at Bilbao, he having only about four thousand
men, while there were as many Christino inhabitants armed in the
town, and Espartero was near it with seventeen thousand. But as
the relief of the English merchants was a pretext for the interference
of the British naval force, and especially as the Carlists were incau-
tious enough to fire on the Saracen English ship of war, lying in
the river, the forces under Lord John Hay had a pretext for active
retaliation. On the morning of the 22d of December, at day-break,
the Carlists opened a long twenty-four pounder from a battery thrown
up during the night on a causeway, above the bridge known by
the name of Luchana. This was principally directed against the
Saracen, and the Spanish war schooner Maria, lying near by. These
vessels, being too low to fire in return, a party of seamen from the
Saracen, and the Ringdove, which was lying farther down, went
ashore, and manned the battery of Anglo-Hispano with a thirty-two
pounder, and gave the Carlists a tremendous return of heavy shot.
Espartero was, in the meantime, on a range of heights called Esandia,
and was kept back by a heavy and unremitting fire from the Carlists.
Colonel Colquhoun had, a short while before this, returned from
England, and had command now of the Royal British Artillery. He
and they had been ordered to Bilbao, and with the field-artillery and
mountain-howitzers, (which last are carried on mules' backs,) he
took up a position on Esandia with Espartero, and in a short while
silenced the Carlists' battery at Luchana bridge.

At day-break a pontoon bridge, (that is, wooden boxes with a gang-
way of planks,) was thrown across the Gilando, a branch of the Ner-

vion, by the seamen of the Ringdove and Saracen, on which Espartero's troops crossed; and, supported again by Colquhoun, took
possession of a rising ground, and directed a heavy fire on one of the
strongest positions of the Carlists, Monte Cabras, and in a short
while silenced their guns in that quarter.

A long eighteen pounder brought from one of the vessels, Colquhoun's detachment, and a battery of Spanish artillery, commenced
a concerted fire, and did great havoc, so much so, that the Carlists
withdrew their artillery: but the dreadfully cold stormy weather, and
the flooded river, did not permit Espartero and Colquhoun to cross
and take up the positions till next day. In the interval, launches
and rafts had been prepared, and when the flood-tide was rolling up,
these, manned by sailors, English and Spanish artillery approached
to Luchana and Monte Cabras, the Carlist positions, during a heavy
fall of snow. The snow was so thick, that they landed before the
Carlist sentries could give the alarm. A bridge of boats was immediately laid across the river, and Espartero's army filed over, and
speedily took possession, the Carlists retreating towards Durango.
All their artillery, and a great number of prisoners, fell into the
Christino's hands. Among the latter was an Englishman, who had
been a sergeant in the Legion artillery, and had been taken prisoner
by the Carlists on the heights of Arlaban, when on a reconnoitering
excursion with Cordova, about twelve months before. He served the
Carlists all that time, and it was seen that he could have escaped
with them when they fled from Bilbao, but gave himself up to
Colquhoun. In consequence of that he got all his pay from the time
he had been absent from the Legion. The citizens of Bilbao, thus
relieved, were in an ecstacy of joy, and the soldiers, English and
Spanish, who had been out night and day in such bad weather, were
as well pleased at getting into warm quarters. Espartero remained
in Bilbao, and planned a movement with Saarsfield, who commanded
the other division of the Queen's army, near Pampeluna, and Evans
at San Sebastian, that they were to make in concert as soon as the
weather permitted; and let this be kept in mind, that these three
Chiefs occupied positions triangularly situated, and that the agreement was, when one of them moved, the others would do so; and
we shall in the next chapter see how these combined movements
were performed, and what was the Legion's share in them.

But it is necessary to notice a few occurrences in passing, and among others our Christmas, and our quarters at the merry season. The snow that came on and lay two feet deep on Christmas morning, drifted in the ruins of Antigua convent among the 6th. That regiment had decidedly the worst quarters. The 7th Irish occupied their city of huts, in which they were crowded, drinking and making merry. These huts, which they had built, were too small for the fighting and dancing, indispensable with the 7th, so that took place outside. If any one of another regiment went near them, he was sure that one of two things would happen to him—he would either be dragged into the hut and forced to drink and be merry, or he would be knocked down outside, perhaps both; but it was certain he could not go through *Irishtown* unmolested—drinking, dancing, and head-breaking, every visitor to the boys of the 7th had to calculate on. On the other side of the Urimea, there were the 9th and 10th Irish, with many a genuine Irishman full of frolic and mischief; and farther on, the English regiments lay in a village and some scattered houses. They had their quarters made into a little London : there were a Westminster in the village, a Cheapside, and a Constitution-hill. Perhaps few will believe, from being accustomed to hear such woful tales of the Legion, that the holidays were held so well with us as they were. Some extra money was allowed in addition to the daily mite, and every thing done by the General to admit of the men getting a few good dinners about the time that these were rife in England, and when it was supposed that the appetite would cause a retrospective sigh for the Christmases of former years. He was right, and both Irish and English vexed the drowsy hours with holiday mirth.

The advance that took place on the enemy's lines in March, had been talked of before its occurrence. We had read in the London newspapers that all preparations were now ready, and that the concerted movements of Saarsfield, Espartero, and Evans, from their different positions would take place in a few days, &c. These reports were often heard, and we had prepared so long for the coming hostilities, that new preparations became necessary. This was not causeless delay on the part of General Evans; he was bound to move in concert with the Spanish Generals; and for some months the snow embedded Espartero in the western mountains of Biscay, so com-

No. 24.

pletely that he could not move, but up on mountains of utter desolation. At last March came with fresh blowing winds, and the snow melted; Evans was informed that he would hear Espartero's cannon on the 10th of that month, on the southern front of the Carlists; and that he on the northern front, would, by pushing on, possess himself of Hernani, and thereby the high road leading to the frontier, and that the enemy thus hemmed in and forced to a combat of strength, or a surrender, while Saarsfield menaced their divisions at Pampeluna, would necessarily end the disastrous war.

I remember the 9th of March, it was a calm, clear cold, day, and regiments were parading in their full strength, no men absent. Regimental surgeons gave permission to the weakly and the useless to to go into San Sebastian, to the hospital, or if not entitled to be on the sick-list, they were sent to the different batteries on the lines to assist in garrisoning these, but in reality, to be as much out of the way as possible, for no one knew the extent of what was to be done next day. Two day's rations came out to each regiment; and mules after mules loaded with ammunition. General Chichester issued an order to his brigade, enjoining men and officers to pay respect to the life and property of all who were not actively fighting. "If you are kind to the people," he said, "they will remain in the towns and villages, and you will get what you want; but if they are not protected and kindly treated, they will flee to the mountains. Do not burn houses—we never yet burned a house but we had reason to regret it,"—and so on went his injunctions. The Lieutenant General's (Evans) orders principally related to the arrangements for the carrying of wounded men off the field; and positively forbade any of the same regiment to assist another who might fall, as an hospital transport corps had been formed for the purpose of carrying the wounded. During the afternoon groups of soldiers in all parts, in and out of quarters, were heard discussing the probabilities of to-morrow. The Legion artillery at one place, and the Royal British and Royal Marine at another, were out, and, with the Rocket Brigade, were paraded and getting their field artillery as near the lines as possible, there to be ready. Some of the heavier guns, that could not be taken where we were going, were planted on different positions where they would be effective in case of a reverse. Two of these were laid on carriages at the new wooden bridge, close to San Sebastian;

and I recollect that a friend with whom I walked, remarked as we took a stroll round to see what was going on, that there was something dispiriting in conceiving the bare idea of these guns being required. Still prudence demanded all preparations to be made. A pisetta—which is four Spanish *reals*, or equal to tenpence-halfpenny British—was advanced to each man, to buy tobacco and other necessaries with, and in all the streets of San Sebastian, crowds of soldiers were in the shops making their purchases—a number joining together and taking a quantity of coffee, chocolate, and such things with them ; for it must be observed that the fight was not expected to be all over on one day. Experience had told every one how valuable anything warm, such as coffee was, when laying out on the open fields at night, and the greater part, instead of spending their money in spirits, were buying those articles. I thought, however, it would not be amiss to have a small *drop* with me ; so a bottle of cogniac was got, and put very secretly into my haversack, while I thought that I could be able to serve myself, and surprise my best friends around the picquet fire some night with it ; but, alas ! I was disappointed—however, *its* fate will be known hereafter.

Presuming that the other regiments of the Legion spent the night similarly to that in which I was, it is deemed unnecessary to particularize them. Officers packed up what trifling articles they meant to carry with them, and deposited what they did not intend to carry, with the inhabitants of the town on whom they were billeted. Servants prepared their master's dinners and their own for next day. Men in quarters cooked their two-day's rations ; beams of wood being taken from the roofs of the old convents to make blazing fires, and in some cases the boards were burned that had served for temporary beds and doors in the frail habitations; those who complained that it was a shame to burn these things, being answered by " Oh we'll never see this place again, let us live when we can ; if we beat them we'll get quarters in Hernani, and if they beat us there'll not be many of us to come back," &c. Some smoked, and sung by turns; some damned, and some sat silent and looked wistfully at the burning fires and boiling kettles. One might be heard saying " I'll carry no more beef than I'm to eat, I'm sure of a bullet, and I'm d—d if I carry beef wi'me." Another would answer that it was a shame to speak that way ; it was enough to tempt Providence, to be swearing at such a time; and then two or three would strike in with "Providence! what has Providence to do wi' the Legion? Providence 'ill not keep the bullets from your head to morrow if they are marked for ye," &c. &c. Others said "whisht; it is as well to be decent." Very few thought of laying down to sleep, for, besides the time being short, the blanket and greatcoat were strapped up by each man, ready to put on, the moment the order to accoutre went round. No knapsacks were to be used, these being ascertained by this time to be of great hindrance to fighting on the broken hilly ground, of the North of Spain.

"On your accoutrements, men and turn out," was the word passed quietly through the quarters at an hour past midnight, and this was quickly obeyed. Every man had been ready; and each put on his belts, took up his musket, and walked out, where Captains f companies, and non-commissioned-officers were telling off the companies into the usual subdivisions, sections, right, and left files, and proving them with as little noise as possible.

At a short distance from us, the Lancers were turning out; they having been in readiness, and like us, aroused without the usual "turnout" sounds of their trumpets. On the glacis before San Sebastian, were the Field Artillery, and Rocket Brigade, with large quantities of ammunition on mules. The hospital Transport Corps with stretchers for the wounded, and all the other various appurtenances were ready. Spanish regiments marched along in the dark, and passed English ones, in taking their different directions to the positions allotted to them. We crossed the Urimea by the bridge, and on going up its bank, met the 10th, and other regiments moving off like us to join their respective Generals of Brigade at points appointed.

About four thousand Spaniards, the 9th and 10th Irish, and the 1s and 3rd English, with the Lancers Artillery &c., moved to the southward of the Ametzagana, the most of the Spaniards as far as Alza. The 6th and 7th, remained for some time longer by their respective quarters; on the western extremity of our lines, we being all towards the southern extremity. General Chichester's brigade, which consisted of the Rifles, 4th and 8th regiments formed in close column behind one of the newly erected batteries, (Queen's), and there we awaited in anxious suspense the first peep of daylight, with which it was said, we were to break the peace of the morning, and rush in on the lines of the enemy.

CHAPTER XX.

The morning of the 10th of March—The fight during the day—The mountain on fire at night—The Legion bivouacing—Outrages committed by men of the 4th regiment—Crossing the river on the 12th—Sketches of character and incidents Attack of the 14th stopped by bad weather—The Carlist military accoutrements contrasted with the English equipments—Extract of a general order relative to cowardice among the Spanish troops.

At last the dawn appeared, the black east was transformed into a thin grey, and the shapes of the hills were becoming discernible. The whispers that had prevailed all the morning, became gradually lower in expectation; and at last died into silence, as General Chichester's tall figure was seen approaching us from the battery, where he had been standing watching a signal. " Gentlemen," he said, addressing himself to the Colonels of the three regiments under his command, " call your columns to attention, and load."

The orders of " prime and load" were given, and while the ramrods were giving their stifled sound above the cartridges, a flash of fire shot across the sky, and a loud burst of Artillery shook the air, and told that the work had begun. These cannon had opened at Alza, nearly a mile from us; but in a few moments the guns along other parts of the lines followed, and the fire flashes illuming the clouds, and the trembling firmament quivering by the shock of the heaviest pieces, spread an awfully grand illusion over the commencement of the action. " Rifles! forward!"—" 4th! forward!"—" 8th! forward !"—" double !"—" the whole double !"—and other orders were mingled together, and by sundry movements of right-wheels, and right-turns, then left turns &c.; to preserve the best ground, and preserve the proper front; we, at double speed were on our way to be met in the fight, as the foe deemed best to meet us.

At the same moment that Chichester's brigade moved forward on the Ametzagana, the Irish Brigade from a more southern point, rushed forward on it also; the 9th regiment particularly, commanded by Colonel Cannon went boldly up, with the hero in front of them, who had in every action distinguished himself; who was now impelled by the irresistible force of his nature to be in front, though his place assigned by rank was in the rear; who, swayed by the same heroic gallantry, fought on the successive days of which this was a beginning, until his career closed in that awful but glorious manner which will be hereafter detailed :—I mean Major Cotter, formerly Captain of the light company in the 9th, and afterwards Lieut. Colonel. Cotter headed the party first in ascent on the Ametza, and the Carlists from seeing themselves beset on all sides, save their rear, and not only beset, but surrounded with an enemy rushing in on them. gave way; and leaving a quantity of ammunition on the hill, betook themselves to other positions ; where from having more time to make a stand, or where having from the first intended to make their stand ; they received, and returned the fire, of those regiments that were ordered to advance on them. The 9th being first on the Ametza; on the south side where the ascent is easy, and no resistance having been made, very much to our satisfaction, (I speak personally), we, ascended more leisurely on its north-western side, and piled arms.

" General, we'll get nothing to do, I think," one of our officers observed to Chichester. " Yes," he replied (hesitating), "I think we'll get *something* to do ; I did not expect that they would stand long here, but they are falling back on ground where they will stand, Do you see what they are doing yonder ?" This was towards a high rocky hill, and great clouds of smoke, mingled with the thunder of artillery and musketry, were rising, and shewed the place and determination of the combatants. Below us, in the valley of the Urimea, the female inhabitants were hurrying away into the interior of the country, carrying the more valuable and portable parts of their property with them, such as bundles of linen. All the men between childhood and old age were fighting. Many of the young women also were engaged with the Carlist army—carrying ammunition working with picks and shovels, throwing up breastworks, or assisting to carry the wounded. Therefore the people left in their houses were mostly old women, very old men, and young children. These we saw driving off their cows and bullocks (each family has two bullocks for working their small farm). The elder children helped the younger over the ditches ; and the aged and infirm crawled as they could. However, some of these last did not go away, for, being

either unable to go, or willing to trust to the mercy of the English
they remained; and as we passed their houses, the poor old people
stood at their doors and cheered the "Inglises." General Chichester
stood before the houses till we passed, and assured them that they
had nothing to fear. This was before we got up to the Ametza, for
when it was seen that the Carlists left it, we were taken by a circuitous road round it, and there being no more of the Carlists on the
same side of the river, near us, we were marched to the top of the
hill to look at the others fighting. Some poet has said of a battle—

> " By Heaven, it is a lovely sight to see,
> For him who has no friend or brother there."

It was a lovely sight ; but I had those whom I esteemed my friends
there. The wounded were brought in our direction, and they
thickly crowded the narrow road. For some hours they were chiefly
Spaniards, a great many of them Chapelgorris. Sometimes half-a-
dozen were carried along at once, and as they passed us, they
cheered and hurrahed, covered with blood.

Colonel Shaw of the Artillery, opened his guns early in the
morning from Alza, on the extreme left of our positions, and
under cover of these, three regiments of Spaniards advanced on
the enemy, and began, what to them was as sharp a day's work as
ever they encountered. The usual impetuosity of the brave, lawless,
undisciplined, intractable Chapelgorris, shone out on this occasion.
When they and the Carlists meet equal in number, the fight is equal;
when the Carlists meet any other corps equal in number to themselves they are vastly superior ; for on the mountains of the North
of Spain none but themselves are their parallels at a mountain fight,
and the Chapelgorris being a part of themselves, but fighting on
the Queen's side, are the only match for the Carlist enemy.
This remark, however, refers only to Infantry. As to Cavalry, the
ground is impracticable, and for artillery, it is often impossible to
bring guns of heavy calibre to bear on those, who, like goats skip from
one cliff to another, and bound across the mountains, sporting with
their enemy as if playing at *bo-peep* ; yet on this occasion—the 10th
of March, as on some others, the advantage was greatly on our side,
and the advantage was the effect of our artillery. The Carlists can
accommodate themselves to round shot ; even common shells become
customary to them, and they learnt to be more steady when these

fall among them, than they were at former periods of the campaign; also rockets, though always more effective in startling them from their positions than either shells or round shot, became in some measure less terrible by frequent use, because they could sometimes elude these missiles by shrinking behind walls, or clapping in ditches; and these sometimes striking against a wall in their course were rendered ineffective, or as at times, they were overshot. But there was one awful missile of death, which, from the universality of its destructiveness, spread unmingled terror into them, and when it could be brought to play with effect on any Carlist position it quickly dislodged them, as it well might, from the safest intrenchments in which they ever protected themselves; this was Spherical Case shot. Those whose profession is *war*, know the singular effects produced by this article of mischief, and therefore need no explanation. Those who are ignorant of what it is, may form an opinion of what the alarm among an enemy would be when the Spherical Case bursting slew men in all directions. The small shot with which it is charged, flies destructively on every side and to a wide distance; forwards, backwards, upwards, downwards, and all alike is death and ruin where it bursts. The Carlists therefore, who dexterously fire from behind trees, or stones, or any cover however slight; which cover affords them always some protection, less or more, from an enemy in front, are utterly confounded, and, as said before, may well be, when these Spherical Cases burst in their rear, or above them scattering death in every direction.

On the 10th of March there were not many of these used, perhaps from the impracticability of the positions; but what were used produced those effects that never fail to follow them. The Spanish regiments on our side sustained the hottest part of this day's engagement, and they stood manfully to their dexterous opponents, yet it is doubtful if they would have fought so well, had they not been so well supported by our artillery and rocket-brigade, as also by the 1st regiment of the Legion, some companies of which were posted across a ravine, to compel the Spaniards to stand to the enemy; to prevent the cowardly from skulking away from their regiments, and to take them prisoners if they were found skulking. For this necessity—the necessity admitted by the Spaniards themselves, see the order of General Oraa, issued to his troops after the battle of Barbastro, the noblest fight that ever the Carlists and Christinos fought, and yet full of disgrace to the Queen's troops;—that fight where Carlos and the best of his troops were hemmed in, where he must have been prisoner, and the war ended, had the Spaniards of the Queen stood firm,—that fight where their gallant General Irribarren stood hand to hand until he fell, the first General, it is believed, in the world that was killed fighting hand to hand! all other Generals, so far as records serve, having been slain by some missile thrown from a distance. This was that fight where the gallant French Legion fought when the Spaniards ran away, and stood until every field-officer fell, not even one being left. Relative to this fight, the general order of Oraa, referred to, was issued, and for which, see the concluding paragraph of this chapter. That will be a suitable commentary on the dreadful recitals of the 16th of March, that will appear in chapters following this.

To return to the 10th, the first day of the hostilities. Colonel De Lancy who commanded the 1st regiment by itself, independent of the other brigades, was engaged with the enemy for a short time in the morning, but having taken a position on the extreme left he remained there to support the Spaniards if necessary : but in the meantime to prevent them from retreating without orders. This duty on the ravine through which a good many had skulked from their respective regiments, was performed by Captain Rae and his company, an old veteran of whom honorable mention will be made soon. And while these precautions were made in the rear of the Spanish regiments to make them fight, it must be mentioned that General Evans with his usual gallantry, was in front. Time after time, he headed the Spaniards, and sword in hand, led them up the hill-side against their adversaries. It tells well for his magnanimous conduct in commanding on that occasion, that though the steadiness of the Spanish troops was not to be depended on, even so little to be depended on, that an English regiment was stationed behind them to prevent flight; that though this was done in their rear, he took the front personally, and led on to the fiercest combats of the day. He had altogether three horses either killed or severely wounded under him on that occasion. And though not wounded himself, he saw many of those that surrounded him fall. Some of these behaved most gallantly; but being mostly Spaniards, their names are neither in my possession, nor are they interesting to English readers.

From the Ametza hill on which our brigade (Chichester's) had piled arms, and from which we were spectators of the night raging towards our left, we had an opportunity of seeing the wounded as they were carried along to San Sebastian. During the whole day a continuous line of wounded Spaniards passed us, which for the first time gave me an opportunity of judging accurately of the evil arising to an army when soldiers are allowed to quit the field carrying off wounded comrades. Here humanity, and professional prudence are at variance, as in warfare they always are. Where so many were falling wounded every minute during the day, it was readily prompted by humanity, that they should be carried off the field, and ordinary means of taking them off were not practicable, the ground being so rough. Yet for soldiers—perhaps two, three, or sometimes four, to be allowed to carry away a wounded man was a great error in military economy, and one that produced results often dreadfully severe on those who from choice, or from being compelled, were still fighting.

A ridge on the contested ground of that day, was taken, and retaken by the two parties five times, each time with a severe loss to both sides. The importance of the position was its command of the road from Hernani to the frontier, which the Carlists were interested in retaining, and General Evans equally interested in wresting from them, as along that line of road their secret assistance came from home, and as along that road they would retreat should they be defeated, as expected to the westward. The road was to both parties important to be contended for, and the height commanding it on which the hot engagement took place, would have been ours, but for a circumstance not intended by either party, which did more than either could have done to decide the conflict. The fields of furze and brush-wood that surrounded its base, and the plentiful covering of the same kind that was spread on the rising ground took fire, and the wind being favourable to a conflagration, there was speedily one, on a scale grandly magnificent beyond anything we had previously witnessed. We had seen the same lines of smoke emitted from the combatants, and heard the same heavy unvaried roll of thunder during the day, while the sun had risen to the meridian, and descended on the unvaried conflict—unvaried to the eye and the ear, but varied often to the parties engaged, the ground being alternately in the possession of both parties: but as night drew on we saw the immense clouds of smoke thicken, and as twilight fell the volumes of fire that spread over the mountain before the hurricane of wind with which the day closed—was, the sublimity of grandeur.

We saw the sparkling musketry on the outskirts until a late hour, and that, had there been nothing to overcome its effect, would have been a fine scene for contemplation. It was the dying battle expiring in sparks as if human fuel was exhausted, or, as if the darkness had scowled on the combatants, and bade them cease, and all but an expiring rebellion against the reign of night had been quelled. That is, the scene would have been such, but for the mighty conflagration of the mountain. Contemplating it, the mind sought in vain to measure its magnificence! Immense piles of flame rose along all its breadth, of two miles or more, and seemed to be setting the clouds on fire;—as the clouds scudding along on the gale of wind, now and again reflected the illumination. Mankind had fought and ceased, and it seemed as if the elements in love with strife, had waged war and ran a race to desolation.

But while we beheld this as merely a spectacle. There were those to whom the spreading flames must have been awfully terrible. On various parts of the ground, wounded-men were lying, who by having fallen when the last change of positions occurred, were not rescued by their party; and who, being on the neutral ground over which the two parties fired, were left scattered about in various parts when the furze took fire; they must have been distracted with dreadful apprehension on seeing no possibility of escape. They perished more painfully, beyond measure, more dreadfully than if they had been slain in the fight,

The 6th, 7th, and 10th regiments, were slightly engaged at times during the day; but nothing remarkable occurred with them, save a few casualties which will be found referred to hereafter.

One incidental occurrence of that day, may be related however, as we pass, for it grew into an event in the life of some persons, and these persons have unfortunately for themselves, become rather celebrated since.

The Adjutant of the 1st Lancers, Lieut Disney who was, since his return to England, engaged in an unfortunate matrimonial specula-tion, for which, he having broken the law, is now doing penance in the neighbourhood of Woolwich; Disney had thought fit on the 10th

of March in front of the enemy, to flog a man for some act of misbehaviour. Often as the punishment was inflicted in Spain, there
were few Officers who ventured on its infliction, while close on the
enemy, when the person punished with smarting flesh and irritated
mind, could have almost immediate opportunities to retaliate an
unseen bullet on their punishers. Yet Lieut. Disney armed with the
authority of the Adjutancy, punished the man alluded to in front of
the enemy, and that too, when the soldiers emboldened by their
situation called out *shame*. The person punished, however, was
not one of the most amiable characters, his name, real, or assumed
was Steinson, and by the assumption of some other *alias* since he
came home, he contrived to mystify himself in the neighbourhood of
Manchester into a highwayman. He was tried and sentenced to
colonial transportation, and it is only pardonable to have alluded
to him at all, from the necessity of explaining that his story to the
judge and jury, which they according to newspaper report, listened
to with great attention ; that story which in a long rigmarole way,
he told about his having learnt the art of highway robbery in Spain,
that the Legion were so used to robberies, that he could not throw
off old habits ; that the pistols with which he was armed, had been
loaded in Spain; that he had travelled with the charges undrawn &c.
This was a generally received tale, and eagerly caught at by persons
who wished to stigmatize the Legion. But it is only necessary to
state, that he was a bad character when abroad, and that though a
good many such were in the Legion ; he was not a specimen of the
majority of men who served in that corps. Having received a
punishment as mentioned, he vowed vengeance on Disney, and was
afterwards transferred as a bad character from the Lancers, to the
10th regiment of Infantry. In that corps he had an opportunity to
retaliate on Disney, which he embraced on the 14th of May following as the troops attacked, and entered Hernani. Disney was in
front with the cavalry, when Steinson fired at him and shattered his
arm ; as it was not generally known from whence the bullet came,
it was put to the credit of the enemy, and Lieut. Disney got the
cross of Fernando for it.

On the night of the 10th, nearly all the regiments bivouaced, that
is, lay on the ground in the open air, during the night. I was on
picquet, and was therefore not altogether a voluntary observer of the

flaming mountain, for the duty of keeping a look out, turned our faces in the direction of the fire. The night was cold and tempestuous, far from being comfortable to those who lay in the open air, and I grieve to write, that some who had the privilege of good quarters; for a roof between their heads and the stormy sky, was good quarters; I grieve to write that those committed some of the crimes, that unhappily are too common in warfare; but which common as they are, never occur without exciting disgust in some, I would hope, the most of men.

The people spoken of in a preceding paragraph, who remained in their houses, assured of protection by General Chichester, admitted as many men (mostly of the 4th regiment) into shelter as the house could contain; but these had not been long in, until the domestic animals were seized and sacrificed. As these were all paid for by the Brigadier, and the amount stopped out of the men's pay, the injury was in some measure remedied, but the heaviest crimes were inexpiated and inexpiable; violence to the defenceless blots the record of that night, and would the names, of those who were guilty, were these worth mentioning. A riotous night, with killing and eating two cows a calf and a pig, with bonfires, made of the garden-gate, harrows, carts, wheel-barrow, chairs, stools, barrels, and tubs, with other articles of husbandry and household furniture, as a hand-bill would express it, accompanied the more infamous deeds of the spoilers.

Next morning the sun rose in his usual way. The Urimea, with its clear deep water, winded through the valley in its usual way; and all was quiet, as if nothing unusual had taken place. But the black burned mountain looked dull and dreary; and the hospitals were filled with men, groaning in their wounds. Upwards of one thousand, out of a comparatively small force, were killed or wounded. The Chapelgorris alone lost two hundred men, and the Carlists must have had many more, as they were exposed to artillery and rockets, which our side were not exposed to.

This day, the 11th, passed over without anything being done; and the next, the 12th, was a pouring rain. However, we advanced; for the day before had been spent in getting artillery up to the heights that had been taken, and making other preparations; and these being made, and General Chichester being to take the lead, that officer would go, heedless of weather. In fact, he saw what could be done ; for the artillery opened a heavy and united attack on all the houses within reach, and where the Carlists were ; knocking them down with shot, and blowing them up with shells. The Carlists being dislodged from these, could not fire in the rain, more than we could ; therefore, our brigade got across the river, and took possession of a space of ground under cover, and considerably beyond the cover of the artillery. The regiment most conspicuously forward was the Rifles.

To explain, how the river required so much crossing, I must mention its windings. It washes the walls on the east side of San Sebastian. Going up, you proceed to the south-west, about a mile, take a round of half-a-mile, and then go south-east nearly another mile. The direction is then south. It is above this last turn, where the ruins, which have been the beautiful village of Layola, stand ; and it was there we re-crossed on the 12th, from the side to which we had crossed by the bridge at San Sebastian. Half-a-mile above Layola, and then at the same distance from the river, is the Ametza hill, eastward. There is nearly a gradual slope from that to the river-side ; and scattered on this, and also on the Layola bank, many fine villas are situated. These have been the residences of gentry and nobility, now joined to the respective parties of the Queen and Carlos, and which, with their gardens and orchards, must have been part of a lovely landscape ; but at the time we crossed the river, all the houses were more or less dilapidated, the roofs broken by bursting shells and the fine stone carvings outside, and oak carvings inside, battered with balls.

The river has various small windings ; but its valley is straight about a mile from Layola, and then there is a turn to the west for two miles, to the little rural town of Hernani. Near the last mentioned turn is the village of Astigarraga ; and I beg the reader's attention particularly to these localities, as it is important for our movements towards these places to be understood. The main road from San Sebastian bears rather to the south-west, till it comes to a conical hill, five hundred feet high, called the Venta, or Advantage hill. This is two miles direct west from Layola, the intermediate space being heights and hollows, partly wooded, and partly bare. From the Venta to Hernani, the road descends for nearly a mile to the south.

It then divides— one branch leads south to Tolosa; the other goes east, leading to France, and keeps the river for two miles, crossing by a bridge at Astigarraga, for no other purpose, apparently, than just to go over and take the other side. This river, the bridge, the road on its bank, Hernani, and the road leading up to and around the Venta hill, and a wooden bridge on the lower and south side of Hernani, must all be kept in view ; and my reader must fancy himself looking at these places, else the events of the 14th, 15th, and 16th of March, will not be understood as they should be. Hitherto, these have been partially misrepresented, described, and commented on, by persons who by no possibility *could* know the localities ; and by others—the " foreign correspondents"—who could not see these situations without being in the heat of the fight ; and they had all as much good sense as to keep at a respectful distance.

Having got over the river, on the 12th, at Layola, by means of stepping out of one boat into another, a row of boats being laid between the two banks, where it was about a hundred yards wide, we advanced, and driving the Carlists back, as was mentioned, getting a few wounded, and all thoroughly drenched to the skin, we took up quarters in the houses which the Carlist soldiers and the other people scared from their houses, had left; and then there was a stir made. None were allowed to enter the houses, until the regiments were regularly told off to them—twenty or forty men to a house according to its size; but, before time was taken to put off knapsacks or accoutrements, presses were opened or broken up—the chests of drawers tumbled down on their faces—the old inhabitants of unmolested corners turned out to see if any stray treasure had deposited itself there. Fires were kindled in the large chimnies of the kitchen : down came shelves, smash went chairs, and crack went tables. " Stand back ; let's get a share o' the fire ;" " on wi' mair wood, some o' ye :" " stand aboot ;" " I'm as wat's ye are ;" " hurrah ! —there goes—down wi' the bedsteads, on wi' them ;" and they were thrown on; and such were parts of the sounds that were intelligible in the noise of breaking and burning. The fire blazed and illuminated the black kitchen as it roared up the spacious chimney ; the old household soot seemed unwilling to survive the profane demolitions of its ancient companions—the chairs and stools, and it took fire and burned too. The wet clothes steamed ; the kitchen, overcrowded, caused new fires to be kindled below; the smoke choked those above; and then fighting and swearing took place. If any one thinks that I could not work myself into a warm corner, and keep it in spite of all the fighting that went on, that one is in a mistake.

I had got a very comfortable corner, was steaming and drying my-self, but watched with apprehension the preparations that were making to put me out; for there was only one human contrivance that could be put in force to do it short of charging bayonets; and alas! that was going on. Wood was heaped upon wood; and the *Champion*, who occupied the other corner, looked with a full-moon face at me, and said, " Oh! Sandy, what'll oo do when that bleezes ?" I sat still, however, and fell into a reverie, contemplating the house, and turning in my mind the probable history of the family that inha-bited there. Amongst the kitchen furniture, there was one species of fixtures that seemed to be unmeddled with, because not worth breaking down to burn. These were a number of wooden pins, with two, three, and four hooks pointing reverse ways, nailed to the joists of the kitchen. An abundance of onions, garlic, bacon, and other things of domestic use, were indicated by these, else there would not have been so many of them : they were roughly made, no doubt cut from the coppice-wood that grew about; and I fancied, from seeing a number of them ready-made, tied together by a bit of their own bark, and hanging on one of their kindred, that the old man must have had his knife always ready, when he saw a piece of notchy wood, to cut a peg with it. This shewed that he had been a man of fore-sight and economy; he had not been a man of taste, for they were not well formed; but he had been an old man, for while some were new, many of them, apparently made by the same hand, wore the venerable soot of half a century. In a little wall-press, on which a black sooty door, closed with hinges that had been often mended, and which I opened as I turned round to endure the fire a little longer, with my back to it, I saw his old hat—his old dun hat!—Poor body ! I thought to myself, he has been in a hurry when he went away : he could not carry two, and he put on his best one. On the same shelf was a black box, about a foot square; it had no cover on it. I put in my hand, and it contained a little salt. " What's in that box, Sandy ?" James M'Queen, a very decent man, asked, " It's the *saut box*," I answered, " Hand it down and let's see't," he said, I did so. James looked at it, and into it; and probably being in a train of thought, similar to my own, said, when he saw it nearly empty, " *I think they've been near oot o' saut afore they've gaen away.* Here, Sandy, pit it up again." I did so, and laid my hands on the old man's hammer, and something else that was lying beside it; but three or four voices bawled out—" Somerville, ye're burnin' !" and another added, " let him burn ; he'll no come out 'til his hide's off. But finding the first exclamation true, I proved the other one false and roared, " let me out," making my way furiously to the door, where I only got time to hear—" d—— ye, if ye come back that way knockin' fo'k owre, oo'll burn ye to death."

A messenger came in bursting with tidings and for the want of breath.—" Chaps, chaps, rin—mercy, rin— a' the regiments is there but ours—up the water, up to yon houses—pang, wine, akadentc, —I've com'd rinnin'." No more of his tale was heard. The plank that was built for a seat tumbled over, and some fell, calling, "murder, murder ! ye're trampin' my hands off, tak' time ;" but that was nearly drowned in the cries of—" my haversack, where's my haversack,"—" gie's a camp-kettle ;" and then the splashing through the gutters, knee-deep, or any way for the shortest road.

This was a house where a good deal of provisions were found, but our informant had rather exaggerated ; the quantity was limited, and the quality of the wine bad ; and the knowing ones had been there before us, even those of our own regiment, The operation of "rumpying the casa," a term that had become universal in the Legion, from a word used by the Spaniards, but which I cannot explain, from not being able to find it or a similar one in any Spanish dictionary : however, the word *rumpy* was a common one ; and "rumpying a casa" was a term for taking every thing that was worth taking, as quickly as possible. The " knowing one" who figured at this kind of work, was not that sort of person that some will suppose him to be. The *keely* of Edinburgh, or them 'ere coves wot have seen the interior of Newgate, displayed no ability at a *rumpy* past others. Where the genius, with the practical experience of theifcraft were required in a clever way, to cut the sash from a Spaniard's waist or keep him in amusement until his dollars were fingered politely, they were distinguished, but in " rumpying the casa" they made no figure. Nor was it the fighting, thorough-going, stick-at-nothing

No. 25.

soldier that flourished there ; it was the " knowing one," a sly dog who never was found going out without his haversack, or something that would be of use, should any thing turn up. He was a person who, in all probability, had been a poacher at home, or a pedlar, or in some kind of small way of doing for himself, and went out to Spain for some reason which he never mentioned. He smoked his own tobacco out of his own pipe ; neither borrowed nor lent : cooked his meat by himself ; never lost any of his regimental necessaries, though it was suspected that things went amissing oftener in the neighbourhood of his berth than anywhere else, yet he was seldom found in a fault. There were "knowing ones" equally gifted in Scotch, Irish, and English regiments, but it must be admitted the Scotch " knowing one" was rather the most knowing.

I met one of these near the house where I with others had run to. I asked him where he had been ; he answered, " danderin' about.' He had not been putting off time drying himself at a fire like us. "Where are ye going ?" I farther inquired. "Nae place," he answered. He was dangling a calabash, a kind of small jar, in his hand, that had a string attached to it. " What are ye going to make of that ?" I inquired. " I'm going to make naething o't," he replied. " What's the use o't ?" I continued. " It's of nae use at a' that I ken of," *he* continued. I knew what use it was for ; so I asked if there were any more of them, but he replied—" maybe there is, I didna look ;" and one who did not know him would have supposed he would toss it into the river as soon as he came near enough. But immediately the cry was up that a pipe of wine was found in a house farther on than we were. All joined in the race. It was set on end ; the head knocked in : but the only things that could be got to drink it from were the forage caps. Those who could get near enough were dipping in their caps—filling them—retiring— drinking and spilling at the same time. Some attempting to put in their heads to drink, were tumbled head foremost, and drawn out again half drowned ; but the "knowing one" with the calabash wrought no frolic, but dipped it in, filled it, and went away by himself to drink it. I believe he invited another to have "a wee drap o't ;" but that was more for self-protection than friendship ; for he knew there were some there who would not scruple to take it from him. But he did not drink it all then. When it was nearly half empty, he said, " It's 'doost aboot toom, and I'll keep this wee drap to gie away for a bit 'bacco, for I'm near oot."

A short while after I saw him with a shirt—a great quantity of these and other things having been found in a house. I offered to buy it from him, he would sell it, he said, when he got home, but not then. I insisted that he would give it to me then, but uselessly. Presently a quantity of flour was discovered in a house. I was at it, but had nothing to put any in. The "knowing one" came, tied the collar and sleeves of the shirt, and made a bag of it. It was proposed not to let him get any, for he was always so cunning, and I, to my shame, seconded that proposal, and was using coercive measures by drawing him back, but he whispered, "I say, man, let's get it; I'll bake a *scone* to ye." He got his flour; but the poor fellow was obliged to bake scones and make puddings for the half of the company.

The river had risen to a red flood. The sailors of the Phœnix were laying a pontoon bridge to get over artillery and horses, and until that was finished, the mules with our rations could not get over, and we had got nothing that day; for when rations for three days were served out, they were generally all done the second day, and with some on the first. But the time was passed off with us by making flour puddings, boiling turnips, and so on, and partly by getting sport with a man of the 9th, who had got astride a wine-pipe, and come down the centre of the broad rolling river, working a right course for himself with his feet, first on one side and then the other. He had come nearly a mile that way, but ran foul of one of the cables of the bridge that the sailors were making—the barrel tumbled, and Pat disappeared. After going down some distance, he got his head above water again, and when the sailors tried to pull him into their boat, he offered to box as well he could, and called out, "oh! J——s, wont you let me alone wid ye's," and swam after the barrel, tried for a long while to remount it, but fruitlessly, as it kept turning round with him, and, exhausted at last with his exertions to keep above water, he landed on the bridge, sat down, and cried. On being asked what he cried for? he started up and exclaimed, "och! what will I do, that am bate in it? by the *book* I'll fight wid ere a one of ye's that made me lose me wager—och, Pat, o Pat, o Pat, that ever you came from the bottom that time you went down, to be seein' this o' yourself," and so on, Pat mourned over himself, being barrel wrecked, for, as one of his comrades said, "there's ne'er a boy in all Cork itself would be after doin' 't like him."

The Royal Marine Corps occupied a part of the same village with us ; they had crossed the river during the afternoon, and were now as like the Legion as the Legion was like itself. There is not a better drilled corps—better appointed in every way, or one that looks better in the British service, than the Royal Marines do ; indeed, for some years past, since their uniform has been altered, they have been proverbial as a good looking corps : but when they marched where the Legion marched—when they fared—(no, they did not *fare* as the Legion, for the Marines had their tea made for them twice a-day whatever went on, and they had their rum regularly, and extra, at such times as that, and rations always of a good quality :) but when they were exposed to make-shift quarters, or the toil, and tear and wear of the Legion, they looked no better than the Legion did at these times, and when the Legion had nothing to do but mount guards and attend parades, they turned out with as white belts, as clean muskets, and as much under the awe of discipline as the Marines did, or as any other corps do. On the 13th, though it was still wet, and an order to advance expected, yet our regiment was paraded twice with white belts, clean-washed gaiters, polished shoes, buttons and brasses, while the Marines had no dress parade at all, and I believe, their commanding officer was the wisest, for if the muskets were cleaned at such times, it was enough ; only this will shew what kind of military order was observed with us.

The 13th passed over with these parades only, and by dividing and partly smoking a quantity of tobacco, which was given to us as a present, but which we afterwards found charged in our accounts. Excepting the getting of that, and a pisetta each, to buy chocolate,&c. which we did from the Spanish women, who followed us from place to place with groceries, nothing else occurred that was remarkable. On the 14th, about mid-day, there was another turn out, and a fresh movement to the front made.

The morning had been wet, and by twelve o'clock the fields where regiments had marched through, and mules carried ammunition and light artillery, were wrought into a state of deep mortar. About a hundred seaman had landed, and were assisting to carry rockets and ammunition, there being such deep sinking swamps, inaccessible hill-sides, obstructing bushes, hedges, &c., that even mules, that can almost go any where, could not be relied on. But the sailors were not merely there to carry burdens, the cutlasses by their sides made it apparent what they could do. They appeared to glory in it, and yet it was seen at once that they were out of their element. Though not marching in order as we did, they sunk in gutters, splashed themselves over head with mud, while regiments marching even through, without turning right or left, were comparatively clean. General Evans was splashing through the soft ground, his horse sinking and springing out again. His aides-de-camp followed, sinking, splashing and springing out again, and all the other mounted officers splashed, sprung, and sunk.

These having passed, and having followed as we best could among the water and knee-deep mire, we at last halted. Expectation being on the stretch, we were soon relieved from uncertainty, by hearing such sounds as, *"forward, the Rifles; double." " Colonel Fitzgerald, move up the 4th!" " 8th, forward"*—hearing these mingled with the sound in rear, of Colonel's calling their regiments to " 'tention," ordering, " prime and load," &c.—these, combined with what the eye saw among the Artillery—the mountain-guns and rockets being hastily taken from the backs of mules, and the guns charged, while slow matches were brought forward; these and other symptoms told us there was a beginning. The rockets blazed off; and along with them the light Artillery, while in front of them we scrambled through briars and other bushes, considerably more excited by the volumes of fire and smoke that rolled on us from the slightly elevated bank from which the rockets and shells took their flight, knocking sundry of our men to the earth with their concussion as they passed over our heads;—more excited by these than we had any visible reasons to be by the enemy, we scrambled through the hedges. Exclamations were mingled of " through the ditch; never mind being half drowned! into the field! the Rifles 'ill get before us! round the field and take them prisoners," &c. while the other regiments, in advance, were scrambling in like manner over the nearly impracticable tract of road that they were forced to take. We had scarcely been fired on, when we had the satisfaction—(some said *mortification·*

but I always doubted *them)* of seeing the startled Carlists breaking cover and bounding off to a more distant position. The Rifles followed, and after them, the light Artillery moved farther to the front, while, as we were not intended for a pursuit, which, from the state of the weather was useless, we came up more leisurely. The pouring rain and the sinking clayey soil rendered progress impossible, more especially, as the Carlists could easily elude any attempt of ours to make them prisoners. There were, however, two or three of them wounded, whom we came up with and sent into our hospital ; but the greater part of those struck by our shells and rockets were, as usual, carried away by their retreating comrades.*

The Rifles kept up a long-shot fire during the afternoon, and the Artillery continued at intervals to fire a shell, but nothing farther could be done. The Carlists did not like to expose themselves to rockets and shells at any time, and much less when the rain prevented them from using their fire-arms with that quickness and effect which is common to them. When evening came on, the Rifles and 4th regiment mounted picquets on the out-posts and accommodated themselves to the inhospitable quarters afforded by the deserted houses of the peasantry. The regiment I was in had the satisfaction of occupying for one night the house of a minister of state ; and though the most valuable furniture had been removed there was still enough left to shew what the rank of the family had been, and more than enough for the mob that inhabited for the night to exercise their faculties of destructiveness on.

It has been often observed, that General Evans, on such an occasion as this, the 14th, should have followed up the enemy, and if they would not stand to fight, he would have at least possessed him-

---

* How is it that the *Rev. Thomas Farr,* who has written and published a volume the most generally correct and interesting on Spanish events, yet published ; how is it that he asserts two or three times, that the Legion only took *two wounded* prisoners during the whole campaign ? Mr Farr is generally correct, but in this he is far from facts. We did not take many wounded prisoners certainly, because it is the most peculiar part of the Basque character, that they allow few of the wounded, and rarely any of their dead to fall into an enemy's hands ; but if the reverend gentleman had said *two hundred,* instead of *two,* he would have been nearer the truth.

self of their ground. Those, who make such observations know nothing of the North of Spain and little of the Northern Spaniards, of whom the Carlist army is mostly composed. A Carlist regiment would cut a sorry figure at a Hyde Park review; but send all the Guards, or three times their number into a Spanish province against only five hundred Carlists, and the Guards would cut a more sorry figure. Even the Spanish Guards, from Madrid—all fine looking, well drilled, and well appointed soldiers, could do nothing in the mountains, with mountaineers to fight against them. The Legion was also, much more ineffective than it might have been, in contending with the Carlists from its superabundance of accoutrements. The following passage, from Mr. Farr's work will put the value of accoutrements in proper estimation. Though the Reverend Author has not experienced, in his own person, the effects of British military equipments, in a mountain warfare, he has formed the same opinion which I have, who carried them. He says,

" See the lightly-armed Carlist soldier ! helmet, he has none ; not a strap or bit of leather of any kind has he to encumber him. On his head he wears a small, light, round cloth cap, of the country —called the *boyna*, or *beset*, which has been, for a long time, and is, even now, a fashionable head-dress with English ladies ; only, when a woman wears it, it is generally made of silk or velvet ; for uniform, he has a plain metal button, on a grey cloth frock coat, and a pair of linen or cloth trowsers—but there is little uniformity in the colour of the coat or trowsers, as it depends entirely on what the Jews, at Bayonne can smuggle over the French frontier. He is armed with a musket, and his cartridge pouch, or *canana*, as they call them, being fixed round his body with a strap, it rather supports than fatigues him. Not one man in five appeared to me to encumber himself with even a scabbard for his bayonet ; in the strap which he fixes his *canana* round his waist, he would make a hole, and in that stick the bayonet. On their feet they had sometimes shoes, but oftener the string-made sandal of their country—*aspargatas* ; which travellers, who have been no further than the baths of Bagneses de Bigone, or de Luchon, in the French Pyrenees, must have observed was worn by their mountain guides in preference to the shoe.

" While the poor fellows of the Legion—heavily and stifly armed, with their sack-clad backs, and a bangling strap over their shoulders, to hold their cartridge pouch, and another to hold their bayonet—are panting, sighing, and almost dropping from exhaustion—scarce able to move for want of breath, either when attacking, or pursuing the enemy—the Carlist soldier—the bravest, the most terrible, the most active mountain enemy in the world—lightly equipped, and with no encumbrances, with impunity attacks or retreats, as best suits his inclination, from his heavy-clad foes, with a consciousness of superiority which he is not wrong in possessing."

" With what perfect contempt do the Carlists treat their enemies ! they can allow themselves to be apparently surrounded, and when there is just one little open corner left, they run off at last, dashing up the mountains, without ever losing a man ; while artillery, cavalry, and every engine of war is of no avail. The only thing a Carlist fears, is to be caught on a high-road, or level ground, where cavalry can act ; or be exposed in the field to spherical shells—for as they burst in the air, they shoot backwards and forwards, right and left, upwards and downwards ;—but it is the power of backward firing that utterly disconcerts them ; as getting behind a tree, parapet, or barricade, not only gives them no protection, but makes them a surer mark. It is exactly this hide behind something warfare that they delight in, from which they can either pounce on their enemy or spring away from him, as best suits their purpose."

The following General Order was referred to some pages back. Its perusal will inform the reader of another species of difficulties—the most dreadful of all—which we had to contend with in Spain. It should have been mentioned too that the two hundred men of the Chapelgorris that fell on the 10th, were mostly lost in consequence of the other Spanish regiments not supporting them in one of their bravely resolute charges—and yet *all* the Spaniards fought better that day than they commonly did.

Order of the day, issued by General Oraa, after the battle of Barbastro, and published in the official Gazette of Madrid, in June 1837.

" The General-in-chief of the army of the centre has published, in an order of the day, the following dispositions, with the intention of terminating those disorders too frequent in the battles, and of which the consequences may be fatal.

" I. Every time that a brigade, or a battalion, commences firing, the Commandant-General of the division, or, in his absence, the superior officer shall place in the rear, half a company of artillery and a picquet of cavalry, with orders to shoot any soldier, who, without being wounded, or furnished with competent authority for so doing, shall quit the field of battle.

" II. The officers of any company which a soldier shall have abandoned, shall be suspended from their rank, and sent prisoners to some fortress until they have proved that they took all necessary measures, and done all which depended upon them to keep the man at his post.

" III. The Commandants of battalions, or chiefs of troops, who shall be dispersed, or fly coward-like at sight of, or under the fire of the enemy, at the moment when they come into action, shall be instantly suspended from their rank, and incur the penalties decreed against them by a Council of War, which shall be held within twenty-four hours.

" IV. During the battle, the most profound silence shall be observed. It is forbidden to cry, " forward," " cavalry," or make any other cry, which might disturb the good order which ought always, and particularly during a battle, to reign in the ranks. The man who makes any cry, shall be punished as the competent officers may judge proper. The penalty of death may be applied to those who have cried, " we are cut to pieces !"—" lost !"—" treason !" or any other cries which may create disorder, and cause the position to be abandoned. The chiefs of battalions, and officers of companies, who shall have heard, and permitted a cry, shall be suspended from their rank.

" V. Conformably to the plan already established in the Army of the North, and according to the temporary regulations here made, there shall be a company formed to carry away, and take care of the wounded in each brigade, in consequence, no other individual is allowed to quit the ranks. This abuse having been tolerated until now, the third part of the disposable force, has been sometimes lost in the midst of a battle. Every soldier who infringes on the present order, shall be instantly shot, unless he returns to his ranks, on being ordered to do so by his officer.

" VI. As the ordnance forbids firing without the orders of the chiefs, they, and the officers of the corps, will employ the greatest energy to avoid the accidents occasioned by useless shots. They will economise the munitions as much as possible, and will only permit batteries, and entire companies to engage with the guerillas or isolated men, and never but within musket shot. These abuses discourage the troops, who uselessly consume their cartridges, which they ought to preserve for more decisive occasions.

" VII. The commandants, generals of divisions, and chiefs of brigades, are responsible for the execution of the present dispositions, which shall be inserted in the order of the day of the army, and read before going into battle.

" CASTELLANO."

CHAPTER XXI.

The Commencement of the Action of the 15th—1st Regiment and Colonel De Lancy—Remarks on Mr. Alcock, relative to wounded men being left in the enemy's hands—Conduct of the Irish regiments in the engagement—Anecdote of Captain Coyle—Taking of the Venta Hill—Preparations for the sanguinary engagement of the 16th, &c., &c.

THE night of the 14th passed dismally for those whose duty was keeping watch in the open air, and cheerfully for those who were in quarters. These extremes arose from the tempestuous weather and pouring rain to which the outlying picquets were exposed, and from the unceremonious appropriation of every article in the shape of furniture to what the soldiers deemed comfort;—that comfort consisting of good fires to generate warmth, and a sound sleep to renovate from the fatigue of the previous day, and to qualify for the day to come. For that, the carved oak, and the mahogany—the chairs, tables, pianos, and guitars flamed in, and around the mansion; saints and heroes on canvas—*Raphaels*, for any thing that was known or cared, were torn from their frames, and from the walls on which they had hung, the oracles of family, or national history for generations, and were used for the night as covering to some half dozen soldiers who had acted the Vandals on them, and next morning were in the hurry and bustle of accoutring and turning out, trodden under foot.

There was cooking and eating of salt beef in the morning, and cleaning and spunging of muskets. The rain towards noon cleared away, and as we turned out no doubt could exist in any one's mind that *now* we were to have something hot. The regiments, that had since the 10th—the first of the hostilities, lain in rear—crossed the river and advanced to where the regiments of Chichester's brigade were. We were all paraded, and moving forward towards our outposts, two pieces of cannon of large calibre from Oriamenda or Venta hill opened on us. The distance was by far too great for any execution being done; yet they excited unpleasant apprehensions, for as we moved onwards we got more within their range, and balls were now and then lopping off the branch of a tree, or plunging into the earth amongst us; though I believe not a single casualty to any regiment occurred. Having moved forward in columns as far as it was deemed probable we could go without receiving the 'enemy's fire, a halt was made for a few minutes, and then the Rifles and 1st regiment of the Legion, with three battalions of Spaniards proceeded to skirmish on the extreme left, the 9th and 10th regiments waited to attack the centre, the 8th advanced to skirmish on their right and to discover where the enemy was likely to be met in full strength. Farther to the westward and to the right, the 6th and 7th regiments covered the Royal British Artillery; the Royal Marine Artillery being with the Rocket Brigade of the Legion near the centre.

We shall leave the regiments on the left, which were second in point of time, in making the attack, and give a few paragraphs of its commencement towards the centre of our positions.

We had gained a point, when from intervening heights and trees we could not be fired on from the Venta; in consequence of that the enemy's large guns were silent for a short time. General Chichester was heard giving the order to our regiment (the 8th) to advance in front, which was immediately obeyed by our scrambling over ditches flooded with water, and through briery hedges. Our commanding officer, Lieutenant Colonel Hogg, then ordered the two flank companies to extend and advance in front of the regiment to discover where the Carlists were. These two companies the *Grenadier* and *Light* extended over a field of furze, and all yet silent, momentarily expected a volley to meet them from some concealed picquet or battalion. The regiments in rear looked forward with intense apprehension to see when the first shots would raise the report and smoke of the combat, and we, going through the furze, which furze rose as high as the middle of the body and occasionally the shoulders cast our eyes before, and around us anxiously, to detect if possible the lurking foe, before we had walked deliberately into their position The Captain of my company (Sheilds) observed to me in a whisper—that he did not think any of the enemy were there, and I was about to reply in some other whisper which died in the birth—when the tops of the furze bushes fell off their stalks—quick whizzing sounds resembling the spit of an angry cat passed our heads, and one of the men close beside us uttered a stifled exclamation of " Oh I'm—I'm shot!—I had been about to answer to the captain's whisper when these sounds arrested me, and the same moment on looking to the front, from which I had withdrawn my eyes but for a few twinklings, a cloud of smoke was whirling itself upwards ; in a moment more a burst of thunder rattled on the ear.

" Steady you men—steady there," the captain exclaimed, as some symptoms of an alarm were observed among them, " fire! " He continued, " what are you looking at," addressing himself to some of the men, who seemed trying to descry an object of aim before they fired.   Nothing but the smoke of the enemy's volley was visible ; but much more was soon heard ; the bugles in all directions sounded the *advance,* and the other field calls, ordering us to push on and make the attack, and the regiments in rear to move up.   At the first impulse of our being attacked, I had fired, though I confess I did not know what at : and the next moment, as a matter of course, I was re-loading.   The cartridge was put into the muzzle, and the ramrod was drawn to ram it down, when, as if by the trick of a juggler, the ramrod disappeared, but by what means or to where, I did not know. There was no difficulty in getting another, though some time afterwards, I got my own about twenty yards from where I lost it.   It was bent and slightly flattened, with a small portion of skin attached to it, which on taking off, I found to answer to a cut on the edge of my hand, which the unseen emissary had been content with, when it chipped the ramrod from me, but which I had not previously discovered.   " Forward," and " hurrah" were the cries! we got into a low road-way, and for a short while played at long shots, from that into a wood, at three hundred yards distance, to which the out-picquets of the enemy had retreated, and from which they fired at the different regiments as they came up to our line of position. The object was now, on our side, to make the light artillery available, and for that

purpose, we got the command, " cease firing," and strict orders not
to fire a shot until ordered.   I mention this strict injunction, in order
that an incident connected with it may be understood.

A man belonging to the company in which I was, named Charles
Scott, a restless being, though a good rough-and-ready soldier ;—a
description of soldier which was by far the best suited to the Spanish
campaigns.   Charles, or Charlie as he was vernacularly called, was
peeping over the ditch bank, behind which we were ordered to keep
silent and unseen : he saw a Carlist General advancing at the head
of some battalions through the wood.   The thickets allowed them to
be seen only indistinctly, but there being no doubt of their intent on
us, Charlie was anxious to give their leader a bullet as soon as possible.   The Captain seeing him level his musket over the bank,
ordered him not to fire ; and as a part of my duty, I urged the order.
" I tell you sir, if you fire, I'll send you to the rear a prisoner," repeated the captain.   I heard Charlie mutter to himself that "there's
no fear o' bein' a prisoner on a day like this ;" and in answer to some
one who whispered that the distance was by far too great, he replied ,
" I've won at a raffle when the target was as *fer* as yon."   The Carlist
leader emerged from the wood, and waving his sword, seemed
cheering on his followers to attack our position ; but unmindful of
the order not to fire, Scott, took aim—discharged his piece, and
though nearly three hundred yards distant, the Carlist tumbled from
his horse, and the animal scampering rearwards, the troops who were
following their leader, fell back into the wood.

There is nothing singular in the forgoing incident, such things occurred frequently, and that is only mentioned now to be borne in
mind as a prelude to other incidents of Charlie's military career which
occurred subsequent to that, and will be found mentioned hereafter.

Our repose at this place was short.   We had only halted there
until other regiments manœuvred on the flanks of the enemy so that
the attack might be simultaneous and forcible.   I had here an opportunity of observing closely the excellent practice of the Marine
Artillery as they wrought the mountain guns—guns, I believe, carrying balls of nine or twelve pounds weight—which in light skirmishing warfare, are by far the most efficient instruments of conflict·
Through the enemy's balls came thick among them they continued
throwing shells into the opposite intrenchments with as complete

regularity in loading, firing, and spunging, as if they had been merely at drill practice. At one of the guns, the gunner, who did the duty of elevating (taking aim) was struck on the shoulder with a musket ball; he was looking along the gun when the shot struck him and lodged in his shoulder, but he continued taking his aim, until satisfied, only having put his hand to the wound. He then stepped back straining his eyes as usual to the point where the shell was expected to go to, while the man with the match received his order to fire; and the messenger of death being obediently destructive as desired when it fell among the enemy, the gunner with apparent satisfaction turned his head to his wounded shoulder, and said " well I have paid them for this more than cent per cent."

On the left, the 1st regiment was severely engaged, and the brave Colonel De Lancy was as usual displaying all that bravery and consummate skill for which he was distinguished. It should have been stated sooner that he did duty on the staff as Deputy Adjutant General, in the discharge of which duty he had gained the respect of all persons connected with him—the friendship of his superiors and equals, and what was more difficult to obtain, which few officers of high rank can obtain, because their duties are diametrically opposed to it—the respectful esteem and friendly wishes of inferiors, especially the multitude of inferiors who composed the ranks. He was a favourite officer even with the men, and yet he was a strict disciplinarian; but his favour arose from his never having punished men excepting for substantial crimes, and his having uniformly studied in his practice to be obeyed by love and respect, rather than by fear. Colonel De Lancy has family connexions in England; I know nothing of them; I am not even aware if they are, any of them, in, or connected with the army; but if they are, and though they may move in the higher ranks of society, which I believe they do, it should not cause a prideful pain in any of them, to be informed that their gallant relative paid more respect to the good will of his inferiors, than he did to the friendship or favour of his equals and superiors in rank; it should not pain his relatives to know, that though brave until he was the admiration of all who saw and heard of him in fight, he had the more vulgar merit of deserving that notice which the author of this work studies to pay to every officer who deserved it—the merit of being the soldiers' friend.

Major Talbert, at the time of this engagement holding the Brevet rank of Lieut. Colonel, was conspicuously forward during the afternoon, and while with De Lancy received a dreadful wound which though not fatal, rendered him incapable of farther service. Lieut. Colonel Hicks also at the same place,` had his horse shot beneath him, and many brave but ill-fated men bore testimony to the heat of the strife by their blood. No abatement of the conflict had taken place, indeed, on all sides it had increased—when, in reconnoitring the enemy's position, in rear of a house from which Colonel De Lancy had formed the resolution to dislodge them if practicable, he was struck on the head by a musket shot. He was carried off the field, and alas, in a short while the brave De Lancy was no more.

The house near which this lamented officer received his death wound, was taken with a loss proportionately severe with its importance, it being situated in a commanding position, and it became next day remarkable in the history of the campaign, as being the place of a dreadful massacre of wounded English prisoners. By whose neglect these wounded were left to fall into the enemy's hand cannot now be satisfactorily ascertained ; *and it was not officially enquired into at the time,* but in the absence of evidence to trace the neglect to the underlings of the Hospital Transport Corps, we must let blame attach itself as it naturally does to the officer of that corps, Lieutenant Smith, or rather to the Medical staff, for the wounded left to perish in this house, were out of the hands of the regimental surgeons. It is scarcely possible here to refer to this melancholy affair without remarking that the Deputy Inspector General of Hospitals, Mr. Alcock, in his work recently published, omits all allusion to the immolation of these wounded men ; indeed it must be admitted that Mr. Alcock could not have reported the matter impartially without in some degree implicating himself, yet, though it may be thus understood that he was *one* of those, even the acting *chief* of those whose duty was to convey the wounded from the field to the general hospital; it must also be stated in qualification of this charge, that Mr. Alcock was a medical officer possessing a character deservedly high and popular. Professional skill and industry, combined with generosity and humanity, were testified to, by many officers and men who underwent the operation of surgical cures, as being the special characteristics of Mr. Alcock. To say less than to repeat that I believe him to be justly entitled to the high respect paid him by persons of all ranks, would be saying too little for his general character; and yet a number of men, amounting to sixty, as many persons well informed on the matter assert, were after bravely fighting on the afternoon of the 15th left in an unguarded house to perish the next morning by the enemy's bayonets. Such was the end of some of the really brave 1st regiment, and a few who were mingled with them from the 4th, and Rifles, who were left to repose in their wounds, on the " pallet of straw." Alas ! the to-morrow of that night was pregnant with disasters for the ill-fated 1st ; but for the present we shall leave them. They piled their arms and lay during the night, officers and men, on the cold damp ground that had been so recently flooded with rain, all anxiously looking forward to the dawn, when a grand trial of strength was to be made for better quarters on the enemy's ground. Until I can state that the regiments, fighting towards the right, piled arms and lay down on the open fields, which they ultimately did, waiting for the morning of the 16th, I must lead the reader through the yet unfinished record of the fight towards the Venta.

At various points, the 9th and 10th Irish regiments contested the ground with the Carlist opponents ; at various parts they were for a time successfully opposed ; and frequently, but for the indomitable resolution of such officers, as Beckham, Cannon, and Cotter, and a few other choice spirits that commanded companies and did *sub* duty— not forgetting the many O'Rourkes and Ryans, O'Callaghans, Rafferty's, Kelly's, and a numerous etcetra of Mac's and O's that filled the ranks—but for their indomitable resolution to *have* the ground and to *force* quarters for that night, the astonishing rapidity with which the Carlists were driven from successive positions would not have been displayed. A number of particular persons, and their particular incidents, compiled from the testimony of individuals belonging to these regiments, will be found in subsequent pages ; but it is necessary to state, in a general way, that the 9th regiment, particularly, were eminently forward and successful on this occasion. Then, having said that, it is not possible to omit stating, that they received and claimed undivided honors, for doing what they did not do that day, namely, take the Venta hill. To the *home* reader this may be un-important ; but to those who were engaged in that fight it is of importance to give each corps its due ; especially, as the account of the affair as given by General Evans was not correct—*intentionally incorrect !*

Having the authority of the General on their side, the 9th regiment at all times gallant and efficient in fight, trumpeted their own fame, Colonel Cannon particularly, and on this occasion they were more than usually loud, and the remnant of them continue to boast yet to their brethren of ill-fate, that—" Och sure dthe boys o' dthe nint took dthe Venta when no other would go to it." There was a regiment numbered the *eighth*, to which General Evans took a dislike unaccountable, ungenerous and unjust ! His dislike was unaccountable because, though the regiment was *Scotch*, he shewed as much favour for Scotchmen as he did for Englishmen or Irishmen individually, though he certainly gave most favour to the Irish regiments ! but a majority of our officers *were* Irish. Nor could his dislike to the regiment arise from any want of respect for the superior officers ; for we had at that time Colonel Hogg commanding us—than whom a more brave—a more skilful—a better drill, or more generally efficient officer, did not at any time, and does not now adorn the highly adorned British Service,—making some exceptive allowances for a rather full quantity of self-importance, the natural fruit of rapid promotion. Then, the General's manifest dislike to the regiment, must have had a source of action that poisoned his good-will in some other way, and by some other means than what was visible to common observers. It may have been the recollection of the mutiny, and the successful result on the part of the men in forcing more regular pay. It may have been the recollection of the impertinent, meddling, mischief-making General Shaw, whose honour like the Leopard's skin— whose character like the Chameleon's hues—had led the unfortunate Scotch regiments to commit irregularities, which, he was not only the first to punish himself but the first to urge the General to severities, for which he soon repented acceding to.—These circumstances, and the unqualified eulogies that appeared in a London newspaper, lauding General Shaw to the disrespect of others, may have induced General Evans to look lightly on the ill-used regiments that had been at first raised, and then disorganised by General Shaw. Or another circumstance may have distorted his fair dealing ; perhaps the military secretary and other persons about him filled his ear to the prejudice of those who were not close enough to have a private whisper ; No. 26.

for it was often said and universally believed, that those who had the General's ear, had the command for the time being, and this makes him suffer now for acts not spontaneously his own. But let his neglect of *our* regiment have proceeded from these or any other supposed causes or from no cause at all, it is certain that we were not favoured with his approving notice as other regiments were; and yet the coming account of the taking of Venta hill—true and uncoloured, will contrast strangely with his general order, and the stories commonly told by persons of the 9th regiment from Colonel Cannon downwards. Overlooking many details of the fight which I could record relative to my own regiment, and not of any other, solely because the same species, or rather class of details in other regiments are unknown to me;—passing over these, I shall notice one circumstance previous to leading the reader to the storming of the Venta, which to omit would be an injustice to the memory of a gallant, much esteemed, and much lamented officer, namely, Captain Coyle.

We were this day the companions, in arms and in fight, of the Chapelgorris. Several dislodgements of the enemy from their strong places had been accomplished, when, having joined in one of those wild hurrahing shouts, and running across a woody declivity, with fixed bayonets, led by General Chichester—the Colonel of the Chapelgorris, and Colonel Hogg—where we had a number of men killed and wounded; the 1st company of the 8th was detached under Captain Coyle, to command a narrow pass at the bottom of a ravine. In this position he was with his company completely detached from the regiment; the fire between us and the enemy being over their heads; but yet, though firing over them the depth of the ravine precluded their having any easy or immediate communication with the regiment. Captain Coyle's orders were to oppose the enemy should they attempt to pass down the ravine, through which they might flank or come in our rear. Though such a manœuvre was an unlikely one, still they might, had they been sufficiently resolute annoyed us by such an attempt, and the precautionary details in the distribution of our forces will therefore be the more readily apparent when it is known that strict attention was paid to such places as this ; particularly when it was considered unnecessary to send any force to this point by some officers. Captain Coyle's company had fired up

the ravine to where a party of the enemy were stationing themselves
for nearly three hours until they had expended all their ammunition,
and the combat being at its height at that time in other parts attention was not paid to their want of ammunition. The Carlists seeing
the fire cease at the bottom of the ravine made an effort to pass down,
and for any thing we could have done on the banks they might have
gone down, and had they been sufficiently numerous would have
baffled us in the rear. Coyle, seeing the impossibility of holding his
position when he could not meet them by a fire, and seeing the utter
ruin to the advantages already gained by the main forces on the
heights should the enemy displace him, ordered his men to fix bayonets and charge. He was reminded by some of his old soldiers that
no charge was ever made without being previously loaded, and that
they had not a round of ammunition in the whole company. Perhaps
he never heard of the once successful call of Colonel Cadogan, when
he was the means of routing Joseph Bonaparte, by exclaiming to his
regiment, the 71st, who were mostly all natives of Glasgow, " *charge
down the Gallowgate ;*" the Gallowgate being a homely street, closely
connected with the domestic recollections of youths, fresh from home,
such as the 71st were at that time, had a talismanic effect in inspiriting them to the charge.—And I say that Captain Coyle, perhaps, knew nothing of such an historical event—it was an *event*, not
an incident—of the Peninsular war—but if he did, his appeal to his
handful of men, when threatened by the Carlists, was still original ;
for to perform a successful act of bravery against an enemy, when the
case is desperate, is as meritorious, though a *copy*, as if *original*.
Coyle, on hearing the complaint that the ammunition was expended,
and seeing the imminent danger, exclaimed, " Charge, you Glasgow
Keelies," and running in front with his drawn sword, continued,
" give them through the wood, laddie !" Captain Coyle was not a
Scotchman, but he had been long enough familiarized with his men
to have observed some of their slang ; and *Keely*, though literally
thief was yet so appropriate to a considerable number of those he
commanded, and the two facts of the *Keelies*, being often the best
fighting soldiers, and bravery being the constitution of respectability
at such fighting times as these—to be a *Keely*, or even called a
Keely, was to be classed in the highest estimates of military worth.
The effect of Coyle's appeal, an effect quickened by his personal ex-

ample of resolute gallantry, was to turn a battalion of the enemy, or parts of battalions, amounting to at least twelve times their number ; and not only turn them but clear the whole ravine, which admitted of the other regiments getting more speedily forward to the positions from which they stormed the Venta, than they would have done in any other case.

Shortly after this the Royal British, the Marine, and part of the Legion Artillery, being on the main road within eight hundred yards of the Venta ; all the Infantry save the 6th regiment, which waited to cover the Artillery if necessary, being to the eastward or left of the main road ; we received orders to move up to a position, from which it was understood we were to storm the intrenchments on the hill, but first the barricades at its bottom. Three hundred yards to the south, and at the same distance from the base of the hill as the 8th were, the 9th, 10th, and three Spanish regiments were about to move forward. That force was there at the moment more by accident, than for the purpose of moving in concert ; indeed the opposition at that point being much more feeble than on the northern side, where the Artillery 6th, 7th, and 8th were, it was not intended that any corps should go forward but the 9th to the storm, that the others in that quarter should only support them ; but the resistance to the 9th having been slight, the other regiments (10th and Spaniards), rushed in also to share in the easily won glory, this was the amount of what they did, having among them all *two men wounded.* Yet let them not be robbed of their reputation by the negative tone in which I write, they went forward impetuously—their impetuosity startled the enemy, but they would have gone, had the enemy resisted them ; and with the brave Cotter, who as it was, dashed over the barricades in front, they could not have failed to be successful while he lived.

If that portion of the attack was easily successful, different, very different was that to the northward of the hill, were it was the lot of the humble sketcher of these events to be stationed. But I must go backwards in point of time half an hour. The Artillery had been throwing shells for more than two hours, and had thinned the Carlists at the barricades considerably, when for a short time they partially ceased. The 7th regiment, who had fired a good deal from advantageous positions ; but who had not been engaged very re-

markably during the afternoon, were now keeping up a fire over a
wall, and from a height which was intended to serve as a covering
protection to those who were to descend to the road beneath them
against the barricades. The Chapelgorris were also at hand, and
the Artillery waited for orders to vomit the shower of shells, that
were to go over our heads, and by falling in front of us, make our
progress more practicable than it could be, were we to march against
the unchecked fire of the enemy from behind their intrenchments.
We had formed in close column immediately, in rear of the left flank
of the 7th regiment, round which we were to wheel. I may mention
that I had just got a bullet in my left arm, bad enough to have
warranted my falling to the rear; but I saw Major Wilson who had
been wounded, come and rejoin the regiment, declaring he would not
lose the glorious opportunity,—the opportunity I supposed of winning
promotion and honor; and I hesitated also, though it may just as
well be told that I would have rather not seen the *opportunity* that
was now so close at hand. Making this admission however, something more must be said; it may throw some light on those ambiguous terms *courage* and *cowardice*, both of which are the effects of
causes strongly complicated in their physical and intellectual nature.
The impulsive wish to purchase safety by staying behind, strong
as its suggestions were, was overruled by another feeling, not the love
of approbation, but perhaps more akin to that quality called self-
esteem; it was the dread of afterwards being made the butt of scorn.
I got many persons to confess their secret thoughts to me, and it
might perhaps be useful at some time to compare these with their apparent courage or cowardice, and by testing them with the commonly
received principles of moral science, ascertain how far our estimates
of character are correct; but at the present it is enough to say, that
I would most willingly have availed myself of a chance to fall to the
rear, had I not dreaded the potent power of what might be called
the "public voice;" but, when seeing that once in the way of being
shot, I might as well join in the hurrah, and being able, run in front
as not, I did so with a full conviction, that hundreds like myself
had their duty been to command, would have from choice been as
forward, and *apparently* as brave as those whose *rank* made them conspicuous. To *be* and to *appear* brave, are widely different circumstances in forming from them an estimate of courage; but *appear-*

ances being all that can be taken as evidence, save where personal confessions are made, we must abide by that evidence, unsatisfactory though it be. In my own humble case I make a confession, because I believe the great majority of officers and men on that occasion, and on all similar occasions to have felt similarly with myself. With no hope of reward ; with a certainty that however we might distinguish ourselves, (I speak of men not of officers), with a certainty, that however distinguished, we would have *no* place in the Gazette —*no* place of promotion if we survived and no share of praise if we fell —with that certainty of giving all our energies for nothing, we yet assumed unimpeachable appearances to say the least; but in reality appearances that in a greater battle or a more *successful* cause, would have received the approbation of an admiring world.

The foregoing represents the thoughts, or feelings, rather when about to enter, or on first entering a fight, than it does those feelings that govern, when the individual finds himself completely and irretrieveably in the midst of death. *Then,* the fire, and the smoke, and the blood, and the thunder that deafens the ear and temporarily distracts the brain, have a strange influence in producing that species of madness called bravery, often shewn by individuals, sometimes by sections, and sometimes by whole regiments of men. Madness, is said to be contagious ; if so in ordinary life, and the fact is now generally admitted, how peculiarly is the contagion manifested in a battle ; you see your Colonel, or Captain, or your comrade, or it may be all of them, and many more suddenly become insane ; you knew that they, like yourself were in dread of death, and would have saved themselves from danger could they have done so without dishonour ; but according as they were morally and physically constituted, so did their dread of dishonour overcome the dread of death, till with quaking hearts they yet raised the shout, and the cheer, and you see them now literally mad. Involuntarily their madness communicates to yourself, and *you* spread the disease. Yet you do not all manifest insanity in the same degree, nor in the same manner : One, the thicker he sees the fire and smoke, and the louder he hears the roar of slaughtering guns, the more eagerly and wildly will he run forward, he being mad through the mere confusion of excited passions. Another equally maddened to the forward rush by his confused brain, has yet such a predominance of some particular faculty, that he does something that distinguishes him from others.—All *might* do something, but all *cannot*—their insanity at the moment being in some, productive of nothing but the mere display of heroism—they being incapable of doing aught but rushing on death—while others, by the strength of some faculty, will seize an enemy, make him a prisoner, comprehend instinctively the utility of rushing to a certain point to secure a piece of cannon, or if they can, they will rush even against greater danger to slay an officer instead of a common soldier.—Another, his equal in the heedlessness of danger, will not rush forward to make choice of a prisoner, or a cannon, or choose the rank of a victim ; if he has *destructiveness* predominant, he will kill the first he meets as an enemy, merely because madness unbalances his mind, or that being excited until unbalanced in mind he is mad, and desstructiveness prompting him to kill, he runs his bayonet into the man he might have taken prisoner ; and having slain that one, he rushes on another from the mere desire to slay ; and yet at other times, that man could talk as humanely as the most benevolent, and when unexcited would never suspect himself of being capable of killing so ferociously as he now does;—as he now does, but is not conscious of until his temporary insanity subsides, and then he knows that he has been mad, but does not confess his madness because the world insists on calling it bravery, and he is willing to be called a brave man rather than a mad man.

All men have not those reflecting powers to know, and many men, are so constitutionally deceptive, that they will not confess even though they know, that they were mad.   Others have had the reputation of bravery forced on them by circumstances, that were they to confess their real feelings, and their real merit it would so injure national interests, by stripping national pride of the glory it has been pleased to fancy as peculiarly its own, that they are justified in retaining what has been forced on them : so truly is the reputation of bravery gained from circumstantial, and often accidental incidents in a campaign, or in a man's life, that the bravery of most men, and most actions are measured, not by the merit of those who fought, but by their success ; not by the degree of the bravery, but by the degree in which it ministers to national vanity.

If a man's house were on fire, and he were surrounded by the flames and about to perish in them, the death would be as dreadful

to him as it would be if the whole metropolis were burning; so was
the battle of five thousand men as great to the five thousand as ten
times the number would have made it to the fifty thousand. Yet in
the latter case, how much more gratifyng would it have been to the
lovers of the marvellous; how much more pleasing would it have been
to those who every day decry war, but are disappointed to find in the
news from Spain that the numbers killed and wounded are so small.
How much more gratifying would it have been to such, if we had
been all slain as the remnant who fought at Andouin were,—who
could not fight because they were not in a situation to fight—who
were put to death because they could not escape, and who were
applauded by all parties—newspapers of all creeds—pronounced to
have been heroically brave, merely because they were killed. How
differently would the world have spoken of us, had we been all killed,
and yet our madness was as impetuous, and in many cases as destructive in proportion to the numbers engaged, as was the insanity
of the heroes of Waterloo.

This *insane courage* is however evinced only in some parts of warfare. It is common in all charges, stormings, pursuits &c. It is not
so common when battalions fire in squares and lines, and it is scarcely
known when soldiers lie under partial cover, or skirmish by Light
Infantry manœuvres. These last, though not commonly supposed to
be, are the most painful performances of a soldier's duty. Mostly all
military writers extol the bravery of British soldiers when describing
the *charge*: Such and such places were taken at the point of the
bayonet &c. and as often as the *bayonet* can be written in the history
of British warfare, so often is the eulogy on British bravery renewed.

It may startle some unthinking readers and those hitherto unin-
formed on such matters, but it is nevertheless true—that instead of
it being an act of superior bravery—instead of greater resolution
being required to charge with the bayonet, than to stand and fire, if
exposed to the enemy's fire—soldiers will not only call for the charge
but having charged they will, as has often been the case, *run voluntarily on the enemy*. The historians of Waterloo, record cases where
whole battalions of men demanded of their Commander to be led to
the charge, and he has been said to answer, "not yet my brave soldiers, not yet." We have associated the words "charge bayonets"

so closely with courage and gallantry, that one almost regrets to be obliged to strip them of their glory. Though it may not administer so much to our national vanity, it is much more rational to suppose, indeed, more consistent with facts to say, that those men who demanded of the Duke to be ordered on, were standing under the painful—overwhelming apprehension of being shot; many of them falling by French cannon shots at the time, and being exposed without any of that excitement that not only makes them comparatively heedless of danger, but more certain of success—that excitement which immediately animates the minds of men when they hear the word "charge," they called loudly for the command.

Take as an instance two men trained to boxing. If what are called scientific pugilists, they will stand with courage to each other, being controuled by the pugilistic laws until the one or other falls senseless, or it may be dead! but if one had run in—had he at an unguarded moment of his opponent *run in* and stabbed him, or strangled him, it would not only have been pronounced foul play, but every spectator would have pronounced it an act of *cowardice!* Two armies standing firing at each other are in precisely the same circumstances as the pugilists; were it possible that two armies could have seconds or umpires to controul their mode of fighting to certain rules of fair play, there would be no running in with bayonets; not unless they ran in on equal terms, which equal terms in the history of the bayonet practice was never yet the case. It was always a part of military tactics, and accounted a proficiency in a commander, to be able to throw an enemy into a temporary confusion, and to take advantage of that temporary confusion by charging bayonets. It may be accounted too much for an inexperienced person such as the author of this, to attempt to unsettle the commonly adopted opinions about "British bayonets," but he nevertheless makes the assertion with the utmost confidence of being supported by the testimony of all intelligent, or impartial minded soldiers who have been in active warfare, that they never saw, and never knew of a British regiment rushing with their bayonets on a French regiment drawn up in line, and ready to receive them; yet these are the commonly received notions. No, no, the Duke of Wellington was too good a tactician to order, or permit anything so wild and reckless to be ordered on the field. Storming of fortresses, is an exception—but the bayonet should not be then used as will be hereafter shewn. When a charge is about to be made by a battalion in line, which indeed is the only real *charge*, though many other advances from *divisions* down to *fours* and *threes* if made by a *double* and the *bayonet*, have been called charges by persons writing more to produce effect, than to correctly inform. When the charge is about to be made, the battalion is ordered first to load, and it is the duty of officers, and especially the supernumerary sergeants in rear, to see that every man is loaded, more particularly at this time than at any other—if degrees of strictness are admissible at all, which they should not be. Each soldier knows that he is not to fire until he comes up with the enemy and stabs a man if he is able—but these hand-to-hand encounters have always been very rare. When he is likely to be overpowered by a man wrestling with his bayonet he is to fire; but not until then, unless the scattered enemy is running before him and he cannot come up with them : in this case he fires if the bugle sounds the order. Now to any one who will reflect, here is proof that a battalion would never be ordered to *run in* on another battalion ready to receive them ; because were the battalion of the enemy on equal terms they would be loaded, and being loaded, might stand and kill almost every man as the battalion at the charge came up. This fact of a charging regiment being ordered *not to fire* until they grapple with the enemy, and are in danger of being overpowered, is itself a proof that the enemy are never supposed to be in a condition to fire when a charge is made on them. It is the commander's duty—a duty always strictly observed—to mark when a column, or line of the enemy are thrown into disorder by the fire of artillery or rockets, and then if the ground admits, to charge them with the bayonet. The boldest charges on record, were those made when the enemy in line had discharged a volley, and being unloaded were thus taken advantage of—even these though far from being an equality of strength—were rare—rarely attempted, and more rarely successful. It evinced the greatest skill in the commander of a divison, when he could manœuvre so as to cause the enemy to attempt to change front hurriedly, and during their change, to charge on their flanks and throw them into confusion. Next to that it was considered skilful to draw the enemy under the fire of artillery, and by shells, or other missiles to throw them into confusion and then charge, and put them to the rout, which charging any individual soldier, or any regiment would at all times choose in preference to a standing steady fire; for though it is almost a national crime to hint, or in the most distant manner insinuate *fear* to British soldiers, it is yet true, that British soldiers are men, and it is peculiar to the constitution of man for him to suffer fear on the approach of death, unless he becomes so excited that passions overcome reflection.

Nor does even the cool, the apparently natural courage of the great Nelson contradict this theory. Though he was not maddened to rage, he had still a strongly acting stimulus! " Now for a peerage, or a tomb in Westminster Abbey!" said he, at the commencement of a battle; and this, to a man who troubled himself very little about a spiritual futurity,—who, whether he did or not, was actuated by a vaulting ambition—to such a man—the peerage and the hero's tomb were powerful stimulants. And farther, when he urged his men to gallantry, by saying, "England expects every man will do his duty!" he only expressed a stimulant, more peculiarly his own—more peculiarly that of his officers, whom England was likely to reward, than that of the thousands of seamen and marines. The love of country may be something, but God knows, the love of the service could be no stimulus to these impressed, flogged, slavishly treated men; and yet they fought in every action more like furies then men. Why was this? simply because the fire, thunder, carnage, and disaster crowded into a small space, drove them mad. Each and all of them were, perhaps, in fight, as reckless of life as their great commander; but they differed in this; he had a multiplicity of objects before him, some of them distant ones, such as the peerage and the Abbey, and these forced exercise on the various intellectual faculties of his mind. They, his seamen and marines, had no such objects to balance the faculties of the mind; the combative man fought furiously because his predominant faculty was excited—the destructive man fought furiously because of his raging desire to kill; other men were furious, merely because they had caught the contagion of madness; and though, awful as the strife must have been to them, on reflection when it was over, and dreadful though it seems to us on contemplation, there was not a seaman who was in a broad-side action, but would always choose it to the less *excitement* of distant and less destructive firing.

Now, the broad-side battle, and the boarding, the storm, and fortress scaling, are similar ; the only difference—if the carnage is equal, is, that the officers, on the quarter-deck, in a naval engagement, observing and giving signals—giving, receiving, and repeating orders· are beyond all comparison more painfully situated, and if they never flinch while the bullets fly athwart their decks, they display incomparably more courage than the officers do, who lead forlorn hopes—mount the breaches hand to hand, with the enemy—lead on the charge, or than they themselves do in boarding their enemy hand to hand, with cutlass and pistol.

Give a man, led to execution, who trembles on the steps of the scaffold, the freedom of his hands ; and suppose him not to have been influenced by anything the *Chaplain* has said to him—let him have the smallest hope of escaping death if he is successful, *to induce him to the attack,* and there are many chances in favour of the supposition that he would attack and board the whole crew of the *gallows*—magistrates, clergy, and executioner! he would attack the whole for his life—and having attacked them, he would feel himself ---*powerful, resolute, and manifesting less fear of death*---beyond all comparison, less fear of death then when *unexcited he trembled* in apprehension of it.

This may be a vulgar, and to some it may appear an unjust comparison to *British valour.* Yet, if we take the trouble to enquire of *ourselves* we will discover a great similarity. The man at the gallows, with his hands bound, if he does not sink down in terror is displaying infinitely more courage than he would do were he to attack the forces around him and meet death by fighting. On the very same principles, the soldier, be he a Colonel or a Drum-boy—if he stands unmoved, which he has no alternative but to do, or shew himself a coward---if he stands unmoved, in line, in column, or in square, and exposed to an enemy's fire, he displays courage, though he may not feel it, infinitely stronger in quality than he does when he fixes the bayonet, raises the shout, and rushes into close quarters ; for then, besides being heedless of death through passion, he is not so ready to be slain as before, and the enemy has at least got a partial defeat.

This then, is the theory and practice of bayonet fighting. And this to any one, who will put themselves to the expense of a few unbiassed thoughts, will throw some light on what bravery is. Let us strip ourselves of national prejudices, and we will find bravery stripped of much of its glory. Some will say, why labour to do anything so unwelcome, so much undesired? I answer, it is less dangerous to know an unpleasant truth, then to dally with an agreeable delusion.

Let it be borne in mind, that in the foregoing paragraphs, I have pronounced no negative on the frequency of the use, and the often successful effects of the bayonet, during the French war. It seems some military writers are at present disputing about its efficiency. Colonel Mitchell for something he has said, is apparently severely dealt with, by a writer in the United Service Journal, who evinces more impetuosity of feeling, than skill in disputation or knowledge of his subject. His article has been reprinted in a widely circulated newspaper,* and is, long ere this humble sheet sees the light admiringly read by thousands, who will never take the trouble to enquire if he is right or wrong. The writer asks many questions † of, was not such, and such places taken at the point of the bayonet, and thinks he overturns his opponent; but he is fighting with himself. He might with nearly as much propriety have asked, was *not* some of the streets in Badajos, as well as positions in many of the battles taken by the *hurrah?* The *cheer,* is nearly entitled to as much credit as the bayonet; for it is the moral effect of both combined, that has established its fame. He repudiates the testimony of medical officers of great experience, who say they rarely saw any bayonet wounds, even among the dead or wounded of the enemy, during the sanguinary French war; and by asserting that certain places were taken at the point of the bayonet, he concludes that there must have been a great slaughter by that weapon, and that there must have been bayonet wounds. Now had a *hurrah,* been capable of producing a physical impression, as it did a moral one, there might have been many wounds produced at charges, which was not the case, though

* Weekly Dispatch, September 9th, 1838.

† By the bye, these questions are asked in a most unmilitary style; if he is a military writer, which his enthusiastic *bayonet charges* against his opponent, would make him appear to be; why does he use the negative *not* in his questions, especially when he expects an affirmative answer. He should know that *not* is an unmilitary word, strictly prohibited in putting questions in all military courts :— the question there being *was* such and such a thing the case. I admit that military courts are not the best models; but in this case, the ungrammatical slang of the lawyers is properly dropped, and this writer should have dropped it also ; because his inconclusive general assertions on the uses of the bayonet, would lead us to suspect that he never saw a bayonet charge, and his unprofessional string of interrogatories, would almost turn that suspicion into belief.

great advantages were often gained. The practical effects of the bayonet, were invariably seen in connection with shot and shells. An enemy was first thrown into disorder by these missiles, and then the mere sight of the bayonets, accompanied with the deafening shouts—which shouts are carefully taught as a part of drill, generally served to make the startled enemy betake themselves to flight ; until they could re-form ; if not—if they stood and shewed front, the bugle was invariably sounded for the charging battalion to retreat to their own ground. If the case was the storming af a garrison, then the showers of bullets and shells thrown over the heads of the storm-ing party into the breaches in front, committed the slaughter, and in almost every case where soldiers went forward on such occasions with fixed bayonets, the bayonets wrought those who carried them more mischief, than they did the enemy.

These statements are made, not alone from personal opinion ; but from an intimate knowledge of the opinions of intelligent old soldiers, many of whom, were in the ranks, and some of whom were officers of the British army, during the fiercest campaigns of the French war. To be sure they are not ready to admit that bravery should be ana-lysed as I have attempted it, nor are they willing to lose any of the fame of the bayonet ; but all will readily admit they would charge into the thickest fight, rather than stand and be fired at. Let the cause of why they would do that, be enquired into.

Perhaps I have kept the battalions of the Legion standing too long waiting for orders to charge on the Venta hill. But as some omis-sions were made in the earlier descriptive paragraphs of this chapter, it is necessary here to supply them, before taking the hill which finished the work of the 15th of March.

The 7th regiment were drawn up early in the day under the Puyo battery awaiting orders. About twelve o'clock an Aid-de-camp arrived from the Brigadier, ordering the right wing of the regiment under Major Brennan, to make a diversion to draw the enemy from a large fortified house in front of the battery, at which Colonel Fitch com-mandant of Puyo had been keeping up an ill-directed fire during the entire of the morning. The left wing remained in their position until three o'clock, when General Godfrey went up and ordered Colonel Beckham to move forward and take the fortified position. The men were ordered to advance without firing a shot, and they did so under a heavy flank fire on the right. Having descended a steep hill and crossed a ravine, they ascended the other side still exposed to the flank fire from the right; but these, the left wing, reaching the top of the hill were agreeably surprised to find their right wing taking possession of the fortified house. Having formed column there, and waited an hour for the assistance of the Chapelgorris, the 7th advanced, and with considerable loss to themselve, drove the Carlists backwards near the Venta hill. At this time the 6th regiment, and Royal Artillery (British), with the Legion Artillery and part of the Rocket Brigade were gradually moving forward to the ground from which they intended storming the Venta; the rockets, and occasionally a shell, clearing the way before them, the 6th had therefore little to do at that time.

To the left of where the 7th were, the 8th and Chapelgorris were engaged, and further to the left the general action with all our other forces was going on. The 7th being ordered to advance by companies to a position, from which they could fire on the barricades at the bottom of the Venta, they advanced but received a peppering until they gained a partial cover. At this time they had a considerable number of severe wounds though only a few killed, and as they were not farther exposed that evening their loss did not then increase much. About the only subsequent casualty, was a wound received by Lieut. O'Brien.

This officer loved his bottle, and on this occasion was said to have partaken freely, still no one suspected that he drank from cowardice, for in truth, there were few braver officers than Jack O'Brien—"Honest Jack" as they called him in the regiment. He was amusing himself by standing rather conspicuously, and as the bullets struck on the ground around him, cutting at the place he saw them strike, as if he would cut them. Colonel Beckham ordered him to move forward his company, on which he exclaimed,—" By Jasus will I Colonel! and I'll go forward till I take quarters for my men in Hernani; —I'll let the rascals see what stuff Irish Boys are made of." At this moment he got a ball through the leg, which cut short his threat. He called loudly for the " Docthor," who on turning to assist him, received a bullet in the left shoulder. Jack O'Brien was taken from the field. He was afterwards killed in the murderous disaster at Andouin.

The 7th were now in that position where they were to fire over the 8th as we advanced on the Venta. We were standing in close column, when General Evans came up at a gallop, his horse swathed in foam, occasioned by the unceasing energy with which he was riding to and from different positions; positions, that by the intersection of heights, rocks, ravines, and woods were separated from each other. I heard him address our commanding officer with the words "Colonel Hogg, you must halt here until I get you more assistance." The Colonel answered, "pray General let me go, nothing can oppose us. Men!" addressing himself to the regiment, "will you take the enemy's defences yourselves, or divide the honor with another regiment?" A loud yelling cheer answered him as he expected; but whether from the consciousness that the *General* heard us, or from knowing that we must go whether voluntarily or not, or from the mere desire to be brave, I cannot say; but there was an inspiriting cheer; and when the General heard it, he said "well, go then, and let me see your determination take you across every barricade!"*

It was twilight. We emerged from our temporary cover, bayonets fixed, right in front. There had been for a short while a comparative cessation of fire; but the moment we were seen by the enemy, red gleamed the flashes, and loud roared the rattle. Whiz, whiz, went the bullets past our ears; chip, chip, came the pieces of stones, and earth among our feet, as the wrathful bullets battered on the ground; Colonel Hogg, Majors Wilson, and Shields; and Captain Shields, with other officers led the front, cheering the men onwards, and dashed along. None of the front section had fallen, though we could hear the thick flying shot was taking effect behind us, when a grand illumination lighted all around, the firmament quivering, and the ears deafened as if the world had burst into fire and thunder. It was the Artillery. In our rear was the thunder of the discharge, over head was the trembling concussion of the bullets on their ourse, and in front was the succeeding rattle of bursting shells, terrible to the astounded enemy; but animating to us who knew the

---

* How can the General reconcile this, with his studied omission of the regiment in general orders. How does he reconcile this, and the manner in which the regiment *did* go forward, of which he was an eye witness, with the eulogy heaped on the 9th regiment, that was on another line of attack, supported by the 10th, and three Spanish regiments, all of which went forward almost *without opposition;* was it true that General Fitzgerald, and Colonel Herman, could do anything they chose with General Evans at this time.

the friendly sound of our own thunder. The cannon had been all ready for that moment, and when the signal of our advance was given, they emitted in one awfully grand volley their shells and spherical cases, which, with the rushing rockets, fell among the enemy, slaying all around. For a few seconds the bullets that met us slackened, the momentary confusion of the enemy was overcome, and again, the fire on our right flank, from behind intrenchments was received. Our Artillery fired on ; and we were getting towards the first barricade where there might be some momentary shelter, but no time could be lost, for success or utter disaster awaited us. Rushing to this, but still fifty yards from it, a loud whizzing sound passed over head, accompanied by such a concussion, that many of the men staggered though none were struck; it was a volley of canister shot from a large gun on the Venta. Fortunately for us it was too high, saving in the rear, where a few persons were knocked down by it. Our Adjutant had his third horse, for that day, killed; and General Godfrey was unhorsed although his duty was not in this part of the action. But that shot passed, and we in front felt at every step that we were getting lower than the musketry, and we felt that was getting thinner, owing to the pouring vollies of shells that came over head from our Artillery, and fell in front among the enemy. " Come on my lads ! come on," Colonel Hogg, exclaimed, as the canister volley alluded to went over us without harm ; " they can't touch us with that" he continued. As he uttered these words I had glanced my eyes for a second to the top of the Venta, to satisfy myself if it had been a cannon shot from that direction, when I saw a second flash from the battery. I saw it at the moment that the Colonel said, " they can't touch us." Oh God ! the next moment where were we ? They did touch us ! they had seen the other, half a minute before, to be too high, and this met us fair in our front. A man at my side was ripped open, another made a stifled exclamation as he fell ! Major Shields, staggered to the side of the road and short as was my glance of him, I could see the scabbard of his sword broken, or nearly broken in two pieces—others were sprawling, still the Colonel was safe, and still the cheering shouts were kept up. Another glance at the battery ! another flash ! another horrid sensation of whizzing sounds, and with others I lay flat on the road.

My ears rung and my eyes quivered; yet I could hear groans and

No. 27.

prayers, and wild shouting hurrahs mingled with furious oaths, uttered as men running, *damned* others running with them, to look at their bayonets; some of these weapons, now and then being run into a comrade, amid the confusion of men falling—falling, both by wounds and by reason of the uneven ground on which many had to scramble, the roadway being narrow. I could also see wild-like faces, at one moment dimly seen, at another, terribly visible by the lurid light that flickered and quivered from rockets and shells. I do not know that I marked, but I might have marked, as some did, the glaring eye, protruding from a blazing face, red with insane stupidity; a mouth gaping as the panting lungs laboured to inhale breath; I might have seen these exhibited by some poor wretch who knew not whither he ran! but still, with outstretched neck, protruding eyes, deafened ears, and labouring lungs, kept a direct course forward, like the hydrophobial dog, until it might be, perchance, some bullet, in mercy struck him down. Or, I might have seen men bounding lightly forward from companies in the rear, and by the agility of their limbs springing to the front. I might have seen those who were loud with the shout, whose life was youth and lively vigour, who, though the prodigal sons of grieving mothers, were yet the fondly cherished objects of maternal love. Ah! poor Barr! you were one of them, and the bullet that cut you open, left you no time to send even one sigh of affection to your mother, in return for her ceaseless prayers; but though the hopeful son, you were affectionate; you were the pride of your regiment too, and I told your mother where and how you died. I might have seen these—these, throughout youth, gay and reckless, falling with shattered limbs, to return armless and legless beggars to their own country. I might have seen, things that will perhaps be deemed strange but which in war are common,— I might have seen those who were supposed brave and who boasted loudest of how they would like a glorious fight.—Many of these were seen, both officers and men, shewing themselves *cowards*.

All these and many other incidents might have been observed, and I did observe some of them; but though I have here filled a considerable space with these observations, I did not then remain long enough where I had fallen, to mark the varied incidents around me. When I had been nearly a minute on the ground, half stupified,—not knowing why I had fallen; but yet on a piece of even ground where nothing could have tripped me over, and being certain no person had come in contact with me, I concluded that beyond doubt I must be shot. The whirling of the world round and round, with a consciousness of being half stupified, and a recollection of having heard wounded men say, that they were insensible to pain on first receiving their wounds, made me suspect that I was wounded, and a pain which I began to feel in my left side confirmed my opinion. I must farther state, and run the risk of being laughed at,—for I would gladly know what other people have thought on such occasions ; therefore though ridicule, be ready pointed as I can fancy I see it, when the reader discovers the real nature of my fall—I must state that for a period long enough to allow of some revolving thoughts, though I am uncertain of what the exact length of the period was, it could not be long, I strongly suspected I had got a pass into the next world. It will be easily supposed, that *appearances* did not warrant me to form the most favourable conclusion of where I had landed. Long tailed rockets vomiting fire and smoke in their rear, with the belching of big guns, and the rattle of small ones; the dawning of red lights and blue, above and below; (I was at the time lying on a road where the ground rose on one side, and sloped on the other) ; these *appearances*, I must confess, I beheld as rather alarming. The men were still hurrying on, and as they passed, now visibly red, by the lurid flashes of the guns, and then indistinctly dark, they to an excited imagination passed away like a troop of " black spirits and grey," and I perhaps, being conscious enough, that I had deserved the *down-hill* road as well as most of my neighbours, formed a very unpleasant opinion of my new companions. Among the spiritual troop that seemed running a race to their new quarters, or to prepare a billet for me, was my friend the *champion*, whom the reader will perhaps remember. His face as usual beamed forth its good nature, had I been able to see it in a less deceitful light ; but as it then appeared, it was as like the region where I supposed we were, as any other. He saw me, and though not halting to receive an answer, uttered the enquiring exclamation of " oh Sandy are ye dead." There can be nothing wrong with me I thought, as I began to stir myself, and found all my limbs entire. My hand attracted by the pain to my side, I felt that my fingers went into a hole, and I knew no hole had been there previously ; I drew them out, and

there was blood on them ; can it really be that a bullet has gone into
me, and I not know, I again enquired of myself.   As I put this self
interrogatory, I saw a man coming backwards with his intestines in
his hands !   They were falling out of his belly, and he was still
walking and holding them up !   At sight of him I started half up,
and taking off my waist-belt, found one of the causes of why I was
lying there.   A bullet had gone through my haversack, which was
girded firmly by my side by the belt ; it had broken my brandy bottle,
which I had always preserved from all accidents, and even from the
suspicions of any one about me, that I had such a thing.   It had
served me in good stead for six days, and now it was gone at a time,
that with the mountains for a bed, and the clouds for a covering, it
was to be most useful.   The *blood* I had seen on my hand, was occasioned by cutting my fingers on it ! and the pain in my side, was
caused by the bullet making its way through a piece of salt beef, an
orderly-book of an inch thick, and twenty rounds of ammunition ; which we all carried extra for contingencies.   It then took a
slanting direction through a few hundred folds of paper, on which I
had written some notes of the campaign, and coming in contact with
my knife and spoon, it was arrested much to the safety of my interior.
But yet with such violence did the spoon and it contend, that the
spoon which had been used to a more legitimate place of entrance,
was, by offering opposition, knocked with such violence against a rib,
as to break it,   Yet none of these could sufficiently account for my
falling, far less for the momentary insanity which had overcome me.
But having discovered that a shot had carried off the heel of my boot,
and that another struck me, but barely, on the forehead ; I found a
cause for being tripped up and stunned, and getting a glance of what
was going on in front, I started up, and learned from circumstances
afterwards told, that I had been barely more than a minute down.

The grandeur, and the disaster of the scene was now at its climax.
Colonel Hogg, brave even to a fault, had first reached the barricade,
that fifteen feet high, crossed the road.   He was on the top of it,
and some of the men were scrambling up to him.   From behind
intrenchments the shot of the enemy flew thickly around them, and
was even battering down the earth of the turf-built defences in our
faces, as we, who were not yet up, were climbing to the top.   It was
evident that none of the enemy could take an aim, or they might

have struck every man of us as we got up, especially the Colonel and the younger Shields, who stood on the top, fairly exposed, waving their swords and cheering the companies who had not got forward to come on. They, and indeed all of us who mounted, were saved by the incessant falling of shells, which coming over our heads, fell between us and the enemy.

Our gunners, perhaps, not being aware how near we had got, threw them with unabated zeal, and so narrowly were they missing ourselves, that we could not get farther forward. The men not yet on the barricades, saw the danger we were in, better than we did ourselves, indeed the confusion of fire and noise was such, that we did not know which fire proceeded from the enemy, until one of the shells coming in contact with a barricade, carried a piece of it away, and immediately after exploding, covered some of our men with earth, which harmless covering, was fortunately occasioned by it having fallen into a trench before exploding. Then following it, another came, that by the violence of its concussion only, threw us from the top of the barricade, to the enemy's side. It being evident by these, that our Artillery did not know we were so close to the enemy, the Colonel immediately ordered all of us to fire, and keep up the fire foeward so that we might be observed. This had the effect desired; the Artillery ceased, and we tearing for some minutes to pull down the barricades to admit of the main body of the regiment who had not got over, re-formed with what men we had on that side, and rushed forward to keep our ground good, and get more.

How long the remainder, who wrought at the defences took to pull them down, I do not know.—" Forward ! forward, men ! " was the cry, and we ascended the hill, but under great disadvantages ; for the ascent being in some parts perpendicular, we had to wind round towards the side where the Spanish and Irish were going up, and this allowed them to get partly in front of us. The Carlists were lying about without heads, and pieces of heads without bodies, some of them torn to pieces by the rockets : I only saw one lying who was not dead, he was an officer, and had both his legs shot off. One of the Spanish soldiers fired a ball into his forehead, which was no doubt mercy, whether it was intended for such or not. The first one who mounted the fortification on the top , I believe, was Lieut. Conlonel

Cotter of the 9th (a short while before Major) ; immediately following him was a mixture from all the regiments that had been engaged in the assault. Our bugles sounded "halt," but some of us were determined to see the top of the hill, and pushed on. The Carlists had precipitately left it, and our first act was to get in and take possession of four pieces of cannon, and pull down the flag. This, of course, was easily done, but all was not quite over then.

The battery was formed by a substantial turf wall, built circularly, enclosing a space about sixty feet wide. The wall was fifteen feet high, but the sudden slope of the cone-shaped hill, caused it to be much higher to those who made a risk to leap over it, and that was done. A barrel containing half a pipe of wine, and another with spirits, were found, and, of course, there was an immediate scramble for them. There was only access from the outside by a ladder ; but the interior was speedily crowded even by it. A part of the ground beneath our feet was boarded over, and one particular spot was covered so as to be bomb-proof; in this there was a magazine of powder. The cry rose, " there's a match burning in the magazine ! " Heavens, what a scene ! no rush could be made, for the whole place was gorged full of men, and those on the outside were crushed to the wall so, that very few of them got the chance of breaking their necks by going over. A crowd overloaded the ladder by which we had come in, and smash it went with a score tumbling down. I was wedged in a crowd near the centre on the very top of the magazine ; some one said there was no powder there. An Irishman looked down and started up, calling, " Holy Saviour, save me, there's twenty of them, and the straw's afire." A Spanish soldier who was next the opening, looked down, he vociferated " feugo" (fire,) crossed himself, and mingling with the roar that the others set up, leapt over their shoulders. A mixture of prayers, oaths, Spanish and English, and crushing from the centre, ensued. Then there was a stillness—I saw smoke issuing from amongst our feet, and almost at the same moment, up with a blaze and a burst, came a volume of fire amongst those who crowded at the wine-pipe. They were not drinking, but they had been, and an instantaneous crush was then felt from that direction. The Spaniards prayed, and the former mixture of interjections was again heard. I observed one man of the 9th, who had been frantic in his utterance of a string of saintly words, and who was the

first one I had heard giving the alarm ; he went forward to the pipe
of wine, filled his canteen, which held three pints, commenced
drinking, and turned to another one, who beheld him with horror,
said, "be the *Book* man alive, is it a fool you are always to be
didn't ye see me adoin' it ? och, now, fill it, or the match 'll be after
going out, and ne'er a one of us 'll get going near it again." Mike
very coolly filled his own canteen and other two, and then, as the
magazine was not likely to go off, some others ventured to the wine
also, and the hubbub around it became worse than ever. Mike was
making his way down the hill at the same time I went, and was loud
in the praise of his experiment ; he continued, "ne'er a snuff of a
magazine is there itself nor be me sowl was there a lit, till I lit it ! it
was agoin' out on me more nor t'ree times, by the blessed trut'."
The real state of the affair was, that the Irishman got up the cry of
the magazine, and then scattered his own ammunition about, put a
light to it, and exploded it amongst those at the wine-pipe, so as he
could get at the wine himself !

When I came down to the bottom of the hill, I found the regiment had been re-formed from the confusion, and that all those who
were absent were estimated as lost. It being dark, I was not seen,
and I had therefore an opportunity of hearing what many have
desired to hear, but few ever heard, *namely*, what people said about
me when I was dead ! There were some who would not be contradicted, one said, "but I tell ye I saw him killed on the road afore
ever we came to the foot o' the" "yes," another added, "I saw a
ball gang through 'is haversack an' in till him when yon awfu' *sough*
gaed o'er us." "Weel" said another, "ye may say as ye like, but I
saw him come to this side when the first o' us came o'er." "Hets,
let *him* gang," said another, one by the bye, that had often been
esteemed by me as a friend, "let *him* gang, we can spare 'im ! there's
better nor him lyin' doon i' the road." "My ghost 'll haunt you
my friend," said I to myself, "but go on, this is a very interesting
part of personal occurrences, I shall not interrupt you," I thought·
But to be short, some proposed to go and look for me, and when one
re-urged that it was of no use, that "he's as dee'd's a herrin'."
Another added, "we'll go and bury 'im at at any rate, that's the
least we can do, he would 've done that to any of us."

I was then discovered by my going to the assistanec of Major

Shields, who was endeavouring to make his way to the regiment from where he was mentioned to have staggered to the side of the road. A grape shot had struck the scabbard of his sword—had flattened it with such violence against his thigh as to injure the limb severely.

The other regiments came all forward, and were sent along into different fields to lie for the night. We were now on a range of heights facing the south, with the Venta hill on our right, and extending nearly two miles eastward, near to the river where it turns to the north, below Astigarraga. Hernani lay down below us about a mile, with a high rocky hill overhanging it on its west side. This hill is called Santa Barbara, and cost the English, under Wellington, a six week's siege, with nine thousand men, to take it from the French, and it is not to be supposed that the Carlists were going to throw its advantages away for nothing. There was a common enquiry amongst both men and officers, of why the General did not go on to Hernani when we had the Carlists on the run? and though these questions were easily answered, still the " correspondents," and the " news from Spain," inquired why did Evans not go? I will answer. Though the passage had been free to the town, which it was not while the walls stood, and the gates were shut against us, though we had forced our way into it by storm that night, which it was possible to have done, the town would have been taken, and the garrison and all the Carlist army would have retired from it to the height of Santa Barbara, while our army would have ravaged and plundered, as all soldiers have done in all times on such occasions, and they would have therefore been incapable of defending it next morning, when the Carlists would have poured down from the hills above. Evans would have been then denounced, and then with justice; as it was, he acted discreetly, and I never saw such resignation to circumstances with any men, nor such cheerfulness with us as was manifested that night in taking up our quarters on the hill-side. Arms were piled—that is, the muskets were put up in rows, three being fixed together by the ramrods crossing at the muzzle, the butts being set triangularly at about thirty inches from each other. Apple-trees were cut down , and fires kindled. Some made beds with the branches of the trees to keep them above the wet saturated ground, others sat round the fires, and all congratulated themselves on the day's fighting having been so successful ; and were saying, " we'll have nothing to do to-morrow, but just go down and walk into Hernani:" so some people thought, but it was found to be otherwise.

CHAPTER XXII.

Morning of the 16th of March—and re-commencement of the fight—1st regiment abandoned by the Spaniards—Rifles, their fate, bravery of Colonel Fortescue and cowardice of Lieut. Col. Boyd, death of Capt. Feilding &c.—3rd and 4th, Colonel Fitzgerald—General engagement—Prisoners taken and slain by the enemy—Colonel Cotter and the 9th regiment, bravery and death of Cotter —Retreat—Rallying—Abandonment of the Venta, &c. &c.—with numerous incidents.

FROM province to province the reports spread, with a rapidity scarcely credible, that Evans had forced the Carlist positions, and was within a skirmish of being able to command the main road that leads to France.   To stop his career was a matter of the utmost importance to the Carlists, and every energy of theirs was put forth that night, to arrest his progress at daylight.   The prayers were offered up ; the priestly benedictions were pronounced ; and the peasants, under their influence, ran through the glens, and crossed the hills, at a rate of speed performable only by the mountaineers familiar with the goatpaths, and full of passionate devotion to the cause of their party. By eight o'clock, on the evening of the 15th, the news arrived at Durango, that the Venta fortifications had been taken ; and it was seen that if any thing could be done to repel Evans, and save the Carlist cause, it must be done, and that immediately.   Messengers were again dispatched, ordering every inhabitant of the country to fly towards Hernani, to assist in its defence; and imploring the garrison to hold out, and the retreating army to rally round its walls to defend it till ten o'clock next morning, and by that time powerful re-inforcements would arrive : above all, the positions commanding the main road towards France were to be maintained, if possible.   Espartero lay with his army in and around Bilbao, and had engaged himself to move against Durango, the Carlist head-quarters, at the same time that Evans attacked Hernani.   General Saarsfield, who commanded the Queen's army in another part of the country, was to move at the same time ; or, at least, he was to menace the enemy with a movement, to occupy their attention in that quarter.   But he did not do so.   A week previous to the 15th, the Carlist army was withdrawn from before him, and brought to strengthen the force against Evans; and during the night of the 15th, about ten thousand men were withdrawn from before Espartero, and hurriedly marched across the mountains to assist the army, already twice our number, at Hernani. Espartero is not an indolent man, nor does he want energy and decision. His military executions formerly put in force, by shooting every tenth man of the Chapelgorris, prove him to be a man that can act with energy : but he is a traitor, and a knave. I saw him once, arm in arm with the good-natured Evans. Their size, age, shape, mustachios, whiskers, and general features are so very much alike, that they might have been believed to be twins, had not the serpent cunning that lay lurking in the Spaniard's features denied the affinity. When I saw them, they had just met, for the first time, at San Sebastian. The multitude gathered to see Espartero land on the quay. Evans met him; and the crowd caused them to take their rout by a private street which brought them close to the window of a house where I had, for a time, the felicity of being a family visitor. Evans seemed delighted, and directed the stranger's attention to surrounding objects, by conversation and gesture. The listener also *seemed* pleased : and I know Evans was unbosoming his soul without reserve, for I saw it in his look ; and they stood a while close to the window where I was, none of their staff-officers presuming to come near them. There was a leer in Espartero's eye, that stole scanning glances at Evans, while pretending to look at something else : it was a serpent twisting its cunning round the open-hearted Irishman, charming its unwary prey. I said to myself, "that man's a villain!" and continued to think him so; even though an enchantress that looked through the same pane of glass, with a pair of uncontradictable eyes, whispered in a tone of soft persuasion, that " el meger hombre," &c. ; that he was the best man in Spain. Evans did not know me; nor was he aware, so far as I know, that such a person was in the Legion, but he will remember that afternoon ; and I am doubtful if there was one of the gaudy train that followed him gave their soul's silent sympathy a license in his behalf, as the humble soldier, looking through the window, did. I had seen, before that time, that General Evans was a victim to his own easy nature; and again, at that moment, he shewed himself what he really is, too honest, generous, and open-hearted in his own character, and unsuspicious of others, in fact too much of a good man to be capable of standing on any of the giddy pinnacles of ambition! This is the true character of General Evans; and let him get credit for it, in spite of all political hostilities.

These are the characters of two men—Espartero and Evans; from whom the sanguinary conflict of the 16th of March drew its character. The first acted the part of a traitor; and the other, true to the union of effort, as jointly planned, led on the continued attack at daybreak, on the morning of the 16th, fully depending on the co-operation of the other two faithless chiefs.

At daylight I felt some one shaking me, where I was lying across the broken branches of an apple tree, which I had spread to keep myself above the gutters of mud and water. "Start, rise; d' ye no' hear what's gaun on?" saluted me, and I woke to hear cannon and musketry rolling on, the same as it had been the day before. Hesitating a moment to think whether it was still yesterday, or a new morning, I *gaunted*, rubbed my eyes, felt myself shivering with cold, ravenously hungry, saw the clouds on the frontiers of France panoramically changing into red, and then started to my feet, joined in the cry of "up men, up!" saw the Colonel rise from *his* dyke-side, put on his sword, heard him call for his horse, and then I, with others, drank as fast as it could be served out, one *tott* of aquardiente, about two-thirds of an imperial gill. Oh, it was a delectable mouthful! my recollections of past enjoyments recur to it as one of the most sensually delightful moments of my life! the chilling frost of teetotalism would have melted before it into *dew!* for the soul that lies purely cold in its moral snow, had it inhabited any poor carcase on the Venta hill, that night, would have thawed natural ice from the body, by dispelling the artificial winter of the mind: or, if I may venture on the opposite side of the moral creed, I will say the liquor was partly drunk in anticipation of the demoniacal performance of the day; it was the devil giving his children a sweetening mouthful to please them, while he sent them out to play on one of his holidays! However, it was swallowed; the old charges were drawn from the muskets, these were reloaded with fresh cartridges, the wet frost wiped off the locks; and we, with other regiments, were commanded to march forward to the renewed fight. But before entering it, we must make a few prefatory remarks."

One of the common reports in the newspapers has been, that General Evans neglected to fortify, destroy, or in some way command the bridge, so as to prevent the Carlist reinforcements from crossing the river. Every one finding fault with Evans, has taken up this as a proof of his incapacity : amongst others, General Shaw. Now, that officer (Shaw) could not, by any possibility, know the positions around Astigarraga bridge : he never saw the village but at a distance; and he never saw the ground on the north side of it at all, where the action of the 16th was fought, because it was in possession of the Carlists all the time that he was in the neighbourhood of San Sebastian. And for the justice of other reports, let the following explanation suffice.

Had Evans been able to destroy the bridge, there were reasons for not doing so. But before he could do it he must have battered down, or been in possession of the village; and if he had possessed the village, or the site of its ruins, there was no necessity for destroying the bridge. Also, Evans had every reason to believe that he would beat the Carlists that day, as he had done before, trusting, as he did, to the plan of co-operation before explained. Now, there, is an incontrovertible apology for General Evans, with regard to that universally quoted mistake of his. And the situation of the other wooden foot-path bridge, behind Hernani, admits of a similar explanation, but shorter. Evans could get no artillery within cannon shot of it, excepting guns that were on the main road, having rising grounds intervening between them and the wooden bridge. Also, with regard to that artillery, Evans rode up to Colonel Colquhoun, while the latter was throwing some monstrous shells and balls, from his heavy battering guns, into the town—balls that set chimnies and steeples spinning into the air, and shells that gutted and unroofed houses at one explosion—while Colquhoun was doing that, Evans rode up to him, and ordered him to desist. He made observations to this effect : " let us fight their army, not the inhabitants of the town ; I know you could level it in half-an-hour, but I would rather remain where I am, than take possession of the ruins of the town and villages ; besides, Colquhoun, there are none in it now but women and children ! "

The 1st regiment of the Legion was posted on the extreme left of our positions. Their work began early, and it was not long till they found themselves, at least, two companies of them, in a fatal position. These were the two flank companies, which having advanced considerably farther than any of the other positions held by the Legion—being as far respectively as two houses by the river-side, when it was intended they should check the Carlists, should they *advance*, which was not expected—being there, these two companies were cut off from their regiment by a battalion of Spaniards having given way near them. The slaughter, consequent on this was dreadful, for nothing being apprehended, the men were having their rations, and when the alarm spread that they were nearly surrounded, some of them it was said ran out without their muskets, and by the time they returned for them they were too late to make their escape. If such was the case it was about the only irregularity with which they could be charged, and they atoned dearly for it. These two companies made their way through the bushes to rejoin their battalion by literally forcing their way through the enemy's ranks. The gallantry of the officers, who commanded them was nobly displayed.* Of one company, only about twenty men reached the regiment, the remainder, amounting to nearly fifty men were shot dead or wounded ; if wounded, they were immediately bayoneted as the enemy closed on them. The other company was scarcely so severely dealt with, but still lost nearly a ha'f of its men. It may not be improper to note an incident of that slaughter which might by some be magnified into something greater than it really was were I not to mention it. Two Sergeants, in serving out the company's rations had tasted more than their own share of aquardiente and were sitting on the boxes that had contained the biscuit. At the retreat of the Spaniards and the consequent pressure of the Carlists in the rear being discovered, these two worthies were informed of the necessity of instant exertion ; but they declared they would not stir until they had another *drop !* they being in that state when neither court-martial or any other threat frightened them. They sat still, and I dare say they were at last considerably surprised to find that the *pot boys* whom they supposed themselves calling to, came and *served* them by running their bayonets into them !

---

* At the time of this being written I am not to a certainty informed of their names. I know who were there ; but as there were some exceptions to the conduct of one or two of them I shall name them hereafter.

The fight began to look lively ! The thunder to which we were now accustomed was again begun from right to left, and those who were spectators, such as I was at that time, beheld with profound interest the growing battle. When the first derangement was manifested on the left among the Spaniards and 1st regiment, the Rifles, under the gallant Fortescue, an officer, whose bravery can never be over-rated, played a conspicuous part. That corps was stationed near the 3d and 4th, these being now joined in one battalion and under the command of Lieutenant Colonel Fitzgerald, an officer, formerly distinguished for bravery, but who, at this time, either neglected or was accused of neglecting his duty as a commanding officer. The Rifles being near them and Colonel Fortescue making a dashing charge down a ravine with one wing of his regiment—a charge in which, however, he lost a considerable number of his men, and had some of his best officers wounded.—Colonel Fitzgerald,* was accused of having disobeyed orders in not doing something similar. As it was, Colonel Fitzgerald stood with his regiment under a heavy fire and met the enemy ; indeed, his position was such, that the loss of his regiment and coolness in sustaining it, was greater than that of the Rifles in the same time, for the latter having gone down the ravine were considerably lower than the enemy's fire. Therefore, Fitzgerald was not guilty of cowardice, if he was guilty of a breach of orders, for which he was afterwards tried by a court-martial. It is even likely, had he not remained where he was, that the Carlists would have got in the rear of the Rifles and cut them off altogether ; but still, as he was declared guilty of a breach of order, and as the honorable Chichester, against whom no officer or soldier ever breathed blame from the beginning to the termination of our service---as he was the accuser of Colonel Fitzgerald, there must have been something wrong.

The remainder of the Rifles were under the command of a person named Boyd, who had once been a private soldier in, and who was and is yet a deserter from the 11th foot, British service. The subsequent rise of this man to be a Lieut.-Colonel, was perhaps as remarkable an instance of the perversion of justice, as ever was recorded. But not to digress from the narrative of the engagement, the

---

* No relation of the General of that name.

reader is referred to the foot note,* for other matters relative to this person, and to follow out the sketch of the fight, I shall quote a paragraph written soon after its occurrence; written while we were yet on the ground of our disasters; but written with that strict accordance to truth, which renders it even at this cool period, needless of alteration. The paragraph says :—

"The Rifles, especially, stood with obstinate determination; and it is a pity that those who like to hear of daring bravery should have only sneered at the Legion for that day's work, for the Rifle regiment alone merited praise, which, though other regiments had merited none, should have counterbalanced the common obloquy. There was one person of note, however, in that regiment, that proved himself, what he had been often suspected to be—a coward! He was a person who, by some most unpardonable oversight of those high in rank, got promoted to be next in command to the gallant Colonel Fortescue of the Rifles. At a moment when the Carlists were overpowering them, General Chichester, who galloped furiously across their front, and who different times rode forward on the enemy sword in hand, and the English regiments following him, dispatched an imperative order for the left wing of the Rifles to charge, and that instantly, adding, "they must go down yonder, and stand till the

---

* Boyd was a policeman in Glasgow, about the year 1831; and went out to Portugal with the renowned Shaw. He was there made a Sergeant, and ultimately Adjutant. He performed many services to his master, of a character, that the law of libel forbids a publisher who has anything to lose, to publish ; suffice it to say, he was one of the council of *three* who levied fines on the men, and sold the regimental rations to the regiment; first pretending there was a scarcity, and then *generously* obtaining an *extra* supply, for which they stopped the pay. He was one who knew what came of the *funny box !* that in which the fines were deposited ; and then, for these and innumerable other odds and ends, not quite mentionable ; he was made a Captain in Spain, afterwards Brigade-Major, ultimately Lieut.-Colonel. He now hangs on the rear of *Sir* Charles Shaw his patron, threatening to inform or *snitch*, which is nearer the phraseology of both gentlemen ; if the gallant *knight* does not get him into something, through his *friends* the Government. At the same time, *Sir* Charles Shaw *would* do something to save consequence if he could ; but he has been heard to declare, that the honor of knighthood has materially injured him ; for before he was gazetted, he could at times borrow eighteen-pence or half-a-crown, which he cannot manage so well now ; and Boyd *will* keep tormenting him so for a place, when God knows he hasn't one to himself.

It is such persons as these, who cause an impression to prevail, that men raised from the ranks, are unfit to be officers. But it so happens, that almost every man, who misconducted himself as an officer on promotion from the ranks, were persons whom a conscientious commanding officer would not have promoted. The error was therefore in the *bad choice*, not in the badness of the materials from which the choice was made.

last man falls ! Officers, use your swords—and men, your bayonets !"
At the same time, the old fellow headed a part of another regiment,
and slashed the leaders of the Carlists down with his own hand. His
Aide-de-camp instantly delivered the order to Colonel Boyd. That
worthy suggested the propriety of sending a young officer, Captain
Fielding to lead them on, using the words, " he wishes to distinguish himself, and you know that I have proved that I could go long
before this." " Go yourself, Colonel Boyd ; that is the General's
order," continued the Aide-de-camp. " Oh, permit me to go," said
the young officer. " Yes, sir, go," said Colonel Boyd ; " I am not
able, I'm so dreadfully knocked up." The young man led out two
companies, and rushing forward on the enemy, fell dead in front of
his men. The other, who did not go, of course saved his life, but
he ought to have lost it, for when a man goes to be a soldier,
whatever rank he may hold, no compromise should save him in such
emergencies."

" About this time the Carlists were becoming more bold and
forward. Don Sebastian, arrived from Durango with ten thousand
infantry and three hundred cavalry. These, as they came to Hernani,
were liberally supplied with spirits, and had promises made to them
that their arrears of pay would be forthcoming next day, to induce
them to go forward. It was now that column after column marched
up in front of us, and had they come in front only, then they would
have stood or turned away ; but, unfortunately, the vast superiority
of their numbers, and a wide extent of country in their possession,
compared with the ground that we occupied, enabled them to come
round on our flanks, which no power or plan could have avoided with
the comparatively small force that was matched against them.

Our brave Irish brethren were not idle then. Sad pity it is that
the reckless manner in which they let themselves be slaughtered
should have been so unworthily estimated at home by the lovers of
the magnificently bloody—for could these have seen the Irish, or had
any one reported their conduct but those who dared not go near
enough to see it, their true character would have become known.
Colonel O'Connel, of the 10th, repeatedly led on his men, and met
the Carlists hand to hand. Colonel Cotter, of the 9th, was equally
resolute and reckless, and his " Cork boys" did not give him it all to
do himself. He was, after repeated personal encounters, engaged in

close quarters, and when, by a furious No. 5 cut, he had half-severed a head from a body, he gave the primary thrust, and ran his sword obliquely into another man's breast-bone, where, in drawing it out rapidly to defend himself on his other side from those who were round him, he broke it, leaving eighteen inches in the victim's body. Though showers of bullets played about him as he wheeled his horse and retreated in search of another sword, he escaped with nothing more than one ball through his left leg—but could *he* go off the field with that wound ? No ! his tragedy was not played out—he wanted a sword, and the next paragraph must tell how he got one.

A Carlist Colonel had been taken prisoner by some of the Lancers ; the real merit of which capture however, belonged to a man named Robert M'Intyre and partly to another, named John Leckie, both of the 8th regiment. These two, with some others, while the regiment lay in reserve, had crept through the bushes, and unseen by the Carlists taken a few marked shots at them. The Colonel alluded to, advanced as if reconnoitring, and one or both of them shot his horse, and wounded him slightly in the neck. M'Intyre rushed forward, but at the same moment some of the Lancers also and the latter carried away the prisoner. M'Intyre got his sword, and meeting soon after an officer of the 7th, named Kenny, of whom something amusing will be heard soon—he sold the sword, and the latter observing Colonel Cotter without one, furnished him.

Shortly after, Cotter, at the head of some companies of his gallant regiment, was seen in close quarters with the enemy. We of the 8th were by this time hot at it near to where he was; but I shall say nothing more of ourselves until I tell out his story. Nearly a whole company of those who had rushed forward with him were killed or taken prisoners. Three thousand men, at least, were in front of them ; for the Carlists at that point were three regiments deep; the battalions in rear pushing up those in front. Cotter played a noble part. With the sword of their own General, he dealt about blows that split heads, and knocked the muskets and bayonets as they came against him, to the ground. He was completely surrounded ; but, in front and rear of his body, with his horse springing wildly amongst clashing bayonets, smoke, and fire, he dealt his blows about. At last the charger fell, and the gallant rider, exhausted with wounds, sunk below as many bayonets as could be dashed into his body at once !

No. 28.

There, and thus fell Colonel Cotter! I have not overcharged a sentence—A thousand eye-witnesses still live to testify the truth of what is here written. That day has been called national disgrace! I should like to see what page of history contains a name more honorable to his country, if the death of a hero is any honor. But that is one of the first who bravely fell—there are others to be recorded.

Reserve regiments have sometimes the best, and often the worst luck. If their side is successful, then they do not fight. If a town is taken and plunder got, they seldom get a share, for they are kept outside; but if a retreat occurs, the reserve regiments come in for the worst part of the fight. It was so with the 6th, 7th, and 8th, on the 16th of March. The 7th were a considerable distance from us, and I did not see what they did, but all the reports which we heard of them spoke favourably, and, no doubt, though driven back by being completely flanked, they made their opponents pay well for the advantage gained.

When the Carlists began to gain ground, the 6th regiment was moved off first, to strengthen the positions towards the right. They had gone a very short distance, when the whole of the Carlist Cavalry came boldly upon them, for there was only one company of the 6th exposed to view, and no doubt, the leader of the Cavalry thought he would easily cut off that company. Unluckily for him, and fortunately for the 6th, the whole regiment was there, and being ready to receive them unseen, they discharged a volley, that sent riders and horses overhead, in a confusion never excelled, in slaughter. Horses gallopped back without riders, and riders without horses, and many of both did not go back at all; but that volley wrought but a part of their disaster. Two howitzers of the marine Artillery sent showers of grape shot on them, and rockets and shells had all gone helter-skelter amongst them, before they could go back to re-form. And they never re-formed: that one charge completed their work for that day, and, with a trifling exception, for ever. They came up a dashing, gallant-looking corps; in five minutes they went back to where they had started from, a mere remnant, the greater part of men and horses being left dead and dying.

On the left positions the 1st regiment after its temporary repulse was again engaged, and again left unsupported by the most of the

Spaniards—I say the most of them, because some of them stood gallantly even until two hundred or more were taken prisoners.* Of the officers of the 1st, who distinguished themselves at this time, were, Lieutenant Colonel Ramsay, Captains Harris, Rae, Stapleton, and others. With eighteen men only, Captain Rae and Lieutenant Dupont (the latter afterwards killed) maintained a position with heroism, which in a more successful fight would have made their country proud of them. What would have been the fate of the regiment, had Colonel de Lancy, who fell the evening before, lived to command that day, it is not easy to say. Certain it is, at least, that had he lived no one would have dared to cast that reproach on the regiment, which, as it was, every one anxious to shield themselves from blame, threw liberally on the 1st; declaring that that corps was the primary cause of the day's disaster. General Evans seemed to entertain similar opinions; but as he did not know the conduct of the regiment by personal observation he must have followed the information of others; and I repeat, that had De Lancy lived, and had he commanded that day, none of these aspersions would have been cast on that corps; for all knew that the officer who succeeded to command it, namely, Colonel Thomson, had not spirit enough to resent an insult to himself, far less to his regiment.

The 1st was engaged for a time near the house which they had taken the previous evening, and close to which De Lancy had received his fatal wound. It was in this house that the wounded of the previous day, to the amount of, some say sixty, others a hundred, and some a hundred and fifty, were lying and being left there, were, in a few minutes after the positions about the house had been abandoned, all put to death.

During the morning the cavalry of the Legion attempted to charge at various times, but the utter impossibility of meeting the enemy

---

* These prisoners were taken to the rear of the Carlists and stripped naked, and were marched to the town of Hernani, in that state. It is a common practice with both parties to strip their prisoners; as by doing so they make discovery more certain should any escape, and beside, they get some addition thereby to their own clothing. The prisoners, Spanish as well as English, taken that day, were all put to death. The Chapelgorris on our side would have made a similar sacrifice of the Carlist Colonel—he being about the only prisoner we got on the 16th; but a party of the Lancers guarded him into safe keeping. He is, or lately was in the castle of San Sebastian, still a prisoner.

successfully on the rough ground, rendered their charges for a time
ineffective. Yet though ineffective so far as slaughter was concerned,
they produced good effects by causing the advancing Carlists to be
less bold than they otherwise would have been. By the time the
retreat became general, however, they had an opportunity to display
the bravery and good discipline which in all former actions had cha-
racterized them. The Artillery was nearly cut off from the retreat,
the heavy guns having been taken from the main road to an advantageous position for firing—but a position from which a hasty retreat
could not be made. The enemy seeing this, took prompt advantage
of the situation of the English gunners, and against shells, canister
grape, and even spherical cases with which the dexterous Colquhoun
battered them down, they advanced, and all but took the Artillery.
They all but took it, because, it was for a time entirely cut off, and
but for the assistance of the two companies of the 6th Scotch the
enemy would have established themselves in such strength around
the guns, as to have made their ultimate retreat impossible. It was
at this moment that the resistance of those who were really brave
was displayed as the very climax of heroism. If I cannot express in
language sufficiently just,—language which may not be just, because
not sufficiently forcible—if I cannot be just to the bravery of Major
Maclaine and others around him at that trying period, it is only
because description becomes powerless in my attempt to tell what
was their situation, and what was done by them. All were not
equally devoted to their duty, else Maclaine and those with him,
would not have been situated as they were ; for with thousands
closing around them, with retreat about to be cut off—with death
and disaster on every side, and with the last chance of personal escape about to close, Maclaine, Colquhoun, and other officers, as well
as men, remained by the guns ; and when the enemy closed on them,
and when loading and firing was no longer practicable, they, but
Maclaine particularly, battled the enemy with handspikes hand to
hand. The victors were too close to load and fire, and therefore, the
battle was hand to hand, one party thrashing with their muskets,
and where they could, stabbing with their bayonets; the other party,
namely, the defeated, smashing the heads and breaking the limbs of
their opponents. Defending themselves thus, these brave fellows
kept the enemy at " off hands," though no more, for a period of time

longer than can be supposed the most valiant could have done with such powerful odds against them. At last the cavalry cut their way through the enemy, and keeping them at bay by hand-to-hand encounters allowed the artillery to escape from their perilous situation.

In the encounter mentioned in the foregoing paragraph, the Lancers as may be supposed had a severe loss. Being exposed to a cross fire, both in their advance and retreat—a fire, which as they charged on the main road, and the road being higher than the wooded ground on each side of it, came with fearful effect from their right and left, and that from adversaries who stood behind the ditches and other natural defences against whom cavalry was harmless : being exposed to this cross fire, besides the personal encounters in releasing the guns, they sustained a loss proportionably heavy to their dangerous daring in meeting it. Had the bravery of these troops been displayed in a successful engagement, how well would it have told! how lustrous on the page of history would it have shone! while, as it was unsuccessful, words wither as the pen writes them, and conscious though the writer may be that the most fervid language would be but bare justice to the heroism of the defeated Legion, he writes with dull hopelessness, because he writes uselessly! he writes uselessly, because his description be it warmly fervid, or coldly tame, will with the most of readers only meet the response of ungenerous contempt. The gallantry of these Lancers would have been applauded in a successful battle, and yet to be gallant as they were in a defeat—to go forward and charge with no hope of gaining a victory; but to charge with defeat on every side, and with a certainty that if they came back at all, they must come back defeated—even heartlessly beaten ;—to charge in such circumstances, was displaying a courage powerfully stubborn and unbending—to a great degree more meritorious, than if they had charged into the fight on equal terms with the foe, animated by the hope of victory.

At the extreme right of our positions a part of the 6th regiment were engaged and severely contested the ground on which they stood. The force of numbers at last overcame them and they, like others, gave way. In doing so they left some men dead behind them whom they buried hurriedly in a ditch; and it may illustrate, if any farther illustration is wanting—the horrid barbarities of the war, to note here, that two months afterwards, when we retook the same ground, the Carlists, in making a hasty retreat took time to dig up the bodies and with a hatchet or some similar instrument cut them to pieces so that we might see them.

In the heat of the action an incident occurred in the 3rd regiment that may be worth noticing. The subject of it was a Sergeant Cotton, or Cotter; perhaps there never was a case altogether its parallel in warfare; certainly there have been few of such sudden transitions from active life and health to the grave. He had been in hospital, and like some others who were deemed sufficiently recovered to join their regiments, he came out that day and joined his company during the fight, and at a time when his regiment was about to retreat. A hastily performed funeral was closing over the dead bodies of some of the unfortunate men, and he had just got forward to see the bodies and lament that some of his comrades were killed, when the Captain observed to him that he was glad to see him recovered and able to join his company. The same moment the luckless Sergeant was shot dead, and his body, clothes, accoutrements, and all thrown into the hole that contained the others. Though necessity urged a speedy retreat, a minute was stolen to throw some earth over them; and the Sergeant thus died and was buried, in little more than that brief space of time. Another minute passed and the triumphant foe was standing on the grave.

The most of the circumstances alluded to up to this part of my sketch, occurred previous to eleven o'clock, a. m., and at the time the regiment to which I belonged was still lying in reserve. We were in a hollow, with an elevation of no great height between us and the enemy. In this hollow we were concealed, just enough to be ignorant of the real state of affairs; and yet exposed enough to be rather uneasy at visits of cannon balls, that had now and then come dashing among us. The first intimation we had of a retreat, was by seeing some Rifles, two or three, come running into the hollow; one of them being met by an Aide-de-camp, who coming galloping to our regiment with orders, exclaimed " go back you coward;" but at the same time prevented this luckless wight from going back, by almost cutting his head off! inflicting such a wound as left the poor Rifleman to perish. Two more of these were seen at a little distance, in rear of us; one had got a bullet in his arm, and was carry-

ing on his back a comrade, who had got both feet shot off by a
cannon ball. A short while after I saw the first shot dead, and the
poor fellow without the feet unable to escape, was holding up his
hands; but was quickly dispatched by the furious victors stabbing
him with a dozen bayonets.

To our astonishment, on marching out of the hollow in which we
had been all this time concealed, we were fired on from the front,
and both flanks, the Carlists having completely outflanked us. We
saw too, the dreadful state of the conflict. Some of the Spanish regiments were in full flight; their officers thrashing them back with
their swords, but fruitlessly. Others were standing fast, and in all
directions save our direct rear, the fire of the enemy was bursting
out of bushes, hedges, ditches, and from behind stone walls on us,
and others who at this point were now a central attraction to their
fire.

The Adjutant-General Le Marchant came gallopping up, and
ordered the Colonel to charge; at the same time he went gallantly
on in front with Colonel Hogg. We saw nothing very alarming in
the charge; for we did not see where we were going, owing to an
orchard that intervened between us, and the enemy immediately in
front. The branches of the apple trees spread, at about four feet
from the ground; hence in running through the orchard with fixed
bayonets as we did, it was necessary to stoop almost two-fold, and
this stooping prevented us from seeing as well as from being seen,
until getting near the top of the orchard, we were met by a dreadful volley from behind a low stone wall. Behind this wall a battalion
of the Navarese, the best Musqueteers in the Carlist army, perhaps
the most dexterous in the world, were ranged; and in rear of them
another battalion stood high enough to fire over them, while behind
both, other columns pressed them up. Our men as will be readily
supposed were scattered on the ground, and a glance at them saw,
legs, arms, heads, and bodies bleeding. We were close on the enemy
before receiving their fire, and now a stone wall about three feet in
height intervened between us. What could we do? retreat—as a
matter of necessity, as quickly as possible and this was done; but
so destructive was the fire, that at every step some poor fellows were
falling, we being struck by bullets from three sides. A veteran of
the 79th, named Shearer, who had been in the wars of Wellington,

and for whom I entertained a high respect, got a shot in one of his knees close by my side. He fell, and another man tried to lift him ; but he at that moment being shot dead or nearly so, Shearer was left as many others were, not mortally wounded; but to be immediately bayoneted by the enemy. Robert M'Intyre a young man belonging to the Light Company of our regiment, displayed a bravery, that though almost unmatchably mad was still so heroic, that I must record it ; and the readers will admire and regret, that such a man died in such a cause.

M'Intyre was taken prisoner; but not before he had defended himself by setting his back to a tree, and resisted the efforts to take him alive, with a determination that struck even the Carlists with amazement. He was at last disarmed, and, as we learned afterwards from undoubted authority, was with other prisoners taken to Astigarraga, and their doomed to be shot. I had an account of his death, both from Spanish and English eye witnesses, who agreed in their accounts as to his insane enthusiasm. The party of soldiers who were loaded, and who stood ready to fire on the prisoners, got the order. They fired, when it was discovered all the victims were killed but M'Intyre ; he had only received a bullet in his thigh. Amid the smoke that rolled over the slaughtered heap, he was seen to take of his cap, and throwing it into the air, vociferated the *vivas* of the Queen's party. A pause succeeded the work of the executioners, who stood uncertain whether to repeat their shots or no ; when a Serjeant more zealous in the cause of death, and perhaps more callous in the feelings of admiration than the others, went up. and putting the muzzle of his musket into M'Intyre's mouth, discharged it, and blew the head to pieces.

One of our bravest and best officers, Captain Coyle, was, when at the head of his company, and standing nobly as he always stood in the front of danger, encouraging his men to resist; the now impetuous victors ; this gallant, and highly respected officer got his death wound, of which he died almost immediately. Lieut. O'Drischall, another good officer, succeeded in command of the company ; but he also received his mortal wound. Ensign Durkin, a youth, and a miniature of a man in body, but hero in mind and courage ; behaved gallantly with that company, an anecdote of him will be found hereafter.

About this time I saw a man belonging to the 6th regiment in a very unenviable situation. He was surrounded by the Carlists, but for a time was concealed from them behind a tree, in the nook of a stone wall. We saw him there at intervals for the space of half an hour, taking deliberate aims at Carlist officers, and bringing them down in a direction which they must have supposed was from their own men. Retreat for him was impossible, so he seemed to be making the most of his time. A great volume of fire and smoke rose in that part of the wood, and when it cleared away for a few minutes the red coat was not seen in his corner, and of course he was by that time either dead or a prisoner.

A part of the 8th had been ordered to keep a post in the corner of a wood at all hazards; and they kept it, and still defended themselves after being cut off. I am able to testify how that was done. It was one of those situations where hope is extinguished, and where all the minor passions are overborne. It is a situation that no philosopher can pretend to explain by rules of theory, and so very few who have been so situated have ever made their escape, practical illustrations are seldom met with. All I can say of it is, the deadlier passions took the command. I observed some of those who, famed for bravado on other occasions, were the only ones shewing symptoms of nervelessness. Amongst others who seemed to have more than ordinary courage was one who said, " die here, men! die here! fight to the last! don't be prisoners!" and another young man named Wilson, formerly one of those members of society that are very humbly estimated, that is, those who drive old hacks, and cry, " canal coals" in Edinburgh, with sometimes a small shade of the *keely* character about them.—Wilson responded to the other one, "prisoners! every man that gangs a prisoner 'ill be shot after they take him, as he deserves to be; die, you ———, die like Britons !" The Lancers came up, and the Carlists who had essayed to take us prisoners, had now more than their match, for they not being prepared for cavalry, fell into the finest disorder that hands raging for slaughter could desire. There were a few moments of mutual destruction; then one of the Navarese regiments and the Tolosa Volunteers of the Carlist force, advanced from behind the stone wall mentioned before, and would have given the Lancers a volley and *ended our share* in the war, but just as they rushed forward, a rebound, then two, three, and four bursted loud above the other noise, and that dreadful new invention, spherical case shot, from our artillery, then just got to that part of the road, mowed down the Carlist regiments. Never was a sound so sweet as that burst of our own cannon to our ears. Our eyes looked with mad delight on the disaster and death wrought by these volleys. The opposing combatants seemed all at once as if a wild whirlwind had passed over them, and laid them prostrate dead and dying. Still the numbers on our flanks were at all points, save that of the main road, in possession of the ground which we had been on half an hour before. There was not one moment to think. From where we were a retreat or a useless death was inevitable, and a good many of us were only brought along by getting hold of the Lancer's stirrups.

Our regiment, shattered as it now was, had another severe attack. The appearance of Colonel Hogg, and other officers, at this time, was almost demoniacal, and so was that of many of their men; being wild and seemingly careless of what became of them. It should be mentioned, that Captains Shields, Dalrymple, and Roberts, were conspicuously brave and zealous, Captain Roberts, particularly; who, for his gallantry, got, what to him was the justly due, order of Fernando a reward he should have had sooner; he was likewise remarked in general orders for a service at a subsequent part of the campaign, which will be mentioned hereafter. The Chapelgorris, whom we now joined, had got a great number killed, and the first time that that corps had ever made a retreat, since it was known in Spain, was then. They refused to move or fire a shot if the Spanish regiments were again put alongside of them, having been three times deserted that day by regiments of the southern Spaniards. But the moment they were told to go alongside an English regiment they hurrahed, fixed their bayonets, and impatiently waited to begin again. They and the 8th, and some companies of different corps, were ordered to keep a position, and they did so, but with dreadful loss. We were inspirited considerably by the determined drumming of a little old fellow of the Chapelgorris. He was about four feet in height, and had been a drum-boy, soldier, guerilla, outlaw, and drummer again, for a period of forty years; never having been done with war in some shape all that time. He rattled his drum before his regiment, standing fully exposed, and they as well as we firing over his head. His comrades vociferated " beuno chico! beuno chico!"

that meant something like well done, little fellow! well done, &c.,
and the more they cheered him, the more furiously did he rattle.
One of their buglers also joined him, and the two stood in front
answering the Carlist " advances," which at this time were heard in
all directions, right, left, and in front of us. The bugler tumbled
dead, and almost at the same moment one of the drummer's sticks
was shot away. Seizing the bugle, he rattled with it in one hand,
instead of the lost drumstick, and was cheered more than ever, and
more furiously did the firing go on; but all at once the drum went
one way and he another; and there ended his career, dead in a
moment. A Carlist, a few yards off, had done it, having crept up a
ditch before the others of his party. The moment he was observed
popping up his head a Chapelgorri dashed forward on him to bring
him prisoner. They wrestled for a few moments, but the Chapelgorri was strongest and stabbed the Carlist, at the same time seizing
the side of his face in his teeth, and tearing it like a wolf : even when
he had torn one mouthful, and the Carlist still writhing, he bit again
and shook the head of the vanquished foe till his own face was be-
smeared with blood. He brought off the Carlist's white cap, and
had just retreated about four yards, when he fell, I saw no more
of him, but was told he lay there.

A few minutes after this, I was attracted to my friend M'Lelland,
with whom I had exchanged congratulations that we were still safe
a short while before. He had observed to me that he thought he
would live us out, (in reference to what Lewis, another friend then
wounded, himself, and I had said about which of the three would
fall first,) for he was sure his head was ball proof; the balls having
touched him first on one side of the head and then the other, without
doing more injury than a slight scratch. Poor fellow! he was now
lying with a gash above one of his temples—a ball being buried in it,
and his head steeping in a pool of blood.

At this part of the retreat the Royal Marines were engaged for a
short while. They had been standing on ground to the right of the
Venta, and rather in front of it all the morning, and the time was
now mid-day. They were never within shot of the enemy until then,
and their share of the fight was performed by discharging a few vollies from the ground where they stood, and then going forward
about twenty yards, into one of the narrow cut bye-roads, and firing

fifteen or twenty rounds from that, partly under cover of its bank.
Now, in stating the assistance of the Marines, in this negative tone,
it is not intended to depreciate anything respecting them, thereby to
enhance the character of the Legion. Far from it. They had
eighteen men wounded, and *none* killed, out of between seven and
eight hundred ; but had they been ordered, or had Lord John Hay
thought fit to permit them to be ordered to stand where they were,
or to go earlier into the fight, when it was at its hottest, of course
they would have done so, and they would have stood until they were
slaughtered or ordered to retire. But Lord John Hay, said, "no,
the Marines shall not be engaged any longer. General Evans, while
three thousand Spaniards have turned their backs on the enemy, and
while so many have not been engaged at all, but are lying there on
the heights looking on ! You of course, will order your own English regiments as you choose, but I shall withdraw the Marines."
This is a part of the conversation that passed between his Lordship
and General Evans, about mid-day. For the precise words I cannot vouch, but this was the meaning conveyed, and immediately
acted on. I am as sure, as I was then of existence, that Lord John
Hay thus addressed Evans, for at the time of their conference I had
assisted in carrying a dying man to the surgeons in the rear, and
while I was holding him until an attempt was made to take a ball
from his inside, the two chiefs stood for a few minutes within five
feet of the operation.

Therefore the Marines did not "*cover the retreat of the Legion*,"
as has been often said by those who had some other object than truth
in saying so. I am a lover of my country ; and though I may be
chargeable with indelicacy in saying so, I must farther assert, that
the national pride in, and admiration of the great men and great deeds
of British fame, beats as passionately warm in my breast as it can do
in any other.

I hope, therefore, it is no compromise of national feeling, nor will
it be deemed a wish on my part to depreciate the merit of the Royal
Marines, when I say, that they are not entitled to the credit of having
covered the retreat of the Legion, and arrested the Carlist victors.
They did not do so, because they were not required by the extremity
of the case, and because they were not ordered though they had been
required, excepting that half-hour before-mentioned, and then they

fronted a space of one-hundred yards, or rather less, while the engagement at that time was spread over a distance of two miles from right to left, and Evans compelled to distribute his small force to oppose the enemy on all that extent.

We continued fighting three hours after the Marines were withdrawn towards San Sebastian, though it was not the same unremitting slaughter all the time, for we had fallen back to the Venta, and the heights on a line with it—the same heights which we had taken the night before, and on which we lay until making our descent towards Hernani and Astigarraga that morning. From this we opposed the Carlists all the afternoon by a heavy upstanding fire; and it was here where the most of the confusion of regiments was observable, and where unmilitary conduct amongst them, if any, prevailed. Many of the regiments had been hurried from the west side of the Venta hill, some companies taking its south, and some its north side, in order to get as quickly as possible to the eastward of it, as that was the most important place to oppose the now assailing Carlists. In doing so, some were sooner at the east side than others. There were bushes, and all such obstacles as are to be seen on a steep and craggy hill-side to be passed, and not a moment of lost time being allowable, those who got first along the steep began firing, while others joined them as fast as it could be done. Also it will be borne in mind, that an army retreating must either carry their wounded with them, or leave them lying; and I suspect all efforts to save the wounded men from falling into the hands of those who invariably put them to death, will be excusable with people of all opinions. Therefore, what could the appearance of the roads and the fields be, when men tried to save their dying comrades by carrying them hurriedly out, instead of leaving them to the care of those who look after the wounded in more successful engagements.

Near the top of that hill, while sharply firing, I happened to get near a Cockney friend, named Oliver. He had recovered from the bruises which he sustained on the morning of the 1st October, when the cannon shots knocked down the Westminster picquet house, and was now in the action without any fresh wound. General Evans was standing with his horse close in rear of us; and as vollies were always specially directed against him wherever he appeared, so those near him came in for a share of the danger. I had just nodded to

Oliver in recognition, and he had bawled out to me something, part of which I heard amongst the noise to be—"hah! haint this'n a flare up, Som'wille?" A man was carried behind him with a shot through his belly; Oliver looked to me, and said, "do you know that 'ere covey as has cotched it in the ty'ipes just now?—that's Old 'Oskins that 'ere is, wot vunce had the Tom and Jerry in Shoiditch, called the Cat and Fiddle; hah! he's done for, poor old feller; he's tu'ning up the vite on 's hyes; I 'spects some more on us 'll be in the vay by—." Now, Oliver's greatest peculiarity was his never ceasing conversation as soon as any one would begin with him, or as long as any one would listen. All that day his greatest pain, in my opinion, must have been the want of some one to talk to, from the impossibility of them hearing him. I did not stop him with the words "by and bye," third part uttered, for the sake of effect; he was actually at that part of his observations, when a ball struck him in the neck, going through his coat collar, stock, and throat, making its exit at the back of the neck. He fell down, and two of his comrades carried him to the rear, and stripped him of his accoutrements. Before leaving the position, which was shortly done after that, I assisted in digging down a piece of a turf wall above his body, that of " Old Hoskins," and another; they lie, the three together, on the east side of the Venta hill.

Shortly after this, at about six in the evening, the Venta, and all these adjacent heights, were abandoned, and the Legion returned to the quarters which they had occupied before the 10th, and again mounted their picquets on the same lines which they had kept during the winter. On going from the Venta, our regiment, and any others that I saw, marched as regularly home as if we had come from a parade, excepting those who were assisting to carry the last of the wounded, amongst which number I was, for a part of the way one. I cannot pass from this without mentioning the great kindness of the inhabitants of San Sebastian towards us. The women of all degrees had been out during the day meeting the wounded with cordials. Poor old Madri, or mother, as we called her, who made a living by selling articles to the regiment, sat on the road-side, giving every one wine, or anything they wished for, and would take no payment. Other females, old and young, acted in the same way; the English women only, being exceptions.

General Evans, in his "general orders," issued soon after this and republished in all newspapers, gives an account of the affair which is not strictly true. This may seem a bold assertion of mine, but still it is consistent with facts; for I believe it to be one of the weakest parts of the General's character, that of striving to be popular by conciliation. He did not throw the entire blame on the Spanish regiments that retreated, as he ought to have done, and he did not denounce the Queen's generals as he might have done; but for this I excuse him, in his wish to have another engagement, or from a wish not to stand in hostility with the authorities until he could honorably withdraw the Legion from the country: also, from a wish to flatter Lord John Hay and the English government, even, I believe, to conciliate political enemies at home, he attached more importance to what the Marines did than was consistent with strict truth; and, amongst other inconsistencies, he never mentioned the 8th regiment at all; but, on Colonel Hogg and the other officers going in a body to him with their resignations, he issued an "after order," apologising for having been misled with reports about the 8th regiment, but that, on farther inquiry, he had found that the conduct of that regiment had been strictly honorable, and their services most efficient. There was something in all this that I did not admire in General Evans; but his wish to be popular by conciliation was a foible, and about the only one which I observed in his character as a military commander. The greatest military chiefs have been men who at once decided, and, right or wrong, abode by their decision. As a proof of what he thought of the Spanish soldiers, there were a number of them that he never brought into action at all, after having seen how the others retreated, but relied solely on the Legion and the Chapelgorris. It was said that Evans was seen on the banks, by the river, that night, giving way to the most poignant grief; and I can well excuse him if that was the case; for *I can testify* of one who, with not the thousandth part to grieve for that he had, laid himself down in his casa, buried overhead in his great-coat and blanket, vexed to a degree, that cannot be expressed in writing.

OFFICIAL DISPATCH

OF

GENERAL EVANS TO COUNT LUCHANA ESPARTERO.

" *San Sebastian, March* 16, 1837.

Ten o'clock, P.M.

" MOST EXCELLENT SIR,

" I regret to inform your Excellency that my hopes from the successful operation of yesterday have not been realized. At a little after day-break we drove the enemy from their last entrenched height over Hernani, and were then employed in preparing for a general attack, when it appeared that considerable reinforcements arrived from the side of Tolosa. The enemy immediately commenced an attack on both our flanks. They pressed three battalions into the rear of our left by the bridge of Astigarraga. We had a more considerable force on that part of our line, and if these three battalions had been immediately attacked they would probably have been completely destroyed; but the 1st battalion of the Auxiliary Legion that was nearest the enemy was seized with a panic and fell back in total disorder on a battalion of Bastile, which imitated its example; and their demoralization communicating to several other regiments on our left a great confusion immediately ensued. The more advanced heights on our left were in a very short time abandoned; the troops falling back some hundred yards towards the fort of Oriamendi. The attack on our right was made with a more considerable force, and our advanced posts in that direction were drawn in. *But the extreme point on that flank was occupied by the battalion of British Royal Marines, which by its admirable steadiness and firmness immediately repelled the enemy and checked all further attempts in that direction. The enemy threw themselves into the rear of that flank also;* and the 6th battalion of British auxiliaries advanced, and drove them from some heights, which they had occupied in our rear.

"The enemy continued their attempts in front, as well as round both flanks; but not as appeared to me in a vigorous manner. All the essential parts of the position, were still in our possession, and the confusion first caused had been remedied. But the great proportion of the regiments had been so intermixed, that the officers for the most part had lost all power of re-forming their men; and I therefore considered it best to withdraw from the points we there held (first having destroyed the guns, and in a great degree dismantled the defences of Oriamendi) to our previous positions, including the Ametza. Our loss in killed and wounded, will probably amount to 800 or 900 men; besides a company of the Oveida regiment, which, having been posted in a picquet-house at some distance, was surrounded and made prisoners.

" I have now only time to express to your Excellency my expectation, that the check we have experienced, will be remedied as soon as the corps of Navarre shall be enabled to form a junction with this corps ; which I trust General Saarsfield will be in a condition to effect, when we shall again assume the offensive.

" I have the honor to be, &c.

" (Signed) DE LACY EVANS, Lieut. General.

I shall have a few remarks to make, on the foregoing dispatch ; but first let the "general order" be read, and then we may discuss them together.   In the meantime, let the reader notice the passages in italics.

GENERAL ORDER.

San Sebastian,

March 21

" The Lieut. General, avails himself of this brief interval to address the Legion, on the event of the last few days.

" On the 10th, 13th, and 15th of the present month ; your courage and good order at once merited his high approbation, and inspired him with unlimited confidence in victory.   Nor has that confidence been impaired by your less steady conduct, and the less fortunate results of the 16th instant ; because he can trace these results to causes not likely again to occur.   On the 10th, you attacked in three columns, the formidable position of the Ametza ; the enemy fled in dismay, as they will always do, when you march straight at them with the bayonet ; attentive to the orders of your officers, and without stopping to fire.   The 9th, 10th, and Rifles, led on this occasion, in a manner worthy of the distinguished character of those corps.   On the 13th, the Rifles, 4th, and 8th, and the British Royal Marines, crossed the Urimea ; and rapidly drove the enemy from the village of Loyola, and the adjacent heights.

" On the 15th notwithstanding the inclemency of the weather, and the almost impracticable state of the country, victory again crowned your efforts.   ₍The whole of the enemy's fortified. positions, and the fort of Oriamenda (Venta) fell into our possession, in accomplishing which you took a brilliant part.   *The* 1*st* 9*th and* 10*th, and Rifles*, were fortunately conspicuous in conjunction with the Princessa regiment in carrying the enemy's last position under a heavy fire, and without returning a shot.

" On the 16th, when on the eve of following up our success by still more signal operations, the enemy received large reinforcements.   Our troops fatigued by the extraordinary exertions of the preceding days, and attacked by a superiority of numbers, retired on the extreme left in some degree of disorder ; imagining that they were about to be cut off by a movement of the enemy to their rear ;— while it was the enemy, if our troops had better preserved order and discipline, who would have been probably destroyed.   The position we were on, was of the strongest nature, and one of which the enemy could not have deprived you ; but when men lose their formation, or separate from their companies, or battalions, or are inattentive to the voice of command, valour becomes useless, and every other

No. 29.

advantage neutralized. This was signally proved by your General being under necessity, in consequence of the irregularity alluded to, to withdraw the forces to their former positions, at a moment when the enemy's attack was repulsed at all points.

" The unshaken firmness of the Royal British Marines, under Lieut. Colonel Owen, in repulsing, as they did, four times their number ; afforded you a noble example of the irresistible force of military organization, and discipline ; which the Lieut. General feels confident on some future occasion, you will be found to emulate.

" *The corps, which during these different operations distinguished themselves: were the British Royal and Legion Artillery, the 1st Lancers, and the 6th, 9th, 10th, and Rifles.*

" Thus a portion of the fruits of our previous success, were relinquished, the whole of the faction having concentrated to resist us ; but the enemy have suffered an immense loss,—a loss far more severe and irreparable than ours, and has spread terror through their ranks.

" But a check in your career of victory, though it may for a moment obscure, cannot obliterate the fame of former deeds of bravery, and particularly that of the 15th instant ; an achievement of which, the best soldiers of any army might be proud, and one, too, which your General assures you, will win for you the admiration of England, and the gratitude of Spain."

(Signed)   DE LACY EVANS.

LIEUT.-GENERAL.

In another general order issued about the same time, similar to the foregoing, there is a passage which I have transcribed ; it is the following :

"The soldier is never so formidable as when he is called upon to vindicate his honor. Let us, then, once more march onward to the combat, and shew that we are worthy soldiers of liberty ! Let him who is not animated with these sentiments, separate himself from our ranks ; for your General does not choose to be surrounded by any but those who are resolved to conquer."

This last passage is not worth any remarks, save a mere notice. Some similar bombastous effusions in the Cæsar and Pompey style appeared at times in General Orders ; and to troops lying on the bare floors of convents, and shivering among snow on parade, we, non-commissioned officers read them from the books.. As newspaper paragraphs, or future historical material, these General Orders do very well ; but to the common every-day-life of soldiers, the big sounding sentences had no charms.

Some other passages in the foregoing " Orders" require more particular notice. In the first one,—that addressed to Count Luchana. I have marked a passage in italics, which first compliments the Royal Marines at the expense of truth, and then contradicts itself, He says, " the extreme point on that flank, was occupied by the battalion of British Royal Marines, which, by its admirable steadiness, immediately repelled the enemy *and checked all further attempts in that direction;* and the beginning of the next sentence says *" The enemy threw themselves into the rear of that flank also!"* and proceeds to shew that the 6th regiment of the Legion advanced and drove the enemy back. It is painful to pick out these discrepancies; but why is the character of the Legion to suffer that mere compliments —decidedly unmerited—may be paid to the Marines? How could they repel the enemy and check all further attempts, and immediately have their flank turned? The truth is simply this: the Marines were not at any time within twelve hundred yards of the extreme right flank. The statement, that the 6th regiment opposed the enemy then, is perfectly correct; and as it will be evident to the dullest intellect, that has the power of connecting ideas, that this part of the General's statement could not be correct, I assure the reader, that the incorrect part, is that where the dishonorable sacrifice to national prejudices is offered in favour of the Royal Marines. The Spaniards are also spoken of in a tone that lessens the real services of the Legion. Major Richardson observes relative to this, that " The anxiety of the Lieutenant General to court favour with the Spaniards, is a matter of notoriety in the Legion. On all occasions has he adopted a tone of charity and condescension towards them ; and in order to ensure popularity, made the sacrifice of every thing English to obtain this, his paramount object." Thus far goes the accusation of Major Richardson ; but the Major is also an idolator of the *regular service*, and suffers any injustice to the Legion without complaint, when the Marines is the theme of praise.

I have said it is painful to pick out these discrepancies in the official documents ; and having picked them out, perhaps those who are unfriendly to us will eagerly catch at them and fling them back as a reproach. But if so, let them bear in mind that General Evans is not original in his style of dispatches ; for mystery—dissimulation— bombast and falsehood, he has in the art of making up a dispatch or General order, the precedents of nearly all former commanders.

In another passage marked by *italics*—that, where he mentions the regiments that most distinguished themselves—there is an error that I cannot omit correcting. He passed over the 8th regiment in silence; but subsequently issued an "After Order," wherein he makes ample apologies for the omission. This After Order not being in any newspaper, and no copy of it being within my reach, I subjoin here a letter, which appeared in the *Times* of 17th April, 1837. It will explain itself.

San Sebastian, April 2.

SIR,

"Although perfectly aware of the inability, of attempting to contradict the generality of those reports, which are so plentifully to be found in most newspapers; I am, nevertheless, induced to make an exception to this rule, in order to correct an inaccurate statement, regarding the conduct of my regiment, which appears in the "Times" of the 24th March. The mistake I allude to, occurs in a letter, giving an account of the action of the 16th, in which it states that the 1st, 4th, and 8th Regiments, were the first to retire. This, as far as regards the 8th Regiment is incorrect, and as the letter of the "Times," contains not only the most accurate, but in a military point of view, the most intelligible account of the operations of the 16th, I have yet seen, I am particularly anxious, that the share borne by my regiment in those operations, should be properly represented.

The ground occupied by the 8th, on the 16th, at the time the retreat commenced, was immediately in advance of our left centre, and close to Hernani, halfway between Astigarraga, and the Oriamendi redoubt; at the base of the range of heights, the summits of which formed the left of our position. Here I was left alone, (the 6th and 7th regiments having been previously withdrawn), in a very isolated and unsupported situation, and with orders from Brigadier-General Godfrey to retire, if necessary to the heights in our rear. This necessity was not long in arriving; our troops were driven from a hill on our left, thus completely exposing our flank, while at the same instant, we discerned the enemy on those very heights in our rear, to which we had been ordered to retire. Thus, with the Carlists on our left rear, the only possible method of retreat, was by a flank movement to our right, whereby the high road might be gained. This movement we attempted, and succeeded in performing; exposed not only to the fire of the battalions, who turned the left of our position; but to that of the continually accumulating numbers descending from Santa Barbara, which were directed against the centre of our line, and threatened to cut us off from the main road; so vigorously were we pressed in this direction, as to be obliged for a few minutes to to assume the offensive, which we did with success; and headed in the most brilliant manner by Brigadier-General Le Marchant, drove the enemy some distance to the rear. In this rally, the conduct of Captain Gurrea, Aide-de-camp to the Lieutenant General, was highly conspicuous. Having thus checked the 'enemy, the regiment then continued to retire, one wing by the right, the other by the left of the Oriamendi Hill, until the wings incorporated themselves with the general line of defence ; where they continued to combat on different flanks of the hill, until again reunited, in the evening previous to the evacuation of the redoubt. From this statement, you will perceive any blame which may attach to those regiments which were first to retire, can in no means be shared by the 8th Highlanders ; as our retreat was subsequent to, and a direct consequence of the troops on the left giving way. The moment the left was threatened, our position became extremely critical ; but when our flank was actually turned, had I delayed my retreat, the battalion must have been infallibly lost. As it was, we were the last to retire ; even the Rifles, whose gallant conduct is so deservedly eulogised, having been previously forced to give way ; and a part of that regiment, under Lieut. Colonel Boyd, the second in command, having retired within my view.

" I trust, Sir, that you will oblige me, by giving these facts early publicity, in such a shape as you may think proper, and with such explanations as may appear to you best suited, to render intelligible the local details, into which I have been obliged to enter.

I have the honour to be, Sir, your most obedient Servant,

GILBERT HOGG, Lieutenant Colonel,

Commanding 8th Highlanders.

To the correspondent of ' The Times,' San Sebastian.

CHAPTER XXIII.

The defeat of the Legion, and its general character compared with other armies—A few historical parallels from the Peninsular War.

I might address this chapter to all young men and lads who are fascinated by the scarlet coats or glittering bayonets which they see on a parade, who are dazzled with the glory of battles, and think no soldiers can fight like *their own;* but as they are not the only idolators of the matchless British—as all classes and all creeds, aristocratic and democratic, hug the opinion that no army is like their own British, I leave this chapter to the perusal of every one who chooses to read it. I shall shew the Legion to have been as like British soldiers, as one British army has been like another.

First, let me take a passage from a work written by the Reverend Thomas Farr, who is also one of the laudators of the Royal Marines now in Spain, who saw the faults of the Legion and the merit of the Marines, with as clear eyes, and a bias as willingly inclining to the *regulars* as any one. Let it be borne in mind how often the Legion climbed over mountains—how every engagement they fought was mountainous warfare, and this passage which I quote will shew the difficulties we contended with in carrying loads of belts, ammunition and knapsacks.—Mr. Farr says relative to the operations of the 16th May, 1837 :—

"As Lord John Hay wished the Marines to arrive before high-water, on the heights above Feuntarabia, as at that time Her British Majesty's steam frigates—the Phœnix and Salamander were to open their immense one-hundred-and-twenty-pound guns of ten inches diameter on Feuntarabia, to cover the entry of the Spanish gun-boats into the bay, who were to invest Feuntarabia on the French side, should it eventually be necessary to bombard it—the first two hours march was rather quick and pressed. A sergeant of the Royal Artillery had very kindly mounted me on a horse, that had been taken not many weeks before from the enemy, having strayed into Christino ground. We were still on the Passages side of the convent of the Holy Virgin of Guadaloupe, and on ground that had never been occupied without resistance. There was a nasty hanging, high rocky hill in front, where the Carlists might have concealed themselves without being perceived until close on them, and they might from an ambuscade have fired a volley and then escaped with impunity into Feuntarabia, without our being able either to punish or catch them. To prevent any accident of this kind, Colonel Owen, who commanded the Marines, without halting the main body, ordered the company in advance to throw themselves forward, and extend right and left as skirmishers, and thus get to the top of the rising piece of ground to be sure that there was no concealed enemy either on its summit or behind it. It was necessary for the company so employed to march at a quickened pace, commonly called double quick time. Having just been mounted, I rode forward with the skirmishers. They certainly had not been employed at this quickened pace much more than ten minutes, when I heard an officer call out, "Sergeant, keep up your men : look at those men behind, keep them up ;" "Sir, he replied, the men say they can go no further ; they are falling down, they beg to be halted." "They cannot be halted," was the reply ; "the ground must be made good." Those that had sufficient strength moved on ; but three or four men fell down from exhaustion and rolled on the grass : one man completely fainted away. Not to break up the line of march, I staid with him, and got off my horse, and in a few minutes mounted him on it.

"The other four men, who were not able to march on, were forced to drop into the rear. In about ten minutes the ground was skirmished over ; there was no enemy to be seen, and the troops halted to take breath on the summit of the hill, just above the Convent of Guadaloupe."

What would have been said by our newspapers, if some correspondent had written that he saw the Legion falling down with ten minutes of fatigue ! It would have been the immoral character of the men—the want of discipline, or something or anything but the true causes that would have been blamed ; and had it been the Legion, a comparison would have been made between it and the heroes of the Peninsular War. Let us take a review of some of the recorded incidents of these glorious Peninsular campaigns. The official dispatches of Wellington in describing the battle of Fuentes D' Honore are big with victory, and all the historians follow the tone of his dispatches, filling up their accounts with those details only which minister to the glory of the army,—especially Colonel Napier, who, more like a special pleader than a historian, makes it appear that British soldiers never were beaten,—these having all the effect of producing a false excitement of admiration, I shall make a short quotation from one of the best written works on the Peninsular War, that entitled " *Vicissitudes of a Scottish Soldier ;*" reminding the reader however, that the soldier is not writing to expose faults, but on the contrary, is exulting in the valour of the British army. He says :—

"Next morning, (5th May, 1811), the enemy being firmly determined upon obtaining possession of the village, they attacked that part of our army which was posted to the right of us. Having succeeded in compelling them to retreat, the French now advanced upon us. *Not calculating upon being hus flanked the whole regiment was dispersed throughout the streets and houses of the village,*[*] in expectation that the enemy must needs cross the river before coming at us. *Lulled into security* by this means, we were suddenly surprised by the entrance of the French on the right ; the rest of them then crossed the river, and broke furiously through the barricades. Surrounded thus on all sides, and finding it useless to withstand, in our dis-.

---

* How exactly is this like the two campaigns of the Legion at Astigarraga bridge which caused the commencement of our retreat.

ordered state the attack of the numerous force which was pouring into the town, *we thought it no disgrace to take to our heels: I must confess that our flight had something the appearance of rabbits running from their holes.* All of us succeeded in gaining the outside of the village, with the exception of half a company, who were hemmed in and taken prisoners."

Had the Legion been in a similar state of disorder what would have been said of it? yet on the 16th of March—the day of the Hernani retreat, we retreated fighting and disputing "every inch of ground." Besides, at Fuentes D'Honore, Wellington had no justification for being surprised, because he had been fighting on the 3rd, resting on the 4th with the enemy before him, and should, on the 5th, have been prepared for them. But that helter skelter retreat was not the only one. Other regiments retreated in the same manner. Wellington states in his official dispatches that the "cavalry retired in disorder." The writer that I quoted knew nothing, of course, about the cavalry, but of his own brigade, when part of his company and others had been again in disorder at a subsequent part of the battle,—he says

"The heat of the battle *and the confusion** enabled us to join the regiment."

And again he says :

"The Light Brigade came to relieve us ; but the fight was completely ended—*chiefly through the interposition of night.*"

Yet this was one of the great victories against which we dare not whisper a breath of suspicion ; one of the great victories won by soldiers to which we, of the Legion, cannot be compared without incurring the displeasure of tory, whig, radical, republican, christian, jew, and infidel ; for all would be shocked at the comparison being made between the Legion and the soldiers of Wellington. But what says the great historical work called "*Annals of the Peninsular War*" of this battle ? let the following answer :

• • • Lord Wellington decided on withdrawing his army to a more concentrated position and giving up the communication by Subagal. • • • • This retrogressive movement was executed with the most perfect regularity, though pressed by the enemy's cavalry, &c.

Now see the difference : a soldier who was in that "retrogressive movement ;" "run-a-way retreats" these movements were called, when performed by the Legion--this soldier says his regiment, the

---

* Who ever heard of *confusion* in Wellington's battles ?

71st, one of the most famed for bravery in the British service "*took to their heels*" and confesses that their "*flight had something the appearance of rabbits running from their holes!*" Had this been written of the Legion, by any of the soldiers, how greedily would Sir Henry Hardinge have grasped at it in the House of Commons. But I am not done with the battle of Fuentes D'Honore. We have seen how historical records can colour—even falsify a retrogressive movement. By referring to Lord Wellington's dispatches, lately published, it will be seen how conveniently he found " the communication by Subagal;" to be unimportant, when he could not retain the positions commanding it. It will be seen too, how all the historians have covered this retreat with honor and glory! nay, made it into a great victory.

Sir Walter Scott, among others has poetized on this battle in his " Vision of Don Roderick"—a poem, to say even the best that an admirer of his genius as I am, can say—a poem very frothy, yet dull and exceedingly stupid—Scott in this, descants on the matchless bravery of the British at Feuntes d'Honore, and as he cannot get rid of the slaughter committed by the French, he generously fills the triumphant foe drunk! I would not refer to Scott at all, were it not that it is from such as he that the nation takes its opinions; —were it not such as he that distort facts to make victories out of defeats,—were it not that similar writers have distorted facts to prejudice the public mind against the British Legion, and were it not that Scott and his co-historiographers by unduly exalting the fame of the Duke of Wellington's army, while the political animosities of partizans have unduly depreciated General Evans's Legion, were it not for these, I would not seek to unsettle the dearly beloved prejudices that our national vanity has hugged and nursed into realities. Scott says—

> "O vainly gleams with steel Aguada's shore,
>   Vainly thy squadrons hide Assuava's plain,
> And front thy flying thunders as they roar,
>   With frantic charge and tenfold odds, in vain !"

Scott is here summing up the power of the French to a climax, to dash it down; and he does so by the following five frothy but false-hood-telling lines: the stanza continues—

> And what avails thee that ?   For Cameron slain,
>   Wild from his plaided ranks the yell was given—
> Vengeance and grief gave mountain rage the rein,
>   And, at the bloody spear-point headlong driven
> Thy Despot's giant-guards, fled like the rack of heaven.

In this, there are more mistakes than one.   But let us notice first the fulsome adulation of Colonel Cameron, an officer, perhaps more cordially cursed and hated by his men, than any other that commanded a regiment.   In a note Scott says—

"The gallant Colonel Cameron was wounded mortally during the desperate contest, in the streets of the village called Fuentes D'Honore.   He fell at the head of his native Highlanders, the 71st and 79th, who raised a dreadful shriek of grief and rage.   They charged with irresistible fury, &c.—• • • • The Frenchman who stepped out of his ranks to take aim at Colonel Cameron was also bayonetted, pierced with *a thousand wounds,* and almost torn to pieces by the furious Highlanders !"

Good God ! who counted the wounds ? what would have been said of Frenchmen, or of the *Legion* had either of them been the savages, the Highlanders are vauntingly represented to have been ? But the truth is simply this, Scott is stating what is not true, I have spoken to old soldiers who are said to have shrieked with grief and rage, and they assuredly deny it.   Besides, they were not Highlanders who are thus said to have given "Mountain rage the rein," they were the greater part of them Glasgow and Paisley weavers who knew nothing about either the Highlands or Colonel Cameron.   Here is what the "Soldier" of the 71st says relative to this—

"Several egregious errors are contained in the words of Sir Walter Scott. He has made the 71st all "Native Highlanders," whereas, to say that there were forty or fifty of them in the whole regiment, would perhaps overrate the real number.   The proportion of Lowlanders in the 79th was not so great; still there was no small quantity of them in that regiment.   Sir Walter has made the 71st yell, shriek and grieve, at the fall of a man who was an entire stranger to them.   I can assure him, that such demonstrations of woe were never shewn by any of us.   I cannot think either, there could be much yelling on this occasion by the 79th, the alleged cause of it being a complete martinet in practice and disposition, and consequently not precisely the idol of the men"

Sir Walter Scott says—

"The grand mass of the French Cavalry attacked the right of the British position, covered by two guns of the horse artillery, and two squadrons of cavalry. After suffering considerably from the fire of the guns which annoyed them in every attempt at formation, the enemy turned their wrath entirely towards them, distributed brandy among their troopers, and advanced to carry the field-pieces with the desperation of drunken fury."

These two ungrammatical sentences have venom and falsehood in them beyond what any rabid partizan, perhaps, ever gave expression to, and yet it is from the pen of our adored countryman, Sir Walter Scott! The facts are these. There was a river between the French and British. The British were neither defending themselves, nor were they prepared for defence, they were as a writer says, who was one of them, and whom I have already quoted,—"lulled into security," and the right flank being suddenly driven back they *" took to their heels"* and ran *" like rabbits running from their holes."* Scott would make it appear that *after* the French crossed the river, and when not being able to form because of the fire of the British artillery; they, the French, stood there, under the fire, and distributed brandy, until drunkenness excited them onwards. Shame on thee Scott! Posterity will hiss you as the stocking makers of Hawick did, and when party politics will have allowed your mercenary prostitution to be seen in its deformity, your natural generosity of mind will, be forgotten, and even the lustre of your mighty genius will shine dimly in the eyes of generations that have none of your prejudices to blind them.

You are dead, and being so I ought to let you alone; but there lives behind you writers possessing all your littlenesses, at whose hands the British Legion in Spain, officers and men, as truly valorous, and honourable to their country as any that lifted arms with Wellington, have been made to suffer every imputation that is odious, merely because such perversions of truth as yours have deluded the public mind in estimating martial achievements.

Lest any reader may suspect that I am unduly severe on what Scott says, let him refer to the Wellington Dispatches and he will find that Scott is not correct in what he states this battle to have been; let the reader consult the *" Annals of the Peninsular War,"* and he will see that though every thing that is plausible is said there to put balm into the wounds that British pride received on that occasion, the historian yet does honour to the French by saying, " they came on boldly marching to their martial music," &c. Scott says they were drunk. The Duke of Wellington says he " repelled the attacks of the enemy," and knowing the real facts on his side, he contents himself as an honorable man, with vaunting very little, but as a commander-in-chief, he *must* conceal every thing dishonorable and he does so. The " *Annals*" say that " towards evening the fire on both sides gradually slackened, and the village as if by mutual consent, was divided by the combatants, the upper part being occupied by the British, the lower by the enemy." The " *Scottish Soldier*" says " they fought, both parties, until night divided them" *Scott* says " the appearance of some small reinforcements, notwithstanding the immense disproportion of force, put them to absolute rout.

I am afraid I have discussed this engagement at too great a length; but as it is one of those great victories, from the height of which we humble soldiers of the Legion, are to be knocked down, I consider it only just, not only to ourselves, but to the public who are guided by those over-wrought rhapsodies of Scott and others, to anatomise it. I am sorry I cannot take up these pages, by examining it, and some other victories at greater length.* But there are some other comparisons that must be made in justice to the Legion.

The troops of General Evans were " buccaneers ;"—they plundered the Spaniards—they were " mercenaries," &c. &c. These charges stand out black enough certainly, beside such as the following, which I take from Sir Walter Scott :—

" Even the unexampled gallantry of the British army, in the campaigns of 1810—11; although they never fought but to conquer, will do them less honor in history, than their humanity; attentive to soften to the utmost of their power, the horrors which war, in its mildest aspect, must always inflict upon the defenceless inhabitants of the country in which it is waged, and

---

* The discussion in the United Service Journal for this month, October, 1838, gives a map and analysis of the battle of Toulouse, and concludes by saying, that they hope they have set the disputed victory for ever at rest. Now, as it is one of those victories, like Fuentes D'Honore, that no party could exactly claim; but where both were brave, and both were partially defeated; it will not be set at rest by any such unjust twisting of circumstances. I observe they dwell with delight on those parts of *Soult's* Dispatches where he uses the word " confusion" in speaking of his troops, while they in giving *Wellington's* Dispatch, omit the word " confusion" though he in allusion to his retreat, says " I was sorry to observe them retire in considerable confusion." This ungenerous, but strictly English omission on the part of the U. S. J., will be seen by referring to the edition of Wellington's dispatches, edited by Colonel Gurwood.

which, on this occasion, were tenfold augmented, by the barbarous cruelties of the French. Soup kitchens were established by subscription among the officers, wherever troops were quartered for any length of time. The Commissaries contributed the heads, feet, &c. of the cattle slaughtered for the soldiery; rice, vegetables, and bread, where it could be had, were purchased by the officers. Fifty or sixty starving peasants were daily fed." &c. &c.

What a set of patriotic, generous, well-fed, good fellows must have been in the British army in those days! Let us see what the " Scottish soldier" says in his book, and I suspect he is as likely to be correct as Sir Walter Scott. The " Soldier" says, page 214 :—

" The sight of a large flock of sheep awakened every appetite ; but how to get at them was the question ; no reasonable pretext for so doing, being at hand some bright genius or other raised a cry that they were " French sheep." This was enough; for with one accord, the whole brigade rushed upon the flock and seized every one of them, the poor Spanish shepherds standing all the while mute with astonishment, at such an act of superior power."

This is one simple case of *generosity* to the inhabitants : read the following from the same author, page 142 :—

" Often have I seen a private pay a dollar for a small biscuit, thinking himself happy to get it at any price. This time enabled the butchers of the army to reap a golden harvest, they having the offals of all the bullocks they slew as perquisites; the most nauseating garbage was sold at enormous prices. The greasy rogues, knowing their power, held tenaciously at the prices they had laid down; and rather than do otherwise, they would sometimes actually go and bury the carrion under ground. Many of the men were detected here in stealing honey from some hives in the neighbourhood." &c. &c.

At page 55, he says—

" In ransacking the village which we came to, some potatoes and honey were found ; this allayed the pain of our gnawing stomachs a little : scarcely any of us slept during the whole night ; the cooking of potatoes engrossing all our attention."

At page 54, the " soldier's" want of shoes, and his *generosity* to the inhabitant who had a pair standing empty, will be seen.

At pages 60 and 61, hunger, and the greediness with which the houses were ransacked, will be observed ; and at the 140th page, he says ;—

" In bivouacking at this place, we had to endure the combined miseries of a wet night and hunger. Next morning one of the men who had been foraging[*]

* More appropriately, *stealing from the inhabitants.*

brought in a bag of Indian corn; with this inestimable treasure he generously
went round the whole company, giving each of us a handful."

and at page 256, he says—

"One of the men succeeded in abstracting a loaf, from the knapsack of a
slain Frenchman ; the generous finder, coming to satisfy his own appetite,
immediately distributed his treasure through the whole company ; each had
only a morsel,—but keen hunger, rendered such a gift sweeter than honey."

In the Legion we had many persons who deserved the severity
of martial law, and perhaps I have not over-coloured a single incident
that speaks of plunder or thieving, but at the same time, I have assuredly omitted no species of crime committed by the Legion, save
one which I have not yet come to—that is the pillaging of a town
taken by storm. And against it is the ravage and murders on the inhabitants of Badajoz by Wellington's army to stand for nothing?
Scott says in Don Roderick, relative to the generous humanity of
British soldiers in the campaign of 1811—

"The rudest centinel in Britain born,
With horror paused to view the havoc done,
Gave his poor crust, to feed some wretch forlorn,
Wiped his stern eye, then fiercer grasped his gun."

The " *Scottish Soldier* " says something of the same campaign,
which proves himself and comrades to be more like what all soldiers
have been, and while they are soldiers, ever will be,—than what Sir
Walter would make appear they were. The " *Soldier* " does not
look on " with horror at the havoc done," but tells the truth, thus
page 131—

"The French had only evacuated the nunnery the night before our arrival,
they had with the mischievous taste of monkeys, torn and destroyed a number
of books and papers, belonging to the nuns ; and in short turning every
thing topsy-turvy : it must be owned however, that we were not backward
in completing the work of destruction."

Then about giving " his poor crust to feed some wretch forlorn."
The " *Soldier* " says page 68—

"I contrived to hold on my tottering steps for a short distance, and saw
by the way four men, of a certain gallant Scotch regiment, robbing a poor
Spanish woman of some bread, although she was protesting in the most
piteous manner, that she had nothing else to give her starving children."

Again, at page 91, it will be seen how the British soldiers of these
days cheated the inhabitants of Holland with vending farthings in the
shape and colour of silver coin, and eyeless buttons for shillings·

The same thing was done in the Legion, and I have given it due notice. The same thing would be done again by any regiment of Her Majesty's Forces, were they among people poor enough and ig-norant enough to be cheated. Then at page 183, mark the humanity and honor of Britons! though a picture of Wellington's soldiers, it is as truly a picture of General Evans's Legion as could have been given, and therefore it is strictly British; for the Legion lost none of the British peculiarities. He says—

"There were some thirsty rogues, who contrived to cheat the Portugueze out of a good deal of liquor; they (the Portugueze), having a polite custom of asking us to taste it out of their horns before a bargain was concluded. By this means, the mere tasters always outnumbered the buyers; and special care was taken by them not to say a word, till a hearty pull was obtained from the horn; then the rum was sure to be bad, or watered, and an affecta-tion made of spitting it out with disgust. In this manner, every horn that came in their reach, was pretty sure to be nearly emptied of its contents. Many of the fellows got drunk upon the *pruevas*, that being the name the Portugueze gave the trying of the liquor; *prueva*, or proof, having the same meaning."

In reference to the above, the *soldier* states that all the men were not alike; but neither were they all alike in the Legion. Why then is the Legion to be maligned, while soldiers, neither their superiors in martial gallantry, or moral honesty, are lauded as matchless? Many readers will admit at once, that the moral characters of Wel-lington's army and those of Evans's were the same: but few, indeed none, will admit their martial gallantry to have been equal! why is this? merely because the amount of the stake for which the two armies contended was not equal. Public opinion, on matters that require the exercise of sound judgment will generally be found on the side of justice; but, when measuring those events that excite the feelings,—that inflame the passions, and quicken prejudice, pub-lic opinion has been nearly always on the side of injustice. The great mass of the British public did not understand the merits of the quarrel between France and England, and they could not check the quarrel, when it was once begun, though they had known its merits. Sons and brothers were away in thousands, and were slain in battle by the French. A Commander's account of the battles, told only of how he was attacked—how he disposed of his troops—how many of them were slain, and how gallantly they fought, concluding perhaps with an apostrophe to the effect that " the enemy though beaten is not yet tired of shedding blood ;"—" we must again meet the foe and avenge his cruelties," " the army has only one desire, and that is, to conquer the blood-thirsty French, &c. &c."

As these were read in conjunction, with news of dear relations being wounded and killed ; and as every writer, save a very few who were accounted an anti-national faction, wrote purposely to inflame the public mind,—it was inflamed; and perhaps never in the history of mankind, were more egregious errors of opinion prevalent, than during the time of these wars. The French on the other hand, had an opinion of the British, that filled the people of France with horror. When Wellington's army entered France, all writers agree in saying, that the people regarded the English with astonishment, at seeing they were like men, and not the demons, that French writers had represented them to be. We had the same opinions of the French ; and our writers scrupled not to tell lies,—either in ignorance themselves, or knowingly to keep the people in ignorance, of the true character of their artificial enemies. Scott says—

"The hoary priest, even at the altar shot,
    Childhood and age given o'er to sword and flame
  Women to infamy ; no crime forgot,
    By which inventive demons might proclaim
  Immortal hate to Man, and scorn of God's great name !"

He gives this as the character of the French; and there is no question but some crimes enumerated in the first *three* lines were committed by them ; but those crimes that he implies in the last line were not the objects of the French : they were the mere expression of Scott's heated imagination and ungenerous prejudices, which in poetry may be pardoned, and which I would take no notice of, had he confined himself to poetry ; but whenever he, in his prose writings, alludes to the subjects of his own day, he does not only colour his statements with prejudices, but hesitates not to give out as facts— statements that are absolute falsehoods ! As for instance, his statements relative to the battle of Fuentes D'Honore. We thus see the eulogies on the Peninsular armies overdone, while with the poor Legion, there were the different correspondents of political factions, to gather up the most trifling incidents, and send them home for publication. At home there were the most active political hostility, to cause exaggeration. When the gallantly fought action of the 5th o

May, 1836, was fought by the Legion and the news came home, it being a complete and indisputable victory—the opposing parties in the political periodicals at home, in the words of Major Richardson, "stormed—fumed—abused—all in the most incoherent manner. It was according to them an affair of brute force, neither skill nor judgment were displayed—the troops owed their success entirely to intoxication which had blinded them to the magnitude of the enterprise—it was a mere mob attack—an affair of blood-thirsty ill-guided mercenaries ; and last not least, came the consolatory assurance that the day would never have been won, but for the co-operation of a solitary English steamer which chanced to throw a few well-directed shells."

But the want of military qualifications has not been the sole amount of the charges against the Legion. The pity of Sir Henry Hardinge and others, was poured out in the House of Commons, in commiseration of the unhappy case of those poor misguided men, as they called them, who were neglected and starved in Spain ;—the same hypocritical pity assuming a tone of contempt as was more natural to the persons who talked of the Legion, generally ended by a sneer at what they called the filthy and ragged Legion. The Legion was sometimes filthy and ragged, but never was it at any time so wretchedly destitute of clothing and comforts as was the British army under Wellington, notwithstanding he could drain the Exchequer, and the faster he drained, draw money the faster into it. Notwithstanding these advantages to the Wellington army, the Legion under General Evans was never so wretchedly ill-clothed as was his soldiers in the greater part of their campaigns. Lest then, some youth who may burn with enthusiasm for the *field*, should think contemptuously of the Legion, and all-gloriously of the Wellingtonian armies, I shall draw aside the veil of glory and let him see the heroes of the Peninsula as they were. My conversations with old soldiers being only verbal evidence, I shall dispense with them, though these are plentiful and powerful in evidence. I shall quote the "*Scottish Soldier's*" excellent little book. He says page 25, the battle of Vimeira having just ended—

" We were much amused when resting from our gory toil, by seeing one of our men taking *the remains of a shirt off his back*, (he had only a piece of a shirt like some of the Legion) and then drawing on a dead Frenchman's
No. 30.

smock-frock in its stead : his own shirt it seems being in anything but good condition."

Then at page 29, he says—

"Next day new tartan tro.vsers were served out, our old ones being in a miserably tattered state owing to the effects of our campaign. They were now thrown away; this produced a fearful scuffle among some of the lower orders of Portugueze, every one of them contending with the utmost noise and fury for the possession of a pair of *breeks* ; to their honour it must be said, however, or rather to free them in some degree from the national reproach I must say, that when it was discovered that the clothes were filled with myriads of those disgusting insects which are usually companions of poverty and campaignings, they threw the rags down with every sign of aversion. Perhaps it is necessary here to apologize or account for our seeming uncleanliness, this is an easy task. Figure to yourself, reader, men landing from a crowded transport without receiving the luxury of clean linen, marching and bivouacking for weeks together without ever putting off their clothes, and your wonder will then cease "

Yes, so say we of the Legion ; we were in a state of filth not much better than what has been commonly represented ; but that arose, not from any peculiar habit—not from the want of proper discipline, not because we were the *Legion*, but because we were exposed to the inconveniences that all soldiers in active warfare have been exposed to, and because we were not better provided for, though thank God not worse—than the soldiers of Wellington. How truly did one of the great mischiefs that befal an army, operate equally against the British in 1809, and the Legion in 1836. The " *Scottish Soldier* " says page 79—

" I believe that the cause of many deaths, and incalculable sufferings to those who survived their miseries, was owing solely to the bad shoes which were furnished by the army contractors: it was thought a good shoe that would last a week ; but the far greater part of them was destroyed in a day or two! of course a constant supply could not be kept up at that rate. Many a soldier, poor as he was, would have paid a guinea out of his own pocket to get a good pair of shoes."

So would many of the *Legion*. I alone wore out *thirty-two* pairs of English made shoes, and three pairs of *boots,* during twenty-three months ; and several of our men destroyed more in the same space of time, only justice demands the admission that some of them were sold, or otherwise made away with. The manner in which the army is cheated by swindling contractors, is disgraceful to the character of the nation; but it cannot be otherwise, so long as the trafficking situations of first Colonelships are kept up as they now are. In this respect the only thing dishonourable to General Evans was, that he adopted and practised, or allowed to be practised, the same swindling practices that are carried on in the British service.

Again the matchless Peninsular heroes, may be seen in a state certainly as low as even the most wretched of General Evans's invalid detachments ever were. The soldier at page 242, says :—

" Removing to the town of Coria, we received some arrears of pay, which were immediately squandered away upon wine ; the kettles of that fascinating liquor never standing empty, so long as the means of supplying them lasted. Our prodigality elicited a remark from a Spanish landlady, which would have done no discredit to any " auld thrifty Scotch wife."—She expressing her surprise that we spent so much money in wine, and never thought of buying shirts to our backs ; in fact it must be owned that we were as ill, if not worse off in this respect, than Falstaff's famous crew,—they possessed a shirt and a half, but we could not boast of one at that time !"

What! the army of Wellington worse than Falstaff's crew! I made mention in an early part of this work, of the state that some of our invalid detachments were in; and how Colonel Renwick was ashamed to go into Santander with them, he having parodyed the words of Sir John, to the effect that " I'll be ——, so and so——, if I march into Santander with you;" and this passage of mine was seized on by those who deal unfairly in party strife, and re-published by them, as a specimen of what the Legion had been. What like were the British, when they entered Toulouse? my authority already quoted frequently, says—

" Fortunately for the 50th, and 92d, they had lately got new clothes,—their appearance therefore was passable in the eyes of the French ; but as for us, and most of the other regiments, magnificent costume was out of the question. Our clothes were in fact worn out ; but not a rag hung pennant like in the air, strict orders having been issued to that effect, although full liberty had been given to mend the holes with any sort of cloth. This indulgence was acted up to in the fullest extent; patches of canvass, and of blankets covering us from head to foot, interspersed throughout with other patches, of all the colours of the rainbow: such habiliments had a very harlequin mendicant effect, &c., &c."

Now these poor fellows with their patched habiliments, could not help themselves, and they were not the worse soldiers for the field, in having patched up their clothes; but neither were the men of the Legion, whose clothing, though never so worn and tattered in appearance, as that of the soldiers of Wellington has yet been held up to ridicule, by those who may have seen at times a patch on a pair of trowsers; I make an exception of those who are seen covered with red rags about the streets of London, and also of all those who at times came home in tattered regimentals, because they commonly sold every saleable article to the Spaniards before coming away; and a passage on board of filthy vessels, on the decks of which the men lay over-crowded, rendered what remnants of clothing they possessed, extremely filthy. Bad as those of the Legion were in appearance, they were not worse however, than the regiments coming home from the Peninsular war. Numerous instances, such as the following might be adduced. The soldier says, in speaking of his passage homewards.

" We derived some amusement from an officer, who was seldom or never absent from the side of the capstan: during the whole voyage, he was continually rubbing his back against it, having long since given up as a hopeless task the idea of freeing himself from the innumerable hordes of vermin, by which we were infested."

And of cleanliness, he at another part says—

" We generally pursued the antedeluvian system of washing, that is to say, walking into a river, and scrubbing only externally."

We of the Legion, notwithstanding all that has been said of our unsoldierlike conduct, could very seldom—indeed never—get off with any such rough cleaning. One day, during the summer of this year 1838, when the Duke of Wellington, or rather Her Majesty, was reviewing the troops in Hyde Park, it was remarked by a Colonel, who commanded a regiment in Spain, that the Guards went through their duty in a very slovenly manner, and the same Colonel having dined in the evening with a General officer of the British army, and a number of military guests, repeated the remark, and added that if his regiment at San Sebastian, had made the same blunders that he saw the Guards make, he would have gone off parade, leaving it to punishment drill. When informed of this officer's remarks, which I was by an authority of unquestionable veracity, I noted it the more readily, because my humble knowledge of military evolutions, enabled me on the same day to detect some mistakes, and a good many loosely performed manœuvres, of which, I remarked to a friend, that had we, on the glacis of San Sebastian, made even one such mistake, we would have been punished for it. I had a few months before, seen the 42d Highlanders, reviewed by Lord Cathcart on Glasgow Green ; and were I to make a mere assertion, that I did not think much of their evolutionary precision, I might be answered now, as I was then by a person to whom I made a remark,—" what of that ? that is only your opinion." But I will state now, what I pointed out then, what indeed, any spectator knowing what military exercise is, must have observed that during one hour's manœuvering, eleven different mistakes were made by pivot-men of sub-divisions and sections, facing reversely from what they should have done ; that when a company was ordered out to skirmish by the sound of the bugle, there was a double-quick, and an extend-from-the-centre, sounded at the same time, and instead of following the sounds, both the flanks got into confusion, by not giving instant obedience to the bugle ; besides when they were extended, they neither formed a regular line, nor were they equally distributed, though there was no local necessity for being confused. Again in firing a volley, it went off in two pieces, with a crackling connection between them. The line was frequently not very well dressed, though never extremely ill ; but the supernumeraries were frequently very negligent. In taking up distance, two Sergeants were seen to run to one point, which caused one to come back ; an officer changed his flank by the front, when he should have gone by the rear ; and another changed his flank about half-way, and was put back by a Sergeant, who I supposed told him he was going wrong. In this style, did the 42d manœuvre with &c., &c., &c.

Now there is nothing extraordinary is these mistakes, they will occur at times with the best disciplined regiments ; and I do not think the 42d is worse in that respect than other regiments, yet neither are they better in *other* respects, than other regiments.*

I speak of that Highland regiment in the last sentence in comparison with other regiments of the British Service not of the Legion. The facts of the 42d having been nearly cut to pieces in different battles, gives, in my opinion, a very contrary character to the regiment from what it generally bears. For instance,

Had any regiment of the Legion committed the blunders, or one half of them at San Sebastian, before General Chichester—and yet he was a mild officer ; that the 42nd committed on Glasgow Green, that regiment of the Legion would have been kept two hours on

---

at Egypt it was eminently successful; but by what means ? why, by disobedience of orders and inattention to strict discipline : It stood under fire of the enemy, as it was being formed, when landing from the boats ; and on Major Stirling giving the word " fix bayonets," and following it with " prime and load," a private named Donald Black called out " charge baignets" and the narrator, a General officer of the army goes on, and says.—" The entire regiment as one man instantly obeyed this energetic command,—ascended the heights at the charge and carried the French position with cold steel in the most gallant style   *   *   *   * General Moore arriving at the spot told the 42nd their bravery was beyond all praise, but that not obeying their commanding officer was a great breach of discipline, and on the present occasion the movement might have had a fatal termination ; and at the same time turning to the colonel he admonished him for the irregularity of his men. Colonel Dickenson replied, " I might have held one man, but by —— General, it was impossible for me to hold a whole regiment." But Donald Black's (in Gælic Dhu) Highland blood was in a flame, and being quite indignant at what he considered unnecessary loss of time, his impatience to close upon the foe in the Scottish manner," &c. &c.—Now this twaddle about " Highland blood being in a flame," amounts in reality to nothing more than the well known facts that the Highlanders of Scotland are a race of persons possessing strange animal passions, their prevailing propensities being what phrenologists call Combativeness, and Destructiveness—passions which are only controuled in them by two equally strong propensities—Self-esteem and love of approbation, with these and an undue share of acquisitiveness, with the faculties that lead to superstition we find the Scotch Highlander making his way over the heads of his superiors in intellect, in many of the petty situations in life, more particularly in the army, where he is the best provost and non-commissioned officer that wears Her Majesty's uniform, merely from his obsequiousness to all above him, and his contempt for all beneath. These qualities of the Highlanders have made them always furious in battle, but not always successful. In the case of Egypt, the cause of their running in on the French, was not that of Donald Black being " quite indignant at what he thought an unnecessary loss of time." it was because Donald Black was afraid of the bullets that were flying thickly around him, and killing some of the men, while he and they, could not gratify their desire to combat, destroy, and revenge. I refer the reader to what was said of bravery and bayonet charges at some previous pages of this work, and I again repeat, that from personal experience,—from the experience of others—and from the study of the animal and moral constitution of mankind, I am right in

parade behind others, or it would have had a week of extra picquets—
or it would have been paraded in heavy marching order, twice a day
for a week, had the regimental ration of wine stopped, perhaps had
all, or more than these punishments : yet such punishing of regiments, was very rare in the Legion ; and the punishment was rare,
not from an inattention to discipline, but from the complete state of
discipline, and perfection in every movement to which the Legion
was drilled.

I have digressed into the question of discipline, from the notice
which I took of the Peninsular army's cleanliness : on that point
General Evans's Legion, and Wellington's army, seem to have been
much alike ; as indeed any soldier, who has seen active warfare would
admit ; but justice to the Legion, demands that I should make a
more obvious comparison with it, than that of the Peninsular army.
I see soldiers of British regiments, going about London at times,

---

stating that the eagerness of soldiers to close on an enemy with their bayonets
is not an effect of courage, but an effect proceeding in a great measure from the
want of it.

Relative to the 42nd regiment, I may also mention their destruction at Waterloo. They were said to have been in the corner of a field, and the cause of their
not seeing the French cavalry coming on them until too late to form a square was
the tall wheat that over-topped them. Gratification of our national passion for
the marvellous, makes us admire the numbers slain, and the excitement of our
peculiarly-easy-excited national sympathies together with the eminently successful result of the battle causes us to pity and forgive the Highlanders for their
fault, or rather prevents us from seeing any fault in them ; but there was a fault,
and for a less one—one many degrees less—a British Admiral was once brought
to execution, solely because the national sympathies so highly gratified by Waterloo
had been disappointed by his failure ; we find that a fault—that of the 42nd not
keeping a look out for cavalry at Waterloo, is rendered glorious merely because
that regiment was killed in heaps without even being able to fight. Query—has
discipline, that first, and most important quality of military virtue—that, which
is said to have been difficult in the Legion—has that been at any time, or is it
now conspicuous in a regiment the most boasted of in the British army, the 42nd ?
Again is it true that while the 42nd is not very well disciplined, which I assert it is
not, that more court-martials have of late years been held in that regiment, than
in any other of the service? and is it true that Lord Hill through the Adjutant
General sent a cautionary order to Glasgow Barracks to that effect ; this last
I answer firmly is true.

who, so far as cleanliness goes, would not have been permitted to enter the gates of San Sebastian, so strict were the orders to our sentries there, to allow no soldiers to enter, who were not properly dressed, and yet with these orders strictly obeyed, few men were ever refused admittance. Those English visitors or "correspondents," who may have reported the appearance of the Legion, must have been, or should have been aware, that hospital orderlies and invalids, whom they may have seen, are a species of *soldier*, that nobody ever saw, or expects to see in the best order of cleanliness. Pioneers on their daily duty of carrying rations, and serving them out, are also an exception. But there are points of comparison to be made, more important to the Legion's character, than the subject of cleanliness; and these points are of such importance, that I consider myself but performing a duty to my fellow-countrymen of civil life, in discussing them. Those who are contentedly wrapt up in the allusions of national glory, will call me anti-national! but if so, let them bring to mind the loud laughter of contempt, that responded from a majority of the nation, to the claims of sympathy from the soldiers, in the hard fought campaigns of the British Legion; let them bear in mind the gratification,—aye, the publicly proclaimed gratification, with which the news of a defeat of General Evans's troops were received; let them bear in mind these things, the enmity of a large portion of the British public, to their own countrymen; and then let them wince or submit to have the veil of national delusion torn, and have unpleasant truths exposed, as they can best bear them.

We are a generous nation, when our sympathies are excited; but we are seldom generous from a sense of justice. Our fathers were the same; they shot Admiral Byng, because a French fleet escaped from him, and because the French to prevent his pursuit, fired into his rigging, demolished it, and did not kill himself, nor enough of his men; yes, history, tells with shame, that England demanded the blood of Admiral Byng; because like a spoiled child, the nation was disappointed in something to please it.

The same people lauded to an undue height, the then first Lord of the Admiralty, Anson, one of the accessaries to Byng's murder; because he had in a South Sea expedition, lost all his ships with a trifling exception; because the unhappy wretches that perished following him, suffered dreadful calamities; and because he and the survivors, robbed some South American merchantmen at sea, and brought home the spoil.

It would be improper for me to take up my limited space in this work, by going over the numerous parallels of national folly, that present themselves in history; although every care has been taken by the historians to flatter national pride, by the mystification of facts. Few indeed, could give facts for until lately nothing was ever known of warfare, but what the General's dispatches told, or what some officer wrote as a return, for the favour of promotion, and then he was perhaps intoxicated with success, or what was as likely to pervert truth, galled by defeat, and was twisting circumstances to please the nation, as a nurse sings lullabys, and tells lies to the child, when she has not been able to procure a toy.

Some will say this is making too light of national feelings; but I repeat it is too true. What could we not say on this point of the Duke of York's army in Holland, and the more recent expedition to Walcheren; what of Sir John Moore's disastrous retreat, or the more lately suffered defeat of the British at New Orleans? But these shall lye unmeddled with, save by one or two passing remarks on Sir John Moore's retreat.

The retreat of Corunna exemplifies in a glaring light the fantastic prejudices of our nation. In the first place, no historian has yet been able to justify General Moore in making such a retreat, though all have attempted to do so; the sunny south of Spain was open to him; but because he led a helter skelter retreat to the north, conducted as well as any General could have conducted it, but yet wretchedly disastrous to his army, and because he was killed, because he did not survive his disgrace—he has been lauded as a General of consummate bravery and wisdom. Perhaps he was both wise and brave—perhaps he excelled all his contemporaries; but though he had excelled them nothing would have saved him from becoming another Byng, from being another immolated sacrifice to appease public disappointment had he not fortunately fallen in battle. But he fell and monuments have been erected to his memory.

Much more could be said of that affair, the philosophy of courage deduced from practical examples of bravery proves, that in that retreat the pursuers exhibited by far the greatest resolution and prowess.

if provisions were wanting to the fleeing army, where could the pursuers find them ? the English by their own account ate up what could
be found on their route ; if mules and provisions could not be kept
along with them, how were the French who kept at their heels to
be better provided ? if the mules could not keep up with the British
one day, how could they keep up with the French the next, and that
for weeks together ? To turn about and fight at the last moment
when farther escape was impracticable, seems very doubtful courage ;
and though they repelled that day the Van of the French, who must
have been exhausted with fatigue like themselves, and who had not
the impulse of *do or die* to goad them on, but who fell back waiting
on their main body coming up, to repel the attack of the French Van
in such circumstances, and then make off in the night on board English vessels, and that in the most disorderly and headlong manner,
seems indeed a very parodoxical victory. The French retreated from
Toulouse in good order without a shot being fired on their rear, and
the English claim the victory. The English retreated from Corunna
in the most disorderly manner ever recorded of an army, and got the
protection of British ships, while the French fired on them, and yet
the English claim the victory ! But let these defeats alone ; opinions
have been, and are yet divided on them ; let us see some of Wellington's campaigns, which no one calls in question.

The battle of Busaco is one of his victories; and his historians
knowing that he did not put the French off their ground, say that
" this battle had powerful moral effects although the situation of the
armies was not materially altered," and they record it as one of the
great achievements, its name is on the colours of the regiments who
fought there &c. Now the British army with Wellington at its head
retreated the second day after the battle, and abandoned all that
part of the country to the enemy. Can any man deny that ? yet Busaco is one of those glorious victories that we of General Evans's
Legion are to be " weighed and found wanting" by. It was wise
for Wellington to retreat when he could not hold his ground, but
why does justice prostrate herself at the name of Wellington, and
stand with a falsehood-telling face in opposition to the claims of
others ? A private soldier may not be considered a respectable authority, in opposition to Generals, but when it is notorious that these
last have never given us a correct version—not even an intelligible

version of the war, and when soldiers have produced intelligent accounts of at least some part of it, may we not compare the two classes of authors, and by also allowing the French to give us some information—form an estimate from among them equally ? Is it unfair
in me, when the Legion of Evans has been depreciated by a comparison to the army of Wellington—when all details and incidents have
been carefully collected and published in the newspapers, and by
persons encouraged and abetted in traducing General Evans and his
soldiers, by persons who held these up contemptuously for comparison
with the armies of the late war, is it unfair in me to seek justice for
the Legion's character in the manner I now do, by exposing those
details of the Wellington wars, which have been as carefully concealed,
as those of our campaign were carefully published ? No impartial
reader will give a negative ; but the subject is one on which I do
not expect many impartial readers. It is but six days since a leading newspaper of the liberal daily press said relative to the United
Service Journal having an article on the expedition to Walcheren—
" why can they not let Walcheren alone ! we wish it were expunged
from the pages of our history !" Now this arises from the national
aversion to know the truth, if that truth does not flatter our vanity.
Is it just to future generations to hand them down the history of our
wars partially recorded ? If war is to be avoided as an evil which
these same liberal papers will readily admit, why should we dally
with the pleasing parts of its history, and seek to expunge all those
events which are most likely to prevent its recurrence ? Why should
we injure the national honor by claiming a character not fairly ours,
—that of never having failed in any warlike enterprise—" never
meeting an enemy but to conquer him," as Scott says ?— Glorious
as is the fame of Wellington—great as his military talents are, and
unquestionable as some of his victories were—*he* even *he* was not
always successful—nor did *he* always meet the enemy to conquer
him.

The battle of Salamanca is well known ! but it has not been so
often trumpeted that Wellington possessing, afterwards, the same
ground that the French fought on, declined to engage them, and
made a hasty and sudden retreat to avoid their attack. The soldier
whom I have quoted, and am about to quote again, is not writing be
it remembered, to depreciate the army ; far from it : he tells of many

hard-contested and honorably-fought battles—many successful enterprises, creditable alike to the commander and the men commanded that will always maintain the honor of the Peninsular armies in a high position of military fame; but with these he tells circumstances that impresses his narrative as an undisguised and instructive tale of truth, and it is therefore preferable to most of those works of higher title that do little more than reprint the Dispatches of the Commander-in-chief.

One prevalent error of opinion relative to the Legion's warfare is, that it did not fight in the regular stand-up-style, but adopted the guerilla system. Now this is to a certain degree true; because the nature of the country, and the mode of fighting in the mountains rendered other styles of warfare at times impracticable; but on the other side it is an erroneous opinion that most people have—that of thinking the British army was always manœuvred in front of the enemy as regiments are seen at a review, or on a parade. Many passages could be quoted from different authors to prove that the British army fell into the loose mode of fighting and marching which was virulently charged against the Legion, which was said to have been much more loose than it really was. I take a passage from the "soldier" at random; it will answer the statement of a correspondent of a certain English newspaper, who spoke contemptuously of having seen regiments of the Legion in reserve, the men of which were lying down to save themselves from the shot of the Carlists! the Soldier says, page 56—

"The French had been long hanging on our rear, like a cloud, which now, however, seemed as if it were about to burst,—as on the morning of the next day, they attacked us in earnest; • • • • I was among the party that was placed as a reserve: in this situation, the enemy began peppering us with cannon-balls, upon which we had recourse to our old system of sitting down.'

There we see the British army sitting down, and that according to their "old system." At the time of the attack, we find the army in a dreadful state, worse I presume then those of Evans's Legion ever was for hunger, for in every page, and in every movement of the army, the soldier is recording the sufferings of himself, and comrades from hunger. In page 57, he says "grim hunger was again preying on our vitals, without an prospect of drawing him out." And

again, page 58, " in the middle of the day, we halted in a turnip
field : even that miserable vegetable was considered delicious food;
and the whole regiment attacked them, as eagerly as famished wolves
would have done a dead horse * * * *. A party of us having
been sent to a farm-house for straw, to litter ourselves in our muddy
beds for the night, we received intelligence that apples were discovered up in the loft. This was indeed joyful news, &c."

Then in another page he says, " some of our men having been
sent down to a farm-house for straw, met there with a number of
French soldiers on the same errand. Reciprocal civilities passed
between them, giving the direct lie to any national antipathy." This
may be valued with the commonly received reports of our *natural*
enemies. Natural! they were artificial, knowing and caring as little
for the *cause* of the quarrel, as any poor fellow of the British, did.

Of this retreat, the "*soldier*" farther says, page 63. "Order
in the march was now totally disregarded, every regiment in the
army being intermixed, owing to the best walkers pressing on, and
keeping as near the van as possible." Now the Legion would have
become similarly disordered, if it had ever retreated in that style ;
but though it did not suffer such disasters in retreating, it has been
branded with every imputation of disgrace. The same writer, says
again, page 68. " I arrived at the town of Batanzas, in a very helpless condition. Colonel Pack was looking out of a window, when I
entered, apparently watching the arrival of the stragglers of his own
regiment ; seeing me, he asked what was the number of my company;
and on my reply, pointed out the house destined for its reception.
I entered with the full expectation, of being the last that would ever
arrive of the whole company, which once consisted of eighty men ;
but now to my astonishment, nine only out of that number stood
before me." The continuation of the same paragraph, shews how
they stole from each other, and that, under circumstances which
could have been but rarely matched in the Legion.

Sir Walter Scott, writes of the French kindling fires, and making
them blaze high to hide their retreat. I would have quoted this passage, but for its extremely gross language ; speaking of " ignominious flight, damned with double shame, &c." But what says the
soldier of the 71st, page 72. " The ships having arrived, we rose
silently in the dead of the night, and leaving some men to keep up

the fires, in order to deceive the enemy, we marched off." This is a well planned honourable stratagem, when performed by the British, and an ignominious flight, when performed by an enemy, so much for national generosity ! we of the Legion may thank our stars, that we did nothing of that kind, or it would have been deep national disgrace. Immediately after the foregoing quotation the "soldier" says "The scene of confusion that took place baffles all description; near the whole of our army was assembled here in the most tumultuous manner, and every one rushed indiscriminately into the boats. * * * All controul and order were now lost, every one shifting for himself without regarding the order to keep by his own particular regiment." I am aware that in quoting these passages, I will be answered with the "peculiar circumstances" in which the army was then placed, but these circumstances not being unavoidable cannot be admitted in palliation of such misconduct.

The writer whom I have quoted proceeds to give an account of their landing in England, and certainly a more sorry figure was never cut by any regiments as these; they seem to have been like the remnants of the Legion at Portsmouth, or rather worse. He also gives the expedition to Walcheren, but it is so full of disasters that it is needless to particularise them. We shall see what he says of Wellington when he has joined the army in Spain a second time, page 113

"We now saw Lord Wellington for the first time since the battle of Vimeira; and soon after we arrived at the town of Sobral. Here we met our army in full retreat from the field of Busaco."

As it is undeniable but Wellington was the conqueror at last, I would here remind the reader again, that these retreats are only quoted to show that there were defeats and retreating in the British army. This having been so often denied, I am under the painful necessity of picking them out of the catalogue of great *victories*. Busaco, is one of them; let us see the retreat from that field of *victory*; a little farther, the "Soldier" says—

"Towards the close of the next day, the enemy made their appearance; we were purposely left alone to engage them, being supposed to be fresher than the rest of the army, who were much knocked up by their laborious retreat. * * * Notwithstanding our best efforts to the contrary, the French drove us out of the town though not without a good deal of difficulty; they at length retreated in their turn. We bivouacked that night midway between the French and British armies, but marched back in the morning and occupied Sobral again. Half of our company were sent out on picquet; I remained along with the other half, in a house where a quantity of dried fish was found; this in addition to plenty of rice and Indian corn, contributed materially to making us all very merry; for the immediate prospect of food draws forth cheerfulness at once from hungry men. An oven being in the place, many set to and baked abundance of bread, not only with the intention of filling their bellies, but their haversacks besides; our " here to-day and gone to-morrow " sort of life putting us under the necessity of breaking the Christian's mandate of " take no heed for to-morrow ;" But alas! we were unexpectedly roused from these *intellectual* enjoyments, by orders to turn out and join the picquet on the outside of the town ; catching up our firelocks with some reluctance, we issued forth and effected the junction. Scarcely had we done so, when General Erskine rode up, and ordered us to retreat, as the enemy were advancing. By the time we had retraced our steps back to the town, we found the rest of the regiment drawn up under arms: the General then ordered two companies to post themselves on a neighbouring hill, which was thickly covered with vines. The intention of this was to amuse the enemy as it were, while we were effecting our escape • • • we were therefore, again obliged to suffer ourselves to be driven through the town, at double quick time • • •. At length we halted from our race, &c."

The author goes on, and says of the following day, that—

" A continual skirmishing was kept up the whole day, from behind walls, and other places of ambush. At one time, the enemy came on in such overwhelming numbers, that we were obliged to retreat rather precipitately over a wall, &c."

Those who have been accustomed to read of the Peninsular battle-fields, and who have talked of fighting in tones that sound highly though inconsistently with realities, will not be prepared to hear that British soldiers fired from behind walls and other places of ambush! they will be prepared certainly to hear of " overwhelming numbers " coming against the British, because " overwhelming numbers " was a convenient expression to cover every retreat. I have, or rather I should say, we, of General Evans's Legion have used the same covering for our retreat from Hernani ; but it may not be inappropriate to point out that the fact of " overwhelming numbers " was admitted by *our* enemy, whereas the *French* deny on their national honor, that at the time the foregoing extracts relate to, they had superior numbers! they assert, and we generally allow the French to be actuated

by military honor, that the British estimates of Massena's army as
well as of Soult's was often over-rated.   Indeed a careful reader of
history will perceive that there a.e errors in the opinions of English
writers, because, no two historians of the Peninsular Wars coincide
in their statements ;   all of them are less or more led away by the
enthusiasm felt at the moment they contemplate the war in its general
character ; and no doubt many of these writers have put down a
number with their pens, and with the same pliable but irresponsible
little instrument, an instrument subservient alike to falsehood and
truth, they have recorded an expression of overflowing nationalty,
and though detecting its injustic: in the course of a temperate perusal
of what they have written, they have still left it unscratched, because
say they " it will give no offence, it will tend to inspire the nation
with martial enthusiasm, which it is our business to promote." Yes,
if this has never been audibly expressed by the historians of the late
war, it has been seen in almost every page of their records ; they
have written a few of them for the nation, the greater number of them
for a party—none of them for mankind.

Indeed if there is one, whose words have come to the public,
more honorable than another, it is Wellington himself ; for a
careful reader of the numerous commentaries, that have been
written on him, will discover that almost all the writers labour to
force success on him, when he does not ask it ; and yet h·, takes it
to himself where truth stands pointing to the foe.

I have laboriously searched for facts, and though I could tell the
tales of old soldiers, in support of what I have here written ; I shall
choose rather to bring supporting testimony from writers. that others
can refer to.   The " soldier" of the 71st goes on, and while taking
due praise to his own regiment, and the whole army—says, in an
honest manner, that they retreated before the French ; that Massena
came frequently forward in order of battle, but that from some cause
or other, which he as a soldier could not explain, Wellington did not
stand to engage him.   There is no doubt, but the prudence of the
sagacious commander of the British, forbade the hazard of battle ;
but why will history not admit the truth ? why does history not
admit that hunger, cold, disease, disaster and defeat, were sometimes the attendant circumstances of the British, as well as of their
foes ? why does history deny that these circumstances weakened the

French and ultimately caused them to evacuate the Peninsula? why will history continue to assert that *battles* decided the war, when facts, standing broadly, prominent and undeniably stubborn, point to other circumstances? why do both parties in the Peninsular strife raise the shout of victory, and each raise to themselves a canopy of national glory out of campaigns, the moral infamy of which will for ever be a disgrace to England and France? The ' soldier' says page 137.

Had the British been placed in the same predicament as the French were, —that is to say, had they been the enemies and invaders of Portugal, they would have found it to be a very different thing from being friendly allies; they would have found that they had to contend with a treacherous and ferocious set of people, who neglected no means, however base or unworthy, to cut off an inoffensive straggling soldier; besides having, in addition, to cope with an army of foreigners as valiant as themselves. These grievances would have, in consequence, roused and goaded them on to revenge; the nature of war also having a tendency to render the heart callous and to brutify the mind, they would, excited by blind fury, have been induced to go farther in their retaliation than the rules of justice prescribed: in short, I have little hesitation in saying, that the British would have committed the same enormities as the French did, had they been in the same situation."

It is almost needless to follow these facts of warfare farther. Many passages similar to the foregoing could be quoted to prove that the Peninsular war, was not a war of that spotlessly honourable kind to Britain that has been always represented; it was the war of a modern tyranny against ancient despotism on one side, and the war of despots against what might ultimately generate into systems for the common welfare of mankind on the other! — it was a war in which both parties engaged, endured dreadful privations, in which both spread havoc and murder on every side of them, wasting blood and treasure without mercy, that the world might be enthralled for another century in kingly bondage. This was the cause, for which the thousands of young men yearly shipped from this country, and who neither knew, or thought of a cause—fought and fell in Spain. This was the cause of the Peninsular war. The war of the British Legion under General Evans was an attempt to oppose the revival of absolute despotism, and an attempt to crush the Inquisitorial tyranny of superstitious Spain, a tyranny now struggling for mastery in Europe and which, but for the Legion of Evans, would have been, ere this, triumphant in the Peninsula, and when triumphant, farewell pro-

No. 31.

gressive reform—farewell rational liberty, Spain will be the depot of
European despotism and the focus of plots hatched, and for ever
hatching against freedom,—even the well-being of England. The *cause*
for which Evans fought was for the good of mankind. The *cause* for
which Wellington fought was to rivet more firmly the already galling
chains of physical and intellectual slavery. The difference is, that
the army fighting against liberty was successful, while that fighting
for liberty has failed.

To substantiate what has been just said, I shall quote a passage
from the Rev. traveller, Mr. Farr, the passage with which his book
concludes; and I will say in quoting that passage, that all who wish
to arrive at the true character of the Spanish war, and those who are,
and *have been* engaged in it, should read Mr. Farr's "*Reminiscences.*"
he having possessed the best means of obtaining information, and
having in an extended sphere of observation gathered up, and im-
ported his information impartially. He says, speaking of the manner in which General Evans and his soldiers were spoken of in England, and the manner in which they were treated in the war; that
they were—

" Not taken in the fair upstanding fight; but first way-laid and entrapped
unarmed, were butchered by an order signed by his own hand, (that of Don
Carlos), murdered by him, contrary to the laws of God and of nations—and
(villified by a party), whose two-hundred-and-forty-two recorded names,
horribile dictu—members of a British Parliament; have by their recorded
votes, so *nobly* espoused against the interests of humanity, against the interests of religion, and the precepts of their Redeemer; but vain shall be
the attempt, whatever may be the motives, and from whomsoever it may
proceed, to restore Spain once more to a state of stupid monkish despotism;
the fagots of the Inquisition have been extinguished, never again to be
lighted."

At another part of his work, Mr. Farr says, relative to the mis-
statements of the party press.

"In the month of September, I was conversing on the Spanish war with
Monsieur Zea Bermudez, well known as the famous prime minister of Ferdinand, the last he possessed; * * * *. Among other things I was relating the acts of forbearance, humanity, and noble conduct of the British
Legion which I had witnessed; defying any one to charge them with even
a single act of cruelty, under the greatest provocation. His answer was
natural: good God! is it possible; and that their countrymen should have

been guilty of telling such lies of them? For he could not suppose that British officers, and members of Parliament, could be capable of uttering such accusations, and yet be utterly untrue."

It may not be out of the way to state here, how Sir Henry Hardinge got *some* of his information about the affairs of the Legion; he got the most of it indeed from discarded officers of no very high reputation for either military or moral worth, officers, who, though they had possessed the highest military qualifications, were still aliens to General Evans, being dismissed by him, and therefore not very sure evidence; as witness Major Richardson, who in a first edition of a work lauded Evans because he, Richardson, was then an officer of the Legion, and in a *second* edition of his work denounced Evans because he, Richardson, was *not* an officer of the Legion;—but the case that I wish to state here, is one, that no person perhaps, in London knows but myself. It refers to the charge brought against General Evans in the House of Commons and in the newspapers of having *flogged women*.

As we had women with us in the Legion, much the same as those following the British army under Wellington, of whom the "*Scottish Soldier*" says, page 80, "Their profligate lives were not only a detestation of their own husbands, but even of many other soldiers," and as these women were a source of much mischief to many men not their husbands, it was necessary with us to keep the unruly ones in check. This so far as I knew, or have been able to learn since, by strict enquiry, was never done by flogging them, at least by order of an officer, where as in the Peninsular War women were flogged, and that in the very division commanded by the now Lord Hill; of course he and the Duke of Wellington were not the perpetrators of that punishment, but though not, it was done beneath them by command of an officer, while in the Legion it was the infliction of the women's barrack room acquaintance, in one case, and that of her brutal husband, for which *he* was punished in another. *Sir John Moore*, also *ordered* this punishment on refractory women more than once or twice; what is to be said of that? But to return to the Legion.

A woman of the 5th regiment, had at Vittoria carried on an extensive plunder by carrying out *accoutrements and muskets* under her cloak, and selling them to the Carlist agents, who were to be found in almost every town, and plentifully in Vittoria. This woman had been the cause of several men being flogged; because when one appeared on parade without his musket or without his bayonet, or it might be his ammunition, what was said? and what was done? Sir Henry Hardinge need not be told that for " losing or otherwise making away with, &c." a soldier is liable to receive, aye, not only liable, but *must* and *does* receive, a heavy punishment, as his military connections about Woolwich in this present year 1838, know very well and need Sir Henry be reminded that *he* would not, as an officer have listened to a soldier's plea, that the articles lost were stolen from him? Need Sir Henry be reminded that as it is highly criminal and dangerous at all times for soldiers to dispose of their "necessaries," that it was peculiarly so with us lying before an enemy, and more especially when the articles disposed of, found their way *to the enemy?* He may, perhaps, need to be told that the danger was much greater with us in the Legion than it was with the British in the French war; because then, the French did not hold correspondence with the British army through agents, as the Carlists did with the Legion; nor did the French need to collect arms and other munitions of war, as the enemy opposing us did. The difference of the necessity for strict measures being taken on this point was on the side of the Legion; therefore, if more crimes were committed and more punishments followed them in the Legion than in the Wellingtonian army, (the truth of which is still questionable) there are plain and obvious causes that tend to produce such consequences. And if the punishments were severe in the Legion, it was the system of war—of all wars — of all armies — not of any peculiar mode in the Legion, that made it severe. True it is, that the most of European armies are free of the stain attaching to the British—that of the lash;—but it is either not known, or if known it is forgotten, that no soldiers are such slaves to drunkenness as the British—no nation, from its highest to its lowest inhabitant gives way to beastiality as we religious Britons do: hence, among our soldiery, drunkenness is the only stimulus and the only object of life. The British soldiers — I speak of them as a whole --- place before themselves no object but to devise means how they can get a bellyful of liquor, every thing is sacrificed to that: whereas, a French soldier views drunkenness with horror; — he sips his coffee, and plays, and dances, and sings, and makes love like an intellectual being,

and he is loved again, and he is respected by his fellow countrymen
of civil life: a British soldier is the reverse of all that. Now,
though it is in part true, that the mode of punishment common in
the British army, having a tendency to degrade the soldier, causes,
or disposes the soldier to commit crime, or at least, causes him to
lose self-respect; though that is true, it would be unjust to say
that the mode of punishment is the only degradation of the British
soldier. No! the real cause must be out—it is *not* flogging, but
that which causes so much flogging — that which leads to the
crimes for which soldiers are flogged—it is the national addiction to
intoxicating liquors.

I will throw no shield over flogging! it is a disgraceful punishment
—but the alternative is not on earth, unless it be something worse
than the lash, by which British soldiers can be kept in subordination!
I am prepared for the storm, I know from whence it will come; but
it is experience—not so much the experience of having suffered the
punishment in my own flesh, or of having seen a hundred other persons suffer it; but it is the experience which I have of those persons
who fill the British army, of the peculiar habits and constitution of
my fellow countrymen; it is the utter impossibility of governing a
body of men by moral means, so long as they are kept in physical
bondage; and that physical bondage, being partly occasioned by the
nature of the duties required from soldiers, and partly rendered necessary by the previously acquired habits of the men transformed into
soldiers, moral influences are completely ineffectual.

I repeat that I know from whence the storm will come; but it
must expend itself at will, I have only one object in making the declaration I now make, and that is to establish truth, in spite of all
errors of opinion, no matter whether these errors are a party's, the
nation's, or even the world's. I say therefore, that the degrading
and beastly punishment of the lash, or something equal to it in
severity, can never be dispensed with, so long as an army of British
soldiers is kept up for the purposes of war. Because, if there is to
be war, there must be an exact and unvarying mode of discipline;
indeed if soldiers are to be used for any purpose, under command of
a chief, there must be implicit obedience; and as soldiers are, and
have ever been recruited from the fairs—the streets—the pot-houses
—or the whisky-cellars, making as a whole a mass of loose morality,

their subjugation to order, is not easily effected. And what means
are to be taken to effect it ? If the civilian sits all night in the tap-
room, and disobeys the moral law, that bids him go home to his wife
and his children, what follows ? Why, merely that he being a free-
man, a free-born Briton ; and under no physical restraint, he sits
until he is gorged, or if it is Saturday night, he sits until the
church-bells ring, and the landlord turns him out, then what like
is he in the streets ? Who has seen Westminster, Drury Lane,
Whitechapel, or Spitalfields ? Coventry, Birmingham, Liverpool,
Edinburgh, Glasgow, and Dublin—I speak of places best known to
myself—who has seen the public-houses in these places on Saturday
nights and Sundays ? who has seen the men of all these and every
other town, who do *not* work in factories, and who therefore drink,
or as they more complacently term it—make holiday on Mondays
and Tuesdays—who has seen these acting in disobedience to the
moral law, and the strongest of all its clauses—the domestic affections
—and will say that they could be soldiers, and could be governed by
a moral influence ? God forbid that I should say, that the industrious population of our towns are all of this description ; were such
an assertion made, it would be a falsehood ; but there are a
very great number in each town of this description, and it is from
among them that recruits for the army are generally taken ; and
again, though they may be a minority in the population—they make
a very great majority of the army—such a great majority indeed
that almost every soldier devotes himself to the sole, and all prevail-
ng desire—that of insinuating himself into the acquaintance of
:ivilians, where he can procure intoxicating liquors.

The consequence then is the soldier gets in debt with his pay-
,ergeant ; and as is commonly the case, the pay-sergeant or the cap-
:ain, perhaps both, being not so honest to the soldier as they should be,
he finds himself continually in debt ;—he then sells a shirt or some
other article, and on an inspection he is served with another for which
he is charged, and the system continues ; but while it continues it
grows. Frequent intoxication, besides a variety of physical evils,
produces that most dreadful of all diseases, mental depression ; and
it is at this point that two great evils meet ; the moral abandonment
of the soldier is completed, because whatever is yet sound in him
is soured by the severity of martial law. The conflict then

lies between martial law and a kind of moral despair; the two great
evils have met, and between them a British soldier is lower than a
brute. Among the French this immorality is unknown; the French
soldier has sometimes committed a robbery when the stake was worth
a risk; he has committed a murder for he will brook no insult; he
commits crimes, but all of them have some portion of intellectual
exercise mixed with them, and it is not too much to say that there
is even some degrees of *dignity* in crime; the French soldier may
gamble—he may seduce innocence—he may slay his fellow-soldier
in a duel—he may be a traitor, but he is never drunk; he manifests
an intellectuality in the commission of his crimes, and he is therefore responsible—he can be punished by an affront—he can be re-
claimed by leniency—he can be stimulated by honor, and where
these were supposed to be inefficacious, the French commanders
have put a criminal to death, so that others might be affected by it,
because they *reflected,* when they committed crimes. But the British
soldier beastifies himself, and then commits crime; he never
reflects, for he commits crimes when he is drunk; when sober, he
is the most humble of dogs---observing an obsequiousness to an officer,
and daily paying a reverence, altogether derogatory to the mind of a
man. The French soldier pays respect to his superior, but nothing
more. We of the British, know that we are prostrating ourselves
beneath the dignity of men; but we do it, reserving for ourselves a
future period of drunken rebellion, to shew that we do not submit
willingly. In fact the British soldier does nothing, but pays obedience until he is intoxicated, and then he has a long catalogue of
petty mean crimes that he goes through. His first begins with that
which in all regiments is nearly alike; but which I remember was a
very prevalent one in the *Scots' Greys,* it is that of catching a "*nat*"
---a *natural*---or in other words an idiot or fool; by which term they
designate all, no matter who they be, that will give them drink. The
cleverest fellow was in that gallant corps---not as some may suppose
---the best horseman or swordsman, he was the one who had most
ability in hooking a "*nat,*" for the beastification of himself and comrades. Then the next step from this moral littleness in men, is to be
drunk and absent from barracks—and if absent, put in the guard-
house on coming home. Crimes follow thick; the soldier is in
the "horrors," he sells something from his kit---by which he gets

drunk again, and that drunkenness gets him confined again; then comes nine days---or it may be three weeks in the " discipline room" ---a week at " pack-drill"---or a month "confined to Barracks." While he is intoxicated, he will not only not suffer to be spoken to, but he seeks out some Sergeant or Corporal who has given him offence—who has perhaps behaved very unjustly—but one that he does not think of correcting until he is drunk. Martial law makes a sulky look, a crime; but the drunken soldier performs what he calls " emptying his stomach," that is saying all that he can to the offence of his superior. This superior puts him in the guard-house, then comes a punishment. The soldier is sour, sulky, and discontented, and perhaps ultimately slays that superior, when a new fit of drunkenness overcomes his reason. Many, very many, are the crimes that the soldier goes through when intoxicated. He breaks out of barracks---he steals---he fights---he is robbed of his clothes---he is afraid to come home when too late, one night;---he stays out two;---he is more afraid;---he deserts;---he is taken;---brought back and punished; and deeper discontent preys on his mind, until he again seeks the oblivious or maddening draught, to drown for a few hours his sad realities; he drinks---is drunk, and awakes again in the guard-house---another degree deeper in crime.

Now many are the modes taken to impose restraint besides corporal punishment. There are pennies a day stopped—there are extra "fatigue" duties—there are in cavalry such things as taking a good horse from a man and giving him a bad one. There are rings worn on the arm for good behaviour, and Bs for bad. There is turning out every hour, half-hour or quarter, during the day, in heavy marching order. There is marching in that order all the day. There is a discipline room—a severe house of correction, in which defaulters are kept at various employments for days and weeks together, there is pack drill. There is extra guard-mounting. There is solitary confinement, there are the tread-mills—the county prisons, and the bridewells ,—there is transportation—there are hangings and shootings, but what does it all produce? what does it prove? nothing but an eternal truth—that the whole system for keeping up warfare is an outrage on man's nature, and that a Briton of all men, is the most irrational soldier.

Then it is here where those who apply the lash take their stand

and say " we try every thing, but nothing will do," it is here where
I say that *if*—let *if* be observed—we are to have war, and an army
to be obedient, no mode of discipline could ever keep it in subjection
but the lash! and if the French maintain discipline without flogging,
it is because the crimes of the British army are unknown among them;
and these crimes are unknown in the French army, because the causes
leading to their commission are unknown among the French people;
whereas these crimes are common in the British army, because their
root—an addiction to drunkenness, is common among the British
people.

I may have said enough to prove that the whole system of punishments is ineffectual—that is generally known, and I beg every reader
to read me correctly, and not say that I stand in favour of flogging
soldiers—I denounce the punishment :—and when future generations
become morally elevated, nothing will mark the depth of degradation
more distinctly from which the nation will have arisen, than the fact
which will be then a historical record, that the people of this age
were kept in subjection by soldiers—and these soldiers by the
lash.

Those who exert themselves to obtain the abolition of flogging,
do it from the best of motives, but they do it under the influence of
partial opinions on military subjects. How often does the same
newspaper contain a paragraph denouncing corporal punishment, and
on the other side a column filled with extracts of Peninsular or Nel-
sonian glory! How often is the youthful mind excited by these
tales to admiration of fighting heros—and detestation of barrack-yard
officers, when these are, in profession and practice, one and the same
class of persons! abolish flogging, and you abolish the hero :—exalt
the hero, and you establish flogging. Those " British Tars" that
fought the " Nile" and " Trafalgar" were once young lads—soft-fin-
gered—soft-hearted youths, who did not leave home without a tear;
what made them man the " wooden walls" and " brave the battle and
the breeze" was it for the nation—or the nation's cause? Cause!
what cause had the thousands of men stolen from their homes—and
forced on board a-man-of-war to fight for? cause, truly! there was a
cause,—but it was the lash laid unsparingly, and frequently on their
backs. Oh! if we but knew the history of the transformation of the
youth of tender years, to the rough veteran of many battles! could

we follow the plough-boy who because his sweet-heart affronts him at the fair, goes and takes the shilling from the recruiting party merely that he may vex her, with their ribbons on his hat ! or it may be the young man who forces himself to swallow liquor even against desire, that he may cut a swagger and look manly ! were we possessed of the history of these transformations, how many chucks beneath the chin to hold up the head ! how many " silence-sirs " " off-to-the guard house-with hims"—" court-martials"—" guiltys"—" strip sirs"—" do your duty drummers"—' lay it in I'll teach the scoundrels" how much of that would we see, and a thousand other maltreatments, and insolences that this unhappy being that makes one of a band of heroes has to endure ? Cause ! who thinks of *causes* when they go into the army ?

It is then, the duty of every journalist to strip war of that delusive power that its history has over the mind; let its ingredients be laid bare ! let the lash and its concomitant severities be laid bare ; and let the whole moral disgrace and infamy of heroism be exposed. There is no middle course !—it is not merely flogging, that is to be done away with ! it is a system that is insupportable without flogging, that must be destroyed.

When speaking in a general sense, as in the foregoing paragraphs, and to the effect that the lash cannot be dispensed with, I allude more particularly to an army in active warfare. It is true that in a barrack-yard substitutes may be found for the punishment, though I question if many of them are more humane. It is certain at any rate, that some men who have received a corporal punishment by the *cats*, would choose it again in preference to six months new fashioned bread and water imprisonment. But if there is to be war where are the prisons ? where, and how are all the modes of punishment which I have already enumerated as *now* in use, or almost any of them to be inflicted before an enemy ? If the nation will have glory, it must be paid for, and the price is humanity.

When Sir Henry Hardinge accused General Evans of undue severities, he was only complaining of what was the practice of his own party. There is some utility in military honor, it sometimes serves as a representative for a moral value; but most unfortunately those who possess it and make most show of it, are woefully destitute of moral honesty. We find gentlemen of the highest military

respectability, standing up in the British Parliament, and charging
an opponent with doing those things which they did themselves, and,
would do again were they in active warfare as they were once; but
not only do they charge their own crimes against an opponent—they
have no hesitation in adding falsehood to their charge. This recalls
to my recollection the case from which I have made perhaps a rather
lengthened digression, namely, the flogging of the women. I had
observed, how well officers of the British army knew that a soldier
coming on parade without a part of his accoutrements---and these
lost—was liable to punishment, how readily too *they* would have
punished him; for if it is necessary to flog as they now do at Woolwich, what must it have been in such a case as ours in Vittoria,
where every facility was afforded to the dishonest soldier to steal the
accoutrements or necessaries of his comrades and sell them, for he
knew better than sell his own, and these sold to the agents of our
enemy. The men who lost their muskets and accoutrements, were
tried and punished on the well known section of the "Articles"
namely, "for losing or otherwise making away with &c.," and when
this woman was discovered carrying off articles for sale beneath her
cloak, she was taken before Colonel Swan, who knowing he had no
magistrate to send her before, no mode of punishment whatever to
inflict on her, said to his regiment, or to the company she had stolen
the articles from;—" Men, I leave her to your discretion, nothing
shall excuse a man from punishment if he comes on parade without
even the smallest article of equipment; if it is your misfortune to
have your things stolen, you must look to the thieves; if your
women are thieves, it is yourselves that must be answerable for them.
I shall not admit this woman into quarters where she can be kept
out, but in being billeted as we sometimes are through a whole street
of houses, who can keep you from the ravages of these women but
yourselves. Now do with this one as you think proper; but remember, if you lose your accoutrements nothing shall save you from
punishment." The men then took this woman, and picking out all
those who had suffered, as supposed innocently, for losing necessaries,
these were appointed to try her and award a punishment. I admit
they were not likely to be the most impartial of judges, but whether
or no, there was a great degree of justice in doing something to deter
this woman and others, from getting the men punished. The sen-

tence against her was to be drummed out of quarters, with the threat that if she returned she would be flogged.   But all the drummers were unable to drum her out, and she was ultimately dragged out giving battle to all and sundry who approached her; but she returning again, the same men took it upon themselves to flog her out, and she was flogged, and such was the case and character of one of Sir Henry Hardinge's proxy correspondents.

Now the means by which Sir Henry Hardinge came to be informed of this case were these.   This woman after ekeing out nearly two years of a life in Spain of the most disgusting profligacy, during which, her husband several times suffered on her account, and ultimately died of vexation, got home to Glasgow, to which place she belonged, and was one day in one of those dens, called " *Spirit Cellars* " among a congregation of spirits similar to her own ; and to these, she had it appears told her story of ill-usage.   A person in Glasgow, who calls himself a " *writer*," (attorney) but whose writing amounts to doing any thing for a " dram," was among the company ; and on the ill-used heroine of the Spanish campaign complaining of her woes, but, expressing a kind of threatening hope that she would get justice—she would get some one yet to take up the case of a broken-hearted widow! when she uttered this plaintive hope and the tears mingled among the whisky, Mr. Gibbie said, " Whisht my dear, tak aff your dram an' comfort yoursel, I sall mak it a' right for you! "   So, Mr. Gibbie meeting me in the street one day, and knowing that I had been in Spain, enquired if I had seen the London papers to-day; on being answered with *no* he told me to go and see them immediately, for, continued he " *I have* brought the case of Mrs. Hatterick before Parliament! I kent the Parliament would soon tak up the case when *I sent* it before them &c."   And sure enough there was a case of woman flogging in the report of Sir Henry Hardinge's speech; but which I might not have suspected as regarding Mrs. Hatterick at all, had not Gibbie— Gibbie is the christian, not the surname—shewed me a London letter *franked*, and written in acknowledgment of his, and requesting *further particulars !* mentioning also, that the case would be attended to in the " *proper place*."   Shame upon the honor of a General of the British army! in the British Parliament to be so employed! to be in such a correspondence, merely that he might

muster ungenerous strength to overturn a political opponent! Not
a political opponent: no, there might be some extenuation for that;
but it was worse—it was dishonorable—it was to traduce a brother
soldier! I could account for Sir Henry Hardinge or any political
ally attacking the "Member for Westminster," and as political strife
goes, they have a right to do so; but it was meanly ungenerous to
attack "General Evans," as they did.

I have, perhaps, said enough, or more than enough, on this subject; but there is one point more, that I would have the reader to be
informed on before passing onwards to the narrative of the Legionary events:—it is the character of our officers, viewing them
generally. My own opinion was always, that taking them as a
whole, they were just as gentlemanly and respectable in character
and family connections, as the officers of the British army are; but
as *I* am not likely to be credited on this point, having been unin-
formed of any character, save that of the rough, hard-working, porridge and potatoe eating ploughmen of East Lothian —who, though
industrious, honest, morally honorable, and happily ignorant of the
world, are yet too much on an outside corner of the earth to know
any thing of the genus "gentleman," I, of course knew nothing of
it, nor have I become skilled in *gentlemanology* yet; but I will quote
what Mr. Farr says of the Legion officers; and when it is borne in
mind, that birth, Cambridge education, the clerical profession, emo-
lument without industry---great experience in travelling through the
world---through the world, both in a social and geographical sense
are Mr. Farr's, and that he is an author that writes against promotions
from the ranks, he will perhaps be credited. He says,

"I left San Sebastian, with the impression that I never saw a set of men
more gentlemanly, or less mercenary in their ideas, than the officers of the
British Legion, who were members of the Garrison Club there. They were
very good specimens of the age, we belong to. The old habits of swearing
and drinking, which were supposed to form part of a camp, were utterly
exploded; and their conduct in every way equal to officers of a British army,
when on foreign stations. It is true, there were some " incomprehensible
vagabonds," amongst the officers of the British Legion, and I will tell you
sooner or later who they were; and several who did not do much credit to
the Legion, had been got rid of in one way or other, before I saw them.*

* These I have often alluded to, as the traducers of the Legion, and its commander.

They were in the language of the Legion, called "Q. H. B's.," that is, Queen's hard bargains—good for nothing. You may ask me by what comparisons, and on what models I have formed my judgment? I will tell you; —I passed about a month at Malta in 1835. Colonel Considine was kind enough, to give me a general invitation to dine with his regiment when I pleased. I dined likewise with the 5th, and 60th regiments. I dined also several times with the Governor, Sir Frederick Ponsonby. I passed a great deal of my time at the Garrison Club, which threw me into constant contact with the officers. The British Legion, had no regular regimental messes at San Sebastian, but I had a general invitation from General Evans, to dine at his table every day. We were in the habit of sitting down, from ten to eighteen persons; the General, his Aides-de-camp, and myself ; the rest were persons invited, such as the different Spanish Generals, and their Aides-de-camp, the officers of Her British Majesty's Navy, and the field officers of the Legion, &c. There was also a Garrison Club, where you found the French and English papers, reviews, and periodicals, the same as at Malta, which threw you continually into the society of the officers. I saw them under much excitement, at the very time of their defeat; and nothing could be more correct than their conduct, or more gentlemanly, &c.

I can make another comparison which will stand considerably to the advantage of the officers of the Legion, and as it will be instructive I shall make it. The fact of my having been once in the 2nd Dragoons or Scots' Greys, is perhaps known to most readers of this work, and lest any may suppose that I retain a feeling of hostility to the officers of that corps, I make a solemn assurance that I do not, but I shall state a few plain and incontradictable circumstances.

First, of military capacity to command. The then Lieutenant-Colonel of the 2nd Dragoons was Lord Arthur Hill, an officer of a mild disposition, much given to gaiety, indeed oftener by a great deal in the Clubs and at the aristocratic soirees in London, than with his regiment ; he was respected and beloved by the men of the regiment because of the easiness of his orders, but when he came and took the command on a field-day, he had no more notion of how to manoeuvre troops and squadrons in proper style, than the youngest recruit of the corps, and he never could do it. He has a Waterloo medal.

Then there was Major Wyndham now the Lieutenant-Colonel of the regiment, whose name was some years ago before the public as a party to a certain celebrated case ;—if there was any difference be-

tween him and Lord Arthur Hill, it was that Major Wyndham was
the easiest, mildest, good-natured, and most incompetent to command
of the two. The Major was a tall and particularly fine looking man ;
one of the best looking soldiers in the British army, but without a
match, perhaps the most ignorant, or rather the most incapable of
learning military exercise of any field-officer in it. When the public
have believed that I could only look back on him with vindictiveness
when newspapers made war for themselves and me, and made him
a party, how often have I sincerely pitied him, knowing as I did that
his simplicity of character, and very innocent abilities had made him
the dupe of two or three of his officers, who were the *real* causes of
that *rumpus*, and who, the Major being commanding officer, screened
themselves from the storm they had conjured up behind him.
Few officers ever enjoyed the warm esteem of his soldiers more than
Major Wyndham did and does now. The Scots' Greys has been in
fact commanded by a *republic* ever since Lieut.-Colonel Grey retired
in 1830 ; *he* was a tartar, but since then every officer in the regiment
has had a share in the command. There were two or three clever
Captains, a dexterous Adjutant, and a first-rate regimental Serjeant-
Major and these kept the regular duty going. There was an ascendancy party and a party out of favour, and these among them kept
poor Major Wyndham continually on the verge of a boiling pot,—
they tumbled him in at last poor man !

Now should there be any hesitation in believing that the gallant
Scots' Greys were so commanded I shall state a proof or two, and
Sir Charles Dalbiac, and Major General Campbell, and their respective Staff, may be appealed to for the correctness of what I say. As
Major Wyndham could not give the words of command without a
prompter, he took care to have one ; and as this happened to be the
last officer of the regiment who had anything to do with drill, namely,
Captain Crawford the Pay-master, the assistance rendered by him, and
by the Adjutant at times, was noticed by the General ; and one time
the General seeing that all three were engaged in commanding a
manœuvre, exclaimed " give the word of command Major Wyndham
I presume *you* are commanding officer !" can Sir Charles Dalbiac
deny that ? Then the next day when inspecting the men on foot, the
Major seeing the General and his staff approaching called the regiment to " attention," and gave the word of command " draw swords."

Sir Charles seeing the mistake, called to the regiment, without making a remark to the Major, " as you were" and added " rear rank, take open order," then turning to the commanding officer, he said admonishingly, "now Major go on." A few days after, paragraphs appeared in the newspapers stating, that Sir Charles had made his inspection, and that he had reported the regiment in a high state of discipline. Sir Charles Dalbiac must recollect this, but it is only one of many similar cases. For instance, before Major General Campbell the regiment was " left in front" and the commanding officer not perceiving it, threw it into complete confusion, in making a charge and retiring, so much so, that each troop was broken up on the field, re-formed, told off, and all begun again as if they had just turned out of stables; that is another memorable truth. I shall cite no more of these cases save making this remark, that it is a historical fact, that the Scots' Greys were dreadfully cut up at Waterloo, and it is in the regiment a traditionary fact that their greatest slaughter occurred at the time when they, the 1st Dragoons, and Enneskillans were intermingled in confusion with each other! Must all these circumstances go for nothing? I readily admit that some of the officers of troops in the Greys were clever soldiers, but the field-officers were not.

Then I must compare these with the officers of another regiment, every one of which I knew well; that is the 8th regiment of the British Legion. I compare these because they are the regiments of the respective services, best known to myself, and I have no doubt but others could make similar comparisons of their military acquaintances.

First, Colonel Godfrey then, was an officer of experience, having a full knowledge of military matters, and one who would neither trifle or be trifled with; he knew his duty, and he compelled every officer and man beneath him to know theirs.

His successor was Lieutenant Colonel Apthorpe, an officer of the E. I. C. Service, whose character as an officer and gentleman stands high, immeasurably high above anything I can say for it.

Our next commanding officer was Colonel Hogg, who though not possessing a lengthened experience, was yet so completely master of his duties, and being master of them performed them with such superior ability, that he was even admired by his more ex-

perienced contemporaries; indeed, I fearlessly assert that in activity
and ability, he has no superior in any service; and if enthusiasm is
part of a clever officer's qualifications, he had that to a degree, that
kept him in a continual personal exercise. He was not an old officer,
but what of that? Sir Henry Hardinge, in the House of Commons,
stated one of his complaints to be, "that young officers could order
an old Waterloo man to be punished." How will Sir Henry like to
be told that the only commanding officer of a regiment that shewed
a *white feather*, and incapacity to command in the Legion, on the 16th
of March was one wearing a Waterloo medal on his breast? and that
is fact; this officer went to the rear, before the half of his regiment
had withdrawn! yet he was a Waterloo veteran.

Then to measure officers by their birth and family connexions,
those of the Scots' Greys will not stand higher than those of the regiment in which I served in the British Legion. The Lieut. Colonel
of the Greys was a younger son of an Irish Peer. In the 8th regiment we had the heir of an Earldom for one of our officers, and he
succeeded to his estate and titles, while in that corps! And besides
that one, there was a scion of the most ancient peerage of Scotland,
—a scion within one degree of being the heir to the present peer.
Then if the want of high family connexion is any discredit, it may
not be amiss to state that an officer of the Greys was the son of an
Edinburgh Ironmonger, and five others belonged to families who in
respectable language, were nobody; three other officers had been
private soldiers, and two who had some family descent, were yet so
poor, that they have stood for years holding lieutenancies, while
cornet after cornet being possessed of cash, have gone over their heads.
The other regiments of the Legion could afford a comparison of their
officers with the British, equally advantageous to themselves: but
these being best known to myself may suffice for my task.

CHAPTER XXIV.

Comparison between the battle of Toulouse, fought by the troops of Wellington
and Soult, and the battle of Ayetta, fought by the troops of Evans and the Carlist
General Segastibelza—Character of General Saarsfield and more causes for the
defeat of Evans at Hernani explained—Narrative of events in the Legion from the
morning of the 4th of May, 1837, to the evening of the 14th, in which many
incidents are related.

In the preceding chapter, the tone of controversy has been assumed, and kept up to a much greater length then was intended
No. 32.

when making the first few controversial comparisons. The importance of the subject must alone be my excuse for entering upon a discussion, which perhaps to some friendly and good natured readers may be unpleasant; and the vast amount of matter, similar to that already quoted, which presented itself in the course of ransacking various authorities, was the cause of lengthening my observations: there is indeed so much of that matter, that I almost regret having entered upon it without the ability to quote more fully, and enter more extensively into the discussion, than I have yet done. But notwithstanding the limits of this work, there is one point more that cannot be omitted—a point which I am confident will, in being discussed afford instructive information to all readers, but which will more especially interest my military friends. The point is a comparison, which by the information of old officers who fought under Wellington, and my own knowledge of Evans's battles, I have been able to make between the battle of Toulouse fought by Wellington, the victory of which, is disputed by the French, and the battle of the 5th of May, fought near San Sebastian by Evans, the victory of which, all Wellington's *friends* have laboured assiduously, and ungenerously to tarnish.

Relative to this, I would refer the dissatisfied reader to an article in Blackwood's Magazine, for August, 1837—an article which, but for its appearance in a periodical of high character, is altogether beneath my notice : for even as a literary production, it is meagrely written, while as a review, which it pretends to be of Major Richardson's "Journal of the movements of the British Legion," it is full of malignity and falsehood. I would refer the reader then to that article, and to the common out-pourings of certain newspapers, in which Evans's engagements have been criticised, and let what follows here be, read; this will then be read to advantage. There is not a military club in London, but will discuss this—there is not a military reader, who will not read it, and it deserves to be read; for as it will be readily observed, that I, the author of this work, could not give the information which is here supplied, relative to the battle of Toulouse; but that I must have procured it from the veteran officers who fought with Wellington, I readily acknowledge that, to be the source of my information; and as every incident which is here referred to, is given without colour or exaggeration, so will every veteran officer recognise a true statement of the battle of Toulouse, in what is here given. For the information of those who are still sceptical of the merits of General Evans's Legion, I have made a comparison of the two commanders—the two armies—the two opposing enemies, and the two victories—namely, the battle of Toulouse fought between Wellington and Soult—and the battle of Ayetta, near San Sebastian, fought between Evans and Segastibelza.

The similarity of these engagements—of the elements of attack and defence—of the number of belligerents on both sides, taking a reduced scale to measure the latter by the former—of the difficulties opposed to each of the engagements—of their duration, and the numbers of killed and wounded, is a similarity as singular as it is correct.

The troops of Soult were posted on the heights of Guillemeri, with the town of Toulouse in their rear, to protect them in case of a reverse.

The Carlists were posted on the heights of Ayetta with the town of Hernani, also in their rear to which they could retire in the event of a similar contingency.

The troops of Wellington were of three countries — English, Spanish, and Portugueze,

The troops of Evans were also of three nations, or at least three distinct kinds of men—English, Spanish, and Biscayan.

Soult had been carefully fortifying his positions, anticipating an attack for some time previous to its occurrence ; and had intrenched himself within four redoubts, well defended by cannon, and well garrisoned, by veterans of the nation fighting for their wives and families.

Segastibelza had for months previous obtained every requisite for his defence, which was in a finished state : consisting of stone walls and strong houses, equal to Soult's, erected under the superin tendance of the Carlist engineers—the best engineers for raising defences of that nature, in Europe—which defences by the addition of cannon, were converted into redoubts of a more dangerous nature than those of the French Marshal. They were well garrisoned by troops ; veterans, and also civilians or Paysanos fighting for their fueros and privileges.

The forces of Wellington were Beresford's corps, 12,000 men— Spaniards, 10,000 and Portugueze, 4000. And the troops to oppose these were about 18,000, which gave Wellington nearly *nine* men, to *six* of his enemy.

The troops of General Evans were about 5000 English; 3000 Spaniards and 600 Biscayans, the latter commonly called Chapelgorris. The opposing force of the Carlists was about 7000, making the difference of superiority in numbers, less on the part of General Evans over Segastibelza, than on the part of Wellington over Soult.

The weather during both battles was precisely the same— a pelting rain; and the ground was equally difficult for successful aggression.

The attack was at day-break with Wellington. It was at break of day with Evans.

The troops of Wellington were unsuccessful on all parts, being driven back by the bayonet—particularly the Spaniards and Highlanders—with frightful carnage; and at last, after four hours' fighting were dead beaten, being obliged to retire out of the reach of musketry though not out of the reach of the redoubts, which being armed with 18 and 24 pounders, from the foundry of which the principal establishment is at Toulouse, caused a heavy cannonade to fall on the line which was formed singly and directly in front of the whole length of the heights; its right being on the high-road from Croix d'Orade to the town over the bridge of Montabieu.

The troops of Evans, though opposed by heights of a steeper nature though encountering equally, artillery and the greater disadvantage of troops protected by loop-holed walls, still rushed onward to grapple with the terrifying difficulties; and despite the violence of the elements—their inexperience of the soldiers opposing them, assaulted and carried the first line. Here they have evidently a prior claim for honor to the troops of Wellington, measuring these last by the battle of Toulouse.

Wellington after his first defeat, and the slaughter of a great number of his men in retreating, had to send for his artillery, which notwithstanding all his splendid abilities he had *left behind* on the other side of the river Ers. The absence of this indispensable arm in the battle of Toulouse, cost the lives of 3000 veterans, which, but for the want of foresight, or by criminal neglect, either in Wellington or Beresford, would never have happened. During this pause in the battle the English had to stand and be knocked down like *nine-pins*, by Soult's artillery, which we may be sure was not idle or unproduc-

tive of effect. The steadiness displayed by the troops exposed to
this dreadful cannonade without the power of returning a shot, excited the admiration of the French : and so far the French historians
are honest, for while they deny Wellington a victory at Toulouse,
they acknowledge the steadiness displayed by his troops after rallying
from the first disaster, to have been admirable.

Evans's troops had also to stand exposed to the hail of musketry
from the loop-holes as well as the fire of artillery, which they did for
some time waiting for the assistance of the 4th and 8th regiments,
which corps landing from the steamers, were marched unhesitatingly
into the heat of the action.

Wellington, at length brought up his artillery about three in the
afternoon; and then by the united attacks of British, Spanish, and
Portugueze on the French, the latter *evacuated* the redoubts; the
redoubts were not carried by storm, for only *one* gun out of *twelve*
which were in the redoubts, was taken, and no live prisoners.

Evans, waited till the artillery of the Phœnix breached the wall of
one of the fortified houses, and then his troops rushed to the assault
---stormed the redoubt---captured the guns---killed the General who
fought gallantly to the last, and carried away in triumph the *red flag*
which the enemy had hoisted as a proof of their determination to
conquer or die.

Wellington occupied only a portion of the field of battle, which
was all the advantage he gained ; for Soult retreated into the town,
holding the tete du pont de Jumeaux which had defied on the other side
of the town, all the efforts of the terrific Picton ; and he was in possession also of the fortified post of the Patte d'oye beyond which Lord
Hill could not advance, and though there was no obstacle between
the field of battle in rear of the redoubt and the town of Toulouse
lying at the base of the heights of Guillemeri, except a canal about
as wide as that in the Green Park, yet for reasons obvious to all,
Wellington did not push across and achieve a victory which, could
he have done, would have surpassed in utility, even that of
Vittoria.

Although the Spaniards and Biscayans deserted Evans, as those
of Iriere did Wellington, yet he made his victory complete, for he
drove the Carlists out of sight. Here again he claims an advantage
over the Peninsular troops, at the battle of Toulouse.

Wellington's loss was about 5000, and the loss of the French about 3,500.

Evans lost about 1000 and the Carlists 1,200.

General Harispe who lost his leg at Toulouse, complimented Evans on the glory his troops had acquired in overcoming the obstacles of redoubts and fortifications, which he knew both by report and his own recollection, to be almost impregnable.

General Harispe denies that, summing up the defeat and success of both parties, the battle of Toulouse fought as it was on a Christian holiday, (Good Friday), when no battle was expected—was gained by the English. For if Beresford gained an advantage on the heights of Guillemeri, the reverse met by Hill, who attempted to turn his demonstration into a positive attack, and also the utter failure of the fighting division under Picton, on the bridge Des Jumeaux; and the convent of Minimes on its front, might be advantageously opposed to the success of Beresford.

Wellington cannot conscientiously assume to himself any glory by this battle, because he suffered Soult to escape harmless, immediately afterwards; and though he entered the town on the following day, yet had Soult determined to make a stand, his entry would have been questionable; and considering the resources of Soult, and the circumstance of only one side of the town, being practicable for the admission of Wellington's Artillery—for the other three sides are surrounded by the Garonne, and the canal—Wellington shewed more prudence than most Generals, in forbearing the chances of a fight, which must have been for a time disastrous to both armies, though ultimately he might have succeeded.

The small advantages gained, arose wholly from the obstinacy of the soldiers, and not from any scientific movement or stratagem, either on the part of Wellington or Beresford. What little there was of *ruse* or plan in the 1st division of Beresford, winding its way unperceived round the right of the heights, by the *Colombier* or Pigeon-house, and attempting to carry secretly about eight o'clock the Pont Des'Demaiselles, was instantly perceived and defeated on its approach. And though the accounts of the battle, published by the newspapers of Toulouse, two days after its occurrence—were highly flattering to Wellington and his army; and though the United Service Journal, and similar publications have vauntingly copied these—this fact should be remembered, that the English were

then in the town of Toulouse, where it was not very prudent for
newspapers to publish anything else, than a report flattering to the
English; for even to be generous to our countrymen, and suppose
the press of Toulouse to be free—so far as the English were concerned—the Duke of Angouleme had come in after the troops of
Wellington, and neither he nor his attendants were likely to be very
lenient to a newspaper that would have offended them, by a compliment to the soldiers of Soult, or Napoleon his master. Also this
circumstance, so much dwelt on by the Wellingtonian periodicals in
this country, namely, that the inhabitants welcomed the entrance
of the British into the town, is easily accounted for, by stating
another circumstance common to all wars, and that is, the readiness
of the people to purchase favour from an enemy by kind words
and services. Were this a criterion to judge of the favours of a
people, not favourable to an army; then might we of Evans's
Legion proclaim the high esteem we were held in, by the inhabitants
of Carlist towns through which we passed. The people brought us
pails of water and cider, offering us these and other favours, at the
very time they knew us to be marching against their fathers and
husbands. The "Scottish soldier" says also that, he was one day
attracted by the *vivas* (cheers) of a blind woman, who supposing his
regiment to be French, cheered for the French; but on being told
by her daughter that the regiment was English, cheered for the English; and the soldier adds that that circumstance might have given
them some amusement, only it had become too common wherever
they went. I say, therefore, the United Service Journal must not
attempt to "come the old soldier," with any such palaver as that
of the cheers from the populace of Toulouse, being any criterion of
the real estimation in which the entry of the English into their town
was held: far less must they vaunt of what the newspapers published.
It is neither the genius of the United Service Journal—nor the
parties whose fame it advocates, and who were then masters of Toulouse, to be quiescent to an offending press; and the *editors* of
Toulouse like many nearer home, knew their own interest.

Then if some of the divisions of Wellington succeeded after a
severe defeat at Toulouse, and if some of them were uniformly unsuccessful—we must follow a little farther our comparisons between
that battle and Evans's at San Sebastian.

The three divisions, or brigades of Evans's army, succeeded equally on all points, although no combination of manœuvres or plans was executed.

Beresford led his men on frequently, but he could not by his example or exciting address, make them follow him to the redoubts.

Evans ran forward when his troops were hesitating, and placing himself on the wall of an intrenchment, exposed to a literal shower of bullets, with hat in hand, and by the exciting address of "Englishmen! there are people of all nations surveying our actions to day—do not make me or our country ashamed of you" took them headlong on the foe, and by his address and courage contributed most heroically to the victory. Here Evans places either Wellington or Beresford at an immeasurable distance beneath him, to estimate them by the battle of Toulouse.

In short, we admire the exertions and tact of Soult and his small force much more—than even nationality of feeling will allow us to admire Wellington's; and we think the Marshal's fame for consummate skill will survive that of his antagonist with military men, even in this country : for since Soult's visit and the opening of this discussion, which the indiscreet friends of Wellington have provoked, conjointly with the exposure, by military historians, of many barefaced mis-statements recorded during the Peninsular war, we are not disposed to consider the Duke's slovenly Dispatches as remarkable, either for purity of grammar, fidelity of report, or evincing much accuracy of operation. While Evans, from policy and necessity of circumstances, gave an undue portion of his praise to the Spaniards and British Royal Marines, he still diminished rather than surcharged any report of the Legion's successes. And his Dispatches, as much surpass those of the Duke in the three aforementioned requisites—purity of grammar—fidelity of report and accuracy of operation as he does any of the Duke's advocates, in personal prowess—urbanity of manner—or steadiness to an adopted principle. To the judgment of those military men qualified to decide on the justice of the foregoing comparisons ;—to those who have moral courage enough, or ability and courage, to form and maintain opinions of their own, I leave the issue of this contest. Having suffered the ungenerous attacks of our countrymen, we of the Legion are bound in self defence to retaliate, and if we cannot honestly exalt ourselves as soldiers to the height of our veteran contemporaries, we can make our want of success less, and consequently raise our character higher, by taking away some of the unjustly conferred and dishonestly appropriated, glory of the army of Wellington. That more has not been done by me to that effect is not the consequence of any existing difficulty ; but simply that I must now pursue the narrative of those events not yet detailed ; the events which succeeded the severe defeat suffered by the Legion on the 16th of March, 1837.

As I mentioned the names of Espartero and Saarsfield, when accounting for the causes of our defeat on the 16th, it is necessary to state here, that I have subsequently obtained some valuable information relative to these two Generals, which throws some light on their character, and the causes of Evans's defeat, at a time that he depended on their co-operation. My authority is a gentleman who travelling in France and Spain, but not serving in either of the rival armies in the latter country, had the best opportunities to gather information ; and as he has not published any book, nor been the correspondent of any newspaper, nor intending yet to publish, I gladly avail myself of his information relative to the character of Saarsfield ; he having an opportunity to learn more of that General than any one who has yet written of recent Spanish affairs.

This gentleman absolves Espartero from any personal blame in not coming up according to appointment from the neighbourhood of Bilbao. And he absolves him because of the want of provisions—the sickness and death among his troops, they being badly clothed, while during three days that he was on the advance, the rain and snow fell incessantly ; and beyond these hindrances which were dreadful enough, there were the numerous rivers fordable in moderate weather, but at that time flowing in unfordable floods. It would therefore seem, that though the Legion suffered the severity of the weather during the continuous fight that commenced with us successfully on the 10th, and ended disastrously on the 16th, we had still the advantage of provisions, ammunition, hospitals and medical assistance, which Espartero was at that time woefully in want of. And to this cause rather than to lukewarmness was his non-arrival near Hernani attributable. The following sketch of Saarsfield is in my informant's own words, he says —

" Of Saarsfield, whose subsequent death in Saragozza, from the hands of his infuriated countrymen brought public execution on many a brave soldier, and also on the chivalrous Don Iriarte, called the Escudo de Navarre—(the shield of Navarre,) you may deem some particulars of importance, particularly as he was the main cause of the Legion wanting Spanish co-operation at the time of its defeat before Hernani. This officer, unquestionably the best qualified to command in Spain, was the grandson of an Irish officer, who had adopted Catalonia for his residence, and Spain for his country. He was made a General by Ferdinand VII., on the latter returning from captivity, in 1814 ; three names were presented to the King in the palace Ildifonso with reasons for advancing them to the rank of General. The first was qualified because he deserved to be a General ; the second, that his nobility entitled him to be a General, and as Saarsfield possessed neither qualifications, the minister said he ought to be made a General, porque ha nacido serlo (he was born to be one.) Saarsfield was always a firm adherent to the *servile** party ; and when Riego proclaimed the " Constitution" in Cadiz, he was sent to re-establish the Inquisition and despotism, which unfortunately to Ferdinand's beloved subjects and the Spanish nation, he successfully accomplished. Since that period his notorious admiration of absolute government made him a great favourite with the Queen, and consequently as decidedly opposed to the people. When Don Carlos arrived in Biscay, in 1835, Saarsfield was earnestly entreated to join his standard ; but the fear of being too precipitate in his plans, and the danger of hazarding his fortune and life on the ultimate success of the Pretender, caused him to pause ere, he embarked in so ticklish an adventure. His principles were those of the Pretender ; but his conscience told him these were not principles of humanity, while experience added that no success can follow a principle not founded in justice.† His position was one of difficulties. Should he oppose the Pretender he would be exiled and outlawed if success crowned

---

* The term *servile* is used with the greatest complacency in Spain : it means a kind of mixture of " place hunter," adherent of the strongest party" together with what is called " conservatism" in England ; so that excepting some few qualities in the Spanish servile adherent, which are not applicable to English conservatives—the term servile is nearly the same in England and Spain, only in this country we do not boast of the term as the Spaniards do.

† The author of this work begs to be understood, as not adopting every opinion that may be incidentally introduced, by those whom he at times quotes as authorities on a particular subject. In this case, he differs entirely from the gen-

his exertions : and if he drew a sword in his defence his estates would be immediately confiscated, and all his property entirely ruined, like that of many others of those nobles, who now repent when too late, their rash alliance with Don Carlos. Saarsfield, therefore adopted a secure kind of policy; he held with the King and hunted with the Queen : adopted the true Whig principle of courting popular opinion and voting with the Tories. His friends were chiefly to be found in the Carlist's ranks, and during the time that he commanded the army opposed to Zumalacarregui in Navarre, so far from ever obtaining any advantage over the Carlist General, he made all the early success of that chief, by giving out a week previous to a movement, the object for which he moved, so that his opponent could be ready for him, and ready to give him a gentle beating, which was always done, and returned in the shape of a feeble attack, and new information relative to the Christino army. He thus enabled the Carlist chief to gain all his celebrity of name, for skill, valour, and assiduity, while one vigorously executed movement might have at various times annihilated the Carlist bands. This was not done ; the Carlists gained strength, and Saarsfield became weaker wholly through his duplicity and treachery."

"The Carlists all knew the opinions of Saarsfield, but some knew him better than others, one of whom, was Colonel Marti, the Aid-de-camp of General Maroto, the present commander-in-chief of the Carlist army. Saarsfield was of a naturally silent reserved disposition,

tleman he is quoting, on an incidental point—and on the same point from many other good-natured people, who are in the habit of paying compliments to the supremacy of justice; he thinks that the experience of Saarsfield who had made his fortune by an adherence to absolute despotism and the Inquisition, must have told him that success had followed principles, *not* founded in justice. Indeed the history of mankind proves the contrary, of what some people are often so generous in ascribing to justice. It is not the justice of a good principle that makes it triumph, when it is triumphant, it is the weakness of the bad principles that oppose it ; and when the *good* is not successful, the cause of its failure is the strength of the *vicious* opponent. If the bad qualities of a man's mind overpower the good, there is a law in nature that will punish him—and a majority of mankind suffer under the law. If society is founded on bad principles, instead of good—the same law of nature punishes society—and society *is* punished. If nations are governed on bad principles, instead of good—the same law punishes nations—and nations *are* punished : this law, is the law of God, just and immutable ; but not that freakish caprice that divers well meaning, but unthinking followers of many religious sects, would ascribe to the Divine Being; so when General Saarsfield made his calculations, a good principle had no influence on his decision—he calculated whether Carlos or the Queen was likely to be strongest, and by whom he would suffer most in case of failure. Had a good principle ruled him, he would have sided with neither.

and like all Spaniards, extremely distrustful; the inevitable consequence of the Inquisition and absolute government. When the
Queen was compelled to the constitution of 1812, for which circumstance Louis Phillipe withdrew from the Quadruple alliance, the
successor of Isturitz still kept Saarsfield in command, more through
a fearful courtesy than confidence in his principles. And when the
latter left Pampeluna, to operate with the division against the right of
the enemy, he continued to bivouac his division on the bleak summit of the two Hermanas (sisters) mountains covered deeply
with snow, and where in two or three days he lost two thousand
men who were either frozen, or compelled by fatigue to enter the
hospital. And when he again advanced, the Carlists had made a
back movement and had so completely got into his rear, that only
the unexpected arrival of General Cairad and the German or foreign
Legion, formerly belonging to the French service, saved his division
from utter destruction. His antecedent, conjointly with these, palpable
blunders, from a General of the abilities of Saarsfield, leave no doubt
of his treachery, as it was the body of the Carlist army left unoccu-
pied by his retreat that came and re-inforced the army opposing Evans
at Hernani."

Such is a sketch of Saarsfield, by a gentleman who had better information on these subjects than almost any person in Spain. He
continues his account of this General up to the time that the populace
and his own soldiers revenged themselves on him by putting him to
a dreadful death; but I have quoted enough to prove why General
Evans was defeated at Hernani.

From that time, the 16th of March, to the beginning of May,
nothing remarkable occurred; but for some days during the latter
end of April and every day during the early part of May, thousands
of men were poured into San Sebastian from the steamers and other
vessels that carried Espartero's army from Bilbao to make a joint
movement with Evans. The Spanish soldiers looked miserable, only
some allowance had to be made for their being mostly landed in wet
weather, and standing for hours, sometimes days, even lying whole
nights about the streets, without quarters. They were under strict
discipline; each musket was burnished with the lock polished to a
brightness that contrasted strangely with the filthy appearance of
their uniform. This consisted of the long light blue coat, made in

surtout fashion, into the breast of which they stuffed oakum and other soft stuffing, until their desire to shew a manly chest became most unnatural. Their shoes were generally in bad condition, many of them being made of canvas and only kept on their feet by thongs warped round the ancle. These kind of shoes are common in Spain and in dry weather answer the mountaineers very well, but for soldiers in wet weather they are neither durable nor comfortable. Many of the Spanish soldiers have watches, and most of them some gold or silver trinket which they carry about with them, and which no hunger will induce them to part with. Most of them possessed small trifles of money, which was likewise preserved never to be spent until they might reach their homes, from which the laws of conscription, not their own will, had forced them. They were a different kind of men, and a very different kind of soldiers from the Biscayans who were with us, and of whom the most of the Carlist army are formed. The Biscavan is mirthful, active and zealous in whatever cause he takes up ; the southern Spaniard seems either spiritless or sullen ; whichever he may be, the one or the other or both, he makes a bad soldier. If he has a quality that a good soldier should have, it is his sobriety and hatred of intemperance !

As the first movements made after the arrival of Espartero's army have been very minutely detailed by Mr. Farr, and as I was at that time in Hospital suffering from the injuries, though not severely, sustained in the fighting days of March, I shall quote some particulars of the movements to obtain quarters, as written by that gentleman. He says—

"On Thursday, the 4th of May, a few days after my return to St. Sebastian from Bilbao, so many fresh troops had arrived that it was impossible to lodge them, without occupying some new ground : orders were given to that 'active, excellent, and highly talented officer,* Major Humphreys, who commanded the engineer department of the Legion, to give the necessary directions, and to superintend the construction of a pontoon bridge to be thrown over the Urimea, opposite the small village of Loyola, and which was to be finished at two o'clock p. m., the hour of high water. Some blue jackets from Lord John Hay's squadron lent their assistance, as usual. The pontoons began to move up the river at about twelve o'clock, having about a mile to be towed. The hills above were bristling with thousands

---

* Many people had a different opinion of Major Humphreys' talents.

and thousands of Christino bayonets. A small party of Carlists about thirty in number, who were there, instead of running away, when they saw so large and superior a force, immediately covered themselves by a mud bank on the other side of the river, and even drove away our men, who were towing up the pontoons, in the face of thousands of their enemies, and an immense quantity of artillery. The business of this day must be dwelt on, to shew that the Carlists, when *in the mountains*, however imposing the force is, however sudden the attack, are never seized with a panic, and never give way until they are really beaten; and when they do retreat, it is rather from calculation than fear; the proof of it is, that the Legion, and the Spanish army acting with it, have never taken but two wounded prisoners in *the field*, although most desirous to effect it. *

" The Carlists were able, with thirty men, for a short time to delay the construction of the pontoon bridge, owing to some mistake in the orders that were given to the Legion and Legion artillery that were to form the covering party, and protect the passage of the boats up the river. The pontoons were ordered to be put in motion at twelve o'clock, and the force which was to protect them did not get their orders to be on the ground until one o'clock. I am glad it was so, as it gave me a proof of the great superiority and greater courage of the Carlists. A short time after the men towing the boats had been driven off, Captain Howe made his appearance on the ground appointed to him, with his field battery of the Legion artillery; the second spherical shot that was fired in spite of the protection afforded by the mud bank, killed a Carlist and his faithful dog, and wounded another man. The wounded man they carried off, but, contrary to their usual custom, left the dead body of their companion and did not even stay to strip him, which was the more extraordinary, as they never like to allow any thing belonging to a Carlist to fall into the hands of their enemies: but spherical shot, being the most destructive engines in the world, they very properly got out of their reach as fast as possible. The pontoons now moved up unmolested, in front of the village of Loyola, while Major Humphreys gave his orders to fix them across the river. One man, a single Carlist volunteer, entirely alone, had the courage to come down and place himself behind a mound of earth, at about the distance of from three to four hundred yards, and stood with the most perfect coolness, firing shot

---

* Mr. Farr is not correct on this point.

after shot at those constructing the bridge, and succeeded in wounding a Spanish officer of Marines in the shoulder. When the bridge was nearly finished, he walked away from the thousands opposed to him with the greatest composure and steadiness, not hurrying himself in the least. It was delightful to see so very cool, brave, and gallant a fellow get away unhurt. I was standing at the time in the Queen's battery, commanded by Colonel Shaw, and the embrasure of the extreme right gun was not quite wide enough to allow it to be pointed where he stood, and it was not thought worth while to move a thirty-two pounder to kill one man, or the first or second spherical would most likely have destroyed him. The bridge was completed at a few minutes after two, and some thousands of troops passed over, under the protecting fire of the Legion artillery, the Legion rockets, and Royal Marine Artillery rockets, as well as the fire of the Ametzagana, the Queen's, Rodil's and the Puyo batteries, which had long thirty-two pounders and smaller guns; there were also the field batteries of the Legion, the Royal marine, and the Royal Woolwich Artillery, which threw spherical shells, common shells, and cannon balls, in addition to the rockets; but the distance was too great to use grape shot. The Carlists, though few in number, and with no artillery, taking advantage of every mountain spot that was favorable to them, kept up a running fire, and retreated in the greatest order; a single prisoner, either living or dead, was not taken, except the one dead man already mentioned; though a deserter, who came over a few days after, said their loss in killed and wounded was eighty-five men: the loss on our side was, I think, one killed and two wounded.

" The ground and houses that it was thought necessary to occupy, in order to lodge the newly arrived troops, to make room for Espartero and his regiments of the Guards, which were to make their appearance in a few days, was taken possession of, extending about a mile and a half on the other side of the river. On the following day, Colonel Shaw very kindly mentioned that Captain Howe would cross the river after the soldiers had got their dinner, and would take up a position in front of the enemy's fixed battery; that if I went up with the Legion guns, I should most likely witness a little artillery affair. Being particularly desirous of seeing how the Carlists could point their pieces, I accompanied the Legion field battery, which was

put so quietly in position, that the enemy in the fort knew nothing
of its arrival. At the back of the village of Astigaraga the enemy
had a large working party, who were commencing a new fort, about
one thousand five hundred yards from the guns. Generally before a
spherical case shot is attempted, a round shot or two is fired, the
number of degrees given by the tangent scale, telling pretty nearly
at what length the spherical fuses ought to be cut : but not wishing
to disturb the working party, Captain Howe, trusting to his great
skill and accuracy in measuring a distance and in pointing a gun,
immediately commenced with two sphericals, and most successful he
was ; for they both burst exactly over the centre of the astonished
working party, who scampered off as fast as they could. We had
only two long six pounders to work with, for it was above the range
of the two short twelve pounders ; and the Carlist fort, armed with
two long twelve pounders and two long eighteen pounders, now
opened its fire on the Legion artillery. The extreme precision with
which the Carlists pointed their guns after they had once ascertained
the ranges, was astonishing ; though it was afterwards discovered,
that it was not *Spanish* firing, for they had eight French artillery
men to point them. Two cannon shot buried themselves in the
ground at a very few feet from the muzzle of the guns ; but as they
did not come horizontally, but were fired from a height, the field
battery being placed on soft ground, they did no mischief. Had the
Carlists possessed common or spherical shells, fired with equal precision, they must have killed every one about the battery, instead of
hurting no one. The Carlists were about nine minutes in loading,
pointing, and firing each gun ; when with the long six pounders,
Captain Howe could average, in case of necessity, a fraction more
than two shots in a minute, which makes full eighteen shots to their
one : or, he could fire more than one hundred pounds weight of
exploding spherical case shot from a six pounder, while they fired one
of their comparatively harmless non-exploding eighteen pound round
cannon shot, only having a long six pound field piece against long
eighteen pounders in a fixed battery ; such is the quickness with
which light field artillery is fired. As soon as the range was ascertained, seven of the six pound sphericals burst one after another in
succession over the Carlist redoubt, the Christino Spanish troops
cheering most lustily at every explosion amongst their enemies. On

our side not a man was hurt, though some deserters, who came in afterwards, reported, true or false, that the enemy had lost fifty-seven in killed and wounded from the sphericals during the evening.

"This comparatively harmless affair is dwelt on, as it led to one of the most important events of the war—an order to surprise the Legion battery the next morning : and the failure of that attack, and the tremendous destruction caused by the artillery, was the *real* cause of the evacuation of the lines of Hernani by the Carlists, and the movement on Valencia and Madrid : for the Infant Don Sebastian—finding that eighteen-pound cannon balls, fired from elevated positions, could not contend even against six pounders with sphericals, on account of the great rapidity with which they are fired, and their tremendous execution—gave an order that an attempt should be made to surprise and capture, at all risks, the Legion artillery the next morning. Captain Howe having gone himself with one gun to the extreme left of the advanced house, which formed the key and terminus of the new position, the Carlists made a most gallant and determined rush on the gun. Here a company of the second light Spanish, which had been placed on the flank of the gun, to protect it in case of attack, immediately on seeing the enemy, and the vigour of their attack, ran away without firing a shot, while other companies of the same regiment behaved very well, and repulsed the enemy from the house. It is impossible to make any calculation about what Spanish troops will do. The same regiment will run away without firing a shot one day, and, placed in about the same position another, will fight with the most determined bravery : for that reason, nothing are so difficult to command as Spanish troops."*

* It appears that even the Carlists, who are volunteers, are not always to be depended on. Captain Henningsen, who ought to be a good authority, says : " How necessary this prudence proved to have been, those who have seen the unsteadiness of volunteers, who fight only for their opinions, can appreciate. Even the inhabitants of La Vendee were, we read, also subject to this fickleness ; although their astonishing resistance was the admiration of the world, and to this day fills a page which is unequalled in the history of devoted heroism. The men who one day took the cannon of the Republicans with loaded sticks, the next, were seized with an unaccountable panic, and fled before the slightest danger without firing a shot.

" The impetuosity of their chief was evidently a principal cause of their perdition. If they had not made their rash attempt on Nantes, or crossed the Seine, till they had become completely organized and disciplined, they might have met with signal victories, and have chosen their moment to march into Paris."

No. 33.

" The Carlists now, in obedience to the orders left by their Prince, and with a devotion worthy of a better cause, attacked in front, with the greatest bravery, the other three guns of the Legion artillery.   Captain Howe having got away in safety with the gun from the left, the four guns opened a most well-directed and extraordinary quickly served fire of sphericals; but so determined was the courage of the Carlists, that one house was taken and retaken three times although under the protecting fire of the artillery; and they got within three hundred yards of the guns, near enough for the short twelve-pounders to fire common grape-shot among them with immense execution.   The Carlists found themselves also under the fire of some very large pieces of Royal Woolwich Artillery, which were stationed close to the Puyo Fort, and which took them in flank, several shells being seen to burst in the midst of them, fired from very large howitzers.

" I will mention here, that when General Evans entered Oyarzun, on his way to attack Irun, he was told that two Navarrese battalions, the fairest way of counting a battalion is at the average of about seven hundred men—had orders to throw themselves into Irun and Fuenterabia, and defend them; but they had refused, declaring they would not shut themselves up in towns to be blown to pieces by English shells and rockets.   A field officer of the Legion, who spoke Spanish perfectly, asked General Soroa, the Governor of Irun, why he refused to surrender the first evening, (a summons having been sent in,) as he had so small a garrison, and was apparently cut off from all relief? He replied, he had received a dispatch, announcing to him that two battalions were on their march to reinforce his garrison; and his orders were, at all risks, to defend the place; and that when he first saw the head of the Christino column advancing, he had no idea that they were enemies, but conceived they were the two battalions promised to him.   Although he soon found out his mistake, he was astonished at their not having made their appearance; and he managed, during the darkness of the night to communicate with them in the mountains, and ordered them to cut their way through, in some direction, and enter into the town, according to their instructions; as it was of the greatest importance to hold out as long as possible, to give Don Sebastian time to continue his march without being pursued.   The officers commanding the two battalions sent him word that they would fight for Don Carlos in the mountains, where they could be of service to his cause, but they would not shut themselves up in a town to be blown to pieces by English artillery; such tremendous panic and dismay had the spherical shells struck into the Carlists since the affair of the 5th and 6th of May."

" So great is the devotion to Don Carlos amongst his mountain adherents, that I confess, it is the first time I have heard of any order, or even wish, of his not being obeyed with the greatest alacrity and enthusiasm : this determination not to face the spherical shells, was the real and only cause of the march of Don Sebastian taking place so suddenly, and the almost instantaneous evacuation of the Hernani lines without defending them. It is true that the expedition on Valencia and Madrid was planned long before, and agreed upon in concert with Austria, Russia, Prussia, and Sardinia, the three former powers not only furnishing the funds necessary to liquidate some old standing debts with the Jew contractors and furnishers at Bayonne, but advancing money to pay the troops, and buy new clothing, and equip the army with various necessaries : but at last their departure was so sudden and unexpected by all parties, that even the leading inhabitants and municipality of Hernani knew nothing about it, as I shall hereafter prove. In the affair of the 6th of May, above mentioned, the Christino loss was, not counting scratches, eighty-one men, sufficiently wounded to be carried into hospital, and twenty killed. The Carlists were said to have shewn in front as many as seven thousand men, and their loss was known to be at least four hundred in killed and wounded in only two hours hard fighting. A deserter coming in shortly afterwards, gave information that their loss was even more than four hundred men, which they themselves eventually confirmed and avowed, in the intelligence that came round by Bayonne ; and some deserters likewise stated that the troops had declared they never would face the English artillery again ; that they would retire and fight where the spherical shells could not follow them : this information not then believed, ultimately proved true, from the facts I have just related."

" It has always appeared to me that there has been a determination, on the part of certain organs of the Carlist-Tory press, never to publish a true statement of what really takes place in Spain, even where truth would have suited their purpose better than falsehood, with the intention that the public might be sure of having at least *two* different statements, and that the readers, being at a distance should not be able to judge which was true and which was false, and by that means keep the British nation in entire darkness, concerning the real result of any event or occurrence in Spain, political or military. Although the affair of the 6th of May was finished by nine in the morning, yet the correspondent of the *Morning Post* thus concludes a letter giving an account of the loss sustained, dated St. Sebastian, May 6th, wherein he says, "the loss of the Carlists is supposed to be about the same as the Christinos," when the contrary was publicly known to every one in San Sebastian, even on the day; and the letter dated the 6th not being sent off, he writes another on the 7th, giving various details, and he in nowise corrects or alters his assertion of the former day, though I may safely say, no one could be blind enough or foolish enough really to suppose, under the circumstances I have related, 'that the loss could be about equal.'"

In writing this work I am in no manner anxious to make myself conspicuous as an author; therefore, though I could appropriate much of the contributed information, by rewriting it as my own, I choose rather to give it to the world in the words of those, to whom I am indebted for it. The following is from an officer of high reputation, who has published nothing, nor manifested any intention of publishing; his account of those events just detailed by the Rev. author contain further details. He says—

"It was on the morning of the 6th of May, 1837, that the Carlists, as if awaking from a sleep which they seemed to have been in, while Evans had pushed forward during the previous day to obtain quarters for the increasing troops, attacked us on the heights above the village of Layolo with about 3000 of their picked troops; which troops, it appears, had been made drunk for this particular occasion.* So well

---

* It is true that some of the prisoners taken by us were intoxicated; but there can be no certainty of the whole being drunk: I should like, therefore, to remind the gallant Colonel from whom the above is quoted, that, he knowing well that no soldiers on earth, are braver than the Carlists, and that commonly, no people have a greater aversion to drunkenness than the Spaniards—though to be sure, the Biscayans are not *real Teetotallers*—so nothing is more unlikely than the truth of that assertion, that attributed their daring bravery at that time to intoxication. It is probable that they had a ration of spirits served out before daybreak, which all soldiers should have, when like the Carlists at that time, they stand shivering during a part of the night under arms—sleepless and hungry, waiting for the order of attack. Had we of the Legion received more regularly

had the enemy managed their advance, that our advanced picquets were attacked before they were aware of an enemy being within their vicinity ; for a short time our Spaniards gave way and the Carlists had every thing to their own mind, until Evans arrived on the spot and made the Spaniards advance, and take every inch of ground from the enemy. His prompt and cool orders put every soul in their proper places for further defence should it be requisite. The Carlists were so furious in advancing to the first attack, that a gun of ours was nearly falling into their hands ; but old Howe was there, ever ready and cool, and had time to retire it to the temporary battery in the rear, from where he opened such a fire as soon made the rebels retire in all directions ; the fire from Howe's guns was tremendous. As day set in it was a beautiful sight to see every rising ground, covered with our cannon and troops, the latter anxiously waiting the

---

a small allowance on such occasions we would have been more energetic than we were, or could be, when sleepless and accoutred for a whole night—or perhaps for days and nights together—we followed our leaders, chattering our teeth—unable with benumbed fingers to unbutton the pouches—bite a cartridge—shake the priming—and draw the ramrod ; unable with nerveless toes to pick our steps in the dark or on the mountain sides without stumbling ; seeing that an officer *had* some brandy, by the flask slung over his shoulder, and knowing that we had none, though perhaps two regular rations might be due to us ; I repeat, therefore, that nothing should be more studiously observed than to give, on all such occasions, an allowance of spirits or wine within moderation to all soldiers—making commissioned as well as non-commissioned officers responsible that none received more than the strict allowance. A refreshment in the shape of food with warm tea or coffee would be very desirable, and could it be obtained, would suit the circumstances of the men better than spirits ; but it is needless to write one word to military readers on the impossibility of procuring that exhilirating beverage before an enemy. You may come two or three miles—stealthily and slowly so as to gain your position unperceived ; you do this in the darkness of night ; you wait for hours, all regiments not being got to their positions at once, and while you wait, you starve, you have been accoutred all the night, perhaps longer, and you are in the most unfit condition possible to move on to fight—from the weariness of limb, and the coldness which benumbs every part of your system—even intellectual ; it being impossible then, to make fires to have coffee, or any similarly prepared refreshment, and from all the regimental mules being required to carry ammunition, &c. thus making even wine too bulky to be carried for the use of so many men ; it will appear that spirits become absolutely necessary. Some may say that a drunken courage is no courage ; but the use of a small quantity of spirits does not imply drunkenness ; it is not to stimulate the system beyond its natural temperament that spirits should be given on such an occasion, but to stimulate the system to its natural temperament; anything beyond that, is too much. Military men know very well the great responsibility that would devolve on those serving out such allowance, and that is why military men see the necessity for severe laws, which civilians never see ; but as all warfare is an outrage on that soft sympathy called humanity, and as glory cannot be obtained but at humanity's expense, and as people *will*, believe, that it is glorious to be great in slaughter ; so we must submit to severe restrictions—restrictions, which in a campaign, must amount to death or obedience :—if not, there must be no campaign.

sound of the " advance," but the Carlists contented themselves with
trying our left. Their loss must have been very severe; thirteen
deserters come over, and all of them agreed in stating that our
cannon had wrought dreadful havoc among their companions.

" Lieut. Hamilton of the Artillery, was actually made a prisoner by
a Carlist officer, and one of his men bayoneted through the neck,
before they were aware of their trying situation. A Mr. Dickson,
who had been made a prisoner a short while before on suspicion of
being a spy, came up at the time, and shot the Carlist officer dead,
by which means the brave little Hamilton got off.*

" I met the Artillery man, who had been wounded in the back part
of the neck, a few minutes afterwards, and was much amused with
the poor fellow as he put his fingers into the wound—which passed
clean through, and said to me, " look here what they have done to
me, what a murdering set of thieves they are ! by my soul, I would
kill the whole bunch of them !" Those who were with him, had a
little trouble to keep him from setting to, to box some two or three
prisoners who were standing at the time.†

It came out afterwards, that the Carlists had crept up during the
night of the 5th, round a house in which were too companies of the
2nd Spanish Light Infantry, who were only aware of the circumstance on turning out in the morning before day-break—the custom
of war,—for the purpose of being ready for anticipated attacks—the

---

* The gentleman who is here spoken of, as " A Mr. Dickson," will be farther
explained hereafter. He was the most extraordinary of any Englishman that
was in Spain. He refused to serve under Evans, or under any one ; but he was
often in the front of a fight ; and that peculiarity of behaviour led to his being
suspected as a spy. He is an officer of the British army, and the son of Admiral
Dickson, whose professional fame is associated with the history of Trinidad :—
The extraordinary adventure of Mr. Dickson, by which he fell into the hands of
the Carlists—his escape from execution under the Durango Decree—an escape as
awfully interesting as anything devised by the imaginations of our novelists—will
be found in a future chapter.

† This man might probably be a very brave soldier, but it was none of that
bravado that evinced bravery ; though there are such incidents as this that are commonly recorded, to tell of the bravery of British soldiers. This officer whom I
quote, was himself as brave as ever drew sword—and besides he was skilful—he
was intelligent—none knew the good and bad qualities of soldiers better than
he ; but in writing, he falls into the error that all—the most intelligent—military
men fall into ; that error which causes us as a nation to have a false opinion of
ourselves : the angry expressions the man used—the contempt of pain—and the
desire for more strife—might be called heroism ; but the attempt to box with the
captured prisoner, or in other words his manifestations of triumph over the
defeated foe, was ungenerous ; he was as like a British soldier, as his narrator is
like all British officers—ready to turn all incidents, by their manner of relating
them, into glory even though they may have been dishonorable.

Carlists let them parade quietly, and then popped their muskets over the wall, and poured in their volley with most dire effect, as became apparent, by the two companies having lost that morning four officers killed, and eighty non-commissioned officers and men killed and wounded. These two companies behaved nobly, for many cannon balls from the enemy's guns struck the house, and though surrounded, they still held the position. The Carlists must also have suffered severely, as I saw upwards of twenty buried within the compass of a few square yards, just as they had fallen. Around this house was a plantation of young fruit-trees, every one of which were literally cut to pieces with musket-balls, being a farther proof, how nobly the point was defended, and how vigorously attacked.

"Our old friends the Chapelgorris as usual were daringly brave.* This morning the moment they were brought up to the scene of action, nothing could keep them back from the enemy: they, on re-taking one of our picquet-houses, found it in the possession of a Carlist officer, and seven of his men, and a few moments more, was the term of their existence. Before killing the officer, they commenced to strip him; and he was begging hard for his life, when one of the Chapelgorris brought his musket to the charge saying "no podo senor," (impossible sir)—and put an end to the poor wretch's career, just as coolly as if he had been putting his bayonet into the side of a hay-stack. This the unfortunate officer had brought on himself as he was particularly noticed during the morning, murdering with his own sword, all those wounded who had fallen into the hands of his party, when the Christinos were driven back at the first onset. The loss of the Legion was trifling that morning, as they were not brought closely into action; I only heard of some twelve or fourteen being wounded, which were mostly of the 6th regiment, as they marched up the heights above Layolo to reinforce the covering party at old Howe's guns.

"I was particularly struck that morning by the dastardly conduct

---

* It is proper to explain here, that Mr. Dickson, the gentleman already spoken of, seeing the Chapelgorris hesitate, seeing the imminent danger and being perfect in the Spanish language, called out to the Chapelgorris to follow him: and that it was he who led on these terrible fellows on that occasion. Whether Mr. Dickson sought to stop the slaughter of the prisoners I am not informed, but I know the Chapelgorris well enough to be warranted in saying, that had he interposed he would have done so uselessly;—they, like the Carlists, *take no prisoners* "War to the knife" is their motto.

of two Spanish officers, who, during the time the men were engaged, were continually turning to the rear calling out, "adonda los cartou-ches" (where is the ammunition.) To one that was doing the thing too often (as I thought) I rode along, and with a few Spanish and English oaths, with the assistance of a nice little *bleeding* instrument made him proceed to the front, I dare say much against his will—telling him he would get ammunition there.[*] I do not mean to infer from this that all Spanish officers are cowards, far from it, for I have known many brave ones, but I will say, without fear of contradiction, that many of the Queen's officers are not worth a penny a dozen."

The foregoing extracts bring the movements of the Legion up to the 9th of May from the time they commenced on the 4th. I had only witnessed the distant conflict from the roof of the hospital where I was a patient, and though I neither had, nor profess to have any particular love for bullets—I, knowing that the grand advance in junction with Espartero was about to be made—applied to be discharged from hospital, so that I might join my company. This unimportant circumstance is mentioned for two reasons,—the first is, that having spoken of my military enthusiasm, in rather a negative tone, people may believe as I know some do—that because I did not feel on all occasions, or at least do not tell the world that I felt an animated enthusiasm for the deadly strife, they conclude that, not to be animated with a love of the battle, leaves only the alternative of taking advantage of every opportunity to keep out of it ! that, not being a just conclusion, I mention this unimportant incident. My second reason for mentioning this, is a twin brother of the first reason—or the same reason turned upside down—it is, that my asking to be discharged from hospital, so that I could share in the coming battle, was no proof of my love of the strife ; nor are the same desires expressed by others, any proof of their devotion to a cause or a campaign. In my humble case I had no particular object in view, I had no hope of promotion depending on being in the fight, nor had I any rank, or honor to lose, if I stayed away. My strongest motive was perhaps to preserve the esteem of my comrades ; for in the respect of giving or with-holding good-will, we were tyrants to each other ;

---

[*] To explain why this officer could use such authority—I must state that he was an Aide-de-camp, and one that not only did his duty—but was never back-ward, whether authorized or not, to compel other persons to do theirs.

indeed no tyranny that a soldier suffers from his superiors is greater in illiberality than that which he suffers from his comrades. Not to be in the fight, is to lose all rights of manliness; you might be on other duty, or you might be sick, but if you were not in the battle you were nobody, you had no right to speak on any subject. This is carried in all regiments far beyond anything that a civilian will believe. In British regiments of the regular service, it is now put down by the superiority of numbers, the superiority being on the side of those who know nothing about war; but at one time a soldier who had enlisted subsequent to Waterloo, dared not open his mouth to an old one, no matter what the subject of conversation might be; he was nobody at all---altogether contemptible in the eyes of the old soldier. Now that the heroes are dying away, others are taking up the same high position, only they estimate themselves by some other standard of superiority. With us in the Legion, the qualification was some important event; you were nothing if you were not on the "long march," or "on the heights of Arlaban among the snow," or in the "5th of May." Now as I had not been in the "5th of May," and as I had been many a time out-voted and put down in a conversation, though that conversation might relate to whether the Glasgow weavers, or the Paisley weavers were the best weavers; whether pease-brose or yit-meal-brose were the best brose, if you talked with Scotchmen; or if the boys of the County Down could stand against the boys of the County Antrim, were you talking with North of Ireland-men; or if Bristol Bob, or Brummagem Bill were the best men in all England, should it be to their friends you were talking; even you might be on more elevated subjects; you might be on tithes and corn-laws, intervention, or non-intervention, it was all one, you knew nothing about any of these matters, if you had not been in "the 5th of May!" This peculiarity belongs to mankind. It developes itself in other shapes in other classes of people; but this was how it developed itself among us. Now though there might be, and there were, other causes operating with me, that was one of those that induced me to keep up my equality with my comrades as a soldier; therefore I made application to get out of hospital.

Having joined them, I was in the movement of the 14th of May, when we proceeded to recover the ground taken on the 15th, and lost on the 16th of March. We were all under arms by midnight, and were turned out two hours before daylight. It was as usual a pouring rain, and as usual we stood, drenched and shivering with our muskets beneath our armpit at the " secure." The vast number of troops that studded every height and hollow, had an imposing effect, as daylight broke and revealed about thirty thousand all under arms. There was not an enemy equal, or half equal to cope with this force; but as the ground did not admit of the whole, not even of a whole battalion moving in a body, we had to make our way among ditches—down slippery hillsides—and up others in detached parties; therefore we were not actually stronger—nor so strong, as those, who protected behind their mountain defences, fired on us as we approached.

While we were standing under arms, we had an opportunity to envy our Marine brethren who were encamped on a sloping hill, and were having a good warm breakfast of tea and its etceteras. They are a fine looking corps on parade, and they certainly looked very well at their breakfast, while we stood protecting them; but in a short while we saw them look very unlike what British soldiers are supposed to be : they could do nothing among the mountains. Indeed nothing is more utterly ridiculous than the reports, that they were a support to the Legion, or at any time a protection; we never moved in their company, but we found in them a hindrance. And though they as one corps could take a comfortable breakfast in such circumstances, it must be borne in mind, that we could not have begun to cook a breakfast, though we had had one to cook, for it was our duty to attend to the enemy; therefore it must not be supposed, that when the Legion was without a breakfast, and the Marines had one, that it is always a part of British campaigning to have hot tea in the mornings to make the bivouac agreeable. Oh no—we had people who took a dislike to the Legion, and in the same proportion became in love with the *regulars,* and there are a great many people at home of the same sort; but these must be told that in the Peninsular war, there were no such pleasant enjoyments " of a morning" as a breakfast; and the Marines only enjoyed their's on the mountain-side, because the Legion was between them and the enemy. Mr. Farr, says " as a body of reserve, the Marines are excellent; when attacked superior to anything ; but no troops however gallant and perfect in discipline, are efficient if they have to march over mountains, or send them to attack an enemy with their

knapsacks on their backs." Mr. Farr's opinion of what they are
when attacked, is only a conjecture, for he never saw them attacked ;
yet I believe his conjecture is just, for there can be nothing to hinder
them from being as good soldiers as other men ; but at the same time
there is nothing in the circumstance of their being *Marines*, or
regulars, to make them better than others ; they never shewed any
superiority at any rate along side the Legion.

Mr. Farr says, that British soldiers are more ready to pay obedience and respect to an officer who has been born a gentleman, than
to one who has been made a gentleman ; I am sorry to be obliged to
express a coincidence of opinion : I remarked the truth of that frequently amongst soldiers ; but it does not belong altogether to soldiers ; it is a national trait in the people of this country, and as even
the thing called an *author* is not exempted from this estimation, it
is no doubtful supposition in me to say, that an *Esq.* or a *late of
Trinity College*, would have made this humble work of mine very
instructive, and much more respectable than it can possibly be from
the pen of one who has laboured with a pick and shovel. Believing,
therefore, that it will be gratifying to the most of those who read
this, to be relieved by a few extracts from a scholar ; I shall quote
one who was a spectator of our movements on the 14th of May, 1837.

" It was on the 9th of May that Espartero arrived from Bilbao at
San Sebastian, and the army was eventually increased to about
thirty-two thousand men : the attack on the Carlist lines, which had
the appearance, in all probability, of being a most bloody affair, was
to have taken place on Monday the 15th, or Tuesday the 16th of
May ; but a trusty and well-paid spy, having early in the morning
of the 13th, brought the information that the Carlists had withdrawn
their artillery, and evidently did not dare to run the risk of the loss
of it, by defending the numerous strong works they had lately thrown
up, where they were known to have put eighteen pieces of cannon
in position, orders were given to lose no time, and the attack took
place on Sunday the 14th of May, being Whit-Sunday. The Carlists, with the most determined coolness and bravery, defended the
heights of the Venta, and the redoubts on the left side of it, with
only musketry and a few hundred men against thirty thousand of
their enemies, and a mass of artillery, and only gave it up when they
saw their right flank had been turned, and their retreat would be

cut off, if they did not evacuate the position. During the attack, several sphericals were observed to burst over the redoubt which flanked the Venta. I was riding along with General Fitzgerald, when he went up with his division to occupy it, and the first thing visible was at least the brains of two men lying on the ground, but the entire extent of the Carlist loss was never known."

" I do not remember whether the Venta was taken at eight or ten o'clock ; but, about two hours after, the gates of the town of Hernani were forced open, and the Carlists driven out ; the village of Urnieta, just a mile and a half in advance of {Hernani, on the right road to Tolosa, was then attacked : it is situated at the bottom of a hill, and entirely commanded by the heights around ; its formation is about six hundred yards long by four hundred yards wide, and the great road going through the centre of it. Here the Carlists, not the least intimidated at seeing the tremendous masses opposed to them, instead of runing away, with musketry only, defended most gallantly the houses and church against spherical shells, rockets, and artillery and only retreated when their flank had been turned, the right half of the town being carried by a very brave and well-executed charge of the bayonet made by the 6th Scotch regiment ; and the movement being pushed on, they found themselves threatened in the rear, when, seeing the danger of being cut off, they at once retreated, running up the mountains as fast as their legs could carry them, not losing a single prisoner."

" It must here be observed that, when the 6th Scotch regiment executed their charge and occupied the right-hand side of the town, a similar charge was ordered to be made by the Spanish on the left side ; but when the quick and lively notes of the bugle repeatedly sounded the charge, nothing could make them move forward against not a hundred and fifty men, although supported by thirty thousand and every implement of war; yet when the Carlists found it necessary to run away, on account of the movement of the Scotch regiment, who were getting in their rear, the Christino Spanish regiment *most bravely* ran after their nimble and gallant adversaries, the instant they turned their backs on them, but not before. In vain now did the dull, heavy notes of the bugle continue sounding the retreat to call them back, as long as they had a flying and non-resisting enemy to contend with : it did put me so much in mind of the pointers and a flock of sheep when field-shooting in England; as long as the dogs look at them, the sheep stand still, or run away; but the moment it suits the inclination of the dogs to move off and retreat, then the sheep, with great boldness, immediately run after them, but should the dogs turn round, the sheep run away once more. Two Spanish aides-de-camp were sent after them before they could be induced to stop running after those, who ran away from them, not from fear, but calculation : if the Christino regiment had only had the courage to execute the charge when ordered, and had but acted on calculation and laid aside their fears, they might have had those they were so bravely pursuing in their possession as prisoners, without running after them to no purpose—for a light armed mountaineer, as long as he is unwounded, is not to be caught in his own mountains except you surround him."

" Fervently desirous of a speedy termination of this war, disgraceful to Christian nations and the age we live in, the events of this day have left a continued painful impression on my mind : here about seven hundred men defend every spot which is capable of defence, inch by inch, with only musketry, against more than thirty thousand men, with cavalry, with rockets, common and spherical shells, round and grape shot, playing on them, against the Legion, the Royal Woolwich, and the Royal Marine Artillery, perfectly fearless of the array brought against them, and not a single prisoner either dead, wounded, or alive is made, except you unburied those who had been deposited in their graves. Even if General Evans had chosen to sacrifice a great many lives by attacking the Venta in front instead of outflanking it, the utmost he could have done would have been to have taken a few wounded prisoners, for the Carlists would have waited until their enemies came within a hundred yards of them, and being mountaineers in their own country, and so lightly armed, it would have been impossible to overtake them and make prisoners in ground where cavalry could not act. It is almost as difficult to get possession of dead Carlists as living ones; for their custom is this, if a redoubt or any spot is to be defended, and where death must ensue, at some short distance in a woody and retired spot they dig a long trench, before, or at the very beginning of the conflict, then with incredible quickness, almost in an instant, even when the enemy are advancing on them, they strip the body of the

dead man to prevent any of his clothes, &c. being employed and rendered serviceable by the enemy, and immediately deposit him in the
ready-made trench, under the idea that the body would be mutilated
if it fell into their enemy's hands, though the Christinos have not
the disgusting habit of mutilating in the field the dead bodies of
their enemies, and cutting off their noses and ears, as the Carlists
have.*

At the back of the redoubt mentioned, Colonel Wylde's aid-de-
camp discovered a grave with several Carlists in it, who had been
buried but a few minutes; and there was likewise a ready-made
trench in the churchyard at Hernani. The Carlists rarely lose their
wounded, as the Legion had only the opportunity of taking two in
the *field* during the whole war : the moment any one is wounded, the
numerous volunteer peasants carry them away on a wooden stretcher
into the mountains, far out of the reach of the foe, even if victorious,
for the Christino troops dare not enter into the recesses of the mountains, even when they occupy the high roads below them. At about
two o'clock Urnieta was taken, and no further advance was made."

Another authority whom I have before alluded to, gives some
details of this movement which the author just quoted, does not
give ; and although it requires more labour to transcribe some of
these kindly but confusedly written communications, I shall give
them in the words of their writers, so that I may not have the whole
story of the campaign to myself—or that I may not be supposed
to have led people's judgment astray, by having it all told my own
way. This gentleman, a Lieut.-Colonel and Aid-de-camp, says—

" On the morning of the 14th, we were formed on our several
positions by two o'clock. The day had well dawned before we commenced operations owing to heavy rain—which seemed to attend the
Legion in all its movements ; for it was an understood thing, however fair the weather might be the evening before, we should go into
action with a good wet skin ; and however extraordinary such a
thing may appear to the readers of these cursory remarks, should
they ever be published, the Legion never had a dry day to com-

---

* " The bodies of the British fouud after the action were generally stripped to
the skin, the nose, tongue, and ears cut off, and otherwise horribly mutilated."—
Twelve Months in the British Legion.

mence work—no, not from the first commencement of their actions
in Spain.*

The Legion was formed in close columns on the right, of the right
division of the army which placed us exactly opposite to a redoubt and
breast works of the enemy, being their advance picquet on the Hernani road, which must be taken before we could get one inch from
the lines of San Sebastian.   As soon as Espartero and Evans made
their appearance, we moved through the fields close to the high road,
but were obliged to wait until the guns had closed the breast works
across the road &c. This was but the work of a few minutes, as the
Carlists had no guns to return our *compliments* sent to them in *round
numbers*.   The Chapelgorris led the division to which I belonged,
with a few English in advance of them, who had strayed from their
respective corps on purpose, one of which was a Lieutenant Scott of the
6th, who was here wounded through the thigh ; the Carlists retired very
quickly from this to their breast-works on and around the Venta
hill, which commanded completely the high road to Hernani ; we
followed, and a halt took place within musket range of this place,
for the purpose of allowing old Howe's guns to come up to clear
another breast-work thrown across the road immediately at the foot
of the hill, a few men behind which, possessed full command of
every point within musket range.   The enemy here seemed to take
things very coolly, which assured me they were all prepared for a
retreat with ease to themselves as soon as they were forced, which
they saw must be the case from our numbers.   I was much amused
with two of their buglers, who having placed themselves on a conspicuous part of the hill, were serenading us with " Ay ! Ay ! Ay !
Mutillae," (a well known party song) but old Howe soon put a stop
to their music, as he broke a shell right over them at a distance
of a thousand yards.   We heard no more bugling after this—we
could just see the caps of the enemy over the tops of their parapets and field works, and I had just left the spot. (I was induced to
do so by very salutary advice) when Evans, Chichester and Staff,
made their appearance on the same spot ; the Carlists no doubt considering them better game, pounced in a volley instantly ; the Staff

---

* The actions of the 6th June, 11th July, and 1st October, 1836 ; were
all dry at the commencement, but they might all be said to have been drowned
out by rain.

turned about, and Chichester remarked on passing, " *how very un-gentlemanly &c.*" The 4th, and 6th, felt the effects of this volley, seven men having been killed and wounded ; although they were drawn up on the slope of the hill from the Carlists, and considered out of danger, the staff escaped—such is the fortune of war.

Espartero was close by in a house, viewing the enemy's positions and the beautiful practice of our artillery, he was in the house on account of the rain for few are braver than " little Espartero," while on the other hand, I think, none so unfit to command an army, requiring a good head to perform operations. I have always understood we were intended as the reserve this morning, to the right attack ; but some how or another, on things appearing to become serious, we found ourselves—Legion in front as usual. The 6th and 8th were ordered to the extreme right for the purpose of turning the left of the enemy ; this we found no easy job, from the country being perfectly saturated with the rain of the morning, not to mention every inch of ground being commanded from the enemy's breast-works ; we could not go faster up the hills than at a very slow pace; but having to pass through a woody country, many lives were saved on our side, while the tops of the trees were cut to peices from the sharp fire kept up from the enemy's breast-works ; it was quite laughable to behold the tumbling that now took place, in gcing up and down the slippery sides of the hills, rendered more difficult, as it had been trodden on ; many of the men actually sat down and slided from the top to the bottom, and such pictures of misery it was impossible for a Cruickshank to have depicted, as some of them exhibited after arriving at the bottom of each valley, poor Count Meerisole, a General Commanding a division, but not much higher than a drummer boy ; by the bye, talking of this, put me in mind of his having been made a prisoner by the enemy, at the first siege of Bilbao, of which place he was then Governor ; he is a brave little fellow, and had on this occasion headed a sortie out of Bilbao, to cut off a working party of the Carlists, who were turning a ditch within some few yards of the gate of the town ; they were repulsed by the superior number of the enemy, and he became a prisoner in the mèlee, ere he had time to strip himself of his clothing ; a huge Carlist laid hold of the little fellow and asked him what he was, on which he pretended to be very frightened, and put his hands "*a kimbo*," as if beating a drum, on which the Carlist, taking him for a drummer, gave him a kick in the— and the little governor cut his "*stick*," with many others, back into Bilbao, being, it is supposed, in appearance so much below the notice of the enemy. But to return, he was obliged to dismount, and for every pace he made forward, he rolled half a dozen back, and at last I was obliged to leave him behind, he having literally rolled down some seventy feet, into the bed of a rivulet, where he appeared with his legs up, with a "*full front*" to the stream which rolled over him, and more like a "hedge-hog" than a General commanding a division, he was covered from head to foot with mud; our onward movements soon left him far behind us in the "*valley below.*" Many were the enquiries after the little General on my arriving at the top of the hill, but I kept his true position to myself, well knowing had I hinted my seeing him, it would have been a job for me to go after the little fellow, I was too old a soldier for that. The 6th managed to get up first, and I found them drawn up behind a house within 200 yards of the enemy's breast-works, waiting for the 8th, and Chapelgorris who were moving after them, but with much more difficulty, as the ground became worse the more it was walked over: they soon arrived, and we found ourselves in a difficult situation, in fact a very awkward position for a short time, inactive and exposed, being obliged as was ordered, to remain at this point for a reinforcement. No such thing arriving, and still, no word of Meerisole, Ross moved off to the right and rear with the 8th and Chapelgorris to take a hill called Ross's mount (from his having taken it from the enemy on the 16th of March before with his own regiment the 6th) being the extreme left of the enemy's position: the Chapelgorris and 8th were trying who could ascend first, although from the top of it, two companies of the Carlists kept up a heavy fire while they were advancing, the 8th never fired a shot, except, at a hare that was trying to get out of the way; four of them turned round and shot at poor puss, as coolly as if no enemy were near them, and only left off their amusement on seeing their Colonel (Hogg) and the head of the regiment near the top of the hill, and the Carlists running away; at this period let me tell the reader, the bullets were flying thick enough. The rebels fled before we could cross bayonets with them, but as the men had just come over two high hills and through as many slippery valleys,

No. 34.

we could not attempt to follow them, they retired right under their own breastworks, which fairly bristled with arms.

"It was at this moment that Howe's artillery had cleared the breast-work on the road at the foot of the Venta. on which our Lancers were pushed along the road, while the Infantry flanked the hill, the enemy then gave way in every direction, retiring quickly to the other side of Hernani and the heights of Santa Barbara, where they had other field works thrown up, behind which, they left several companies of their skirmishers to await our advance; even here Espartero showed his want of dash, for had the cavalry and the divi-sions of infantry been pushed forward in proper time, many prisoners must have fallen into our hands, as it was at least a mile and a half from this to Hernani, open road and open country, he had no reason to fear being turned in flank, allowing the enemy even to have had a superior force, which was not the case, as our own brigade had worked its way to the extreme left flank of the enemy, and the left division had turned the Carlist's right flank early in the morning by entering both villages of Astigarraga, so that Espartero had nothing to do but to push straight to his front; no, another halt now took place to bring up the guns to burst open the gate of Hernani, whereas the troops might have advanced, rounded it, and entered from Urineta gate, which was fully proved by the Lancer officers, who had ridden round the town, and only turned back on seeing the superior force of the Carlist cavalry formed up on the roads to Tolosa, ready to march off if forced, another proof that no person was in the town although Espartero kept our guns plying shot after shot at the gate, was this, Capt. Hamilton then in command of the rockets, who always liked to see the enemy before he sent his " *Barbers poles* " in among them, had proceeded close to the gate of the town, so much so, that one of our shells burst right over him, and he fell on his horse's neck as if killed, from the effects of the explosion—he was stunned---but only for a moment or so.

" About this time the 8th were pushed forward to take Santa Bar-bara, as the Carlists had shewn an inclination to make a stand on this very strong position; the men of the 8th were now much knocked up, having had a running advance the whole morning to the several positions of the enemy, and to add to their difficulty, their road lay through fields in many places knee deep with mud ; Hogg was a long

way in front calling " come on men,". he was on horse-back and had
been so the whole morning ; * but the poor men had been obliged
to run for miles up and down hills with knapsacks, brown bess, and
60 rounds of ammunition tied to their backs . Hogg is a brave man
every one must allow, but I should be sorry to be one of his battalion
in front of a cool enemy. I happened to have orders to carry that
forced my going past the 8th, and I never felt for men more in my
life, they were perfectly exhausted ; a great deal of inquiries were
passing from one to the other as to what they were *rinin'* for, with
complaints from many as to their inability to go further, while others
were crying " stop men ". and received for answer, " stop !
ye'll no stop till Hogg gets up to the Carlists;" " ah, man, but
Hogg's in his glory now." I spoke to them and cheered, some remarked, " if I had a horse like you, I might gang' ; facks death, I'm
nearly dead." I took off my cap and said to them, " come on 8th,
it is only a few yards now, just a wee bit down the Saut-market,
and a bit turn to the right brings you to Samuel Dow's in the Brig-
gat." Although worn out in appearance, my appeal had its effect,
the 8th gave a cheer, and the next moment found them round the
Santa Barbara, and the Carlists retiring in all directions, over the
range of hills leading to Andouin on the Tolosa road. I was much
pleased with the Chapelgorris who were coolly advancing up the
most precipitous face of the Santa Barbara, in the very front of the
Carlist breastworks under a galling fire, and no doubt the movement of the 8th saved these fine fellows, as the enemy gave way,
when they found their flank about to be turned, which was the case
the moment the 8th had rounded the Santa Barbara ; that regiment
moved after the enemy for half a mile to the right, and occupied
some farm houses, throwing out picquets to the front, who kept up
a partial skirmishing with the enemy for some time ; the Chapelgorris had come down on the road on the Urineta side of Santa
Barbara and formed, while the 6th with the pipes at their head, were
seen winding their way to occupy some farm houses on the heights
within 300 or 400 yards of the village of Urineta ; such were the
positions of our Brigade when waiting further orders from the
General, not having learned the fate of Hernani.—But we heard,

* Only part of the morning.—AUTHOR.

" the Irish are in Hernani;" and to our Brigade such a thing did not require confirmation, as it was enough to us to see the enemy cutting away in every direction, right and left of the village of Urineta, and meeting on the road to Tolosa, where they were trying with each other who could go the fastest, never for a moment supposing Espartero would remain quietly in Hernani, which had cost him but a few men killed and wounded. Nothing should have prevented his entering Tolosa this day, but more of this in its proper place.

" About 400 Carlists remained in the village of Urineta, the houses of which and the church wall on the Hernani side were loop-holed, these fellows kept up a complete serenade of musketry, on our advanced posts and sentries, and woe to the straggler that dared to shew his nose near the village, yet Espartero at two o'clock in the day intended to set quietly down in Hernani, and let the enemy annoy his out-posts, when he had a force sufficient to have detached 15,000 direct to Andouin that evening, without the risk of losing a single man, I mean had he followed up the enemy as he ought to have done, but instead of which he gave the Carlists confidence by his un-military movements; at last necessity brought the order " the village of Urineta must be taken;" a Spanish regiment was sent out of Hernani who proceeded to the left of the road through to the fields, while the 1st Lancers were on the main road ready to charge through the streets, after the enemy might be driven from their loop-holes; from our position moved the 6th under the brave Clarke; (whose right arm was then in a sling from a wound received on the 16th March), as we were moving down we could see the enemy watching every move of the 6th; Clarke took them down in close column, wheeled a " quarter circle" to the left in beautiful style, which completely deceived the enemy, as it was done so rapidly; the 6th were under cover of a house at the very entrance of the village, and within 100 yards of the Carlists having only lost three men wounded, &c. of the last company of the column; next moment, Clarke at their head, made a dash into the village, the enemy gave way, then came the Lancers down the road, all was the work of five minutes—poor Clarke! he is now no more, having fallen at Andouin. I must not pass over the gallant conduct of Lieutenant Morgan of the 6th regiment, who with six of his most active men never stopped until they had driven the enemy clean through the village, one of his men (Homan) I saw fall by his side, with a ball through both temples, within twenty yards, of at least a hundred Carlists : should Lieutenant Morgan ever hear of these note taken on the fi eld, he will remember his having received the *Fernando* for his conduct which others would have robbed him of.—The 6th and lancers began to open every house in the village, and I must say, I would defy any company in London to shift goods with so much dispatch ; I have no doubt they were quickened in their movements by perceiving the Spanish troops coming down the road to occupy the village ; it was not "first in, first served ;" but being first in they took good care to leave little for the last ; as the Queen's troops relieved us, we proceeded back to our several positions in the heights and took up our quarters for the night, tired with being at work, of which the marching was the severest part, from 2 a. m. to 4 p. m.

CHAPTER XXV.

Incidents and reflections—Movement to Irun—The attack opens—Disposition of the Regiments—Particulars of the 1st, Rifles, and Royal Irish—Major Macduff killed—Captains Linton and Hornsy wounded by a treacherous flag of truce —Particulars of other parts of the attack and defence—Flag of truce—Cuckoo —Night—Morning—Evans sends a flag of truce to allow the women and children to leave the town—Dreadful cannonade—The fort surrenders, and the town taken—Descriptive account of the pillage, with numerous incidents, pleasing, fearful, and disgusting.

A GREAT portion of the foregoing chapter being quotations from persons who knew the circumstance of the Legion's progress to Hernani better than I did, I had no hesitation in offering them as good authorities, but I shall now take up the narrative of my own observations ; leading the reader forward to an event which has hitherto been very much underrated at home, but to which I shall endeavour to give that justice of description that it so much deserved, and which the " correspondents" from ignorance, or other motives so ungenerously with-held.

The 15th of May was passed in cleaning our arms, accoutrements, and clothes,—in cooking our rations for the anticipated early move-

ment of next day, in parading to shew that we were clean, and in
looking after other matters which are common to all soldiers situated
as we were, and which therefore could not be forgotten by us, namely,
making spoil, and appropriating it to our own uses. It is necessary
to state however, that the people left us very little either in the town
or in the vicinity of Hernani to appropriate; in all the houses there
was furniture, in some of them the furniture was very good, but
though it might have suited a broker, it was not to be disposed of in
the knapsack of a soldier; therefore unless what was burned in making fires to dry ourselves—which fires, however, were by no means
insignificant in size,—the furniture was mostly all saved, indeed to
do justice to the Legion I must say it was in most cases very much
respected; for I was a witness to various interferences of men in behalf of saving the people's furniture, "let it alone," they would say,
" the people will come back to it." You would see at times, one going to kindle a fire outside the house to cook ; a dozen men looking
out at the windows above him would call " shame to you! to take
the chairs to burn!" and they would pelt him until he procured
something less sanctified to the domestic associations of the mind.
This man would retort that he must have a fire ; and then he would
be asked if he did not see fires large enough for him,—to which his
reply would be, " they are too large I can't get near them." This
was the difficulty to be encountered; the logs of wood piled above
logs, sent out a heat as if rebelliously defying the approach of those
who kindled them ; and thus all who wished to cook, had to make
fires for themselves.

As I watched some of these individuals, I fell into an involuntary
train of philosophising thought. There were those who might be
called at home " the off scourings" of society, who were certainly not
very correct in their morality but who gave proofs then, that to have
a bad character is not to be bad without some redeeming quality. I
saw a man breaking down a cradle, and he was one, as correct in
his general deportment as any man could well be in the society of
soldiers; he was a good soldier and in common phrase an amiable
young man. A swearing, half drunken fellow, who possessed none
of the most amiable of reputations in such matters as not being backward to help himself to any thing he wanted whether it was his own
or another's—passed, and seeing the destroyer of the cradle at work,

said, with a few rough oaths, that it was a shame to break the cradle, that nothing melted his heart sooner than the like of that ; and then he went on to persuade the man who was breaking it to desist, he appealed to the recollection of the man's own childhood and home, and supposed that it must be an old family piece because of its ancient manufacture, and deduced therefrom that generations must have been " *rockit*" in it, that a curse could only fall on us when such a sacred relic of the domestic home as the *cradle* was destroyed, and he concluded with an oath, saying, that he would look on a man as no more than a brute who could not cast his thoughts back and think, " how vexed he would be if soldiers were to come and break and burn his own mother's things that way." Now this man was not the moral wreck of some once well educated or what we would call " better informed but misguided" young man. He was an Edinburgh hawker of coals—belonged to a fragment of the community locally celebrated by the name of " Gilmerton Carters," and had no school education— was altogether ignorant of the very first rudiments of learning ! and yet he was possessed of those qualities of mind which from their natural strength shone out in spite of circumstances. The attendant circumstances conduced to put down all such feelings as this man possessed, and in the next paragraph I will shew how ; but in the meantime I must remark in continuation of the foregoing, that mankind are nearer an equality in virtue than we are often willing to believe. A man in one situation of life might not have the same reputation in another situation of life, and were we to look narrowly into many of the motives that give the appearance of virtue, and that which is commonly an accompaniment—virtuous indignation at the vices of others—we would be more restrained in denouncing those whom we deemed inferior to ourselves. Among the heterogeneous mass of moral and animal materials, of which the Legion, like all other armies was composed, there was a wide expanse of observation for those who chose to observe ; and I made some comparison of different men in different circumstances, which perhaps might be useful to the student of human nature, and which after arranging, I may at some time publish ; but at present I detect myself, wandering from the narrative of Legionary occurrences, and must therefore return.

While drying ourselves around a great fire, and watching the progress of its greatness, I could not help noticing the similarity of destructiveness as developed in the animated and inanimated destroyers. The men who kindled it first, had perhaps no intention of doing more than making a fire to dry themselves; but vast quantities of wood being at hand—there being something like a builder's timber yard—logs were brought and piled above logs, and some men at this were satisfied. Others who up to this, had looked listlessly on, had their passion of destructiveness suddenly excited, and called out "how glorious! we'll have a fire!" and immediately ran off to get more wood. I knew some of them to be persons who would not, on any account, have gone to kindle a fire either for the good of themselves or comrades, and who were always the last to do any thing that they were ordered, if the nature of the obedience required, admitted at all of procrastination;—these, like the hard invulnerable logs of oak that one might strive in vain to kindle with a moderate appliance of combustion, raged in destruction when once on fire, setting at a rebellious defiance all attempts to controul them. If we suppose the passions of the animated, to be like the fuel of the inani- mated fire—then the moral faculties may be to one, what water is to the other; and education, which should train and direct the moral faculties may be in the one case, what an engine and its hose with energetic firemen are in the other case. Some fires extend to an awful breadth of destruction because of the want of water, and these re- marks are made here because I saw all those who figured most con- spicuously at this great fire—were persons whom I had previously noted to myself as most destitute of the moral faculties. Now they were by no means the persons most frequently detected in the com- mission of crime; some of them were well behaved soldiers; but when the more moderately destructive men were satisfied with making a great blaze—these others ran to the wood-yard—rolled up the logs, and because they could not go near enough to lay them on the fire, raised them over end by an exertion of strength that nothing but an extraordinary excitement could have called into activity, and let them fall on the fire. Then the wood being piled and no more at hand, some one took a gate from its hinges, and another seeing that, took the humble, old fashioned, and rudely made plough, and threw it on: in another minute the bullock-cars crowned the bonfire, and then the cry for more wood was louder than ever. One, whose organs of destructiveness and wonder were probably only catching their first excitement, then exclaimed "Let us have a good fire at once" and ere the more moderate knew what more he and his compeers could have, the house was on fire! And the men who had been asleep, who were cleaning themselves, or who sat peacefully at some necessary employment inside, were seen rushing out while those who had their knapsacks and accoutrements in the house were seen among smoke and fire, trying to save them. Happily for the most of us, we . were cleaning ourselves outside, and had our belts hanging on the trees of the orchard, bleaching in the sun.

When contemplating this last act of destructiveness, I was led into another reverie of comparisons on seeing the fruit-trees which surrounded the house;—all of them being in the highest luxuriance of blossom. "How like are these" I soliloquised to the softening beauty and tender affections of woman; and these nearest the fire, how like are they to woman in dire adversity! The wetness of the frequent showers has not yet been dried by the sun, and when the fire burst out of that house, around which these sweet cherry trees have been long peacefully associated, how their little drops glistened like tears, as tears glisten on the face of a woman at the first approach of calamity; when the fire grew redder and the oaken beams that are the support of the walls,* became in imminent danger how the growing disaster made the little drops painfully vivid and visible, until the strong oak has caught fire. The dry oak is now the prey of a destroyer and the tears of the sweet cherry tree are dry;—there is calm despair—the lovely flower shrivels itself up—there is no mercy and it asks none; it will not survive the more stubborn companions of domestic life, and it stands against' the wrath of its destroyer with a defiance of unnatural fierceness;—it resists and will not burn, for the softness of its heart that made it at first, tender and lovely, and even affectionate to those whose affections were towards it, makes it more insensible to, and immovable in adversity now. But the destroyer will have his prey; and the fountains of its heart being dried up, and life no longer desirable, it resigns, dies and is consumed away; it is consumed all but the root, which for a time will stand black and scorched like the memory of the dead; but new summers

---

* The most of the houses in Spain are an immense piece of oaken framework which in making a house is first set up, and the masonry amounts to nothing, more than filling up spaces between the beams of wood.

will come, and new trees, this root will be taken up, and like the memory of those that were, will pass for ever away."

I had soliloquised in the foregoing mood, when orders came to stop the whole regimental allowance of wine, for having set fire to the house ; but it being represented that only one company was charge-able, the punishment was restricted to that company, and terrible punishments were threatened if the names of those who set it on fire were not disclosed. Names could be given in ; but as there was only one mode of punishment which could be inflicted—we being there only for a night, and being to march against the enemy next morning—and which punishment would have been inflicted on any one whose name was revealed—that is, the punishment of three or four dozen lashes—the more easy and more common method of get-ting over the disaster was taken,—that of every man offering to prove that the house was burned by accident.

It may be here proper to say, why the only punishment that could have been inflicted was three or four dozen lashes.   This was the punishment of the Provost, and in a place where there was no time for imprisoning—no time for extra drilling—no time in fact for any punishment but a summary one; what I would ask, *could* have been done? Rations of food or wine might have been stopped from a cri-minal, but experience proved that measure, of no effect when the criminal was at large, because his comrades contributed their shares to make up an allowance for him.   Had a whole company's rations been stopped, they might not have raised a supply so easily ; but then, to punish a body of men for the fault of one or a few, was unjust, and always productive of evil consequences ; while to have stopped a company's rations until the company would discover and punish the offenders themselves, was bringing the offender to a fearful punishment, for nothing was so severe—as company punish-ments.   A criminal would at once call out for a regular court-martial or punishment from an officer, rather than take the chance of receiv-ing mercy from his comrades.   It is true, that a man was scarcely ever turned over to his comrades, but when his crime was such that the Colonel, or the Captain knew would draw on him the severity of the other men ; and therefore it might be that all company punish-ments were so severe—I believe that was the cause, but whether it was or not, it is beyond question true, that there was less mercy in barrack-room court-martials than in any others. Then at such a time as that when we were in Hernani, ready for the field, and preparing to move, what was to be done? To give a man extra duty, which duty could only be to mount picquet or guard, was nothing; — 'for,' said the criminal, 'I am as well on duty as off—those that are off are lying in the open air with their clothes and accoutrements on, the same, and not any better than me;—I can stand my sentry-go and then I can bid them defiance;—they can't keep me on picquet more than four-and-twenty hours—thank the 'Articles of War' for that; or if they do, they can't punish me for falling asleep,' thus a man would comfort himself after committing any species of crime; what then was to be done? discharge him from the army? flog him? shoot him? or what?—if you let him go at liberty and unpunished what became of discipline or obedience to command? if a relaxation of law is once made, when is it to stop? then if you would discharge the man what would become of him? besides how many unwilling soldiers would follow his example to be similarly dealt with? If you would flog him with the *cats,* as is commonly done in the British service, or bruise him with *rods* as the Germans—Spaniards—Portugueze and others do, you would outrage humanity or if you would put him to death, you would outrage humanity still more: besides, crime being much more common among British soldiers than any others, *recruiting* would barely keep pace with shooting:—what then is to be done? We saved the man who burned the house for the amusement of himself and others from punishment, by denying design in the origin of the fire; but such an excuse on the part of comrades, was neither at all times prudent, nor at all times practicable. Some will say—as others have said, and said against their own knowledge of facts, that the Legion was composed of worse moral materials than other armies;—but this is not true; and so far were the Legion from over matching all precedents, that it was common to hear on every extraordinary occasion—the old soldiers of the Wellington campaigns, say — "oh that was nothing; — if you had seen our plundering! if you had seen our regiment at such a time, then you would have seen something! but here! here there's nothing to be had—we can never get liberty to forage for ourselves like soldiers in any other war," &c. Then these old soldiers of the Peninsula armies would launch out into long tales of their former cam-

paigns, that put our petty plundering into the shade. Even that
night when the house was set on fire, and when some began to call
it a shame, the old veterans soon put out the memory of such a humble solitary blaze, by the recollection of former glories of a similar
and more magnificent kind.

The night of the 15th passed, and the morning of the 16th, one
of the loveliest of the infant summer, dawned in all the richness of
Spanish beauty, and we prepared to move onwards to the attack on
the fortress and town of Irun. We marched through Hernani amid
all the bustle of regiments "turning out," "falling in," and moving
to the muster of their respective brigades or divisions;—amid the
choking crowds of forty pieces of field artillery with horses and waggons, and a thousand mules getting loaded with ammunition and rations—amid the noise of drummers and buglers, a dozen or a score to
each regiment rattling and routing in all quarters—amid all that din
and bustle, we contended for marching room on the gorged streets,
and ultimately found ourselves two regiments abreast, on the road
to the frontier of France with five or six thousand men in front and
twice as many in our rear. The main body of Espartero's army remained in, and around Hernani, and nearly two thirds of the numbers who started with General Evans, filed off at various points of
the road taking up positions on the heights and in the villages, so
that they might advance if required,—prevent a manœuvre of the
enemy, to cut off a retreat—or be ready to move with Espartero on
the town of Tolosa should Evans be successful without their assistance. At two miles distance from Hernani, we all filed off into a
field, and had the half of our aguardiente served out, the half was
small, but though in ordinary cases it is a disgusting spirit, worse
even than raw unmalted whisky, it was on such an occasion as that,
and at such a time, deliciously sweet; our bread and beef had been
given out the previous evening, and though intended to last until the
following day, many had made, and were making an end to it then;
"for" said they " we may as well eat it when we're able there 'ill be
a dozen or two in every company dead before *dinner time* so we may
as well eat it at once !" Some of these who had the misfortune tosur-
vive their rations, were commonly the first to raise an outcry of the
" infernal shame" of men having to fight without something to
ate.

It was, as has been said a lovely morning, and we moved forward, leaving in our rear the valley of the Urimea. As we left it, and looked back, the beauteous river seemed lying in its green meadows and blooming orchards as if oversleeping itself. The sun had melted the morning mist into thin air—the larks were mounted—the linnets and the cuckoos, with innumerable myriads of other songsters—all were begun, all were rich in the melody of a new summer. The forests of fruit-trees in their full blossom, were on each side of us, all green, odoriferous and luxuriant, and the showers which now and again came scudding along, putting out the sun for a few minutes, left every bush as if weeping,—looking up in his face when he came back to shine, as if complaining that something had meddled with them, and then he dried their tears, and the little birds hopping on the branches began to sing again.

Amid this scene of peace, the clustering bayonets bristled along the line of the tortuous march; but where we would see or meet the enemy, was uncertain, and we kept moving on, coming into villages that the Carlists had left on our approach. We saw no male inhabitants, save one or two, but the houses had all women in them, who crowded to the windows to see us, and most readily gave answers to any questions which those in command put relative to the Carlists; and at every house, and at nearly each hundred yards distance, there were females, young and old, with pails containing water and cider for us to drink. Poor things! it was impossible that it could be kindness that prompted them; but they no doubt did it from a wish to propitiate us as much as possible, and they were successful, for not a man dared to stir, or in any way molest them: whoever had done so, was to have been punished with instant death.

We at last halted on the brow of a rising ground, and we of the ranks could surmise that the commencement was near, for the movements of aids-de-camp indicated that our halt was made preparatory to getting up the heavy artillery—getting cavalry to the front &c. The time that we thus halted was a period of a soldier's life in which he feels a sensation that no civilian has felt or can feel. The author of the *Subaltern* who has in all his works depicted with minute fidelity the anatomy of a military life, gives a description of this anxious sensation felt by soldiers in the following words.—

" It would be difficult to convey to the mind of an ordinary reader, anything like a correct notion of the state of feeling which takes possession of a man waiting for the commencement of a battle. In the first place, time appears to move upon leaden wings; every mi-nute seems an hour, and every hour a day. Then there is a strange commingling of seriousness and levity within him—a levity which prompts him to laugh he knows not why, and a seriousness which urges him ever and anon to lift up a mental prayer to the Throne of Grace. On such occasions, little or no conversation passes. The privates generally lean upon their firelocks, the officers upon their swords; and few words except monosyllables, at least in answer to questions put, are wasted. On these occasions too, the faces of the bravest often change colour, and the limbs of the most resolute trem-ble, whilst watches are consulted till the individuals who consult them grow absolutely weary with the employment. On the whole it is a situation of higher excitement, and darker and deeper agitation than any other in human life; nor can he be said to have felt all which man is capable of feeling who has not felt it."

We had halted as was said, and the General with his staff proceeded to reconnoitre the enemy's positions. It was while they performed that indispensable duty, that we suffered all that anxiety which the author of the *Subaltern* speaks of, as common to soldiers. The wander-ing thought—the serious ejaculation—the whispered jest—and the foul oath, were mingling among us, when the rebound of a cannon at some distance, gave indication that we were within hearing of the enemy's fort. In another half-minute, a tree was shivered in front of our columns, and a second rebound following that, proved that we were within cannon range. The guns from the battery of Irun fired on; and the coolness displayed by Evans and his staff in standing fairly exposed, spying with their glasses, while bullet after bullet whirled past them, and in a few instances, among them, must be specially noticed; for no courage—no cool unexcited courage was ever seen superior to it in any soldier. He stood till satisfied in taking observations, and then turned to some of his Aid-de-camps to give orders in the same calm manner, while near him, a cannon ball was making its way through the horse of one of his attendants—and another covering him with mud, amputating the arm of a Spanish officer, and whirling into confusion the picks and shovels of our Sappers who were throwing up temporary works for our cannon; while such shots as these were playing around Evans, one of which also took off the arm of a groom who was holding his master's horse—and then the head of a servant (a man named Norman, belonging to the town of Leicester), who had striven hard to get into the staff service, that he might be out of danger! this ball passing from an arm to his head, dashed a piece of his skull with such velocity against another man that one of *his* limbs had to undergo amputation; yet amid all these, Evans, and the equally brave and more usefully active Chichester—stood making choice of position as if the balls had been the mere spitting drops of rain that were at the time falling from one of the travelling clouds that idled through the sky.

"Make way for the artillery there!" we heard an Aide-de-camp say to the colonel of some infantry regiment. "Make way and let the artillery pass!—d——n these drivers, why don't they spur on." Then there were others coming with orders such as "Rifles to the front!" "1st regiment by the right of that house," and "Move on the Irish brigade by the corner of that field." "Colonel Ross, take the 6th and 8th by that foot-path in rear of the General, &c., &c" There were also orders to Spanish regiments which I am neither sufficiently learned in to be able to write, nor sufficiently enthusiastic in recording to consider them of much interest; suffice to say, we all moved onwards—the most of us rather uncomfortably exposed to the cannon shot of the Carlist fort that commanded the town of Irun.

Passing along and exposed to this battery, we were only saved from a number of the deadly twenty-fours, by watching the flashes of the guns, and then bending ourselves to the ground, beneath a bank of about two feet in height, which rose on the left hand side of the rugged pathway. Though a few of us were occasionally half-buried with earth as the angry missile dashed up the soil seemingly vexed with being cheated of a more legitimate blow—we were not without mirth. The falling of some in the way of others, and the falling of some who fell when there was no bullet coming, drew forth the sarcasms of those whom the presence of death himself could not prevent jesting.

While thus scrambling along to a position which at the time, we supposed was to be ours, the English artillery opened with tremendous effect on the fort. This artillery was cleverly put in position and practice by Colonel Shaw, indeed that officer distinguished himself eminently on that occasion ; but Captain Howe and Adjutant Skedd, were as usual the officers who above all deserved praise.* Skedd's second or third shot carried away the staff of the fort, on which the red flag of defiance or " no surrender" was hoisted ; and the fall of this emblem of mortal hostility was acclaimed, by the shouts of the whole army; even, it was said, by the French troops, and the people crowded on the frontier of France to witness the storm.   France was about a mile distant from Irun, and the knowledge of the brave battalions of that country being witnesses of our conduct, was not without its effect in producing a warm energy, and determination on the part of the Legion not to disappoint them.

The 1st regiment, under Lieut. Colonel Samuel Shaw, an officer whom I have not hitherto spoken of or alluded to; but who did his duty well on this occasion, moved towards the south-eastern side of the town, our approach and the commencement of the attack being on the western side.   The Rifles, and the Royal Irish regiment—for so the 9th and 10th being now joined together, were called, proceeded in the same direction to make their way in the best style they could to the eastern barriers of the town.   The 1st took a circuitous rout, and came inwards by the road, as if coming from the French frontier. There they were exposed to a heavy fire of musketry from the loopholed walls, and also from light cannon---six and twelve pounders,

---

* As the reader must have felt some interest in old Howe, from the frequent occurrence of his name, it is necessary to say a few words of who and what he was.   Captain Howe had served in the ranks of the Royal British Artillery, and received a commission on going to Spain.   He was perhaps unsurpassed in dexterity ; and in the common routine of military duties, he was one of the most useful *working* officers in the Legion ; but his grossly outrageous tyranny was insufferable.   In the same corps Lieut. and Adjutant, Skedd maintained a creditable proof of what officers raised from the ranks could be.   If there was any difference in the degrees of merit between Howe and Skedd, its settlement may depend on the difference of other people's judgments.   One thing at least is certain—Howe could draw on him the admiration of his fellow soldiers, but he could never command their love.   Skedd was admired as an excellent practical gunner—always in the field, and always at his duty ; besides which, he was beloved and esteemed by all his men.   Howe has been appointed by Sir Hussey Vivian, to be master gunner of Stirling Castle, and he well deserves the respect the Master-General of the Ordnance, has thus paid to military merit.   There may be others waiting for, and deserving something similar, and it may not be easy to do what justice would dictate ; but Mr. Skedd being grey in the military service of the country, and having recently done as much for the honour of the corps, and the cause in which he was engaged, as any man could do, and more than most of his contemporaries—there will be a part of Sir Hussey Vivian's duty unperformed until he places him in one of the numerous situations at his disposal.

placed at the second and third floor windows of the houses. The cool bravery of General Chichester was conspicuously seen at this place, both by his own men and by the enemy. Lieut.-Colonel Ramsey who commanded the left wing of the 1st., was also remarkable for his gallantry, as indeed all the officers of that regiment were at this time. It would be invidious to name one or two and omit the others, but Captain Rae a veteran of other wars, by his steady and skilful judgment became the object of admiration to his men, and of thanks to his superiors. Rae, with his company made his way gallantly to one of the gates; but it is necessary to state that he was preceded by Captain Linton, and the grenadier company.

Having with great difficulty obtained a partial shelter under the walls of a convent, which stood at the outskirts of the town, the 1st regiment remained there inactively, waiting on orders to storm, as the necessity or propriety of such orders might occur. While at this convent a number of their men were killed, and among the officers, Captains Linton and Hornsby were severely wounded. These officers received their wounds at a time and in a manner which reflects the foulest disgrace on the Carlists, of any deed, which as soldiers, they have committed.

A white pennant was hung from a window, and the officers believing, as it was intended to make them believe, that it was a flag of truce and that the garrison would surrender, went forward to speak to those who had displayed the emblem of peace. There were several officers advanced, among whom was Major Macduff, the gentleman spoken of previously in this work; they went forward confiding in the flag of truce; but when approaching the place where it was exhibited, a volley was poured out on them. Macduff fell dead, and some others, non-commissioned officers and men, lay beside him. A greater number were wounded, among whom were Captains Linton and Hornsby, and some officers of the Rifles.

While the 1st had made their progress to that barrier farthest from the point of commencement, the Rifle corps which now consisted of what has been previously named the 7th regiment, as well as its own original materials—were taken forward in gallant style by their ever brave and dauntless hero, Fortescue. The measure of punish ment which they met for their temerity in going up to fortified houses—from the windows of which and innumerable loop-holes—
No. 35.

showers of bullets flew from the vomiting musketry, this punishment was severe. Fortescue about this time, when his men were falling around him, by the thickly flying shot, received at once three bullets through the collar of his jacket, which he only noticed by a smile, and the observation of " rough work boys !" But more of the Rifles hereafter.

The Irish regiment was also engaged near the same part of the town, and similarly with the others, made a lodgment in some of the exterior buildings; but save getting a few men killed and a considerable number wounded, nothing remarkable occurred with them until next day.

While the eastern approaches to the town were thus invested, two Spanish regiments, and the 8th of the Legion proceeded towards the fort—the fort being situated at the opposite side of the town, from that where the 1st, Rifles, and Irish were.

We proceeded some distance among bushes, which screened us from the view of those who might have showered grape and cannister on our front; and emerging from the cover, we saw with no great satisfaction that there was no way of approaching the town on our side, without encountering the garrison of the fort. A Spanish regiment which was posted about three hundred yards in our rear, opened fire, not having seen us advance because of the wood, and we being enveloped in the smoke that rolled from the cannon on both sides, our uniform was indistinguishable; they therefore concluded from our situation that we were the enemy, and having so concluded, they treated us accordingly. In vain, by sounding our bugles, and exposing himself to view, did the Colonel try to make us known ; for some time the bullets came pouring into a hedge that skirted the low roadway in which we were screened, and whenever any of us made ourselves visible, additional vollies came hissing over our heads. The fire on both sides was at this time terrific, for the fort which was about a hundred yards to our right plied eight pieces of cannon incessantly, the balls from which went directly over our heads, and were smashing down the houses and walls, among which the Spaniards were partially sheltered. Our artillery in like manner plied without intermission, and shell after shell, sometimes two and three at once took same the tract over our heads, only reversely, and exploding above and in the fort, kept up an incessant thunder. Amidst this

the small arms were a mere crackling noise, and the smoke from both
hanging thickly on the air, we from our situation found it no easy
matter to make a farther advance. In addition to all that, the rain
fell during half an hour that we lay there, in torrents. In a few
minutes we were all drenched, and no position in which the musket
could be held could keep it dry; the only article of dress about us
that approached to waterproof, was the "blue bonnet," and most of
the men, were seen wrapping their bonnets firmly round the locks
of their firearms, while their bare heads received the storm. This
was the more vexing, as we knew that there was hot work waiting
on the muskets, and that there were but a few yards to advance until
that work would begin,

The Spaniards who had mistaken us for the enemy, were at last
apprised of their mistake, by General Evans, I believe, and the order
"fix bayonets!" was given, while following it, the cry rose " now for
the town !" and the Colonel led on at a pace exceeding considerably
that of double quick. I remember to have heard him say, as he gave
the order to advance, " now my men, we're the first in this direction,
—let us *be* the first; don't let these d——d Spaniards get before
us !" and a loud yelling cheer responded to this appeal. We really
thought at the time that we were about to enter the town, and that a
determined rush would be all that was required to carry the defences,
whatever or wherever these might be. We had no knowledge of
being so very near the fort as we were, nor had we any information
of what the defences were round the town; I mean we of the ranks,
including also the greater part of our regimental officers, had no information. Hogg, led away "left in front ;" and having given particular directions to Captains of companies, to take their men onwards
by the most practicable openings that might be discovered; he raised
the cry as mentioned, " now my boys for the town !" seeing him
take the left of the regiment, Captain Shields of the grenadiers, (the
company in which I was,) said to us—" through here men ! follow
me ! the Colonel wishes to shew off the *Light Company*, let us cut
them out ! here, through the orchard, this is the shortest way !"

We followed Shields ; and having gone a few yards through the
orchard, and turned the corner of the bank of earth, on which grew
a thick thorny hedge, we, to our consternation, found ourselves beneath the walls of the battery. To go on was impossible ; there

was a ditch ten or twelve feet deep, and as many feet in width,
while the walls of the fort rose about eighteen feet perpendicularly
from the verge of the ditch.   Nor could we immediately retreat, for
the passage through which we had come was narrow, and the men
in the rear hearing nothing but thunder and seeing nothing,
were not aware of the situation of those in front, therefore, to turn
suddenly back, was, as to go forward, impossible.   It appeared that
the garrison had suspected the possibility of our approach in that
direction, for a gun charged with grape was pointed to the spot we
were on, as if ready to be fired when necessity demanded.   The moment we were observed by those, who amid fire and smoke were
working like furies at the different embrazures, one of them ran towards this gun with a match.   Captain Shields exclaimed to those
beside him " fire men ! d—n you fire !"   Every musket was instantly to the shoulders of those who were in view of the embrazure;
but *snap* went one fireless lock, the priming being wet, —and *flash*
went another where some of it was dry ; the most of them either
" snapped" or " flashed" and a moment more would have made all
attempts to fire too late— it was only soon enough, as it was, because
the breech of the gun on the fort had to be uncovered ere the match
could be applied to the touch-hole—the showers of rain and the
showers of fire having caused it to be covered as it waited for a necessity, it was, therefore, only time enough to fire, because of this
momentary delay.   The rain had put many of the muskets out of
firing order, but there were some of them that made no objection to do
their duty.   I had a fusil, the fire of which was at any time to be
depended upon, and it was so then ; among a score or so, two or
three pieces went off, and I cannot, by that means, say whose bullet
shot the hapless Carlist as he was putting the match to the gun; but
he was shot ; and I was both sure that my fusil went off, and that I
intended to shoot him.   He staggered backwards, and as he fell
another took the match, and ere he could be popped down, he and
the match did their duty ! what a crash of fiery wrath it was ! and
yet that discharge did not kill even one man.   In the first place, we,
whom they could see, were too low for it, and they were not aware
of the proper level, or could not take the proper level for those in our
rear.—But though not killing any they must have frightened those,
who hidden from them did not know that there was any shot coming

for a part of the hedge and some branches of the trees were cut down, while a number of the bayonets and two or three muskets were smashed to pieces, throwing the men who carried them in a heap on the ground. We would have had another discharge from a gun in the next embrazure which was, as we supposed, similarly loaded; but as the gunners about it were levelling it for us a shell from our artillery struck among them and exploded. Two or three more followed and during the confusion that ensued, we made good our retreat. Going back a short distance we were enabled to follow the remainder of the regiment, and we came up to them at a post where by a stealthy approach, they had got under cover on the main road, within fifty yards of the fort. Lieutenant Colonel Martin, who acted as Aid-de-camp at that time to our brigade—says in some notes which I have been favoured with, and which were taken when the town had fallen, that.—

" 'Towards evening Evans appeared to wish to take the Fort by storm, for which purpose the 8th were ordered to advance near the fort, and to wait for the scaling ladders &c.; fortunately for the regiment the country was very woody through which they had to pass, so much so, that it was only now and then that the garrison could see them, and to add to their farther security, they were perfectly covered on their nearer approach to the fort, by a house within seventy yards of it, which had been left standing by some mistake or other of the Carlists; from this very house a few of the 8th, and Chapelgorris silenced two guns, by the sharp fire they kept up on the embrazures, by putting their muskets through the top of the roof; they were perfectly safe and none of the enemy had courage enough to attempt re-loading the two guns after the house was occupied as related; I will ever remember going through the apple orchard in getting up to this house, I can compare the shower of balls to nothing I ever heard before, but the flight of a covey of patridges. I really thought of them at the time and fancied I should have been much safer on the *moors*— with a different music to be sure, but very like it. From this house we found a road leading to the right of the fort; it was a regular covered way, the bank on the right being some five feet or more in height, which we moved along perfectly secure, although within 100 feet of the fort: a few minutes showed us the stupidity of the enemy, in leaving the houses standing perfectly loop-holed and commanding the side of the fort they were within 70 yards of the muzzle of the guns, as if they had found out their mistake, they opened a most galling fire on the 8th, but too late to do much harm as our fellows commenced such a heavy fire through the loop holes, which it then appeared had been made on purpose for them, that the enemy found they were obliged to content themselves with the first shots ; for such a fire was kept up on their embrazures, that it was perfectly impossible for them to get to the guns to re-load.   The garrison still had the power of annoying some of our troops who were drawn up behind some houses on the Hernani road ; it was in one of these houses that a poor lad of the Lancers (servant to Mr. Moore, a reporter), was holding his master's horse, when a cannon ball entered and carried off his head !   To-wards sun-set, Evans wishing to save blood, sent Col. Cottenor of his staff with a flag of truce, offering the enemy terms if they would surrender.   During the parley we had an opportunity of looking into the ditch of the fort, and for myself, I was perfectly satisfied we had got out of a good thing so far, in not being forced to storm after our first advance to our present position : the entrance to the fort on our side must have been through the embrazures, the ditch being very deep and the sides built of stone ' straight up and down ,' it is true we might have got over the roof, but to get there was the query.

" After an hour spent in useless parley, the town refused to give up, although I suspect the fort would have been too glad of the chance, as far as the soldiers were concerned.   We had a good deal of conversation with the garrison who came out on the embrazures, glad to have an opportunity of smoking their paper segars, so essential to every movement of a Spaniard ; we were for a time the greatest friends in the world ; but at it again we went, and the firing did not cease before late at night ; when no doubt some took to sleeping, others to cooking, and I dare say a greater number prepared for ' to-morrow,' as the first break of day would be sure to commence the strife again, unless we retired, or they chose to give in ; it would take too much space, and perhaps he considered ' coming. it rather too strong,' or I could enumerate many acts of individual bravery that had taken place before the close of the 16th."

While on the march in the early part of the day, we had been cheered by the kindly voice of the Cuckoo, and when the flag of

,ruce was sent in by Evans and the firing had ceased, one of these musical ministers of peace and summer, having thought the war was over, put forth a note, as if on trial, and hearing nought but its own egotistical melody echoing through the vacuum of silence, it went gaily on. The voice of this bird had a softening influence even on the war-hardened soul of a Chapelgorri. With his mouth blackened by biting his cartridges, and his face scorched by the incessant firing of his musket, he was fixing a new flint, and as his vengeful eyes followed the officer who bore the flag, he grinded his teeth and muttered curses in his fierce Biscayan dialect against all who would give or take quarter. His scowl and his curse—his blackened lips and his scorched hair—his new flint and the trimming of his lock and barrel, were an union of appearances that spoke the depth of his hatred to the foe with his desire and determination to be slain or have more slaughter. While he cursed those who lost time in parleying with a flag of truce, the sweet voice of the Cuckoo came melodiously from the adjoining wood, he listened, and after hearing a few notes he turned to some of our men, and in a softened tone said, in the Biscayan tongue, " Ah the Chapelgorris should never hear the Cuckoo till the battle is over." The flag of truce being rejected, five of the guns on the fort bounded off, the bullets from which scoured the road, working havoc as they scoured, and were a signal for our artillery to recommence the thunder of shells and rockets. The disappointed songster broke his melody, and the Chapelgorri loaded his musket.

Night came on and we lay on the road side all the night keeping anxious watch on the fort and road leading to the town. For our own safety we were not permitted to kindle fires and being wet, with nothing but the mud to stand upon, we were not so comfortable as the most of us wished to be. Still we were patient, for we looked forward to the morning—the scaling ladders—the forlorn hope and the certainty of our being employed in the storm—with no great desire for daylight. I was the object of envy for a few hours, having by industry gathered some stones of which I made a bed to keep above the mud, and on which I enjoyed a sound sleep while hundreds were standing on their feet amid the wet all the night.

Next morning a most exciting incident occurred. The reader will observe that from our position we had no direct communication with the troops in our rear, for we had got to where we were, in a great measure by stealth under cover of smoke, and the road with all the fields behind us were now clearly seen, and commanded by the guns on the fort. The Commissary's boxes of biscuit were about half a mile from us, and the question arose " whether would we be without our ration of biscuit, or run the risk of going for it." Volunteers were soon found who stole to the rear by the way we had advanced, and day-light not having set in clearly, they succeeded in getting to the biscuit stores without molestation ; but to come back the same way was not practicable, owing to the load that had to be carried and obstacles that had to be scrambled over, besides the light was gleaming, and a great part of the way was visible to the battery. A consultation was held among the orderly corporals who were drawing the biscuit, and it was decided that they should " toss up," to determine who of them should venture with his four men and company's rations to go along the main road. This, some of them urged was safe, because as they said, there was not a gun on that side of the battery now, that they were all demolished the day before, and that the garrison would not fire along the road owing to the musketry they would be exposed to from our men. The lot fell on a corporal Macgregor to make the venture. We saw him approaching, and his voluntary fatigue men carrying on their shoulders a box of the precious hard-ware for which our teeth were well whetted. The other companies seeing the grenadiers' fatigue-men only, made sport with us to the effect that " Oh the *sand-bags* couldna take time to come with their rations like the men of the other companies, &c." This was because they, poor hungry fellows, thought their biscuits were coming safely and quietly in some other direction, and to tell the truth the *sand bags* (as the grenadiers of each regiment are familiarly called) trembled for the safety of their corporal and the four men, perhaps the safety of the box which they carried increased the trembling anxiety, at any rate, we looked along the road in acute expectation of seeing a cannon ball whirl the box and men into destructive confusion. They had come within twenty yards of a corner, which if they gained, would cover them from any farther danger—but off went the box, a part of it whirling high into the air ; while the corporal, the men and the biscuits lay together on the road. The eye saw that disaster and the next moment the ear caught the shock of the cannon on the fort which had destroyed the hungry hopes of the grenadiers. It was a discharge of grape shot that had thus direfully met them in the face, but with the exception of breaking the box, and by the force of the concussion making them stagger to the ground it did no more harm; for while two of them started to their feet and ran inwards, the corporal and the other two dragged the box which still contained the most of its contents, and to our great satisfaction we got the expected teeth exercise. The others seeing this did not venture in the same direction, and thus the *sand-bags* had their biscuit and their laugh, while the others had to breakfast on expectation.

I have been favoured by a very intelligent, and acute observing Rifleman, with an account of what occurred with the regiments on the eastern side of the town during the evening, and the morning of next day; and have copied his notes without alteration. They are as follow :—

" Our regiment (the Rifles), took to the fields, south of the main road passing at four deep, within a few hundred yards of the Carlist battery, which commenced a smart fire of musketry and round shot from the heavy pieces. We passed however without accident, and formed on a height close by under cover of a wood; here we remained some time; the 1st company then advanced extending under General Chichester, and the remainder of the regiment soon followed; we then halted and formed close column on a hill near the main road, which leads from the east gate of the town into France. A small body of the Carlists made a hasty retreat from the adjoining fields and road, at this moment, into the houses near the town. This was followed by a direct movement on our part to the same houses, "come this way, 8th company," said Major Atkyns, running with full speed across a field, and jumping into a lane which led to the enemy; the men closely followed, but before we could gain the lane, several of them fell severely wounded. The Carlists having commenced a sharp fire from every window in each house, down the lane we went, and in a few moments we came to the road, and close to the Carlists who fled to the gates of the town, and gained the inside. A heavy piece of Artillery now opened upon us, from a fortified house at the corner of the gate, and every loop-hole round the walls blazed in defiance, yet on we went, men still dropping. In

vain did General Chichester give the halt, whether in mistake or
wilfully, I cannot say. But our buglers sounded the advance, and
two of them were shot dead while yet sounding; 'for God sake
Riflemen, get under cover, you will every one of you be [shot,' cried
the General, as the bullets fell thick around him, and the rushing
whiz of the still more dreadful grape shot passed his ear; we ran
forward to the gates, but to enter without scaling ladders was impossible, or I am sure we should have been into the town at that time;
we turned to the right, and found our way into a church; here
100 of us rested for the night, the remainder occupying the houses
adjoining.

" Several men got wounded in attempting to get to an hotel, close
by where there was plenty of wine from Madeira to Bordeaux; I
bought a bottle of champagne for 4 coppers ($2\frac{1}{4}d.$), which the seller
had risked his limbs, perhaps his life to get. The Carlists being so
close, and we once outside the Church having no cover, stood a hundred chances to one of getting shot; yet in spite of this, we had
wine in abundance that night, as many by their looks next morning
told.

" The interior of the church this night might have been matched
against the church of Passages on the 12th July, 1836. Some men
found their way into the belfry, and the ringing of bells was kept
up to a late hour. The organ did its share of noise and discord,
and what with fatigue, wine, and uproar, I fell fast asleep; daylight
was peeping, when I was roused to fall in ; the lads in the belfry
had already commenced their amusement, and the Carlist gunners
theirs, all to the same tune as last night. I must confess I felt very
much pleased on being told I had no occasion to leave the church as
I had possession of the company's papers, for even then I would
sooner have saved a Carlist than have shot one, so I contented myself
with munching a biscuit, and thinking on all I had seen and was
likely to see; this continued a short time, when amidst the confused roar of musketry and artillery I heard loud cheering.—I could
remain no longer, and ran towards the gates, they were already
partly opened, and some of the 1st regiment and Rifles were scaling
the outsides to get into the windows of the houses adjoining, I
passed in with some trouble, numbers trying to do the same, each
striving to be first into the town. Major M'Intosh here lost his cocked

hat, a musket ball carrying it clean off his head, *and he may thank me for not getting one through his head*—it was promised him, and at this moment it was all but carried into execution.

"The second barrier was then carried, and at that moment I saw a comrade named Swan running, with his cap in his hand full of coppers, calling to a chum, 'Take these—I've got plenty of silver;' while he yet spoke a bullet closed his lips and eyes, and the coppers lay scattered on the ground.

"A Carlist was taken from one of the houses between the barricades; he was torn from an old woman, a young woman and two children that clung round him, hurried down the stairs and shot at the door; the Carlist had fought bravely from house to house, and I suppose he had been the last to fly, he never spoke a word, nor uttered an exclamation.

" We had now gained the second barricade, our men still dropping without a chance of returning a shot with effect; as the Carlists had now retreated to the townhouse, which held out to the last. We lost a brave young officer named Wheat, who was shot in gaining this point, one much regretted by all the regiment; our bugle-major fell here also, severely wounded, and a young bugler named Crawley was shot through the head; the bugle-major died the next day. A Carlist soldier, the last that retreated, died bravely, he was wounded in attempting to gain the townhouse with three others, and before he could get to the door the others had entered and closed it; one of our shots struck him—he knocked against the door for admittance; but the Carlists were too much in danger to open it, and the poor fellow became the mark for forty rifles and muskets; finding he could not escape he turned his face to us and died, crying ' *Viva Carlos Quinto ! !'*

" I had now made my way into a house, where finding an old lady and her two daughters in the greatest terror for their lives, I assured them they had nothing to fear from me, and there being no time to doubt me, they at once placed themselves under my protection, nor had they reason to regret having done so, as the treatment some women met with from our troops proved afterwards. The conflict still continued, the Carlists keeping up a determined fire from the town-house, and an adjacent line of buildings, our men returning fire from every house opposite, from the doorway to the top window;

at last a rush was made to force the strong barricaded door of the town-house, and instantly the Carlists ceased firing, and put the butt ends of their muskets out of the looped stone walls, and windows of the building; while a white handkerchief was seen extended to us from an upper window."

Of the taking of this place, Mr. Farr has also an interesting sketch, the concluding part of which is as follows.

" A very short time after the town was taken, the fort surrendered at discretion : here again the British Legion in an instant obeyed the voice of their chiefs, and spared every life. General Evans took another very humane precaution, being aware that the Chapelgorris never gave or received quarter, that they put every one to death as every one put them to death ; he had the fore-thought before the assault took place, to send them to a distance to occupy a hill, under the pretence that two Carlist battalions, who where known to be in the neighbourhood, might during the confusion of the attack and assault, make a sortie from some woody and mountain height, and try to turn his positions ; and as it is the invariable custom when a town is taken by storm to give it up to plunder, had the Chapelgorris arrived before the guards had been put in different houses, a few women who remained most foolishly in the town, would most likely have been put to death or maltreated. About what and for whom had General Evans taken these humane precautions ? About a town and for a garrison commanded by General Soroa, the very general who, at Fuenterabia, when the English on their first attack were driven back, and when eleven of them were taken prisoners, signed and ordered the execution of these our unfortunate countrymen.

" To close the line of operation, it was now requisite to get posses- sion of the very strong town of Fuenterabia : to spare the unnecessary effusion of blood, General Evans sent a summons to the town—their reply was a very natural one, ' As we put you English to death on all occasions, of course you have put to death the garrison of the town and fort of Irun, and will put us to death likewise ; we may as well die fighting, as be butchered in cold blood.' When they were told that not an individual of the garrison or fort had been hurt, al- though taken by storm, they received the intelligence with an ironical smile of mockery and incredulity ; protestations and assertions were in vain, not a word would they believe ; but they said, if it reall be true, we will surrender the town, but we must have occular demonstration of the fact, before we can credit it;" and occular demonstration they had, for two of their officers were allowed to ride into Irun, accompanied by Colonel Lezama, where they found the garrison alive and well treated.

Having no idea that any act of kindness could proceed from any other motive, but that of concealed or avowed fear, they now begun to shuffle and hesitate, and try to get out of their contract. To my surprise, an aid-de-camp came galloping to report they could not surrender unless an article should be inserted in the capitulation, that they should be the first prisoners exchanged. I was standing close to General Evans at the time, and he immediately said, addressing himself to Generals Seoane, Jaurregui, Lord John Hay, Colonel Wylde, Generals Chichester and Fitzgerald, and the officers of the staff, ' as the town of Irun was carried by storm, by the laws and usages of war the garrison have forfeited their lives, and therefore I am of opinion, we can grant the terms :' and they were accordingly granted, and which was looked upon as a final settlement; but the surprise was increased when again an aid-de-camp came back, bringing a message, ' that they would not surrender, unless one of their officers, accompanied by an English officer, went to the head-quarters of Don Carlos, to have his consent to the capitulation.' This was evidently carrying the joke too far; the answer of General Evans was at once prompt and decisive. ' To spare blood, all that one soldier can honourably ask or grant to another, has been accorded ; in five minutes, if the capitulation is not brought here signed on their parts, and the gates of the town opened, the five minutes once expired, the fire from our batteries commences.' Nearly four minutes had elapsed, when General Evans, ever thoughtful of the safety of others and regardless of his own, turned round and said, ' As the time is nearly expired, and you are all standing here very much exposed, you had better separate to the right and left, for however bad shots they are, they could not well help hitting some of you, were they to open their batteries.' We were standing on an eminence exactly before them, within point-blank range. To me it was a most interesting moment. In a few instants the gates of the town once more opened, and shortly after the garrison began to file out and deposit their arms on the glacis. The 6th Scotch regiment, under Colonel Ross, was

ordered to march into the town and take possession of it. I walked
down with them, Colonel Ross very kindly allowing me to accompany
him ;—when we were within about an hundred yards of the prisoners,
General Chichester having ordered Colonel Ross to halt his regiment,
the general addressed them, saying, 'Now, my brave fellows, I have
a request I feel convinced you will grant, that you will not cheer, or
shew any sign of exultation ; I am sure you have no wish to triumph
over, or hurt the feelings of a fallen enemy.' In Roman or Spartan
history a finer trait of real, noble, and chivalrous feeling does not
exist ; and this honourable feeling was displayed to a town where
eleven of our countrymen, having fallen into their hands as prisoners
had, contrary to the laws of war and nations, been most foully murdered.

" I now entered the town with Colonel Ross and the 6th regiment ;
not a living soul made their appearance. Having seen the
regiment drawn up in the Place d'Ames, at the further end of
the town, in about half-an-hour I returned down the main street.
Owing to the quiet and correct conduct of the regiment in taking
possession, in that short space of time a sort of confidence began to
exist, for several women were visible at the windows, and one seeing
me descend the street, opened the door of her house, and thinking
I looked tired and thirsty, which I really was, offered me a glass of
wine, which I received with thanks. The property of the different
officers was also most religiously respected. On my return to the
glacis, I found those that had horses to dispose of, selling them and
receiving ready money. What odd exchanges take place in time of
war ! I was very tired, and a friend of mine having made a purchase,
I got on its back, and what should I find myself seated on, but the
horse that belonged to the Carlist priest, who was chaplain to the
garrison of Fuenterabia, and had been made prisoner. Delighted at
being once more on horseback, I rode it to Irun to sleep ; the cause
of my being reduced to make a campaign on foot, was, that the horse
that I originally came out with from San Sebastian received a hurt
the first day, when Urineta was taken.

" Immediately after the capture of Irun and Fuenterabia, I inquired
of Colonel Shaw, who commanded the artillery, the number of guns
and the quantity of ammunition taken, as I was writing to a General
who was much interested in the Legion, and had never quitted the

Duke of Wellington's side in any one battle in Spain, nor even at Waterloo. He said, ' Tell the general when he and I were in Spain together, it took the Duke three days to get his army in order after Badajoz was taken by assault and given up to plunder; now you have seen with your own eyes, the day after a town has been taken by storm and given up to plunder, the men of the British Legion perfectly sober and steady, and under the completest order and discipline, and ready to take another.' No language can express the humanity, bravery, and excellent order of this much abused British Legion, although they were under the excitement of having taken a town by storm, and having plundered it the day before.

" Nothing is so difficult as to let loose the reins of discipline and all at once draw them tight again; and yet only two hours after the town was taken, the Royal Irish, one of the regiments who had formed the storming party, marched out more than seven hundred strong, drums beating and colours flying, only thirty men being absent when the muster roll was called over, perfectly sober, and under the most perfect order and control. Could the Duke of Wellington with his army ever do anything of the kind? Hear what Colonel Napier, their gallant historian says, after the glorious assault of Ciudad Rodrigo, in 1813. ' The allies now plunged into the streets from all quarters, for O'Toole's attack was also successful; and at the other side of the town, Pack's Portuguese meeting no resistance, had entered the place, and the reserves also came in. Then throwing off the restraints of discipline, the troops committed frightful excesses. The town was fired in three or four places, the soldiers menaced their officers, and shot each other—many were killed in the market place, intoxication soon increased the tumult, disorder every where prevailed, and at last the fury rising to an absolute madness, a fire was wilfully lighted in the middle of the great magazine, when the town and all in it would have been blown to atoms, but for the energetic courage of some officers and a few soldiers who still ' preserved their senses.' After the fall of Badajoz, Colonel Napier thus narrates the dreadful scene that ensued :—' Now commenced that wild and desperate wickedness which tarnished the lustre of the soldier's heroism. All indeed were not alike, for hundreds risked, and many lost, their lives in trying to stop the violence; but the madness generally prevailed, and as the worst of men were leaders here, all the dreadful passions of human nature were displayed. Shameless rapacity, brutal intemperance, savage lust, cruelty and murder, shrieks and piteous lamentations, groans, shouts, imprecations, the hissing of fires bursting from the houses, the crashing of doors and windows, and the reports of muskets used in violence, resounded for two days and nights in the streets of Badajoz! On the third, when the city was sacked, when the soldiers were exhausted by their own excesses, the tumult rather subsided than was quelled. The wounded men were then looked to—the dead disposed of!'

" ' Such unfortunately was the conduct of these troops.' says the pamphlet on Spanish policy, ' veterans in comparison to those of the Legion, commanded by experienced officers, and under a system of discipline severer than that of any other army in Europe, but which was inapplicable to the Legion ; they, moreover, had no Durango decrees rankling in their minds, and no mangled corpses of their comrades had been exposed in insult to their view just before the storming of Badajoz ; but at Irun the very same " injudicious officer" alluded to by Lord Carnarvon, commanded the garrison ; and how does he, for himself and for his companions in arms, speak to Don Carlos upon the conduct of the British Legion ? He surely cannot be a suspected historian of what took place on that occasion.

" For a proof of the humanity and generosity, as well as the bravery and sobriety of the Legion, I will quote the declaration of the bloody General Soroa himself, extracted from the pamphlet I have mentioned, in confirmation of my assertion.

" This memorial, addressed by the governor of Irun to Don Carlos, after stating the dispositions taken for the defence of the place, continues ; ' but, notwithstanding the prodigious valour all displayed, the exterior fortifications being demolished, it was impossible to resist the impetus and valour of the English division, which, with fixed bayonets and a tremendous fire, attacked us on the 17th—the few soldiers (for the greater part were already *hors de combat*.) having fallen back with the armed peasants upon the consistorial house, our last point of resistance, we considered our death inevitable, as the assault was to be made by the British Legion. Resolved to perish among the ruins of the edifice, we beheld the battalions advance, the ladders prepared, and ourselves surrounded on every side. The fort whose artillery might still have protected us, was no longer able to resist the attack, and surrendered at the moment when the English, in the market-place, reinforced on every side, passed the fosse, and were about to force the outward gate. In this most critical situation some officers of the Legion advanced, and with the greatest generosity offered us quarter. Sire, an offer so unexpected surprised us for a moment; but they pledged their honour, and resistance being madness, we laid down our arms.

" It would be prolix, Sire, were we to extol, as it would be our duty, the delicacy and the regard we received from men, who, on our part, have been treated with the utmost rigour of war, and at a moment, when, in the fulness of our hearts, we see every attention heaped upon our officers and soldiers, we should be wanting to the noblest dictates of gratitude, if we failed to make known this heroic conduct to your Majesty.

"Sire, your Majesty's troops, although beaten, are not dishonoured, for it is certain, that, in the whole of the war, no fortified place has defended itself with equal valour against such superior forces, our conduct being even qualified as fool-hardy by those to whom we owe our lives.

" The officers and soldiers, Sire, who are prisoners, are worthy of every consideration, and we, as their chiefs, in their name and at their request, earnestly solicit that your Majesty will command the generals of your royal army to treat with all humanity the individuals of the above-mentioned Legion who may fall into their hands—for justice requires it as well as the gratitude of your vassals, your royal and never-failing clemency, and the interests of your Majesty's service: near seven hundred families of those who composed the garrison of this town and Fuenterabia, would have mourned the death of their fathers, brothers, relatives, and friends—they all live, and live for your Majesty, by the noble generosity of their enemies. May your Majesty listen to the voice of these unfortunate individuals, who have been snatched from the brink of the grave, and benignantly receiving our petitions, may your Majesty grant them."

No. 36.

CHAPTER XXVI.

Anecdotes and reflection s arising from the capture of Irun—Conduct of Col. Arbuthnott—Captain Peirce—A private soldier—Captain Roberts—Chapelgorris and slaughter—Entrance into the houses—Anecdote of a Fiddler—Reflections—Charlie Scott and the piano—Drinking Wine—The Priest—Sketch of Captain Dickson, and other incidents.

In addition to the foregoing narratives of Mr. Farr, Colonel Martin, the Rifleman, and my own, which make up the previous chapter, and which give a plain account of the taking of Irun, a plain account far from being exaggerated by descriptive flourishes, I find that not to add a few more incidents out of many, which are in my possession, would be to leave this part of our campaign imperfectly narrated. What Mr. Farr says, relative to the good behaviour of the soldiers of the Legion after the capture of the town, compared with the Wellingtonian army in a similar situation, is true; but the causes of the difference must be stated. There was no difference in the men:—as soldiers, the two armies—those of Wellington and Evans, were the same, and to them the spoiling of a town had the same exciting stimulants. The causes why the Legion did not commit the same horrible atrocities, will be gathered from some of the incidents related in this chapter. However we must be just; we must not make a veil of partiality to cover those enormities which were committed by the Legion ; for we *had* a share of pillage, and its attendant crimes ; and all we can say in favour of ourselves is, that we were not so awfully monstrous as our fathers-in-arms who sacked Badajoz. The following paragraphs have no order of arrangement, I give them here, as they occur to me.

Colonel Arbuthnott, brother-in-law to General Evans, and who had up to the time remained in a quiet official situation at Santander, was put in command of the storming party at the Behobia gate of Irun. Whatever opinions might have been circulating about his love of personal safety, which opinions did circulate, and which I mention only to shew their injustice; these were honorably confuted as ground-

less. The self devotion of Colonel Arbuthnott, was the admiration
of all those, and they were many, who beheld him. He was most
peculiarly conspicuous in attempting to blow up the gate. This
was only an attempt, so far as destruction to the gate ensued; but
the explosion overturned part of the barricades, and for the moment
startled the defending garrison, so much as to cause them to retreat
to the inner barrier.

This gave an opportunity for another officer, possessing the highest
qualifications for such work, to shew his bravery to advantage.
Captain Pierce of the 1st regiment, was that officer; and he will
perhaps pardon me, if, in addition to the Fernando cross—the compliments paid him in general orders—and the unmixed sentiments of
admiration from all his fellow countrymen in arms, as well as the
Spanish witnesses of his bravery, he will perhaps pardon me, if in
addition to all these, I add my humble mite of approving praise.
I have not the honour of knowing Captain Pierce, I was not even
acquainted with his person in Spain, for his distinguishing deeds
were performed near the close of our service; it is only by the oft repeated stories of his gallantry, then told among the men, and which I
have since heard confirmed by some of his brother officers, that I am
enabled to speak of him. He was the first officer—in fact the first
person, who mounted the barriers by the scaling ladders at the Behobia
or eastern gate. Exposed to the full fire of those who lined the
inner barriers, and showered small shot through their loop-holes,
the gallant Pierce stood on an elevated position waving his sword,
and cheering those who struggled on the ladders to support him.
The houses too, on each side of the street, emitted their obliquely
flying shot from the windows, which took deadly effect on some of
the poor fellows who mounted the barrier. The first who gained the
elevation of his gallant officer, was shot dead, and it betokened the
presence of mind as well as courage of young Pierce, to take the
body of this man as he did, and drag it inwards, so that it might
not fall down among those who were mounting the ladders, and
produce discouragement. The men as they got up stepped over the
body of this soldier, and others stepped over some of their bodies,
until a party sufficiently strong was mustered to go forward to the
renewed storm. Pierce continued to be distinguished as a leader of
the foremost, until the last shots were fired : his name will be again

heard of in connection with the wonderful capture of Mr, Dickson, among the Carlist prisoners.

The man who was shot on first mounting the barricade, left behind him a considerable excitement relative to the circumstances of his death. He did not belong to Captain Pierce's company, but as the storming party were not only men of different companies of the 1st regiment, but a number of them volunteers from the Rifles, and the royal Irish ; and as this man had been taunted by his comrades the previous evening for cowardice—Captain Pierce on seeing him join the forlorn hope volunteers, ordered him to go to the rear, and stay with his company, adding " go you coward, I heard your comrades tell you to your face last night, that you had been skulking." The man replied, "then the comrades you heard say so, were liars, and were they near enough the front, I would prove them so ; it is because of that taunt that I am here, and I shall not go back; you can try me by a court-martial—or provost me for disobedience of orders, should you have it in your power to do so ; but the officer or man who calls me a coward, and who would prove me one, must come to the front for evidence, for it is not to the rear I will go to argue with them what I am." " Well spoken my good fellow, you are the the kind of man I want,"—was the approving response of Pierce. This martyr to the enmity, or at least the jokes of some of his comrades went on, and as was said, he was the first that mounted the scaling ladder, and was the first shot on the top of it.

While these resolute fellows made an entrance on the eastern side of the town, the 8th regiment, and a mixture of Spanish regulars and Chapelgorris, attacked in like manner the western barriers. Mr. Farr states, that to avoid a wholesale murder of the garrison and inhabitants, General Evans ordered the Chapelgorris to occupy an out-post unconnected with the storm. It is quite true that the General ordered them, and that they were marched to that position as a reserve ; but no Chapelgorris will remain inactive, if there is the slightest chance of killing a Carlist ; and their brothers and fathers the Chapelchurris, are always actuated by the same feelings, when the death of a Christino comes within possibility—therefore the Chapelgorris though ordered, did not remain on reserve as some of the successive incidents will shew.

After a good many obstacles, my regiment the 8th, made its way through gardens, and over the walls to the gate ; one of the obstacles was rather remarkable however, and it must be mentioned. We found ourselves exposed to the cannon shot of a heavy piece, stationed at about eight hundred yards to our left, in the direction of Feuntarabia. A garden wall of ten or twelve feet high opposed us, and it was supposed that we must either get the ladders, or the Sappers to get over it; all of these being employed otherwise, and each bullet from this gun coming rather nearer us than was comfortable—we stood, every man from the Colonel downwards, vexed at this baffling stone-wall. " Mind your heads !" some one exclaimed, who was looking out to watch the flash of the cannon, so that we might crouch beneath a partial bank to save the smashes of the bullets, that were throwing the earth about us. We had bowed to save this one, and we had good cause, for it coursed across us at about the level of our heads, had we been standing upright, and to our great satisfaction made such a gap in the wall, that ere they could send another, the whole, or nearly the whole of the regiment had entered in the direction we had been wishing to go.

After passing this and a few other obstacles, we were at the gate. Here an officer, whom I regret not to have mentioned earlier—for he had distinguished himself before this, (particularly on the 16th of March)—here this officer—Captain Roberts, was conspicuously brave. Though we found it necessary to scale the defences ; Captain Roberts had mounted and was bravely leading on some men, who made their way through the partitions of the adjoining houses, exposed to the shot of those defending them, and in a fearful position was preparing to burst the gate. Fortunately for his party, and perhaps for us all, an inhabitant came, and as we were afterwards informed, gave up the keys in the hope of purchasing safety by the good officer. Poor old fellow ! his two daughters were looking from a window, even though they were exposed to the shot—anxious to see what became of the official venture of their father. Captain Roberts got the keys from him, and as the gate opened, and we were admitted, we cheered the old Carlist. I was near enough to see that he trembled at first, but that as we cheered him on passing, he began to gather confidence ; and we deemed him fortunate in having purchased our good graces, while many of his unhappy towns-men, were still fighting, or lying as some were, wounded and trampled among merciless feet, I had glanced at him and deemed him fortunate, and so perhaps were he and his daughters thinking of themselves, when a party of the Chapelgorris crushing in among our men, dashed their bayonets into him ere, by us, the atrocious deed could be prevented. This was the first blood on our entering; the shells and muskets having killed those lying on the street, and so far as I witnessed, there was not a great many more killed in a similar way; still there were some.

The next object that attracted my attention, was a Chappelgorri with the foot of a man, which had been severed by a shell, stuck on his bayonet, and the bayonet fixed on the muzzle of his musket; he capering merrily along the street with it.

Though there was still battle farther down the street for those fond of fighting, many took an early opportunity to burst open the doors of shops and dwelling houses, and help themselves; some, however, were not immediately fortunate in their choice of houses; for, while many houses were undefended, others had those in them, who perhaps expecting no mercy seemed unwilling to take the chance of receiving it. I, with others, entered a house of this kind, and when we had passed through the first apartment of the ground floor and saw nothing but the furniture, we were hastily pursuing our inclination to go up stairs when a shot came down from the second floor, and a Spanish sergeant who struggled to get before me fell dead. The next moment I was struck by a bullet which barely missing my shoulder entered the folds of my great coat, which was strapped on my back, and passing through it, lodged among my books. Its force nearly hurled me overhead, and those behind supposing perhaps, that I was shot, and seeing the Spaniards done for, in reality—commenced firing up the stairs : when one fired he was a signal for every one to fire, and the smoke, with the falling plasterwork brought down by the bullets, so choaked the narrow stair-case that we were almost suffocated. The cry behind us, was, "fire up the stair!" "shoot them in front if they wont go on!" while we in front being forced up and not knowing where we were going, groped among thick darkness with musketry ringing above and below. What was most alarming, were the bullets coming through the floors from the lower apartments after we were up; the men who fired them, not knowing that we were above them. At last a cessation of the firing enabled us to

see what was around us, and to our satisfaction we were in a house,
which by appearance seemed to be well worth a short fight. A man
was lying dead at a back window, where it was supposed he was
making his escape when the first of our men got up stairs, by whom
he had been shot. Just as I took a glance at his body and its death
wound, I saw another man trying to escape through a garden, three
or four muskets were discharged at him from another house, and ultimately he fell.

It was an awful picture of war that was now unfolded to us, and
yet there were many pleasing traits of character observable in different men. I could not help remarking on the various propensities
which were following their impulses. Among other oddities, when
I entered one apartment where no spoilers had yet been, I saw the
barber of my company playing on a violin. He was a good natured
young man, named James Galbraith ; and while others made havoc
and raged for plunder, *Jamie* was indulging a desire which he had long
cherished when thinking on home and its merriments, namely, that of
having a "jig on the fiddle" as he termed it; another "Glasgow
chappie" came into the same apartment looking for spoil, but seeing
nothing sufficiently valuable or portable, stood inactive for a few minutes surveying himself in a splendid mirror that hung on the wall.
The sound of smashed glass in some other rooms reached his ear, and
kindled in him the contagious propensity of destructiveness ; " hets !
to h— wi' yer fiddle !—break it !" he uttered in a contemptuous tone,
and at the same time taking the butt of his musket, dashed the mirror to the floor in crackling fangments. The bayonet which was
fixed on the muzzle, came slightly in contact with the fiddler's arm,
but the latter took no further notice—indeed he was so absorbed in
the music of " *Corn riggs are bonny*," that he had neither heard nor
seen the one who broke the mirror, he took no further notice than
merely to step a pace to his rear, and say, " tak care min, ye'll break
the fiddle.".

Thus, were exhibited the varied leading propensities of the human
animal. One being susceptible in a high degree of the charms of
music, forsook the pillage even the wine and the brandy though there
were an abundance of these, and though at other times he was by
habit partial to the stimulus of either —this man having never heard
the notes of a violin during his two years' foreign service, was to a

high degree excited by the sound of that instrument, and as he told me afterwards "wanted to get up a dance" he having lost all consciousness of present realities by trying as he said if he " still minded his auld tunes." The other, was a person on which music was charmless noise; and in the absence of those qualities that delight in the " concord of sweet sounds," he had no particularly developed moral faculty to counteract his very powerful propensity of destructiveness. As the musical man is suddenly infected with a desire to be musical when he hears the harmony of pleasing concord;—as he will involuntarily move his feet, his fingers and his head to the sound, and be animated to ardour by the martial march—or subdued to affection by the softer-souled notes of love;—so is the man whose nature is unmusical, ready to be excited by the contagious influence of propensities kindred to his own. The one who broke the mirror would have perhaps spared it, had he not heard the sound of glass and earthenware breaking in another apartment; he hearing these sounds had his ruling faculty infected, and he smashed the glass to pieces, urging the musician at the same time *" to break the fiddle."*

I may mention another case almost similar, which came also under my own view five minutes or less, after that just mentioned. We being in a house which belonged to a rich inhabitant, there was a drawing-room with elegant furniture, one article of which was a pianoforte and nothing less than one of " Broadwood's" too all the way from London. There are no carpets on Spanish floors; but the wood is polished to a brightness that makes you feel as if you trode something richer—something that makes your feet prouder than a carpet does; and this floor with the surrounding furniture, and curtains,--- which I suspect from the nature of their manufacture and which will be explained hereafter, would put any upholsterery goods in London to the blush—this apartment from its unusual display of richness was· to those who sought plunder, like the magnet to the steel, while to some others it was full of inspiring veneration that almost forbade their entrance. Among the latter was a young man named Charles Scott a native of Hawick—the person who shot the Carlist officer at the beginning of the engagement on the 15th of March as mentioned previously in this work, and a person who would be mentioned more frequently for his good soldiership, were I able to give all the incidents which deserve notice; this man familiarly styled " Charlie" was one who thought it a great shame to "break things," and he was one who was also charmed to a reverential respect for the fine furniture. Charlie, had probably never been in such a room before, most certainly, according to his own confession, he had never seen a piano-forte until then, far less had he ever dreamed that *his* fingers could make such sounds as he heard produced when he *brizzed* them as he said (pushed) against the keys. The instrument was now profaned by one whose vulgar hands would have been horror to the delicate fingers of the Senorita which had with fascinating grace swept it with their fairy touches. Nothing perhaps could have been at greater variance than the certainty that the embodicement of the angelically lovely and earthly loving being that is sometimes singing and playing and making thraldom for the masculine world on a piano, had been the priestess of that spot where now sat in capering glee the unmusical Charlie : nothing could have been at greater variance than the certainty that *she* had been there, and the certainty that one whom nature had not designed to be, and art could never make, a musician, now defiled in vulgar sport, this most refined cabinet of refined elegance. Yet Charlie was an amiable young man of his kind; he was perhaps the very antipode of any being that had ever been seen at one; but though the genteel aversion of vulgarity, or the aristocratic repulsion of plebeianism, has seldom been seen in such justifiable grounds, as when the painful exhibition of the Hawick stocking-maker at Irun; still here are, as will be seen, a species of beings far beneath Charlie.

While he enjoyed himself making as he said "bonny soonds" another man of the same company came behind him, and having brought up a twenty-four pound cannon ball purposely from the street, stood ready to make sport of the innocent Charlie. The latter was laughing in an ecstacy of delight at the "funny noise he was making with his fingers," when, down plunged the cannon ball through the instrument, carrying with it the musical interior, and falling with no gentle weight on Charlie's toes. Those who had time to see this, set up a shout of laughter, and Charlie turned round and said "man, yer a spitefu niggar! what ill was the bit moosic thing doin' t'ye? an' ye've shauked (crushed) my taes into the bargain." About half an hour after this, I saw Charles with a ham rolled up in a sheet, he was eating a slice with sugar on it, having been as I supposed in a grocer's shop.

We had not been long in this house until a dozen or more of us were seated around a table, drinking wine which we found bottled in considerable abundance. We had all the necessary decanters, glasses, and appurtenances of genteel wine drinking save a cork-screw ; where that was kept we were not able to discover, and none of us were disposed to lose time by looking for it. The necks of the bottles were broken off by a sharp stroke on the edge of the table, and when one broke farther down, and the wine was by this means lost, the person breaking it, was comforted by two or three voices calling " never mind that ! here's plenty more." We were at our wine when some of the Chapelgorris entered, who, though on ordinary occasions willing enough to drink with the English, were otherwise employed then. They upbraided us for sitting idle, and one of them who had been as he doubtless believed, well employed, came forward swinging a Carlist head by the hair. He had severed it with his knife which was still open in his hand, and his comrades set up a savage shout as he came indignantly up to the table and swept the glasses off with the bloody head holding it by the long black hair. A mirror similar to the one broken by the " Glasgow chappie" in another apartment, was hanging in this, and the Chapelgorri demolished it by throwing the head with a vehement force, perhaps deeming that its reflection rebuked the fearful realities of the scene.

About this time, an incident was in the progress of occurrence outside, which has been told me by some of the eye witnesses. A jolly fat priest had been discovered hidden somewhere, and was dragged out to the daylight of the street. He was surrounded by a host who demanded his money, and having got all he had, demanded more. They also took from him the keys of the Sacrista which to fall into the hands of heretics—and they were heretics indeed—was a cause of greater pain to the poor old man, than even the loss of his dubloons, three or four of which as was said, were the amount of money taken from him. My informant came up to the relief of the reverend gentleman, shortly after his money had been taken from him, and he then found him wearing a straw hat which an Irishman was officious enough to put on him, in place of the legitimate clerical canoe, which he—the Irishman himself wore. Two were laying a bet as to whether a bayonet could go through him ; one said if it went in at his belly, the point would not be seen at his back, another urged it would. A third was setting him on a tub turned bottom upwards—saying, when the poor old man was duly elevated—" there now ;—there now ;—prache us a sarmon on the advantages of a pihyous life !" The interference of an officer, saved the holy man from farther indignity.

The ever active, and ever usefully employed, Chichester, had, after exposing himself to the hottest of the engagement in the streets, and holding up a white pennant repeatedly, to induce the garrison to surrender, gone forward and was the first, or at least the most conspicuous in fighting against the Chapelgorris, and other Spaniards who sought to kill the Carlist prisoners. Having secured the safety of these, he was next employed in running from house to house, and street to street, causing the wine and other liquors to be run out to prevent drunkenness. Generally, a ball was fired into a cask of brandy, or a pipe of wine beneath, and another above, leaving it to empty itself at leisure. A man inclined to drink, might be seen with a china or chrystal vessel, which he threw away when satisfied. Another would come, and say " ah ! this is just what I've been looking for ; lend me one of these shoes—no, give me that boot, its new and cleaner than the shoe, and then he would fill—as I myself, saw one do—the boot with wine, and drink till satisfied.

At various parts of the streets officers were seen guarding the helpless prisoners, who were found hiding in cellars and houses, and who, but for the exertions of our officers and men, would have been put to death by their own countrymen. I saw one surrounded by Colonel Hogg—Captains Roberts, Shields, and Forbes—the prisoner was, as if leaning on the back of one of these officers while the others covering his body on the two sides, and in his rear kept off the Chapelgorris, one of whom sprang from one side to the other, trying to poke his bayonet into the trembling Carlist. The same was seen in all other parts of the town ; but all were not equally successful in saving their prisoners· I was told of some of the 1st regiment who had one in charge, and who seeing two Chapelgorris following them, closed round their man, telling the red-caps to keep off : the latter said, in the Basque tongue, that there was no need to keep them off, for they would do him no injury, that they were also following to guard him. This put the Englishmen a little off their guard, seeing which, one of the Chapelgorris plunged his bayonet into the prisoner saying " the English do not know how to take care of prisoners."

A variety of incidents occurred at the time of ransacking the town, many of them honorable to the soldiers, and a considerable number not so honorable—a few even fearfully atrocious ; but as I find the materials of this work swelling it beyond the size I wished to preserve, I am under the necessity of omitting them, as there are many important events yet to mention, which cannot be omitted.   I must first, however, give a sketch of Mr. Dickson, who distinguished himself so much in rescuing Captain Hamilton of the artillery, in a former engagement with the Carlists, and who was found among them in the town of Irun.   I copy the following sketch from the " Mirror of the World" to which it was communicated by a correspondent, who had an account of Mr. Dickson's adventure, I believe from his own lips, this correspondent says :—

" Captain Dickson was not one of those who served under De Lacy Evans, nor was he one of those few Englishmen who, at times, left this country to join their fortunes with the cause of Don Carlos ; he was a half-pay captain of the British Service, the son of an English admiral, and went out to Spain, it would appear, merely to see what was passing between the contending parties, for he declined to accept an appointment under the English general.   He was perfect as a Spanish linguist, having resided a number of years in Trinidad, and other of the south-western colonies where the Spanish language is spoken, and that qualification, with a restless activity, led him into contact with some of the military personages in the North of Spain, even though his intention on going out was to be a mere spectator. We shall pass over his adventures, such as rescuing an officer of the artillery from the enemy, and various other acts of intrepidity, and confine our sketch to his adventure among the Carlists, when the English Christino general attacked the town and fortress of Irun. The reduction of this place was looked forward to with considerable interest by those concerned either as actors or spectators, and among the latter was Captain Dickson.

" The attack began on the 16th of May, 1837, at about one o'clock, p. m., the battery firing the first shots at the English general and his staff, as they drew near to reconnoitre.   One of these shots killed a horse of the staff, and carried away the arm of a servant who was holding a horse for his master to mount ; but they were immediately

responded to by opening of the English artillery, the first ball from
which carried away the flag-staff of the battery on which the red flag
of " No Surrender" was displayed.   In a few minutes the flag was
again hoisted, and the battering of about thirty pieces of cannon continued to and fro between the attack and defence.   At four, p. m., a
flag of truce was sent by Evans, offering to leave off hostilities if the
town would surrender ; but the gallant officer, Major Macduff, and
those who accompanied him, were, contrary to the usages of war
and the law of nations, shot by the enemy, to whom they offered
terms. At the same time, a Spanish officer was sent in with a similar
emblem of warlike faith to the battery ; and the garrison of that,
being either more respectful of the laws of war than the garrison of
the town was, or more respectful to a countryman than a foreigner,
listened to what he had to say, but refused to surrender.   The cannonade then recommenced, and went on without intermission on both
sides, until night stopped the strife for that day.

    " It was about four o'clock, P. M., when Captain Dickson passing
through the town of Hernani, on his way to Irun, he having gone
the evening before rearward to San Sebastian to provide himself with
what was required to live in the open air for a few days and nights,
the town being expected to hold out for a considerable time.   Dickson having thus gone back to San Sebastian on the 15th, was not
with the army when it marched from Hernani on the morning of the
16th, nor did he know it was to move so soon, else he would have
been with it, for he did not intend to lose any of the fighting.   As
it was, he had lost the commencement, and he was now on his way
from San Sebastian, when passing through Hernani, he was accosted
by General Gurrea, the commander of a division of the Queen's
army and asked if, as a favour, he would carry a letter to General
Evans.   He hesitated, and observed that if the letter was of importance, that it would be advisable to send it by some one under an escort,
as he, though intending to be at the head quarters of Evans that night,
was by no means sure that he would be there, owing to the probability
of the communication not being clear.   He was answered that the
road was clear, but that on going forward to Astigarraga, a village
about a mile farther on the road, he would be furnished with an escort on applying to an officer who was stationed with a battalion
there , and farther, the general begged of him to undertake the deli-

very of the letter, " for," said he, " I have just been informed that two Navarrese battalions, of seven or eight hundred men each, are in the mountains above Irun, and will descend during the night, surprise General Evans, cut their way into the town to reinforce the garrison, which, being so reinforced, may sally out and produce consequences fatal to the investing army. It is therefore imperative that this letter which contains information of this, should go forward immediately, and my knowledge of your energy, Senor, makes me anxious to commit it to your care, knowing that you, beyond any one I can send, will not fail to push forward." Captain Dickson being thus pressed to undertake the delivery of this letter, being promised an escort, and having no objections to do the favour required by probabilities of such importance, took it, and proceeded onwards.

On arriving at the village where he was to have the escort, he applied for it, and was told that he might be escorted if he chose, but that there was no necessity for such caution—that the road was perfectly safe, General Evans having picquets on parts of it, and Spanish regiments being in all the villages, with picquets on the heights, besides, that there were five English Lancers mounted, and about twenty men on foot belonging to the Legion, who had just come out of San Sebastian, and were going on to head-quarters. This intelligence was perfectly satisfactory—indeed, he wished no other escort; for what he was most particular about, was to have some one to show him the way.

The party moved onwards, and arrived at the little town of Oarzun, a place rather more than half way to where they were going, measuring the distance from where, as a party, they joined together. On coming to that place, they met a few more Englishmen, who, under an officer, had been left in rear, during the early part of the day, unable to march. This officer taking command of the whole party, and some of that party being sick, had more than a common difficulty to get them put in motion ; and though he might have got quarters for them all night, there was no food nor medical assistance, and, beyond that, it was necessary to push on to join the army, for the Spanish picquets had just communicated that the regiments of the enemy seen among the mountains, were supposed to be approaching, and that it was intended to allow them to enter Oarzun if they chose—that the Spanish picquets were to close in on Evans rear, so that no midnight attempt might be made to break through his positions, to gain the town or fortress of Irun. These reports rendered it necessary to warn all detached parties to beware of taking shelter in houses on the roadside; and Captain Dickson being aware that this was the news contained in the letter, urged the party onwards, knowing the necessity of getting out of the way, though he saw that the importance of his trust was partly obviated, the intelligence of the reinforcement having come to that place from General Evans. He had previously been riding, but as he chose for a short distance to walk, he gave his servant, who was mounted on a mule, his cloak to carry, while he put one of the sick men on his horse. He had not gone far, when another man fell behind, declaring that he could not go on—that he would rather die where he was quietly, than be tortured by going any farther; and Dickson, seeing that this man was really sick and unable to walk, tried to bring him along to have a ride on his horse. This he attempted for a short distance, but the inability of the sick man to walk rendered the possibility of overtaking the party hopeless; and Dickson, giving him a half dollar to purchase something for himself, told him to go back to Oarzun, and get into some of the houses where there were women; "for," said he, "it matters not what the Spaniards may be, the kindness of women is universal, and no woman will give you up, even to an enemy, if you go and beg her protection;" and turning his face to his own journey, he commenced running to overtake the party. He ran onwards, and at every turn of the road where he thought he would come up with them, he found himself still alone: he ran on and on, but he never saw or heard of them again.

Having travelled a considerable distance, perhaps four miles, he supposed that the army of Evans must be close to him, and yet it did not seem to be there, for he expected to see occasional rockets, or shells, or hear a shot; but all was dark, and still as death. "Where shall I go?" said he to himself; "we were to keep the main road—I have kept it; we were to find the army at a less distance than three miles from Oarzun—I must have travelled four." While he thus soliloquised, a shot flashed before his eyes! and another—and another, until five went off, and the bullets cut the air with a sharp whiz past him. Startled for a moment by these, and observing a bank of earth considerably higher on his right hand than the road, he bowed himself for shelter beneath it, and the firing ceased. By that, he concluded that he was the object fired at ; but he was not, and, before we go farther with him, we must tell what these shots were fired at, and where he was.

" The forces under the English general had been, during the afternoon, on and near the main road ; but, with the exception of one English and one Spanish regiment, they had removed artillery and infantry, after the darkness set in, to other positions, from which the bombardment and the storm were to commence in the morning. The two regiments spoken of were, however, left, and they being nearly beneath the enemy's battery, closer indeed than the enemy was aware of, and to prevent suspicion of their proximity, being all quiet and withdrawn behind a wall and some houses on that side of the road opposite to the bank already mentioned. Captain Dickson was thus permitted to advance as far as their position, without seeing aught of the enemy. He passed even farther, for though some parties of these regiments must have seen or heard a person passing, they had no orders to challenge any one coming from their own rear ; and as different officers on duty, and corporals relieving sentries, were occasionally passing softly along, and all vigilance was directed to one point only—that which constituted the front of the position, a point where a double sentry was posted, and near to which Captain Dickson had just got —no notice was taken of him. No notice was taken, until perhaps the noise of his footsteps sounding on the acute ears of the Carlist sentries at the embrazures of the battery, caused them to turn their eyes with a keener discernment to that point where the bank ended, and which keenness discovered the double sentry keeping its watch, with the men's heads visible over the bank. Captain Dickson would have been stopped at this point, but, just as he approached it, the enemy discovering the two men on their post, shot them dead. So instantly mortal were the bullets, that not even a groan followed their wounds, and he was not aware that any person was fired at but himself. Before the picquet to which the two men belonged had crept softly up to the spot, which softness of approach they were obliged to observe to avoid being fired on, he concluded that the shots were not fired at him, and that, though they seemed by the flashes to be near, they might still be at a considerable distance ; he therefore moved slowly and softly forward. He was now past the outposts of the Christino army, and this was the time and the means by which he passed. He believed he had yet to meet them, and a few yards bringing him again under a wall which covered him from the battery, he went onwards with that expectation.

" In about five minutes he found himself where the road separated into two branches; one was little more than a bye-path, and the other seemed the continuation of the high road. He hesitated there for a short time, questioning whether he could be right in taking the road or the path, but he took the road, calling to mind that he had been instructed not to go off it, until he came to the head-quarters of the English general. Looking carefully before him to see if there was any appearance of a town, he discovered, on suddenly emerging from betwixt two walls, that he was entering a street. He continued to go on at a smart walk, and his footsteps were resounding through the vacancy of the still night, when, with a thundering voice in front of him, a sentinel vociferated, " Quien viva ?" (who comes here ?) Supposing that this was the first sentry of one of Evans' Spanish regiments, he answered boldly in the Basque tongue that he was a Spaniard, knowing how easily, from his ability to converse in their own language, he could satisfy them about who he was when he would get up to them. However, instead of being told to advance, he was ordered by two or three voices to halt, and one of them again uttered in a fierce tone, which sounded as if there was no time to be lost, ' Who are you ?' Dickson, still believing it was a picquet of the Christino Spaniards, (the Queen's party,) answered ' English — a Spanish Englishman.' He saw at the same moment above a dozen muskets make their appearance through the loopholes of a barricade, and he heard a voice say in the Basque tongue, " No, hold your fire for a moment," and then the voice continued by inquiring through one of the loop-holes, ' What do you want ?' Dickson knew by these repeated questions that he was wrong ; for if he had been where he at first thought he was, the first answer would have sufficed. Thoughts flashed through his mind, all urging contrary means of escaping. It was but a few yards to run back, but then a dozen or a score of muskets were levelled at him through the loop-holes. Then he thought if he hesitated they would fire, or if he went forward without being ordered to advance they would fire, and he could hear them speaking in Basque within, of the propriety of shooting him or allowing him to

No. 37.

approach.   Not to give them any chance to suspect from his hesitation that he was an enemy, he told them that he had brought important news for them.

" News," said the person, that from his manner of speaking appeared to be the officer, " what is the news ?" " You will see by this
paper," said Captain Dickson.   He was then ordered to advance, and
doing so, handed in the letter addressed to General Evans, at one of
the loop-holes.

" Captain Dickson was not perfectly satisfied of their being Carlists,
although he strongly suspected they were; but, as he had not yet
betrayed himself either way, he considered he was safe in giving
in the letter ; for if they were Christinos, he was right in doing so ;
while if they were Carlists, he had no means of safety, not the lightest shadow of hope, but in giving them this letter under a pretence
that he had brought it to them out of friendship.   The officer perhaps not having light to read the address, or perhaps being unable
to read it, inquired of Captain Dickson who it was for.   " For General Evans," was the reply.   " Where did you get it ? was the next
question.   " From an orderly," was the answer.   The officer, from
the silence that ensued, seemed to have gone away with it, and meantime one of the sentries asked Dickson if he was a soldier or a civilian : the answer was " a civilian."   The next question was, " Have
you been with the king ?"   " No ; but I'm a friend," was the reply.
" A friend of whom ?" was the continued interrogation.   " Oh, God !
what am I to say ?" ejaculated the perplexed adventurer to himself ;
and as he thought of what he would say, and shifted his head a little
to a side that it might not be touching the muzzle of the musket
levelled at him by the interrogating sentry—a touch which was very
unpleasant when he called to mind that a sentry could shoot a suspicious man beyond an outpost, and the Carlist sentries were not
particular on that point, whatever their orders might be ; knowing,
indeed, that they would most positively shoot him if they had the
slightest suspicion of his not being a true friend—he felt rather uneasy at the muzzle of the musket following every motion of his head,
while another lay stationary, pointing to his breast.   Knowing that
on his answers, and the skill with which he might parry unpleasant
questions, depended alone the possibility of averting the fingers that
trembled at the trigger with the keenness of suspicion, he felt acutely

uneasy at the last question, namely, " whose friend are you ?" He
was about to say " Carlos Quinto," (Charles the Fifth, Don Carlos,)
when one of the sentries, not being so very knowing as Captain
Dickson had dreaded, said, " You see the friends of the king are well
fortified here." This strengthened his hope of being able to avoid
making a mistake, and he ventured to say he was the friend of Carlos, and that his friendship had inspired him to risk all dangers in
bringing them the letter, which he understood contained important
information.

" Some further conversation was kept up, and at last Captain Dickson found that, by shifting his body a little during the process of
question and answer, he got himself between two loop-holes, which
were about two feet apart, so that, by standing close up against the
wall, he was safe from an immediate death ; he saw they need come
out before they could kill him. But the officer returning, drew his
attention again to the proper line of defence to be observed against
unpleasant questions. Several of them ensued, and the answers
amount in all to this :—that he had been coming out of San Sebastian, when, meeting with a drunken lancer, who was an orderly on
duty, he saw this letter fall from him, and supposing it to be important, from several inquiries made about the orderly by different aid-
de-camps sent to look for him, he brought it to them.

" Captain Dickson, perhaps, had cause to depend more on this made
up story than will be immediately apparent to every reader ; because
the Carlists were really favoured at times with information from gentlemen of easy conscience, who made it their business to get acquainted with one side, to convey information to the other, The
Christinos were in the same disreputable receipt of information ; and,
whether honorable or not, England has the credit of having furnished
a considerable number of adventurers practising on both sides. The
circumstances attending captain Dickson's different adventures make
it plain, beyond doubt, that his was not an intended visit to the
Carlist camp.

" Having told his story, he was asked if he would come in, or if
he wished to go away ? Knowing well that, had he expressed a
wish to go away, he would not have gone far, he instantly answered
that, as a matter of course, he would come in. There was now a
fearful difficulty to be obviated. It was mentioned that his servant

had carried his cloak, and his horse having gone with the servant, the most of his travelling property was behind him, or somewhere that he was ignorant of; but he had still a haversack slung over his shoulder, and in this was a quantity of papers and letters, a few books and newspapers, all anti-Carlist, besides different things that would betray him. As it required some time to remove the heavy barrels of sand placed against the gate, especially these being casks, that, when filled with their legitimate contents, contained some a thousand, some fifteen hundred, others two thousand gallons of cider; these being filled with sand, and placed against the barrier gates, opposed all attempts to work them back by a lever for a period rather tedious, supposing any thing urgent had depended on their removal; but as it was, the time required to open the gate gave Dickson an opportunity of putting off the haversack, and putting it as far to a side as he could reach, without exciting, as he thought, the suspicions of the sentry, who still watched him through the loop-hole; but these suspicions were excited, and the sentry asked what he was doing ? Dickson replied that he had put his foot on a stone and stumbled.

" The gate was opened, he was admitted ; the gate was again closed, the mighty casks of sand set firmly against it, and he was being led away, when a rough, growling voice, that he had not hitherto heard, broke on his ear, with the question of, " Where's the English prisoner?" This was the voice of General Saroa, the governor of the place, who, it appears, had been sent to, and who had just now arrived to question Captain Dickson about the letter. The sound of his voice, the fierceness of the tone, and the expression of " prisoner"—a prisoner with the Carlists ;—these, and the reflection that instantly followed, were not calculated to please Captain Dickson with the interior of the barrier-gate. Seeing him, the governor asked, roughly, " Who are you, Sir ?" Dickson began to tell him the story told to others, but was interrupted with—"How did you pass the outposts?" This was also answered; and Dickson, assuming airs of great unconcernedness and affability, seemed to lighten the interrogator's brow a shade or two. Saroa scanned his man for a few minutes, and then proceeded to put a variety of questions, to all of which Dickson gave answers to the best of his ingenuity and information. But he was to undergo another ordeal of examination. The governor went away; he was ordered to follow, which order three armed men obeyed for

him, by pushing him rather unceremoniously along in the wake of
the governor. This was not very like as if they believed in his friendship, and notwithstanding all his coolness, assumed and shown off
with considerable skill, the coward fear still rebelled; but an officer,
the one who had spoken at the barricade, slapped him on the shoulder
with his hand, which is a sign from a Spaniard that you have his
good wishes; even so much respected is this sign of protection if
given to a man in danger, that a Spaniard is rarely known to violate
the honor understood to be pledged by this slap on the shoulder:
Dickson, receiving this gratuitously from the lieutenant, was some-
what eased in his apprehensions, but then he reflected that a lieutenant was a small officer beside a general.

They went into a house, up stairs, into a large room, and there he
was told to take a seat. Another officer began to question him—an
officer whose face looked soft and pleasant beside that of the governor
but whose eye, quick and intelligent, seemed to worm itself into his
innermost thoughts, and showed by its glances, which seemed to cut
a way into his palpitating breast in search of answers, that this was
a far more dangerous questioner than he had yet met. It turned out
so; all the former answers, and many more, were given, when a
pause ensued as if enough had been asked. This pause lasted until
it became silence: then the governor asked the other officer what he
thought about the matter. "I think he has made a mistake in coming here—a very great mistake indeed!" ending this inconsolatory
observation with a leer at poor Dickson. The two superiors rose,
whispered for a few minutes at the door, glanced back at the Englishman, then at the lieutenant, and told the latter to take care of
his prisoner. The lieutenant sat silent; he looked at Dickson, and
Dickson made himself appear cheerful, until, in about five minutes,
two men entered in the rough, dirty uniform of their corps, and,
with lips blackened by the powder that they had bitten from the
cartridges of the previous day's battle, they glanced at Dickson, then
to the lieutenant, as if inquiring is this their man; and, pulling from
beneath their loosely-hanging great coat each a bayonet, they stepped sternly and roughly forward. Dickson having now but one apprehension, felt the crisis; he had no doubt but these were his butchers—in fact they were, for they came up to drag him out in fulfilment of the governor's order; and they would have instantly done

so, had not the lieutenant prevented them.   He stepped forward,
told them he had the charge of the prisoner, and he was to remain
with him until a further examination.   This sufficed for the moment
—the two men went away ; the governor in a few minutes called for
the lieutenant, demanded why he had sent away the two soldiers,
and the lieutenant and the governor continued in conversation, sometimes audibly and sometimes whispering, for nearly ten minutes. At
the end of that time Dickson could hear that it was arranged that he
was to have a trial, or, at least, that he was to undergo another examination, but that it could not be proceeded with immediately, as
the other officer, and those who were to form a council, were at that
time otherwise employed.   The lieutenant, therefore, took him back
to the guard-house at the barrier gate ; and just as they got there,
the sentries challenged some person who was coming in the same
direction in which Dickson had come. This person immediately gave
the appropriate answers, and the requisite countersign.   He had come
from the battery, and others were about to follow him, to get a supply of ammunition.   When Dickson heard him at the loop-hole, he
thought on his haversack, which contained such incontestable evidences of his anti-Carlist connexions, that he almost trembled with apprehension.   His worst fear was realised ; the man outside took up
the haversack, and the fearful owner heard him exulting at the loop-
hole on his prize.

   " To Dickson there was a period of dreadful suspense between the
time that the soldier found the haversack, and the return of a messenger, who had gone for the governor.   His papers, he knew, were
such as would inevitably condemn him in a case where so little evidence was necessary to condemnation.   He saw death before him, in
hopeless certainty ; and that death was more dismal when he reflected
that none of his acquaintance or relatives would know how he came
into the Carlists' hands, even supposing his body to be discovered
among the heap of dead which he knew would lie on the streets ere
the English Legion could occupy the town ; but the more probable
misfortune would be, that, when murdered, he would be stripped,
and his countrymen would never know when, where, or how he disappeared.   " Have I then," said he, within himself, ' survived the
wars of the Peninsular army—dangers of adventure in useful and
professional travel —tropical suns, and deaths that were courted, but

were unwilling, when I might have been honorably respected; have I survived all these, to die dog-like here, leaving either no record of death, or one that will be a reproach to my family?" He thus ruminated in thought, when the old governor again made his appearance, and questioning the person outside, through the loop-hole, told him that he could not spare any ammunition for the fort, and that, though he could, it was impossible now to open the gates With this answer the messenger went away, very probably questioning himself how the prize he had found came there, but at the same time resolving to maintain the credit of his Biscayan guerillaism, by making the most of a favourable accident, and holding his tongue.

" Dickson was thus relieved from this immediate danger, but then there were other chances of the same evidence condemning him; the town might not be taken: or, if it should, it might be some days, and the chances of his being alive then were few. These and a multitude of thoughts filled his brain, as he was taken away to a house by the lieutenant, and given over to the custody of what seemed to be another garrison guard.

'' About four hours, as he surmised, had passed, when a serjeant came into the dully lighted apartment, and, inquired for the English prisoner, took off a cap with a gold band, and showing it to Dickson, inquired if he knew it; but on the latter professing ignorance, he replaced it on his head, and went out. When he had left, the soldier who stood sentry over Dickson, said that, that was a brave soldier; that he had yesterday shot an officer of the English, and afterwards leaped over the wall, unbuckled his sword, took off his cap, and returned to the garrison unhurt, though the English were pouring vollies on him. The serjeant, returned with the sword, showed it to Dickson, and the latter immediately recognized it to be Major Macduff's. This officer was, with others, fired on when under parley of a flag of truce, and this was the first intimation that Dickson had of how near the English troops were, or had been, o the fortifications of the town. He entered into conversation with his serjeant on the subject of the attack and defence, taking special care not to commit himself by remarking on the matters of which he was ignorant; but, to his disadvantage in conversing with them, he was ignorant of all that had occurred on the previous day. He learned, however, that their hatred and dread of the English Legion were equally strong; that they were determined to hold out to the last man, because they expected no mercy from soldiers who, as they had been informed, put every prisoner, without discrimination, to death.

" It was a dull, prison-like apartment, imperfectly lighted by the reluctant fire of green wood, that now and again received a Biscayan oath and a poke from a bayonet, whose owner never intended his steel to preserve a gloss of idle brightness; it was a dismal apartment, for the occasional glare of an unsteady blaze only served to show the powder-blackened lips, the sullen brows, the scorched hair, and the war-worn uniform of soldiers, who seemed, exactly as they were, enjoying a brief respite from the strife of battle. The vacillating flame that shot up declined and fell, making darkness by the contrast more black, and which again rose in alternate changes, seemed to Dickson as if an accompanying vision followed the issue of prayer and curse, that then, as they commonly do with Spaniards, exchanged places on the same lips. He was questioned by one party, who came in to warm themselves, and again by those who succeeded, all being astonished at finding an English prisoner in the safe keeping of a guard; such an unusual precaution taken by the butcherous Soroa was to them wonderful, and they had all a desire to hear the story of the Englishman.

" While engaged in reciting the story of his kindly services and wishes on behalf of the Carlist cause, a loud rebound broke overhead and shook the walls, massive though they were, that enclosed this apparently subterranean guard-house. The soldiers started to their feet, and again another shock, louder than the first, trembled over the building. An officer entered, and with the flat of his sword struck the nearest soldier on the shoulder, uttering a violent oath, and the exclamation of " Villain ! to your duty!" Another got the same unceremonious exhortation, and another, and another, until the vivacity with which every one sprung to his musket left the officer nearly alone; seeing which, he also disappeared leaving only one man, the sentinel, with Dickson.

" The cannon now rebounded above, and also, as the sound seemed, around the place in which he was confined. He was in the lower part of a large building, called the consistorial-house, or town-hall, and the cannon that first broke silence was a 'twelve-pounder, three of

which were on the third floor of the building, and were firing from
the windows on the advancing English.

" They had not fired many rounds, when, by the sound of other ex-
plosions in the streets, he could understand that the English artillery was throwing shells into the town. At the same time he
heard the bells of some one not far distant church ringing, on which
he inquired at the sentinel, who had ventured to look out for a few
seconds, what the ringing meant. 'It is the English,' was the
reply, ' but they are yet beyond two barriers, and they can never
force them.' Dickson was willing to acquiesce in the expressed
hope that they would not, but secretly he prayed that they would;
knowing well that by their entry, and that only, could he save his
life.

" The firing went on, and on ; for a time he heard nothing but the
continuous thunder of cannon, and the inferior crackle of musketry.
At last he perceived through a crevice, that the houses on the opposite side of the square which fronted the house he was in, were
battered down by the incessant bursting of shells ; and while he still
watched at the crevice, a shell entered at a window in the floor above,
and bursting, forced down a part of the floor above him. That shell
was followed by others, and those who had wrought the guns at the
third floor windows, were now battered by the bullets from the English artillery. Dickson could hear, by the irregular fire, that those
who directed the guns above him were suffering severely ; but it was
not until another shell came in, tearing the partition walls of an
adjoining apartment, and which caused some wretchedly mutilated
then to be brought into the place where Dickson was, that he learned
the progress that the English troops had made, and were then making. At this time he heard cheering in a neighbouring street, and
he knew the cheers to be those of the English.

"They were still beyond the inner barrier, and that was still plentifully served with musketry. There was, however, a necessity, of
those who supplied ammunition, to make their way across the square,
and this every minute became a passage more and more perilous.
Shells and rockets fell incessantly, and a number of boys, whose
duty was to carry cartridges to the different guns and garrisoned
houses, were ordered to cross the square with ammunition to those
who defended the inner barriers. The poor little fellows dared not

refuse, for old Soroa ordered them himself; one of them, therefore, took up the cartridges he was to carry, and looking at the falling missiles for a moment, crossed himself with the holy sign, and dashed along—he went safe. Another made the same attempt in the same way; but ere he was many yards from the doorway from which he emerged, he and his ammunition were blown to pieces by a rocket. The next that was to follow seeing this one's misfortune, hesitated, but a fierce, growling order told him it must be done, and he went. Another was following on the same errand, when the soldiers who manned the barricade were seen returning inwards.

"The English had made their way from house to house by cutting through the walls, and they were now entering the square. The first who came there was an Irishman, who was quickly shot for his temerity; but it should be stated, that the brave Captain Pierce had led on the storming party, and that to him the highest share of credit was due. As the front of the assailants came into the square, the Carlists betook themselves to the house, and barricaded the doors. There was one poor fellow, however, too late, and he was left to be shot at without mercy. When he saw there was no escaping, he turned his breast to the advancing enemy, and waving his cap, cheered for the success of the Carlist cause. While he yet cheered, he sunk beneath the battering shot.

"In the interior, the most frantic imprecations and vows of vengeful defiance were heard amid the mixing fire, thunder, and smoke; and though there were not, out of the whole, one-fourth part of the muskets in firing condition, owing to the foulness with which the dreadful morning's work had choaked them, there were still more at the different ranges of loop-holes—all striving to fire fast—than could get room to do so with advantage.

"Dickson now heard the expressed determination of 'no surrender;' and, further, he heard that some of those who were not aware that he knew the Spanish language, were talking of making sure work of him, or, in other words, killing him, before there might be a chance of his escaping. However his well-assumed horror at the approach of the English, and his apparent energy in assisting to barricade the doors, disarmed those who were about him of their intentions. Besides, some of them said that he would be of use as an interpreter, should the English not put them to immediate death. The small shot was now entering at various openings, and though he knew that a surrender must soon be made, that they would soon be taken prisoners, or buried in the ruins of the house, he felt great anxiety to make some signal to the assailants, and yet dared not propose it to the defending garrison.

Two men, an artilleryman and a rifle, made their way, unscathed, to that part of the barricade in rear of which Dickson was standing, and he saw, by their gestures, that they were encouraging others to come on. For some time he endeavoured, but in vain, to let himself be heard through an indistinct opening; for the fear of attracting the Carlist to that part against which the adventurers were unconsciously standing, prevented him from taking readier means to discover himself. Captain Pierce, with some other officers and men, came up to the same place; many of their followers, however, dropping as they crossed and fronted the fire from the loop-holes. Measures were in active progress to blow up the door, and the light artillery were also brought up the street to be directed against this house. Dickson, seeing that they must all inevitably perish in the ruins' resolved to make himself heard; and, fortunately, the artillerymen, who came first to the spot, and who kept close to the wall, to save himself, probably, from the fire of the loop-holes and the upper windows, heard the voice of one within who said there was English in the house. He drew the attention of his comrades to the voice, and Dickson had the satisfaction to hear that they wondered to themselves "who the English can be that are inside." He heard one say, that, "perhaps they were the deserters, and that he would like to take them prisoners, and not to kill them by blowing the house down."

At that time, the officers in this desperately garrisoned house came to Dickson, to take his opinion on the propriety of surrendering. He told them that he was sure they would be spared their lives if they made no further resistance; and the whole of them, on hearing that, ran to the upper floors, and ordered the men to put the butts of their muskets through the loop-holes, as a sign of submission. He was still endeavouring to make himself heard through the aperture spoken of, to those outside, and therefore did not observe the disappearance of those around him, until, turning his head, by accident, he discovered, as he thought, that every one but himself had gone to the rearward departments of the building. At seeing this, he tore at the barricading planks to get the door opened : but some of the wounded, whom he had not seen lying in the darkness of the apartment, exclaimed, ' Villain! traitor !' and swore vengefully at his apparent treachery in opening the barricade. One of them made a desperate effort to reach him with a bayonet, and another fired a musket, both of which, however, missed their object ; and the necessity of a desperate energy gave additional strength to remove the oaken legs from behind the door, which, but for removal, must have been set on fire, or battered down by cannon, either of which would have been fatal to those within.

" In a few minutes Dickson was among the English outside, and the artilleryman exclaimed, ' Why, as I live, this is the gentleman that saved our guns, our officer, and our men, by leading on the Chapel-gorris last week.' One officer said, ' Mr. Dickson !' and another added, ' Mr. Dickson!' ' Dickson! how the devil came you there ?' But the capture of prisoners had to be proceeded with, and those who first saw Dickson open the doors, left him to be interrogated by others, and a few minutes were only necessary to spread the story of his capture. ' Ah! the rascal ! put a bayonet in him ! he's a spy !' ' Kill him !' ' Off with his head !' ' No quarter to spies !' ' An English Carlist ! a Tory !' ' Kill the Tory! down with the rascal,' &c. &c. These were some of the exclamations that Dickson heard ; and if he was in danger with the Carlists, it was in a tenfold degree more violent and un-assuageable now. Bayonet struggled with bayonet to reach his body, and he was not fired at, only because he was surrounded on all sides by English officers. It was to Captain Pierce, and afterwards to Colonel Ramsey, that he owed his life at that time, for Pierce, knowing him personally, and believing him incapable of being a traitor, defended him. He and one or two other officers were, with their swords, keeping off the riot of bayonets, when General Evans appeared. Dickson attempted to address himself to the general, but the noise that prevailed, and the ecstasy in which the general rode up, followed by the cheers of a battle-excited soldiery, prevented all attempts of explanation from being attended to.

" ' Away with him! away with him, he's a traitor !' was the exclamation of the general on first discovering who he was; and this being in consonance with the belief and excitement of the soldiers, nothing more was wanted as a warrant for instant execution.

" To the accident of Colonel Ramsey coming up, Dickson owes his life, for Ramsey swore that he himself would die before Dickson; that he was not a traitor; but that, whether he was or was not, he ought to have a fair trial.

"Captain Dickson got safe from among the infuriated soldiers: General Evans afterwards believed his explanatory defence, and permitted him to go into France. There, a few days after, he saw the sentinel who had first challenged him on his approach to the outer barriers on the night of his mistaken adventure.

" This sentinel told him that he attempted to shoot him, but that his piece missed fire, and ere he could again cock, the officer had told him to allow the Englishman to approach, and then to blow his brains out, if he could not give an account of himself. This soldier had escaped being taken prisoner, as all the others of the garrison not killed in action were, by having a place of concealment in his house, in which he had a store of wine and bread, and where he subsisted five days, until all had become quiet; he then came out, and appeared as a returned peasant. He congratulated Dickson on his escape, for he said it was fully intended to put him to death next day, had the town not been taken by the English."

If Captain Dickson escaped so narrowly from the wrath of the Legionaries, it must be a matter of painful reflection to contemplate how narrowly the "correspondent" of a London morning paper escaped. He, poor fellow, would have had greater difficulty in finding protecting friends, than Dickson had; for all that was against the latter, previous to his being found in Irun, was merely a suspicion, and to balance that, there were several noble feats of daring, that had gained for him the admiration of all beholders. The "correspondent" on the other hand, while he might have found those who from the innate generosity of their nature, would have saved him from violence,—among whom beyond doubt, would have been General Evans himself, for none were so ready to do a generous action, though not much deserved than he: yet the chances I must confess, would have been greatly against the fugitive scribe of foreign news, had he not made himself clever in flight. It is much better that we were saved the discredit of taking the head off this person, but how-ever discreditable such an act might have been, his would have been the most justly shed, of any blood that has been spilt in Spain. We had undeniable evidence, and I have had that evidence strengthened since our return to England, by the additional testi-mony of those who were for a time in the Carlist ranks; that this same correspondent with others, was not only a witness of the Du-rango Decree butcheries on the English prisoners—but was one of those who continually represented to the Carlists the savage disposi-tions of the Legion, and fabricated the stories of our putting pri-soners to death. We found this gentleman's luggage in Irun, he having made his escape on a mule, or as some said a donkey, without his traps, on the approach of the Legion.

I shall quote what Mr. Farr says, of this person's correspondence with his employers:—it is as follows.

"The kindness and humanity displayed by the Legion at the taking of Fuenterabia and Irun I have already shewn, in the facts put together to refute the charges of cruelty brought against them. As the other details of the bravery and good conduct of the troops before Fuenterabia and Irun have all been so lately published in the newspapers, I will not repeat a more than thrice-told tale: yet in spite of their humanity and good conduct, the *Morning Post* of Sa-turday, announces the intelligence, and comments on the conduct of their brave and kind-hearted countrymen, by saying, that the ' scenes of massacre and pillage which took place disgraced the Bri-tish name,' and, in addition to these false accusations of cruelty, the Tory press had the impudence to state, after the places were taken, that the Carlists never thought of defending Fuenterabia and Irun and therefore there was no merit in taking them. Now in the *Morning Post* of May the 10th, what letter does the *Post* itself publish, written by its correspondent, who had been in the Christino-camp, and had passed over with what he learnt there to the camp of the enemy? These letters are a rich treat, and well worth reading. In one of them, dated Fuenterabia, Thursday night, May 11th, only a few days before it was taken he says ' As General Evans is very anxious to enter the place, and as I believe he will not have that chance, perhaps he will be contented to learn the description of its present condition from the latest English visitant;' and he then goes on giving various details of its great strength; and in a letter dated Irun, Friday morning, May 12th, describing Irun, he says, 'There is a fort irregularly constructed, but still of immense force, commanding the approach on one side; the streets are effectually barricaded, so as to retire from one point to the other; the houses are well loop-holed and fortified for mischief, if any be intended on this side. The projected attack is the constant theme of speculation, and great confidence is expressed as to the result; although the numerical force of the Christinos is admitted to be far superior, the deficiency in numbers is made up by ardent feeling—even the women and children have volunteered their aid: the care of the wounded, by the irremoval from the field of strife, in order not to diminish the strength of the troops, will be undertaken by the women.' It must have been a bitter pill for the *Morning Post* to swallow, for all these prophecies were published on Friday, May the 19th, and on the very next morning, on Saturday, May the 20th, it was forced to announce, that a telegraphic dispatch had arrived, and that both places had been captured. When I read the letters on my return to San Sebastian, I could not help thinking once more of the advice of my friend, the correspondent of a leading Morning Journal, given me at Madrid:—'Let no man ever think of writing home any prophecies of what is likely to happen in Spain, these Spaniards are such an incomprehensible people; for one morning your prophecy is announced with much solemnity and commented on, and the very next day, if not the same day, perhaps in a second edition, a telegraphic dispatch proclaims to the public your ignorance, and covers you with ridicule; let every one in Spain content himself with relating past events, without trying to prophecy about the future.'

"It was on Sunday, the 14th of May, that General Evans quitted St. Sebastian, and on the Sunday following re-entered it, having taken Hernani, Irun, and Fuentarabia. The distance from Irun to St. Sebastian is about eight miles. While on the march, one act of Carlist audacity and impudence amused me much: we were about ten thousand men, with cavalry, artillery, and rockets, and had about eight hundred prisoners with us, who had formed the garrison of Fuentarabia and Irun, and a good many of the wounded men were in the hospital carts. I was riding by the side of General Evans and General Jarregui (the Pastor, as he is called, from his having once

been a shepherd) ; if I remember right, it was between Oyarzun and
. Astigarraga, where 'a single Carlist peasant had the audacity to stand
in a kind of garden, a few hundred yards from the line of march, and
let fly a single shot at the Generals and their staff, and then start off
into the mountains : owing to the nature of 'the ground, the whole
ten thousand men could not have made him prisoner.

" After a week of most extraordinary inactivity, as every hour was
precious,—it being known that the object of Don Carlos was an attempt on Valencia or Madrid, most likely both,—at daylight, on the
morning of Monday, the 29th of May, the troops, about thirty thousand strong, were ordered to march from Hernani towards Andoain,
and make a forward movement. The plan laid down was this :—
Espartero was to advance with about twenty thousand men, consisting
of the Spanish Guards and best regiments, and march towards Pampeluna ; then manœuvre his force in any direction he might think
most likely to counteract the plans of Don Carlos in his projected
march.

" It is with these troops that Espartero has since entered Madrid
and eventually has forced Don Carlos to recross the Ebro. Andoain
was taken without much resistance, though General Gurrea was
killed by a volley from a parapet, exposing himself, I thought without
any necessity. His loss was most severely felt by General Evans,
Lord John Hay, and Colonel Wylde, as they had, most deservedly,
the highest opinion of his bravery, his honesty, and his talents.
One of his sons was aid-de-camp to General Evans ; he has every
requisite for making an excellent soldier. General Evans had four
Spanish aides-de-camp, all extremely brave and active in the field—
' *similes cum similibus.*'   No man, that did not possess a perfect
disregard of life, could remain on the staff of a general who exposed
his person as General Evans did, on every occasion.

" My instructions were, not to be tempted to pass Andoain to
witness any of the fighting in the mountains, for as the army was to
separate in two divisions there, if I went on, I should most likely
not be able to get back again to St. Sebastian with the division that
returned, in order to remain under the orders of General Evans.

" For full three hours I was lying on a hill, within three hundred
yards of the church of Andoain, where our countrymen, one hundred and twenty-seven men and thirteen officers, have, since that

period, after having capitulated, been most foully murdered. I long
to hear the Carlist-Tory defence of it in the House of Commons, or
a Carnarvon defence of it in the House of Lords.*

" On this hill I witnessed the distant fighting in the mountains;
about three thousand Carlists, with much gallantry and perseverance, hanging on the rear and annoying the flanks of Espartero's
twenty thousand men. I then took great pains to inquire into the
real strength and situation of Andouin, as a military post; because I
was told that it was not our intention to continue to occupy Andouin.
At first the resolution struck me as extraordinary, knowing that
there was scarce a single Carlist at that time in the neighbourhood,
as the three or four thousand men had followed Espartero, to harass
his rear, on their march over the mountains, to Pampeluna; but it
was clearly explained, that Andouin being seated in a hole, and having a narrow river within four hundred yards of the church, over
which they could not throw an advanced post and keep a look out,
owing to the superior bravery and activity of the Carlists, that it was
liable to be attacked in the rear and the communication with Urnieta
and Hernani cut off; in fact, that it was as a military position, perfectly untenable."

CHAPTER XXVII.

The disbandment of the Legion—Formation of the new force under Colonel
O'Connell, &c., &c., &c.

In taking a retrospective view of the incidents recorded in these
rather desultory sketches of mine, I find many more crowding on my
recollection, and with claims for a place equally strong to any that
have appeared; they must however for the present lie aside, as we
proceed now to disband the Legion.

---

* The correspondent of the *Morning Chronicle* says, in a letter, dated Madrid,
November 11th, 1837 " I have just seen a letter from an officer, who has read,
at Logrono, all the correspondence found on Messrs. Gruneison and Henningsen,
when taken by the National Guards and confined in prison there. One of the
letters, he states, was from Arias, Minister of State to Don Carlos, addressed to
an English Lord (Carnarvon), thanking him for his "book," and great exertions
in his "majesty's behalf" *in parliament*. The letter is written in the minister's
own hand-writing, in indifferent French, and concludes by apologies for the
" Durango decree." The document was found in the possession of Mr. Henningsen, and is now in the hands of Espartero.
    No. 38.

The term of service expired on the 10th, or rather the 9th of June, and previous to that, preparations were made to pay off the regiments.　Had there been no intention of raising a new force out of the old one, it would have been more prudent to have kept up the money and paid the men on their arrival in England, but as a re-enlistment was going on, it became necessary to resort to the common modes of recruiting—that mode which was always, when levies of men were required, pursued with militia regiments in Britain, in order to get them to volunteer into the regulars, namely, that of giving men money, and every facility to wallow in drunkenness until it was all spent.　This mode was put in operation in the Legion, and as had been the case with many thousands of militia men who are said to have volunteered for their *King and Country;* and who afterwards became the heroes of the Peninsular campaigns—many of our men, the unwary ones of the Legion, found themselves enlisted, attested, and new-made soldiers when they became sober.　Others, who, during the tumultuous debauch had either kept out of the snare, or had been too drunk to get into it, found themselves in such an awful state of burning horror, that in their madness they recklessly went—though when sober they had sworn to their comrades and to themselves not to go, and took the bounty.　This purchased a temporary re-excitement, but when that miserable price of life was swallowed in a new intoxication, they awoke and found themselves soldiers—deeper in horror, with no money nor means of obtaining it—prostrated beneath martial law and unavailing repentance; envying those who were embarking for England, but strictly watched and sternly restricted from the possibility of getting home themselves.

But though a majority were of this description, there were a number of men who remained from other causes than being entrapped in drunkenness.　I knew some who refrained from drinking but who were robbed, and rather than come home pennyless re-enlisted; others stopped from the mere love of the life they were leading, and some from a dread of what would befal them if they came home.　I recollect one to whom I put the question of "why have you ' taken on ? ' " that being the phrase denoting enlistment; his answer was "take on !" I may as well take on here as be 'lagged' (transported) when I get home.

Of the officers who made up their resolution to stay in the new force, I have a much higher opinion than of the men. Many of the officers remained from strict principles of honour, being determined that they would not return to their own country where they knew they would be branded with reproach, until they had seen the last of the war. There were other officers who had been induced to leave good situations at home to go out at the beginning; and some who had no situation having gone out, were with these, on the unhappy equality of not knowing what to turn themselves to should they come home, at least until there might be some assurance of being paid their arrears. These last, however, I venture to say were few, compared with those who remained from an honourable wish to maintain and carry out the military credit of the expedition they were engaged in.

It is necessary that the subject of arrears of pay should be unravelled here; for many of those who have told their tales of woe in the metropolis and other towns of England, who go about in old red coats, and who complain of receiving no pay, are persons to whom no pay is due. On the very day that this is written, (in December, 1838,) I saw three of the Legionaries in ragged red, whose claims I knew well did not justify their common story. One of them received through my own hands nearly four pounds sterling on the 9th of June, 1837, which was the full amount of his pay up to the 10th, on which day his service ended. The second had received to the amount of twelve shillings more than his pay entitled him to, in clothing, as many others had; indeed nearly the half of the whole strength of the Legion had not only no arrears to receive, but many of them were in debt, having received clothing and necessaries above their amount of pay. The third of the three men, was one whose case I was not familiar with, but whatever his claims might be, he had like his two companions, been sixteen months in England, during which time, had they desired they might have transformed themselves from the remnants of a military uniform.

I find it incumbent on me to explain these matters, because badly as our military enterprise may have terminated in respect of serving the national interests of Spain, and frail as the faith of that country may have been towards us, these persons who go about as the ragged representatives of this Legion's distresses, cause a feeling to prevail in England against those who are not blameable, as well as a very exaggerated prejudice against those whose just share of blame is not understood in this country ; I allude first to the officers of the Legion, and lastly to the Spanish authorities.

It is common with those persons wandering from street to street or from town to town, to tell stories of being cheated of their pay by their officers, thereby impressing on the minds of the people who have no means of obtaining information, and who do not care whether they are rightly informed or not, but who in forming prejudices against a body of individuals such as the officers of the Legion, should care ; these travelling reciters of their Spanish sufferings, generally give their tale in nearly the reverse ratio of truth.   The real state of matters stands thus :---

The officers who served up to the 10th of June, 1837 — the period at which the service of General Evans terminated—have twelve months' pay due to them ; some of them may be liable to a deduction for various items of over-expenditure on their companies or regiments, such as giving their men more supplies of clothing and necessaries than their pay amounted to—but all of these officers have an arrear of twelve months' pay.

The non-commissioned officers and men who served up to the same period, and who returned to England when the General returned, were all paid up to the last day of their service : none of these, therefore, have an arrear due to them.   There were however, numbers of men invalided and sent home at various times during the two years of Evans's command ; and they stand in this position.   Those who were " hospital birds,"—that is a kind of impostors very well known to all military people, who manage to get into hospital in spite of all the vigilance of their superiors, and who assume ill health and remain incurable in spite of surgical ingenuity—or who are sent to hospital, if only admissable at all—in order to rid a regiment or a company of their pernicious influence, should they happen to be dirty intractable men, inveterately stubborn and unsoldierly—which they often are ; this kind of persons who constitute a majority of the " hospital birds" are mostly claimants for a large balance of pay ; for, being in hospital they were not served with clothing, neither did they receive money when that was paid to the duty men of their respective regiments. The men who were wounded in the various engagements and invalided, are, some of them paid, and some of them not paid. They have been ruled by the following accidents. They were perhaps in debt to their Captain when they were wounded, and if they were severely wounded, they were soon struck off the strength of their regiment as unfit for farther duty; hence, though they might remain in the country six, or even twelve months—for Mr. Alcock the excellent and most worthy medical gentleman who was chief of the practical department in the surgical hospitals—he had a superior, but he was himself the *working* chief, and he enjoys and eminently deserves to enjoy the high esteem of all who came under his skilful treatment, and whose wounds were within the possibility of cure—this gentleman permitted men to re-main in hospital where they could get a few months good quarters and living, after they were cured, rather than send them to England legless, penniless, homeless, and friendless, as not a few knew them-selves to be when they lost their limbs;— therefore these men are not entitled to pay, because they were allowed to remain in the coun-try as a *favour* long after they had been struck off the regimental strength. These have been put on a pension list and all of them have received payment of their pensions on a scale equal to that of the wounded of the British army. Some of these wounded men, however, have an arrear of pay due to them; because they were, per-haps, creditors to the amount of three or four months at the time of being wounded; or as was sometimes the case, they may have remained a considerable time on the strength of their regiment after being wounded, and have been invalided at last, without being paid, as the money issued to regiments was only according to the strength of the regiment at the time of the issue. Again, numbers of these wounded men were paid their arrears on landing in England, so that it is ex-tremely difficult to know from looking at their mere outward appear-ance, or listening to their story whether they are paid or not.

The whole of these---all the invalids---whether invalided through imposition, sickness, wounds, or any other cause, are, as well as those discharged at the 10th of June, 1837, in consequence of the term of service expiring, entitled by the "conditions of service" to receive a gratuity, or compensation of two, four, or six months pay, according as they might be recommended by their commanding offi-cer. Therefore, the very worst soldier, whatever his behaviour or service may have been, even though he may have been indebted to the company's ledger, is entitled to receive at least two months' full pay, and none of these gratuities have yet been paid.

These are the circumstances in which those stand who served un_ der Evans, and who terminated their service, either previous to or at the time of his return to England, namely, the 10th of June, 1837.

But at that time there was a new force raised under Colonel O'Connell, which consisted of 250 Lancers, 200 Artillerymen, 810 Infantry and 130 Sappers and hospital Staff.   The bounties paid to these, were six dollars to the Cavalry, Artillery, and Sappers ; and five dollars to the Infantry ; the dollars being reckoned at four shillings and fourpence each. The officers of that force received only in the whole, three months pay, and as neither clothing nor money could be obtained for the men, and as the field allowance of the officers, which during Evans' command, had been paid, was also stopt by the Spanish government --- General O'Connell (for he obtained rank though there was no pay) demanded that vessels should be provided to carry his men to England, as their contract had not been fulfilled ; what that contract was, will shortly appear. These officers and men therefore, form distinct sets of claimants from those who terminated their service with General Evans.   The men who served under O'Connell have nearly all their pay for that period of service still due to them.   And in addition to all the arrears of pay, the officers who were not dismissed for any misconduct, or who did not resign without due permission—are, whether having served in the old or new force, entitled to receive a gratuity of pay to the amount of one half of their respective periods of service.   Those, for instance, who served during the two years of Evans' command, have a claim for twelve months' pay in addition to their arrears, and those who served with O'Connell are entitled to a further gratuity in the same proportion.   Such are the claims of the officers and men of the Legion on the Spanish government.

There is another claim put up by a few individuals which I am, as I think, justified in taking notice of, more especially as a recent case in the sheriff's court, and the decision come to by the sheriff, is likely to call forth a number of similar cases.   I have learnt nothing of this case as pursued, and defended, save from a newspaper report ; yet knowing the merits of the claim much better, I humbly venture to assert, than the sheriff could possibly know them—I beg to put all those on their guard against similar impositions whose views of justice, or sympathy for what they may conceive an injured party—leads them to decide in favour of this new set of claimants.

The case referred to, was that of a man who had been groom to an officer, pursuing that officer for wages. In judging of this case it is necessary to consider the legal claim, and the moral claim of the individual separately ; both of them are insupportable—but whatever may at first appear just in a mere legal point of view, is altogether neutralized by the moral injustice of the circumstances that enabled the claimant to pursue.

Legally, the groom had no claim on his master, for both were the servants of the Spanish government : the groom was a soldier, he was liable to do what he was ordered ;—as in the British army. He could be taken off parade, sent to an officer's stable to groom his horse—kept there a day—a week—a month—a year—or not an hour —he could be taken from and sent back to his duty, without having the right to ask a question, why he was so taken away, or so sent back. If this is an arbitrary law, it is the fault of the British legislature —it is a British law, and in Britain no civil magistrate has a right to interfere with it. But the interference of the Middlesex sheriff in this case was illegal on a stronger point than even this. Officers in the British service pay their military servants—though legally they are not bound to do so, and on active service they have, what is termed, a field allowance, from which it is generally supposed to be paid. But as the Spanish government thought fit to strike off this field allowance, the English magistrate should have compelled the payment of that to the officer before he decided for the groom. If he had no power over the Spanish authorities to compel the payment of that allowance, which, suppose him to have, would be a gross absur-dity—neither has he the power to interfere between two persons who were by the order of the King in Council permitted to enter into the service of a foreign country, where, for two years, they were without an exception on any legal point—the servants of the Spanish govern-ment. Although subjected to the British Articles of War ; the Le-gion was only so by permission of the Spanish authorities—and that was permitted simply because British officers and British soldiers understood it best. The Spanish government could, at any time during these two years, have ordered the substitution of Spanish martial law for that of the British. The Spanish government could at any time have given us Spanish pay instead of British, and in some allowances they substituted their own customs for ours—as in the case of the field money—the weight of bread and beef, &c. If otherwise—if the Spanish government were not wholly and entirely our masters, then the question is—who were our masters? The English government disclaims the responsibility, and it disclaims justly; because all that the King and his Privy Council did, was to give British subjects leave to put themselves under the laws of Spain.—The laws of Spain were our laws, and they were only for convenience exchanged for the British Articles of War by a contract between two individuals; who then were our masters? The English Government declares itself incompetent to interfere on any single point between the defunct Legion and its late employers. The British parliament decides by a resolution that however desirable it may be to have an adjustment of the Legion's claims, it is not competent for parliament to interfere. Then if the Secretary of State—if her Majesty and her Privy Council—if even the British parliament, cannot interfere between the Spanish government and the Legion's claims, is a mere provincial magistrate to decide? is the sheriff of Middlesex competent to take cognizance of a matter that lies beyond the power of the very highest authorities of the country? The sheriff no doubt looked at the case as one of a simple small debt class; but he is grossly in error. The debt was, in the first place, never legally contracted; because, as a soldier, the groom was bound to do any thing he was ordered by a superior, leaving remuneration at the mere option of the officer served. And, in the next place, as even the custom of payment, was altogether altered in Spain from what it is at home, by the arbitrary contingencies over which the commander-in-chief of the army had no control, it went at once far beyond the ability or power of an English magistrate to decide on it.

But I would not have said the hundredth part of what I have said, on such a claim, so far as regards its legality, were it not that I have the strongest impression on my mind that the claim is unjust—that remuneration for such services as this groom is said to have performed, is altogether undeserved—and not only undeserved, but that the groom is a deep debtor to his master for having conferred the very great favour of, taking him from the ranks and hard duty, to make him a servant. I know nothing of either the master or the groom; I have never heard an observation made about them; I neither know their names nor the number of the regiment to which they belonged; but as I intended devoting a few pages to a description of what *servants* were in the Legion; though this case had not come under observation, I do it the more readily now to put people, more especially magistrates, on their guard against such claimants in future.   I believe it is common in all debt cases for the circumstances under which the debt was contracted to be taken into view, in making any order for its payment; assuredly that rule should never be more closely followed than in the case of *servants* from the Spanish service setting up claims for wages.

Had I a choice of any situation in a campaign—from the General commanding down to the private soldier—and were I to set the question of honour aside—I would choose to be an officer's servant without wages.   There is a great difference in being a servant, according to the rank of the officer, and his personal disposition, but even to serve the worst of them, is easy and agreeable, when compared with the duties that soldiers are ever liable to have imposed on them in the time of war.

We saw,—and what we saw, was what all soldiers in active warfare have seen—we saw the spare rations—we saw the keen looks of the hungry—we often felt hopeless hunger, and the officers in some situations were in no way better provided, than the men of the ranks.   There might be no possibility of helping ourselves, but if there was, the officer dared not at any time look for *forage*, nor take it if it fell in his way;—nor could the soldiers of the ranks, save at rare times; but the servant was always first, when anything was to be had.   The officer's servant had a right of entrance into houses, and once in the houses, he could use a freedom that the common soldier could not use;—he was the servant of an officer, and he would get every favour from the Spaniards which they had to give. He was not obliged to march in the ranks—and on those burning marches, when a soldier, from the necessity of keeping the men up —is not allowed to fall out of the line to lap a mouthful of water— nor the officer, from the necessity of shewing an example of forbearance to the men; the servant comes up somewhere, or anywhere between the baggage guard and the rear of the battalion, with a mule or a horse carrying his master's baggage and his own, whistling, or singing careless of any restriction. Going off the march into quarters—he can secure at least the second best bed, or corner—should there be no bed—and he is always sure of an undisturbed rest, having no dread of being one of the guards or picquets, which are mounted from the tired men of the battalion. Though it may rain or snow, his master must take a turn of outline duty, but the servant can stay at home.

If in quarters, where no permission is given to the soldiers to go out of, or into a town without a pass, the servant is always free. This freedom of motion which he possesses, makes him always a consequential being, both in his own eyes, and in the eyes of others, especially in the eyes of the Spanish inhabitants ; who have all great faith to put in the honesty of a servant—than in another soldier ; because, as they think, were he not the most honest of all the company he belongs to, he would not be a servant.

Now as any person who has read those books, which have been written in considerable abundance, since the close of the Peninsular war—such as the " Military Sketch Book," or those of its class, which afford an insight into the details, and as we may say, the interior of a campaign—those who have read these books, must have found that the best qualification for an officer's servant, was his *foraging,* or in other words plundering ability. The distinctive qualities that would mark a soldier out for a good servant in a garrison town, are altogether of secondary importance in the daily bustle of a campaign. Hence instead of the good servant being the most honest—he was the man who could at any time—if at any time it could be done—get up a dinner for his master, and force a good berth, and good provender for his master's horse ! no matter how these might be accomplished, so as he could do it all without coming into the clutches of the provost. But being an officer's servant, the provost did not see *his* doings so quickly, as those of an unpatronized soldier.

The officer who was pursued by his groom before the sheriff, must have been either a field officer, or an officer of cavalry, as none other kept grooms ; but which ever he was, there is nothing more probable than that this servant had sneaked, and hunted, longing and beseeching to get into the glorious privileges of servitude. If he was fond of the battle, he would generally find means of getting into it; but if he wished to save his head, he like all servants of his class, could keep out of the thick fight, which privilege to some serving men, was a great matter indeed. When the boisterous blasts of Biscay have battered on the lines, where shivering picquets, and benumbed sentinels stood, this groom lay in warm quarters. When the daily drill—the fatigue duty—the picquets and the guards, which for ever kept the duty men employed, and often prevented the small breakfast, which to them would have been comfortable—this groom has toasted his toes and his bread, and drank his chocolate and coffee, at his unmolested ease. How often have I seen the fatigue parties day after day, to the amount of five or six hundred men, working laboriously—unloading ships, carrying ammunition in murdering weight, to and from the magazines—building batteries —dragging guns—making roads and bridges—parading, and being drilled in heavy marching order, all on the same day—and all in the name of soldiering—all for a soldier's pay; and besides, tearing and wearing their clothes so much, that new ones were served to them so often, that they had no pay to receive—how often have I seen these men so employed, and the *servant* lounging at his ease—riding out his horses, or smoking his cigar on a balcony—a more independant and easy man by a great deal, than his master; yet these, who had the incomparable privileges of officer's service; are those in favour of whom, English magistrates are stretching the law—and stretching it against officers, who are almost the only and real sufferers themselves.

It will become the sheriff or any other magistrate to pause ere he gives a similar decision in favour of this, the only well fed and well treated class of men that were in the service.

The claims of those who served only during the first two years are grounded solely on the conditions of service as contracted between the Marquis Alava on behalf of the Spanish government, and General Evans on behalf of the Legion. But those who re-engaged to serve a third year under General O'Connell, have a claim for which the British Government is responsible. The commissioner, Colonel Wylde, pledged himself in the name of the British Government that the Spanish authorities would deal fairly with the new Legion, and he

even made an indirect promise that the old claims would be settled'
through the interference of Britain if we would only renew our term
of service.   For the particulars of this, the reader is referred to pages
274—5, where this subject was introduced in connexion with a sketch
of the character of colonel O'Connell.

Those who saw the raw material of the Legion embarking for Spain,
and who have also seen its ragged remnants return, have an opinion
that nothing but rags was at any time to be seen on it.   This may
be pardonable in persons who never called to mind that they only
saw its two extremities.   I must make a few remarks, and state a
few circumstances to set people right on this part of the subject.
The whole of those recruits that are congregated at the Ship
public house, Charles street, Westminster—and which are destined
for all regiments of the British service, are in every respect as inferi-
orly clothed as the men for the Legion were ; the one party had disposed, and the other now disposes of all their clothing if they had
anything that could be disposed of, ere they are seen in gathered
numbers ; and this is done in expectation of a speedy and entire
change.   There is only this difference ; the recruits for the Legion
were seen in greater numbers, and they were therefore noticed the
more readily ; while the recruits for the national army, are seen only
a few at a time, and being among the motley crowds of a street, they
draw forth no notice.

The second extremity of the Legion, has been seen after the men
disposed of all their disposable uniform, and in many cases a great
deal more.   I must tell how this was done.

At the period of the Legion being disbanded, those who had
money, spent it with those who had none, so that, as has been already
mentioned, there were some whole days of drunkenness :   Men
who would have saved their money were robbed, and as there was
scarcely a possibility of putting down a riot, from there being a complete break-up of military restraint, and from the unwillingness to
take harsh measures with those who were indulged as much as possible
as an inducement to re-enlist, in consequence of that, robberies and
riots went on for some days unchecked ; and thereby many a man
had his clothes destroyed who wore a good and perfect uniform a few
days before.   And as they expected to embark almost immediately,
never dreaming but the gratuity of six months' pay would be payable

on our first landing in England, many gave away and threw away every article but what covered mere nakedness. But as we did not embark for a month after our arms were given in, being kept, as pretended, for the want of vessels, but in reality to afford as much time as possible for recruiting from the unwilling mass, and, as our blankets had all been taken from us at the disbandment, the whole lay in the old unfurnished houses night and day in their clothes. The belief still continuing that every man would have money to purchase clothes as soon as he landed, made them less careful than many might have been during that month. Again, had we embarked immediately on being released from discipline and duty, the dirty ships into which most of the men were gorged in over abundance, and in which they lay packed up like pigs in a Drogheda steamer, a passage in these ships was enough to produce the appearances which the Legion wore on coming home. In addition to all that, the time became so tedious while we waited for vessels, or to be recruited, that many despaired of them coming at all; and when vessels did come they were for a time merely small trading craft on board of which a hundred men were packed with the greatest difficulty. This produced mighty squabbles among the different regiments as to who should go first. General Fitzgerald was charged with the embarkation of the men : but he devoted no attention to the matter, indeed he threw every obstacle in the way of both officers and men, and therefore it fell in some cases to the awful contest of mob decision.

When a vessel came into the harbour to discharge a cargo, and when it was ascertained that she would be reloaded with Legion, parties would go and take possession of the sea shore. They would work with the greatest energy at getting out her cargo—carry sand for ballast—get in her water, and least any others should get into her, and she sail and leave them behind—they who thus bespoke her, lay on the shore, and on the quays for nights together, in some cases a week.

I remember seeing two vessels go out of the harbour into the bay, each having a load of about two hundred persons, all burning with high hopes for their own country, and deep hatred for the land they were leaving. Their anxiety to get on board, had been made a subject of mirth by the seamen, and it was certainly ludicrous for any one to behold, who was not one of themselves. They lay three or four days on the quay, to make sure that no others would precede them, and when the ships were ready, and the weather did not permit them to sail, the ragged crowd were seen clinging to the rigging, drenched with rain, and starving by hunger and cold, rather than they would run the risk of losing their passage, by coming on shore.   When parties were working at getting in the ship's water— others were keeping possession, by sitting astride the bowsprit, yards, and shrouds ; and when these two vessels cleared the harbour, and got into the bay—the wind being unfavourable, the Legionaries manned the boats and pulled, until relief after relief gave up the task in hopeless exhaustion.   The wind was not favourable, yet not so contrary, but the vessels could have got clear of the bay, but the Captains, with their crews, seeing the anxiety of the hope-worn Legion, to get out of Spain—kept them pulling in desperate energy during a whole day and night, as if to get out to sea; while in reality, the steersmen brought the ships back at every tack, to where they had been half an hour before, to the great amusement of their own sailors, as well as the crews of five or six English and French vessels of war, lying at anchor close by.

As an illustration of the recklessness that provides not for the future, I may mention one or two cases which came under my own observation.   When the balance of pay was issued, immediately before our being disbanded ; an Irishman, whose arrears by his having been in hospital with a wound for two or three months, amounted to about five pounds—was greatly puzzled for a few hours, in questioning what he would do with it.   At last in a military clothing establishment, a cocked hat stood before his eyes, and he purchased it with feathers, for something more than three pounds. He gestured about in it for a few days, declaring that though he had been a private, he would go home a " bould gineral;" but the linger- ing stay gave his pride time to cool, and his stomach time to make so many hungry appeals, that he decided at last on going home a private, and of course sold his hat and plumes for about one tenth of what he gave for them.

Another whom I have seen begging in the streets of London, cut a swell for a few days as a gentleman, keeping two servants in livery. He did not last long of course.

Some bought donkeys to ride on—some, guns and pistols of curious

workmanship. Some arrayed themselves in Spanish dresses, richer
or more common according to their amount of cash; but as all those
who had been non-commissioned officers, pioneers, servants, &c., had
large sums of money—having had few stoppages—great numbers of
fancy uniforms were seen flaunting about. Had the whole been
taken home immediately, or soon after being paid—the appearance
of their arrival in England, would have been very different from what
it was; or, which was once intended—had the money been kept
up until landing at Portsmouth, a very different state of appearances
would have been seen. This was not done, solely, because of the
means taken to raise a new force out of the old, already explained.

For six months, Colonel Hogg of the 8th, and I believe some
other Colonels also, caused the regimental coatees (or dress coats,)
to be saved from wear, so that the men might have a soldier-like appearance on going home. Only six weeks before the disbandment,
he drew a new shell jacket for every man of his regiment from the
stores, at the rate of seven shillings and sixpence each, to save the
coatees. Even these jackets were not absolutely requisite, for every
man had a good jacket; but because some of them, were soiled by
the March campaign—he got these new ones to be worn on parades
while the coatees were never worn, but at an extra field-day or
review. As soon, however, as it was decided on, to raise a new
Legion, the clothes were given to the men, to do with them
what they chose, and the riot and drunkenness consequent on
getting money in the absence of restrictive discipline produced precisely those effects that were desired, namely, the
destruction of the clothes so that they might scare themselves
from going home to England. These clothes destroyed, it was supposed would prevent many from going home when a new bounty
was offered. And it did prevent some, but many knowing ones took
the bounty and got home notwithstanding.

There was a bank in San Sebastian and if Don Jose Brunet who
was its chief, told me correctly, I was the only individual in the Legion from top to bottom of it who put money in the bank. He gave
no interest, and that might be a cause for those who were saving
their money, to keep it themselves or give it to private individuals.
I lost that money at last, but the very loss of it has, I believe done
me great service—I will explain how.

During the time we lay in teazing expectation of vessels coming to ship us off, we had but a very bare allowance of rations, and a number of my associates who had small sums of money, expended a daily portion on our mess, and we having nothing to do but to mess—messing was perhaps, more expensive than it might have been. I was banker for a number of them and in my name and amongst my own, their cash lay with Jose Brunet. It became necessary from our continued stay to draw some of it; and the fact being known through my company that I had money---many, indeed almost all of the men came praying that I would lend them some on security of their papers. The men were on the verge of starvation, and having no apprehension of the failure of the gratuity payments—indeed, I went that day to Colonel Wylde the British commissioner, and he told me that agents *were* appointed to settle with us whenever, and wherever we landed, and more particularly I remember what he said as he told me five hundred of us would be sent to Glasgow, which was the case ; believing then, that no hazard could be run in giving credit to the value of the gratuity certificates, I lent my money--- all but the price of a suit of clothes, which money, I need scarcely say, is not repaid, and from the men being scattered over the kingdom, never will be repaid to me. Were I disposed to believe in fatality, I might attempt to trace it out in this circumstance, and the following. When about to embark, I sent a parcel of luggage on board before me in keeping of two or three persons whose honesty was not to be suspected, but in the crowd and bustle of boats heaving and dipping in a rough sea around the ship, my parcel went, as was ultimately supposed, overboard. I was then on the shore, and an officer, Colonel Martin, came to me and urged me to change my purpose and stay with the new Legion. His offers were enticing, and some men whom I knew, and who were part of the new force, coming and expressing a similar desire, I certainly would have relinquished the homeward bound passage for another year, had my money not been before me, and especially my clothes. I went on board with the intention of returning to join the new Legion, but an hour was spent in looking for my lost luggage,—and as no persons were allowed after that, to go on shore—I was too late. Those men and officers, upwards of two hundred, amongst whom I would have been, were all bloodily murdered two months afterwards.

I may presume that the moral and physical misery on board of
those vessels that carried men to Portsmouth, was not less in amount
and severity, than that which five hundred and twenty persons, of
whom I was one, endured on board the *Prince Regent* transport on
our passage to the Clyde.   It is probable indeed, that the mass of
the Legion which came by way of Portsmouth, suffered most; because many of them lay there for weeks, even tedious months on
board the *Swiftsure* hulk ; and some of the ships were wrecked on
the coast, both of France and England with their wretched cargoes.
On the main body arriving at Portsmouth, many of them enlisted
into British regiments.   Also on coming to the metropolis, and in
various towns of England through which they travelled in search o
home, or the means of subsistence, the recruiting parties of the British depots filled up their strength with the fragments of the Legion.
How these might be received at their respective head-quarters I cannot say; but this I am well assured of, both by my own experience,
and by the opinions of those officers and soldiers, who from being
old campaigners in the national wars are well qualified to judge,—I
am well assured that whatever sneers might be cast on the Legionaries who entered British regiments, by the soldiers of these regiments,
the latter will have a fearful amount of real soldiering to perform,
ere they be hardened and made war-proof to the same degree, as
those Legionaries were, who they may affect to despise, or who at
least have been despised. *

---

* The British army is now at the first chapter af a campaign, the result of
which will probably—far too probably—give the soldiers of old England a fearful chastisement for their insolence. I speak of that insolence which sets them
up self-satisfied with their own unmatchable prowess in the field, and which
through all their public writers and partizans poured contempt on the unsuccessful Legion in Spain.

English soldiers will find a subtle , wary, and unconquerable enemy in the rifle-
warring *habitans* or peasants of Canada, compared with what the loose rolling
masses of Napoleon in the Peninsula were. That warfare, now so contemptible
in Spain, will be opened in Canada; and the over brightened gloss of military
glory worn by Britain will be ill suited to the tedious marches and countermar-
ches that the Canadians will lead them for a few years. The English military
partizans affect to laugh at the *feeble* energies of the Spanish belligerents; they
treated with scorn the arduous enterprises of General Evans among the mountains of Biscay, and they assumed over and over, and do yet assume, that they,

No. 39.

Presuming then, that the misery endured by those sailing to
Portsmouth, was similar to that suffered by us on board the *Prince*

---

even though less in number than Evans's Legion, would have scoured Spain.
They will have now, unhappily for the British Empire, an opportunity to scour a
country not by any means so difficult to traverse as the Basque mountains; but
they will scour that country in vain. The gathered hosts of Junot, Soult, and
Massena were weak in Portugal and Spain compared with the scattered *habitans*
of Canada.

It is not for me to say aught of the justice or injustice of their cause: nor of
the factious wrangling at home which has rendered the peaceful efforts of Lord
Durham valueless; it is not for me to enter on an enquiry into that unhappy spirit
of opposition that pervades men of all ranks and professions in this country; but
I may be allowed to make a few remarks on the military part of the Canadian
subject as its character—the character it will in future assume—is intimately
akin to that of the Spanish war.

It will be a disastrous day for Great Britain, when Canada succeeds in declaring a national independence. It will be a fearful precedent for other colonies.
There is a deep crime committed against the British nation, by those who have
in this country fostered or abetted the Canadian revolt; either as sharers in their
misgovernment, or sympathizers in their appeal to arms; because every subject
of the British crown if he expects to live, and leave his children in this country,
has an interest in keeping the empire from falling in pieces. He may see desirable changes in its Government; he may even deem an organic change absolutely
necessary, but let him possess what opinions he may on British Government, if he
is a British subject, and *not* a Canadian, he has the most vital interest in the
prevention of any colonial revolt.

But Canada has revolted, and the revolt is beyond military controul. The
Canadians want no leaders of great name to concentrate them—their numerical
strength is not important; but leaders *will*, as in other wars, rise from amongst
themselves. The newspapers will annihilate the rebel hands, many a time; but
they will still continue to level their rifles from behind the stump, and the tree—
and the bush. The rock—the river, and the island, will have their bands over and
over again, when British "Despatches" have as many times put down the in-
surrection.

Those persons who expect the Canadians to come out, and meet the royal
troops in a pitched battle, have poor notions of warfare.

The Canadians will vex and wear out the British army with fatigue. They
will care nothing for being called "*Brigands*" and "*Robber-bands.*" They
know that Washington was called all the ill names that British partizans could
devise. They know that Britain called the French by the same opprobrious
names; and some of their more intelligent soldiers will say—"these names are
all to our advantage, the British people call us robbers and brigands because they

Regent, I shall follow in my description as I did in person, the returning fortunes of those who landed on the Clyde.

---

wish we were only these; and what they wish, they are more ready to believe than what is true. They will give us strength, just in proportion to the time they continue to keep their eyes shut." I have been led to say something of the Canadian revolt here in consequence of the opinions that the great mass of people entertain relative to warfare. They suppose that because Napoleon took vast numbers of men into the field of battle—because his battles made him the great conqueror that he was—because Wellington marshalled the British masses to oppose Napoleon's, and because he became great, because of these things, they suppose that some great man, and great army, and great battle must be seen, ere the Canadians can be called at war with the British ; whereas in truth they are at this moment more powerful lying in their scattered ambush, than they would be drawn up in battle array with a mighty commander at their head. The British would in the latter case have a fair chance in an encounter, while as matters really are, they will be reduced to the necessity of chewing the bit—galled by a fickle enemy, bearing the opprobrium of defeat alternately, with the inglorious reputation of conquering or dispersing a small band. *Let it be borne in mind the Canadians are at home—like the Carlists. Napoleon and Wellington fought in foreign countries which obliged them to join in battle.* And are the British people and the British press to denounce the murderous reprisals in Spain, and the slaughter of prisoners and the cries of no quarter : are we to denounce these in Spain, and cry out for military murder in Canada ? If Espartero were to shoot Merino or Cabrera at Madrid ; suppose he got them, and were Colborne to put Nelson and Bill Johnson to death at Montreal, what would be the difference ? I can see none. In both countries there is a civil war, and the parties contend in both for the control of their respective governments. Then if we send out Lord Elliot to Spain to make a convention between the two parties of that country in respect of prisoners, and if, as a nation, we are to sound through the world our praises for having done so, are we to denounce Lord Durham for having acted on the spirit of that convention in Canada *without* the " Elliot " of some foreign power coming to remind us that we were butchers ? What questions does that awaken ? Many :—too many of a too painful nature for me to enter on.

But one word more. The British soldiers are committing gross outrages on the religous prejudices of the Canadians. A party of the 71st regiment had a donkey dressed in the holy robes of a Catholic Clergyman. Now as General Evans allowed no such enormities in Spain, it becomes my painful duty to raise our Legionary reputation by shewing the misconduct of others. The British army will have a war alike in every respect to that in which we were engaged in the mountains of Biscay : they laughed at the little battles of the Legion, but let them beware that they never engage *their* slippery enemy with less success than we did ours.

The *Prince Regent* is one of the best transports employed in the service, and yet she is a vessel wretchedly rigged, manned, and accommodated to her trade of carrying troops. Out of her whole crew, there were only two able-bodied seamen ; the remainder having been, as usual with transports, picked up at under wages. She had been up the Mediterranean with troops, and was on her passage home *uncleansed,* when she took up five hundred and twenty of the Legion. Some of our non-commissioned officers went on board, to distribute the men to the berths as they arrived, and the filth and stench then, was intolerable. Fleas and lice, bugs, and other vermin, nestled in every seam and splinter ; not because the Legion was on board, but ready to devour the men of the Legion when they came on board ! yet this was a British troop ship.

The wreck of the Barrossa in the early part of this month, (December, 1838), has drawn forth discussions on the transport service ; and the opposition journals are all hurling their wrath at the ministerialists, for not having a better conveyance for troops, than these transports. Now as it is best at any time to arrive at the truth, it may not be improper for me to state, that the system of Government hiring ships from companies, for the conveyance of troops ; which companies, are commonly a gang of favoured jobbers, who buy up the hulks of old merchantmen, rigging them with the refuse of the dock yards—this system by which money is supposed to be saved, but by which dreadful sufferings and dangers are imposed on the soldiers—is old—very old—much older than the present ministry —even so old as to have been in existence, and slovenly practice during the whole period of the ministerial reign, of that party which is now so sensitive on the subject of the inefficiency of the troop ships. Still the breaking up of these dirty bulks, or at least their discontinuance as troop ships, is such a desirable object, that to obtain it, we should not quarrel with the parties or their motives who are battering at the system.

The *Prince Regent* logged and rolled in the Bay of Biscay with us, for a period of three weeks, and as we were not aware during that time of what port in the British island we would land, our anxiety was teazing enough. We had been told that Glasgow was our destination ; but by some means a scepticism on that point prevailed ; and some of our men for their own amusement. having spread a report that the ship was sailing for the West Indies, where the whole cargo would be sold for slaves ! the consternation among the ragged crowd in the hold, was indeed ludicrous to witness. It will scarcely be credited that men from any part of Great Britain, even though they *were* in the Legion, could be so very ignorant of possibilities as to believe, that such a thing as stealing five hundred and twenty men, and taking them to a foreign market, could gain believers ; but such was the case. Parties of those who lay cooped up in corners, were heard at times discussing such matters. One would laugh at the ridiculousness of such a notion, while others would shake their heads and say, " I'm not sure about that ; I'll believe anything now ! After they took us away, telling us faithfully as they said, that we were to be back in three or four months at the very most, and keeping us two years, and putting some of us in confinement for six months at hard labour, and starved and naked, because we refused to stay more than one year, which was their own bargain—after that I would believe that they could do any thing."

Though I heard these conversations, I could scarcely conceive that any could credit what they said they believed ; but one day when I was on deck, three men who had been part of the community that inhabited some dark buggy corner, came to me and asked seriously what my opinion was. I could not resist the tendency of my mind to pity, and I, willing to have something myself to talk about, explained how such occurrences as they dreaded were impossible ; at which they returned to their dens beneath decks, much comforted, and comforting those about them.

To have studied the various phases of mind that were observable during these three weeks, might have been interesting and instructive to—either a moralist or pathologist ; for certainly the disease of mind was produced by a disease of body. When the ship pitched and rolled about, that was the time for an alarmist to gain proselytes to the belief that they were not sailing homeward. When the weather was fine, then the gratuity money was discussed : the kind of clothes they would buy with it, what they would give for this article of clothing, and what for that. One said " pies and porter" would be the first thing he would taste on landing ; another said he would have a " beef steak," a third would have " oatmeal porridge" because he had been so long without them, and a fourth would have a whole *half-Mutchkin* of whisky to his " own cheek," at the very first. Poor fellows ! they were doomed to a sad disappointment.

When some one would come beneath decks and say he had seen land, then the most animated discussion would arise, as to what land it was ; and if another said there was no land seen, the mob tenaciously adhered to the report of the first speaker. One day there was land seen, and some one pronounced it to be the Isle of Man. Immediately the most lively conversation arose about fustian jackets— pies and porter—looms and yarn, and gills of whisky. Soon after, the report came down that we were putting out to sea again, and that we were tacking to and fro on the coast of France ; on which almost every man discovered that he was crushed by another ; that the ship had a horrid smell—that the fleas were beginning to bite again, and that it was a cursed shame for any one to talk at that time of the night, keeping them from sleep.

At last one of those snoring breezes that drives along even the most unwieldy hulks, sent the *Prince Regent* dashing through the Irish channel one day. Never, I believe, will five hundred beings—as dirty and forlorn as we then were in appearance, wear such light hearts as we, when the shores of Ireland on one side and Galloway on the other flitted past. It was a battering rain and boisterous wind, but that was all nothing, the Craig of Ailsa got three cheers as the bending masts groaning beneath their canvas carried us along. There was not a height or hollow in the land on either side which was not described by some one or other who claimed acquaintance with the locality ; and with gladness though rough and wet, that night passed over.

The next morning was a lovely one. The ship had anchored during the night, and as she weighed in the morning a gentle breeze sprung up, and bore her into the Clyde. There were such hopes expressed as " we will be paid on board," and " oh yes ! they'll never let us land this way." One would say, " there'll be enough of the brokers along side selling clothes, and thank God we'll have nine pounds three shillings to buy them ! that's one consolation." There were all kinds of hopes, but the pleasing ones prevailed ; and there was brushing and washing, and shaving, and combing ; but more particularly there were criticisms on the alterations that had taken place. Steamers were seen on the river, that none of them knew ; others had red funnels instead of white ones; there were new stacks of chimnies on the public works, and new houses built on the river-side all of which events with many more, gave rise to animated discussions. But there was among all these and amid the joy that prevailed, one deteriorating reflection and that was the sad one of what had become of all the men that went away two years before. There had been two thousand three hundred men in all, taken out to Spain from that place; of these, there were two hundred still serving,—two hundred had gone by way of Portsmouth, and five hundred and twenty had come home. Such was the proportion of numbers which shews the dire loss sustained by the Legion.

Many indeed were the enquiries by relations for those who were not among us, but the rush of enquiry was not set on until we reached Glasgow. At Greenock where we landed, some people enquired why we had not "killed Carlos" before we came away, and a few looked at us with apparent astonishment and exclaimed "oh the blackguards! have they come back again?" To a lady, whose dress seemed to rank her among the respectables, and who lamented that any such vagabonds should have returned, and that she had hoped they were all killed,—an old man who stood near her said "whist Ma'am;—ye have na a son there, or ye wadna speak that way." A few minutes afterwards, I heard some of the towns people say to this old man, "William, is your son among them?" "No," he answered, "my son is not among them; they've left my son in his grave, but though I kent that lang syne, I cam doon here to see them for they're a' the sons o' somebody." "Atweel are they William," was the response of one of his hearers.

The magistrates of Greenock hired two steamers to convey us up the river to Glasgow; and though I confess that fears for the non-payment of the gratuities were beginning to take hold of me, I with a few others endeavoured to keep the spirits of the main body afloat, by directing their hopes, to the *agents* who were to pay us, being in Glasgow.

I would be telling a painful story that may as well sleep in forgetfulness were I to proceed with ourselves any farther.

CHAPTER XXVIII.

Affairs of the new Legion—Slaughter at Andouin, &c.

THE neglect of the Spanish government was again so vexatiously oppressive, that General O'Connell proceeded to Madrid to represent the sufferings of his troops, and to make arrangement for their regular payment, or in failure of that, to procure means of conveying them home to England. He was therefore absent when the most disastrous event occurred that had happened at any part of the Legion's service. This was the massacre at Andouin.

A Spaniard of Irish extraction named O'Donnell, had the chief command in the north at that time; and having determined on making a forward movement from Hernani in the neighbourhood of which town the troops had been quartered from the departure of General Evans, he put his force in motion on the 9th of September 1837. He crossed with a Spanish brigade at the bridge of Astigarraga taking the high range of hills to the left of Hernani, having the Artillery— Lancers and Scotch battalion with the Chapelgorris along the main road as skirmishers under Jochmus late quarter-master General of the Legion;—while Santa Cruz wound along the range of hills from the Santa Barbara with another Spanish brigade. The Irish regiment was in the different forts about Alza, and the Rifles at Orimendi, both having refused to march until they got some assurance of pay. They did not refuse to do duty where they were, but they would not move forward. The Rifles however, with the exception of thirty-five men were induced to move after the main body, which they joined at Andouin.

The Carlists were not in great force, but they stood behind their several breastworks until their flanks were turned by O'Donnell, and Santa Cruz. Jochmus made his way by the main road, pouring destruction into the enemy from the Legion Artillery, which under that brave old fellow Howe, and his not less dexterous Adjutant, Skedd, wrought heavy and fearful work in front of the advance. The whole of the movements were beautifully conducted, and the advancing troops arrived early in the afternoon at Andouin, having suffered very trifling loss. But the slaughterous artillery had cracked many a shell over the heads of the enemy, and their dead and wounded were seen strewed at those points where they had made a stand, in considerable abundance.

The Lancers particularly distinguished themselves; I am not informed of what officers were there; but three of them, Captains Hogreve, Henderson, and Baron Stutterheim were conspicuous. "These three brave fellows" says an eye-witness, "let no opportunity slip of charging the enemy." On one occasion, they espied the Carlist cavalry drawn up on the road. "Come on" said young Hogreve, "there's the cavalry, let us at them." At them they went, gallantly followed by their men, and crossing a field for a near cut, they came upon a column of infantry. This they supposed was a regiment of their own Spaniards; and having called to it, to move out of the way, they galloped through its openings. This corps was rather astonished, and so was the enemy's cavalry, for they wheeled and retreated at the gallop before the English Lancers. But if the Carlists were at first astonished, the English Lancers were not less so, when they found themselves fired on in rear by those whom they had supposed were their friendly allies. The latter were in their turn charged by the Lancers, but they were in a great measure protected by running down a steep hill-side covered by the trees. The commanding officer—Lieut. Colonel Wakefield, was not with his regiment of Lancers that day, nor the days immediately following on which there was slaughter, which has occasioned a variety of free remarks to be made on his professional character; all of which are however sufficiently balanced by the many proofs which he at other times afforded of unquestioned bravery.

As soon as O'Donnell entered Andouin, he began to fortify the place, intending it to be the centre of his line of operations. During the progress of the fortification, a considerable number were wounded while working, as the Carlists occupied heights which completely commanded the town. These heights being on the opposite side of the river Urimea, and being intersected with deep trenches, it was next to impossible for the working parties to make any defence. Several reports got into circulation, relative to the Carlists having got a reinforcement; but O'Donnell did not seem to care much whether they had, or had not; he went on with his works as usual, feeling his situation secure.

The disposition of his forces were certainly the best that could have been made, and supposing them to have possessed immoveable courage, there is no ground to believe that his positions were not perfectly judicious. His right was protected by a brigade of Spaniards on the hills, to the right of Andouin; while another brigade formed his left on a corresponding height. Both wings commanded the fords of the river in the front, and had thrown up breast-works for their protection from the enemy's musketry.

The position at Andouin was strengthened on the 11th by the Rifle Corps, which as was mentioned, refused to march on the 9th, but which was now induced to proceed to the front under Colonel Wilson. An officer who held a high rank in the service, has informed me of some particulars of that movement; among which he says, " the Royal British (Woolwich) Artillery and Marines were brought forward, as far as Hernani; but for what reason, I never heard explained. They did nothing as usual, save giving us the name of their numbers; thus making it appear in England that we were at all times assisted by the Marines, when in fact none of the Legion ever saw the latter, excepting far in the rear, on some distant hill, looking on and eating their breakfasts and dinners, which fighting soldiers are never much in the habit of tasting." This informant, says also, that—" up to the 12th, our loss in skirmishing and protecting our working parties, was eleven officers, and about two hundred men killed and wounded." And he adds, " Nothing could equal the beautiful practice of the Legion Artillery, while remaining at Andouin. It so completely cowed the enemy, that they were obliged to relieve those in their trenches, cne at a time; and then it was quite amusing to see the way they ran in and out; doubling until their heads nearly touched the ground; for if old Howe took it into his head to lay a gun, he was always sure to bring down his man, I have often been an eye-witness to his splendid practice, more particularly at this place. And while mentioning him, it would be unfair not to mention Skedd along with him."

The morning of the 14th, proved to O'Donnell the truth of the Carlists having got a reinforcement, for immediately after day-break, they opened a heavy fire from their guns, which had been brought up during the night, and placed in battery on the hills, opposite to the left of his position, and which completely commanded the town of Andouin. Howe was soon at work, and dismounted their guns, killing and wounding nearly every Artilleryman who worked, or attempted to work them. He put an effectual stop to their practice; after which everything became quiet, and the troops that garrisoned Andouin, returned to their usual work—when they had piled arms, of entrenching and fortifying.

It is supposed that the Carlist General had thrown forward his troops, under cover of his guns, for the purpose of being ready to advance, and they not hearing their Artillery firing, and not seeing any reason why they should not go forward, about 300 of the Chapelchurris (a Carlist corps corresponding in character to the Chapelgorris of the Christino party), were thrown across the river, at the ford in front of the Infanta regiment to feel their way. This regiment had piled arms, and was going on with the usual duties of a camp around them : but the moment they saw the Chapelchurris cross the river, they ran, their Colonel leading the way.

This gave courage to the enemy, and column after column crossed the river at this point, while the Infanta regiment was running away, and calling to the other Spanish regiments, that "the whole of the Carlists had crossed the river, and they would all be murdered if they did not retire." In this dastardly conduct, the greater part of their officers were the first to set an example. The Spaniards are never backward in a steeple chase, and the "tally ho" was soon heard from them, from the one extremity of the camp to the other. The Infanta regiment had left their arms standing in pile, and some of the other Spanish regiments threw away arms, ammunition, and every other article that would have impeded their progress in the race to Hernani.

At this time every thing was going on as usual in the village of Andouin ; the Artillery, Scotch, and Rifles, never for a moment suspecting that they were deserted by the cowardly division of O'Donnell. The greater part were in the trenches working as usual ; and a company of the Rifles under Captain Courtney, was working near the bridge, below the town and fronting the centre of the enemy's position. It was merely remarked by some, that "there is a little skirmishing going on to the left ;" and their true position only became known to them, by seeing the enemy among the tents and pile of arms, left by the Infanta regiment, and by hearing and feeling the bullets that came battering among them.

On perceiving this, the order, " stand to your arms!" was quickly given by the officers in command of the working parties, and two companies of the Scotch were immediately ordered to ascend the hill. These brave and devoted fellows went gallantly up, and drove the enemy, many times their number before them; but it availed nothing; for on ascending and taking an elevated position, they perceived that the Carlists were thickly crowding in their rear, while the Christino regiments were flying in every possible direction from the scene of action. What could the small Legion do? the only way by which they could have returned, was blocked up by the enemy, and they were surrounded on all sides. They were called to, to lay down their arms, and that by doing so, they would receive quarter. In this they could place no dependence, as at the very time of that promise of quarter being made, they saw some of their comrades who had been detached a short distance off, and who had surrendered—they saw them murdered; and this main body of the unfortunate Legion, determined therefore to sell their lives at the highest price.

It would appear by what could be gathered, from the very few that escaped from the village, that a considerable number of them succeeded in forcing their way back to Andouin: but not before the village was beset on all sides. They were hemmed into the square, and there without exception put to death. It is worthy of remark, that some of the Carlist officers most forward here, and most liberal in distributing murderous death, were those whose lives had been saved by the English at Irun, they having been exchanged for other prisoners, a short while before this Andouin affair.

The exact numbers killed there, were :—of the Scotch, Colonel Clarke ; Major Shields, Captains Shields, Larkham, and Dalrymple ; Lieut. Carnaby, and sixty non-commissioned officers and men.

Of the Rifles, there were Captains Courtney, and Forbes; Lieuts. O'Brien, Sims, Haslem, and Townsend, with fifty nine non-commissioned officers and men.

Of the Lancers, there were Major Mackellar and two men killed, with three wounded. Five horses killed, and fourteen wounded.

Of the Artillery, there were three officers wounded. Two gunners killed, and four wounded, one of the two gunners, had his head carried off by a cannon ball from the enemy's guns, when in the village.

There are many, and various accounts given of the time, and manner of their deaths; but the following may be relied on, as nearly correct, so far as regards the officers. I add also a short account of those officers, whose lives, characters, or peculiarities, were in any way known to me.

Colonel Clarke went out to Spain originally as Adjutant of the 6th regiment under Colonel Tupper. He was a clever practical soldier, not much in favour with those beneath him in rank, because of his unceasing attention to the details of discipline and duty. He was always in danger when it was possible to get into it; being without exception the most daring and reckless officer that was at any time in the Legion, and had been several times wounded. On the 16th of March he got a ball through one of his arms, and he had that arm still in the sling when at Andouin. He was killed by being torn from his horse by the bayonets of the enemy, at a time when having endeavoured to rally the Spaniards, and not having accomplished, he was making his way by himself back to where the Scotch were surrounded, to die as we are warranted by his character to suppose, with his comrades.

Captain Dalrymple and Lieut. Carnaby, were taken together and killed a short way from the village: they having tried to escape when too late. Some of the men who have escaped, say, that Dalrymple begged to be carried along with them being exhausted, but that there was no possibility of assisting any one, from the distance to run, and the nature of the ground to be run over. Dalrymple had been always a favourite with his men; he was one of those who would at any time give a refractory soldier a box on the ear with his own fist rather than send him to a court-martial. He was not supposed to be greatly in love with soldiering, but having a family at home he had been induced to remain in the new Legion, until there was some certain provision made for those who went home. It is supposed that Lieut. Carnaby was assisting him along, when both were taken and killed.

Captain Larkham was a youth, the nephew of a British officer of high standing. The young man had gone to Spain in conformity to his own and his uncle's wishes. He had inclined to be a soldier, and his uncle sent him to see some active service in the field previous to his entering into a British regiment. He was wounded two or three times during General Evans's service : and at Andouin he was wounded and was seen to defend himself, with his sword, on his knees. Being at last overpowered he was slain, and the tartan plaid which he wore was held aloft by his slayers, as a trophy.

Captain Courtney and his company defended themselves nobly near the bridge. They fought to the last man.

Captain Forbes was killed in the village, charging in front of his men. He was a native of Aberdeen, had once been a merchant in a prosperous way at that place, but failed. He had tried various unsuccessful schemes until in hopelessness as I believe, he went out to Spain as a private soldier, sending, as I recollect, his two pounds of bounty money to his wife. Being an excellent accountant, he was appointed by Colonel Godfrey of the 8th, to be Orderly Room Clerk. He afterwards got a commission, and rose to be Adjutant and Captain, under Colonel Hogg. In a little work which I wrote and published in Glasgow in the latter part of 1837, entitled " *A Narrative of the British Auxiliary Legion*", I gave several sketches of him under the nick name of *Humphrey*, which he bore in the regiment. These sketches were then given, because, he being a man very vain of himself, I intended him to see the weak parts of his military achievements. However, he was then dead though I did not know it, and I have only mentioned those seemingly ungenerous sketches here, in order to express my deep regret that they were ever published. His last act, was one that covered a multitude of former unsoldierlike sins, for he fell as has been said in front of his company, charging the enemy.

Lieut. O'Brian, was what the language of a camp would call a good fellow. Some people have said that he was once a "fancy-man" of the celebrated Mrs. Clarke, the *natural* Duchess of York. Be that as it may, he was not much more than the wreck of a man in Spain. Hard living, and a braggadocio spirit that led him into frequent adventures, in which he was a sufferer, had impaired his physical constitution ; and his intellectual one expired in a manner to be deeply regretted, both by his friends and foes, and he had a goodly number *of* both. O'Brian had got some distance from the village, by the assistance of a friend, but he was obliged to drop from exhaustion ; he was not down a minute, when his brains were dashed out by the butt ends of the Carlist muskets; his cries were horrid.

Lieutenant Sims was killed, it is believed, with Captain Courtney, and Lieutenant Haslem fell a sacrifice to his own generosity in trying to save Lieutenant Townsend. The last time they were seen, Haslem had Townsend on his back; the poor boy having been wounded.

Major Mackellar was a native of Port Glasgow. He had been in Portugal and went out to Spain under Colonel Tupper in the 6th Scotch regiment. He was, in manners, a perfect gentleman ; and in courage and conduct a soldier. In every engagement of the Legion, either general or partial, Mackellar had been in contact with the enemy, and the Lieutenant-General had more than once, in orders, expressed a high opinion of his meritorious services. On the 5th of May, 1835, and 16th of March, 1837, he was particularly distinguished. In the retreat on the last mentioned occasion, he rendered essential service in saving the guns ; and unfortunately it was a similar service on the 14th September, that cost him his life. He was at the head of the Lancers at Andouin, and seeing the enemy's cavalry about to cut off the retreat of the Artillery, he charged to save it, and was slain in the charge.

The saddest part of my melancholy record has yet to be written. It is sad in itself, but doubly so to me, as the subjects of it were the officers with whom I had the honour to be intimately connected during the whole period of my service. I speak of the two brothers Major and Captain Shields. They were the sons of an officer of the British army, who, with the eldest went out to Portugal. The father was killed, and the son returned, not wearied of warfare, but as appeared, willing to engage in the first campaign that would again offer. He then with his younger brother Robert, went out to Spain, he as Captain, and Robert as Ensign of the grenadier company of the 8th regiment. I was always with them, having acted as their clerk in keeping the company accounts previous to being promoted to the Colour-Sergeantcy, which promotion was obtained for me at their immediate instance; and as a matter of course, I continued to keep their accounts. Both were dangerously ill of fever in Vittoria during which, I was often beside them. On the 5th of May the Captain was severely wounded : in consequence of which, and being senior Captain of the regiment he got a brevet Majority, and shortly afterwards the full rank ; while his brother was promoted to a Lieutenantcy, and some months after to the Captaincy of the same company. Both were gentlemen of the most amiable disposition, strict disciplinarians as soldiers, but yet so honourable in every circumstance and transaction with their men, that the most scrupulous superior could not have found a fault in them, while the most discontented soldiers were often heard saying that they would rather have their " own two Shields's" though they were more strict, than any other officers.

They were the only brothers of a family of sisters who with their mother live as I am informed, in the neighbourhood of Dublin, their native place.   I am enabled to speak of the warm brotherly affection that subsisted between themselves, and between them and their family.   I know frequent appeals from the warm sources of motherly and sisterly love, besought and urged them to return and make a home happy by their presence; and I knew that the desire was strong in both to leave the turbulent strife of the campaign, and rejoin the domestic life of home.   But both were soldiers ; and though the impulse of affection beat homewards, the desire of adding something more to their rank and consequence prevailed with them, to renew their services under General O'Connell.

They renewed their services and on the 14th of September, they were, as they had always been, foremost in the fight.   When endeavouring to force a retreat into the village, after having led up their companies to the height spoken of formerly, the Captain was mortally wounded, or at least so severely that he fell.   His elder brother the Major, stood over his body defending it from the savage assailants, and he also fell. It was near the place of their death, that Captain Larkham was killed, and it is said by some, that the two brothers and Larkham were seen all wounded, and all defending themselves in prostrate conflict at the same time.

The Lancers behaved nobly during the retreat, charging the enemy in every direction, and sticking close to the Artillery.   " Too much" says an eye-witness, cannot be said for the brave old Howe, and those with him ; he literally skirmished every inch of the way to Hernani, dealing destruction on all sides as the Carlists ran in parallel lines with the retreating army. On the first movement towards a retreat he was when ready to start, induced by the thronging numbers of the enemy to halt, and give them a volley of spherical case shot : he remarking that though it was time to be off, he could not think of missing such an opportunity for a good shot. The Adjutant of the Artillery, Mr Skedd, was nearly left a prey to the devouring enemy, he being left by his servant without a horse. When the guns had given the discharge just spoken of, and were ready to gallop off, he ran to the spot where he expected to find his horse, but the servant thinking it was time, or more than time to be off, had mounted and was away in front on the road. Mr. Skedd had thus to follow on foot, and though the guns were supposed to be the last of the retreat there was at least one behind them and that was Mr. Skedd himself. He came up with them at last, and had an opportunity to return a few shots on his pursuers with more precise and destructive effect than those which had been aimed at him.

The conduct of Baron Stutterheim of the Lancers, and Captains Hogreve, and Henderson, was beyond all praise; though it is to be lamented that the most of that credit, which they so richly deserved, was given to Lieutenant-Colonel Wakefield who was not on the ground at all: where he was, or what he was doing to keep him from joining them some time of the day, is best known to himself.

Many brave acts were done by individuals now living during the retreat from Andouin. Jochmus and his A. D. C. Cotter were often conspicuous; O'Donnell had dismounted for the purpose of rallying his Spaniards, and became so exhausted that he was on the point of being made prisoner; and he would have been captured, had not Colonel Arbuthnott dismounted and given his horse to him; they both escaped.

O'Donnell was in a state of partial distraction from the cowardly way in which he was deserted by his troops ; he found it impossible to rally them until he reached Hernani; and then he found that nearly 800 stand of arms with ammunition in proportion, had been thrown away ; also that the whole of the tents, provisions, &c. had fallen into the hands of the enemy. The stores taken, amounted in all to 800,000 rounds of ammunition, and six weeks' provision for 5000 men. The entire loss in killed and wounded was, 20 officers and 300 men, some of the Spanish officers were cut down by O'Donnell himself—and by two Englishmen (officers) whom it may be as well now not to name—for refusing to rally their flying troops.

I must omit many interesting incidents that have been communicated to me, as my prescribed space is now more than over-exceeded, but I may give the following. An officer says— "A most singular thing happened on the morning of the 11th while we occupied Andouin. An officer of the Artillery was wounded, a musket ball shattering his jaw. Dr. Wilkinson of the Scotch was immediately with him, and dressed his wounds. Wilkinson afterwards joined a group of us near the spot, and was describing the course of the ball. He placed his thumb and finger on his own throat, on the place corresponding to that of the Artillery officer's wound; and when telling how the ball had made its entrance and exit by saying,—"look, here is the place"—a ball struck him on the identical spot, wounding also the tops of his thumb and finger. We were astounded when we saw the blood flowing, for although we heard him exclaim "Good God? I'm hit too?" we really thought he was humbugging. Now it was "diamond-cutting-diamond," as Dr Bayne had to extract the ball and dress the wound of his medical comrade : fortunately for Wilkinson none could do it better."

The same officer who relates the foregoing, says,—

Reports were in circulation that many of our poor fellows with some Spaniards, had shut themselves up in the Church of Andouin, and only surrendered on receiving a promise of quarter, but that they to a man, were bayoneted on opening the doors. We had fifty other reports all likely enough at the time, but when we came to compare one story with another, we were clearly of opinion that our brave fellows were butchered in the square of the village and at the bridge."

The Carlists acknowledged a loss from the 9th to the 14th September inclusive—of 700 officers and men ; upwards of 400 having fallen on the morning of the 14th. The excellent practice of the Artillery so admirably conducted by Howe and Skedd, who to their high honour saved all their guns—was one of the causes, not the least effective, in thus punishing the enemy.

The loss sustained by the small Legion at this time, rendered it unfit for any useful operations, and more especially as General O'Donnell returned from Madrid, without having succeeded in his mission of obtaining the protection of the Spanish Government. He issued the following "order of the day" when his troops had continued three months longer in starvation, which had the effect of getting them shipped to England, save about three hundred who with Colonel Wakefield continued, and still (December 1838) as I believe, continue to serve as Lancers and Artillerymen.

GENERAL ORDER.

" St. Sebastian, Dec. 10.

" Fellow Soldiers,—I cannot allow the relationship which has existed between us to cease, without offering to you, in as strong terms as I can express, my unqualified admiration of the unparalleled devotion with which you have endured the no common share of privation and hardship which has fallen to your lot. I congratulate you that you have shown, not alone that daring courage in the field which is the marked characteristic of the British soldier, but that you have shown even more than his wonted patience under suffering.

" The conflict in which we have been engaged has been to you more murderous than to the allies in whose ranks you fought : you were aware that, wounded or helpless, should you fall into the hands of the enemy, you had no mercy to expect ; you knew that no barbarity would be wanting to heighten the sufferings of your last moments. You knew that many of your comrades had been treated with the ferocity only to be expected from the Indian savage ; but your fearless step was ever quicker when it led to the enemy, and your shout the most heartfelt when called to the battle. Your privations I cannot call to mind without a thrill of indignation, in reflecting that many were imposed upon you, not by unavoidable necessity, but by the culpable neglect or the wilful malevolence of the individuals appointed by the Spanish Government to superintend your equipment. To their eternal infamy be it recorded, that they allowed you to meet this inclement season exposed in the lines, most of you barefooted, and many without other covering to your nakedness than your great coats. This cruelty, I repeat, was inflicted on you when the slightest exertion or good feeling might have remedied the evil.

Your pay has been allowed to run with a long arrear; this was unavoidable, from the financial embarrassment of the Spanish Government, and would, I feel confident, have been cheerfully borne by you;
but when accompanied by other acts of injustice and ill-treatment, it
has given me an opportunity of dissolving the Legion, and of declaring your engagements with Spain at an end.

" Three months have elapsed since I claimed from the Minister of
War the fulfilment of the 12th clause of your contract, and since then
you have continued to perform with exactness, all the duties required
from you.   No determination from the Government in answer to my
application has been communicated to me.   I undertake to demand
redress for an injustice offered to you, and I am met by an arbitrary
order that a part of the force should lay down its arms.   No assumption of illegal authority—no matter by what temporary authority it
may be backed—shall induce me to desert your interests, and I will
confidently appeal to our own government for such redress as the
justness of your claims demand.   No exertions of mine shall be
wanting to advocate your rights; and as I am aware that threats have
been held out to the corps of cavalry and artillery, that, in the event
of their discontinuing to serve, they will forfeit their claim to gratuity,
I boldly affirm, that such is not the case: on the contrary, you are
entitled, by the 12th article of the contract of service, to all the
advantages which would have accrued to you had your period of service
extended to the 10th of June next.   This clause was framed by me
for your protection, and now for that purpose will I enforce its
fulfilment.

" It now remains to me to add my warmest thanks to those officers
who served under my command.   I cannot express, in terms sufficiently strong to please myself, my feelings in regard to those whose
generous assistance has materially contributed to enable me to support
the difficulties which have surrounded my situation.

" To Colonel Ross, Assistant Adjutant-General, to the officers of
my personal staff, Colonels Herman and Freestun; to Colonel Clerk,
Assistant Quartermaster-General, and to the Inspector-General of
Hospitals, whose exertions have been unwearied, I feel deeply indebted.
To Colonel Wooldridge, of the Rifle Battalion, I must particularly
address my thanks.   To Major Brenan, my extra Aide-de-Camp,
whose devotion I have on several occasions admired—to each and all

of these officers, I reiterate my obligations ; and, in the peculiar circumstances which have preceded the dissolution of the Legion, I have doubly experienced their manly and unflinching support. To the officers commanding the corps of cavalry and artillery, although in most instances their services have been amongst the most valuable, I regret I cannot in this instance offer my thanks.

" Having thus promulgated in general orders the dissolution of the Legion, I avail myself of the same opportunity to exhort the officers and men to be guarded in their conduct, until the means of conveyance to their own country shall be provided for them, in order to give no opportunity for persecution.

" O'CONNELL."

BRITISH AUXILIARY LEGION OF SPAIN.

ARMY LIST,

CORRECTED TO

1st APRIL, 1837,

BEING THE LAST PUBLISHED.

BRITISH AUXILIARY

GENERAL OFFICERS.	AIDES-DE-CAMP.

Col. Lezama, 6th Regt.

COMMANDANT IN CHIEF. Governor of Passages.
Lieut.-General De Lacy Evans. Lt.-Col. Don Raphael Escudero y
M. P. G. C. St. F.   Alava.

Lt.-Col. Don Fernando Cotoner.
Lt.-Col. Don Ricardo Shelly.
Capt. Don Ignacio Gurrea.
Lt.-Col. Wooldridge.
Lt.-Col. Meade.

Extra.
Major Kent Murray 8th Regt.

BRIGADIER-GENERALS.

Major Townley, 1st Regt.
Capt, Knight, extra, 1st Regt.
Chas. Chichester, 4th Regt.
Major W. H. Fitzgerald, R. I
C. L. Fitzgerald, R. I. Regt.
Regt.

Col. Chas. Wetherall, Acting-
Commdt. attached to Col. Carbonell's department in England.

LEGION OF SPAIN.

Military Secretary's Office, 1st April, 1837,

Military Secretary's Department.

MAJORS OF BRIGADE.

Military Secretary, Lt.-Col. G. F. Herman, Rifles.

INFANTRY.

Adjutant-General's Department.

Deputy Adj.-Gen. Col. M. C. O'Connell, R. I. Regt.
Dep. Assist. Gen. Maj. W. S. Clarke, R. I. Regt.

1st BRIGADE.

Quarter-Master-General's Department.

Lt.-Col. Freestun, 4th Regt.

Dep. Q.-M.-G. Colonel A. Jochmus, 8th Regt.

2nd BRIGADE.

Dep. Assist. Q.-M.-G. Maj. J. M'Intosh, Rifles.

Major Beckham, 1st Regt.

CAVALRY.

Deputy Provost-Marshal, Capt. Thos: Gorman. unattached.

FIELD OFFICERS.

COLONELS.	Date.
A. de Ramon y Carbonell - -	20th July, 1835
A. D. Arbuthnott, Com. Depot, and Chief Agent of Transports - - -	26th Oct. ,,
a M. C. O'Connell, R.I. Regt. D.A.G. -	11th July, 1836.
a A. Jochmus, D.-Q.-M.-G. 8th Regt. -	20th Sept. ,,
a V. Lezama, 6th Regt. S. - -	13th Oct. ,,
W. H. Jacks, 2nd Lancers - -	9th Dec. ,,
Claud. Shaw, Artillery - -	20th Mar. ,,
T. Perronet Thompson, M.P. Honorary -	,, ,, ,,
Charles Wetherall, unattached - -	,, ,, ,,
a M. Ross, 6th Regt. - - -	,, ,, ,,
a R. Cannan, R. I. Regt. - -	,, ,, ,,
M. Fortescue, Rifles - - -	,, ,, ,,
a W. Wakefield, 1st Lancers - -	,, ,, ,,

LIEUTENANT-COLONELS.

W. M. Slone, unattached - -	16th Nov. 1835.
a W. F. Campbell, 4th Regt. - -	5th May, 1836.
a S. Shaw, 1st Regt. - -	,, ,, ,,
F. C. Ebsworth, 4th Regt. -	3rd Sept. ,,
a G. Hogg, 8th Regt. - -	12th ,, ,,
a J. Boyd, Rifles - -	,, ,, ,,
Smyth de Burgh, S. - -	20th ,, ,,
a P. Fitzgerald, 4th Regt. - -	,, ,, ,,
a G. F. Herman, M.S. Rifles - -	,, ,, ,,
a W. L. Freestun, S. 4th Regt. - -	1st Oct. ,,
a J. W. Wooldridge S. unattached -	,, ,, ,,

FIELD OFFICERS—continued.

LIEUTENANT-COLONELS.   Date.

a F. R. Clarke, 6th Regt.	-	1st Oct. 1836
G Fitch, unattached,	-	,, ,,
a G. M'Cabe R. I.	-	7th Feb. 1837
J. Apthorpe, Honorary	-	7th March
a J. Talbot 1st Regt.	-	23d do.
a P. Ramsay 4th Regt.	-	,, ,,
a J. P. Meade. S.—R. I.	-	,, ,,
W. H. Wilson 8th Regt.	-	,, ,,

MAJORS.

a W. N. Bull 1st Regt.	-	5th May, 1836
a W. Shields. 8th Regt.	-	,, ,,
a R. Hamilton 9th do	-	,, ,,
a W. H. Fitzgerald, R. I. do	-	,, ,,
J. W. Newcombe, Rifles,	-	,, ,,
a D. Durie, Rifles,	-	19th do
W. S. Clarke, S.—R. I.	-	13th June,
a T. Shepperd, R. I.	-	1st July,
C. Cumberlege, 1st Lancers,	-	,, ,,
a H. Lyster, 4th Regt.	-	20th Sept.
C. Galway, R. I.	-	,, ,,
T. Humphrey, Engineers,	-	,, ,,
a J. Shaw, 6th Regt,	-	25th do
a R. Atkyns, Rifles.	-	1st Oct.
a E. F. Brennan, R. I.	-	,, ,,
a E. Parke, R. I.	-	,, ,,
a Thos. Askey, 4th Regt.	-	,, ,,
a J. M'Intosh, Rifles,	-	,, ,,

FIELD OFFICERS —continued.

MAJORS.		Date.
T. Maclaine, 4th Regt.	-	1st Oct. 1836
a C. Wood, 6th do	-	,, ,,
W. Peyton, Unattached,	-	30th Decr.
E. Stephenson, 1st Lancers,	-	5th Jany. 1837
R. Baker, do	-	25th March
E. Howe, Artillery	-	,, ,,
a E. Sheppard, Rifles,	-	,, ,,
K. Murray, S. 8th Regt.	-	,, ,,
a P. Allez, R. I.	-	,, ,,

CAVALRY.

1st. Regiment—The " *Reina Isabel* " *(Lancers)*.

Lt.-COLONEL.

W. Wakefield, Col. 15th Sep. 36

MAJOR.

C. Cumberlege,   1st July, 36

CAPTAINS.

E. Stephenson, Bt.-Maj. 1st July, 1835.
R. Baker, Bt.-Maj.   do
F. Hogreve,   5th July, 36.
C. Jennings,   25th Aug.
J. Hanson,   8th Oct.

LIEUTENANTS.

E. Moore,   26th Aug. 35
Baron Stutterheim, 26th Oct.
A. Middleton,   1st Dec.
W. Partington,   5th July, 36
J. Stoddart,   3d Sep.
W. Francis,   1st Oct.
H. Disney, Adjt.   6th Nov.

CORNETS.

R. Henderson, 11th April, 36
H. Byam,   do.
J. Hely,   19th July,
C. Walker,   1st. Oct.

PAY-MASTER,

Wm. Laurie, Capt.1st. July 35

ADJUTANT.

H. Disney, Lt.   6th Nov. 36

RIDING-MASTER.

QUARTER-MASTER.
E. Casey,   23 Sept. 36

SURGEON.
W. Lardner,   1st July 35

ASSISTANT SURGEON.
— Daykin,   26th July, 36

VETY.-SURGEON.
R. S. Bailey,   25th June,

Facings   yellow.

CAVALRY.

2nd Regiment—The "*Queen's Own Irish*" *(Lancers).*

LT-COLONEL.

W. H. Jacks, Col. 31st July, 35

CORNETS.

Chidley Maloney, 31st. July, 35
O'Connell Burke, 8th March, 36
G. Hardman,   16th June

MAJOR

W. Martin, Bt. Lt.-Col.
        20th Mar. 36

PAY-MASTER.

Lou. Lindo,   17th Oct. 35

ADJUTANT.

W. Berry, Lt.   27th Dec. 35

CAPTAINS.

H. Kensington, 27th Aug. 35
I. G. Maturin,   31st do.
I. Marsh,   29th Jan. 36
J. R. Bevor,   9th Dec.

RIDING-MASTER.

T. Murphy, Lt.

QUARTER-MASTER.

M. Nowlan,   11th April, 36

SURGEON.

V. M'Swiney,   25th Sept, 36

LIEUTENANTS.

W. Burke,   7th Aug. 35
W. T. L. Travers,   do.
T. Murphy, R M 11th Ap. 36
W. Berry, Adj.   14th do.
C. Courtney,   9th Dec.
W. H. Ertaminger, 23d Mar. 37

ASSISTANT-SURGEON.

S. E. Piper,   21st. May, 36

VETY.-SURGEON.

T. S. Beech,   4th Feb. 36

Facings Yellow.

INFANTRY.

1st Regiment.

LT.-COLONEL.

S. Shaw, - 20th March, 37

MAJOR.

P. Ramsay, Bt. Lt.-Col.
5th May, 36

CAPTAINS.

Geo. Talbot, Bt. Lt. Col. , 35
1st July
W. N. Bull, Bt. Maj. do.
E. Beckham, Bt. Maj. S. do.
H. Linton, - 27th Dec.
C. Townley, Bt. Maj. S.
25th Sept. 36.
A. Harris, - - 27th do.
F. Durie, - - 16th Dec.
E. Knight, S. - 23rd Mar. 37
D. Allez, - - 1st April
F. Hornsby, - do.

1st LIEUTENANTS.

D. Kelly, Capt. 25th Sept. 36
J. Rae, - - - 5th Aug.
J. M. Stratrusteguy, 8th do.
C. W. Palmer, - 20th do.
W. Stapleton, - 18th Sept.
A. W. Letamundi, 1st April, 37
W. G. Pierce. - do.
P. Dupont, - do.

2nd LIEUTENANTS.

—Gregg, - 20th Sept.
Alex. Lawson, 19th Oct.
W. Phillips, - do.
J. Richardson, - 1st April, 37

PAY-MASTER.

C. S. Bedford, Capt. 5th Sept. 35

ADJUTANT.

D. Kelly., Capt. 13th Oct. 36

QR. MASTER,

A. Ball, - - 31st March 37

SURGEON.

J. K. Walter, - 16th Jan.

ASSIST. SURGEON.

J. Kirkwood, - 16th Nov. 36

Facings Yellow.

4th Regiment, or, "*Westminster Grenadiers.*"

Lieut.-Colonel Charles Chichester, Brig-Gen. 20th June, 1835.

LT. COLONELS.

W. F. Campbell,   5th May, 36
F. C. Ebsworth,   3rd Sept.

MAJORS.

P. Fitzgerald, Bt. Lt. Col.
                25th April, 36
J. Ellis,   -   -   18th Sep.

CAPTAINS.

W. L. Freestun, Bt. Lt.-Col, S.
                3rd July, 35
H. Lister, Bt. Maj. 16th do.
N. Cooke,   -   19th Oct.
T. Askey, Bt. Maj. 3rd Jan, 36
G. M'Donald   -   5th May,
G. Maclaine, Bt. Maj. 10th July
W. Cotter,   -   1st. Oct.
J. O'Sullivan,   -   22d Mar. 37
J. Courtney,   -   do.

1st. LIEUTENANTS.

J. C. Gregg,   -   17th May, 36
S. L. Dustin,   -   23rd July,
J. Firmin,   -   -   do.
— Irwin,   -   -   10th Aug.
C. G. Hodgson,   11th Nov.
I. B. Sparrow,   - 24th do.
C. J. Johnson, Bt. Capt.
                6th Feb. 37
J: M'Intosh,   -   22nd March.
F. H. Brockwell,   23 do.

2nd LIEUTENANTS.

— O'Brien,-   -   24th Feb, 36
C. Morris,   -   15th June,
— Lister, -   -   -   do.
G. S. Siems,   -   8th July
J. Ives, -   -ι -   17th do.
F. Elliot.   -   -   23rd do.
— O'Connor,   -   8th Oct.
J. Brown,   -   - 24th Nov.

PAY-MASTER.

T. Edwards, Capt. 3rd July 35

ADJUTANT.

QUARTER-MASTER.

— Baldwinson,   15th June, 36

SURGEON.

— Kearns,   24th Aug. 25

ASSIST.-SURGEONS.

Facings   white.

6th Regiment, or, " *Scotch Grenadiers*"

LT.-COLONELS.

Malcolm Ross, Col. 13th May 36
F. R. Clarke, 23rd March, 37

MAJORS.

J. Hamilton, 20th Sept. 36
John Shaw, 25th Sept. 36

CAPTAINS.

V. Lezama, Bt.-Col. 15 July, 35
C. Wood, Bt.-Maj. 22nd Sept 36
P. Mackellar, Bt. Maj.
  5th May, 36
—Larkham, 25th Sept. do.
W. Foster, 27th Jan. 37
M. Dellamere, 17th Feb. do.

1st. LIEUTENANTS.

R. M'Leod, - 19th May, 36
W. Nettleship, 8th Oct.
W. Morgan, do.
M. Ridge, Adjt. do.
J. O'Neil, 27th Jan. 37
J. Robbins, 17th Feb.
J. Light, do.

2nd LIEUTENANTS.

J. Scott, 25th Oct. 1835
G. Stewart, 9th Dec.
J. Tinson, 23rd March, 37

PAY-MASTER.

J. Drummond, Capt.
  4th July 25

ADJUTANT.

J. Ridge, Lt. 17th Feb. 37.

QR.-MASTER.

G. A. Howitt, 12th May, 36

SURGEON.

J. Bayne, 23rd March, 37

ASSIST.-SURGEON.

VOLUNTEER.

T. Carr, 9th March, 37

Facings Blue.

No. 41.

8th Regiment.—"*Highlanders.*"

LT.-COLONELS.

G. Hogg,   17th Feb. 37
A. Jochmus, Non-eff. 1st. Mar 37

MAJORS.

W. H. Wilson, Bt.-Lt.-Col.
            20th May, 36
W. Shields,   17th Feb. 37

CAPTAINS.

H. Dalrymple,   11th July, 36
F. Lyster.   22nd Aug. 36
A. C. Robertson, 20th Sept. 36
R. Shields,   21st Jan. 37
K. Murray, Bt. Maj. 2 Aug. 36
P. R. Roberts,   16th Mar. 37

LIEUTENANTS.

J. Roche,   10th July, 36
R. O'Driscoll   do.
A. Forbes, Adj. Bt. Capt. do.
J. B. Cooke,   4th March, 36
W. Butler,   19th Feb. 37
J. Goldriske,   23rd Feb. 37

ENSIGNS.

— Hart,   23rd Aug. 36
G. F. Price,   do.
J. Fragoes,   6th Feb. 37
A. Durkan,   10th do.

PAY-MASTER.

J. Kymer, Capt.   8th Aug. 35

ADJUTANT.

A. Forbes,   11th Dec. 36

QUARTER-MASTER.

H. Groom,   15th Sept. 36

SURGEON.

W. Murphy.   21st May, 36

ASSIST.-SURGEON.

E. Healey,   21st May, 36

Facings red.

CONSOLIDATED ROYAL IRISH.

Lieut.-Colonel Fitzgerald, Brigadier General, 15th July, 1835.

LIEUT.-COLONELS.

M. C. O'Connell, Col. non-eff.
19th July, 35
R. Cannon, Col. - 26th May, 36

MAJORS.

T. Shepperd, - 1st July, 36
J. M'Cabe, Lt.-Col. 7th Feb. 37
E. Brennan, - 22nd Jan. 37

CAPTAINS.

W. H. Fitzgerald, Bt. Maj.
16th July, 35
C. Galwey, Bt. Maj. do.
J. P. Meade, S. Bt. Lt.-Col. do.
J. C. Holmes, - 5th Oct.
E. Parke, - 15th Dec.
J. B. Street, 12th Jan. 36
Thos. O'Dell, - 5th May,
P. Allez, Bt-Maj, 14th June,
W. S. Clarke, Bt.-Maj. do.
J. Feehan, - 1st July,
R. Wright, - 12th Aug.
W. E. Mockler, - 22d do.
J. Keogh, - 1st March 37

LIEUTENANTS.

J. O'Connor, Bt-Capt.
12th Jan. 36
J. Sparrow, - 5th May,
A. Fitzgerald, - 1st July,

H. O'Donnell, - 28th July 36
W. F. Mandeville, 12th Aug.
T. Morris, - 24th do.
H. Fitzgerald, - 13th do.
J. O'Neale, - 11th Nov.
R. Gubbins, - do.
T. C. Bunnett, - 27th do.
T. Lambe, - do.

ENSIGNS.

J. P. Bezant, - 18th Mar. 36
S. Chadwicke, - 15th June,
— Lynch, - 28th July,
— Orme, - 19th Aug.
J. Carmody, - 2d Oct.
P. Kelly, - 17th Nov.

PAY-MASTER.

R. Meagher, Capt. Acting,
8th Jan. 36

ADJUTANT.

P. Allez, Bt.-Maj.

QUARTER-MASTER.

I. Smith, - 5th March, 37

SURGEON.

T. D. Maybury, 1st March, 36

ASSIST.-SURGEONS.

M. O'Connell, 19th July, 35
G. A. Plunkett, 12th Oct.

RIFLE CORPS.

LIEUT.-COLONEL.
M. Fortescue,   25th May, 36.
MAJORS.
J. Boyd, Lieut-Col. 5th May, 36.
David Durie,   27th May, 36.

—M'Dermott,   23rd Oct. 36.
M. Ximines,   5th Jan. 37.
J. Ebbs,   1st Feb, 37.

CAPTAINS.

G. F. Herman, M. S. Lt.-Col.
    11th July, 35.
J. W. Newcombe,   Bt.-Major,
    11th Oct. 35.
R. Atkyns,   15th Dec. 35.
G. Jeffrey,   5th May, 36.
J. M'Intosh,   Bt.-Major S.
    5th May, 36.
E. Sheppard,   Bt.-Major,
    27th May, 36.
R. Durie,   15th Oct. 36.
J. Boyd,   13th Aug. 36.
R. Bowden,   23rd Sept. 36.
E. Burridge.   23rd Sept. 36.

1st LIEUTENANTS.

—O'Brien,   23rd July, 36.
W. Hook,   12th Aug. 36.
R. T. Townsend, Adj.
    12th Aug. 36.
T. Barker,   22nd Aug. 36.
— Phelan,   23rd Sept. 36.
T. Haslam,   26th Dec 36.

2nd LIEUTENANTS.

P. J. Wheat,   17th Mar. 36.
J. Davis,   21st Aug. 36.
T. Kenny,   23rd Sept, 36.
— Boxer,   10th Oct. 36.
—Ludorice,   10th Oct. 36.

PAY-MASTER.
W. Burt, Capt. 12th Aug. 35.

ADJUTANT.
T. T. Townshend, Lieut.
    8th Oct. 36.

QUARTER-MASTER.

A. M'Duff,   18th July, 36.

SURGEON.
G Duplex,   28th Oct. 35

ASSIST-SURGEONS.
A. King,   1st Jan. 36.
J. Mahony,   21st May, 36.

Green—Facings red.

ARTILLERY.

LT-COLONEL.

Claudius Shaw, Col,
8th Sept. 35.

CAPTAINS.

E. Howe.   25th Feb. 36.
J. Wade,   25th Oct. 36.

1st LIEUTENANTS.

J. H. Hamilton,   Bt.-Capt.
    25th Feb. 36.
B. Bagley,   1st April, 36.
T. Muttlebury,   8th April, 36.
W. H. Kenny,   1st Oct. 36.

2nd LIEUTENANTS.

R, Skidd,   17th Oct. 36.
D. B. Shaw,   20th Dec. 36.

ADJUTANT.

QUARTER-MASTER.

J. Clarke,   1st Jan. 37.

SURGEON.

T. H. Crosse,   12th Aug. 35.

ASSISTANT-SURGEON,

J. Croft Roberts, 12th Aug. 35

ASSIS.-VETY.-SURGEON.

Joaquin Briones, 17th Mar. 36.

J. Lazenby, in charge of Stores of Artillery and Depot, Woolwich,
9th Oct. 35.

FIELD TRAIN.

ASSIST.-COMMISSARY AND PAY-MASTER.

DEPUTY. ASSIST. COMMISSARY.

W. Weale,   31st May, 36.
H. Reeves,   17th Oct. 36.
J. W. Collins,   6th Nov. 36.
O. T. Maudsley, 6th Nov. 36.
—Bishop,   6th Nov. 36.

CLERKS OF STORES.

C. Sidley,   14th June, 35·
G. Fenwick,   7th Aug. 35·
G. Aynge,   31st May, 36.
C. Rogerson,   31st May, 36.
J. Bennett,   18th Oct. 36.

Blue—Facings red.

ENGINEERS.

Major Humphrey	-	-	-	11th Sept. 1835.
Captain Hornbrooke	-	-	-	1st Oct. 1836.
Lieutenant Reid	-	-	-	1st ,, ,,
2nd Lieutenant Fryer	-	-	-	5th May, ,,

Commandant of Passages, Colonel Lezama.

DEPOT, SANTANDER.

Commandant, Col. A. Arbuthnott   -   26th Oct. 1835.

Acting Adjutant, 1st Lieut. Stratrusteguy, 4th Regt.   ,,   ,,

Quarter-Master, 2nd Lieutenant Orme, R. I. Regt.

UNATTACHED LIST.

Lieut-Colonel Sloane, Town Major of San Sebastian	16th Nov. 1835.
Lieut.-Col. Wooldridge, A. D. C. -	1st Oct. 1836.
Bt.-Lieut.-Col. Smith de Burgh - -	20th Sept. ,,
Bt.-Lieut.-Col. Fitch, Commandant of Puyo	21st May, ,,
Capt. Chase, attached to Artillery -	,, ,,
Capt. Gorman, Dep. Provost Marshal -	16th Mar. 1837.
Lieut. Purzeski, Cavalry Staff of Br. Gen.	
Santa Cruz - - - -	23rd ,, ,,
Surgeon Rigg - - . -	
,, Bunnett - - -	
,, M. G. Scott - - -	29th ,, ,,
Paymaster, Capt. T. J. Wills, late 2nd Regiment	15th July, 1835.
Bt.-Major W. Peyton, late 4th Regiment	4th ,, 1837.
Capt. Byrne, late 7th Regiment - -	4th ,, 1835.

Surgeons unattached, with pay and allowance of
Assistant-Surgeons.

W. Lambton.	-	-	-	-
W. H. Sholl.	-	-	-	-
M. D. O'Connell.	-	-	-	
William Docker.	-	-	-	

MEDICAL DEPARTMENT.

INSPECTOR-GEN. OF HOSPITALS.

J. Callander, M. D. 4th Aug, 35.

DEPUTY INSPECTOR-GEN. OF 'HOSPITALS.

Rutherford Alcock, 5th May, 36.

ASSIST.-INSPECTOR OF HOSPITALS.

H. J. Bunnett, M. D. 30th Mar. 37, but with the pay and allowance of Staff-Surgeon.

STAFF-SURGEONS.

Alex. Taylor, M. D. 9th Aug. 35.
D. M. Davies,   22nd Aug. 35.
John Gannon,   1st Dec. 35.
A. M. a Beckett,   1st Jan. 36.
J. Dorset,   21st May, 36.
H. Wilkinson,   23rd Mar, 37.
—Johnson,   30th Mar, 37.

STAFF-ASSIS.-SURGEONS.

A. Belmont,   12th Oct, 35.
W. Cruikshank,   1st Jan. 36·
W. Hackett,   16th Feb. 36.
A. Dolce,   25th Mar. 36.
F. Dicker,   5th Sept. 35.

HOSPITAL ASSISTANTS.

R Hendley,   22nd Aug. 35.
H. B. Bunnett,   16th Nov. 36·
W. Smith,   25th Jan. 36.
J Salamo,   21st May, 36,
-- Jamieson,   10th Aug. 36.
— Palmer   9th Sept. 36
W. Nutt,   1st Mar. 37.

PURVEYOR OF HOSPITALS.

DEPUTY PURVEYOR OF HOSPITALS.

Sydney Crocker. 25th Mar. 36.

HOSPITAL TRANSPORT.

2nd Lieut. J Smith,
                   25th Sept. 36.

Facings red.

COMMISSARIAT.

DEPUTY-COMMISSARY-GENERALS.

A· M; G. Faxardo	18th July, 35.
Robert Grindlay	1st Aug. 35.
C. Black . . . : .	20th May, 36.

ASSISTANT-COMMISSARY-GENERAL.

George Service	15th Feb. 37.

Facings black velvet.

CHIEF AGENT OF TRANSPORTS IN SPAIN.

Colonel Arbuthnott	1st Sept. 35.

AGENT TO THE LEGION,—Owen C. Edmond.

OFFICERS OF H. C. MAJESTY'S ARMY ATTACHED.

Colonel R. De La Saussaye, to Quarter-Master-
General's Department . . . 16th Mar. 36.

Major the Baron Burgoldt . . 1st Dec. 35.

Capt. Don Jose Calisto Serrano . . 1st Jan. 36.

Inspector-General-in-Chief of all the Civil Departments of the Legion, Don Mateo Llanos. 1st Mar. 36.

Attached to Commissariat, Don Jose Eizmendi Nov. 1835.

ESTABLISHMENT IN THE UNITED KINGDOM.

Acting Commandant, Col. C. Wetherall, 15th Sept. 35.

Assistant-Commissary-General, D. Ibbetson, 17th Apr. 36.

Paymaster of Invalids, Pensions, and Family
Certificates, Owen C. Edmond ; Office, No 11,
Great St. Helen's Bishopsgate St., London. 10th July, 35

MEMBERS OF THE ROYAL AND MILITARY ORDER OF ST. FERDINAND.

Lieut.-General De Lacy Evans, *Grand Cross.*

3rd CLASS OF ST. FERDINAND.

Brigadier-General Charles Chichester.

2nd CLASS OF ST. FERDINAND.

Brigadier-General Charles L. Fitzgerald.

COLONELS.

M. C. O'Connell,   -   -   -   -   *R. I. Regt*

1st. CLASS OF ST. FERDINAND.

COLONELS.

Alexander Arbuthnott, Commanding Depot at Santander.
A. Jochmus, S. A.-Q.-M.-C.
R. De La Saussaye, attached to Q.-M.-G.

V. Lezama, S.	7th Regt.
Malcolm Ross	6th ,,
M. Fortesque	Rifles.
R. Cannan	R. I.
Claudius Shaw	Artillery
W. Wakefield	1st Lan.
W. H. Jacks	2nd ,,

INSPECTOR GENERAL OF HOSPITALS,

John Callander, M. D.   -   -   -   -

DEPUTY INSPECTOR-GENERAL OF HOSPITALS.

Rutherford Alcock   -   -   -   -

MEMBERS OF THE ROYAL AND MILITARY ORDER OF ST. FERDINAND—continued.

LIEUTENANT-COLONELS.

Don Fernando Cotoner,	A.D.C.
W. F. Campbell	4th Regt.
S. Shaw	1st „
W. Martin	1st „
Don Ricardo Shelly	A.D.C.
Don Raphael Escudero	„
F. C, Ebsworth	R. I. Regt.
G. F. Herman. S.	Rifles.
J. W. Wooldridge, S.	unattached.
G. Hogg	8th Regt.
J. Boyd	Rifles.
P. Fitzgerald	4th Regt.
F. Clarke,	6th „
W. L. Freestun, S.	4th „
Smyth de Burgh, S.	unattached.
J. P. Meade, S.	R. I.
P. Ramsay	4th Regt.
George Talbot	1st „

MAJORS.

W. H. Fitzgerald	R. I.
M. Newcombe	Rifles.
William Shields	8th Regt.
Edgar Beckham, S.	1st. „
R. Hamilton	6th „
T. Shepperd	R. I.
C. Cumberlege	1st Lancers.
J. Humphreys	Engineers.
D. Durie	Rifles.
W. N. Bull,	1st Regt.
Thomas Askey	4th „
W. S. Clarke	D.A.A.G.R.I.
E. Parke	R. I.

MEMBERS OF THE ROYAL AND MILITARY ORDER OF ST. FERDINAND—continued.

MAJORS—continued.

C. Galwey	R. I.
J. Shaw	6th Regt.
C. Wood	6th ,,
C. Atkyns	Rifles
Baron de Burgoldt	Spanish Army
J. M'Intosh, S	Rifles.
E. F. Brennan	R. I.
T. E. Maclaine	4th Regt.
P. Allez, Adj.	R. I.
P. M'Kellar	6th Regt.
E. Stephenson	1st Lancers.
Kent Murray	8th Regt.
C. Townley	1st ,,

CAPTAINS.

F. B. Street	R. I.
C. Jeffrey	Rifles.
N. Cooke	,,
T. O'Dell	R. I.
Don Ignacio Gurrea	A. D. C.
R. Wright	R. I.
E. Howe	Artillery.
T. J. H. Chase	unattached.
Jose Calisto Serrano	,,

LIEUTENANTS.

T. Murphy	2nd Lancers.
John Courtney	R. I.
J. H. Hamilton	Artillery.
J. J. Sparrow	R. I.
J. O'Connor	,,
W. Partington	1st Lancers.
F. C. Byrne	R. I.
H. O'Donnell	,,
W. Muttlebury	Artillery.

MEMBERS OF THE ROYAL AND MILITARY ORDER OF ST. FERDINAND—continued

CORNETS, 2nd LIEUTENANTS, AND ENSIGNS.

F. H. Brockwell	4th Regt.
James M'Intosh	R. I.
C. Courtney	2nd Lancers.
O'Connell Burke	,,

PAYMASTER.

Capt. D. Byrne	unattached.

QUARTER-MASTER.

D. Brookes	Artillery.

———

a Attached to Field Officers' Names, denotes those present on the 5th of May 1836.

OFFICERS TRANSFERRED TO INVALID ESTABLISHMENT, IN CONSEQUENCE OF WOUNDS, &c. RECEIVED IN THE SERVICE.

Officer	Regiment
Major Thoreau	Artillery.
Capt, Oakley	1st Lancers.
Lieut.-Col.-Wyatt	8th Regt.
Capt. and Bt.-Major Brew	3rd ,,
Major Reid	7th ,,
Capt. Duncan	1st ,,
,, Arnold	,, ,,
,, Carnaby	6th ,,
,, Butler	7th ,,
,, Glazier	8th ,,
,, Edge	6th ,,
,, Deacon	1st ,,
., James	4th ,,
,, Costello	Rifles
,, Thornton	9th Regt.
,, M'Donald	6th ,,
,, Gardner	8th ,,
,, Chadwicke	4th ,,
,, Joyce	10th ,,
,, De Backer	6th ,,
Lieut. Macnamara	,, ,,
,, Barker	Rifles
,, Treeve	1st Regt.
,, Woods	9th ,,
,, Burn	,, ,,
,, Dillon	,, ,,
,, Mount	4th ,,
,, Hervey	8th ,,
,, Stack	9th ,,
,, Mackay	7th ,,
,, Carter	,, ,,
,, O'Connell	10th ,,
,, Hinbury	Rifles
Ensign Kempe	7th Regt.
,, Fyfe	8th ,,
Staff-Surgeon Barry	
Quarter-Master Bradford	3rd Regt.

RETIRED LIST.

Br.-Gen. J. G. Le Marchant	A. G,
,, E. L. Godfrey	8th Regt·
Col. A. Cruise	A. A. G.
Lieut.-Col. J. Thompson	1st ,,
,, H. Beckham	7th ,,
Major and Bt.-Lieut.-Col. Hicks	1st ,,
Capt. A. Landers	7th ,,
,, A. Duncan	,, ,,
,, W. Phelan	,, ,,
,, H. T, Brown	Rifles.
,, E. De Burgh	,,
,, P. Harding	,,
,, J. James	4th Regt.
,, R. Fannin	1st ,,
,, M. Rigg	,, ,,
,, — Kirby	6th ,,
Lieut. R. Glenny	7th Regt.
,, A. Nugent	,, ,,
,, J. M'Namara	,, ,,
,, T. Bell	1st ,,
,, Adlum	10th ,,
Ensign Shore	1st ,,
,, Grant	10th ,,
,, W. Campbell	7th ,,
Quar,-Master Bennett	1st ,,
,, Shea	10th ,,
,, Robertson	7th ,,
Assist.-Surgeon W. Kirby	7th ,,
Staff-Surgeon Watson	

At the Court at *St. James's*, the 10th day of *June*, 1835.

PRESENT,

The KING'S Most Excellent Majesty in Council.

WHEREAS by an Act passed in the fifty-ninth year of the reign of His late Majesty, King George the Third, intituled "An " Act to prevent the enlisting or engagement of His Majesty's sub- " jects to serve in foreign service, and the fitting out or equipping " in his Majesty's dominions vessels for warlike purposes, without " His Majesty's licence," it was enacted and declared, that if any natural born subject of His Majesty, his heirs and successors without the leave or licence of His Majesty, his heirs or successors, for that purpose first had and obtained under the sign manual of His Majesty, his heirs or successors, or signified by Order in Council, or by Proclamation of His Majesty, his heirs or successors, and should take or accept, or agree to take or accept, any military commission, or should otherwise enter into the military service as a commissioned or non-commissioned officer, or should enlist, or enter himself to enlist, or should agree to enlist, or to enter himself to serve as a soldier, or to be employed or should serve in any warlike or military operation in the service of, or for, or under, or in aid of any Foreign Prince, State, or Potentate, or of any person exercising, or assuming to exercise, the powers of Government in or over any foreign country, either as an officer or soldier, or in any other military capacity, or should without such leave or licence as aforesaid, accept, or agree to take or accept, any commission, warrant, or appointment as an officer, or should enlist or enter himself, or should agree to enlist or enter himself, or serve as a sailor or marine, or to be employed or engaged, or should serve in and on board any ship or vessel of war, or in and on board any ship or vessel used or fitted out, or equipped, or intended to be used, for any warlike purpose, in the service of, or for, or under, or in aid of, any Foreign Power, Prince, State, or Potentate, or of any person exercising, or assuming to exercise, the powers of Government in or over any foreign country, or should, without such leave and licence as aforesaid, engage, contract, or agree to go, or should go, to any foreign state or country, or to any place beyond the seas, with an intent or in order to enlist or to enter himself to serve, or with intent to serve, in any warlike or military operation whatever, whether by land or by sea, in the service of, or for, or under, or in aid of, any Foreign Prince, State, or Potentate, or any person exercising, or assuming to exercise, the powers of Government in or over any foreign country, either as an officer, or a soldier, or in any other military capacity, or as an officer, or sailor, or marine, in any such ship or vessel as aforesaid, although no enlisting money or pay or reward should have been, or should be in any of the cases aforesaid, actually paid to or received by him, or by any person to or for his use or benefit,—in any or either of such cases every person so offending should be deemed guilty of a misdemeanour, and should be punishable by fine and imprisonment, as in the said Act is mentioned.

His Majesty, by and with the advice of his Privy Council, being desirous of enabling all persons to engage in the military and naval service of Her Majesty Isabella the Second, Queen of Spain, is pleased to order, and it is hereby ordered, that from and after the tenth day of this instant month of June, it shall be lawful for every person whomsoever to enter into the military or naval service of Her said Majesty as a commissioned or non-commissioned officer, or as a private soldier, sailor or marine, and to serve Her said Majesty in any military, warlike, or other operations, either by land or by sea, and for that purpose to go to any place or places beyond the seas, and to accept any commission, warrant, or other appointment from or under Her said Majesty, and to enlist or enter himself in such service, and to accept any money, pay, or reward, for the same.

Provided always, that the licence and permission hereby given shall be in force only for the term of two years from the said tenth day of June instant, unless by Order in Council, made in manner aforesaid, such period should be further extended.

WM. L. BATHURST.

No. 42.

CONDITIONS.

Under which BRITISH SUBJECTS *will be admitted to the service of* HER CATHOLIC MAJESTY, DONNA ISABELLA THE SECOND, QUEEN OF SPAIN.

1st. The time of Service to be for either one or two years, as may be preferred by the individual engaging to enter Her Majesty's Service.

2nd. The Pay and Allowances to be the same as in the English Service, according to the rank and employment of each individual.

3rd. This Force to be governed in conformity with the British Military Articles of War, and, in matters not connected with military discipline, by the laws and institutions of Spain, in all other circumstances.

4th. At the conclusion of the Service, each Officer to receive a compensation equal to the amount of pay of one-half the time of their respective Service, without prejudice to any further recompence which the Government may confer for special services, on the recommendation of the Commanding Officer of the Forces.

5th. The Amount of Bounty for each Recruit, on being attested in the Service of the Queen of Spain, will be two pounds sterling.

6th. Each Non-commissioned Officer and Private to receive, at the conclusion of their respective Service, a compensation equal to the pay of two, four, or six months, according to their conduct, at the discretion of their Commanding Officer.

7th. The compensations designated in the preceding Articles to be absolutely forfeited, in case any Officer or Private should be dismissed the Service, or retire from it without the sanction of the Commander of the Forces, unless on account of wounds or sickness.

8th. In case the Spanish Government should find it expedient to dispense with the services of any individual, he shall receive the compensation corresponding to his time of Service, as determined by the 1st, 4th, and 5th Articles.

9th. The wounded, invalids, and widows of those who may be killed in action, or die on actual Service, shall be entitled to the

pensions corresponding to their respective ranks and employments, according to the Regulations of the British Army.

10th. In all other matters not herein detailed, the Rules and Regulations of the British Service will, as far as the cases admit,
be adhered to.

11th. All the recommendations made by the Commander of this
Force, in favour of the Officers and Soldiers of all ranks composing it, both during the War and after its conclusion, will
be most favourably attended to by the Spanish Government.

On the part of the Spanish Government,

(Signed)   MIGUEL DE ALAVA.

The foregoing is to be circulated to the Recruiting Establishments
of Her Majesty; the original, with the seal and signature of the
Ambassador representing, at this Court, the Queen Donna Isabella,
being in my possession.

(Signed)   DE LACY EVANS.

Bryanstone Square,
22nd June, 1835.

ALPHABETICAL NOMINAL ROLL

Of the whole of the Officers that served in the British Auxiliary Legion, at any time from its commencement to its close, with remarks.

The following roll has been made up from various scattered General Orders and documents by an amount of labour which its appearance does not exhibit save to those who know the confusion in which the continual changes of rank, regiments, and casualties, kept the official returns. It is not even yet perfect; but where an uncertainty existed, omissions have been made, rather than insertions of errors. The letter *u* (uncertain,) will point out the omissions; and any officer or other person will oblige the author by communicating correct information relative to these omissions or information *on any other topic* relative to the Legion. Their communications will be thankfully received for *future* use.

When the remark 10*th June* 37. occurs, it will be understood as invariably signifying that the officer served until the disbandment of the Legion, and no longer. It is believed that all the *names* are here; the wounds are all stated according as they appeared in the various General Orders.

ALPHABETICAL ROLL.

ADLUM, Ensign, 10th Regt. 19th July, 35, promoted Capt. retired 26th May, 37.

ALCOCK, RUTHERFORD, Staff-Surgeon, 4th July, 35, promoted Dep. Insp. Gen. of Hospitals, wounded 5th May, 36, 10th June 37, an excellent medical officer.

ALAVA, *Don* RAPHAEL, Lt. Col. and Aid-de-camp (*u.*)

ALLEZ, J. W. Capt. and Adjt. 4th Regt. 4th July, 35, killed in action 5th May, 36.

ALLEZ, PETER, Brevet Major, 9th Regt. and brother to the former, retired (*u*) 37.

ALLEZ, D. Lieut. 4th Regt. brother of the two former, 17th May, 36, promoted Capt. 10th June, 37.

ALLEN, T. Ensign 3d Regt. 13th Sep. 35, (*u*)

ALVAERIZ, Lieut. 4th Regt. 4th July, 35. (*u*)

APTHORPE, Major, 4th Regt. July, 35, and Lt. Col. 8th Regt resigned Oct. 36, his leave from the E. I. C's Service having expired·

ARIEL, S. F. Commissariat clerk.

ARNOLD, Lieut. 1st Regt. 1st July, 35, promoted Capt. invalided 30th May, 36.

ARBUTHNOTT, ALEX. Colonel 26th Oct. 35, Commandant of Depot at Santander, distinguished at the storming of Irun, brother in-law to General Evans, 10th June, 37.

ARMSTRONG, J. Lieut. 3d Regt. 10th July, 36. (u)

ARMSTRONG, Ensign, 7th Regt. 31st Aug. 35, wounded, 5th May, 36. Promoted Lieut. invalided 24th May, 37.

ARMSTRONG, T. Lieut. 9th Regt. 18th July, 35. (u)

ASKEY, THOS. Qr. Master 4th Regt. 4th July, 35, promoted Major, severely wounded 1st Oct. 36, 10th June, 37.

ATKYNS, Capt. Rifles, 12th Oct. 35, promoted Major, wounded severely 5th May, 36, do. 1st Oct, 36, and slightly 17th May, 37, —10th June, 37.

ATKINSON, Commissariat Clerk. (u)

ARCHER, Dep. Asst. Com. Gen. died by fever, in Vittoria.

A'BECKETT, Staff-Surgeon 14th July, 35, 13th June, 37.

AYNGE, GEORGE, Clerk of Stores, promoted from the ranks of 3d Regt. 31st May, 36, entered New Legion, an active officer, the author of some meritorious but anonymously published poetry.

BAKER, Capt. 1st Lancers, 1st July, 35, promoted Major, 10th June, 37.

BAILEY, R. S. Vet. Surgeon, 1st Lancers, 25th June, 36. (u)

BAILLIE, WILLIAM, Capt. 5th Regt. 16th July, 35, retired 31st Aug. 36.

BALFOUR, Lieut. 6th Regt. killed in action 5th May, 36.

BALL, A, Ensign 10th Regt. 14th Aug. 36. appointed Qr.-Master 1st Regt. 31st March, 37, promoted from the ranks, 10th June 37.

BALDWENSON, Qr.-Master 4th Regt. 15th June, 36, 10th June 37.

BAYNE, J. Asst. Surgeon 6th Regt. 6th Sept, 35, promoted Surgeon 23d March, 37, New Legion.

BACKHOUSE, Lieut. Artillery 15th July, 35, killed in action 1st Oct. 36.

BAGLEY, Lieut. Artillery 15th July, 35, 10th June, 37.

BATTERSBY, R, L. Capt. 2nd Lancers 31st July, 35, resigned at Vittoria 1st Aug. 36, had been Capt. in 15th Foot British Service.

BARTON, Major and Lt. Col. Rifles 17th July, 35. (u)

BARTON, Pay Master, (u)

BASSETT, Ensign, 3rd Regt. (v)

BATES, Qr. Master, 2nd Regt. 29th July, 35.

BAYLEY, Lieut. 4th Regt. (u)

BARNETT, Ensign 9th Regt. 18th July, 35. (u)

BARRETT, J. E. Asst. Surg. 7th Regt. 15th July, 35, promoted Surg. 9th Regt. retired, March, 37.

BARKER, W. T. 2nd Lieut. Rifles, 17th July, 35, (u)

BARKER, T. Volunteer Rifles, July, 35, promoted Lieut. (u) One of these two officers was severely wounded, 5th May, 36, one was invalided, 30th Sept. 36, the other remained till 10th of June 37, and was promoted Capt.

BARRY, Staff Surg. 22nd Aug. 35, invalided (u) 37.

BEEVOR, Jas. R. Lieut. 2nd Lancers, 7th Aug. 35, promoted Capt· 9th Dec. 36,—10th June, 37.

BEECH, T. S. Vet Surg. 2nd Lancers, 4th Feb, 36.

BERRY, W. Cornet and Adjt. 2nd Lancers, Dec. 27th, 35, promoted Lieut. entered the New Legion after 10th June, 37, was considered one of the best drills and swordsmen in the service, had been a non-commissioned officer in the 8th Hussars.

BECKHAM, H. Lt. Col. 7th Regt. 2nd Aug. 36, wounded 5th May, 36, retired March, 37.

BECKHAM, EDGAR, Capt. 2nd Regt. 2nd July, 35, promoted Major, transferred to Staff, 10th June, 37.

BECKHAM, (u)

BEDFORD, G. S. Capt. and Pay Master, 1st Regt. 5th Sept. 35, 10th June, 37.

BEDFORD, Major Staff, 3rd July, 35. (u)

BERTRAND. Ensign 4th Regt. (u)

BEZANT, G. P. Ensign 9th Regt. 18th July, 35, promoted Lieut. severely wounded, 5th May, 35, mortally wounded 16th May, 37, died next day.

BENNETT, Qr. Master, 1st Regt. 21st Dec. 35, retired, (u) 37.

BELL, J. W. Capt. 5th Regt. 20th Sept. 35, (u)

BELL, J. Lieut. 1st Regt. wounded 16th March, 37. (u)

BEATSON, Major 6th Regt. 4th July, 35, transferred and promoted Lt. Col. 10th Regt. 13th July, 36, severely wounded, 11th July, 36, retired March, 37.

BENNETT, Clerk in Ordnance Dep.

BELMONT, J. Asst. Surg. 1st Regt. 2nd Sept. 35, promoted Staff Asst. Surgeon.

BISHOP, Dep. Asst. Commissiary, 6th Nov. 36, 10th June, 37.

BISHOP, Commissariat Clerk.

BLACK, C. Asst. Com. Gen. 22nd July, 35, Dep. Com. Gen. 20th May, 36, served in the New Legion, one of the Commissioners for the settlement of claims.

BLEWETT, B. Capt. 9th Regt. 18th July, 35, died by fever in Vittoria.

BLACHFORD, H· W. Capt. 4th Regt. 4th July, 35, (u)

BLOGG, J. Commissariat Clerk.

BOYD, J. Capt. 5th Regt. 16th July, 35, promoted Lt. Col. and transferred to Rifles, 10th June, 37.

BOYD, J. Lieut. 9th Regt. 16th Sept. 35, transferred and promoted Capt. Rifles, 10th June, 37.

BOYD. C. Lt. Col. Asst. Adjt. Gen. 27th July, 35, (u)

BOWDEN, Lieut. 2nd Lancers, 31st July, 35, transferred and promoted Capt. in Rifles, 10th June, 37.

BOXER, 2nd Lieut. Rifles, 10th Oct. 36, promoted Lieut. wounded 16th March, 37, 10th June, 37.

BOVILL, 2nd Lieut. 4th Regt. 4th July, 35, (u)

BROWN, R. T. Lieut. 2nd Regt. 2nd July, 35, transferred to Rifles, promoted Capt. wounded 1st Aug. 36, retired (u) 37.

BROWN, G. Ensign 8th Regt. 14th July, 35, died by fever at Vittoria, Feb. 36.

BROWN, J. 2nd Lieut. 3rd Regt. 24th Nov. 36, wounded 16th March, 37, New Legion.

BROWN, B. Major 10th Regt. 9th Sept. 35, (u)

BROOKES, D. Qr. Master of Artillery, 29th June, 36.

BREW, W. Capt. 3rd Regt. 3rd July, 35, promoted Major, invalided 30th Sept. 36.

BRENNAN, Capt. 3rd Regt. 31st. Aug. 35, transferred and promoted Major 6th Regt, 22nd Jan. 37, wounded 16th March, and retired 10th June. 37.

BRASH, Capt. 6th Regt. (*u*)

BREARY, C. B. Asst. Surg. 5th Regt. 11th Aug. 35, transferred 4th Regt. 10th June, 37.

BRADFORD, Qr. Master, 3rd Regt. 15th July 35, invalided (*u*) 37.

BROCKWELL, F. H. 2nd Lieut. 3rd Regt. 16th Feb. 36, promoted Lieut. wounded 5th May, 36. 10th June, 37.

BIONES, Vet. Surg. Artillery, 17th March, 36. (*u*)

BURKE, W. Lieut. 2nd Lancers, 27th Aug. 35. 10th June, 37.

BURKE O'CONNELL, Cornet 2nd Lancers, joined as Reg. Ser. Maj. his discharge having been purchased from the 15th Hussars, for that purpose, served in New Legion.

BURKE, Lieut. 2nd Lancers, 27th Aug. 35. (*u*)

BURGOLDT, *Baron*, Major Staff, 1st. Dec. 35, 10th June.

BULL, Capt. 1st Regt. 1st July, 35, promoted Major 10th June, 37.

BUNNETT, H. J. M. D. Staff Surgeon. 4th Aug. 35, Asst. Insp. of Hospitals. 30th March, 37.

BUNNETT, H. B, Hospital Assistant, 16th Nov. 36, (*u*)

BURNETT. H. J. Surgeon 1st Regt. 21st Aug. 35. (*u*)

BURNETT. J. Lieut. 1st. Regt. 4th Sept. 35. (*u*)

BUNNETT, J. C. Lieut. 3th Regt. wounded 16th March, 37.

BURNAND, Fr. Capt. and Pay Master, 9th Regt. 30th July, 35, (*u*)

BURNELL, Qr. Master, Rifles, (*u*)

BURROWS, Adjt. 10th Regt. died by fever, at Vittoria.

BURT, W. Pay Master, Rifles, 12th Aug. 35, 10th June, 37.

BURT, J. S. Major of Engineers, 4th July, 35, (*u*)

BURN, Lieut. 9th Regt. (*u*)

BURRY, Staff Surgeon. (*u*)

BUTLER, Ensign, 8th Regt. 23rd July, 36, promoted Lieut. wounded 15th March, 37, invalided.

BUTLER, Lieut. 7th Regt. severely wounded in a skirmish, 14th Sept. 36, invalided.

BURRIDGE, E. Ensign, 5th Regt. July 35, mounted Capt. 7th Regt. and Rifles, 10th June, 37.

BYRET, Volunteer, 9th Regt. (*u*)

BYRNE, J. Quarter Master, 1st Lancers, 1st. July, 35. (*u*)

BYAM, Cornet, 1st. Lancers, 11th April, 36, a first-rate rider, and first-rate shot; fought three duels in one day, always wounded or killed his antagonist, quarrelling with him cautiously shunned by other officers.

BYRNE, D. Capt. and Pay Master, 7th Regt. 15th July, 35, unattached, 10th June, 37.

BYRNE, Charles, Lieut. 9th Regt. 18th July, 35, promoted Capt. (*u*)

BYRNE, F. Volunteer 9th Regt. July, 35. promoted Ensign, dangerously wounded 5th May, 36.

CANNAN, R. Major 6th Regt. 20th Aug. 35, promoted Colonel 9th Regt. 10th June, 37, wounded severely 5th May, 36, a skillful and clever officer, but capricious in temper.

CARNABY, Lieut. 6th Regt. 4th July, 35, promoted Capt. severely wounded 5th May, 36, a brave and highly distinguished officer, killed in action 14th Sept. 37.

CASEY, Qr. Master 1st Lancers, promoted from the ranks.

CADOGAN, Capt. on the Staff, 1st July, 35, died by fever at Vittoria.

CAMERON, Lieut. and Adjt. 5th Regt. 4th July, 35, transferred to 8th Regt. resigned early in the service.

CAMPBELL, W. F. Major 7th Regt. 15th July, 35, transferred and promoted Lieut. Col. 4th Reg. wounded slightly 5th May, 36, and severely 16th March, 37, 10th June, 37.

CAMPBELL. J. Capt. 10th Regt. 19th July. 35 transferred and promoted Major 6th Regt. (*u*)

CAMPBELL, COLIN, Ensign 5th Regt. July 35. (*u*)

CAMPBELL, Ensign 7th Regt. non-effective 7th July, 36.

CAMPBELL, W. Ensign 9th Regt. (*u*)

CALDER, ARCHIBALD, Capt. 6th Regt. 4th July, 35, wounded 11th July, 36, died by fever arising from his wounds, Nov, 36.

CAREY, WALTER. 2nd Lieut. 6th Regt. July, 35. (*u*)

CARR, T. Ensign, 12th Oct 36 dismissed, afterwards volunteer in 6th Regt.

CARNABY, W. H. C. Lieut 4th Regt 4th July, 35. (*u*)

CARTER, Lieut and Adjt 7th Reg. (*u*)

CARMODEY, J. Ensign 10th Regt. 11th Nov. 36, 10th June, 37.

CALLANDER, JOHN M. D. Inspector General of Hospitals, from 4th Aug 35, to 10th June, 37.

CALDICOTE, J. Commissariat Clerk. (*u*)

CARBONELL, A. DE RAMON Y. Col. 4th Regt. Staff, 10th June, 37.

CHALMERS, Qr. Master 2nd Lancers, 10th Aug. 35, non-effective, 25th Dec. 35.

CHADWICK, J. M. Lieut. 2nd Regt. 2nd July, 36, afterwards Capt. 3rd Regt. severely wounded, 5th May, 36, invalided.

CHADWICK, C. 2nd Lieut. 3rd Regt. wounded mortally, 5th May, 36.

CHASE, J. C. H. Lieut. 6th Regt. afterwards Capt. on the Staff, wounded 1st October, 36.

CHADWICK, S. Ensign 10th Regt. 15th June, 36, (*u*)

CHAMBERS, (*u*)

CHITHAM, E. Ensign 1st Regt. 1st July, 35. (*u*)

CHICHESTER, C. Brigadier General, 20th June, 35, wounded 16th March, 37, an officer who always displayed the highest order of courage, ever foremost in fight, and continually exerting himself in general and detail affairs, for the honour and welfare of the Legion, 11th June, 37, now serving in Canada.

CHRIGHTON, Lieut. 4th Regt. (*u*)

CHURCHILL, Lt. Col. Staff, 4th Aug. 35, afterwards Col. Commanding 3rd Regt. resigned early in 37.

CLARIDGE, Cornet 1st Lancers, (*u*)

CLARKE, F. R. Capt. and Adjt. 6th Regt. afterwards Lt. Col. severely wounded 16th March, 37, killed in action at Audouin 14th Sept. 37.

CLARKE, F. R. Asst. Surg. 8th Regt. resigned early.

CLARKE, W. A. Capt. 6th Regt. and Staff, 16th Aug. 35, afterwards promoted (*u*)

CLARKE, J. Qr. Master Artillery, 1st Jan. 37.

COLEMAN, Asst. Surg. 1st Lancers, 1st July, 35 (*u*)

COURTNEY, (*u*)

COURTNEY, Cornet, 2nd Lancers, 31st July, 35, afterwards Lieut. had his horse killed under him in the affair of Allegria, June, 18th 37, made several Carlist prisoners on that occasion, by promising them quarter if they would lay down their arms, which being complied with on their part, was taken advantage of, by Riding Master Murphy, who slated them, (see MURPHY.)

COURTNEY, J. 2nd Lieut. Rifles, 17th July, 35, afterwards Capt. killed in action, at Andouin, 14th Sept. 37.

CODD, H. Lieut. 31st Aug. 35, died by fever at Vittoria.

COOPER, H. Ensign 1st Regt. 1st July, 35, promoted Lieut. killed in action, 5th May, 36.

COOPER. Lieut. 9th Regt. 18th July, 35, died at Vittoria by fever.

COOPER, H. Volunteer, 1st Regt. (*u*)

COCKER, W. B. Major Staff, 2nd Regt. 2nd July, 35, (*u*)

COCKER, Capt. 8th Regt. (*u*)

COOK, J. B. Ensign and Qr. Master, 8th Regt. 14th July, 35, promoted Lieut. and Bt. Capt. wounded 1st October, 36.

COOKE, N. Lieut. 3rd Regt. 3rd July, 35, promoted Capt.

CROCKER, Dep. Purveyor of Hospitals, 10th June, 37.

CROCKER, G. Lieut. 3rd Regt. 3rd July, 35, (*u*)

COTTER, W. Lieut. 3rd Regt. 4th Aug. 35, promoted Capt.

COTTER, W. H. Lieut. Rifles, 17th July, 35, afterwards Capt. died at Vittoria by fever.

COTTER, J. Capt. 9th Regt. 18th July, 35, promoted Major, and Lt. Col. wounded 1st Oct. 36, killed in action 16th March, 37.

COSTELLO, E. Lieut. Rifles, 17th July, 35, afterwards promoted Capt. wounded severely 5th May, 36, invalided, 11th Oct. 36.

COLQUHOUN, J. N. Colonel Artillery, 1st Aug. 35, performed eminent services.

COLLINS, J. W. Dep. Asst. Commissary.

COLDSTREAM, Ensign 8th Regt. 14th July, 35, promoted Capt. mortally wounded, 6th June, and died 5th Aug. 36.

COWLEY, Ensign 7th Regt. 15th July, 35, afterwards Capt. (*u*)

CORNWALL, Capt. 7th Regt. 14th Aug. 35. (*u*)

COYLE, Lieut. and Adjt. 8th Regt. 11th Aug. 35, afterwards Capt. in the 4th Regt. and again in the 8th, killed in action 16th March, 37, a brave officer much esteemed by the men he commanded, and much lamented.

CONSIDINE, Colonel and Military Secretary, 11th July, 35, severely wounded 5th May, 36. (*u*)

CORFE, Lieut. 3rd Regt. wounded 5th May, 36. (*u*)

COTONER, DON FERNANDO, Lt. Col. Aide-de-camp to the Lieut. Gen. wounded severely 5th May, 36.

CORR, W. Capt. Supernumerary 10th Regt. July, 35. (*u*)

CORR, PATRICK, ditto, ditto, ditto. (*u*)

CREAGH, Capt. 5th Regt. (*u*)

CRUISE, Colonel, Asst. Adjt. Gen. 27th July, 35, retired—37.

CROSSE, Surgeon Artillery 12th Aug. 35, 10th June, 37.

CRUICKSHANK, Staff. Asst. Surgeon 1st Jan. 36, 10th June, 37.

CRIPPS, JOS. Capt. 4th Regt. 4th July. 35. (*u*)

CUMBERLEGE, C. Capt. 1st Lancers 1st July, 35, promoted Major : 10th June, 37.

CUMMING, R. Surgeon 7th Regt. 1st Jan. 36, wounded 16th March, 37. (*u*)

CURZON Ensign Rifles. (*u*)

DADE, Asst. Surgeon 1st Regt. 1st July, 35. (*u*)

DANCE, Qr. Master 1st Regt. (*u*)

DAYKIN, Asst. Surgeon, 1st Lancers. afterwards **Asst. Surgeon** Artillery.

D'AMBLEE, 2nd Lancers severely wounded.

DAVIS, Lieut. Col. Dep. Qr. Master General.

DAVIS, J. 2nd Lieut. 7th Regt. and Rifles (*u*)

DAVIES, D. N. Staff Surgeon 22nd Aug. 35, 10th June, 27.

DAWSON, E. Lieut. Rifles 23rd Sept. 36, killed in action 16th March 37.

DAWSON, Volunteer 8th Regt. afterwards connected with the Commissariat, and imprisoned for a lengthened period, for some real or supposed offence.

DALRYMPLE, H. Capt. 8th Regt. 11th July, 36, killed in action 14th Sept. 37.

DE CAMPO, PEDRO, Vet. Surg 2nd Lancers, died by fever, in Vittoria.

DEACON. M. Capt 1st Regt 31st Aug. 35, invalided 36.

DE KALLING, Capt 10th Regt and extra Aid-de-camp wounded 5th May, 36.

DE BURGH, E. Ensign 2nd Regt, 2nd July, 35, afterwards Capt. Rifles, dangerously wounded, 16th May, 37.

DE BURGH SMYTH, Lt Col Staff corps.

DE BURGH, E. S. (*u*)

DE VINE, Asst Vet Surgeon at head quarters.

DE KOVEN, Capt 2nd Regt 2nd July, 35, afterwards in 1st Regt wounded 5th May, 36.

DE BACKER, H. L. B. 2nd Lieut. 6th Regt. July, 35, wounded 11th July, 36.

DE BRUCE, Lieut. 10th Regt. afterwards Capt. Engineers.

DE CARTARET, C. M. Lieut. 10th Regt. July, 35, (u)

DEALTRY, C. Ensign 19th July, 35, (u)

DE LANCY, OLIVER. Col. 8th Regt. and Dep. Adjt. Gen. 11th July, 35, mortally wounded 15th March, 37, died soon after, one of the bravest and best officers of the Legion.

DELLAMERE, Ensign 6th Regt. 12th Sept. 35, afterwards Capt. 10th June, 37.

DE ROTTENBERG, *Baron* G. Lt. Col. Rifles, resigned May, 36, now in Canada.

DENNIS J. Staff Surg. 8th Aug. 35, (u)

DISNEY, H. Lieut. and Adjt. 4th Nov. 36, wounded 14th May, 37, invalided.

DILLON, LUKE, Ensign 5th Regt. July, 35, afterwards Lieut. 9th Regt, wounded 6th June, 36.

DICKER, E. Asst. Surg 5th Regt 5th Sept. 35, 10th June, 37.

DICKSON, Lt. Col. 7th Regt. 15th July, 35, resigned in the latter' part of that year, came home and fought several duels, has laboured incessantly to throw odium on General Evans, for *ill-using* the Soldiers, &c. while he himself, was without exception the most wantonly cruel, unmanly, and unsoldierlike, in the treatment of his regiment, of all the officers that commanded in the Legion, he is one of those who have supplied *Sir Henry Hardinge* with charges against Gen. Evans, for the House of Commons.

DIGHTON, H. 2nd Lieut. Rifles, 17th July, 35, (u)

DONNELLY, Qr. Master. 2nd Lancers, (u)

DOHERTY, Capt. 3rd Regt, 18th Sept 36.

DOCKER, Wm. Asst-Surg 3rd Regt, 3rd July, 35.

DOYLE, C. M. Ensign 6th Regt. afterwards Lieut. wounded 11th July, 36.

DORSET, Asst-Surg. 1st Lancers, promoted Staff Surgeon, 10th June, 37.

DOWBIGGIN, Capt 10th Regt. and Lt Col. Staff. (u)

DOLCE, A. Staff Surgeon.

DRUMMOND, JOHN Capt and Pay Master, 6th Regt. 4th July 35, 10th June, 37.

DRUMMOND. N. C. Ensign 6th Regt. (*u*)

DURIE, FECTOR, Ensign 1st Regt 1st July, 35, promoted Capt. killed in action, 16th May, 37.

DURIE, R. Lieut 5th Regt 16th July, 35, transferred to Rifles, wounded 5th May, 37, promoted Capt. 10th June, 37.

DURIE, DAVID Capt Rifles 17th July, 35, wounded 5th May, 36, promoted Major, wounded 1st Oct. 36, 10th June 37.

DUSTIN, S. L. Lieut 4th Regt 23rd July, 36, 10th June, 37.

DUPLEX, G. Asst Surg. 3rd Regt. 3rd July, 35, transferred to Rifles. promoted Surg. 28th Oct. 35, 10th June, 37.

DUNSMORE, Lieut. 4th Regt. (*u*)

DUPONT, P. Ensign, 1st Regt. 8th July, 36, wounded 16th March, 37, and killed in action, 16th May, 37.

DUNDAS, ROBERT, Major 7th Regt. 15th July 35, died by fever Dec. 24, 35.

DUNCAN, ALEX. Lieut. 7th Regt. 15th July, 35, promoted Captain. (*u*)

DUNCAN, J. J. Capt. and Adjutant, 2nd Regt. 24th August' 35, transferred to 1st Regiment, wounded 6th June, 36, invalided.

DUNCAN, J. Staff Assistant Surgeon. (*u*)

DURKIN, J. Hosp. Assist. afterwards Ensign 8th Regt.—one of the smallest, but most assuredly, one of the bravest little fellows that ever wore a sword; particularly distinguished before the enemy 16th March, 37.

DUNNE, G. P. Capt. and Paymaster 10th Regt. 16th Aug. 35, died by fever at Vittoria, Dec. same year.

DWARRIS, F. Lieut. 2nd Regt. 14th Aug. 35. (*u*)

EAMES. (*u*)

EBHART, B. W. Capt. 2nd Regt. 2nd July, 35. (*u*)

EBBS, J. Lieut. Rifles, 18th July, 36, wounded 16th March, 37.

EBSWORTH, F. C. Major 5th Regt. and Lt.-Col. 10th, Regt. 15th Sept. 35, killed at Hernani by the Spanish Soldiers of Santa Cruz, when interposing his own body to save that General from assassination in July, 1837.

EDWARDS G. H. Major 3d Regt. 25th July, 35, died by fever at Santander Jan. 35.

EDWARDS THOS. Capt. and Pay Master 3d Regt. 3rd July. 35, 10th June 37.

EDWARDS, J. Commissariat Department. (*u*)

EDGE, Capt. and Adjt. 6th Regt. (*u*)

EIZMENDI DON JOSE, attached to Commissariat Nov. 35.

ELIOT, F. 2nd Lieut. 4th Regt. 23rd July, 36, transferred to 1st Lancers April 37, a brave soldier, celebrated as a duellist.

ELLIES, Lt. Col. 2nd Regt. 23rd Aug. 35. (*u*)

ELLIES, JAMES Major 4th Regt. 18th Sept. 36, promoted Lt. Col. 1st Regt. 10th June.

EMAN, J. E. Lieut. 3rd Regt. 31st Aug. 35, (*u*)

ERMATINGER, W. H. Cornet 1st Lancers 19th May, 36.

ERSKINE, the *Honourable* S. Lieut. 5th Regt. 29th Aug. 35. (*u*)

ERSKINE, A. Ensign, 8th Regt. 14th July, 35, promoted Capt. resigned July, 36.

ESCUDERO, DON RAPHAEL, Lt. Col, and Aide-de-camp.

EVANS, GEORGE DE LACY, Lieut. Gen. Commanding in chief June, 35, 10th June, 37, wounded 1st Oct. 36.

EVANS, R. DE LACY, brother to the Lieut. Gen. and Brigadier Gen. 20th June, 35, resigned early in 36.—now in India, a distinguished officer.

FANNIN, Ensign 2nd Regt. 2nd July, 35, Capt. 1st Regt 17th July, 36, resigned without leave.

FAXARDO, AUGUSTUS M. G. Dep. Com. Gen. 18th July, 35, 10th June, 37.

FAXARDO, M. JOSE Commissariat Clerk.

FEEHAN, J. Capt 9th Regt. 1st July, 36.

FENWICK, G. Clerk of Stores, 7th Aug. 35, 10th June, 37.

FINUCANE, G. Major 2nd Regt. 4th Aug. 35, promoted Lt. Col.

FITZGERALD, P. Capt. 3rd Regiment, 3rd July, 35, wounded 16th Jan, 36, promoted Major and Lt. Col. commanded 3rd Regt. in the action of 16th March, 37, and was accused of neglect of duty, but according to common opinion falsely, resigned.

FITZGERALD, G. Surgeon 7th Regt. died by fever near Vittoria.

FITZGERALD, CHARLES Lt. Col. 9th Regt. 15th July, 35, promoted Brigadier General, 10th June, 37.

FITZGERALD, H. Ensign 9th Regt. 4th July, 35, promoted Lieut. (*u*)

FITZGERALD, HARRY, Volunteer 9th Regt. promoted Lieut. (*u*)

FITZGERALD, W. H. Capt. 10th Regt 19th July, 35, promoted Major 10th June, 37.

FITZGIBBON, Lieut. 2nd Lancers, 7th Aug. 35, invalided at Vittoria, 12th April, 36.

FITCH, Major Commandant of Depot at the Convent Del Corban, early in 36, promoted Lt. Col. unattached and commandant of Puyo battery, retired 10th June, 37.

FIRMAN or FOREMAN, Lieut. and Adjt. 4th Regt. 6th Aug. 36, wounded 1st Oct. 36, and 16th March, 37, 10th June, 37.

FINLAY, Ensign 4th Regt. (u)

FISKE, C. N. Ensign 8th Regt. 14th July, 35, promoted Capt. wounded 5th May, 36, resigned (u)

FITZCOSTA, Ensign 8th Regt. 29th July, 36, resigned (u)

FIELDING, Capt. Rifles, 5th Sept. 36, mortally wounded 16th March, 37, died soon after.

FOX, Capt. 3rd Regt. 3rd July, 35, (u)

FORTESCUE, Capt. Rifles, 17th July, 35, promoted Major, Lt. Col. and Col. Commanded the Rifles with a distinguished headlong bravery, wounded 5th May, 36, 10th June, 37.

FOSTER, J. W. 2nd Lieut. 6th Regt. July, 35, promoted Capt 10th June, 37.

FORBES, A, Ensign 8th Regt. March, 36, promoted Lieut. and Brevet Capt wounded 16th March, 37, killed in action 14th Sept 37.

FRANCIS, W. Lieut. 1st Lancers 1st Oct, 36. (u)

FRYER, Ensign 4th Regt. 5th May, 36.

FREESTUN, Capt. 3rd Regt. 3rd July, 35, Lt. Col. Staff, wounded 16th March, 37.

FRAGOES, Ensign 8th Regt. 3rd Feb. 37, 10th June, 37.

FRANKS, M. Capt. 10th Regt. 19th July, 35, died at Vittoria by fever.

FRASER, Lieut. 8th Regt. (u)

FYFE, H. Ensign 8th Regt 10th July, 36, invalided.

GARDINER, G. C. Capt. 8th Regt. 11th July, 36, invalided (u)

GARDINER, R. Lieut. 10th Regt. 19th July. (u)

GALWEY, C. Capt. 10th Regt. 19th July 35, promoted Major, wounded severely 16th March, 37, 10th July, 37.

GALWEY, Lieut. (Super.) 10th Regt. July, 35.

GARTLAND, Ensign 10th Regt. (u) killed in action 1st Oct. 36.

GARCIAS, Lieut. 6th Regt. July 35.

GANNON, Surgeon 5th Regt. 16 July, 36, afterwards Staff Surgeon,—10th June, 37.

GERDEN, Qr Master 9th Regt. 10th Oct. 35.

GILL, Asst. Surgeon 5th Regt.

GLYNN, —— 2nd Lancers—appointed Aide-de-camp to Gen. Cordova 2nd Dec. 35—resigned at Vittoria Dec. 36—had been in the Portugueze Service, and was severely wounded.

GLAZIER, W. B. Lieut. 3rd Regt. 3rd July, 35 — promoted Capt. —invalided.

GLENNY, ROSS, Lieut. 7th Regt. 15th July, 35— wounded 16th March 37—retired March 37.

GOLDSTONE, Surgeon, 2nd Lancers 31st Aug. 35—resigned— 36.

GOODYER, F. Lieut. 2nd Regt. 2nd July, 35.

GOODYER, F. Ordnance Department.

GOODYER, C. Commissariat Clerk.

GOULD, V. Ensign 3rd Regt. 3rd July 35.

GOULD, J. Ordnance Department,

GORDON, THOS. 2nd Lieut. 6th Regt. July 35—died by fever.

GORDON, Commissariat Clerk, died.

GORDON. Qr. Master, 9th Regt. 10th Oct. 36.

GODFREY, E. L. Lt. Col. 8th Regt. 23rd Aug. 35—promoted Brigadier General — wounded 16th March, 37, retired shortly after.

GODFREY, B. Staff, Asst. Surgeon, 23rd May, 36.

GOLDRISKE. J. Ensign 8th Regt. 23rd Aug. 36—promoted Lieut. wounded 16th March, 37, New Legion.

GORMAN, Dep. Provost Marshall—promoted Capt. attached to 8th Regt.—10th June, 37.

GREVILLE, Capt. 7th Regt. 15th July 35.

GREVILLE, the *Hon.* R. F. Major 1st Lancers 26th Aug. 35.

GREGG, J. C. Lieut. 4th Regt. 17th May, 36,

GREGG, 2nd Lieut. 1st Regt. 20th Sep. 36

GRIFFIN, Ensign, 6th Regt.

GRIFFIN, Ensign, 9th Regt.

GRAY, W. W. Lieut. 7th Regt. 15th July, 35—wounded 5th May 36.

No. **43.**

GREY, Hosp. Assistant.

GREGSON, Lieut. Hosp. Trans. Department, 21st Sept. 35.

GROOM, Qr. Master, 8th Regt. 15th Sept. 36—New Legion.

GROVE, M. Surgeon, 10th Regt.—died by fever (u)

GRANT, HENRY, Ensign, 10th Regt. 28th Aug. 36—retired March 37.

GRANT, Commissariat Clerk.

GREENWOOD, Asst. Surg. Rifles, 17th July, 35.

GRINDLEY, Dep. Com. General, 1st Aug. 35—10th June, 37.

GRUNDEY, E. Staff Asst. Surg. 31st Aug. 35,—died in London while in a fit, soon after.

GUBBENS, R. Lieut. 10th Regt. 11th Nov. 36.

GURREA, DON IGNACIO, Aide-de-camp.

GWILT, 2nd Lieut. Rifles, 17th July, 35.

HANSON, Lieut. and Adjt. 1st Lancers, 18th Sept. 35—promoted Capt. 8th Oct. 36—10th June 37, or, New Legion.

HARDMAN, F. Cadet, 2nd Lancers, Sept. 20th 35—appointed Cornet 10th Jan. 27—promoted Lieut. in New Legion.

HARRIS, H. C. Staff Asst. Surg. 11th Aug. 35.

HARRIS, Qr. Master 1st Regt. 24th Aug. 35—promoted Capt.— 10th June, 37.

HAGGERTY, Lieut. 4th Regt. 4th July, 35—transferred to 7th Regt. wounded 5th May, 36.

HAMILTON, F. 2nd Lieut. 6th Regt. July 35.

HAMILTON, R. Capt. 5th Regt. 16th July, 35, and Major 7th Regt. 20th Oct. 36

HAMILTON, PEDRO, 2nd Lieut. 15th June, 36—resigned Dec. 36.

HAMILTON, A. F. Lieut. 7th Regt. 15th July, 35—killed in action 5th May, 36.

HAMILTON. C. Ensign, 7th Regt. 15th July, 35.

HAMILTON, J. H. 2nd Lieut. Artillery, 5th July, 35—promoted 1st Lieut. 25th Feb. 36, and Capt.—37—10th June, 37 or New Legion.

HAMPTON, T. B. Lieut. Artillery, 3rd July 36—10th June 37.

HACKETT, W. Staff Asst. Surg. 16th Feb. 36—10th June, 37.

HACKETT, J. C. Commissariat Clerk.

HADWEN, J. Clerk of Stores, 15th July, 35.

HARRINGTON, Ensign, (*Super.*) 10th Regt, July 35,—promoted Lieut.— non-effective 16th July, 36.

HARLEY, Major 9th Regt. July, 35—transferred to 4th Regt.— promoted Lt. Col. 5th May, 36—resigned without leave, early in 37.

HAVELOCK, J. Capt. 5th Regt. 31st Aug. 35—died by fever at Vittoria, 31st. Dec. 35.

HARDINGE, F. Ensign, 7th Regt. 15th July, 35—promoted Capt. —retired March 37.

HASLAM, T. Ensign, 7th Regt. 23rd July, 36—promoted Lieut. Rifles, 26th Dec. 36—entered New Legion—killed in action 14th Sept. 37.

HARVEY, J. Ensign and Qr. Master, 8th Regt. Dec. 35—promoted Lieut. 1st July, 36, invalided—37.

HART, Ensign, 8th Regt. 23rd Aug. 36—promoted Lieut. wounded 16th March, 37—10th June, 37.

HALL, G. B., Capt. 9th Regt. and Major on Staff 18th July, 35.

HALL, F. Volunteer Rifles, July, 35.

HAYES, Qr. Master, 9th Regt.

HELY, T. Lieut. 1st Lancers, 1st July, 35—promoted Capt.

HELY, 2nd Lieut. 1st Regt. 12th May, 36.

HELY, Cornet, 1st Lancers, 19th May, 36—10th June, 37—or New Legion.

HEALY, Asst. Surg. 8th Regt. 21st May, 36—10th June, 37.

HENDERSON, R., Cornet 1st Lancers, 11th April, 36—10th June, 37.

HERMAN, G. F. Capt. Rifles, 11th July, 35—appointed Lt. Col. and Military Secretary—10th June, 37.

HENLEY, R. Hosp. Asst. 22nd Aug. 35—10th June, 37.

HEA, E. O. Lieut 4th Regt. 30th Aug. 36.

HILL, VALENTINE, Cornet 2nd Lancers, 10th Aug. 35—non-effective, 14th May, 36.

HICKS, Major 2nd Regt. 2nd July, 35—wounded 30th Aug. 35. promoted Brevet. Lt. Col. wounded severely, 5th May, 36—and 16th March, 37.

HIPPSLEY, Capt. 2nd Regt.

HIND, Commissariat Clerk.

HIGGINBOTHAM, Lieut. 3rd Regt.

HIMBURY, or HANBURY, J. Ensign 4th Regt.—promoted Lieut. in Rifles, 30th Oct. 36—wounded 5th May, 36—invalided, 37.

HILL, Lieut. Rifles.

HINKMAN, T. D. Commissariat Clerk.

HOGREVE, Lieut. 1st Lancers, 1st July, 35—Capt. 5th July, 36 — 10th June, 37.

HORNBROOK, J. 2nd Lieut. 4th Regt. 4th July, 35—promoted, Lieut. and Capt. Engineers.

HORNBROOK, Cadet 4th Regt. July, 35—appointed Ensign.

HORNBROOK, Asst. Surg. 1st Lancers,

HOLDSWORTH, Asst. Surg. 2nd Lancers—died by fever at Santander, Jan. 36.

HORNSBY, Ensign 5th Regt. July, 35—transferred to 1st Regt. promoted Lieut. 29th July, 36—Capt. 1st April, 37—dangerously wounded, 16th May, 37—10th June, 37.

HOWITT, Qr. Master, 6th Regt. 12th May, 36—10th June, 37.

HOWE, E. Lieut. Artillery, 1st July, 35—Capt. 25th Feb. 36—Major, 25th March, 37—New Legion.

HOOK, 2nd Lieut. Rifles, July, 35—1st Lieut. 12th Aug. 36—10th June, 37.

HOLMES, J. G. Lieut. 9th Regt. 18th July, 35—Capt. 5th Oct. 35—wounded 14th May, 37—10th June, 37.

HOLMES, J. W. Ensign, 9th Regt. 18th July, 35—promoted Lieut. —wounded and promoted Capt. 5th May, 36—retired 8th March, 37.

HOCESSAN, Commissariat Clerk.

HOGG, Ensign, 1st Regt. died (u) by fever.

HOGG, G. Capt. 8th Regt. 14th July, 35—wounded 4th March, 36—wounded and promoted Major, 5th May, 37—Lt. Col. 17th Feb. 37—Col. May, 37—New Legion.

HODGSON, Ensign, 3rd Regt, 3rd July, 35—Lieut. 11th Nov. 36, —10th June, 37.

HUNTER, G. Capt. 4th July, 35.

HUMFREY, Capt. Artillery, 20th Sept. 35—promoted Major, and transferred to Engineers.

HURLEY, MICHAEL, Qr, Master Artillery, 26th July, 35.

IBBETSON, D. Asst. Com. Gen. in England.

INMAN, Cornet 2nd Lancers, 27th Aug. 35.

INMAN, Lieut. 1st Lancers,—Capt. and Adjt. 8th Regt. retired 11th Dec. 36.

INMAN, (*u*)

IRWIN, Ensign, 7th Regt. 15th July, 35.

IRWIN, Lieut. 4th Regt. 10th Aug. 36, wounded 1st Oct. 36.

ISDELL, G. Hosp. Asst. 1st Sept. 35.

IVES, 2nd Lieut. 3rd Regt. 17th July, 36.

JACKS, Lt. Col. Commanding 2nd Lancers, 31st July, 35—Brevet Col. Dec. 36—10th June, 37—Commanded the Foreign Hussars in Sicily, till the breaking up of that Squadron in 1814— a half-pay Capt. 20th Light Dragoons. The officer so frequently and honourably mentioned in Mr. Gleig's " *Hussar* " as Capt. Jacks.

JACKSON, J. Capt. 6th Regt. 4th July, 35—died, by fever at Vittoria.

JACKSON, Son of the foregoing; Ensign 3rd Regt. 3rd July, 35— promoted Lieut. wounded 5th May, 36—and killed in action 1st Oct. 36.

JAMES, S. J. Lieut. 2nd Regt. 2nd July, 35 ; and Capt. 24th August, 35—transferred to 4th Regt.—wounded 6th June, 36— and Invalided

JAMIESON, Hosp. Asst. 10th Aug. 36—10th June, 37

JENNINGS Lieut. 1st Lancers, 18th Sept. 35—Capt. 25th Aug. 36—10th June, 37

JENNER, W. H. Asst. Surg. 6th Regiment, 4th July, 36.

JENKINS, G. A. 2nd Lieut. 1st Regt. 24th Aug. 36.

JENKINS, W. F. 2nd Lieut. 6th Regt. 24th Aug. 36.

JEFFREY Lieut. Rifles, 17th July, 35—dangerously wounded 5th May, 36—Promoted Capt.—wounded 1st Oct. 36—10th June, 37.

JOHNSON, C. J. 2nd Lieut. 3rd Regt. 16th May, 36—promoted Lieut. and brevet Capt. 6th Feb. 37—10th June, 37.

JOHNSON, J. Surgeon 4th Regt. 7th Jan. 36.

JOHNSON, W. Dep. Asst. Com. Gen. 1st Oct. 36,

JOHNSTON, J, Staff Asst. Surgeon, 14th July, 35.

JOHNSON, W. 2nd Lieut. 4th Regt. 4th July, 35.

JONES, E. O. 2nd Lieut. 4th Regt. 4th July, 35.

JOCHMUS, A. Colonel and Dep. Qr. Master Gen. 20th Oct. 35—wounded 7th May, 37—Brigadier Gen. New Legion.

JOYCE, S. P. Lieut. 10th Regt. 19th July, 35—Capt. 19th Sept 36—wounded 5th May, 36—invalided—37.

KENSINGTON, H. Capt. 2nd Lancers, 27th Aug. 35—10th June, 36—had been Capt. in the East India Company's Service.

KENYON, G. Capt. 1st Regt. 1st July, 35.

KEAN, O. Lieut. 1st Regt. 27th Oct. 36.

KELLY, D. Capt. and Adjt. 1st Regt. 25th Sept. 36.

KELLY, P. Volunteer 9th Regt. Aug. 36.

KELLY, O. 2nd Lieut. Rifles 18th Sept. 36—10th June 37.

KELLY, C. Lieut. (Super.) 10th Regt. 19th Aug. 35.

KELLY, Commissariat Clerk.

KENNY, T. Ensign 7th Regt. 23rd Sept. 36.

KENNY, W. H. Lieut. Artillery, 1st Oct. 36—10th June, 37.

KEEVIL. Capt. and Adjt. 3rd Regt. 3rd July, 35—wounded 5th May, 36—resigned June, 36.

KEARNS, Surgeon, 3rd Regt. 24th Aug. 35—10th June, 37.

KEMPE, J. G. 2nd Lieut. 4th Regt. 4th July, 35—wounded 5th May, 36.

KEMPE, F. Ensign 7th Regt. 25th July, 36—invalided —— 37.

KEAYS, J. Commissariat Clerk.

KEOGH, Ensign 9th Regt. 18th July, 35—Lieut. 15th Dec. 35—promoted Capt.—10th June, 37.

From what has been said in another part of this Work relative to this Officer, it is necessary to call the reader's attention to the following explanation.

It was a current report in the Legion that Captain, then Lieutenant Keogh had been guilty of deserting his Company : and the informality of the proceedings arising therefrom, together with the extremely unjust manner of treatment practised by General Fitzgerald whose favorite Captain Keogh was, towards other officers, perhaps tended to confirm the reports. The Author of this Work is of opinion, however, that an Officer should scarcely lose his character for such a short period of service as that of the Legion, as sufficient opportunities were not given to afford redemption. The men who were witnesses of Captain Keogh's conduct latterly, concur in giving him the highest praise, and it is only just to observe that anxious inquiries on the part of the Author have tended to prove that an officer may fail at one time and be very brave at another. This appears to have been the case with Captain Keogh.

KINLOCH, J. Lieut Col. 1st Lancers, 1st July, 35—promoted Col. and Brigadier General, resigned Sept. 36.

KIRBY, H. R. Lieut. Col. 1st. Reg. 14th July, 35—wounded severely 1st Oct. 36—resigned ——, 37.

KIRBY, Lieut. 5th Regt. 31st August, 35.

KIRBY, W. 2nd Lieut. 4th Regt. 4th July, 35—Capt. 17th July, 36—retired ——, 37.

KIRBY, W. S. Asst. Surg. 7th Regt. 20th May, 36—retired March, 37.

KIRKWOOD, Asst. Surg. 16th Nov. 36—10th June, 37.

KING, C. M. Capt. Inspector of Transports in England, 7th Aug, 35.

KING, A. Asst. Surg. 7th Regt. 1st Jan. 36—10th June, 37.

KING, A. W. Major 3rd Regt. 26th Aug. died by Fever at Vittoria.

KNIGHT, Lieut. 1st Regt. 31st Aug. 35—appointed Capt. and A. D. C. to Gen. Chichester—killed in action, 5th May, 36.

KNIGHT, E. Ensign 1st Regt. and Staff, 17th Oct. 36—Capt. 23rd March, 37—10th June.

KYMER, Capt. and Paymaster, 8th Regt. 8th Aug. 35—10th June, 37.

LANE, Regimental Commissary, 2nd Lancers.

LARDNER, W. Surg. 1st Lancers, 1st July, 35—10th June, 37.

LAURIE, W. Capt. and Pay-master, 1st Lancers, 1st July, 35—10th June, 37.

LANDERS, Lieut. 5th Regt. 16th July, 35—transferred to 7th Regt—Capt. 6th June, 36—retired March, 37.

LARKHAM, Lieut. 8th Regt. 14th July, 35—transferred to 6th Regt.—Capt. 25th Sept. 36 — wounded 5th May, 36—killed in action, 14th Sept. 37.

LAMBE, Ensign 9th Regt. 3rd July, 36—Lieut. 25th Nov. 36- - wounded 16th March, 37.

LAMBTON, W. Staff Asst. Surg. 7th Aug. 35—retired March, 37.

LAIDLAW, Commissariat Clerk.

LAZENBY, Lieut. in charge of Depot and Artillery Stores at Woolwich.

LATHEY, Deputy Purveyor, Medical Staff—died at Santander by Fever.

LAWSON, A.2nd Lieut. 1st Regt. 19th Oct. 36—10th June, 37.

LLANNOS, DON MATEO, Inspector General of all the Civil Departments of the Legion.

LA SAUSSAYE, Col. attached to Quarter-master General's Department.

LETAMUNDI, A. W. 2nd Lieut. 1st Regt. 21st Nov. 35—promoted 1st Lieut—10th June, 37.

LEAKE, Lieut.,2nd Regt. 2nd July, 35—Capt. 28th Oct. 35—died at (*u*)

LEAKE, R. A. Ensign 8th Regt. 14th July, 35—died at Vittoria by Fever.

LEWIN, Commissariat Department.

LEZAMA, Capt. 7th Regt. and Col. Staff 15th July, 35—10th June, 37.

LEWIS, Asst. Surg. died by Fever at (*u*)

LE MARCHANT, J. G. Adjutant General 11th July, 35—retired March, 37—Major in the 20th Regt. British Service—a distinguished Officer of that Service, as well as of the Legion.

LINDO, LOUIS, Pay-master 2nd Lancers, 17th Oct. 35—New Legion.

LINTON, H. Ensign 1st Regt. 1st July, 35—Lieut. 21st Aug.—Capt. 27th Dec.—wounded 1st Oct. 36 and 16th May, 37—10th June, 37.

LIGHT, Ensign 8th Regt. 14th 'July, 35—promoted Lieut. and Capt.'—'wounded 6th June, 36 — resigned and re-entered the Legion in the 6th Regt. as Ensign—promoted Lieut.'— 10th June, 37.

LIVINGSTONE, Lieut. 8th Regt. 14th July, 35—resigned early in the Service.

LLOYD, Cornet, 2nd Lancers, 14th April, 36.

LONG, H. Capt. 2nd Regt. 2nd July, 35.

LOSACK, A. Capt. 4th Regt. 4th July, 35.

LOMAX, H. Capt. Rifles, July, 35.

LUTTRELL, H. Lieut. 8th Regt. July, 35—resigned Dec. 35.

LUKIN, W. S. Commissariat Clerk.

LUDOVICE, 2nd Lieut Rifles, 10th Oct. 36—10th June, 37.

LYNCH, Cornet, (Super.) 2nd Lancers—died Feb. 36 at Santander.

LYNCH, P. Ensign 10th Regt. 12th July, 35—promoted Lieut.— killed in action 11th July, 36.

LYNCH, Ensign 10th Regt. 28th July, 36.

LYSTER, H. Capt. 5th Regt. 16th July, 35—transferred to 3rd Regt.—Brevet Major—wounded 16th May, 37—10th June, 37.

LYSTER, F. Capt. 8th Regt. 22nd Aug. 36—10th June, 37.

LYSTER, Ensign, 3rd Regt. 15th June, 36—severely wounded 16th March, 37—10th June, 37.

MAITLAND, Cornet 1st Lancers, July, 35.

MARSH, J. Cornet 1st Lancers, 1st July, 35—Lieut. 1st Oct. 35— transferred to 2nd Lancers, and promoted Capt. over all the *Subs* of that Regt. in Jan. 36—10th June, 37.

MACKAY, Assist. Surg. 1st Lancers, 21st May, 36—resigned — 37.

MACKAY, H. Ensign 5th Regt. Dec. 35—promoted from the ranks —Lieut. 7th Regt. 24th May, 36,—invalided.

MACKAY, A. Capt. 9th Regt. 18th July, 35—wounded 5th May, 36—died by wounds and surgical treatment soon after.

MARTIN, W. Capt. 8th Regt. 14th July, 35—promoted Major, transferred to 2nd Lancers, and promoted Lt. Col. 20th March, 36, Pay Master New Legion.

MARTIN, H. J. Ensign, 5th Regt. July, 35—transferred to Rifles, and promoted Lieut. 26th Oct. 35—left the service early, and has since been employed by the political opponents of Gen. Evans, in circulating dishonourable accounts of the Legion, through public meetings and the Press.

MATURIN, G. J. Capt. 2nd Lancers 31st Aug. 35—was on Gen. Evans's Staff at the defeat before Hernani 16th March, 37—was slightly wounded in the arm, and had a part of his pouch belt carried away by the same ball which wounded Capt. Jameson of the *James Watt* Steamer—is one of the French Officers whose evidence is given in the Report for the abolition of corporal punishment—served after 10th June, 37.

MACKENZIE, Major 1st Regt. 21st Aug. 35.

MALONEY, C. Cornet 2nd Lancers, 31st July, 35—accompanied Martin Zurbano, in his expedition, (*See Rid. Mast. Murphy.*) served after 10th June, 37.

MACKENZIE, Hosp. Assistant 31st Aug. 35.

MANDEVILLE, F. W. Ensign 2nd Regt. 10th July, 35—Lieut. 10th Regt. 12th Aug. 36—10th June, 37.

MACLAINE, Lieut. Artillery, 3rd Aug. 35—transferred to 3rd Regt. and promoted Capt. 10th July, 36—afterwards Major—retired 37.

MACLEAN, J. 2nd Lieut. Rifles, 1st Dec. 35—1st Lieut. 21st Sept. 36—severely wounded, 1st Oct. 36—invalided 20th Dec. 36.

MACDONALD, Qr. Master, 5th Regt. July, 35—left the service, without leave in Nov. 35.

MACDONALD, A. Lieut. 5th Regt. July, 35—Capt. 6th Regt. and severely wounded 5th May, 36—invalided 28th Nov. 36.

MACDONALD, W. Ensign 6th Regt. July, 35—promoted Lieut. wounded 5th May, 36.

MACDONALD, G. 1st Lieut. 4th Regt. July, 35—Capt. 5th May, 36—10th June, 37.

MACFARLANE, Lieut. 5th Regt. July, 35—Capt. 8th Regt. from which he retired about June, 36.

MACLEOD, R. Ensign 5th Regt, July, 35—Lieut. 6th Regt. 19th May, 36—10th June, 37.

MACNEIL, Lieut. 2nd Regt. 2nd July, 25—transferred and promoted, Capt. 6th Regt—killed in action, 5th May, 36.

MACKELLAR, Lieut. 6th Regt. July, 35—severely wounded, and promoted Capt. 5th May, 36—afterwards Major—killed in action, 14th Sept. 37.

MACNAMARA, F. N. Ensign 8th Regt. July, 35—Lieut. 6th Regt. 21st April, 36—invalided.

MACNAMARA, J. Ensign 1st Regt. 1st April, 35—transferred to 7th Regt. and promoted Lieut. wounded 16th March, 37, retired·

MAHON, Ensign 7th Regt. severely wounded 5th May, 36.

MACDOWAL, Ensign 6th Regt. 25th Sept. 35.

MACKNIGHT, Qr. Master 8th Regt. 20th Aug. 35—afterwards Capt. Adjt. and Major—resigned Aug. 36. (*for particulars of this gent, see page* 41.)

MACDOUGALL, DUNCAN, Col. 9th Regt. and Brigadier Gen. 19th June, 35—resigned May, 36—his resignation much regretted by the whole Legion.

MARTILLI, J. G. Ensign 9th Regt. July, 35.

MAYBURY, T. D. Asst. Surg. 10th Regt. July, 35—Surg. 1st March, 36—10th June, 37.

MACINTOSH, J. Ensign 10th Regt. 16th July, 36—Lieut, 4th Regt. 22nd March, 37—wounded 5th May, 36—10th June, 37.

MACINTOSH, J. Lieut. Rifles, July, 35—promoted Capt. and Major 5th May, 36—served on the Staff—10th June, 37.

MACDUFF, A. Qr. Master Rifles, 18th July, 36—wounded 16th March, 37—10th June, 37.

MACDUFF, Major, unattached, killed 16th May, 37.

MAHONEY, Assist. Surg. Rifles, 21st May, 36—10th June, 37.

MAUDESLEY, O. T. Clerk of Stores, 14th July, 35—Dep. Assist. Commissary 6th Nov. 36—10th June, 37.

MANCHA, J. M. Clerk of Stores.

MANCHA, J. Clerk of Stores.

MACAULEY, Clerk of Stores.

MACSWEENY, V. Surgeon 2nd Lancers, 11th Sept. 36—10th June, 37.

MACSWEENY, R. Capt, 10th Regt. July, 35.

MACSWEENY,

M'NEES, B. R. 2nd Lieut. 4th Regt. July, 35.

M'CARTHY, Lieut. 7th Regt. July, 35.

M'CABE, Capt. 9th Regt. July, 35—Major 7th Regt. 15th Dec. 36—Lt. Col. 7th Feb. 37—wounded severely, 5th May, 36—10th June, 37.

M'DERMOTT, Lieut. Rifles, 1st Oct. 36—wounded severely, 16th March, 37.

MENZIES, Ensign 6th Regt.

MEADE, Capt. 5th Regt. July 35—Major, and Lt. Col. on the Staff—10th June, 37.

MELLER, H. Ensign 10th Regt. July, 35—promoted Lieut. and afterwards Capt. of Engineers—particularly distinguished with a party of his Sappers in taking some picquet houses from the enemy and destroying them in the latter end of July, 36. It is the more necessary to mention this here as no notice has hitherto been taken in this Work of the hard working, useful, and gallant Corps of Sappers and Miners, a portion of which, Capt. Meller. for a short time commanded with distinguished honour to himself and the service. Other officers to be sure were connected with that department; but it was notorious that two of them, at least, were the most unfit to perform the duties of practical Engineers that could have been selected; and it was no less notorious that one of the smartest off-hand dashes of gallantry performed during the service was that undertaken and performed by Capt. Meller and a handful of men—the credit of which, however, was given to, or rather taken by another officer who did not take one step in the danger, and who was known to be always unfond of Carlist lead—Capt. Meller resigned in the latter end of 36 or early in 37.

MEAGHER, Quarter-master 10th Regt. 10th July, 35—afterwards Capt. and *acting* Pay-master—10th June, 37.

MIDDLETON, A. Cornet 1st Lancers, July, 35—Lieut. 1st Dec. 35—wounded severely 1st Oct. 36—served after 10th June, 37.

MIDDLETON, H. Lieut. 9th Regt. Sept. 35—afterwards Capt.— non-effective 30th June, 36.

MIDDLETON, R. Capt. 5th Regt. July, 35.

MIDDLETON, 2nd Lieut. 4th Regt. 5th July, 36.

MIDDLECOTE, Ensign 8th Regt. 26th Aug. 36—non-effective 3rd Nov. 36.

MILL, J. Capt. 2nd Regt. 2nd July, 35—Major 26th Oct. 35.

MITCHELL, B. Major 5th Regt. 11th Aug. 35—transferred to 8th Regt.—mortally wounded 5th May, 36, and promoted Lieut. Col. —died next day.

MILLER, S. D. Lieut. 8th Regt. 11th Aug. 35—promoted Capt.— resigned July, 36.

MILLER, A. Lieut. 1st Lancers 1st July, 35.

MILLER, Commissariat Clerk.

MOORE, E. Lieut. 1st Lancers 26th Aug. 35—10th June, 37, or New Legion,

MOORE, F. 2nd Lieut. Rifles, July, 35.

MONTGOMERY, H. Capt. 1st Regt. 31st Aug. 35—died by Fever at (u)

MOUNT, E. Ensign 3rd Regt. July, 35—Lieut. 19th Oct. 35.

MOULD, P. R. Asst. Surg. 4th Regt. 4th July, 35.

MOULD, P. R. Capt. 10th Regt. 26th Oct. 35—killed in action 5th May, 36.

MORGAN, 2nd Lieut. 6th Regt. July, 35—Lieut. 8th Oct. 36—10th June, 37.

MORGAN, Capt. 9th Regt. 18th July, 35.

MORRIS, C. 2nd Lieut. 15th June, 36—wounded 1st Oct. 36.

MORRIS, T. Lieut. 10th Regt. Aug. 36.

MORLEY, Lieut. 7th Regt. 31st Aug. 35.

MOCKLER, W. E. Lieut. 10th Regt, July, 35—Capt. 22nd Aug. 36—wounded 16th March, 37—10th June, 37.

MORSS, G. B. Asst. Commissary.

MURPHY, W. Asst. Surg. 8th Regt. 14th July, 35—Surg. 21st May, 36—10th June, 37, and afterward in New Legion.

MURPHY, T. Cornet and Riding-master 2nd Lancers, 31st July, 35—Lieut. and R. M. 10th April, 36—a great character—shot Capt. Smith of the same Regt. in a duel—ran his lance through two Carlist peasants, who were employed by a Christino Officer to place stones for the passage of the Infantry, the bridge having been destroyed by the enemy—Killed fifteen Infantry-men on the 18th June, 37, in the affair of Allegria, some of whom had been promised quarter by those who had taken them prisoners—accompanied Martin Zurbano in the extraordinary expedition into the Carlist country, when Brigadier General Ituralde and all his family were made prisoners—left the 3rd Light Dragoons British Service, in which he was Troop Sergeant Major on his receiving the offer of an appointment as Riding-master in the 2nd Lancers of the Legion—remained after 10th June, 37.

MULLINS, A. Cornet 2nd Lancers, Aug. 7th 35—Lieut. March, 8th 36—resigned on account of ill health—is brother to the Member of Parliament of that name.

MUSTON, J. H. Ensign, 3rd Regt. 3rd July, 35—Lieut. 19th Oct. 35—dangerously wounded 16th March 37.

MUSTON, C. M. Ensign 2nd Regt. 2nd July, 35.

MUTTLEBURY, T. Lieut. Artillery, 8th April, 36—wounded 16th March, 37—10th June 37.

MURRIDGE, Ensign, 5th Regt.

MURRAY, K. Capt. on the Staff, 10th Aug. 36—promoted Major—
10th June, 37.

MUNRO, Capt. 8th Regt.

MUNNS, F. Lieut. Rifles, 17 July, 35.

NASH, Ensign 2nd Regt. July, 35—died by fever at (*u*)

NANGLE, J. Ensign 9th Regt. 5th April, 36—Lieut. 12th Oct. 36.

NEWLAND, Ensign 6th Regt.

NETTLESHIP, Volunteer 6th Regt. July, 35—Ensign, 6th Sept.—
Lieut. 8th Oct. 36—promoted Capt. 10th June, 37.

NEWALL, Surgeon 9th Regt. July, 35—died by fever at (*u*)

NEWCOME, Lieut. Rifles, July, 35—Capt. and Major, 12th Oct.
36—10th June, 37.

NEYNOE, Capt. Rifles, July, 35.

NELSON, Commissariat Clerk.

NICHOLLS, (*u*)

NICHOLSON, E. Ensign 1st Regt. July, 35.

NICHOLSON, T. Volunteer, 2nd Regt. 8th Oct. 35.

NIGHTINGALE, Ensign 1st Regt. 24th Aug. 36.

NOWLAN, Qr. Master 9th Regt. 15th Sept. 35—transferred to 2nd
Lancers, served after 10th June, 37—is supposed to be the only
Qr. Master who did not enrich himself by his office.

NOBLE, C. Lieut. 1st Regt. 1st July, 35—Capt. 29th Oct. 35—
wounded 5th May, 36,

NUGENT, A. Ensign 7th Regt, July, 35—Lieut. 21st Aug. 36—
retired March 37.

NUGENT, C. Ensign 7th Regt. July, 35.

NUTT, W. Hosp. Assistant 1st March, 37—10th June, 37.

OAKLEY, J. Capt, 1st Lancers, 26th Aug. 35—invalided, 36.

OAKLEY, C. Capt, 8th Regt, 1st Sept. 35—died by fever in Vittoria.

O'BRIEN, 2nd Lieut. 3rd Regt, 24th Feb 36.

O'BRIEN, Volunteer, 3rd Regt. wounded severely, 5th May, 36.

O'BRIEN, J. Ensign, 7th Regt. July, 35—Lieut. 23rd, July, 36—
wounded 16th March, 37, and killed in action 14th Sept. 37.

O'BRIEN, P. Ensign, 10th Regt. July 35.

O'BRIEN, Commissariat Clerk.

O'CONNOR, 2nd Lieut: 3rd Regt. 8th Oct. 36—wounded 16th
March, 37—10th June, 37.

O'CONNOR, R. Lieut. and Adjt. 10th Regt. Aug. 35—transferred to 3rd Regt.—promoted Capt. and Adjt.—severely wounded 1st Oct. 36, and 16th March 37.

O'CONNOR, J. Ensign, 9th Regt. July 35—Lieut, 12th Jan. 36, afterwards Capt.—10th June, 37.

O'CONNELL, M. C. Lt. Col. 10th Regt. 19th July, 35—promoted Col. and Dep. Adjt. Gen. March 37—commanded New Legion as Brigadier General after 10th June 37.

O'CONNELL, R. Ensign 10th Regt. July, 35—Lieut. 10th June, 36—invalided March 37.

O'CONNELL, M. Lieut. 10th Regt. July 35.

O'CONNELL, Ensign, Dep. Provost Marshall 4th Sept. 35—died by fever at Vittoria.

O'CONNELL M. D. Asst. Surg. 10th Reg,. 19th July, 35—10th June 37.

O'DELL, T. Lieut. 19th July, 35—Capt. 5th May, 36—afterwards Brevet Major—wounded 16th March, 37.

O'DONNELL, H. Ensign, 10th Regt. July 35—Lieut. 28th July, 36—wounded, 16th March, 37—10th June, 37.

O'DONNELL, M. Ensign, (Super,) July 35.

O'DRISCHOLL, R. Lieut. 8th Regt. 10th July 36—mortally wounded' 16th March, 37—died soon after.

OGILVIE, G. Capt. 6th Regt. 4th Sept. 35.

O'LEARY, Major, and Lt. Col. 10th Regt. July, 35

O'MEARA, Major Rifles 26th Aug. 35

O'NEALE, E. St. J. Capt. 6th Regt. 4th July, 35—promoted Major —served on the Staff as Major of Brigade—10th June 37

O'NEIL, J. 2nd Lieut. 6th Regiment 6th Sept, 35—1st Lieut, 27th Jan, 37—10th June, 37.

O'NEALE, J. Volunteer 10th Regt, July, 35—promoted Ensign and Lieut—wounded 16th March, 37—10th June, 37

ORME, R, F, Capt. 8th Regt, Aug, 35

ORME, F, Ensign 9th Regt, 19th Aug, 36—Qr.-master at Depot

ORIEL, Commissariat Clerk

O'REILLY, W. Lieut, Rifles July, 35—promoted Capt, killed in action 5th May, 37.

O'SULLIVAN, Ensign (Super.) 10th Regt, 35.

OSBORNE, F. Cornet 2nd Lancers July, 31st 35—came home to England on sick leave, in Jan 36, and remained.

O'SULLIVAN, Lieut, 4th Regt, 1st April, 36—Capt, 22nd March, 37—10th June, 37

O'TOOLE, Cadet 4th Regt, July, 35—promoted Lieut

OUTLAW, Cornet 1st Lancers, 1st Sept 35

PARTINGTON, Cornet 1st Lancers, July, 35—Lieut, 5th July, 36, —severely wounded, 1st Oct 36—promoted Capt. and Major in New Legion.

PALMER, C. W. Ensign 1st Regt, 28th Sept 35—Lieut, 20th Aug. 36—wounded 16th March, 37—10th June, 37.

PALMER, H. J. Capt, 4th Regt, 25th Sept 35.

PALMER, Hosp, Asst, 9th Sept, 36.

PARKER, H. Brevet Major, 3rd Regt, and Staff, July, 35.

PARKE, E. Capt, and Major 10th Regt, 15th Dec 36—wounded 5th May, 36—10th June, 37—a great duelist.

PATTERSON, W. 2nd Lieut, 6th Regt, July, 35—Lieut, 25th Sept, 35.

PAGET, *Lord William*, Colonel 2nd Lancers, and Aide-de-camp to the Lieut, Gen. wounded 5th May, 36—came to England on sick leave and never returned.

PAGET, R. Capt, 6th Regt, July, 35.

PEREYERA, *Don J.* Lieut. attached to 1st Brigade.

PEYTON, Capt, and Pay Master, 4th Regt, 4th July, 35—resigned March, 37.

PEARCE, W. G. was appointed Cornet 2nd Lancers, July, 35 by virtue of recruiting for that Regt, in Cork, but was refused his commission on landing in Spain from some capricious and unexplained motive of Colonel Jacks; lost his valuable outfit of regimentals, horse, &c, which like all the officers of cavalry, he had prepared at great expense; ultimately got a commission, 24th May, 36, as Ensign 4th Regt, promoted Lieut, 1st Regt. 1st April, 37—and afterwards Capt. 10th June, 37.

PEIRSE, F. 2nd Lieut, 4th Regt, 4th July, 35—Lieut, 16th Nov, 35—afterwards brevet Capt,—wounded 6th June, 36—retired 31st Dec. 36.

PENTLAND, Commissariat Clerk.

PIPER, Asst, Surg, 2nd Lancers, Jan, 36—10th June, 37.

PITT, H, Ensign 2nd Regt, 2nd July, 35.

PIGOTT, H. 2nd Lieut, 3rd Regt, 27th July, 35

PILFORD, Capt, 5th Regt, July, 35—died by Fever at Vittoria, 27th Feb, 36

PICKTHORN, W. H. Capt, 8th Regt, 14th July, 35—tried for striking a Soldier and dismissed by sentence of Court-Martial, Oct, 35

PHILLIPS, Ensign 1st Regt, 19th Oct, 35

PHELAN, W. N. Capt; 7th Regt, 17th July, 36—wounded severely 5th May, 36

PHELAN, R. Ensign 7th Regt, 13th June, 36—Lieut, 23rd Sep, 36—had both his legs amputated 16th May, 37, at Irun.

PHELAN, G. Capt, 9th Regt, July, 35

PLANK, Staff Asst, Surg, died by Fever at Vittoria

PLUNKETT; G. A. Staff Asst, Surg, July, 35—Asst, Surg, 9th Regt, 12th Oct, 35—10th June, 37

PLUNKETT, Capt, Rifles, 17th July, 35

POCOCKE, Dep, Asst, Com, Gen, died by Fever at (u)

PRICE, W. Lieut. 5th Regt. July, 35—transferred to 10 Regt.—mortally wounded 5th — died the 15th May, 36.

PRICE, W. Ensign 5th Regt. July, 35.

PRICE, G. Ensign 9th Regt. July, 35.

PRICE, G. F. Ensign 8th Regt. July, 35—resigned, and was again Ensign 23rd Aug. 36—10th June, 37.

PRIMROSE, Capt. 10th Regt. July, 35.

PURZESKI, Cornet 1st Lancers, 1st Jan. 36—10th June, 37.

QUARLES, W. Cornet 2nd Lancers, 7th Aug. 35—Lieut. 7th April, 36—left the field of battle on account of sudden ill-health during the affair in which his Regiment was engaged near Arlaban—resigned and returned to England, and was remarked at Brighton for wearing the order of *San Fernando* and calling himself *Major* QUARLES.

QUILL, Ensign, 10th Regt. 19th July, 35 ; promoted Lieut.—noneffective 16th July, 36.

RAMSAY, PERCIVAL, Capt. 4th Regt. 4th July, 35—Major 5th; *No.* 44.

May, 36—afterwards Lt. Col. 1st Regt.—wounded 5th May, 36, and 17th March, 37—an amiable gentleman and brave soldier distinguished on all occasions where duty and danger were allied, particularly on the 16th of March, in the disastrous retreat. Among the many incidents of the battle-field which occur to individuals, a rather singular one befel Col. Ramsay and Capt. W. G. Pearce, on the 1st Oct. 36. They with two or three more officers were seated each on an empty ammunition barrel for a short while that their regiment kept possession of a farm house and court-yard ; and as they were not actively employed though the battle was raging outside, Ramsay amused them with a few of his ex-haustless and mirthful anecdotes. While they were thus amused, heedless of the neighbouring thunder though ready, and expecting to march into it at a moment's notice, a 32 pound shot came through a house, and coming unexpectedly to the barrels on which the officers were seated, carried away the frail supports of the two gentlemen named, on which they fell in the mud, and in their fall brought down the others around them, to the no small enjoyment of the soldiers who witnessed the harmless disaster, and of themselves when they scrambled to their feet. Col. Ramsay died by apoplexy since his return to England, much regretted by all who knew him in Spain, or elsewhere, whether in rank, his supe-riors—equals—or inferiors. He had been a Captain in the 47th Regt. B. S.

RAIT, JAMES, Major; 1st Lancers 1st July 34—promoted Lt. Col, resigned June, 36.

RAE, J. Lieut. 4th Regt. 5th Aug. 36—transferred to 1st Regt.—slightly wounded and distinguished at the taking of Irun, 16th May, 37—promoted Capt. 10th June, 37

RAY, J. Lieut. 4th Regt. 2nd Aug. 36—retired March 37.

RAWSTONE, W. Ensign, 3rd July, 35—died by fever at Vittoria.

RABY, Ensign, 8th Regt. 24th March 36—wounded 6th June 36.—resigned 37.

RENWICK, EDWARD, Lt. Col. 3rd Regt. July, 35—died by fever at Santander.

REID, 2nd Lieut. 4th Regt. 17th July, 36—transferred to, and promoted Lieut. of Engineers, 1st Oct. 36—10th June 37.

REID. (u)

REID, Wm. Brigadier General—a distinguished officer of the British Service, and one who maintained and added to his superior reputation by the gentlemanly and soldier-like performance of his duties in the Legion—joined 1st Aug. 35—wounded 5th May, 36—retired shortly after—now Major of Engineers at·Portsmouth.

READ, R, Capt. 7th Regt. 15th July, 35—Major 20th Sept. 36—invalided March, 37.

REEVES, HENRY, Clerk of Stores 25th Aug. 35—Dep. Asst. Com. 17th Oct. 36—10th June, 37.

RIGG, M. Capt. 1st Regt. 4th Sept. 35—retired March 37.

RIGG, E. Hospital Assistant, 12th Sept. 35.

RIGGE, Surgeon, 2nd Lancers, 1st Jan. 36—invalided Sept. 36.

RICHARDSON, J. Capt. 2nd Regt. 2nd July, 35—transferred to the Q. M. G.'s Staff, and promoted Major—slightly wounded 5th May, 36—a strange incomprehensible character to those who have no means of judging of him but by his accounts of himself and the Legion. He is the author of " *Journal of the Movements of the British Legion,*" in which he has lauded that force and its Commander up to the time that he himself left it, when suddenly discovering that all the talent! honour! virtue! and respectability! had retired from the service, he turned his laudatory writings into dissenting abuse. He left the service shortly after the action of the 5th of May, that engagement having been, as was supposed, too *hot* to warrant his waiting for a repetition of it.

RICHARDSON, 2nd Lieut. 1st Regt. 1st April, 37.

RIBLE, Ensign, 3rd Regt.

RIDGE, M. 2nd Lieut. 6th Regt. 26th July, 36—1st Lieut. 8th Oct. 36—appointed Adjt. 17th Feb. 37—afterwards Capt.—10th June, 37.

RIDGE, W. Lieut. Artillery 11th Aug. 35.

ROBINSON, Capt. 1st Lancers.

ROBERTSON, Dr. E. Surgeon, 2nd Lancers 31st July, 35—resigned at Santander, on being appointed Surgeon to the 47th Foot B. S.

ROBERTSON, HUGH, Qr. Master 2nd ·Regt. 15th Sept. 35—transferred to 9th Regt.

ROBERTSON, A. C. Lieut. 8th Regt. 14th July, 35—Capt. 20th Sept. 36—wounded 1st Oct. 36—10th June, 37—now serving in the 20th Foot. B. S.

ROBINSON. 2nd Lieut. Rifles, 23rd Aug. 36.

ROBINSON, Lieut. Rifles.

ROBERTS, P. H. Ensign, 8th Regt. July, 35—Lieut. 5th May, 36
Capt. 16th March, 37—10th June, 37. This officer was with
Major—afterwards Lieut. Col. Wilson, particularly distinguished
before the enemy, 16th March, 37. It is deemed necessary to
notice this as by an oversight 'their names were .omitted in my
description of that day's fighting, while other officers of the same
regiment were particularized. Capt. Roberts was also gallantly
distinguished at Irun 16th May, 37—for which he got the order of
San Fernando.

ROBERTS, J. C. Asst. Surg. Artillery, 12th Aug. 35—10th June,
37.

ROBBINS, G. 2nd Lieut. 6th Regt. 14th Sept. 35—Lieut. 17th
Feb. 37—10th June, 37.

ROOKE, Capt. 2nd Lancers, 31st Aug. 35—resigned at Santander,
on account of ill-health, 20th Jan. 36—Half-pay 'Lieut. 4th
Dragoon Guards, B. S.

ROOKE, C. Lieut. 4th Regt. 4th July, 35.

ROSS, MALCOLM, Major 8th Regt. July, 35—transferred to and
promoted Lieut. Col. 6th Regt. 13th May, 36—severely wounded,
11th July, 36—promoted Col. and appointed acting Brigadier in
the latter movements of Gen. Evans—appointed Adjt. Gen. to the
New Legion under Gen. O'Connell.

ROGERS, E. Qr.-master 3rd Regt. July, 35—died by fever at (*u*).

ROGERS, H. Capt. 7th Regt.

ROGERS, J. Apothecary to the Forces, 24th Aug. 35.

ROGERSON, C. Clerk of Stores, 31st May.

ROGERSON (*u*).

ROMAINE. 2nd Lieut. Artillery,.15th July, 35.

ROACH, Ensign 8th Regt — promoted Lieut. 10th July, 36—
severely wounded, 16th March, 37—entered New Legion.

ROOSE, Asst. Surg. 18th July, 35.

ROSE, F. Surg. 9th Regt.

SALARNO, Hosp. Asst. 21st May, 36.

ST. LEGER, Capt. 7th Regt. 23rd Aug.

SALMON, Asst. Surg. Artillery, 5th Sept. 35—died by fever at (*u*).

SCARTH, Cornet 1st Lancers, 1st July, 35

SCARMAN, Lieut. 1st July, 35—promoted Capt—killed in action, 5th May, 36.

SCALLEY. (*u*)

SCALES, Ensign 10th Regt.

SCOTT, J. 2nd Lieut. 6th Regt. 25th Oct. 35.

SCOTT, J. Surg. 4th Regt. 4th July, 35.

SCOTT, W. G. Asst. Surg. 4th Regt. 4th July, 35.

SERRANO, *Don* JOSE CALISTO, Lieut and A. D. C. attached to Light Brigade.

SERVICE, Dep. Asst. Com. Gen. 3rd March, 36.

SERVICE, Commissariat Clerk.

SILVER, J. Asst. Surg. 1st Regt. 1st July, 35.

SIEMS, 2nd Lieut. 4th Regt. 8th July. 36—wounded 16th March—entered New Legion—killed in action, 14th Sept. 37.

SIDLEY, G. Clerk of Stores, 25th July, 35—10th June, 37.

SHAW, S. Major and Lieut. Col. 10th Regt. 12th Oct. 35—transferred to 1st Regt. 20th March, 37—10th June, 37—wounded 5th May, 36.

SHAW, J. Lieut. 6th Regt. July, 35—Capt. 4th Sept. 35 Major 25th Sept. 36—10th June, 37.

SHAW, C. Lieut. Col. Artillery, 8th Sept. 35—promoted Col. 10th June, 37.

SHAW, D. B. 2nd Lieut. Artillery, 20th Oct 36—10th June, 37.

SHAW, C. Col. 6th Regt. July, 35—afterward Brigadier Gen.—resigned in Aug. or Sept. 36—wounded 5th May, 36.

SHEPPARD, E. 2nd Lieut. Rifles, July, 35—1st Lieut. and Adjt. 12th Oct. 35—Capt. and Bt. Major, 27th May, 36—severely wounded 16th March, 37—10th June, 37.

SHEPPARD, T. Lieut. 9th Regt. July, 35—Capt. 7th Sept, 35—Major, 1st July, 36—10th June, 37.

SHEPARD, D. P. Purveyor of Hosp. 12th Aug, 35.

SHEA, M. Qr.-master, 11th Aug. 36.

SHELLY, *Don* RICARDO, Lieut. Col. and A.D.C.

SHIELDS, W. Capt. 8th Regt. July, 35—Major, 17th Feb. 37—severely wounded, 5th May, 36—killed in action, 14th Sept. 37.

SHIELDS, R. brother of the former—Volunteer in 8th Regt. July, 35—Ensign, 25th Sept. 36—Lieut. 5th May, 36—Capt. 21st Jan. 37—killed in action, 14th Sept. 37.

SHOLL, W. B. Staff Asst. Surg. 7th Aug. 35—afterward Surg. unattached.

SHORE, S. Ensign 1st Regt. 19th Oct.' 36—wounded, 16th March 37—retired same month.

SKEDD, R. 2nd Lieut. Artillery 17th Oct. 36 ; afterwards Lieut, and Adjt. served in New Legion, had been twenty-eight years, most of that time a non-commissioned officer, in the Royal British Artillery ; was Sergeant Major in the 8th Regt. of the Legion, and promoted for his skilful and soldierlike conduct.

SKIPWITH, Capt. 1st Lancers.

SKURRY, F. H. Staff Asst. Surg. July, 35—died by fever at. (u)

SLEIGH, Lieut. and Bt. Capt. Artillery, Aug. 35—resigned by ill health, ——, 36.

SLOANE, W. M. Major Commandant, 4th Regt. 4th July, 35— Lt. Col. 16th Nov. 35—afterward Commandant of San Sebastian, unattached—10th June, 37.

SMALL, Capt. 1st Lancers, 18th Sept. 35—resigned 36.

SMITH, W. A. Capt. 2nd Lancers Aug. 27th 35—Shot in a duel with Lt. Murphy, in April, 36—had been a Capt. in Foreign Service.

SMITH, Ensign 1st Regt. 16th July, 35—non-effective 31st March, 36.

SMITH, Ensign 1st Regt. 26th Sept. 36.

SMITH, Ensign 8th Regt. invalided March, 36.

SMITH, Hosp. Assistant.

SMITH; J. Qr. Master, 9th Regt. 5th March, 37.

SMITH, D. Ensign 5th Regt. July, 35.

SMITH, Lieut. Hosp. Transport Corps, 25th Sept. 35—10th June, 37.

SNELLING, Commissariat Clerk.

SPARROW, 2nd Lieut. 3rd Regt. 16th July, died by fever in Vittoria.

SPARROW, J. B. 2nd Lieut. 3rd Regt. 16th July, 36—1st Lieut. 24th Nov. 36—10th June, 37.

SPARROW, J. J. Ensign 9th Regt. July, 35—severely wounded and promoted Lieut. 5th May, 36—10th June, 37.

SPENSER, Staff Asst. Surg. 25th April. 36.

STAPLETON, Volunteer 1st Regt. Sept. 35—Lieut. 18th Sept. 36.

STAPYLTON, Capt. 3rd Regt. July, 35.

STACK, 2nd Lieut. 3rd Regt. July, 35—Lieut. 24th Aug. transferred to 9th Regt. wounded 5th May, 36—invalided.

STAUNTON, Asst. Com. Gen.

STAUNTON, Lieut. 6th Regt. Sept. 35.

STAUNTON, 2nd Lieut. 4th Regt. July, 35.

STEPHENSON, E. Capt. 1st Lancers, 1st July, 35—promoted Major—10th June, 37.

STEPHENSON, Lieut. 3rd Regt. 4th Sept. 35.

STEPHENS; Commissariat Clerk.

STEWART, C. Capt. and Adjt. 1st Regt. July, 35—promoted Major—and appointed Commandant of Depot of Del Corban, wounded and resigned 10th Oct. 36—afterwards served in New Legion.

STEWART, C. W. Capt. 1st Regt. 1st July, ——

STEWART, 2nd Lieut. 6th Regt.

STOREY, Lieut. 6th Regt. July, 35—wounded 5th May, 36.

STRIDE, Lieut. 7th Regt. July, 35

STRATFORD, the Hon. G. Lieut. 8th Regt. and Staff July, 35.

STREET, 9th Regt. 16th Sept. 35—Capt. 12th Jan. 36—10th June, 37.

STREET, Asst. Surg. 9th Regt. July, 35.

STREET, Commissariat Dep. taken prisoner and killed by the Carlists, Jan. 36.

STODDART, Cornet 1st Lancers, July, 35—Lieut. 3rd Sept. 36.

STUTTERHEIM, Baron, Lieut. 1st Lancers, 26th Oct. 35—served in the New Legion, after 10th June, 37.

SUTTON, Qr. Master 9th Regt.

SWAN, G. C. Lt. Col. 5th Regt. July. 35—transferred to 7th Regt. commanded that corps and was severely wounded 5th May, 36—afterwards invalided; now serving in Canada.

SWANSON, Qr. Master 6th Regt. —— 35—died by fever in or near Vittoria.

SWIFT, Ensign 6th Regt. 21st Sept. 36.

SYNGE, N. 2nd Lieut. Artillery, July, 35.

TAYLOR, J. R. Surgeon 8th Regt. July, 35—resigned in the latter end of that year.

TAYLOR, Dr. A. Staff Surgeon, 9th Aug. 35—10th June, 37.

TALBOT, G. Capt. 1st Regt. 1st July, 35—Major on the Staff, wounded 5th May, 36—and 16th March, 37—Brevet Lt. Col. 10th June, 37.

TALBOT, Capt. 1st Regt.

TALBOT, Major 9th Regt. July, 35.

TINSON, 2nd Lieut. 6th Regt. 23rd March, 37—10th June, 37.

TILNEY, H. R. 2nd Lieut. 4th Regt. July, 35.

THACKWAITE, Ensign 3rd Regt. 3rd July, 35— died by fever at (u)

THOMPSON, J. Major 1st Regt. 1st July, 35—promoted Lt. Col. resigned March, 37.

THOMPSON, C. W. Ensign 1st Regt. July, 35—promoted Lieut. and Capt. transferred to 9th Regt. severely wounded 5th May, 36. resigned soon after—the author of a work called " *Twelve Months in the British Legion*," son of the well known Col. Perronet Thompson.

THOMPSON, T. P. Lt. Col. British Service, the officer just alluded to ; an honorary field officer of the Legion—unattached.

THOMPSON, M. Ensign 1st Regt.

THOMPSON, J. (u)

THORNTON, Ensign, 9th Regt. July, 35—promoted Lieut. and Capt.—retired—36.

THOREAU, Capt. 10th Regt. July 35—transferred to Artillery, 27th Oct. 35—promoted Major—invalided 36.

THORNE, Dep. Purveyor of Hospitals—died by fever at (u)

THYNNE, Asst. Com. Gen.

TOWNLEY, CHAS. Ensign, 2nd Regt. July. 35—Lieut. 14th Aug. 35—Capt. 1st Regt. and Staff, 25th Sept. 35—severely wounded 5th May, 36—Brevet Major—10th June, 37.

TOWNLEY, (u)

TOWNSEND, 2nd Lieut. Rifles, 17th July, 35—Lieut. 12th Aug. 36—appointed Adjt.—entered New Legion—killed in action 14th Sept. 37..

TOTTENHAM, C. H. 2nd Lieut. Rifles, 17th July, 35.

TRAVERS, Lieut. 2nd Lancers 27th Aug. 35—10th June 37.

TRACEY, Major, or Lt. Col. 1st Regt.

TREEVE, Ensign, 10th Regt. July, 35—afterwards Lieut. 1st Regt. —invalided.

TUHOY, EDWARD, Lieut. 10th Regt. July, 35.

TUPPER, W. Le M. Lt. Col. 6th Regt. July, 35—promoted Col. —mortally wounded 5th May 36.

TUPPER, A. J. Pay Master, 5th Regt. July, 35—afterwards held the same office in the 9th Regt.—10th June, 37.

TYNER, Capt. 7th Regt. July, 35.

VANE, H. Lieut. 2nd Regt: July, 35.

VICKERS, CHAS. 2nd Lieut. 1st Regt. 27th Aug. 36.

VILLIERS, E. J. 2nd Lieut, Rifles, July, 35.

VILLIERS, W. C. 2nd Lieut. Rifles July, 35.

VOGAN, Surgeon 2nd Regt. July, 35.

WAKEFIELD, Capt. 1st Lancers July, 35—promoted, Major—Lt. Col. 15th Sept. 36—entered New Legion after 10th June, 37.

WADE, GEORGE, Cornet, 2nd Lancers 31st July, 35—obtained an Ensigncy in 13th Foot B. S. and resigned the Legion May, 36.

WADE, C. F. Lieut. and Bt. Capt. Artillery 12th Aug. 35—afterward Capt.—10th June, 37.

WALLACE, Lieut. 1st Regt. 1st July, 35.

WALLACE, (u).

WADDELL, W. R. Capt. 4th Regt. 35.

WADDINGHAM, SAM, Lieut. 5th Regt, July 35.

WALKER, C. Cornet 1st Lancers, 1st Oct. 36,

WALKER, C. Ensign 7th Regt. 19th May, 36—wounded in a, skirmish 14th Sept, 36,

WALKER, Lieut, 6th Regt.

WALSH, Capt, 7th Regt, July, 35,

WARNER, entered the Legion as Qr, Master Serjt. 8th Regt. promoted Qr.-master to 7th Regt,—killed in action, 5th May, 36.

WATSON, Surgeon, Rifles, 17th July, 35.

WATSON, Lieut. 7th Regt. 15th Aug. 35.

WARING, E. Staff Asst, Surg. 20th Sept. 36.

WALTER, Surg. 1st Regt, 16th Jan. 36.

WETHERALL, Lt, Col. Asst, Com. attached to Col. Carbonell's department in England from the beginning of the service, and now a Commissioner for the settlement of claims, which employment is likely to last for a few years.

WEALE, Clerk of Stores, 7th Aug. 35—Dep. Asst. Com, 31st May, 36.

WHEAT, P. J. 2nd Lieut, Rifles 17th March, 36—killed in action, 16th or 17th May, 37.

WHITE, Capt. Rifles, July, 35—died by fever at (*u*)

WHITEHEAD, T. Lieut. and Adjt. Artillery 8th Sept. 35—died by fever at Vittoria.

WHITAKER, E. Staff Asst. Surgeon, 8th Aug. 35.

WILKINSON, Ensign 1st Regt. July, 35—was dismissed, and went over to the enemy.

WILKINSON, H. Surgeon 5th Regt. July, 35—transferred to 6th Regt. 6th Sept. 35—entered New Legion, after 10th June, 37.

WILLS, Capt. and Pay Master 2nd Regt. July, 35—afterwards unattached—10th June, 37.

WINDIBANK, Qr. Master, 4th Regt.

WIDDOWSON, Volunteer 6th Regt. July, 35—Ensign 16th Aug. 35—died by fever at Vittoria.

WILSON, Capt. 7th Regt. July, 35—severely wounded, 5th May 36. invalided.

WILSON, Capt. 8th Regt. 1st Oct. 35—Major, 20th May, 36—afterwards Lieut. Col.—wounded 15th March, 37. It is due to this officer to state that his gallantry and skill were conspicuously seen on the 16th of March. There were others, perhaps equally valiant, whose bravery]has not been mentioned in this work, but these were few—very few—and though in fairness these should have been also particularized, it is the more necessary to mention Lieut. Col. Wilson, as most of the officers of the 8th Regt. have been already spoken of ; they, being better known to the Author then those of other regiments, and by an unintentional and unjust over-sight this officer's name and peculiarly destinguished conduct has been hitherto omitted.

WILLIAMS, Dr. T. Asst. Inspr. of Hospitals, 4th Aug. 35.

WILLIAMS, F. A. Staff-Asst. Surg. 5th Sept. 35.

WILLIAMS, Surg. 9th Regt. died by Fever, in or near Vittoria. (Perhaps these two last names allude only to one person.)

WILLIAMS, I. K. Cadet 4th Regt. July, 35.

WINDER, J. Lieut. Artillery, July, 35.

WOOD, C. Lieut. 2nd Regt. 2nd July, 35—Capt. 23rd Sept. 35.

transferred to 6th Regt.—promoted Major—severely wounded, 5th May, 36—and 6th June, 36—10th June, 37.

WOODS, Volunteer, 9th Regt. July, 35—Ensign, 25th Sept. 35—wounded, 5th May, 36—promoted Lieut. and invalided.

WOOLRIDGE, J. W. Capt. 4th Regt. July, 35—wounded and promoted Major, 5th May, 36—Lieut. Col. 1st Oct. 36—served on the Staff as A. D. C.

WOOLEY, G. Ensign 3rd Regt. July, 35.

WRIGHT, Ensign and Adjt. 9th Regt. 7th Sept. 35—Lieut. and Adjt. 5th Regt. 26th Oct. 35—Capt. 10th Regt. 12th Aug. 36—served in New Legion after 10th June, 37.

WRIGHT, J. T. G. Ensign 7th Regt. 29th July, 36.

WRIGHT, Qr.-master 9th Regt—killed in action, 5th May, 36.

WYATT, B. Major 8th Regt. Sept. 35—an officer much esteemed, but who had the misfortune to lose parts of both his feet by frost in Vittoria—invalided.

WYMER, W. Capt. 2nd Lancers. 31st July, 35—invalided by a Medical Board, [at Vittoria, 8th March, 36—had been Capt. in 11th Light Dragoons, B. S.

WYKE, Lieut. 1st Lancers, 1st July, 35.

XIMINES, M. Ensign 2nd Regt. July, 35—Lieut. 26th Oct. 35.

YARDLEY, Commissariat Clerk.

YATES, Commissariat Clerk.

YORSLEY, J. 9th Regt.

YOUNG, G. Cornet 1st Lancers, July, 35.

YOUNGHUSBAND, Major 2nd Lancers, Nov. 35—died by fever at Santander, Feb. 36—In him the Lancers lost a true supporter of their rights—the officers a real friend—and the service a brave soldier. He had been Capt. in the 13th Light Dragoons, B. S.

THE 2nd LANCERS.

THE 2nd Regiment of Legionary cavalry have not been mentioned in this work so frequently as the other regiments, nor so often as they deserve. This arises from that corps having been detached the greater part of their period of service from the Legion, and attached to the spanish army ; by which separation, we were less acquainted with their exploits. This separation was the cause also of their pay having fallen into greater arrears than ours ; because the Spanish General under whom they served considered them as a part of the Legion, and therefore did not estimate for them, while General Evans, or those under him, considered them as a part of the spanish army, or at least treated them as such.

The following letter will explain their situation.

To the EDITOR of the GLOBE.

Brussels, Jan. 6, 1838.

Mr. Editor,—Having seen in the *Globe* of the 1st inst. a letter from Gen. Evans to Col. Wetherall, in which he states that the whole of the non-commissioned officers and men serving in Spain under his command had been paid up to the 10th of June, with some "trivial and unavoidable exceptions ;" I cannot forbear commenting upon so extraordinary an assertion, and will feel obliged if you will insert this in your next number.

Among the "trivial and unavoidable exceptions" alluded to, he mentions a detachment lately landed in Cork, the state of whose accounts he says he is unacquainted with, and gives as a reason that they were upwards of a year detached from his immediate command.

This detachment consisted of a large portion of the 2nd Lancers, the remainder of whom were still at this time, in San Sebastian, unpaid, and in a state of the greatest destitution.

The 2nd Lancers were, it is true, detached for more than a year from the remainder of the Legion ; but by whom ? By Gen. Evans ; who, on leaving Vittoria for San Sebastian, gave them orders to remain. Was it not then his duty still to see justice done to them ? During the long stay of the Regiment in and about Vittoria, Gen. Evans was in the habit of sending orders to Col. Jacks, commanding the 2nd Lancers. Whatever promotions took place in the regiment were given by Gen. Evans; in short he exercised all the privileges and powers of the General commanding them, except those of protecting their rights.

As the 10th June approached, officers and men looked out daily for orders to proceed to the head-quarters of the Legion for the purpose of their accounts being settled. Without these orders Col. Jacks, could not move; however, no orders came, and we were detained in expectation of them till a much later period than the 10th of June, about which time we heard that Gen. Evans was in England, wholly unmindful of the 2nd Lancers. Col. Jacks, then, finding his regiment neglected and apparently forgotten, took upon himself to march it down to San Sebastian, where he heard, on his arrival, that there was no pay nor any chance of pay for the 2nd Lancers, though the other non-commissioned officers and privates of the Legion had nearly all been paid up to the 10th of June, and the officers of every other regiment had received three months' pay.

I myself sailed for Cork in the Columbia with the detachment above mentioned, and saw the men landed, each having received four Spanish dollars, for which they could with difficulty get 15s. A liberal reward truly for two years' service in a regiment, of which Gen. Evans himself, in letters to Col. Jacks, speaks in the highest terms. Be it known that to each private among them an arrear of pay from 10l. to 15l. was due, and to each non-commissioned officer considerably more. A short time before, another part of the same regiment had sailed for England in a small cutter, without receiving any part whatever of their claim, preferring the chance of finding work at home, to the certainty of starving in a foreign land.

Now, Sir, an entire regiment of cavalry taken out by Gen. Evans, looking to his promises as their only security, is left by him in the interior of a foreign country, without orders, without pay, or any settlement of their accounts. I might beside mention many other acts of injustice which the same corps was made to suffer by Gen. Evans, and yet he asserts that the non-commissioned officers and men of his Legion were all paid up to the 10th of June, and instances the case above stated as one of a *few " trivial and unavoidable exceptions."*

I have the honour to be, Sir, your obedient and humble servant,

CHIDLEY MALONY,

Late Second Lancers.

AFFAIR OF ALEGRIA.

THIS was the affair in which Riding-master Murphy distinguished himself by killing Carlist prisoners. The following is the official account of it. Though the stigma of indiscriminate slaughter attaches to the regiment by one officer having misconducted himself it was still a valiant performance; and the revilers of the Legion will be pleased to recollect that Murphy had come from the British Service.

"Vittoria, June, 19, 1837.

"GENERAL—I have the honour to inform you that yesterday, when in command of the rear-guard, consisting of Lieutenant-Colonel Zurbano's corps, and a squadron of my regiment (the 2nd Lancers), and on the march from Salvatierra towards Alegria, at about three p.m., the enemy, consisting of upwards of 300 infantry and 40 cavalry, with a support, commenced firing on the column under my command; but, as there was a river between, it was impossible to advance against them; Zurbano's infantry, and the detachment of the Regiment of Almansa, were then pushed forward and crossed the river by a bridge; the squadron of the 2nd Lancers and a squadron of Portuguese Lancers moved in the same direction; and all immediately advanced towards the enemy, who, as soon as they perceived our intention, quickly marched towards the hills; finding that the Infantry could not arrive in time, I advanced at a brisk pace with the second Lancers, along the crest of a hill near the villages of Langania and Greno, the Portuguese Lancers keeping in a parallel direction on our left on the side of it. The enemy, consisting of upwards of 300 Infantry and 40 Cavalry, formed line with a wood on their right, and their Cavalry on the left, and awaited our approach at about 200 yards in front. I immediately charged them with the 2nd Lancers, when their Cavalry galloped off, and the Infantry broke and fled with precipitation to their left, towards two battalions which were in reserve, and well posted at about 500 yards distance, but too late to avoid the effects of the charge, which was most impetuous and completely successful, having killed upwards of 100 in the field, and taken thirty-seven prisoners; among the former were five officers.

" I cannot speak too highly in praise of the squadron of Portuguese Lancers, or of the commanding-officer of it, who used every exertion to bring his men into the charge with the 2nd Lancers, but which, from their position on the side of the hill, was not practicable; but they arrived on the field most opportunely for supporting the English Cavalry, and 'I believe about eight of them were up almost immediately after the enemy broke, and they as well as the whole of the squadron behaved most gallantly.

" To Lieut. Col. Zurbano, whose knowledge of the country and zeal in her Majesty's cause, is principally to be attributed the happy result of the day. He charged with the 2nd Lancers, and in this, as on all former occasions, displayed the most intrepid conduct: him also I beg to draw under your Excellency's observation: but as you are so well acquainted with his numerous acts of devotion to the Queen's cause, I will merely add that he has, on this occasion, surpassed all other of his actions.

" The Colonel of the Spanish service attached to your Excellency's staff was at the head in the charge, and most nobly and gallantly distinguished himself.

" I now beg leave to draw your Excellency's notice to the brave officers and men of my Regiment (the 2d Lancers) whom I had the good fortune to command on this occasion. The Captains Kensington, Maturin, and Beevor, Lieutenants Murphy, Berry, and Courtenay, and Cornet Malony particularly distinguished themselves; as did every non-commissioned officer and Lancer. The Assistant-surgeon Piper was likewise up and ready for the duties of his profession.

" When your Excellency takes into consideration that we are serving after the expiration of our contract, that I had only sixty-five horses in the field, that we attacked nearly five times our number, I trust I may be permitted to solicit your Excellency's recommendation to her Majesty the Reina Gobernadora of all those who participated in this glorious achievement.

" It will almost appear incredible that this was effected without the loss of a single Lancer killed or wounded, and only three horses killed or wounded. The enemy immediately after their defeat retired to the mountains.

" I have the honour to be your Excellency's most obedient humble servant.   " W. H. JACKS,

" Colonel Commanding 2nd or Queen's Own Irish Lancers.

" To General the Marquis das Antas, &c., &c,. Vittoria."

Omitted in the Alphabetical Roll.

KIRKMAN, Pay-master 2nd Lancers, July, 35.
STONE, T. Staff Asst. Surg.
STRATUSTIGUY, A. D. C. to Col. Arbuthnott.

NOTE.—All persons who are disposed to correct the Author in the Statements contained in this Work, will oblige him by communicating their corrections with any other information to the Publisher, 4 Brydges-Street, Covent-Garden, London.

THE END.

PRINTED BY J. H. STARIE, 59, MUSEUM STREET.